Springer Texts in Business and Economics

Springer Texts in Business and Economics (STBE) delivers high-quality instructional content for undergraduates and graduates in all areas of Business/Management Science and Economics. The series is comprised of self-contained books with a broad and comprehensive coverage that are suitable for class as well as for individual self-study. All texts are authored by established experts in their fields and offer a solid methodological background, often accompanied by problems and exercises.

Bernd W. Wirtz

Digital Government

Strategy, Government Models and Technology

Springer

Univ.- Prof. Dr. Bernd W. Wirtz
Chair for Information and Communication Management
German University for Administrative Sciences
Speyer, Germany

ISSN 2192-4333 ISSN 2192-4341 (electronic)
Springer Texts in Business and Economics
ISBN 978-3-031-13085-4 ISBN 978-3-031-13086-1 (eBook)
https://doi.org/10.1007/978-3-031-13086-1

This Springer imprint is published by the registered company Springer Nature Switzerland AG
The registered company address is: Gewerbestrasse 11, 6330 Cham, Switzerland

Preface

The Internet has fundamentally changed the lives of many people over the last two decades. Digitization also has a significant impact on public institutions and public administration. Nowadays, digital government has become an important competitive factor in the international context. Against this background, this textbook offers a comprehensive perspective on digital government in public administrations.

This textbook is largely based on the textbook *E-Government*, Speyer 2017, by Bernd W. Wirtz and Peter Daiser. It is with great regret that Peter Daiser will no longer be able to contribute to the book project in the future due to his various commitments. I would like to thank Peter Daiser most sincerely for his previous collaboration and his valuable contribution.

In revising this new edition of the book, I received various kinds of support from the former and current employees and the doctoral students of the Chair of Information and Communication Management at the German University of Administrative Sciences Speyer. I would like to particularly thank Ms. Tirza F. Mueller (M.A.), Ms. Johanna Heckeroth (M.Sc.), Ms. Isabell Falke (M.A.), Mr. Paul F. Langer (M.Sc.), Mr. Pascal Kubin (LL.M.), and Mr. Florian Schmidt (M.Sc.) for their dedication to this project.

The scientific development of a subject area thrives through the critical analysis and discussion of concepts and content. Given this, and the still inchoate state of knowledge regarding digital government, we are grateful for any recommendations or comments.

Speyer, Germany
October 2022

Bernd W. Wirtz

Contents

About the Author

Bernd W. Wirtz studied business administration in Cologne, London, and Dortmund, culminating in an MBA (Master of Business Administration). He later served as a lecturer for media management at the Universities of Düsseldorf (Germany) and Zurich (Switzerland). In 1994, he was awarded a doctorate in the field of new media and competition strategies (Doctorate in Business Administration).

After finishing his studies, Prof. Wirtz worked as a consultant with Roland Berger & Partners as well as Andersen Consulting/Accenture (Manager in the field of new media/electronic commerce) and as a lecturer at the University of Zurich. From 1999 to 2004, he was Full Professor (Deutsche Bank Chair for Strategic Management) at the University of Witten/Herdecke (Germany). Since 2004, he has been Full Professor (Chair for Information and Communication Management) at the German University of Administrative Sciences Speyer (Germany).

Prof. Wirtz is an editorial board member of the journal *Long Range Planning*, the *Journal of Media Business Studies, the International Journal on Media Management*, the *International Journal of Business Environment*, the *International Journal of Public Administration*, the *Public Organization Review*, and the *International Review on Public and Nonprofit Marketing*. He has several years of experience in consulting on strategy projects for leading media and telecommunication enterprises and the European Commission. His publications focus on media and Internet management, business model management, marketing, electronic business, and digital government (approximately 330 publications). In total, Prof. Wirtz has published 20 books (e.g., 10th edition of *Media and Internet*

Management in German/2nd edition in English, 7th edition of *Electronic Business* in German, 4th edition of *Direct Marketing* in German, 5th edition of *Business Model Management* in German/2nd edition in English, and 4th edition of *Mergers & Acquisitions Management* in German).

Part I

Concept and Strategy of Digital Government

Introduction

1

Contents

Learning Objectives
By working through this chapter, you will be able to:

1. Describe the evolution of Internet hosts.
2. Explain the major changes brought about by the worldwide use of the Internet.
3. Describe the advantages of digital government.
4. Define digital government.
5. Explain the range differences of different digital government definitions.

For some time, there has been an essential change within the economy and society induced by information technology.[1] This change is mainly caused by increasing digitization: "With the beginning of the 'digital age', also called 'digital revolution', which evolved throughout the development of the multimedia market, there will be a fundamental change of existing structures in the telecommunication, computing, entertainment and media industries" (Denger and Wirtz 1995). This assessment in 1995 aptly illustrates the impact of digitization.

In the modern information society, innovations in information and communication technology have influenced citizens' behavior as well as their desired information requirements by having fundamentally changed the way people work and communicate. This information technology-induced development alters social and

[1] See for the complete textbook the German language version Wirtz (2022). See for Chapter 1 Introduction also Wirtz (2020, 2022); Wirtz and Daiser (2015, 2017).

B. W. Wirtz, *Digital Government*, Springer Texts in Business and Economics,
https://doi.org/10.1007/978-3-031-13086-1_1

cultural as well as commercial and administrative structures. Especially the Internet, which allows various forms of information access, interaction opportunities, as well as knowledge creation and sharing, has intensified this digital transformation.

Digitalization, networking, and globalization connect individuals and organizations on a worldwide level and reduce the importance of geographical boundaries. The consequences affect both the private and the public sector. Concerning the latter, the rapid evolvement from simple information access to providing complex processes and powerful tools and networks changes the public service provision and process landscape (Chen et al. 2006; Dawes 2008). Thus, governments worldwide pursue digital government solutions, which are particularly relevant for themselves and their stakeholders (Wirtz et al. 2001, 2012, 2014; Wirtz and Daiser 2017, 2018).

Citizens, for instance, demand a more flexible and more transparent administration as well as an increasing range of services that are provided online via the Internet. From a business perspective, a consistent, sustainable implementation of digital government is highly relevant for the economy since an unrestricted online availability of public services is regarded as an essential factor in international competitiveness. In this regard, digital government reflects an important starting point for satisfying these requests. And apart from that, governments aim at optimizing efficiency and effectiveness through increased administrative productivity as well as substantial cost reductions (Wirtz et al. 2014).

Stakeholder Relationships

As already pointed out, governments need to consider multiple stakeholder relationships when implementing digital government. Wirtz and Piehler (2010) identified four relevant groups: (1) government-to-government (G2G) refers to the linkage of government and public sector bodies for collaboration and cooperation. (2) Government-to-business (G2B) reflects the provision of information and services as well as interaction between governmental and profit-oriented non-governmental organizations. (3) Government-to-NPO (G2N) relates to the interaction between governmental and non-profit non-governmental organizations. (4) Government-to-citizen (G2C) considers the relationship between the government and its citizens with respect to public service provision and e-democracy. In this context, Milakovich (2012) also mentions employees, which leads to a fifth group, government-to-employee (G2E) representing the digital relationship between agencies and their employees as well as non-governmental contractors.

Meeting these challenges is a key task of the digital government concept. The following discussion therefore explains the reasons why digital government has become so important today and addresses its main features and potentials.

1.1 Digital Government Importance

A key reason for the importance of digital government is the tremendous influence of the Internet as a global networking and communication system. Its rapid spread on a worldwide level (see Figure 1.1, which illustrates the development of worldwide

Internet hosts, namely domain names that are assigned to an IP address) connecting state, economy, society, and citizens also across national borders made it an unprecedented medium. From this point of view, the Internet seems to be an ideal technology to interact and collaborate with all kinds of public stakeholders.

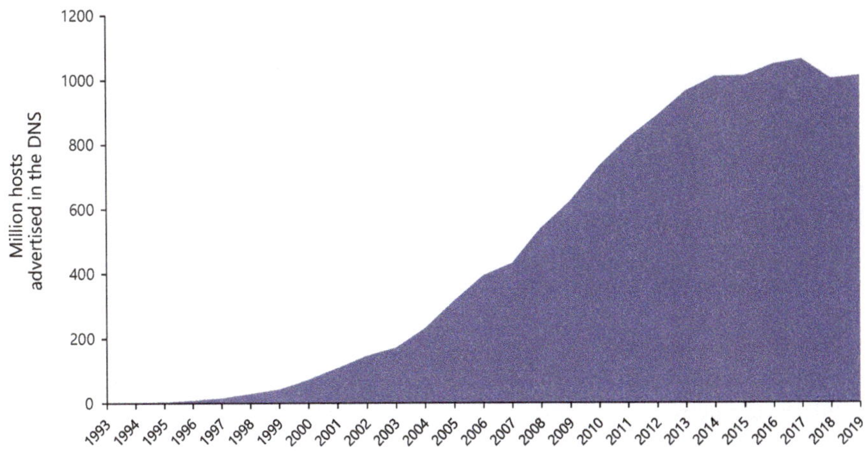

Fig. 1.1 Development of the number of Internet hosts since 1993. Data source: ISC (2019)

Worldwide Spread of Internet Usage

In the private sector, for example, it allows companies to develop foreign markets and to conduct international business transactions more efficiently than ever before. However, it also transforms the way businesses are organized and how they operate, which leads to special needs and requirements that public authorities have to meet from a G2B perspective. The same holds true from a citizen point of view, because the use of modern information and communication technologies has changed citizens' demands, too. In light of the enormous importance that the Internet has reached, governments and public authorities therefore have to account for an adequate adoption and handling of these technologies to meet the respective user needs.

Ongoing Changes Due to Technological Development

The ongoing technological development and the constantly increasing degree of globalization, which in combination caused a massive change in business and society, pose severe transformational challenges to governments all over the world. Here, digital government, which is considered a powerful system if applied effectively, may contribute substantially to stepping up to the plate (Vélez-Rivera et al. 2008; United Nations 2014) since it is regarded to possess remarkable potential for improving the responsiveness of governments and the public sector to the needs of their stakeholders (Vélez-Rivera et al. 2008). When looking at the influencing conditions that exert pressure on governments from a macroeconomic, business environment perspective, these touch on political, economic, social, technological, legal, and environmental factors.

Political Pressure

Political pressure arises from the fact that the Internet has massively influenced citizens' behavior as well as their desired information requirements. The resulting information ubiquity dethrones the state—formerly being the largest data collector—from his information monopoly by increasing the number of relevant information providers which leads to a competitive information authority environment (Im et al. 2014).

Since non-state entities already tend to show network structures that empower individuals, favoring these organizations in terms of benefiting from the rapid development of information and communication technologies, in combination with the "[...] non-territorial nature of today's problems and solutions [...] [, this] strongly suggests that the relative power of states will continue to decline" (Mathews 1997). Thus, public authorities need to effectively deal with this transformational change to stay on top of it and not to lose touch with their citizens by actively and directly interacting with their stakeholders and rethink their role and delivery model within the digital world.

Globalization and the Knowledge Revolution

The globalizing world changes the way individuals and organizations communicate, collaborate, and compete. International cross-border business and available information and communication technologies flatten the world and form new, complex systems of interaction. The resulting knowledge revolution, which is mainly created through interconnected markets and databases as well as a large number of participants that are virtually linked together via information and communication technologies, forces the public sector to revise strategies, management, and operations to respond to increased citizen demands in a more dynamic economic environment (Milakovich 2012).

Demand Pressure

Moreover, governments and public sector organizations, which tend to show long processing times, lack of flexibility, and a focus on processes instead of results, face general demands of reducing costs and improve operations. The upcoming digital native generation demands better public service provision in terms of convenient access and interaction as well as ongoing personalization and customization possibilities. To relieve these growing pressures, they need to move away from traditional bureaucracy and move on to doing business that centers on the client: citizens as well as governmental and non-governmental organizations. This transition requires an uncomfortable shift, leaving behind long-standing public sector culture and work patterns, toward a novel business model that builds upon an open, transparent, and fast digital interaction between all parties involved (Brown et al. 2014).

Global Challenges

Apart from that, complex, interdependent global challenges, such as international conflicts, poverty, or inequality, require an increasingly effective collaboration across borders and across all layers of government as well as with non-governmental stakeholders. Thus, the public sector must provide a well-functioning public administration that delivers the services demanded by citizens and businesses, promotes citizen engagement, participation, and empowerment, and creates an environment that fosters a sustainable social, economic, and environmental future (United Nations 2014).

Companies such as Google, Amazon, or Facebook, which appeared a couple of years ago, have turned many ways of doing business inside out by creating new markets, new opportunities, and entirely new business models, as well as professionally delivering innovation and scalable user-oriented e-services with unprecedented speed. In this context, governments, formerly being among the earliest adopters and largest users of information technologies, could not keep up with the development pace of technology and network organizations since they are partly stuck in complicated and nowadays outdated automation processes (Brown et al. 2014), have difficulties to compete with the private sector in the war for talent, and are bound to rigid procurement procedures (Vélez-Rivera et al. 2008).

Legal Challenges

Although governments are basically forced to act on the digital advancement of public services, there still persist legal challenges, which complicate a smooth flow of this development, since the online provision of information may violate personal data rights and freedoms (O'Hara 2011), existing inconsistent legal frameworks and copyright obligations hinder data transparency (Goodspeed 2011), and incompatible policy-making may lead to incomplete data provision (Janssen et al. 2012).

This situation becomes even more difficult for governmental decision-makers since public provision of information always carries an additional risk of breaching confidentiality or security issues. Thus, governments and public authorities need to balance legal restrictions, transparency values, and data privacy (Goodspeed 2011).

Environmental Challenges

Governments are under growing pressure to consider environmental aspects within public policy-making and to elaborate governance measures and mechanisms that foster environmental protection and promote a sustainable management of natural resources. Furthermore, citizens demand an increase in environmental public service provision and an improvement of environmental stewardship. On the whole, the target is to achieve an environmentally sustainable future for next generations (United Nations 2014).

Taking into account this widespread need for action as well as the various levels involved that require improvement, namely "[...] people, process, technology, and governance" (Brown et al. 2014, p. 4), governments as well as the public sector need to undergo a severe transformation process. This is where the advancement of time and location-independent information and communication technologies, in the form of digital government, comes into play (Wirtz et al. 2017).

Advantages of Digital Government

Digital government promises to provide manifold game-changing advantages. It is supposed to ease access to public sector information and to make interaction with government and public institutions more convenient through online transactions, thus advancing public administration and transforming public service provision (Garson 2004; Welch et al. 2005). Moreover, by shifting the interaction focus from a provider to a user perspective, digital government shall extensively enhance public sector service orientation (Holzer 2004).

The concept embraces the idea of fostering internal efficiency, effectiveness, and productivity, and thus substantial digital government-related cost savings are expected (Parent et al. 2005). Increased accountability reflects citizens' demands for transparency and improves control over government bureaucracy (Ahn and Bretschneider 2011). Furthermore, digital government provides a toolset for e-democracy since the concept promotes knowledge sharing, participation, collaboration, and innovation.

In addition, digital government is expected to generate benefits for social inclusion, employment, health, and education, as well as to help governments to promote effective natural resource management (United Nations 2014). Finally, digital government is considered to have the power to renew the image of the government and the public sector (Ahn and Bretschneider 2011; Arellano-Gault 2012) and thus to strengthen citizen trust in the government (Chan et al. 2010; Im et al. 2014). The potential benefits of digital government are summarized in Figure 1.2.

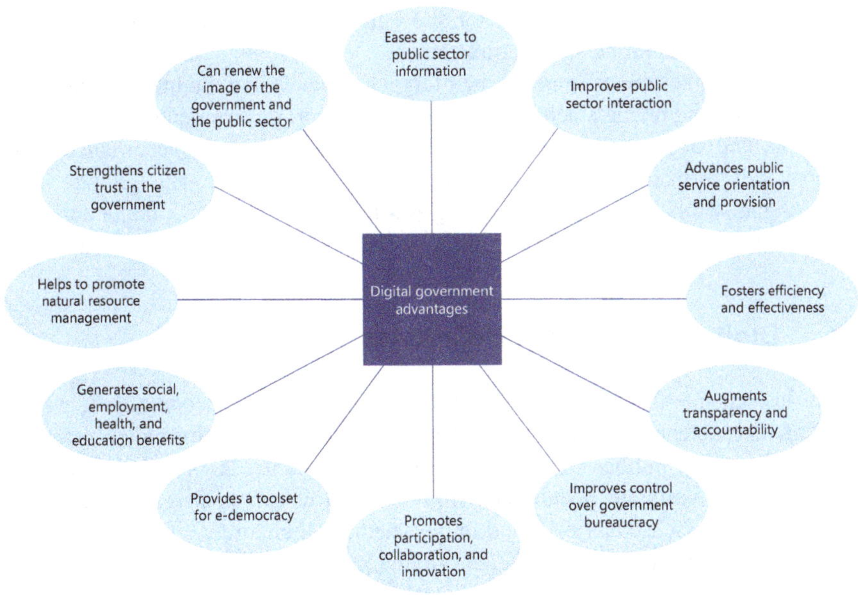

Fig. 1.2 Advantages of digital government. Source: Wirtz and Daiser (2015, 2017)

Digital Government Business Models

Thus, digital government is not just about digitizing existing bureaucratic processes. It should rather be seen as a transformation of digital business models onto the public sector and in terms of how governments operate. This new way of doing business is supposed to allow interactive access 24/7 via one-stop web portals (Garson 2004). These one-stop shop governmental websites are virtual portals that are an integral part of modern public service provision (Liu et al. 2010) and that are organized from a user-oriented perspective, bundling relevant information for citizen–government, business–government, employee–government, or government–government interaction.

This approach represents a major improvement in the provision of government services, since before, citizens often needed to address various agencies for solving different requests. In a worst-case scenario, they also had to show up in person in every agency, making access to public services a time-consuming activity (Milakovich 2012). In this respect, digital government tries to put people online instead of in line (Schellong 2009).

Challenges of Digital Government Implementation

But despite its extensive expected benefits, digital government is still in an emerging state and its full potential has not been developed yet (Arellano-Gault 2012; United Nations 2014). Apart from that, public sector officials face difficulties that arise from the implementation of new technologies (Arellano-Gault 2012). Furthermore, since the private sector and the public sector show inherent differences, existing digital business models cannot be simply transferred.

While companies concentrate on their target customers and the market automatically penalizes and rewards actions in the private sector, governments have to serve all people and organizations and deal with coercive actions in accordance with political will formation within a heterogeneous society (Veit and Huntgeburth 2014). Against this background, digital government has become a major topic of interest to science and public management (Bélanger and Carter 2012).

1.2 Digital Government Definitions

Up to now an interdisciplinary body of knowledge has been accumulated, which covers diverse scientific fields such as business administration, information systems, communication, or public management (Arduini and Zanfei 2014). Since different areas tend to investigate phenomena from contrasting perspectives, quite a few explanation approaches can be found in the scientific literature.

In the E-Government Act of 2002, the 107th Congress explained e-government as "[...] using Internet-based information technology to enhance citizen access to Government information and services, and for other purposes" (107th Congress 2002, p. 2899).

Since the year 2002, the number of e-government and digital government definitions has significantly increased in the literature. Due to the growing integration of new digital technology concepts, in particular IoT, AI, big data, and cloud computing, the term digital government has become more and more appropriate and common in recent years. Table 1.1 depicts selected definitions that illustrate the different priorities regarding digital government.

Table 1.1 Selected definitions of digital government/e-government

Author(s)	Definition
Silcock (2001)	Simply stated, e-Government is the use of technology to enhance the access to and delivery of government services to benefit citizens, business partners and employees
UNDPEPA and ASPA (2002)	[. . .] E-government is defined as: utilizing the internet and the world-wide-web for delivering government information and services to citizens
Carter and Bélanger (2005)	[. . .] the use of information technology to enable and improve the efficiency with which government services are provided to citizens, employees, business and agencies
Heeks (2005)	[. . .] E-government in a broad sense: all use of information technology in the public sector. It covers a broad range of managerial issues: from high-level strategy to detailed tactics; from the technicalities of data flows and process mapping to the politics of e-government
Evans and Yen (2006)	Simply speaking, E-Government means the communication between the government and its citizens via computers and a Web-enabled presence. The advantages in timeliness, responsiveness, and cost containment are outstanding
Spirakis et al. (2010)	Electronic government is the use of Information and Communication Technology in the transformation of government; primarily aiming to the improvement of accessibility, effectiveness and responsibility. It is based on the diffusion of the information and the information policy development. Electronic government guides to increasing citizens' participation and active citizens' development affecting the mechanisms of democracy
Veit and Huntgeburth (2014)	Digital government is defined as the use of Information and Communication Technologies (ICT), in particular the internet, to transform the relationship between government and society in a positive manner
Yavwa and Twinomurinzi (2019)	Digital government is defined as a socio-technical phenomenon or mechanism by which governments provide efficient services using ICT in a seamless and interfaced manner
Twizeyimana and Andersson (2019)	e-Government is commonly conceptualized as governments' use of Information and Communication Technologies (ICTs) combined with organizational change to improve the structures and operations of government

Source: Wirtz and Daiser (2015, 2017)

Range Differences of Digital Government Definitions

Although the definitions head in a similar direction and demonstrate common points, they show differences in scope, subject, and technology, too (see Table 1.2). While UNDPEPA and ASPA (2002) see e-government as a tool for information and service provision to citizens, Spirakis et al. (2010) link participation, development, and democracy mechanisms with this topic and, e.g., Carter and Bélanger (2005) bring employees, businesses, and agencies on board.

Table 1.2 Range differences of digital government definitions

	Minimum range	Maximum range
Scope	Information and service delivery	Enabler for e-democracy
Subject	Citizen	All public sector stakeholders
Technology	Computer and web presence	Internet

Source: Wirtz and Daiser (2015, 2017)

Evans and Yen (2006) define computers and a web-enabled presence as sufficient technology, while most speak of information and communication technologies (Carter and Bélanger 2005; Heeks 2005; Spirakis et al. 2010; Veit and Huntgeburth 2014; Yavwa and Twinomurinzi 2019; Twizeyimana and Andersson 2019) or the Internet (UNDPEPA and ASPA 2002). In this context, Silcock (2001) mentions technology in general without specifying this more precisely.

Veit and Huntgeburth (2014) stress the positive outcome of digital government for the relationship between government and society. By Yavwa and Twinomurinzi (2019) digital government is seen as a socio-technical phenomenon. The desired improvement of structures and operation of government is in the focus of the definition by Twizeyimana and Andersson (2019).

Similarities of Digital Government Definitions

However, there are similarities that are in line with the majority of the definitions. First, a technology-enabled government is assumed. Second, information and services are provided online and unattended to government or public sector stakeholders. Third, accessibility, accountability, efficiency, effectiveness, and government–stakeholder interaction are positively influenced. Before exemplifying the use of the term digital government in this book, we first have to differentiate it from e-governance/digital governance since these terms are sometimes used synonymously, even though they do not mean the same (Saxena 2005).

E-governance[2] refers to a technology-driven administration and control system of formal and informal arrangements to enhance governance structures and/or processes as well as to guide and confine collective activities (Bannister and Connolly 2012; Vig 2012). Therefore, "[…] e-government constitutes only a subset (though a major one) of e-governance" (Saxena 2005, p. 3).

[2] "E-Governance is the use of information and communication technologies (ICTs) in government in ways that (1) alter governance structures or processes in ways that are not feasible without ICT and/or (2) create new governance structures or processes that were heretofore not possible without ICT and/or (3) reify heretofore theoretical ideas or issues in normative governance" (Bannister and Connolly 2012, p. 11).

Definition of Digital Government

Accordingly, digital government constitutes a technology-enabled part of the government or public sector governance model that allows unattended public stakeholder access to information and services, improves government–stakeholder interaction, fosters accountability, efficiency, and effectiveness, and forms the basis for e-democracy from a technological point of view. Thus, we apply the following definition throughout the book in accordance with Wirtz and Piehler (2010):

Definition of Digital Government (Wirtz and Piehler 2010; Wirtz and Daiser 2015; Wirtz 2020)
The term digital government describes the electronic handling of administration and democracy processes in the context of governmental activities by means of information and communication technologies to support public duties efficiently and effectively.

1.3 Aim and Structure of the Book

To start off, we would like to point out that this book is not the Holy Grail to digital government offering all the answers to all remaining questions. We rather present a custom-tailored overview of the current state of digital government for science, education, governments, public administration, and public management.

Aim of the Textbook

The aim of this work is thus to collect and summarize our experiences and state-of-the-art knowledge from these fields of activities to establish a sound knowledge base for academics and practitioners alike.

As laid out in the previous pages, digital government is a topic of paramount importance because it affects many facets of our private and professional lives as digital government applications have already become an important interface for citizen–government interaction (Wirtz et al. 2015). Moreover, the related scientific discourse shows solid optimism about its usefulness and potential for public administration (Bekkers and Homburg 2007), which suggests that a further intensification of digital public interaction can be expected. However, its path is not finally laid out yet, and thus, scientists as well as public managers need to be open to new findings and experiences and stay curious about its development to actively shape the future digital government.

In this context, we intend to make a valuable academic and managerial contribution by providing fundamental aspects of digital government to teachers and students and by creating a firm foundation for development, implementation, and operation of digital government, as well as advancing related knowledge and forthcoming research.

Structure of the Textbook

This textbook is divided into four parts: Part I contains the first four chapters and introduces the topic of digital government. The next chapter presents a comprehensive overview of the foundations of digital government by first referring to the principles and the development of the information society and, second, providing an overview of the evolution of digital government. Chapter 3 outlines the concept and strategy of digital government by presenting the Four Forces Model of Digital Government, the E-Government Value Activity System (EVAS), as well as vital strategic management aspects. A brief excursion on open government versus digital government closes the chapter. Chapter 4 investigates the digital transformation as a macro-oriented phenomenon and explains digital leadership and digital teams as two disruptive implications on the organizational level.

Part II refers to the underlying technology, smart cities, and digital government business models and covers Chapters 5–9. Chapter 5 deals with the basics of digital business technology, technology at the human–machine interface, and security in digital government. Chapter 6 examines the concept of artificial intelligence, big data, cloud computing, and the Internet of Things. Interrelationships between the concepts are addressed. Chapter 7 examines social media and the issue of digital disinformation. Relevant success factors in social media and the digital government potential of various social media tools are presented.

Chapter 8 provides information on the smart city concept, explaining the smart city ecosystem, as well as the services and user structure of smart cities. Subsequently, Chapter 9 deals with digital government business models, illustrating conceptual, process-related, and implementation-related facets of the concept.

Part III contains information on digital government services, channels, and implementation aspects, covering Chapters 10–14. The user-oriented aspects of digital government are presented in Chapter 10. Here, we illustrate demand as well as service preferences from a user perspective. Chapter 11 presents the basics of digital government services, including government-to-citizen services, as well as government-to-business services.

Thereafter, Chapter 12 deals with multichannel e-service delivery and is followed by Chapter 13, which explains the success factors of digital government. Chapter 14 presents the 10 steps of digital government implementation and concludes with the monitoring and audit, as well as with targets of digital government implementation.

Part IV contains Chapters 15 and 16. In Chapter 15, three case studies of the digital government portal offerings of Hong Kong, London, and New York are outlined, representing three top-tier city websites that serve as first-mover examples. Chapter 16 provides an outlook on future developments related to digitization and digital government. Figure 1.3 shows the content structure of this textbook.

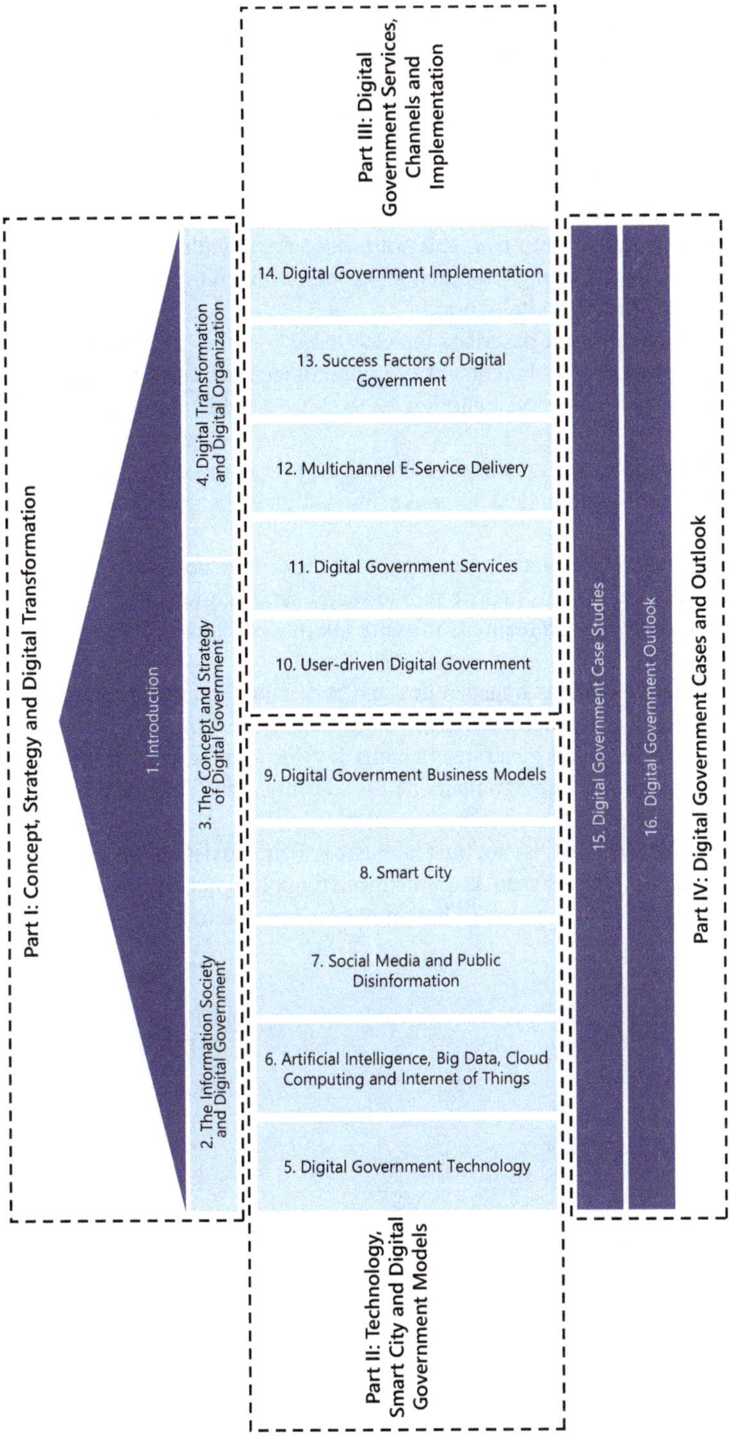

Fig. 1.3 Structure of the textbook

1.4 Summary, Review Questions, Topics for Discussion, and Online Exercises

- A key reason for the importance of digital government is the growing influence of the Internet as a global networking and communication system.
- The Internet is a profound technology to interact and collaborate with all kinds of public stakeholders. Public authorities need to effectively deal with this transformational change to stay on top of it and not to lose touch with their citizens by actively and directly interacting with their stakeholders and rethink their role and delivery model within the digital world.
- The term digital government describes the electronic handling of administration and democracy processes in the context of governmental activities by means of information and communication technologies to support public duties efficiently and effectively.
- Digital government promises manifold advantages. It is supposed to ease access to public sector information and to make interaction with government more convenient.
- By shifting the interaction focus from a provider to a user perspective, digital government shall extensively enhance public sector service orientation.
- The concept of digital government also fosters internal efficiency, effectiveness, and productivity.
- Digital government augments transparency and accountability. It improves control over government bureaucracy. Furthermore, digital government provides a toolset for e-democracy and generates benefits for social inclusion, health, and education. Thus, digital government helps to strengthen citizen trust in government.
- Finally, digital government is not just about digitizing existing bureaucratic processes. It should rather be seen as a transformation of digital business models onto the public sector and in terms of how governments operate.

Chapter 1
Review questions, topics for discussion and online exercises

Review questions

1. Describe the major changes that have been caused by the worldwide use of the Internet.
2. Explain the importance of modern information and communication technologies for governments and public administrations.
3. Describe the advantages of digital government.
4. Define digital government.
5. Describe the range differences of digital government definitions.

Topics for classroom discussion and team debates

1. Discuss the advantages and disadvantages of digital government for your city.
2. Discuss to what extent excellent digital government is important for the development of the information society.
3. Discuss the relevance of digital government for the international competitiveness of states in global competition.

Online Exercises

1. Visit your local digital government website (city website) and explore the structure of the site.
2. Visit www.un.org and explore the different content and service offerings.
3. Compare the offerings of www.un.org and your city's website. What are the differences in content and services (goals, target groups)?

References

107th Congress (2002): E-Government Act of 2002. Public Law 107–347. Available online at http://www.gpo.gov/fdsys/pkg/PLAW-107publ347/pdf/PLAW-107publ347.pdf, checked on 3/11/2015.

Ahn, Michael J.; Bretschneider, Stuart (2011): Politics of E-Government: E-Government and the Political Control of Bureaucracy. In Public Administration Review 71 (3), pp. 414–424.

Arduini, Davide; Zanfei, Antonello (2014): An overview of scholarly research on public e-services? A meta-analysis of the literature. In Special issue on: Selected papers from the 10th Conference in Telecommunications, Media and Internet Techno-economics Special issue on : The development of public e-services: Empirical analysis and policy issues 38 (5–6), pp. 476–495.

Arellano-Gault, David (2012): The Evaluation of Performance in the Mexican Federal Government: A Study of the Monitoring Agencies' Modernization Process. In Public Administration Review 72 (1), pp. 135–142.

Bannister, Frank; Connolly, Regina (2012): Defining e-Governance. In e-Service Journal 8 (2), pp. 3–25.

Bekkers, Victor; Homburg, Vincent (2007): The Myths of E-Government: Looking Beyond the Assumptions of a New and Better Government. In The Information Society 23 (5), pp. 373–382.

Bélanger, France; Carter, Lemuria (2012): Digitizing Government Interactions with Constituents: An Historical Review of E-Government Research in Information Systems. In Journal of the Association for Information Systems 13 (5), pp. 363–394.

Brown, Alan W.; Thompson, Mark; Fishenden, Jerry (2014): Digitizing Government. Understanding and Implementing New Digital Business Models. Basingstoke: Palgrave Macmillan (Business in the digital economy).

Carter, Lemuria; Bélanger, France (2005): The utilization of e-government services: citizen trust, innovation and acceptance factors. In Information Systems Journal 15 (1), pp. 5–25.

Chan, Frank K. Y.; Brown, Susan A.; Thong, James Y. L.; Venkatesh, Viswanath; Kar, Yan T.; Jen-Hwa Hu, Paul (2010): Modeling Citizen Satisfaction with Mandatory Adoption of an E-Government Technology. In Journal of the Association for Information Systems 11 (10), pp. 519–549.

Chen, Peter; Gibson, Rachel; Geiselhart, Karin (2006): Electronic Democracy? The Impact of New Communications Technologies on Australian Democracy. for the Democratic Audit of Australia. Political Science Program. Report No. 6. Edited by The Australian National University. Available online at https://www.academia.edu/1396007/Electronic_Democracy_The_Impact_of_New_Communications_Technologies_on_Australian_Democracy.

Dawes, Sharon S. (2008): The Evolution and Continuing Challenges of E-Governance. In Public Administration Review 68 (Supplement 1), pp. 86–102.

Denger, Katharina S.; Wirtz, Bernd W. (1995): Die digitale Revolution. In Gablers Magazin 9 (3), pp. 455 20–24.

Evans, Donna; Yen, David C. (2006): E-Government: Evolving relationship of citizens and government, domestic, and international development. In Government Information Quarterly 23 (2), pp. 207–235.

Garson, G. David (2004): The Promise of Digital Government. In Alexei Pavlichev, G. David Garson (Eds.): Digital Government. Principles and Best Practices. Hershey: Idea Group Pub., pp. 2–15.

Goodspeed, Robert (2011): From Public Records to Open Government: Access to Massachusetts Municipal Geographic Data. In Journal of the Urban & Regional Information Systems Association 23 (2), pp. 21–32.

Heeks, Richard (2005): Implementing and Managing eGovernment. An International Text. London: Sage.

Holzer, Marc (2004): Restoring Trust in Government: The Potential of Digital Citizen Participaton. In Marc Holzer, Mengzhong Zhang, Keyong Dong (Eds.): Frontiers of Public Administration. Proceedings of the Second Sino-U.S. International Conference: "Public Administration in the Changing World". Beijing, China, May 24-25, 2004. New York, Washington: The United Nations Public Administration Network, The American Society for Public Administration, pp. 6–24.

Im, Tobin; Cho, Wonhyuk; Porumbescu, Greg; Park, Jungho (2014): Internet, Trust in Government, and Citizen Compliance. In Journal of Public Administration Research and Theory 24 (3), pp. 741–763.

ISC (2019): Internet Domain Survey, January, 2019. Available online at https://downloads.isc.org/www/survey/reports/current/, checked on 6/1/2021.

Janssen, Marijn; Charalabidis, Yannis; Zuiderwijk, Anneke (2012): Benefits, Adoption Barriers and Myths of Open Data and Open Government. In Information Systems Management 29 (4), pp. 258–268.

Liu, Yuan; Chen, Xi; Wang, Xiaoyi (2010): Evaluating Government Portal Websites in China. PACIS 2010 Proceedings. Paper 88. Available online at http://aisel.aisnet.org/pacis2010/88, checked on 12/13/2012.

Mathews, Jessica T. (1997): Power shift. In Foreign Affairs 76 (1), pp. 50–66.

Milakovich, Michael E. (2012): Digital Governance. New Technologies for Improving Public Service and Participation. New York: Routledge.

O'Hara, Kieron (2011): Transparent government, not transparent citizens: a report on privacy and transparency for the Cabinet Office. London: Cabinet Office, pp. 1–84. Available online at https://assets.publishing.service.gov.uk/government/uploads/system/uploads/attachment_data/file/61279/transparency-and-privacy-review-annex-a.pdf.

Parent, Michael; Vandebeek, Christine A.; Gemino, Andrew C. (2005): Building citizen trust through e-government. In Government Information Quarterly 22 (4), pp. 720–736.

Saxena, K. B.C. (2005): Towards excellence in e-governance. In International Journal of Public Sector Management 18 (6), pp. 498–513.

Schellong, Alexander (2009): Citizen Government Interaction: The Promise of the E-Channel. In Albert Meijer, Kees Boersma, Pieter Wagenaar (Eds.): ICTs, Citizens and Governance: After the Hype! Amsterdam: IOS Press, pp. 13–20.

Silcock, Rachel (2001): What is E-government. In Parliamentary Affairs 54 (1), pp. 88–101.

Spirakis, Grigorios; Spiraki, Christina; Nikolopoulos, Konstantinos (2010): The impact of electronic government on democracy: e-democracy through e-participation. In Electronic Government, an International Journal 7 (1), pp. 75–88.

Twizeyimana, Jean Damascene; Andersson, Annika (2019): The public value of E-Government – A literature review. In Government Information Quarterly 36 (2), pp. 167–178. DOI: https://doi.org/10.1016/j.giq.2019.01.001.

UNDPEPA; ASPA (2002): Benchmarking E-government: A Global Perspective. Assessing the Progress of the UN Member States. With assistance of Stephen A. Ronaghan. Edited by United Nations Division for Public Economics and Public Administration (UNDPEPA), American Society for Public Administration (ASPA). United Nations. New York. Available online at http://unpan3.un.org/egovkb/Portals/egovkb/Documents/un/English.pdf, updated on 2002, checked on 3/11/2015.

United Nations (2014): United Nations E-Government Survey 2014. E-Government for the Future We Want. With assistance of Department of Economic and Social Affairs. New York. Available online at http://unpan3.un.org/egovkb/Portals/egovkb/Documents/un/2014-Survey/E-Gov_Complete_Survey-2014.pdf, checked on 12/1/2014.

Veit, Daniel; Huntgeburth, Jan (2014): Foundations of Digital Government. Leading and Managing in the Digital Era. Berlin, Heidelberg: Springer (Springer texts in business and economics).

Vélez-Rivera, Bienvenido; Fernández-Sein, Rafael; Rodríguez-Martínez, Manuel; Rivera-Vega, Pedro I.; Díaz, Walter; Núñez-Molina, Mario (2008): Multidisciplinary e-government research and education as a catalyst for effective information technology transfer to regional governments. In Hsinchun Chen (Ed.): Digital Government. E-government Research, Case Studies and Implementation. Berlin: Springer (Integrated series in information systems, 17), pp. 671–695.

Vig, Shinu (2012): Ensuring Better Corporate Governance Through E-Governance. In International Journal of Marketing, Financial Services & Management Research 1 (9), pp. 188–194.

Welch, Eric W.; Hinnant, Charles C.; Moon, Jae M. (2005): Linking Citizen Satisfaction with E-Government and Trust in Government. In Journal of Public Administration Research and Theory 15 (3), pp. 371–391.

Wirtz, Bernd W. (2020): Electronic Business. 7th ed. Wiesbaden: Springer Gabler.

Wirtz, Bernd W. (2022): E-Government. Wiesbaden: Springer Gabler.

Wirtz, Bernd W.; Daiser, Peter (2015): E-Government. Strategy, process, instruments. 1st ed. Speyer.

Wirtz, Bernd W.; Daiser, Peter (2017): E-government. Strategy, process, instruments. 2nd ed. Speyer.

Wirtz, Bernd W.; Daiser, Peter (2018): A meta-analysis of empirical e-government research and its future research implications. Online first 09 July 2016. In International Review of Administrative Sciences 84 (1), pp. 144–163. DOI: https://doi.org/10.1177/0020852315599047.

Wirtz, Bernd W.; Mory, Linda; Piehler, Robert; Daiser, Peter (2014): Measuring eGovernment portal management on the local level: Results from a survey of public administration officials. In International Public Management Review 15 (2), pp. 1–31.

Wirtz, Bernd W.; Piehler, Robert (2010): E-Government. In Bernd W. Wirtz (Ed.): E-Government. Grundlagen, Instrumente, Strategien. 1st ed. Wiesbaden: Gabler, pp. 3–18.

Wirtz, Bernd W.; Piehler, Robert; Daiser, Peter (2015): E-government portal characteristics and individual appeal: An examination of E-government and citizen acceptance in the context of local administration portals. In Journal of Nonprofit & Public Sector Marketing 27 (1), pp. 70–98.

Wirtz, Bernd W.; Ullrich, Sebastian; Mory, Linda (2012): EHealth in the public sector: An empirical analysis of the acceptance of Germany's electronic health card. In Public Administration 90 (3), pp. 642–663.

Wirtz, Bernd W.; Vogt, Patrick; Denger, Katharina S. (2001): Electronic Business in der Versicherungswirtschaft. In Zeitschrift für die gesamte Versicherungswirtschaft 90 (1), pp. 161–190.

Wirtz, Bernd W.; Weyerer, Jan C.; Thomas, Marc-Julian; Möller, Anke (2017): E-government implementation. Theoretical aspects and empirical evidence. In Public Organization Review 17, pp. 101–120.

Yavwa, Y.; Twinomurinzi, H. (2019): The moderating effect of spirituality on digital government in low-income countries: A case of SMEs in Zambia. In Proceedings Annual Workshop of the AIS Special Interest Group for ICT in Global Development (12), pp. 1–25.

The Information Society and Digital Government

2

Contents

Learning Objectives
By working through this chapter, you will be able to:

1. Describe the development of information and communication technology.
2. Explain Kondratieff waves and their underlying principle.
3. Explain the ICT Development Index.
4. List the most important E-Government/Digital Government Acts.
5. Name the World E-Government Leaders.

The innovation in information and communication technology and the resulting advent of the Internet were strong drivers for moving from an industrial to an information society.[1] So far, "technological innovations have always shaped the development of economy and society. The digital age, also called digital revolution, which was initiated through the development of the multimedia market leads to a fundamental change of existing structures in the telecommunications, computing, entertainment, and media industry" (Denger and Wirtz 1995, p. 20). This early assessment of 1995 clearly illustrates the far-reaching impact of digitization.

[1] See for Chapter 2 The Information Society and Digital Government also Wirtz (2013, 2019, 2020, 2021, 2022); Wirtz and Daiser (2015, 2017).

B. W. Wirtz, *Digital Government*, Springer Texts in Business and Economics,
https://doi.org/10.1007/978-3-031-13086-1_2

2.1 The Development of Information and Communication Technologies

To understand the underlying evolution of the information society, we have to take a look at the information and communication technology development over the past 50 years. The development from 1966 to 1994 is illustrated in Figure 2.1 on the following page.

Development of Information and Communication Technology Until 1994

In 1966, IBM introduced the Disk Operating System (DOS/360) for its mainframes. This was the first system that allowed batch processing (executing a series of function commands or programs without rebooting the mainframe or other manual intervention). Only three years later, Paul Baran and Donald Watts created ARPANET, the ancestor of the Internet. This was followed by another milestone in the development of information and communication technologies, the intervention of the microprocessor by Intel.

Based on these previous steps, IBM introduced the first personal computer and Motorola presented the first commercial mobile phone. These were the main technological breakthroughs that enabled the development of interconnected information and communication technologies that we know today.

Given the first network technologies and users, who possessed the necessary hard- and software, information technology in general gained more and more commercial interest. In this context, Microsoft released Windows 1.0, a user-friendly operating system that applied a graphical instead of command line interface, to conquer the personal computer market. At the same time, Steve Case founded Quantum Computer Services, which was renamed to America Online (AOL) three years later, and around the year 2000 was the world's largest Internet provider possessing more than 30,000,000 paying customers.

With the beginning of the World Wide Web in 1989, the starting point of interconnected networks was set and the digitalization trend picked up speed. Big enterprises, such as SAP releasing SAP/R3 in 1993, had to react to provide network-compatible software, and young entrepreneurs like Jeff Bezos, who founded amazon.com in 1994, were first movers in the Internet and digital business world.

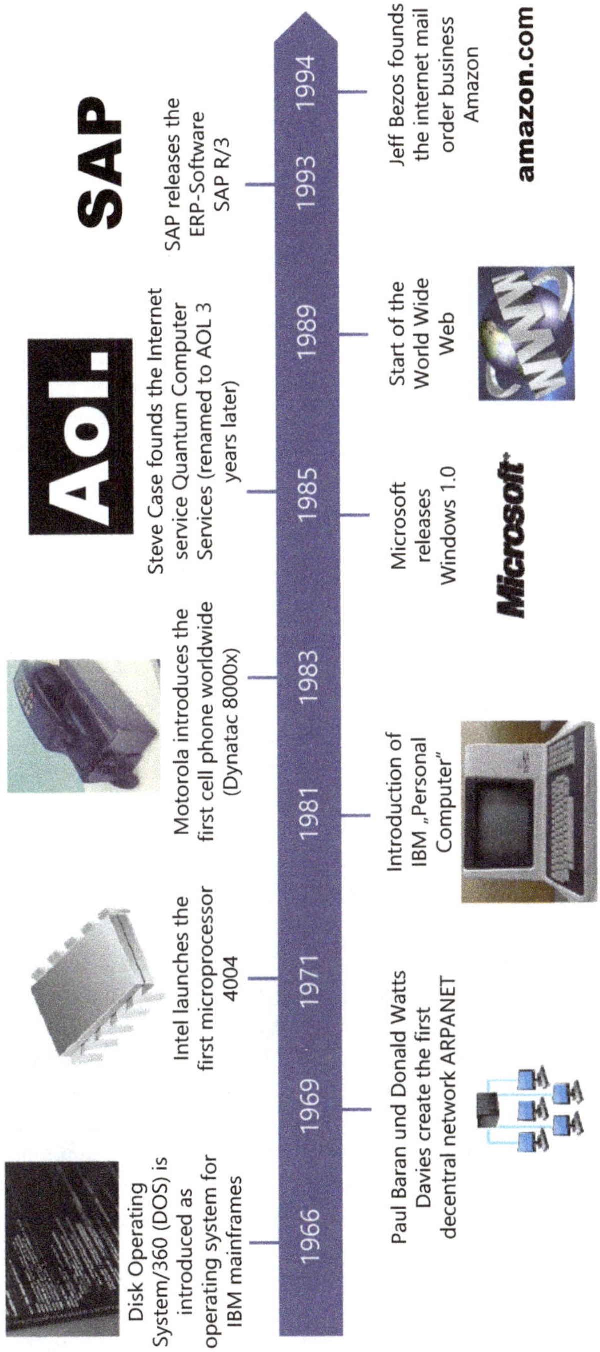

Fig. 2.1 Development of information and communication applications (1966 until 1994). Source: Wirtz (2013, 2021)

Development of Information and Communication Technology Until 2021

A year after the establishment of amazon.com, eBay Inc. was founded by Pierre Omidyar and quickly became the largest online marketplace for private and commercial traders. As people started to use the Internet more intensively, the demand for online mobility increased, too. Thus, in 1996 Nokia introduced the first smartphone, which up to now has become a commodity in the mobile phone market.

In the year 1998, Lawrence Edward Page and Sergey Brin founded the Internet service provider Google Inc. and offered a far-reaching search engine with the same name. In 1999, AT&T started to market broadband in the USA and thus enabled high data transmission rates. The organization launched its service including digital subscriber line (DSL), cable modem, and wireless Internet access for corporate customers. Since the end of the 1990s, the information society has significantly gained in importance, particularly due to the development of the Internet economy.

Therefore, changes in the competitive marketplace and economic conditions resulted in numerous foundations of dotcom companies since the year 1998. This trend has been supported by the further development of mobile networks and the ubiquitous diffusion of the Internet. For instance, the implementation of the first UMTS network at the Isle of Man by the local organization Manx Telecom in 2001 was an essential milestone for the mobile information and communication technologies.

Rise of New Online Services

Ongoing technological progress led to increasing bandwidth and thus a continuing rise in data transmission rates, which allowed the provision of new online services, such as music or video distribution. An important cornerstone in online music distribution, for example, represents the media library and player iTunes, which was released in 2001 and soon became the leading portal in digital music marketing. Moreover, completely new services like Facebook, an online social network, were suddenly realizable.

In the year 2006, AT&T launched their brand U-verse, offering triple-play telecommunications services in 21 states of the USA and using the FTTP, VDSL, and ADSL communication protocols. Already in the year 2009, the Swedish organization TeliaSonera put the first commercial LTE network in Stockholm and Oslo into operation. In 2016, Oculus VR launched its virtual reality headset for customers and Samsung launched the Galaxy S8 smartphone.

In 2021, IBM and Fraunhofer inaugurated IBM Quantum System One, which is currently the most powerful quantum computer in Europe. Figure 2.2 shows the development of information and communication applications from 1995 until 2019.

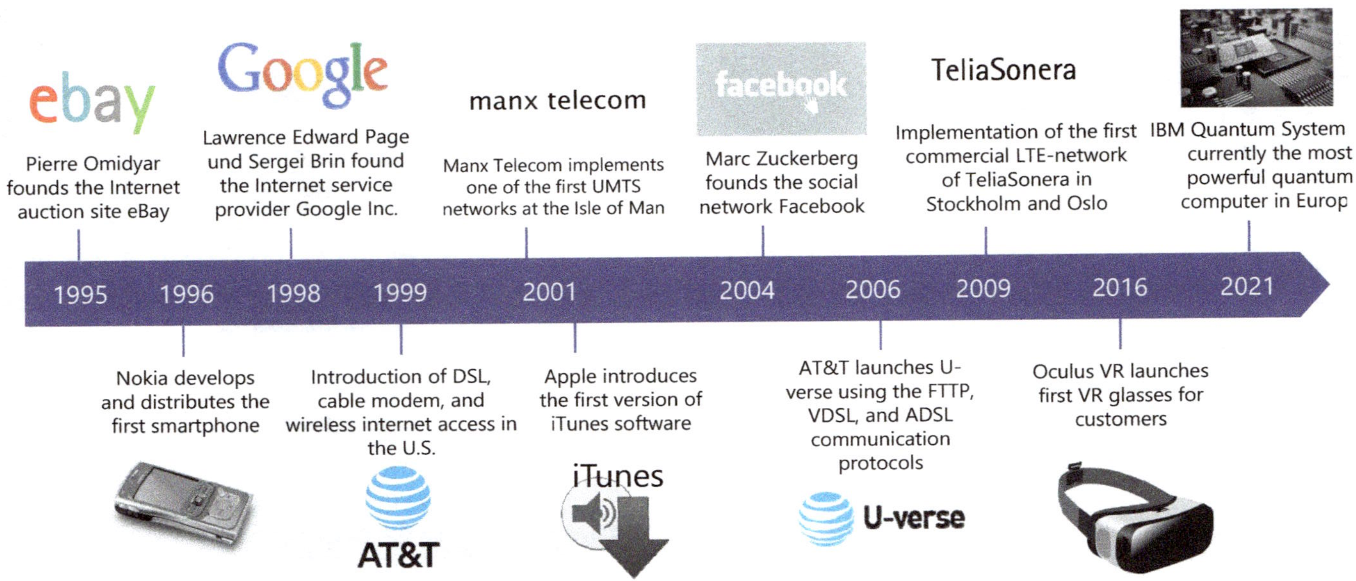

Fig. 2.2 Development of information and communication applications (1995 until 2021). Source: Wirtz (2013, 2021)

So far, wired as well as wireless Internet connections are constantly becoming faster, enhancing online service provision at home and on the way. In the USA, for instance, the T1 cable was introduced in 1956. Then in 1978 ISDN revolutionized communication and in 1993 ADSL and in 1995 VDSL again brought along major breakthroughs in online data transmission. About ten years later, the VDSL2 standard (G.993.2), which promised increased speed and better performance, was defined, and in 2009, the first LTE networks were put into commercial operation.

Rise of the Internet

These information and communication technology developments provided the technological basis for the global system of interconnected computer networks called Internet, which in 2021 already showed more than 5.1 billion users. Figure 2.3 illustrates recent worldwide Internet usage and population statistics.

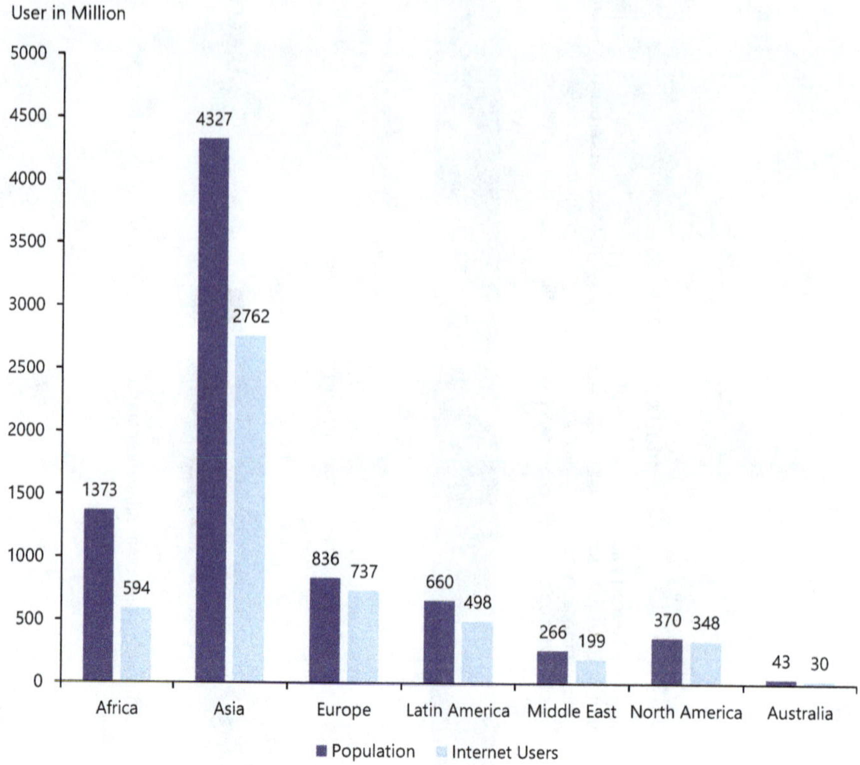

Fig. 2.3 Worldwide Internet usage and population statistics. Data source: Internet World Stats (2021)

This means that already six out of ten people worldwide use the Internet. The respective development and diffusion of modern information and communication technologies as well as the respective repositioning and use of these technologies were key drivers for moving from an industrial to an information society.

2.2 The Information Society and Its Development

Conducting a title search for "information society" in the Social Science Citation Index shows that the topic is of academic interest since the 1980s and that peaks can be identified in 1983, briefly after the introduction of the first personal computer, and around the introduction of the Apple Macintosh in 1984 as well as from 1995 to 1997 when the World Wide Web started to gain popularity (Fuchs 2013). Thus, with personal computers becoming a commodity and the advent of the Internet, the concept of the information society received increasing attention.

Characteristics of the Information Society

Manuel Castells, who is one of the leading authors of this topic (Homburg 2008), summarizes that the world entered a new technological paradigm by making use of globally networked information and communication technologies. This is a key reason for a set of related social transformations that have taken place all around the world during the past three decades. Although these transformations partly have taken distinct forms and show different manifestations due to varying cultural and historical characteristics, they nowadays fundamentally affect a vast majority of societies. However, what has changed is not the role of knowledge or information since these factors have always been playing an important role in societies, but rather the availability and application of new information and communication technology[2] (Castells 2000). According to Castells (2000), this new economy we are living in is characterized by the following three features:

1. It is informational, meaning that information management and knowledge creation capacities are main determinants for competitiveness for all economic participants.
2. It is global, in the sense that economic units can communicate and coordinate their strategic and operative activities in real time on a global scale.
3. It is networked, meaning that economic units are interconnected, which allows the network enterprise[3] to develop a new form of organization.

Kondratieff Waves

The underlying principle of the shift from an industrial to an information society can be partly explained when looking at the Kondratieff waves, also called supercycles or K-waves (Denger and Wirtz 1995). Figure 2.4 illustrates the concept of the Kondratieff waves (content based on Nefiodow and Nefiodow (2014)).

[2]For this reason, Castells later refers to the term network society since information society may be misguiding (Castells 2000).

[3]A network enterprise "[...] is a network made from either firms or segments of firms, and/or from internal segmentation of firms. [...] These networks connect among themselves on specific business projects, and switch to another network as soon as the project is finished" (Castells 2000, pp. 10–11).

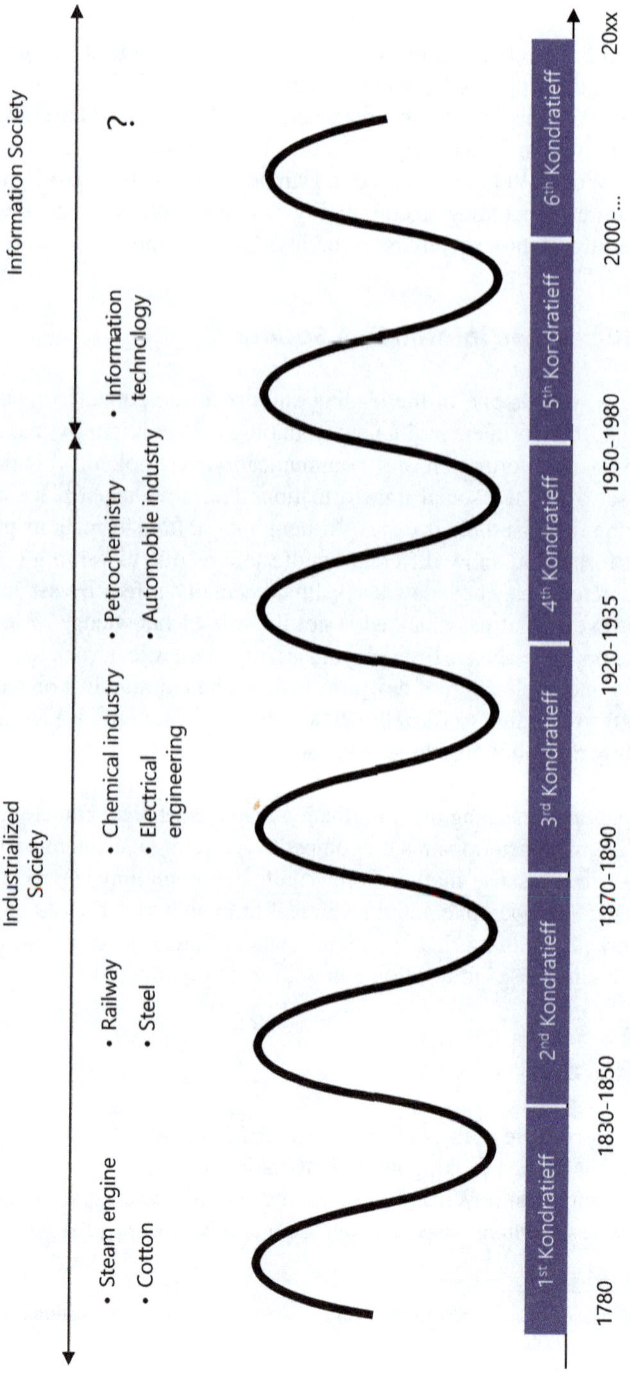

Fig. 2.4 The development of a technological revolution. Source: Wirtz (2019, 2020, 2021)

According to Kondratieff, technological innovations essentially determine the status of societal development through sinusoidal innovation phases (Schumpeter 1939). Innovations such as the steam engine open up new economic opportunities, which are reflected in an increase in investment. As soon as innovation has established itself in society and industry, the associated investments decrease considerably. At this stage, however, pioneers are already developing the next technological advance (e.g., railways) for a further investment boost. This change, currently induced by the dynamics of the development of information and communication technology, is an important driver of the evolution toward an information society.

2.3 Digital Government Development

Applying new information and communication technologies to the public sector environment promised to enhance public administration productivity and to satisfy citizen demands for online information and service provision. This was the starting point for an increasing integration of these technologies into governance systems and processes and public authorities began to digitally provide information and services to citizens and businesses.

This novel form of service provision was called electronic government, e-government, or digital government that—based on its innovative nature and expected potential—quickly received increasing attention in public administration and management practice as well as in science (Dawes 2009). In the following section, we outline its progress in practice and examine its development in different countries.

Digital Government in Practice

In the USA, the High Performance Computing Act of 1991 (HPCA) laid the initial groundwork for making developments like digital government possible and led to the elaboration of the National Information Infrastructure (NII), which was proclaimed in the Agenda for Action of the Clinton Administration (Department of Commerce 1993). Until that time, information and communication policy did not play a major role in US-internal politics (Kleinsteuber 2012).

However, in 1993 the American government started to build up the so-called information superhighway, changing the conditions and the relation between politics, media, and the public. With this initiative, the USA started to make collective, nationwide use of then novel information and communications technologies and popularized as well as commercialized digital networks (Rosenbach 2012).

US E-Government Interagency Taskforce

A major digital government breakthrough from an implementation perspective happened in 2001. The Office of Management and Budget Director Mitchell

E. Daniels initiated an e-government interagency taskforce to elaborate an action plan for implementing the e-government vision as advised by the President.

The e-government taskforce identified 25 high-payoff, nationwide projects with an estimated savings potential of several billion dollars. However, these were not supposed to be exhaustive, but would rather grow or be modified with increasing implementation and degree of maturity.

The projects were allocated to five areas: (1) government-to-citizen, e.g., elaboration of one-stop portals, (2) government-to-business, e.g., e-tax, (3) government-to-government, e.g., disaster assistance and crisis response, (4) internal efficiency and effectiveness, e.g., e-payroll or e-training, and (5) cross-cutting initiatives addressing barriers to digital government success, e.g., as e-authentication. The respective projects came under the responsibilities of competent agencies, such as the Department of Interior, Treasury/IRS, Labor, Education, which performed their role as project managing partner (Forman 2002).

US E-Government Act

On December 17, 2002, the E-Government Act of 2002 was enacted. Its main purposes were the improvement of management and promotion of public online service provision as well as the establishment of a Federal Chief Information Officer within the Office of Management and Budget. It represents the political and legal foundation for all following e-government initiatives in the USA.

In 2009, President Barack Obama signed the Memorandum for the Heads of Executive Departments and Agencies on Transparency and Open Government. In this document, he proclaims a political concept of transparency, participation, and collaboration, as well as an improvement in efficiency and effectiveness.

He further directs the Chief Technology Officer to coordinate responsible departments and agencies in order to achieve the underlying principles of the memorandum. This is a clear statement for the future of digital government from an US perspective. In a similar way, other countries started their own programs to build digital communications networks.

Digital Government in South Korea

A forerunner in electronic government services is South Korea, which already enacted the Computer Program Protection Act and Supply and Utilization of Computer Network Act in 1986 to secure network technology and infrastructure. By doing this, the country set a clear digital focus early and thus became one of the first movers in information and communication technology infrastructure development.

In the beginning of the new millennium, South Korea committed itself to promote digital government by starting various initiatives under the Promotion of Digitalization of Administrative Work for E-Government Realization Act, the Participatory Government's Vision and Direction of E-Government, and the E-Government Roadmap, in which South Korea specifically formulated their vision of attaining the world's best e-government.

This aim was pursued through four specific performance initiatives: increase online public services to 85%, become one of the top 10 countries for business support competitiveness, reduce visits for civil service applicants to a maximum of three visits per year, and raise the digital government utilization rate to 60%.

In 2008, South Korea established the Master Plan for National Informatization, which consists of 12 e-government improvement initiatives. These initiatives aim to further enhance the openness, sharing, and cooperation of the Korean e-government environment (National Information Society Agency 2012).

Digital Government in China

China started its information and communication technology development with the definition of the Golden Projects in 1993, which refers to a pool of initiatives that are carried out by the government to enhance electronic business, government, and governance. Examples are the Golden Bridge Project, which concentrates on the diffusion of commercial Internet service, the Golden Macro Project, which focuses on the advancement of governmental information sharing, or the Golden Shield Project, which refers to increasing police efficiency and public security.

Digital Government in Japan

The enthusiastic discussion of building an information superhighway in the USA and the developments in other countries were closely followed in Japan. Here, the Ministry of Posts and Telecommunications pushed a plan to develop an advanced information and communication network that supports virtually unlimited media transmission throughout the country.

Since Japan believed that they had fallen behind the USA with respect to the broadband Internet infrastructure, this plan became a cornerstone of the information and communication infrastructure development. Thus, in 1995 Japan integrated the Basic Policy for the Promotion of Advanced Information and Communication Society and developed the Master Plan for Promoting Government-Wide Use of IT. The three pillars of this digital communication network plan were multimedia, information infrastructure, and fiber optics (West 1997).

In this context, the government of Japan promoted government digitalization to respond to the society's rising interest in electronic provision of government information and public services. Hereby, the Japanese government made this project a top national priority and also provided interest-free loans to financially support necessary investments.

In 2001, the e-Japan Priority Policy Program was started, which aimed to create the world's most advanced information and telecommunications network. Key targets of this program were the promotion of education, learning, and human resources development, the facilitation of electronic commerce, and the digitization of public administration and management areas.

A year after its initiation, Japan enacted the Law Concerning the Use of Information and Communications Technology for Administrative Procedures, in which the government provided a legal framework for digital government. Given these initiatives, Japan made quick progress in advancing its digital network technologies and is now listed among the top 20 of the most developed countries in the field of information and communication technology in the world (see Table 2.1).

Table 2.1 ICT Development Index

No.	Countries	Rank 2017	IDI 2017	Rank 2016	IDI 2016	Rank 2015	IDI 2015
1	Iceland	1	8.98	2	8.78	3	8.86
2	Republic of Korea	2	8.85	1	8.8	1	8.64
3	Switzerland	3	8.74	4	8.66	7	8.56
4	Denmark	4	8.71	3	8.68	2	8.88
5	United Kingdom	5	8.65	5	8.53	4	8.75
6	Hong Kong, China	6	8.61	6	8.47	9	8.52
7	Netherlands	7	8.49	10	8.4	8	8.53
8	Norway	8	8.47	7	8.45	10	8.49
9	Luxembourg	9	8.47	9	8.4	6	8.59
10	Japan	10	8.43	11	8.32	11	8.47
11	Sweden	11	8.41	8	8.42	5	8.67
12	Germany	12	8.39	13	8.2	14	8.22
13	New Zealand	13	8.33	12	8.23	16	8.14
14	Australia	14	8.24	16	8.08	13	8.29
15	France	15	8.24	17	8.05	17	8.12
16	USA	16	8.18	15	8.13	15	8.19
17	Estonia	17	8.14	14	8.16	20	8.05
18	Singapore	18	8.05	20	7.85	19	8.08
19	Monaco	19	8.05	18	8.03	18	8.1
20	Ireland	20	8.02	19	7.9	22	7.82

Data source: ITU (2015, 2017)

The ICT Development Index

This list is based on the ICT Development Index (IDI), which combines 11 indicators into a single benchmark measure and is applied to monitor, compare, and evaluate information and communication technology developments across countries over time. The 11 indicators are made up of three subgroups:

1. Five indicators measure ICT readiness, which reflects the availability of fixed and mobile Internet access.
2. Three indicators measure ICT intensity, which reflects a country's Internet usage and broadband subscriptions.
3. Three indicators measure ICT capability/skills, which reflects a country's literacy rate and educational level.

According to the ICT Development Index, Iceland is the world leader and scores significantly higher regarding the proportion of households with a computer and in Internet bandwidth per Internet user, than the Republic of South Korea, which is in second place. Denmark, Finland, Iceland, Norway, and Sweden, the five Nordic countries, all ranked particularly highly, with Finland in place 22 (ITU 2017).

ICT Development in the Asia-Pacific Region

In second place on the ICT Development Index is the Republic of South Korea. There are a variety of reasons for this situation. The Republic of Korea was one of the first movers in professional information and communication technology infrastructure development, possesses a rather high population density, has a highly competitive market for companies offering broadband connections, promotes open networks and systems for cheap Internet access, gives subsidies for connecting low-income people, and was a first mover in becoming a highly connected country (Sutter 2010). However, South Korea is not representative for the Asia-Pacific region. In 2014, less than 15% of the population in developing countries of this territory had access to broadband Internet. Based on this situation, the United Nations Economic and Social Commission for Asia and the Pacific (ESCAP) formed the initiative, called Asia-Pacific Information Superhighway, to increase the availability of high-speed Internet and make this technology affordable across Asia and the Pacific by extending the infrastructure with a terrestrial fiber optic network (ESCAP 2014).

ICT Development in the European Union

In the case of the European Union, briefly after the establishment of the single European market in 1992, projects and working groups dealing with the application of information and communication technologies were set up. A key taskforce was the Bangemann group that produced a clear implementation roadmap that included three main targets: (1) destroy public information monopolies, (2) nurture competition, and (3) install pilot projects to reduce social resistance (Commission of the European Communities 1993; Bangemann 1997).

The findings and subsequent actions of this approach were the first steps toward a fundamental change in European Union media and information regulatory behavior (Baubin and Wirtz 1996), which led to various European projects and initiatives that aimed to promote information and communication technologies.

SWAD-Europe Project

From 2002 to 2004, the European Union funded the SWAD-Europe project that aimed to support the W3C Semantic Web initiative through research, demonstrations, and by supporting the development of universally accessible platforms that allow automated and manual data sharing and processing as well as complementing and harmonizing web technologies and languages (Brickley 2015).

EU IDAB Initiative

The IDABC initiative, which was a European Union program and stands for Interoperable Delivery of European eGovernment Services to Public Administrations, Businesses, and Citizens, was launched in 2004. Goals of this initiative were an enhancement of correct use of information and communication technologies for cross-border services for stipulating the development of public e-service provision and an improvement of efficiency and collaboration of European public administrations. The European Interoperability Framework (EIF), which is a set of recommendations for administration, business, and citizen communication, was an outcome of the IDABC (European Commission 2010).

European Commission's ISA Initiative

The program ended on December 31, 2009, and was followed by the ISA (Interoperability Solutions for European Public Administrations) initiative, which was approved by the European Commission on September 29, 2008. The ISA program focuses on back-office solutions that support the interaction of European public administrations as well as the implementation of policies and processes (European Commission 2015b).

EU i2010 Strategy

In 2005, the European Union launched i2010, which aimed at bringing together various information and communication technology initiatives on a European level, to support and deliver a competitive information economy. All member states have agreed and clearly committed themselves to the i2010 strategy: (1) establish a single European information space, (2) foster innovation and investment in technology research, and (3) promote public services and social aspects for more quality of life in the information society (ECDL Foundation 2008).

Ministerial Declaration on eGovernment

The Ministerial Declaration on eGovernment on November 18, 2009, which was unanimously approved by the Ministers responsible for the digital government policy of the European Union and its candidate countries as well as the countries of the European Free Trade Area (EFTA), clearly explains that the participants agreed to deepen their cooperation, to further promote digital government, and to actively support the post-i2010 initiative (European Union 2009).

European Commission's E-Government Action Plan 2011–2015

Based on the ministerial declaration on e-government, the European Commission developed the E-Government Action Plan 2011–2015, which aims to help providing European policy instruments, to support the transition into an information society, and to create collaborative e-government services on a local, regional, national, and European level. To achieve these targets, the following priorities were defined: empower citizens and businesses, strengthen mobility, foster efficiency and effectiveness, and create the necessary environment to support the transformation (European Commission 2015a).

European Commission's Digital Agenda

The European Commission's Digital Agenda was announced in 2010 and forms one of the seven Europe 2020 strategy pillars. The Digital Agenda in turn comprises 132 actions based on seven pillars (I. Digital single market, II. Interoperability and standards, III. Trust and security, IV. Fast and ultra-fast Internet access, V. Research and innovation, VI. Enhancing digital literacy, skills, and inclusion, VII. ICT-enabled benefits for society) and proposes to better exploit information and communication technology benefits and potential to foster innovation and economic growth. The Digital Agenda aims to reduce barriers that block a free flow of information and digital services as well as updating relevant market rules within the European Union (Bertschek and Ohnemus 2016).

Denmark's National Strategy for Artificial Intelligence

Starting in 2019, the government of Denmark has launched "Denmark's National Strategy for Artificial Intelligence," consisting of 24 key initiatives, including several initiatives that are directly related to the public sector (OECD 2020). For instance, case processing is supposed to be quicker and administration to be more efficient through digital sorting of citizen inquiries, which ensures that citizens receive faster replies (Danish Government 2019). Figure 2.5 shows an overview of selected digital government acts and initiatives.

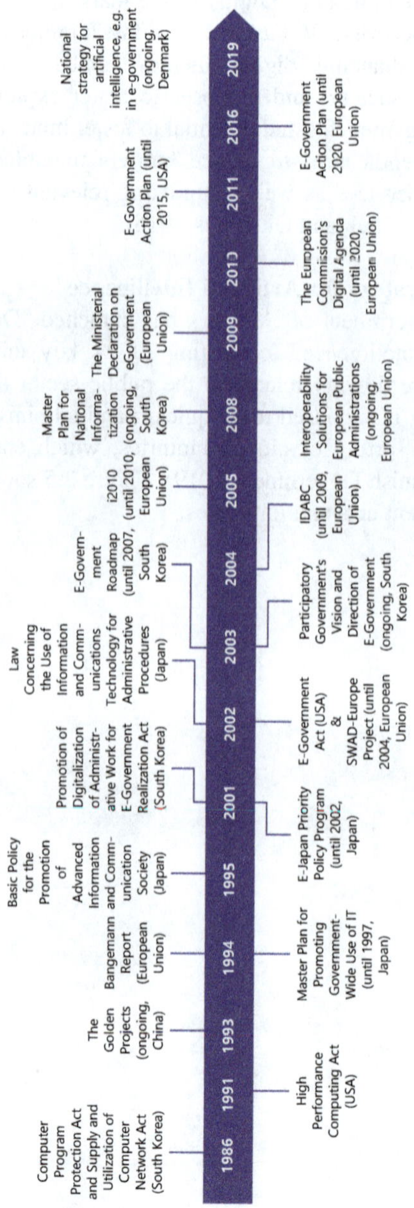

Fig. 2.5 Overview of selected e-government/digital government acts and initiatives (1986–2019). Source: Wirtz and Daiser (2015, 2017), Wirtz (2021)

A similar development, "[. . .] [handling] the most important services of administration through the Internet and therewith to organize all procedures in a more comfortable, faster and less bureaucratic way" (Timm and Kahle 2005, p. 721), can be seen in many countries all around the world, promoting digital government on a global scale.

This is underlined by Karunasena and Deng (2012), who resume that "[g] overnments around the world continuously use e-government for transforming their public service delivery, promoting greater interaction between their citizens and government, streamlining the two-way communication between citizens and governments, improving the efficiency of public organizations, and saving taxpayer money [. . .]."

Country Ranking

However, there are wide disparities among the countries concerning their extent of e-participation and digital government readiness. These indicators are investigated in the United Nations E-Government Survey, which is a comparative ranking of the 193 member countries with regard to their e-government implementation state.[4]

United Nations E-Government Development Index

The United Nations E-Government Development Index (EGDI) is based on three components: the scope and quality of online public services, the status of development of telecommunication infrastructure, and the status of human capital. Furthermore, the United Nations E-Government Survey explores regional trends and prospects, as well as changing focus topics, like requirements of digital government capacity and ways of building digital capacity for the public sector (United Nations 2020). The survey shows a steady global trend toward higher levels of e-government development, reaching from an average world EGDI of 0.47 in 2014 to 0.60 in 2020.

Currently, the European countries play a leading role in digital government development (United Nations Department of Economic and Social Affairs 2020). The results of the United Nations E-Government Survey 2020 are displayed in Table 2.2.

[4]For further information, see United Nations Department of Economic and Social Affairs (2020).

Table 2.2 World e-government leaders in 2020

No.	Country	Region	EGDI 2020	Rank 2020	Rank 2018
1	Denmark	Europe	0.9758	1	1
2	Republic of Korea	Asia	0.9560	2	3
3	Estonia	Europe	0.9473	3	16
4	Finland	Europe	0.9452	4	6
5	Australia	Oceania	0.9432	5	2
6	Sweden	Europe	0.9365	6	5
7	United Kingdom	Europe	0.9358	7	4
8	New Zealand	Oceania	0.9339	8	8
9	USA	Americas	0.9297	9	11
10	Netherlands	Europe	0.9228	10	13
11	Singapore	Asia	0.9150	11	7
12	Iceland	Europe	0.9101	12	19
13	Norway	Europe	0.9064	13	14
14	Japan	Asia	0.8989	14	10

Data source: United Nations Department of Economic and Social Affairs (2020)

In a nutshell, governments have come a long way and have already reached a well-advanced state of digital government, but achieving the level of desired user centricity still requires a further transformational shift.

2.4 Summary, Review Questions, Topics for Discussion, and Online Exercises

- Innovation in information and communication technology and especially the advent of the Internet were strong drivers for moving to an information society.
- Kondratieff waves provide a part explanation for the underlying principle of the shift from an industrial to an information society.
- According to Kondratieff, innovations open up new economic opportunities, which are reflected in an increase in investment. As soon as innovation has established itself in society and industry, the associated investments decrease considerably. However, at this stage of development pioneers are already developing the next technological advance for a further investment boost.
- A forerunner in electronic government services is South Korea, which already enacted the Computer Program Protection Act and Supply and Utilization of Computer Network Act in 1986 to secure network technology and infrastructure.
- In the USA, the High Performance Computing Act of 1991 (HPCA) laid the initial groundwork for making digital government possible. In 2001, an e-government interagency taskforce was initiated, in order to elaborate an action plan for implementing digital government in the USA.

- In the case of the European Union, briefly after the establishment of the single European market in 1992, projects and working groups dealing with the application of information and communication technologies were set up.
- Based on the Ministerial Declaration on eGovernment in 2009, the European Commission developed the E-Government Action Plan 2011–2015, in order to help provide European policy instruments to support the transition into an information society, and to create collaborative digital government services.
- Nowadays, governments around the world use digital government. However, there are wide disparities concerning their extent of e-participation and digital government readiness.
- Currently, the European countries play a leading role in digital government development, with Denmark at the top of the United Nations' World E-Government Leaders ranking 2020. Considering the ongoing technological advancement, the field of digital government may continue to offer dynamic challenges to public managers.

Chapter 2
Review questions, topics for discussion and online exercises

Review questions

1. Outline the development of information and communication technology.
2. Explain the principle of Kondratieff waves.
3. List the countries with the highest ICT Development Index.
4. Name five important e-government/digital government acts.
5. Which countries are the World E-Government Leaders in 2020 according to the UN?

Topics for classroom discussion and team debates

1. Discuss the changes that the Kondratieff-cycle of digitalization causes.
2. Discuss the perspectives of an information society against the background of data security as well as personal and privacy rights.
3. Why are there are such large differences between countries in the areas of information and communication technology and digital government and what might be the underlying causes? Discuss!

Online Exercises

1. Go to https://publicadministration.un.org/en/Research/UN-e-Government-Surveys. Examine how the UN's E-Government Ranking is arrived at. Discuss whether the criteria applied are useful.
2. Enter https://www.ai.gov/. Look at the contents of the initiative and identify its main issues and goals.
3. Visit https://ec.europa.eu/jrc/en/science-area/information-society. Explore what aspects make up the Information Society and what main topics are related to it.

References

Bangemann, Martin (1997): The Information Society–the EU Framework. In Business Strategy Review 8 (4), pp. 13–16.

Baubin, Thomas; Wirtz, Bernd W. (1996): Strategic management and transformation in converging industries—towards the information society. In Walter Brenner, Lutz Kolbe (Eds.): The Information Superhighway and Private Households. Heidelberg: Physica-Verlag, pp. 363–377.

Bertschek, I.; Ohnemus, J. (2016): Europe's digital future: Focus on key priorities. Edited by Centre for European Economic Research (ZEW). Mannheim. Available online at https://ftp.zew.de/pub/zew-docs/policybrief/pb02-16.pdf, checked on 5/19/2021.

Brickley, Dan (2015): SWAD-Europe: Project Fact Sheet. Available online at http://www.w3.org/2001/sw/Europe/factsheet/, checked on 3/18/2015.

Castells, Manuel (2000): Materials for an exploratory theory of the network society. In British Journal of Sociology 51 (1), pp. 5–24.

Commission of the European Communities (1993): Growth, Competitiveness, Employment. The Challenges and Ways forward into the 21st Century. White Paper. Bulletin of the European Communities. Supplement 6/93. Brussels. Available online at http://europa.eu/documentation/official-docs/white-papers/pdf/growth_wp_com_93_700_parts_a_b.pdf, checked on 8/21/2015.

Danish Government (2019): National strategy for artificial intelligence: Ministry of Finance; Ministry of Industry, Business and Financial Affairs. Available online at https://eng.em.dk/media/13081/305755-gb-version_4k.pdf, checked on 5/10/2021.

Dawes, Sharon S. (2009): Governance in the digital age: A research and action framework for an uncertain future. In Government Information Quarterly 26 (2), pp. 257–264.

Denger, Katharina S.; Wirtz, Bernd W. (1995): Die digitale Revolution. In Gablers Magazin 9 (3), pp. 20–24.

Department of Commerce (1993): The National Information Infrastructure: Agenda for Action. With assistance of Information Infrastructure Task Force. Department of Commerce. Washington, DC. Available online at http://eric.ed.gov/?id=ED364215, checked on 3/17/2015.

ECDL Foundation (2008): What is the i2010 Initiative? Available online at http://www.ecdl.org/index.jsp?n=895&a=1902, checked on 3/18/2015.

ESCAP (2014): Reducing Digital Divide: Asia-Pacific Information Superhighway. United Nations. Available online at http://www.unescap.org/news/reducing-digital-divide-asia-pacific-information-superhighway, updated on 10/17/2014, checked on 4/20/2015.

European Commission (2010): IDABC. Available online at http://ec.europa.eu/idabc/, checked on 3/18/2015.

European Commission (2015a): European eGovernment Action Plan 2011-2015. Available online at http://ec.europa.eu/digital-agenda/en/european-egovernment-action-plan-2011-2015, updated on 3/2/2015, checked on 3/18/2015.

European Commission (2015b): ISA. Interoperability Solutions for European Public Administrations. Available online at http://ec.europa.eu/isa/index_en.htm, updated on 3/16/2015, checked on 3/18/2015.

European Union (2009): Ministerial Declaration on E-Government. Approved on 18 November 2009. Malmö, Sweden: 5th Ministerial eGovernment Conference.

Forman, Mark (2002): E-Government Strategy. Implementing the President's Management Agenda for E-Government. Simplified Delivery of Services to Citizens. Washington, DC: Executive Office of the President Office at Management and Budget.

Fuchs, C. (2013): Capitalism or information society? The fundamental question of the present structure of society. In European Journal of Social Theory 16 (4), pp. 413–434.

Homburg, Vincent (2008): Understanding E-Government. Information Systems in Public Administration. London, New York: Routledge.

Internet World Stats (2021): World Internet usage and population statistics. 2021 Year-Q1 Estimates. Available online at https://www.internetworldstats.com/stats.htm, checked on 6/1/2021.

ITU (2015): Measuring the Information Society Report 2015. Available online at https://www.itu.int/en/ITU-D/Statistics/Documents/publications/misr2015/MISR2015-w5.pdf, checked on 6/1/2021.

ITU (2017): Measuring the Information Society Report 2017. Volume 1. Available online at https://www.itu.int/en/ITU-D/Statistics/Documents/publications/misr2017/MISR2017_Volume1.pdf, checked on 6/1/2021.

Karunasena, Kanishka; Deng, Hepu (2012): Critical factors for evaluating the public value of e-government in Sri Lanka. In Government Information Quarterly 29 (1), pp. 76–84.

Kleinsteuber, Hans J. (2012): Der Information Superhighway. Analyse einer Metapher. In Hans J. Kleinsteuber (Ed.): Der „Information Superhighway": amerikanische Visionen und Erfahrungen. Wiesbaden: VS Verlag für Sozialwissenschaften, pp. 17–47.

National Information Society Agency (2012): e-Government of Korea. Best Practices. Edited by Ministry of Public Administration and Securtiy. Seoul. Available online at http://unpan1.un.org/intradoc/groups/public/documents/UNGC/UNPAN043625.pdf, checked on 3/6/2015.

Nefiodow, Leo A.; Nefiodow, Simone (2014): Der sechste Kondratieff. Die neue, lange Welle der Weltwirtschaft : die langen Wellen der weltwirtschaftlichen Entwicklung. 7th ed. Sankt Augustin: Rhein-Sieg Verlag.

OECD (2020): Denmark's national strategy for artificial intelligence. National Strategi for Kunstig Intelligens. Available online at https://oecd.ai/dashboards/policy-initiatives/2019-data-policyInitiatives-24241, checked on 5/10/2021.

Rosenbach, Marcel (2012): Von der Agenda for Action zum Telecommunications Act von 1996. US-Kommunikationspolitik zwischen Deregulation und öffentlichem Interesse. In Hans J. Kleinsteuber (Ed.): Der „Information Superhighway ": amerikanische Visionen und Erfahrungen. Wiesbaden: VS Verlag für Sozialwissenschaften, pp. 89–119.

Schumpeter, J. (1939): Business cycles: A theoretical, historical and statistical analysis of the capitalist process. New York: McGraw-Hill.

Sutter, John D. (2010): Why Internet connections are fastest in South Korea. In CNN 2010, 4/1/2010. Available online at http://edition.cnn.com/2010/TECH/03/31/broadband.south.korea/, checked on 4/21/2015.

Timm, Ulrike; Kahle, Irene (2005): E-Government und andere Zwecke der Internetnutzung. In Statistisches Bundesamt–Wirtschaft und Statistik 7, pp. 717–726. Available online at http://www.destatis.de/jetspeed/portal/cms/Sites/destatis/, checked on 1/31/2012.

United Nations (2020): UN E-government surveys. Available online at https://publicadministration.un.org/en/research/un-e-government-surveys, checked on 5/10/2021.

United Nations Department of Economic and Social Affairs (2020): E-government survey 2020. Digital government in the decade of action for sustainable development. New York. Available online at https://publicadministration.un.org/egovkb/Portals/egovkb/Documents/un/2020-Survey/2020%20UN%20E-Government%20Survey%20(Full%20Report).pdf, checked on 5/10/2021.

West, Joel (1997): Building Japan's Information Superhighway. Japan Policy Research Institute. Available online at http://www.jpri.org/publications/workingpapers/wp7.html, checked on 3/17/2015.

Wirtz, Bernd W. (2013): Medien- und Internetmanagement. 8th ed. Wiesbaden: Gabler.

Wirtz, Bernd W. (2019): Medien- und Internetmanagement. 10th ed. Wiesbaden: Springer Gabler.

Wirtz, Bernd W. (2020): Electronic Business. 7th ed. Wiesbaden: Springer Gabler.

Wirtz, Bernd W. (2021): Digital Business and Electronic Commerce. Cham: Springer International Publishing.

Wirtz, Bernd W. (2022): E-Government. Wiesbaden: Springer Gabler.

Wirtz, Bernd W.; Daiser, Peter (2015): E-Government. Strategy, process, instruments. 1st ed. Speyer.

Wirtz, Bernd W.; Daiser, Peter (2017): E-government. Strategy, process, instruments. 2nd ed. Speyer.

The Concept and Strategy of Digital Government 3

Contents

Learning Objectives
By working through this chapter, you will be able to:

1. Describe the Four Forces Model of Digital Government.
2. Explain the E-Government Value Activity System (EVAS).
3. Describe the individual steps of the digital government development strategy.
4. Explain the goals of digital government strategy.
5. Outline the open government framework and the strategic e-participation framework and explain their components.

The beginning of digital government was set by the development of modern information and communication technologies. With boosting processing power and transmission capacities of computers and networks as well as increasing demand for electronically provided information and services from citizens and businesses, governments and public authorities began to run first electronic service offers at the end of the 1990s.[1] This novel form of service provision emerged as electronic government or e-government (Dawes 2009).

[1] See for Chapter 3 The Concept and Strategy of Digital Government also Wirtz and Daiser (2015, 2017), Wirtz (2019, 2020a, 2022).

B. W. Wirtz, *Digital Government*, Springer Texts in Business and Economics,
https://doi.org/10.1007/978-3-031-13086-1_3

E-government being a technology-enabled part of the government or public sector governance model was quickly regarded as a powerful system that can provide manifold benefits since it allows unattended public stakeholder access to information and services, improves government–stakeholder interaction, fosters efficiency and effectiveness, and forms the basis for e-democracy from a technological point of view. Furthermore, its digital platform character for government stakeholder interaction embellishes unity and standardization and thus reflects citizens' demands for more transparency and accountability.

Today, digital government is an inherent part of governments and public administration worldwide since it is highly relevant for these organizations to address their individual stakeholder desires and requirements. In this context, the implementation of digital government and its associated benefits is a compelling topic for citizens and is especially relevant for the economy since the availability of online public services is an important factor within global competition.

3.1 Four Forces Model of Digital Government

The driving forces behind the situation, requiring change for government and public administration, can be explained by the Four Forces Digital Government Model, which aggregates relevant drivers to four key developments: convergence and technology, state and politics, society and economy, and citizen empowerment (see Figure 3.1).

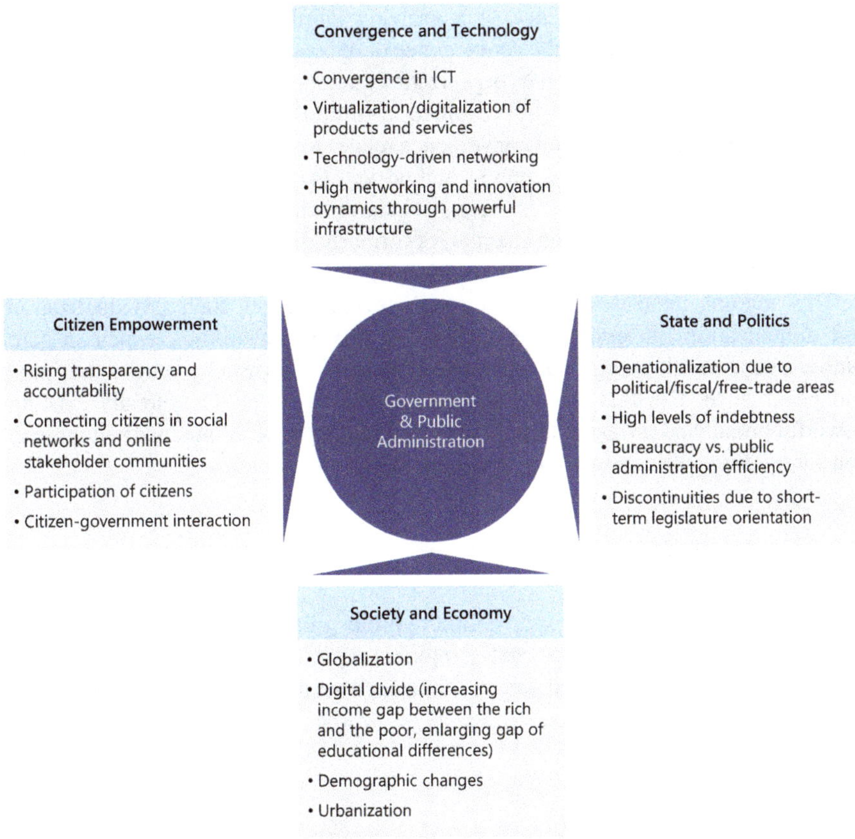

Fig. 3.1 The Four Forces Model of Digital Government. Source: Wirtz and Daiser (2015, 2017)

Convergence and Technology

The first force of the digital government model is convergence and technology. Although all of these developments are crucial, this is the most significant one since it covers the fundamental breakthrough of making digital government technologically possible. Here, convergence describes the approximation of underlying technologies, diminishing sector boundaries, networking of different public and non-public areas of value creation, and finally, an integration of sectors, business units, organizations, products, and services (Denger and Wirtz 1995). This means that the underlying technological innovation leads to a more comprehensive service provision.

Levels of Convergence

Depending on the respective level of aggregation, convergence can be divided into different types (see Wirtz 2016):

(1) Sector level: Convergence of a growing number of organizations within related sectors finally leads to the convergence of the corresponding sector. (2) Organization level: Convergence forces organizations to reposition their value chains and core activities and which results in modified institutional boundaries. (3) Organization unit level: Organization unit convergence relates to various organization units of a public authority or different public authorities. (4) Service and product level: Convergence of services, content (e.g., standardization of formats), distribution channels (e.g., same distribution channel for formerly different formats), or products (e.g., convergence through integration of functionalities).

This ongoing trend was initiated through several drivers, such as virtualization and digitalization of services and technology-driven networking, which in sum caused a paramount strategic and operative change in all forms of electronic business and governance. But this change is by no means over yet. The already existing powerful broadband infrastructure, which itself undergoes continuous development, constantly drives new networking applications and innovation.

State and Politics

The second force is state and politics. From this point of view, ongoing denationalization of countries as well as regional coalescence of markets and nations requires adequate technological preconditions for transnational cooperation on political and administrative level. These have to be created by the respective governments.

Denationalization
Digital government is a suitable answer to tackle this challenge since it is an Internet-based solution and thus provides the possibility to quickly establish an online environment that allows government–user interaction on a global scale.

High Levels of Indebtedness
At first glance, high indebtedness levels seem to contradict the expensive implementation of digital government solutions. However, the expected digital government cost-cutting effects, which are achieved, for example, by automation, standardization, and outsourcing of activities, fit the current need to economize and the cost-saving character of digital government has positive side effects on managing indebtedness.

Public Administration Efficiency
This goes along with the desire for less red tape and the wish for an increase in public administration efficiency. In this context, digital government is a decent system due to its administration process automation and standardization capacities. An example of a comparable undertaking is electronic banking.

While earlier the clients needed to visit a branch of their bank in person to conduct a banking transaction, people nowadays can settle nearly all transactions from home at any time. This form of automatization and outsourcing of activities to the client has led to a significant cost reduction of 70–90% in e-banking service delivery.

Short-Term Legislation Orientation
Considering the prevailing political discontinuities caused by short-term orientation on votes and legislature periods, digital government is—although being an election campaign-friendly topic—not universally supported by decision-makers in the government and the public sector due to its legislature period outlasting character and requirement of profound transformation processes. Thus, political discontinuities represent a negative driver or obstacle.

Society and Economy

The third force is society and economy. Its key drivers are globalization, digital divide, demographic change, and urbanization.

Globalization
The high economic interconnectedness and international assimilation of lifestyles as part of globalization require a stronger public sector focus on superregional and supranational demand aspects as well as on cross-border cooperation of governments and public authorities. As mentioned before, digital government, which is based on Internet technology and thus can be regarded as a global medium, is an adequate system to approach this situation.

Digital Divide
Digital divide describes differences in access to and use of information and communication technologies, especially the Internet, between individual social groups with distinct technical and socioeconomic factors. Key hypotheses are that (1) the use of modern information and communication technology is not distributed evenly within society since its access depends on social factors and that (2) this unequal situation leads to social disparities of opportunity.

In this context, the increasing income gap between the rich and the poor and the enlarging gap of educational differences are frequently mentioned topics. As with the observable polarization of income ratios and differences in education of distinct social groups, the risk of digital divide is also present online. Here, digital government can be used to create similar opportunities in terms of citizen–government or organization–government interaction by assuring direct and uniform access and providing information and services in similar form and equal quality to all users.

Demographic Changes
Another aspect of the societal and economic force is demographic change, which in the context of information and communication technology refers to the situation that a high proportion of older people with only limited Internet skills will face a young

generation that grew up with these technologies (digital natives) and thus demands increasing online information and service provision.

Since the majority of the digital native generation shows Internet usage patterns and is hence believed to individually manage their public administration relevant matters online, this is seen as a chance to massively relieve public administration workload through automatization and outsourcing. In this context, automatization refers to tasks that are run automatically, electronically, and independently of staff assignment and outsourcing relates to tasks that are shifted from public administration staff to the user (e.g., data input, filling in online forms).

However, digital government faces severe strategic and structural challenges because of the generation that does not possess similar online affinity and often lives in regions with only limited high-speed Internet access. Here, the smart country initiative strives to establishing innovative concepts to master this challenge since gaining and maintaining the confidence of the vast majority of the citizens is an absolute necessity for comprehensive, nationwide public information and service provision (Co:llaboratory 2014). In the report of Co:llaboratory (2014), four critical recommendations to address this situation are presented: (1) digital society, (2) digital infrastructure, (3) digital coproduction, and (4) digital location policy.

Digital society means that the regional community becomes a more self-sustaining position and jointly develops (citizens, public administration, and politics) regional solutions. To reduce the burden of limited online access, digital infrastructure—in terms of high-speed Internet and network possibilities—needs to be established.

Digital coproduction serves to enable and encourage citizens to more strongly participate in public administration service provision (e.g., citizens inform citizens about administrative procedures). Finally, public communities of practice foster collaboration across administrations and decentralization, and open innovation networks with society, economy, and science promote local development.

Urbanization

With increasing urbanization and rural depopulation, keeping up today's expensive decentralized public administration infrastructure and maintaining a high territorial presence will not be feasible from a cost perspective in the long run. Cost constraints will reduce the density of public administration resources and local public service provision, requiring more centralized and automated public service provision. In this context, digital government is a reasonable and cost-effective platform to realize these demands efficiently.

Citizen Empowerment

The fourth driving force of the digital government development is citizen empowerment. This change in the public environment mainly concerns the citizens themselves.

Rising Transparency and Accountability

The rising transparency and accountability of public actions and the possibility that citizens can locally, regionally, and nationally unite in social networks and communities, exchanging their desires and opinions, all became possible due to modern information and communication technologies. United they can have a considerable influence on political and administrative processes and can exert pressure in voting networks, which clearly strengthens the position of the citizens.

Participation of Citizens

Furthermore, citizens claim more participation in public policy issues and for a renewed citizen–government interaction. Here, governments have to act, for instance, by providing a more transparent form of governance and integrating citizens into public processes.

In the light of the aforementioned four driving forces of digital government, an integrated management approach is mandatory to handle the multitude of interrelated impacts and related activities. Against this background, the E-Government Value Activity System (EVAS) is outlined in the following.

3.2 E-Government Value Activity System (EVAS)

Value activity systems are based on the concept of the value chain, which describes a set of organizational activities performed to deliver a product or service to the market. The value chain concept was developed in management research and first described by Michael E. Porter.[2]

The Digital Government Value Chain

The underlying idea of the value chain is based on a process view of organizations. From this perspective, an organization is a system made up of subsystems that transform input factors into outputs. The effectiveness and efficiency of the associated activities, which are needed for the transformation process, finally determine the costs and the profit of the organization.

Given an exemplary digital government value chain (see Figure 3.2), its activities may consist of (1) content and service concept, (2) content and service development, (3) technological distribution, (4) marketing and user relationship management, and (5) digital payment.[3]

[2] For further information, please see Porter (1985).

[3] Since it is not common to describe public stakeholders as customers, we refer to user relationship management instead of using the term customer relationship management.

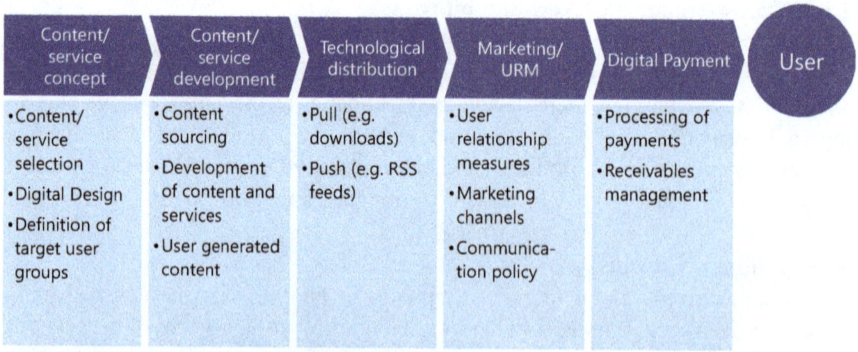

Fig. 3.2 Exemplary digital government value chain. Source: Wirtz (2000, 2020a, 2021)

The first step of the value chain deals, for example, with content and service selection for as well as layout and design of the digital government portal. In the next steps, the respective content and services have to be developed and their technological distribution needs to be set up (e.g., pull vs. push concept).

The marketing and user relationship-related step of the value activity is of vital importance. Here, the access to the user is determined, which requires customer-oriented marketing and relationship measures. Finally, the imposed fees and charges have to be processed, which completes the value chain activity. This exemplary value chain sequence is presented in Figure 3.2.

The E-Government Value Activity System (EVAS) is conceptually built on the value chain approach, but it provides a more differentiated perspective on the entire system as well as its interfaces. From a theoretical perspective, digital government is a technology-enabled part of the government or public sector governance model that allows unattended public stakeholder access to information and services and forms the technological basis for e-democracy.

Therefore, digital government is often referred to as a comprehensive approach to elaborate citizen-oriented public services and enhance public administration effectiveness and efficiency. Thus, it is an important element of public management reform programs across the world.

The EVAS Model

Figure 3.3 illustrates the Model of E-Government Value Activity System (EVAS), which portrays the key value activities that need to be comprehensively planned, organized, steered, and controlled to promote effective digital government within the public administration environment.[4]

[4] A regular and reliable operation of the general public authority infrastructure, such as accounting, legal, administration, management, etc., is a precondition of an effective and efficient digital government.

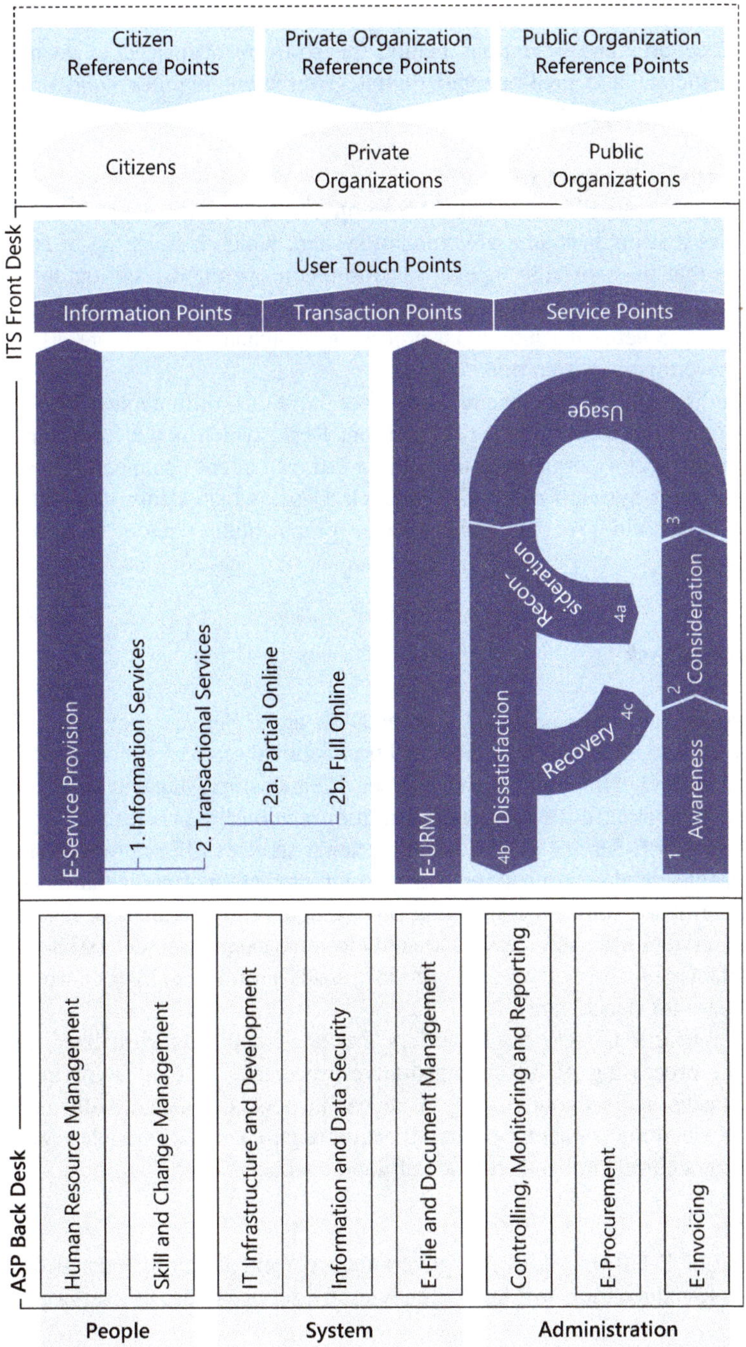

Fig. 3.3 Model of E-Government Value Activity System (EVAS). Source: Wirtz and Daiser (2015), Wirtz (2021)

Despite e-government's online character, it is not a completely virtualized system since procedures and operations behind the software also need to be managed. Hence, efficient and goal-oriented digital government requires solid underlying routines, processes, and structures.

Value Activity Perspective
For this reason, the EVAS model is based on a value activity perspective of public authorities that outlines an e-government system, which is made up of subsystem activities that have specific inputs, transformation operations, and outputs, which involve acquisition or consumption of human, financial, or knowledge resources. Therefore, the better the individual processes are managed, the more efficient the digital government system runs.

Regarding the EVAS model, we first have to differentiate between the Information-Transaction-Service (ITS) Front Desk, which is the front-line part of the public sector organization with a direct client connection, and the Administration-System-People (ASP) Back Desk, which deals with internal or supporting activities of the public sector organization without a direct client connection.

ITS Front Desk

The two key activities in the ITS Front Desk are E-Service Provision, which is subdivided into information services and transactional services, consisting of partial and full online transactions, and E-User Relationship Management (E-URM), showing an integrated digital government user relationship process.

Concerning E-Service Provision, information services offer purely information-based, single-sided services to the user without interaction or participation activities (e.g., information retrieval concerning service hours of departments). Partial transactional services offer services that are only to some extent provided online and thus still contain media breaks (e.g., the user downloads a form to apply for a work visa or completes a tax declaration).

Full transactional services are offers that are completely virtualized and thus allow the processing of full administrative procedures without involving further media breaks and without having to appear in person, which usually requires a qualified electronic signature or identification (e.g., change of vehicle registration, requesting a current police certificate of good conduct).[5]

E-URM
The goal of E-URM in a digital government context is the maintenance of user relations to induce users that have already used a service to use this service again or

[5] For further information on e-services, please refer to Chapter 11.

use a similar service. This process consists of a sequence of phases: awareness, consideration, usage, reconsideration, dissatisfaction, and recovery.

In the awareness phase, the user recognizes the availability of the services provided, which suits his needs. Based on this, an initial user contact is established via information and communication technologies (e.g., visiting the website).[6] In the next phase, consideration, the potential user is presented with the service offerings from the digital government system, which are tailored to the expected user needs.

This requires a profound knowledge of the potential user needs and preferences. In the usage phase, the user should select the desired service and start processing. If the user is satisfied with the handling and the outcome, he may reconsider using the digital government service offering. Therefore, the services offered need to be designed in a way that satisfies the needs of the user.

At this point of the interaction, user satisfaction should be checked through user feedback or monitoring systems that support constant evolution of the services provided. This is of particular importance since a dissatisfied user may not use the service again, may discourage others from using the service, or may leave the entire platform. In this case, measures for recovering dissatisfied users have to be at hand.

User Touch Points

The user touch points (information points, transaction points, and service points) are the ITS Front Desk interface to the digital government stakeholders (citizens, private organizations, and public organizations) and thus are the actual connection between the digital government system and the user. The parallel use of multiple user touch points across all channels has become a regular procedure (e.g., online banking), helping information and service providers to optimize customer-specific service provision and to guide customers toward economically reasonable interfaces (Wirtz 2012).

Apart from the technological benefit with regard to managing server requests, particular user touch points provide users with bundled, customized service offers, leading to an increased overall satisfaction experience. This is important since in addition to economic also user-oriented aspects need to be taken into account in order to achieve a positive value contribution for the online service offering. If only considered from cost-efficiency perspectives, the expected effect may even be turned on its head (Rayport and Jaworski 2004).

The distinction of the different user touch points is based on their primary function. For information points this is the provision of information (e.g., information on opening or service hours on a website). In the case of transaction points, this is the transaction-based service offering (e.g., requesting a police certificate of good conduct). Service points mainly deal with services that are provided before or after a transaction process has been started or inquiries that demand staff involvement (e.g., complaint management, inquiries regarding applications or requests in progress, customer call-backs).

[6] For further information on user relationship management, please refer to Section 10.4.

Reference Points

A further vital aspect are the reference points for citizens as well as private and public organizations. Here, a reference point refers to any source of information that may influence the user in using or not using digital government services. If, for instance, a friend or a colleague has made a dissatisfying experience while using the digital government system, this may influence the intention to use the system, irrespective of the system's actual quality and efficiency. Although these reference points can only be influenced indirectly, their potential user impact needs to be borne in mind.

ASP Back Desk

The ASP Back Desk activities deal with the internal or ITS Front Desk supporting processes of the public sector organization. The primary challenge of human resource management is recruitment, training, and motivating employees. Since people are a vital source of skills, knowledge, and value, good human resource management can create a sustainable benefit in implementing and running an efficient digital government.

Skill and Change Management

Skill and change management are vital aspects to change the current organization and move employees from the status quo to the digital government environment. First, because public administration and management within a digital government setting demand other skills and competencies than past practice and, second, because the shift from old paper-based to new electronically oriented structures and procedures requires a paramount transformation of the entire organization. Therefore, training and accompanying employees as well as professional change management are key factors for successful digital government.

IT Infrastructure and Development

IT infrastructure and development relates to the support systems that allow to process and manage information and maintain daily operations (infrastructure) as well as to the innovation process of developing and integrating new applications and functionalities (development). Since digital government to a high degree depends on well-working IT systems and innovative solutions, the related activities are cornerstones of a rewarding digital government system.

Information and Data Security

Information and data security refers to an important aspect of digital government. Here, we would like to emphasize that the actual security of private user data and the perceived security of individual user data and network-based information processing are crucial factors that need to be maintained by all means (Cavoukian 2010). If people believe that their personal information is not stored or processed confidentially and securely, they will tend to oppose digital government-related online data storage and processing since—especially for transactional offers—a certain level of trust is necessary (Bélanger and Carter 2008).

E-File and Document Management

E-File and document management deal with electronic and paper-based administration of files, documents, and records. In this context, especially the digital government-driven conversion from paper-based work to the paperless organization (e.g., introduction of electronic citizen files) causes complex, extensive conversion procedures in the public sector.

Furthermore, due to an increasing requirement of supraregional and supranational procedures, there is a growing need to exchange objects of the file and document management between state, federal, and local governments, especially concerning IT-based administration processes (e.g., coordination, information, or handling of records in the course of duty shifts) since no subject-specific data exchange standard for these types of transactions is available yet.

The requirement also derives from the legal guidelines for long-term storage and archiving of public records. Apart from that, rising digital government specifications and expectations concerning speedy and electronic handling of transactions and processes further drive this development.

Controlling, Monitoring, and Reporting

Controlling, monitoring, and reporting activities are constantly required for keeping track of the overall digital government workflow system and for a consistent and sustainable management of the involved ASP Back Desk and ITS Front Desk activities. These activities can be broken down into a strategic and an operative component. Key aspects of the longer-term oriented strategic controlling are planning, information, and early warning purposes, while the operative monitoring part focuses on target-performance comparisons for result-oriented steering and control of the overall digital government system.

Controlling, monitoring, and reporting activities require appropriate standards as a basis for measurement and an integrated, automated performance measurement system. Furthermore, a common understanding of the potential implications of downtime due to system crashes, failure, or mistakes should be present throughout the group of responsible digital government officers (Wirtz et al. 2014).

E-Procurement

E-Procurement is the integration of network-based information and communication technology to support operational and strategic activities that are required to supply the necessary inputs that are not self-created by the organization. Its main target is the reduction of procurement cost, which is partly offset by e-procurement system investments and maintenance cost as well as training cost for employees.

However, demand aggregation usually allows significant cost savings and the increase in standardization and automation helps prevent corruption and creates transparency, contract security, and enhanced quality. Nonetheless, this massive transformation implies restructuring and reorganization of existing processes and structures, and thus is a vital activity for digital government (Wirtz et al. 2009).

E-Invoicing

E-Invoicing is supposed to close the payment gap in otherwise consistent transactions without media discontinuity and support compliance in all relevant legal requirements. The widespread introduction of an electronic invoice processing system that allows sending and receiving electronic invoices without media breaks shall ensure significant gains in efficiency and make a notable contribution to sustainable economic and increased competitiveness.

E-Invoicing forms the basis for the next step in electronic payment, integrated e-payment systems that enable users to pay invoices directly from web applications. However, these fundamental changes in processes and procedures need to be implemented and managed on a strategic as well as an operative level for successful and efficient digital government. For this reason, e-invoicing is an important developing activity that requires intensive care.

Given the E-Government Value Activity System, its associated value activities need to be managed in a systematic way. Referring to Chandler (1962), structure follows strategy and thus strategic management is required to effectively and efficiently lead and operate the digital government value activities.

3.3 Strategic Management of Digital Government

The term strategy has Greek roots and was originally closely related to military action.[7] Strategy in this context meant the leadership of an army up to the first encounter with the enemy, as from that point in time, army leadership became tactical. This strictly military view is usually not found in today's business strategy understanding anymore. It is rather the creation of a sustainable rent that can be seen as a key element of modern strategic corporate management: "Strategy can be viewed as a continuing search for rent" (Mahoney and Pandian 1992, p. 364).

In particular, it was during the 1980s and 1990s that two dominant strategy paradigms have evolved within the international management research. On the one hand, there is the market-based view of strategy, which is mainly build upon the notions of Michael E. Porter concerning industrial organization research. On the other hand, there is the resource-based view, which specifically attributes enduring organizational success to organizational resources (Wirtz 2021).

Market-Based View

The underlying principle of the market-based view is the structure-conduct-performance paradigm, which relates an achieved outcome to market structure and behavior: "To explain the competitive success of firms, we need a theory of strategy which

[7] See for the following Section 3.3 also Wirtz (2019, 2020b, 2021).

links environmental circumstances and firm behavior to market outcomes" (Porter 1991, p. 99). In the case of the public sector, this outcome may be seen as a service optimization and benefit maximization for the various public e-service demand groups (citizen, private, and public organizations).

Resource-Based View

In contrast, the resource-based view tries to explain the emergence of competitive advantages through heterogeneity of resources: "Regardless of the nature of the rents, sustained competitive advantage requires that the condition of heterogeneity be preserved" (Peteraf 1993, p. 182). Transferred to the environment of public sector organizations and governance, competitive advantage means that governmental and administrative service provisions on local, regional, and federal level achieve a significant higher added value for their users than comparable service provisions of other public and private digital service providers.

The term resource refers to "[...] all assets, capabilities, organizational processes, firm attributes, information, knowledge, etc. controlled by a firm that enable the firm to conceive of and implement strategies" (Barney 1991, p. 101). However, resources only lead to competitive advantage if they share the following four basic characteristics: (1) valuable, (2) rareness or access barriers, (3) lacking substitutes, and (4) imperfectly mutable and are combined and/or coordinated in a success-pursuing way.

Competence-Based View

The competence-based view, which is often used in a similar manner like the resource-based view, tries to explain organizational success—in the sense of achieving strategic goals—with the creation and use of resources, skills, and competencies. Here, Sanchez et al. (1996), for example, describe competency from an organizational perspective as a target-oriented, repeatable discretion for collective action of an organization. Against this background, we allocate the competency to the resource-based view and thus refer to both when mentioning the latter.

Currently, strategic management, which mainly deals with making fundamental decisions about the intermediate and long-term goals and activities of the organization, is characterized by a dual strategy comprehension taking into account both the market and the resource-based view.

Apart from that, it can be observed that the two different perspectives partly converge to generate a harmonized theory without isolating the market structure and behavior-oriented or resource and competency-based factors: "Strategy is the direction and scope of an organization over the long term. It ideally matches its resources to its changing environment, and in particular its markets, customers and clients so as to meet stakeholders expectations" (Johnson and Scholes 1993, p. 10).

Integrated Understanding of Strategy

Therefore, an integrated understanding of strategy, which brings together the key elements of the market and the resource-based view that are relevant for success, should qualify as a vital basis for strategy formulation, especially in the field of digital government.

On the one hand, creation, combination, and coordination of innovative resource bundles is a key element of an organization's activities. On the other hand, carrying out evaluations and adjustments between the primary internal development perspective of the resource-based view with external market-oriented aspects and factors also represents a key element.

In the light of the above, the development of a digital government strategy requires integration of existing strategy concepts within the organization. But in addition to the classical offline strategic management, digital government also demands success-oriented consideration of innovative technology-based online methods and tools (Chaffey 2009). Although digital government forms a paramount part of the public sector organization's overall strategy, it is not a stand-alone concept and thus requires a subordinate integration into the superior strategy.

Digital Government Strategy Development

The development of a digital government strategy includes all organizational activities concerning the definition, formulation, description, planning, implementation, and audit of the digital government strategy. In the following, the proceeding of the individual steps as well as the related key content that have to be taken into account are explained (please see Figure 3.4).

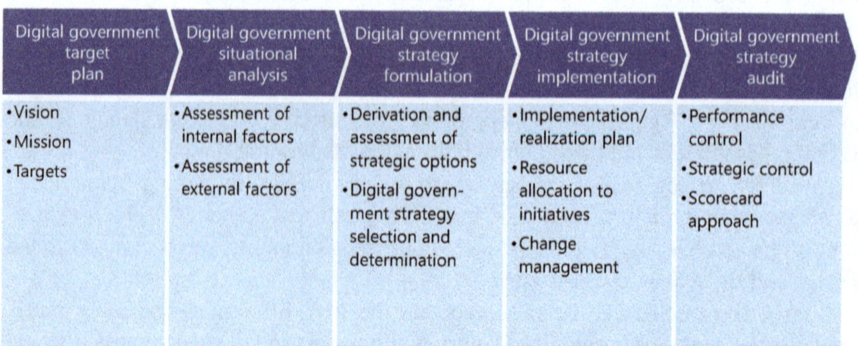

Fig. 3.4 Taxonomy of digital government strategy development. Source: Wirtz (2016, 2020a, 2021)

Vision

The starting point of the digital government target plan is the formulation of the digital government vision. Here, a vision is generally understood as the central theme or the guiding principle of organizational activity, an idea of how an organization should look like in the future and which future reality is pursued for the organization.

Characteristic examples for vision statements are “to make people happy” from Walt Disney or “to organize all of the data in the world and make it accessible for everyone in a useful way” from Google. Thus, the digital government vision is the guidance for the strategic digital government development (Hill and Jones 2013).

Apart from that, a vision should fulfill a meaningful, motivating, as well as action-guiding function. Depending on the content, a vision can be classified into four groups: (1) target focus—pursuing a future target state, (2) change focus—modifying basic organizational principles, (3) competitor focus—outperforming a competitor, or (4) role focus—becoming a role model (Müller-Stewens and Lechner 2011; Wirtz 2021).

Besides the abovementioned aspects, especially the public manager’s assessment concerning the future development of information and communication technology is important. Digital government-related technological changes and breakthroughs that may influence online public service provision need to be considered.

Mission

In addition to the digital government vision, digital government strategy formulation requires the elaboration of a digital government mission statement. The digital government mission differs from the vision in that it does not focus on an aspired future state of the organization, but defines a core statement regarding digital government purposes, values, and standards of conduct (Grant 2005, 2016).

Thus, the definition of these core principles determines the digital government system’s reason to exist as well as which public services are to be provided. This maxim may also be regarded as an expression of a permanent action-guiding set of values that specify a framework of appropriate behavior or organizational conduct for internal stakeholders. Consequently, the digital government mission statement can be considered as the primary guiding principle contributing to meet online public service provision demands of citizens and businesses.

Targets

Based on the digital government vision and mission, the next step is the derivation and operationalization of concrete organizational targets. By using clearly formulated targets, the long-term organizational development can be actively influenced. Thus, concrete targets fulfill a coordinating role within the organization allowing us to focus public activities onto particular planning specifications. In this context, targets may be defined as a normative idea about a future state of the organization.

Effective target setting requires two vital aspects: target formulation and target content. Concerning target formulation, academics and managers usually follow the approach of defining SMART targets (Hill and Jones 2013). Here, SMART is a mnemonic acronym that provides criteria to guide target setting. The letters stand for specific (clearly define area for improvement), measurable (make the objective quantifiable/traceable), assignable (specify the responsible person), realistic (targets need to be achievable with the available resources), and time-related (specify when the target needs to be achieved) (Doran 1981; Grant 2016).

Considering the target content, there is no clear common consensus on this issue since this depends on the overall strategy and targets of the respective public sector organization. Based on the general digital government objectives, these should follow its underlying principles of improving public sector efficiency and effectiveness, reducing overall levels of expenditure, and enhancing accountability, transparency, and responsiveness of the public sector.

Digital Government Stakeholders

Against this background, satisfying stakeholder needs in an effective and efficient way may be seen as the primary goal of public administration, making stakeholder identification and evaluation an important topic for strategic target setting. Figure 3.5 shows an overview of vital digital government stakeholder groups.

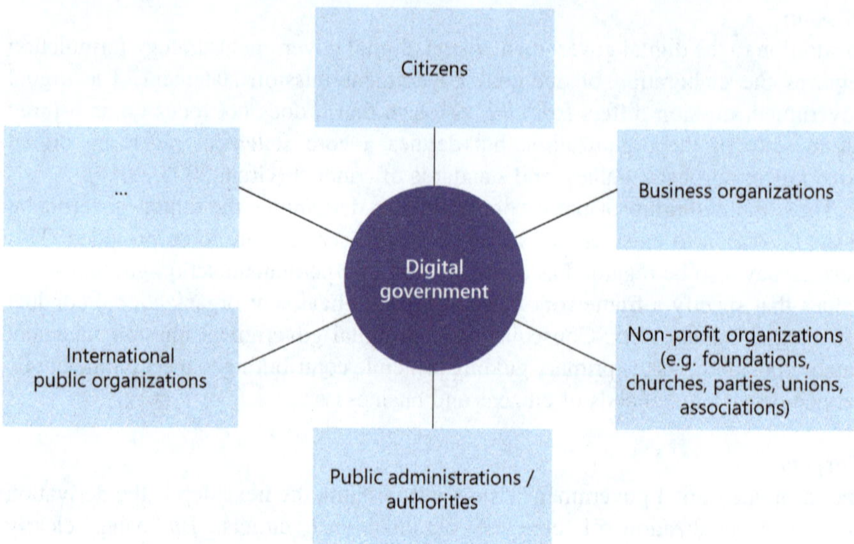

Fig. 3.5 Taxonomy of digital government stakeholders. Source: Wirtz and Daiser (2015, 2017)

Stakeholders of the public sector are persons or organizations that can affect or are affected by its actions (citizens, businesses, public administrators, etc.). In order to systematically consider the interests of different stakeholders in the digital government targets, identifying relevant or potential stakeholders is a first important step.

Since taking into account every digital government pressure group is generally neither constructive nor realistic, the identified stakeholders have to be further specified according to their inherent target and power structure (Welge et al. 2017). The key objective of this task is to identify the agenda of the individual stakeholders.

In addition, it is important to assess—depending on the power structure of the respective stakeholder—the potential influence that stakeholders can exert on the initiative or organization. Based on this analysis, the final step is to determine how stakeholders relate to the overall digital government targets, which in summary defines if they have to be considered in the target formulation.

Goals of Digital Government Strategy

In terms of goal setting, it can be summarized that the primary strategic objective of digital government is to provide direct and convenient digital access to government services. However, there are multiple subgoals in order to achieve these primary goals through digital government.

Each goal should take into account the legitimate claims of all digital government stakeholders (Müller-Stewens and Lechner 2011).

Figure 3.6 shows examples of the goals of digital strategies. These include increasing digital data protection, improving digital transparency, assuming digital responsibility, and promoting digital open innovation. In addition, decreasing the digital divide, digital user participation and loyalty, and its improvement are other crucial digital government goals. Further goals of digital government strategies are the development of digital know-how and the protection thereof, as well as the promotion of digital open innovation.

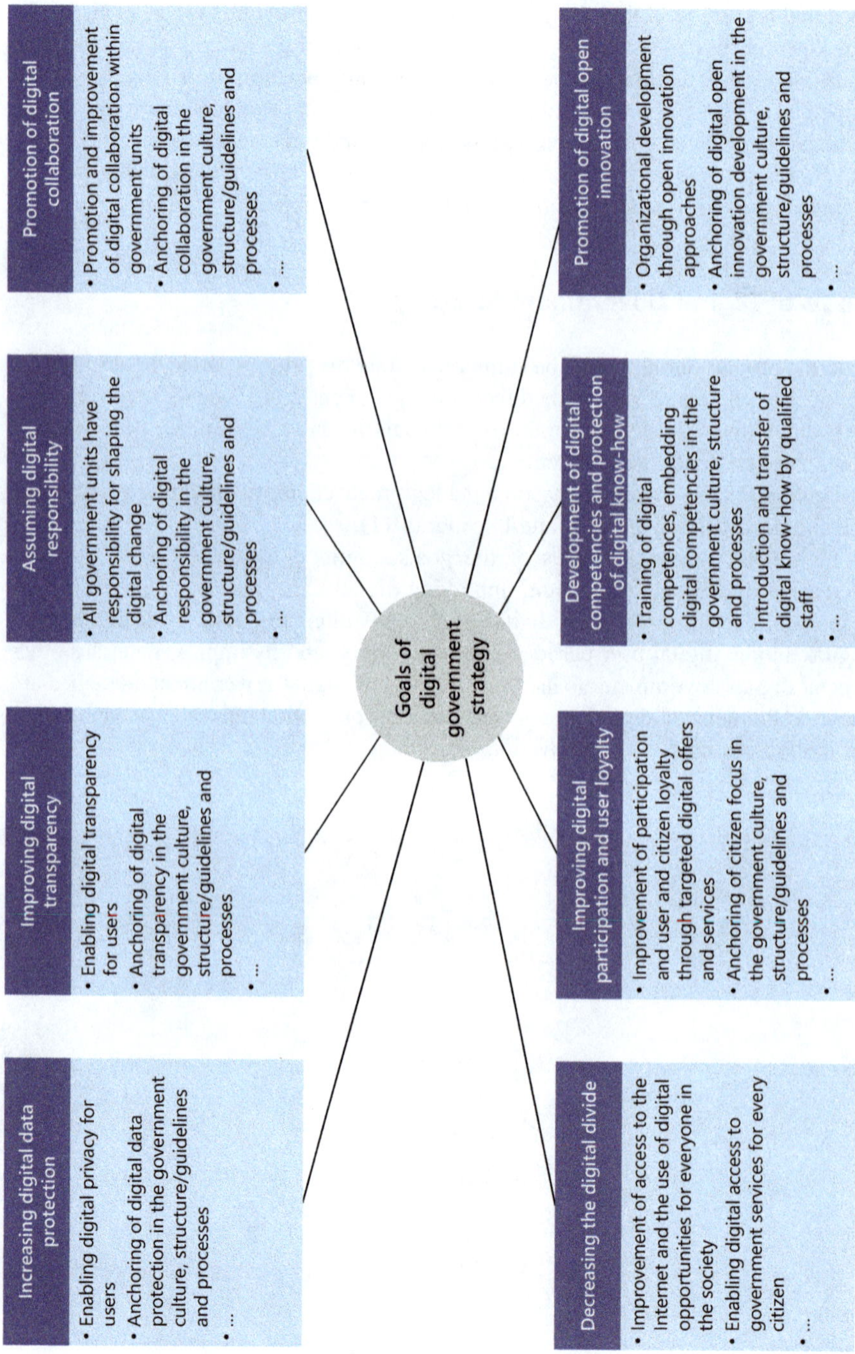

Fig. 3.6 Goals of digital government strategy. Source: Wirtz (2020a, 2021)

Increasing Digital Data Protection
The first goal to be achieved with digital strategies relates to increasing digital data protection. In order to meet the growing privacy expectations of users, it is important to anchor digital data protection within digital government strategy.

Improving Digital Transparency
The second goal deals with the improvement of digital transparency. By implementing appropriate strategies, governments can deal with the growing need for transparency in the digital age. In addition, a strategy based on transparency helps to identify and prevent corporate misconduct at an early stage.

Assuming Digital Responsibility
The third objective concerns the responsibility of government units to shape the digital change. To achieve this goal, governments must become aware of their responsibility with regard to digitalization. In this respect, digital technologies should be used primarily for the benefit of people. In a broader sense, government units should always adopt a critical approach when they implement new technologies.

Promotion of Digital Collaboration
The fourth goal of digital government strategies refers to digital collaboration. Digital technologies enable collaboration regardless of time and place. As soon as government units consider the potential of digital collaboration when designing their digital strategy, they can benefit from significant efficiency gains.

Decreasing the Digital Divide
The fifth goal of a digital government strategy can be to decrease the digital divide. For this purpose, it is necessary to improve the access to the Internet for everyone in society. Thus, everyone has the option to use digital opportunities. Digital government can hence enable digital access to government services for every citizen.

Improving Digital Participation and User Loyalty
The sixth goal that digital strategies can be directed at is improving user participation and loyalty. With the help of digital technologies, services and products can be offered more precisely, thus increasing user loyalty. Furthermore, digital interfaces enable the participation of users.

Development of Digital Competencies and Protection of Digital Know-how
Seventhly, a digital strategy can aim at developing digital competencies. By integrating training into their digital strategy, government units can promote the emergence of these organizational competencies. Subsequently, governments can focus on protecting their digital know-how, which is especially important in the face of increasing competition from the private sector.

Promotion of Digital Open Innovation

Eighthly, the strategic objective of promoting open innovation can also be a goal of digital strategy. In this respect, governments can align their innovations directly with external demands and integrate citizens into the innovation process. Furthermore, by strategically considering open innovation, they can reduce costs compared to conventional innovation strategies and exploit the innovative power of external actors.

With regard to internal processes, the development of digital skills among staff and the promotion of digital collaboration within government units should be mentioned. In addition, the preservation of digital know-how represents a further goal in digital government.

These goals should be reflected and implemented in the government culture, the government structure, and the various government processes.

Digital Government Situational Analysis

The second step of the digital government target plan is the digital government situational analysis (see Figure 3.4). Figure 3.7 presents an overview of the situational digital government analysis.

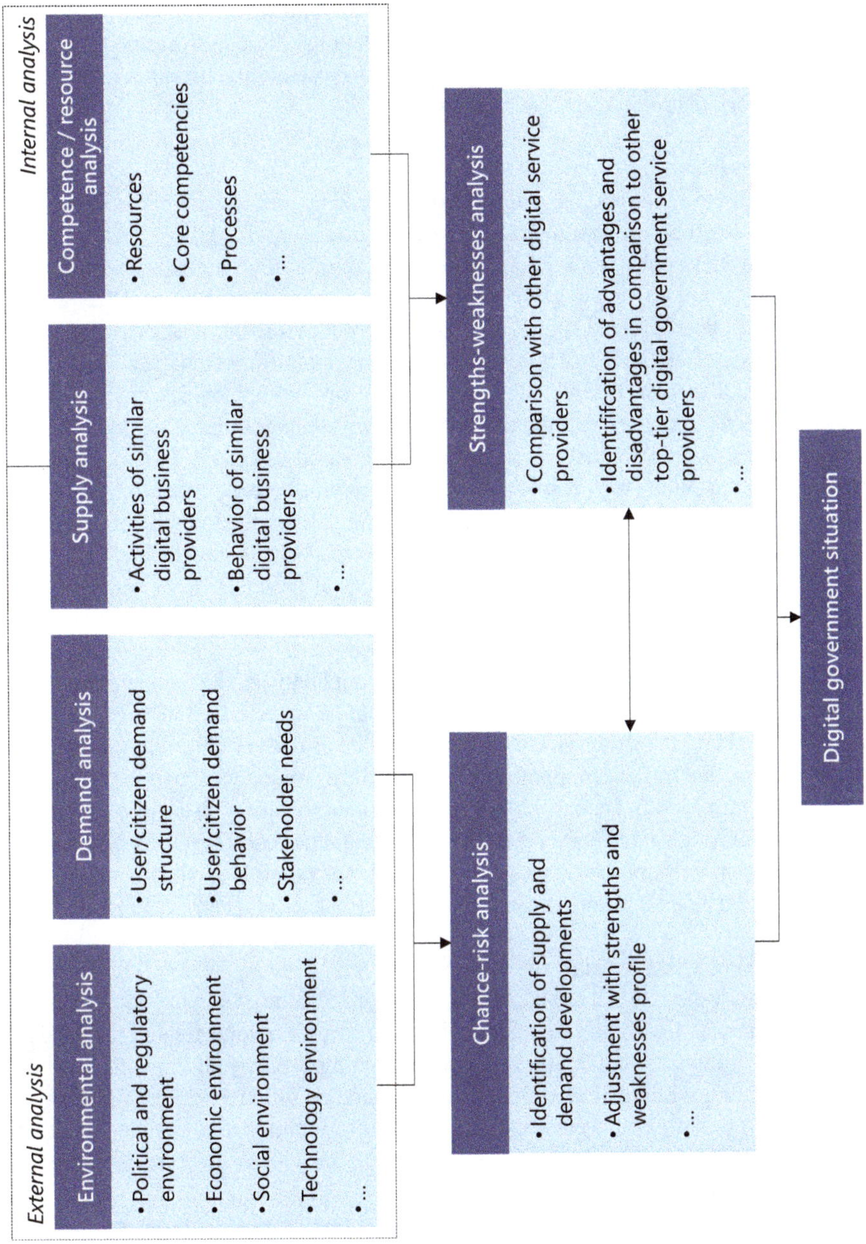

Fig. 3.7 Elements of the situational digital government analysis. Source: Wirtz (2001, 2010, 2021)

Since the situational analysis is a fundamental framework in strategy development, this step requires special attention. The situational digital government analysis proceeds in two streams: an analysis with an internal orientation and an analysis with an external orientation (Andrews 2003).

Internal Analysis

The internal view covers the analysis of internal resources, competencies, and processes as well as the activities and the behavior of similar e-service providers. The external view deals with the analysis of the digital government system from a macro and a micro perspective. Whereas the micro environment refers to investigating stakeholder demands and provider behavior, the macro level relates to the analysis of demand structures and regulatory conditions (Chaffey 2009).

The internal analysis is directed to the organization's competencies and resources. This perspective strives to identify one's own demand-related resources and competencies. In this context, resources are understood as classical factors that are required to provide the respective digital services (e.g., people, IT), and competencies are combining factors that allow the value-added combination of the resources (e.g., specific skills, knowledge). Here, core competencies that are required for an organization's service provision are of particular importance.

Competence/Resource Analysis

In the next step of the situational digital government analysis, the competencies and resources of other digital service providers need to be investigated in the same way and integrated into the analysis. Other digital service providers are private and public organizations that offer comparable digital services (e.g., city portal providers, community providers). Their behavior and activities to satisfy user demand are of paramount importance for defining their own strategic targets. Therefore, all relevant digital service providers should be analyzed—as far as possible—with regard to their targets, strategies, and competencies.

Strengths–Weaknesses Analysis

The outcome of the internal analysis, consisting of the competency/resource and the provider analysis, can be transferred into an organization-oriented strengths-weaknesses analysis, indicating the potential competency-pull impact that the existing digital government organization can generate within its sphere of influence. The aim of the strengths-weaknesses analysis is to identify and evaluate existing advantages and disadvantages compared to other providers in order to derive a reasonable scope of action.

External Analysis

Concerning the demand analysis, the stakeholder needs, demands, and behavior have to be investigated because these influence the demand fundamentally. This step aims at creating transparency to achieve a stakeholder-oriented approach, taking into account their specific requirements. When looking at the environmental analysis, the objective of the investigation is to identify conditions that have a direct or indirect influence on the organization.

Chance-Risk Analysis
The findings of the environmental and the demand analysis are summarized in a chance-risk analysis, revealing the capacities to develop a competency-push impact.

Finally, a comparison of the chance-risk analysis and the strengths-weaknesses analysis allows a meaningful assessment of the organization's situation from an internal and an external perspective. This information establishes a rational and comprehensive basis for choosing the fundamental strategic options for the digital government system.

Digital Government Strategy Formulation
The third step of the digital government target plan is the digital government strategy formulation. The achieved results of the formerly conducted analyses concerning the organization's situation allow us to define the aspired digital government strategy. For this purpose, it is necessary to be aware of the generally available strategic digital government options—how the digital service may be provided from a strategic perspective—to make a reasonable evaluation and determine the deducted strategy in the next stage.

According to Porter (1985), there are generic market and competitor strategies that successful organizations consistently follow. Transferred to the digital government environment, this means that public managers should consider demand and provider strategies in order to achieve a prosperous digital government outcome. In this context, demand strategies refer to the procedures that an organization chooses to satisfy its stakeholder demands and provider strategies refer to the focus that an organization has for achieving a competitive advantage.

Based on this line of thought, demand strategies mainly deal with the question of which digital services shall be provided and which stakeholders shall be addressed. In contrast, provider strategies aim at achieving a competitive advantage through being more efficient than other providers or through differentiating their digital service offer from that of other providers. Therefore, it is reasonable to follow one of the three consistent strategic options, which are summarized in Figure 3.8.[8]

[8] See for the following Section Digital Government Strategy Formulation also Wirtz (2020b).

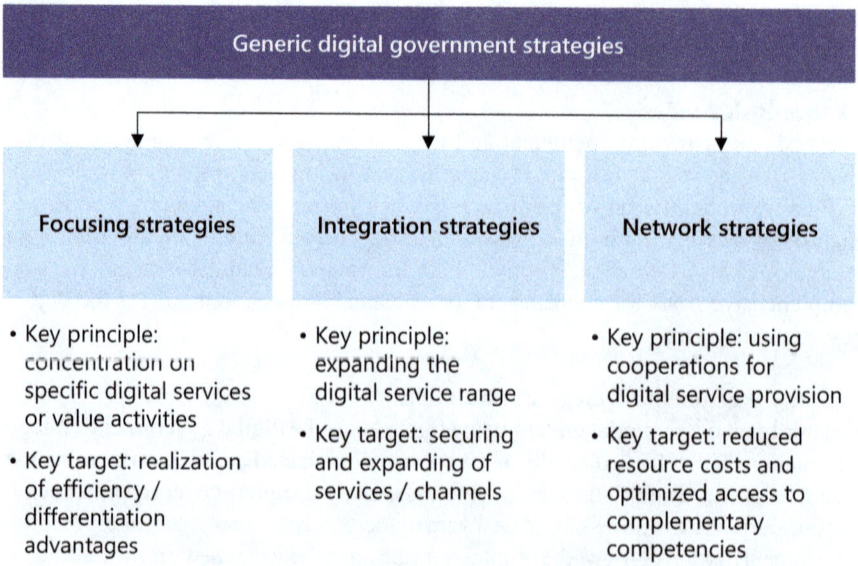

Fig. 3.8 Generic digital government strategies. Source: Wirtz (2006, 2011, 2020b)

1. *Focusing Strategies*

Within the framework of a focusing strategy, a digital government system is laid out to a specific area or set of digital services, in which the organization attempts to achieve a leading position within its field. This form of strategy allows us to gain efficiency or differentiation advantages. A focusing strategy can make sense in complex and innovative environments if the core competencies of the organization facilitate a leading position in the corresponding value stage.

This strategic option may thus, for instance, be viewed as a transitional step for public authorities that just started off with their digital government system and quickly want to address specific stakeholder needs to generate digital service traffic on their servers. This strategy is used by many Internet enterprises during their initial phases. A well-known example of this is Google or Yahoo, which first only offered a search engine to gain market presence before dedicating themselves to offer additional digital services, such as news, email, finance, or location services.

2. *Integration Strategies*

Integration strategies—in contrast to focusing strategies—target to expand the digital service range. This can be pursued through the independent—in-house, outsourced, or a mix of both—development of new services (internal expansion) or acquisition of existing providers or suppliers (external expansion).

This strategic option may be used to exploit an organization's existing core competencies and to reduce its dependency from other providers. In the case of digital government, integration strategies mainly deal with horizontal integration, expanding their digital service range across different administrative subjects. Currently, a massive development and expansion of offered public digital services from various private and public providers can be seen.

3. *Network Strategies*

Besides focusing and integration strategies, network strategies are an additional strategic option. The underlying principle of networking strategies is the formation of two or more organizations that cooperatively work together on a specific service or process. These forms can be observed on horizontal, vertical, and lateral levels. Organizations that cooperate on a horizontal level are called strategic alliances, whereas vertical or lateral orientated collaborations are labeled strategic networks. However, in all circumstances the organizations stay legally independent.

Network strategies allow organizations to benefit from both focusing and integration strategies. First, because the different network partners can concentrate on, develop, and bring in their core competencies and, second, because the network structure supports the integration of skilled highly specialized service providers. Moreover, network strategies enable organizations to better keep up with the increasing innovation rate since service or product development can be shouldered by various partners.

Besides these convincing chances, network strategies also carry risks, such as losing know-how, free-riding of partners, or unpredictable behavior of competing organizations. Apart from that, networks do tend to be unstable, which may lead to uncertainty among the organizations involved and may complicate collaboration and cooperation between the partners in the long run.

Summing up, focusing, integration, and network strategies possess manifold advantages, but may also give rise to problems and difficulties if not applied in a sensible manner. Therefore, the derivation and assessment of strategic options needs to be based on a current comprehensive situational analysis and conducted very carefully, taking into account relevant and appropriate internal and external factors. This is the fundamental groundwork for digital government strategy selection.

Digital Government Strategy Implementation

Having formulated the digital government strategy, the next step of the digital government target plan is the digital government strategy implementation.[9] This step serves to implement the formerly defined digital government strategy and accordingly to pursue the aspired goals of the digital government strategy. Figure 3.9 illustrates the phases that are associated with this step.

[9]For further information on digital government implementation, please refer to Chapter 14.

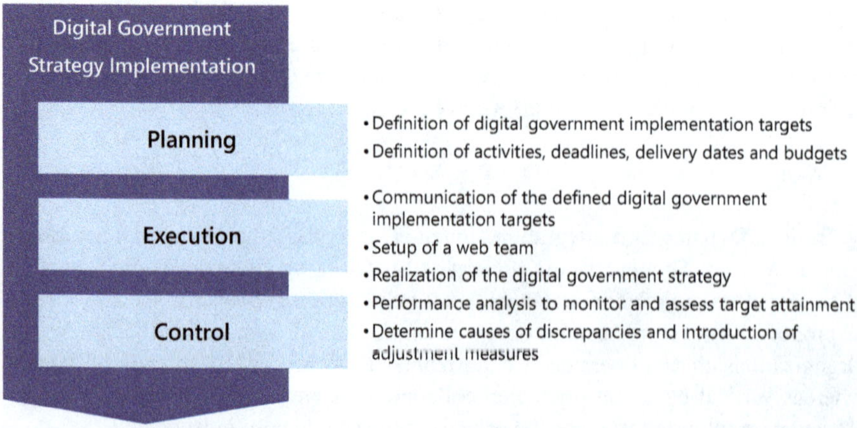

Fig. 3.9 Digital government implementation phases. Source: Wirtz (2010, 2020a, 2021)

The strategy implementation procedure is an interdisciplinary and cross-hierarchical process. Its coordination requires an approach in multiple stages, which are passed iteratively. Although the scientific literature on strategy implementation shows different approaches on this topic, these mainly differ concerning their constituents, but are in general based on a rather similar schedule model.

In the digital government context, subdividing the digital government strategy implementation process into the three classic phases, planning, execution, and control, proves to be useful. Specific success factors arise from the particular characteristics of the digital government online or Internet environment, which should be considered when implementing digital government.

Planning

The planning phase serves to determine the key targets of the digital government strategy implementation. In addition to the specification of the implementation proceeding, expense figures in particular decisions regarding budgeting, deadlines, schedules, resources, and milestones are assessed in this phase.

There exist various instruments, such as network diagrams or detailed workflow schedules, to implement these plans. Due to the typically extensive planning effort that is associated with realizing or implementing digital government strategy concepts, efficient handling of this matter usually requires adequate IT support. Therefore, the corresponding resources have to be considered, too.

Execution

On completion of the planning phase, the digital government strategy implementation enters the execution phase. Here, the strategy targets and the respective implementation approach need to be communicated first. Early communication of these matters can, for instance, support acceptance of the pursued digital government strategy among affected public administration staff.

Once the basic structures for strategy implementation have been created, a project team must be put together that is assigned with the task of implementing the digital government strategy implementation plans. Against the background of the online context, recruiting technical experts who possess an adequate level of network, web, and IT expertise is a mandatory provision. Therefore, the project team needs to be equipped with people who have a relevant set of digital government proficiency.

The core process of the execution phase is the actual implementation of the digital government strategy implementation plans in the public sector organization. This stage of the digital government strategy development process reflects the transition from the planning to the execution phase.

Control

Evaluating the degree of implementation or how well the aspired goals of the digital government strategy implementation have been realized is the aim of the final phase control. In this context, interim results and project progress need to be constantly measured and critically examined. If necessary, particular parts or tasks of the projects have to be rerun if the desired outcome has not been achieved.

Digital government implementation projects usually require certain stages that need to be completed successfully in order to achieve the desired results. In addition, successful project progress requires comprehensive project management on a project leadership level that spans all associated phases.

Success Factors of Digital Government Strategy Implementation

The success of implementing a digital government strategy strongly depends on the specific field of application, numerous environmental factors, and ultimately the respective strategy. Nevertheless, basic factors and parameters can be identified. Their knowledge and conscientious observance can sustainably increase the success of digital government strategy implementation.

Particularly in view of the prevailing dynamic competitive and market environment, it must be ensured that strategy is implemented at a certain speed while still allowing flexible adjustments (Rayport and Jaworski 2001).

In addition to considering the dynamic and competitive market environment of digital government, the success factors of digital government strategy implementation listed in Figure 3.10 can also be mentioned.

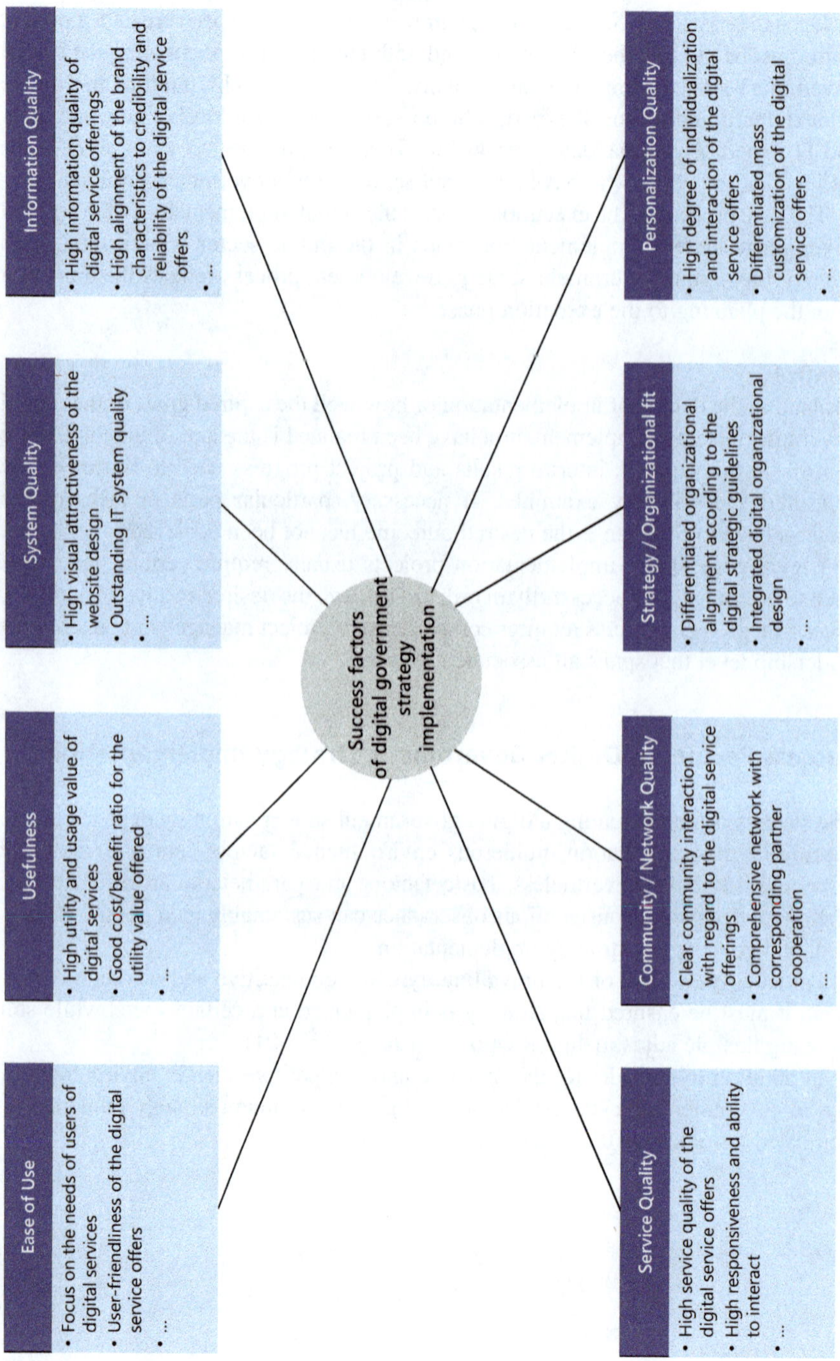

Fig. 3.10 Success factors of digital government strategy implementation. Source: Wirtz (2020a, 2021)

Digital Government Strategy Scorecard

In order to systematically reflect all digital government relevant strategic management dimensions, it is reasonable to apply a digital government strategy scorecard, which is a method to keep track of digital government strategy relevant factors. Figure 3.11 provides an example of a digital government strategy scorecard (Kaplan and Norton 1997).

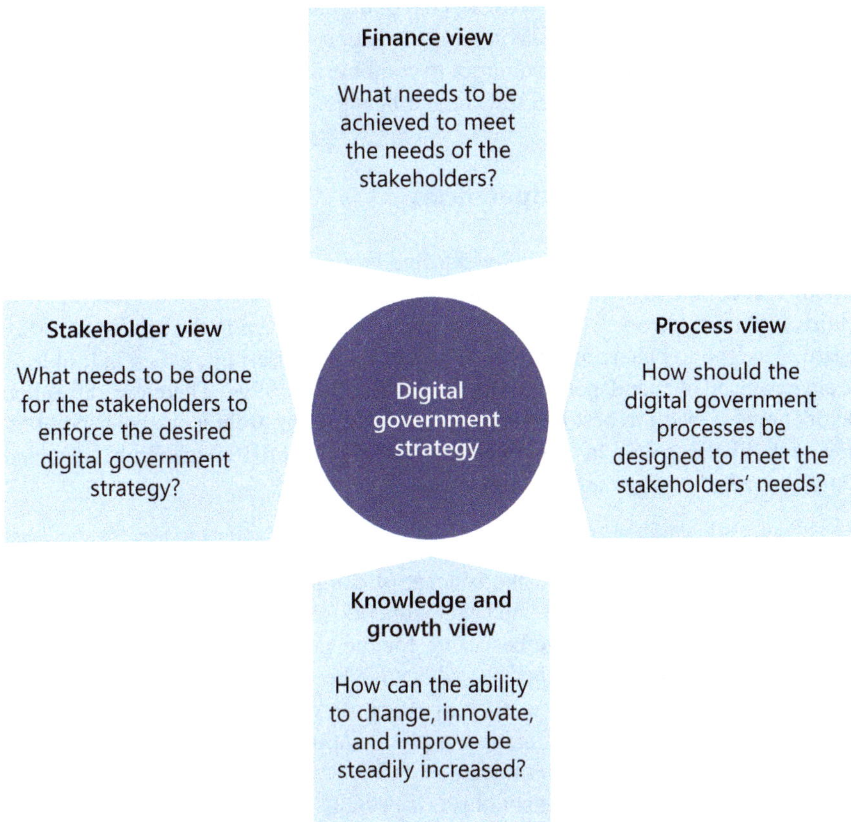

Fig. 3.11 Dimensions of the digital government strategy scorecard. Source: Wirtz (2011, 2016, 2018)

A digital government strategy scorecard allows us to assess the performance of a digital government strategy concerning its formerly defined dimensions, which are measured through a limited number of indicators. There are four dimensions, which should be considered when developing the digital government strategy scorecard—the finance, the process, the knowledge and growth, and the stakeholder view.

The finance view deals with the question: what needs to be achieved to meet the stakeholders' needs? This usually refers to specific investment and cost-cutting targets that should be included in the digital government strategy. The process view is concerned with the strategic design of the digital government processes in a way that these meet the needs of the respective stakeholders.

From a knowledge and growth view, a digital government strategy should provide a clear strategic guideline on how to foster the ability for future enhancement. Finally, it is indispensable to have a clear vision of what needs to be done for the stakeholders, so that they support the desired digital government strategy.

Further vital factors for long-term success of digital government systems are core assets, which take on a central role in service creation, and core competencies, which denote the public authority's capabilities to combine its assets and competencies in a manner that gives rise to special stakeholder benefits.

Core Assets and Core Competencies

In classic management theory, core assets and core competencies give companies a sustainable competitive advantage, which leads to the achievement of superior returns in the long term.[10] Moreover, competitive advantage in the private sector is regarded to lead to better, superior product and service offerings, which in turn lead to an enhanced demand position (Fahy and Smithee 1999). Therefore, all other factors being equal, the best product and service offering from a customer point of view will finally result in a market leadership position by satisfying customer demand in a better way than the competitors.

Competitive Advantage

Transferred to the public sector, the concept of competitive advantage thus allows the respective organization to create better, superior service offerings and to provide its services for society with higher value for the public, supporting their public service remit. In addition, competitive advantage becomes a vital factor for public administration for further reasons, such as efficiency demands of the public and the government, shared services, conducting privatization processes, to maintain and increase citizen trust in the government.

In the case of digital government, this is especially important since governmental providers, for example, face increasing competition from the private sector (e.g., privately managed city or tourism portals) or have to deal with user dissatisfaction and user churn (e.g., users who do not want to use electronic service provision anymore and may switch to other providers or service channels).

Furthermore, local competitive disadvantage will lead to an ongoing centralization of digital government service provision, which in turn results in a decrease of local activities and resources. At the same time, digital government faces intra-channel competition since it should possess benefits compared to the former status

[10] See for the following Section Core Assets and Core Competencies also Wirtz (2020b).

quo (e.g., face-to-face public administration visits to handle administrative matters) in order to attract users for online service provision.

Summing up, competitive advantage is of vital importance for the public sector, too. Nonetheless, considering this work's digital government focus, this concept is referred to as digital government advantage, which can also be achieved through identification and effective management of core assets and core competencies.

Core Assets

Core assets are those tangible and intangible assets that play a central role in the establishment and marketing of digital government online services. In the case of public sector organizations, these include employees, data, or the technological infrastructure.

Core competencies complement core assets and describe the capabilities of the public sector organization, particularly the capabilities of its employees and its management to combine the public sector organization's assets and core assets in a way to achieve special user benefits. Examples of core competencies of public sector organizations in a digital government context are outstanding user relationship management or distinguishing technology and programming abilities.

The concept of core assets and core competencies arises from the resource-based theory approaches of strategic management. Therefore, the resource-based view and its advanced concepts—capability-based, dynamic capability-based, and knowledge-based view—form the basis for the following discussion of core assets and core competencies of digital government management.

Resource-Based Approach

The resource-based approaches are used to explain differences in results between organizations and to derive strategies for the creation of competitive advantages. In this context, an inside-out perspective is applied, meaning that the accumulated internal assets and capabilities of the organization are in focus.

Based on this reasoning, the achievement of sustainable competitive advantage is attributed to the unique and specific assets and competencies of an organization. Discrepancies in these assets and competencies as well as in their management are regarded as reasons for differences in organizational success.

The classic resource-based view is primarily concerned with the assets and core assets of an organization, largely neglecting competencies. The term asset in this context refers to an undifferentiated input factor, which is freely acquirable in the market and forms the necessary condition for all activities of an organization (Teece et al. 1997). Thus, financial resources or human resources are general examples for assets.

If organization-specific assets play a particularly important role in the value chain of the organization, these are referred to as core assets. However, assets can only be classified as core assets if they are valuable to value creation, rarely available in the market, and not easy to imitate or to substitute. Otherwise, they cannot create the potential for sustainable digital government advantage. Based on this proposition, the following definition for the asset and core asset concept concerning public sector organizations is derived.

Digital Government-related Definition of Assets and Core Assets (Wirtz 2011, 2020a)

Assets are tangible and intangible resources that form the basis for the activities and the competitiveness of a public sector organization. Core assets concern public sector organization-specific assets that were accumulated in-house or were at least refined and that have a special intrinsic value for a public sector organization's value creation process. They are relatively scarce and are difficult to imitate or substitute. Core assets form the basis for a lasting digital government advantage.

The resource-based view follows the fundamental premise of imperfect factor markets. This theoretical circumstance is the prerequisite for the asset heterogeneity of organizations, which underlies the resource-based theory approach. According to this reasoning, above-average returns can only be achieved if the value of an acquired asset exceeds its cost.

In addition to imperfect factor markets, there are usually no specific factor markets for highly specific or intangible organizational assets. Citizen trust, for example, cannot be acquired in the market, but can only be built on long-term high-quality service provision. Such internally accumulated assets are generally of far greater importance for an organization's success than purchasable factor markets. Since these core assets are highly organization-specific, difficult to imitate, and mostly difficult to substitute, they usually reflect the largest differentiation potential.

Digital government-related core assets of public sector organizations are for example exclusive alliances and networks, existing and obtained data, employees, IT platform, and technological infrastructure. By building up exclusive alliances with specialized information or service providers, public sector organizations can elaborate unique features of their online service offerings to lure users to their digital government platform and keep them revisiting.

Public sector organizations also have the possibility to create exclusive alliances and networks within the public sector that are difficult to imitate by competitors from the private sector. Moreover, much of existing and obtained data in public sector organizations is either not directly available through other sources or cannot be retrieved at all. Smart application of this data can therefore generate a digital government advantage.

The employees of a public sector organization, being the persons with the relevant know-how and competencies, are essential for value creation. Since their implicit knowledge and expertise is rarely available in the market and difficult to imitate, employees are core assets of the public sector organization. The IT platform, being the interface between the digital government user and provider, and the technological infrastructure, providing the backbone for the functioning of the digital government system, are core assets of public sector organizations.

Competency-Based Perspective

The answer to the question how a core asset-based digital government advantage is transferred into superior services is provided through the competency-based perspective of the resource-based theory. The underlying assumption of this perspective is that organizational skills and abilities allow smart combinations of assets and core assets creating surpassing services, which are different from those of competitors and have thus the potential to create user preferences.

For this reason, competencies allow us to manage core assets in a way to achieve digital government advantages for the public sector organization. Organizational competencies are therefore a coordination capacity that is based on the social interaction patterns, the knowledge, and the individual skills of the public sector organization's employees and its management.

Characteristics of Core Competencies

According to the management-oriented explanation of Prahalad and Hamel (1990), core competencies are characterized by three features: (1) provide access to various business areas, (2) are transferable to a multitude of products/services and/or customer groups, and (3) form the basis for its core products or services. Based on the previous discussion, competencies and core competencies of public sector organizations can be defined as follows:

Digital Government-Related Definition of Competencies and Core Competencies (Wirtz 2011, 2020a)

Competencies form the foundation for the collective action in a public sector organization and facilitate the service creation process, in which assets and core assets are combined into valuable services. Core competencies are a special form of competencies. They are relatively scarce and do not lend themselves to imitation or substitution by the competition. Core competencies make a significant contribution to the perceived user benefits and provide public sector organizations with a lasting digital government advantage.

Automatization and data processing competencies are of high importance for digital government implementation and management. The same holds true for content creation competency, which covers the abilities that are necessary for successfully producing information content that satisfies user demand. An outstanding digital government system further requires collaboration competency since comprehensive service provision usually involves the collaboration among different organizations or organization units.

Experience design competency refers to the ability of creating a satisfying user experience while visiting the online platform. Technology and programming competencies are indispensable abilities for a digital government undertaking since these are needed to set up, maintain, and develop the relevant IT infrastructure.

Running a successful digital government system calls for distinct information and service bundling as well as service development competencies since these directly influence the service offering, which is designed to satisfy the user's demands. Finally, user relationship management is an important core competency since this requires the activities to attract users to the digital government system and to maintain the growing user base. Figure 3.12 provides a summary portrayal of digital government-related core assets and core competencies in the public sector.

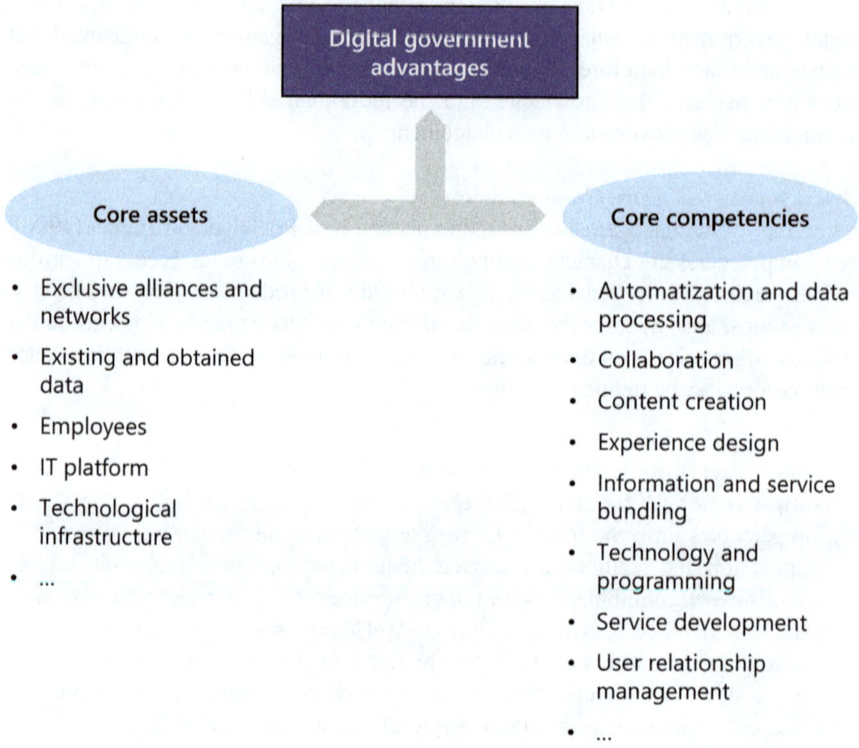

Fig. 3.12 Digital government-related core assets and core competencies. Source: Wirtz (2005, 2019, 2021)

The system to provide digital government services needs to be envisaged like a tree. In this picture, the trunk and major limbs are core services, the smaller branches are service segments, and the leaves are the final digital government services. Since the actual source of sustainable digital government advantage lies in an effective and enduring combination of core assets and core competencies, a superior final digital government service may only result in a short-term competitive benefit but for the most part not in a long-term digital government advantage.

Roots of Competitive Digital Government Services

For this reason, the interconnected "tree system" is based on its roots, the core competencies, which provide the nourishing basis for sustainable competitive service provision. Thus, like a tree, the digital government system grows from its roots and branches out to its final digital government services.

Prahalad and Hamel (1990) exemplify this matter by referring to an organization that possesses the core competency of producing electronic displays. By using its competency, the organization could successfully do business with different products in different markets (e.g., pocket calculators, watches, smartphones, tablets, machinery and equipment).

Transferred to the digital government context, this means that the public sector organization's core competencies can be applied to establish a lasting digital government advantage in terms of superior service provision. Given, for example, the core competencies automatization and data processing, experience design, service development, and service bundling, these can be exploited to develop outstanding core services, like electronic declarations or electronic voting, which are tailored to specific service segments, such as citizens or businesses.

Since both core assets and core competencies are not rigid or stiff objects but responsive factors that can be developed, the resource-based perspective was complemented with the dynamic capabilities view. Dynamic capabilities explain the development of resources and competencies over time and reflect an organization's capability to build up, configure, integrate, and coordinate core assets and competencies (Teece et al. 1997).

Building up or dismantling core assets or core competencies is, for example, required if organizations are constrained to adapt to varying surrounding conditions. This activity demands regular reviews of an organization's assets and competencies in order to decide which, for instance, need to be developed or degraded.

These processes can be controlled by the management of the organization through the definition of specific goals and strategies that support an asset or competency-based development. Here, especially the digital government user needs and requirements should serve as a benchmark for the continuous review of the core asset and core competency profile. The cycle is illustrated in Figure 3.13.

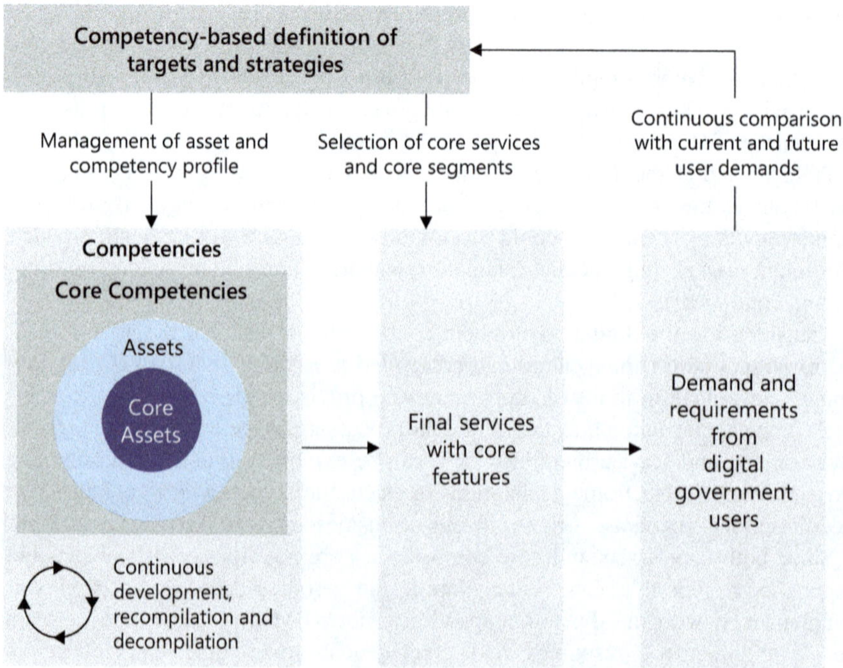

Fig. 3.13 Core asset and core competency development. Source: Wirtz (2005, 2019)

Developing core assets and core competencies requires a systematic analysis and management process since this procedure plays a vital role in the formulation of recommendations for action in order to ensure the organization's future success. First, the core assets and core competencies that possess strategic importance for the organization need to be determined. Here, future scenarios may be analyzed to identify promising core assets and core competencies, i.e., mobility is assumed to become an important topic for digital government provision, and thus, IT platform, technological infrastructure, technology and programming, and service development are promising core assets and core competencies.

Second, the achieved hypothetical target state is compared with the current core asset and core competency profile to identify relevant fields of action. If, for instance, a public sector organization does not yet have access to the required core assets and core competencies to adequately address the previously mentioned mobility topic, these need to be actively developed. In the same manner, core assets or core competencies can be outsourced, reduced, or completely dropped if they do not show strategic or operative relevance anymore.

Finally, the results of the target and actual situation outcome are transferred to derive the respective course of action. Core assets and core competencies that show, for instance, a high future significance, but a low current state should be quickly build up, intensifying investments and knowledge management. However, core assets and core competencies that show a diametrically opposed picture (low future significance but high current state) should be dismantled and disinvested.

Analysis and Management of Core Competencies

If specific core assets and core competencies have rather become obsolete (low future significance and low current state), these may be outsourced or further reduced. If core assets and core competencies, however, show high future significance and the public sector organization already has achieved a high current state, they should be maintained and upgraded by all means.

Having set a clear strategic course of action, the respective core assets and core competencies can be systematically developed or dismantled and thus adjusted to the public sector organization's digital government requirements. Apart from the strategic management perspective, information and communication technologies, which are a key driver for digital government, play an important role in the conception of the digital government system.

Open government is often mentioned as a closely related concept to digital government, which in this context should be taken into account. For this purpose, the concept of open government is explained in the following and compared with the concept of digital government.

3.4 Open Government

The topic open government, which generally stands for the opening of the state and the administration to the economy and the population (Wirtz and Schmitt 2015), has received increasing attention in recent years. A key driver for its growing popularity in science and public management was the Obama Administration's Initiative on Transparency and Open Government (Evans and Campos 2013; Lee and Kwak 2012). Its global importance is underlined by the Open Government Partnership, which was established in 2011 and already counts 78 member countries (Open Government Partnership 2021).

The core of this initiative was to create a transparent, participative, and collaborative government by involving public stakeholders in public policy and public administration processes. In addition, this change should lead to more effective and more efficient administrative procedures and prepare government for the digital challenges (Wirtz and Birkmeyer 2015; Wirtz et al. 2018c).

Making Public Sector Data Accessible

The basic idea behind the open government concept, making public sector data accessible, is neither new nor groundbreaking. These considerations can be traced far back into the past within the context of freedom of information, anti-corruption, or previous transparency initiatives (Nam 2012). US President Thomas Jefferson, for example, already declared in 1789 that a certain degree of information availability and openness is necessary for the people's trust in the government (Yagoda 2010).

However, considering the possibilities that modern information and communication technologies provide and leveraging them "to generate participatory, collaborative dialogue between policymakers and citizens" (Evans and Campos 2013, p. 173) shows manifold opportunities for various areas, such as public policy, public management, governance, economy, and science.

Definition of Open Government

Despite the increasing number of publications on open government in recent years, it is a rather young field of research, and definitions and explanations often still leave room for interpretation. This circumstance becomes clear when looking at popular open government definitions, which are presented in Table 3.1:

Table 3.1 Selected definitions of open government

Author(s)	Definition
OECD (2009)	"Open and responsive government refers to the transparency of government actions, the accessibility of government services and information, and the responsiveness of government to new ideas, demands and needs."
Geiger and von Lucke (2012)	"Open Government acts as an umbrella term for many different ideas and concepts. The narrow definition of Open Government consists of transparency, participation and collaboration of the state towards third actors like the economy or the citizenship."
Harrison et al. (2012)	"Broader access to government data and other documentation, the ability to contribute to decision-making processes within government agencies, and the possibility of responsible engagement with agency leadership in such processes are incrementally more democratic actions that lie at the heart of the open government vision."
Meijer et al. (2012)	"Openness of government is the extent to which citizens can monitor and influence government processes through access to government information and access to decision-making arenas."
Evans and Campos (2013)	"Open government is widely understood as the leveraging of information technologies to generate participatory, collaborative dialogue between policymakers and citizens."
Wirtz and Birkmeyer (2015)	"Open government is a multilateral, political, and social process, which includes in particular transparent, collaborative, and participatory action by government and administration."

Source: Wirtz and Daiser (2017), Wirtz (2021)

The OECD (2009) describes open government as a concept of transparency, accessibility, and responsiveness for government information and action. The understanding of Geiger and von Lucke (2012), who see open government as transparency, participation, and collaboration fostering concept between government and third parties, heads in a similar direction, but does show variations though. Concerning Harrison et al. (2012), their definition focuses on access and participation of public stakeholders in governmental decision-making and actions. Meijer et al. (2012) relate open government to monitoring and influencing government processes through adequate access to information and decision processes.

The definition of Evans and Campos (2013) emphasizes technological aspects and thus sees the development of modern information and communication technologies as key open government enabler and driver. Wirtz and Birkmeyer (2015) view open government more from a conceptual perspective and explain that open government is a multilateral process, which requires transparent, participatory, and collaborative governmental action.

Since to our understanding open government is rather of a philosophical, meta-level nature than digital government, which can be regarded as a modern form of government from a functional and technical perspective that lays the basis for open government, we apply the following definition of open government:

Definition of Open Government (Wirtz et al. 2017)
Open government is a concept that generates a transparent, participatory, collaborative, and innovative government environment by providing existing data and knowledge to third parties and integrating external knowledge into political and administrative processes.

Open Government Framework

The elements and relationships within the open government framework are deduced from the literature, which serves as a guideline for explaining the concept of open government. The framework consists of an internal (the three open government pillars: transparency, participation, and collaboration) and an external part (the external drivers: accountability, technology, acceptance and trust in government, and regulation and law) (see Figure 3.14; content based on Wirtz and Birkmeyer 2015).

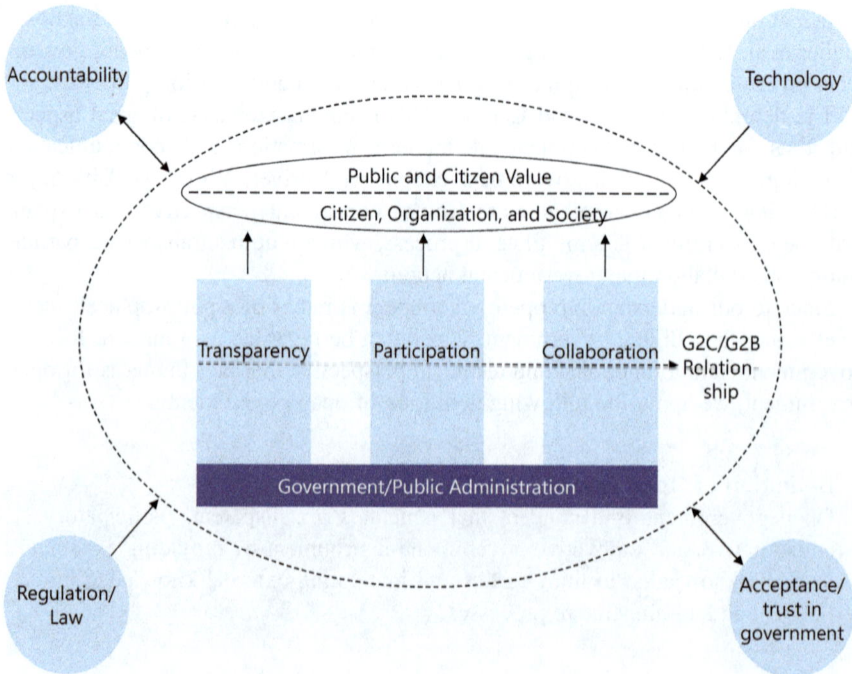

Fig. 3.14 Open government framework. Source: Wirtz and Daiser (2017), Wirtz (2021)

Three Pillars of Open Government

Transparency is one of the most frequently mentioned aspects of open government. According to van Dooren et al. (2012), transparency consists of three elementary components: (1) systematic and timely release of information, (2) an effective role for legislature, and (3) an effective role for civil society through the media and non-governmental organizations. In this context, transparency requires an adequate public access to relevant information, and thus this constitutes another essential element of transparency (Dawes 2010).

Participation, which means that public stakeholders become involved in public policy and public administration decision-making through information exchange, is another essential part of open government. This concept is supposed to encourage public engagement and increase government decisions through additional relevant input from public stakeholders.

The third pillar of open government is collaboration. In comparison to transparency and participation, collaboration has so far not been directly associated with democratic political theory (Harrison et al. 2012). Collaboration aims at actively engaging public stakeholders in administrative procedures and effective cooperation among executive departments and agencies across all levels of public administration, as well as with citizens and private organizations.

The three open government pillars transparency, participation, and collaboration target at creating and increasing public value, which is the key objective of the open government concept. Public value describes the value that the government contributes to citizens, organizations, and society and thus how public activities contribute to the common good (Moore 1995). Transparency, participation, and collaboration have a significant influence on government-to-citizen and government-to-business relationships since high transparency, active participation, and effective collaboration strengthen the relationship between the government and its stakeholders (Geiger and von Lucke 2012).

External Drivers of Open Government

This core of open government is constantly influenced by the external drivers accountability, technology, acceptance of and trust in government, as well as regulation and law. Accountability is a vital factor since a public administration that is accountable and responsible for its actions and decisions can be regarded as a prerequisite for democratic government as well as good governance (Wirtz et al. 2018b). For this reason, accountability is considered to be a central element of democratic governance.

Technology is a crucial external factor for the concept of open government. Web 2.0 technologies and social media, for example, have had a considerable impact on the relationship between the government and its stakeholders (Wirtz et al. 2018a). The associated availability of information through modern information and communication technologies has led to well-informed stakeholders that are enabled to participate in administrative procedures. Since this factor, however, demands implementation and maintenance of adequate information and communication technologies, the associated technological development may require intensified investments.

Acceptance and trust are further important factors for open government. In this context, acceptance can be understood as the degree to which citizens agree with the open government strategy and the government's tools to implement this strategy, while trust describes the confidence of citizens in their government's work.

Especially transparency and public access to information can be conducive to support acceptance, and participation and collaboration can serve to build trust since they allow public stakeholders to become part of administrative actions.

Regulations and laws set the framework necessary for successful open government, because every administrative action requires and underlies a specific system of rules. Considering that open government is a transnational topic and every country has its own laws, open government concepts and systems can vary significantly between different countries. For this reason, regulations and laws are substantial external factors.

Digital Government and Open Government as Complementary Concepts

Summarizing, digital government and open government should be viewed as complementary concepts. While open government is rather a philosophy or strategy on how to increase public value through transparent, participatory, and collaborative action by the government, digital government is concerned with the electronic handling of administrative procedures to support public duties efficiently and effectively.

However, both concepts are mandatory and mutually dependent for government to become more transparent, more participatory, more collaborative, and more efficient, since digital government provides the required technological approach and open government the necessary conceptual framework. Considering the approach of this book, we focus on digital government without special reference to the open government concept, while keeping in mind that a digital government system should also always strive to realize the open government targets.

As previously explained, citizen participation is a vital element of open government. Governments started in the 1960s to use citizen participation as an instrument "to enhance governmental legitimacy, foster public trust in government, and improve transparency of decision-making processes" (Wirtz et al. 2016, p. 1). Given the importance of digital government development for citizen participation, in particular e-participation, this concept is explained in the following.

3.5 E-Participation

The roots of e-participation date back to the 1960s. At that time, citizen participation started to become a topic of increasing interest. Two decades later, first ideas on e-democracy, which involves citizens in political and democratic procedures through the use of information and communication technologies, were presented (Kim 2008). Given these developments as well as the progress of digital government and open government, e-participation gained considerable momentum and became a topic of high scientific and practical relevance.

While the topic is still seen as an evolving concept, there is vast evidence that e-participation expands opportunities for civic engagement, supports sustainable development, and provides several political and societal benefits. It creates an intrinsic value for citizens that may deepen democracy and make governance more responsive and transparent. Moreover, integrating citizens into policy decisions may lead to more informed strategies and more inclusive societies. Furthermore, e-participation may promote effectiveness of public policy and service delivery and may mobilize new resources, capacities, and ideas (United Nations 2016).

In essence, e-participation is about enhancing the interaction between the government and its citizens/stakeholders through active participation. Following the explanations of the OECD and the United Nations, this is can be achieved through three dimensions: e-information provision, e-consultation, and e-decision-making (OECD 2001; PADM 2013; United Nations 2016). This means that the government has to ensure that the relevant stakeholders receive and have access to the required information, to engage citizens/stakeholders in public policy, and to empower citizens/stakeholders through co-design and co-production of policy and public service components.[11]

Definition of E-Participation

Although it is widely agreed that e-participation requires information and communication technology to provide input and exert influence concerning governmental decision-making and actions, there is still no commonly accepted definition of e-participation (see Table 3.2).

Table 3.2 Selected definitions of e-participation

Author(s)	Definition
OECD (2003)	E-participation as an electronic form of active participation is "a relationship based on partnership with government in which citizens actively engage in defining the process and content of policy-making. It acknowledges equal standing for citizens in setting the agenda, proposing policy options and shaping the policy dialogue—although the responsibility for the final decision or policy formulation rests with government."
Macintosh (2006)	E-participation is "the use of information and communication technologies to broaden and deepen political participation by enabling citizens to connect with one another and with their elected representatives."
Sæbø et al. (2008)	"eParticipation involves the extension and transformation of participation in societal democratic and consultative processes mediated by information and communication technologies (ICT), primarily the Internet. It aims to support active citizenship with the latest technology developments, increasing access to and availability of participation in order to promote fair and efficient society and government."

Source: Wirtz and Daiser (2017), Wirtz (2021)

The OECD sees e-participation as an electronic form of active citizen participation, which is defined as "a relationship based on partnership with government in which citizens actively engage in defining the process and content of policy-making. It acknowledges equal standing for citizens in setting the agenda, proposing policy options and shaping the policy dialogue—although the responsibility for the final decision or policy formulation rests with government" (OECD 2003, p. 55).

Macintosh (2006, p. 365) puts a stronger focus on the technology aspect and defines e-participation as "the use of information and communication technologies to broaden and deepen political participation by enabling citizens to connect with one another and with their elected representatives." Sæbø et al. (2008) see e-participation mainly as a technology-driven extension of citizen participation. According to them, e-participation "involves the extension and transformation of participation in societal

[11] See for the following Section 3.5 also Wirtz et al. (2016).

democratic and consultative processes mediated by information and communication technologies (ICT), primarily the Internet. It aims to support active citizenship with the latest technology developments, increasing access to and availability of participation in order to promote fair and efficient society and government" (Sæbø et al. 2008, p. 400).

While these definitions also show differences, there are some substantial overlaps with regard to the general understanding of e-participation. A common feature is the information and communication technology supported or enabled interconnection between the government and its stakeholders. Furthermore, the citizens/stakeholders experience empowerment, allowing them to exert influence on policy content and processes, and thus supporting their active engagement in policy-making. Against this background, we define e-participation in the following way:

Definition of E-Participation (Wirtz et al. 2016)
E-participation is a participatory process that is enabled by modern information and communication technologies, includes stakeholders in the public decision-making processes through active information exchange, and thus fosters fair and representative policy-making.

Although several academics and practitioners attribute significant potential to e-participation initiatives, they often fall short of expectations. Since e-participation requires planning, coordinating, and monitoring, this process should be prepared systematically in order to increase the success of e-participation initiatives (Wirtz et al. 2019). For this purpose, Wirtz et al. (2016) deduced an integrated strategic e-participation framework that serves as a guideline for explaining the concept of e-participation and that helps public officials to identify relevant e-participation factors and drivers.

The Strategic E-Participation Framework

The identified factors (e-participation targets, forms, strategies, instruments, and demand groups) and drivers (accountability, transparency, stakeholders, and technology) are presented in the following and conceptually summarized in an integrated strategic e-participation framework (see Figure 3.15; content based on Wirtz et al. 2016).

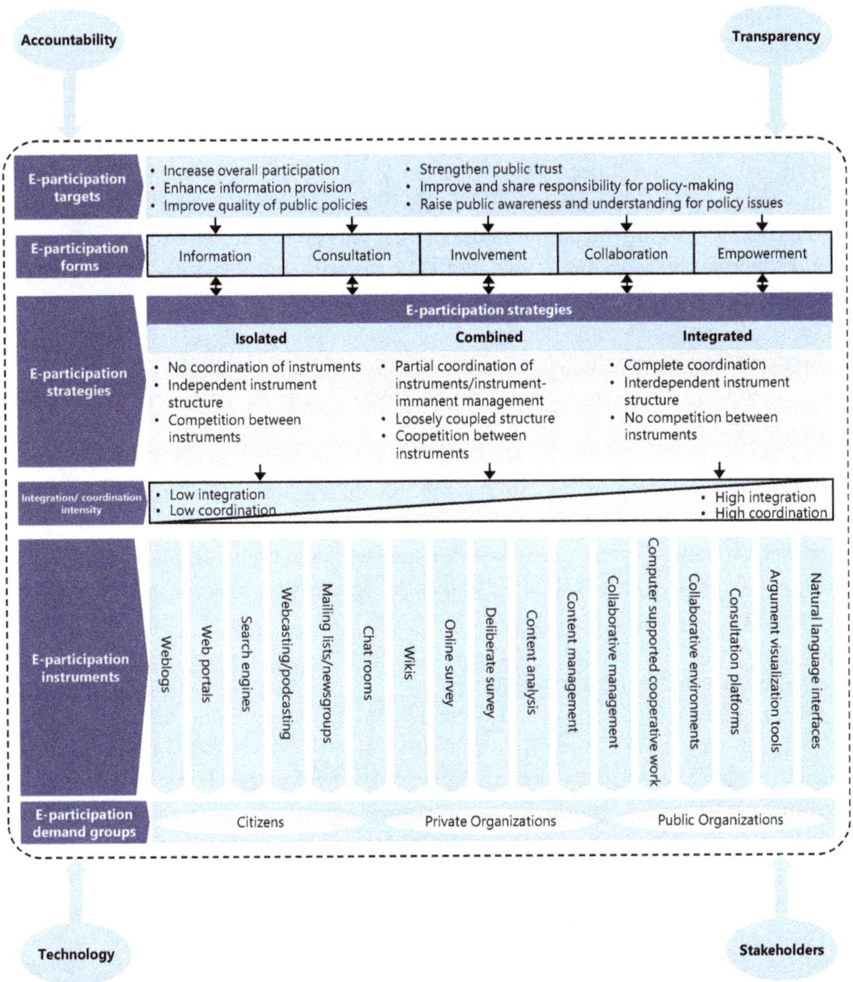

Fig. 3.15 Integrated strategic e-participation framework. Source: Wirtz and Daiser (2017), Wirtz (2021)

E-Participation Targets

The integrated strategic e-participation framework starts with the e-participation targets, which are pursued with the e-participation initiative. In total, six key targets can be identified: (1) increase overall participation, (2) enhance information provision, (3) improve quality of public policies, (4) strengthen public trust, (5) improve responsibility for policy-making, and (6) raise public awareness and understanding for policy issues.

E-Participation Form

Having defined the e-participation target(s), the next step is the determination of the e-participation form. In this context, the International Association for Public Participation provides a widely accepted, sophisticated classification of interactions between government and the community. The five categories are (1) information, provide balanced and objective information to the public, (2) consultation, obtain public feedback and expertise, (3) involvement, consider public concerns and aspirations by working directly with the public, (4) collaboration, incorporate public input by partnering with the public, and (5) empowerment, leave the final decision with the public (IAP2 2007).

E-Participation Strategies

Concerning the distinctive strategic approaches, Wirtz et al. (2016) apply the theory of transaction costs since it can be used to analyze an optimal level of integration to reduce organizational costs (Williamson 1975; Klein et al. 1978). Following this approach, which is based on the assumption that different levels of integration possess different transaction cost, three distinctive forms of integration emerge from which three types of strategies can be derived: (1) the isolated e-participation strategy, (2) the combined e-participation strategy, and (3) the integrated e-participation strategy.

Integration/Coordination Intensity

These strategies differ significantly concerning the integration and coordination intensity of the applied e-participation instruments. The isolated e-participation strategy is characterized by a low integration and an independent coordination of instruments. Thus, the e-participation instruments are managed rather individually, regardless of their respective strengths, weaknesses, and combinatory effects. This impedes the exploitation of synergy effects and may cause competition and cannibalization effects among the e-participation instruments and demand groups.

The combined e-participation strategy constitutes a more sophisticated strategy, which distinguishes itself by addressing particular synergies between the instruments used. Although the instruments are in general still managed individually, they are partially coordinated, and thus, loosely interconnected. The instruments are applied in a coopetitive way, meaning that there is still competition among the applied e-participation instruments, which is, however, alleviated compared to the isolated strategy.

The integrated e-participation strategy is the most sophisticated approach. Here, all instruments are coordinated, meaning that the instruments are used and managed in a complementary way. Thus, the integrated e-participation strategy allows the highest degree of exploiting synergy effects. Given the high management and coordination effort of this strategy, it requires a high level of centralized e-participation integration and coordination competence.

E-Participation Instruments

Having determined the e-participation target(s), form(s), and strategy, the provider of the e-participation initiative should select the appropriate e-participation instruments. For this purpose, e-participation providers can choose between 17 categories of e-participation instruments. This classification is based on the work of Tambouris et al. (2007), who scrutinized various e-participation projects concerning the applied tools and applications and derived a conceptual categorization that provides a suitable frame for classifying e-participation instruments. The 17 categories range from simple weblogs to more sophisticated platforms, visualization tools, and language interfaces.

E-Participation Demand Groups

The e-participation demand groups are the target groups that are directly involved in and addressed by e-participation initiatives. This can be citizens, private organizations, and public organizations. In addition to these internal factors, there are also external drivers (transparency, stakeholders, technology, and accountability), which have an impact on e-participation initiatives.

External Drivers of E-Participation

Transparency is an important driver for e-participation. This driver is expected to have a positive influence on democratic processes (Ala'i and Vaughn 2014) and increase public trust. Furthermore, transparency is believed to have the potential to reduce governmental misconduct (Etzioni 2010). In an e-participation context, the provision of information by the government and the interaction between the government and the citizens enhance the overall transparency of decision-making in public policy (Macintosh 2004; OECD 2003). Here, both adequate general public access to information (Dawes 2010; Noveck 2009) and the timely provision of information (McDermott 2010) are of crucial importance.

Accountability is another important driver for e-participation. This driver is closely linked with transparency since accountability and transparency are mutually dependent and reinforcing. In the context of e-participation, accountability comprises aspects such as answerability, blameworthiness, and liability, which means that the government can be held responsible for its actions (Bovens 2006).

A further important driver of e-participation are the stakeholders of the respective initiative. The term stakeholders covers more than the usual demand groups of the e-participation initiative. It also includes the entities that provide e-participation services, politicians, political parties, and politicians as well as citizens that do not play an active role in the e-participation initiative, but are affected by the outcome (Aichholzer et al. 2007). The pressure of the stakeholder groups is a crucial e-participation driver (García-Sánchez et al. 2011).

Finally, technology is a significant external driver of e-participation. Information and communication technologies provide the technological foundation for e-participation initiatives (Chadwick 2003), and social media technologies facilitate social interactions in the Internet. Especially the advent of social media has accelerated the impetus for governments to achieve the goals of transparency, collaboration, and civic participation (Bertot et al. 2010; Evans and Campos 2013).

As laid out before, e-participation initiatives are a vital aspect of digital government and open government undertakings. Similarly, they require—compared to the traditional approach—new forms of business models for delivering services.

3.6 Summary, Review Questions, Topics for Discussion, and Online Exercises

- The Four Forces Digital Government Model aggregates relevant drivers of digital government to four key developments: convergence and technology, state and politics, society and economy, and citizen empowerment.
- Convergence and technology is the most significant force driving the advance of digital government, since it makes digital government technologically possible.
- The second force state and politics is a driver for digital government, since increasing denationalization requires appropriate solutions, and digital government provides the possibility to establish an online environment that allows government–user interaction on a global scale.
- The third force is society and economy. Its key drivers are globalization, digital divide, demographic change, and urbanization.
- Digital government's forth driving force is citizen empowerment. The rising transparency and accountability of public actions and the possibility that citizens can unite in social networks and communities became possible due to modern information and communication technologies. United they can have a considerable influence on political and administrative processes.
- In the light of the four driving forces of digital government, an integrated management approach is mandatory. Against this background, the E-Government Value Activity System (EVAS) provides a value activity perspective of public authorities.
- In terms of goal setting, it can be summarized that the primary strategic objective of digital government is to provide direct and convenient digital access to government services. However, there are multiple subgoals in order to achieve these primary goals through digital government.
- In order to be successful, core assets, e.g., exclusive alliances and networks and existing and obtained data, as well as core competencies, e.g., automatization and data processing or user relationship management, are crucial.
- Open government is often mentioned as a closely related concept to digital government. Generally, open government stands for the opening of the state and the administration to the economy and the population.

- A vital element of open government is e-participation. E-participation is a participatory process, including stakeholders in the public decision-making process. It is enabled by modern information and communication technology.

Chapter 3
Review questions, topics for discussion and online exercises

Review questions

1. Describe the Four Forces Model of Digital Government.
2. Explain the digital government value chain and the EVAS Model.
3. Describe the digital government strategy development step by step.
4. List the goals of digital government strategy.
5. Explain the open government framework and the strategic e-participation framework.

Topics for classroom discussion and team debates

1. Discuss on the basis of the four forces which force is the most important one. Should citizen empowerment on the Internet be applied more extensively by users in order to make digital government providers aware of their preferences?
2. Discuss whether the fast moving digital society even requires a long-term strategy. Is a short-term adaptation not the more effective approach?
3. Discuss to what extent e-participation contributes to an improvement of political and social processes?

Online Exercises

1. Visit https://open.usa.gov/. Look at the topics of the U.S. National Action Plans and discuss whether these are the essential elements to put open government into practice.
2. Access https://e-estonia.com/. Work out the essential cornerstones of the E-Estonia strategy.
3. Visit https://www.gov.uk/government/publications/uk-digital-strategy. Explore the site. What are the main cornerstones? Compare them to the strategic cornerstones you found at https://e-estonia.com.

References

Aichholzer, G.; Lippa, B.; Moss, G.; Scherer, S.; Schneider, C.; Westholm, H. et al. (2007): Interdisciplinary framework to address the socio-technical and political challenges of eParticipation. Bremen: DEMO-net Deliverable 6.2.

Ala'i, P.; Vaughn, R. G. (2014): Research Handbook on Transparency. Cheltenham: Edward Elgar Publishing.

Andrews, Kenneth R. (2003): The Concept of Corporate Strategy. In Henry Mintzberg, Joseph Lampel, James B. Quinn, Sumantra Ghoshal (Eds.): The Strategy Process. Concepts, Contexts, Cases. 4th ed. Upper Saddle River: Prentice Hall, pp. 72–79.

Barney, Jay (1991): Firm Resources and Sustained Competitive Advantage. In Journal of Management 17 (1), pp. 99–120.

Bélanger, France; Carter, Lemuria (2008): Trust and risk in e-government adoption. In The Journal of Strategic Information Systems 17 (2), pp. 165–176.

Bertot, J. C.; Jaeger, P. T.; Munson, S.; Glaisyer, T. (2010): Engaging the Public in Open Government: Social Media Technology and Policy for Governments Transparency. Available online at http://tmsp.umd.edu/TMSPreports_files/6.IEEE-Computer-TMSP-Government-Bertot-100817pdf.pdf, checked on 5/20/2016.

Bovens, M. (2006): Analysing and Assessing Public Accountability. A Conceptual Framework. European Governance Papers. Available online at http://edoc.vifapol.de/opus/volltexte/2011/2459/pdf/egp_connex_C_06_01.pdf, checked on 5/20/2016.

Cavoukian, Ann (2010): Privacy by design: the definitive workshop. A foreword by Ann Cavoukian, Ph. D. In Identity in the Information Society 3 (2), pp. 247–251.

Chadwick, A. (2003): Bringing E-Democracy Back In. Why it Matters for Future Research on E-Governance. In Social Science Computer Review 21 (4), pp. 443–455.

Chaffey, Dave (2009): E-Business and E-Commerce Management. Strategy, Implementation and Practice. 4th ed. Harlow, New York: FT Prentice Hall.

Chandler, Alfred D. (1962): Strategy and Structure: Chapters in the History of the American Industrial Enterprise. Cambridge: MIT Press.

Collaboratory (2014): Smart Country. Digitale Strategien für Regionen. Available online at https://digital.zlb.de/viewer/api/v1/records/16295063/files/images/SmartCountry_ExecutiveSummary.pdf/full.pdf, checked on 6/21/2021.

Dawes, Sharon S. (2009): Governance in the digital age: A research and action framework for an uncertain future. In Government Information Quarterly 26 (2), pp. 257–264.

Dawes, Sharon S. (2010): Stewardship and usefulness: Policy principles for information-based transparency. In Government Information Quarterly 27 (4), pp. 377–383.

Denger, Katharina S.; Wirtz, Bernd W. (1995): Die digitale Revolution. In Gablers Magazin 9 (3), pp. 20–24.

Doran, George T. (1981): There's a SMART way to write management's goals and objectives. In Management Review 70 (11), pp. 35–36.

Etzioni, A. (2010): Is Transparency the Best Disinfectant? In Journal of Political Philosophy 18 (4), pp. 389–404.

Evans, Angela M.; Campos, Adriana (2013): Open Government Initiatives: Challenges of Citizen Participation. In Journal of Policy Analysis and Management 32 (1), pp. 172–203.

Fahy, John; Smithee, Alan (1999): Strategic marketing and the resource based view of the firm. In Academy of Marketing Science Review 10 (1), pp. 1–21.

García-Sánchez, Isabel-María; Rodríguez-Domínguez, Luis; Gallego-Álvarez, Isabel (2011): The Relationship between Political Factors and the Development of E-Participatory Government. In Information Society 27 (4), pp. 233–251. Available online at http://search.ebscohost.com/login.aspx?direct=true&db=a9h&AN=62823488&login.asp&site=ehost-live.

Geiger, Christian P.; von Lucke, Jörn (2012): Open Government and (Linked) (Open) (Government) (Data). Free accessible data of the public sector in the context of open government. In eJournal of eDemocracy & Open Government 4 (2), pp. 265–278.

Grant, R. M. (2016): Contemporary strategy analysis. Text and cases. 9th ed. Chichester: Wiley.

Grant, Robert M. (2005): Contemporary Strategy Analysis. 5th ed. Malden: Blackwell Pub.

Harrison, Teresa M.; Guerrero, Santiago; Burke, G. Brian; Cook, Meghan; Cresswell, Anthony; Helbig, Natalie et al. (2012): Open government and e-government: Democratic challenges from a public value perspective. In Information Polity 17 (2), pp. 83–97.

Hill, Charles W. L.; Jones, Gareth R. (2013): Strategic Management: An Integrated Approach. 10th ed. Mason: South Western Educ Pub.

IAP2 (2007): Spectrum of Public Participation. Available online at http://c.ymcdn.com/sites/www.iap2.org/resource/resmgr/imported/IAP2%20Spectrum_vertical.pdf, checked on 5/18/2016.

Johnson, Gerry; Scholes, Kevan (1993): Exploring Corporate Strategy. Text and Cases. 3rd ed. New York, London: Prentice Hall.

Kaplan, Robert S.; Norton, David P. (1997): Balanced scorecard. Strategien erfolgreich umsetzen. Stuttgart: Schäffer-Poeschel (Handelsblatt-Reihe).

Kim, Jinbaek (2008): A model and case for supporting participatory public decision making in e-democracy. In Group Decision and Negotiation 17 (3), pp. 179–193.

Klein, B.; Crawford, R. G.; Alchian, A. A. (1978): Vertical Integration, Appropriable Rents, and the Competitive Contracting Process. In Journal of Law and Economics 21 (2), pp. 297–326.

Lee, Gwanhoo; Kwak, Young Hoon (2012): An Open Government Maturity Model for social media-based public engagement. In Government Information Quarterly 29 (4), pp. 492–503.

Macintosh, A. (2004): Characterizing e-participation in policy-making. In IEEE (Ed.): System Sciences 2004. Proceedings of the 37th Annual Hawaii International Conference. Hawaii. New York: IEEE, pp. 117–126.

Macintosh, A. (2006): eParticipation in Policy-making: the Research and the Challenges. In P. M. Cunningham, M. Cunningham (Eds.): Exploiting the knowledge economy. Issues, Applications and Case studies. Amsterdam: IOS Press, pp. 364–369.

Mahoney, Joseph T.; Pandian, J. Rajendran (1992): The resource-based view within the conversation of strategic management. In Strategic Management Journal 13 (5), pp. 363–380.

McDermott, P. (2010): Building open government. In Government Information Quarterly 27 (4), pp. 401–413.

Meijer, A. J.; Curtin, D.; Hillebrandt, M. (2012): Open government: connecting vision and voice. In International Review of Administrative Sciences 78 (1), pp. 10–29.

Moore, Mark Harrison (1995): Creating Public Value. Strategic Management in Government. Cambridge: Harvard University Press.

Müller-Stewens, G.; Lechner, C. (2011): Strategisches Management. Wie strategische Initiativen zum Wandel führen: der Strategic Management Navigator. 4th ed. Stuttgart: Schäffer-Poeschel.

Nam, Taewoo (2012): Citizens' attitudes toward Open Government and Government 2.0. In International Review of Administrative Sciences 78 (2), pp. 346–368.

Noveck, B. S. (2009): Wiki government. How technology can make government better, democracy stronger, and citizens more powerful. Washington: Brookings Institution Press.

OECD (2001): Citizens as Partners. Information, Consultation and Public Participation in Policy-Making. Paris: OECD Publishing.

OECD (2003): Promises and Problems of E-Democracy. Challenges of Online Citizen Engagement. Paris. Available online at http://www.oecd.org/gov/digital-government/35176328.pdf, checked on 5/11/2016.

OECD (2009): Government at a glance 2009. Paris: OECD Publishing.

Open Government Partnership (2021): Members. Available online at https://www.opengovpartnership.org/our-members/, checked on 7/1/2021.

PADM (2013): Developing capacity for participatory governance through e-participation: engaging citizens in policy and decision-making processes using ICTs. Concept paper of the United Nations' Public Administration and Development Management. Available online at http://workspace.unpan.org/sites/Internet/Documents/CONCEPT%20PAPER%20e-Participation%2001.30.13.pdf, checked on 7/24/2017.

Peteraf, Margaret A. (1993): The cornerstones of competitive advantage: a resource-based view. In Strategic Management Journal 14 (3), pp. 179–191.
Porter, Michael E. (1985): The Competitive Advantage: Creating and Sustaining Superior Performance. New York: Free Press.
Porter, Michael E. (1991): Towards a dynamic theory of strategy. In Strategic Management Journal 12 (Special Issue 2), pp. 95–117.
Prahalad, Coimbatore K.; Hamel, Gary (1990): The Core Competence of the Corporation. In Harvard Business Review 68 (3), pp. 79–91.
Rayport, Jeffrey F.; Jaworski, Bernard J. (2001): e-Commerce. Boston: McGraw-Hill.
Rayport, Jeffrey F.; Jaworski, Bernard J. (2004): Best Face Forward. In Harvard Business Review 82 (12), pp. 47–59.
Sæbø, Ø.; Rose, J.; Flak, L. S. (2008): The shape of eParticipation. Characterizing an emerging research area. In Government Information Quarterly 25 (3), pp. 400–428.
Sanchez, Ron; Heene, Aimé; Thomas, Howard (1996): Dynamics of Competence-Based Competition. Theory and Practice in the New Strategic Management. 1st ed. Oxford, New York: Pergamon (Technology, innovation, entrepreneurship, and competitive strategy series).
Tambouris, E.; Liotas, N.; Kaliviotis, D.; Tarabanis, K. (2007): A framework for scoping eParticipation. In Judith Bayard Cushing, Theresa A. Pardo (Eds.): Proceedings of the 8th Annual International Conference on Digital Government Research. Philadelphia: Digital Government Research Center, pp. 288–289.
Teece, David J.; Pisano, Gary; Shuen, Amy (1997): Dynamic Capabilities and Strategic Management. In Strategic Management Journal 18 (7), pp. 509–533.
United Nations (2016): United Nations E-Government Survey 2016. E-Government in Support of Sustainable Development. With assistance of Department of Economic and Social Affairs. New York. Available online at http://workspace.unpan.org/sites/Internet/Documents/UNPAN97453.pdf, checked on 7/20/2017.
van Dooren, Wouter; Caluwe, Chiara de; Lonti, Zsuzsanna (2012): How to Measure Public Administration Performance. In Public Performance & Management Review 35 (3), pp. 489–508.
Welge, Martin K.; Al-Laham, Andreas; Eulerich, Marc (2017): Strategisches Management. Grundlagen - Prozess - Implementierung. 7th ed. Wiesbaden: Springer Gabler.
Williamson, O. E. (1975): Markets and hierarchies: analysis and antitrust implications. A study in the economics of internal organization. New York: Free Press.
Wirtz, Bernd W. (2000): Electronic Business. Wiesbaden: Gabler.
Wirtz, Bernd W. (2001): Electronic Business. 2nd ed. Wiesbaden: Gabler.
Wirtz, Bernd W. (2005): Medien- und Internetmanagement. 4th ed. Wiesbaden: Gabler.
Wirtz, Bernd W. (2006): Medien- und Internetmanagement. 5th ed. Wiesbaden: Gabler.
Wirtz, Bernd W. (2010): Electronic business. 3rd ed. Wiesbaden: Gabler.
Wirtz, Bernd W. (2011): Media and Internet Management. 1st ed. Wiesbaden: Gabler.
Wirtz, Bernd W. (2012): Direktmarketing-Management. Grundlagen - Instrumente - Prozesse. 3rd ed. Wiesbaden: Gabler.
Wirtz, Bernd W. (2016): Electronic Business. 5th ed. Wiesbaden: Springer Gabler.
Wirtz, Bernd W. (2018): Electronic Business. 6th ed. Wiesbaden: Springer Gabler.
Wirtz, Bernd W. (2019): Medien- und Internetmanagement. 10th ed. Wiesbaden: Springer Gabler.
Wirtz, Bernd W. (2020a): Electronic Business. 7th ed. Wiesbaden: Springer Gabler.
Wirtz, Bernd W. (2020b): Media Management. Cham: Springer International Publishing.
Wirtz, Bernd W. (2021): Digital Business and Electronic Commerce. Cham: Springer International Publishing.
Wirtz, Bernd W. (2022): E-Government. Wiesbaden: Springer Gabler.
Wirtz, Bernd W.; Birkmeyer, Steven (2015): Open government: Origin, development, and conceptual perspectives. In International Journal of Public Administration 38 (5), pp. 381–396.
Wirtz, Bernd W.; Daiser, Peter (2015): E-Government. Strategy, process, instruments. 1st ed. Speyer.

Wirtz, Bernd W.; Daiser, Peter (2017): E-government. Strategy, process, instruments. 2nd ed. Speyer.

Wirtz, Bernd W.; Daiser, Peter; Binkowska, Boris (2016): E-participation: A strategic framework. Online first 08 November 2016. In International Journal of Public Administration 41 (1), pp. 1–12. DOI: https://doi.org/10.1080/01900692.2016.1242620.

Wirtz, Bernd W.; Daiser, Peter; Birkmeyer, Steven (2017): Open Government. In A. Farazmand (Ed.): Global encyclopedia of public administration, public policy, and governance, vol. 11. Cham: Springer International Publishing, pp. 1–5.

Wirtz, Bernd W.; Daiser, Peter; Mermann, Marina (2018a): Social media as a leverage strategy for open government. An exploratory study. In International Journal of Public Administration 41 (8), pp. 590–603. DOI: https://doi.org/10.1080/01900692.2017.1289388.

Wirtz, Bernd W.; Daiser, Peter; Thomas, Marc Julian; Schmöe, Myriam (2018b): Open government implementation: an exploratory survey of public administration officials. In IJEG 10 (4), pp. 359–381. DOI: https://doi.org/10.1504/IJEG.2018.097262.

Wirtz, Bernd W.; Lütje, Sebastian; Schierz, Paul Gerhardt (2009): An empirical analysis of the acceptance of e-procurement in the German public sector. In International Journal of Public Administration 33 (1), pp. 26–42. DOI: https://doi.org/10.1080/01900690903188768.

Wirtz, Bernd W.; Mory, Linda; Piehler, Robert; Daiser, Peter (2014): Measuring eGovernment portal management on the local level: Results from a survey of public administration officials. In International Public Management Review 15 (2), pp. 1–31.

Wirtz, Bernd W.; Schmitt, Daniel (2015): Open Government: Konzeption und Gestaltung im gesellschaftlichen Diskur. In Verwaltung & Management - Zeitschrift für moderne Verwaltung 21 (1), pp. 46–54.

Wirtz, Bernd W.; Weyerer, Jan C.; Rösch, Michael (2018c): Citizen and open government: An empirical analysis of antecedents of open government data. An empirical analysis of antecedents of open government data. In International Journal of Public Administration 41 (4), pp. 308–320. DOI: https://doi.org/10.1080/01900692.2016.1263659.

Wirtz, Bernd W.; Weyerer, Jan C.; Rösch, Michael (2019): Open government and citizen participation: an empirical analysis of citizen expectancy towards open government data. In International Review of Administrative Sciences 85 (3), pp. 566–586. DOI: https://doi.org/10.1177/0020852317719996.

Yagoda, Jay A. (2010): Seeing is Believing: The Detainee Abuse Photos and Open Government's Enduring Resistance to Their Release during an Age of Terror. In University of Florida Journal of Law & Public Policy 21, pp. 273–306.

Digital Transformation and Digital Organization

4

Contents

Learning Objectives

By working through this chapter, you will be able to:

1. Define and discuss digital transformation, digital leadership, digital organization, and digital teams.
2. Explain the interactive relationships between digital transformation, digital leadership, digital organizations, and digital teams.
3. Distinguish traditional leadership and organizations from digital leadership and organizations.
4. Explain the composition, structure, and technological features of digital organizations.
5. Define and discuss the different development stages of digital teams and digital organizations.

The diffusion of digital applications has substantially accelerated since the advent of the Internet in the early 1990s. In the meantime, the digitization of the economy and many areas of society has reached an advanced stage. The new technological possibilities of this progressive digitization and the radical market changes caused by new technologies have led to a fundamental conversion of organizational structures and processes.[1]

[1] See for Chapter 4 Digital Transformation and Digital Organization also Wirtz (2020, 2021, 2022).

B. W. Wirtz, *Digital Government*, Springer Texts in Business and Economics,
https://doi.org/10.1007/978-3-031-13086-1_4

This digital transformation is characterized by a change of the value constellation and a digital infiltration of all system-related elements and processes. The digital transformation initially affects the executive level (digital leadership), which then influences the design of the organizational (digital organization) as well as the interaction level (digital teams) of government. Figure 4.1 provides an overview of the key aspects related to the digital transformation and organization of governments.

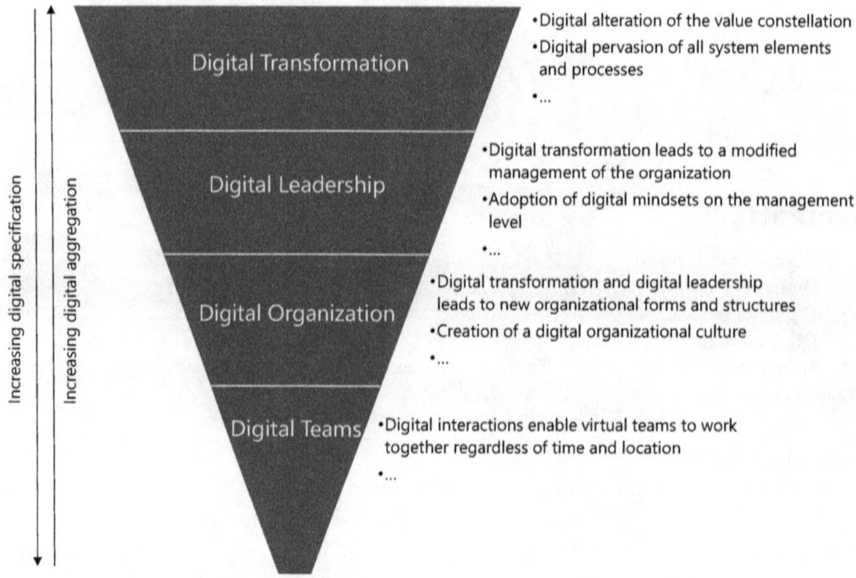

Fig. 4.1 Digital transformation pyramid. Source: Wirtz (2020, 2021)

In this regard, digital transformation represents the driving force that changes the leadership of public organizations and establishes digital mindsets on the management level in the sense of digital leadership. This digital-based leadership affects how work is organized within governments. In addition, it is characterized by the development and introduction of new digital-based organizational forms and structures that lead to the creation of a digital organizational culture.

On the interaction level, the digital networking among organizational units and employees leads to the formation of digital or virtual teams. Digital interactions enable these teams to work together regardless of time and location. Against this background, the following sections are dedicated to the important aspects of digital transformation and digital organization. Section 4.1 begins by explaining the digital transformation as the overarching driving force that shapes society and organizations. Afterward Section 4.2 deals with the specifications of digital leadership. Section 4.3 describes the relatively new phenomenon of digital organizations. Finally, Section 4.4 refers to digital teams and the impact of digital technologies on human collaboration.

4.1 Digital Transformation

Digital transformation is of central importance to governments and companies and offers tremendous potential for almost all industries. It opens up new business models and enables agile management as well as the improvement and development of products and services. At the same time, digital transformation constitutes a dynamic and complex challenge that affects organizational structures and activities of governments.

Definitions of Digital Transformation

Despite a considerable number of different definitions of the term "digital transformation" in the literature, a uniform understanding is still missing. Table 4.1 shows various definitions of digital transformation.

Table 4.1 Selected definitions of digital transformation

Author(s)	Definition
Capgemini Consulting (2011)	Digital transformation (DT)—the use of technology to radically improve performance or reach of enterprises—is becoming a hot topic for companies across the globe. Executives in all industries are using digital advances such as analytics, mobility, social media and smart embedded devices—and improving their use of traditional technologies such as ERP—to change customer relationships, internal processes, and value propositions.
Bouée and Schaible (2011)	We understand digital transformation as the consistent interconnectedness of all industrial sectors and the adaptation of the actors to the new conditions of the digital economy. Decisions in interconnected systems include the data exchange and analysis, the calculation and evaluation of options as well as the initiation of actions and consequences.
Berghaus and Back (2016)	Digital transformation is a technology-induced change on many levels in the organization that includes both the exploitation of digital technologies to improve existing processes, and the exploration of digital innovation, which can potentially transform the business model.
Kofler (2018)	From a societal perspective, the digital transformation is omnipresent and affects every individual—it is irrevocable. We are all affected and actively drive this continuous change in different roles (for instance as customers, developers, employees, scientists) without any foreseeable end.

Source: Wirtz (2020, 2021)

In order to derive a systematic definition of the term digital transformation, it is necessary to evaluate the definitions through a subject-related, functional, and teleological lens and to identify commonalities at the respective level.

When comparing the various definitions in terms of their subject-related aspects, the convergence of some central characteristics is apparent. Many definitions consider the application of technology or a technology-induced change as central aspects. Regarding this, the universally and ubiquitously applicable character of technology across all economic and social areas is emphasized. In addition, the definitions inherently imply an adaptation to the novel conditions of the digital economy.

From a functional perspective, the present definitions underline the profound impact of technology on economy and society. In this context, some definitional approaches also take into account the way technology works at the organizational level and address the changes of business models, customer relationships, and value propositions, as well as the development of new business models, processes, software applications, and systems.

As far as teleological aspects are concerned, the definitions are somewhat heterogeneous. While most approaches ignore teleological aspects or address them superficially in the sense of improving the performance or reach of organizations, others name specific objectives and purposes such as an increase in innovation and improvement of the customer experience.

From this overview, the different perspectives and commonalities in terms of content and scope become apparent. Moreover, many of the definitional approaches show a specialized and narrow understanding of the term. All things considered, none of the definitional approaches addresses the subject-related, functional, and teleological aspects comprehensively. For the purpose of this book, a broad, integrated definition of digital transformation is applied.

Definition of Digital Transformation (Wirtz 2020, 2021)
Digital transformation represents the fundamental change and transformation of economy and society toward a digital-based economic and social system. In this process, all economic and social structures and processes are significantly supported and shaped by digital technologies with the aim of improving efficiency and effectiveness at a higher level of welfare.

Phases of Digital Development and Transformation

In order to develop a basic understanding of digital transformation and its effects on governments, this section provides an analysis of the general digital development process, classifying digital transformation within it. Figure 4.2 depicts the phases of digital development and describes the essential features and implications of digital transformation for governments.

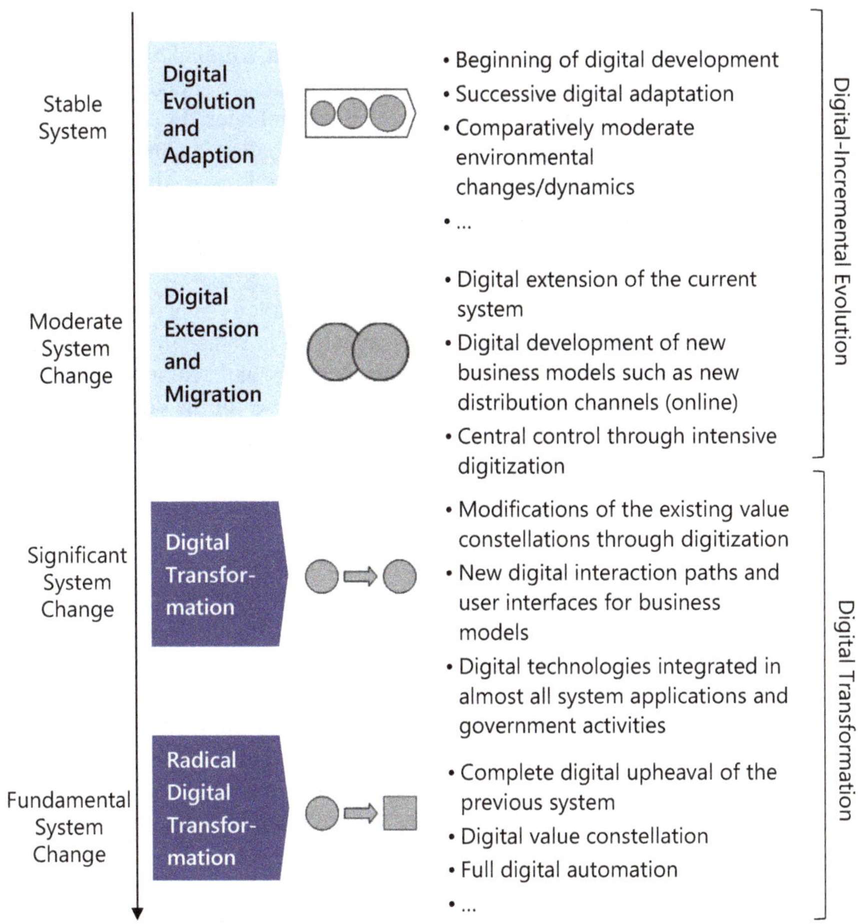

Fig. 4.2 Phases of digital development and transformation. Source: Wirtz (2020, 2021)

The digital development process can be divided into four successive phases: digital evolution and adaptation, digital extension and migration, digital transformation, and radical digital transformation.

Digital Evolution and Adaption

The starting point of the digital development process is a stable system that initiates the phase of digital evolution and adaptation. The digital evolution and adaptation is characterized by the beginning of a digital development and a successive digital adaptation accompanied by comparatively moderate environmental changes and dynamics. As the technological progress and the degree of automation are very low, modern information and communication technologies play a subordinate role in this context. The control and governance of technologies is entirely incumbent upon humans.

Digital Extension and Migration

In the subsequent phase of digital extension and migration, a digital extension of the current system is carried out. The activities of governments are supported by a wide range of modern information and communication technologies. In addition, novel business model characteristics, such as new online distribution channels, are developed. In some cases, the support provided by the technology is already partially automated, i.e., the technology takes over central functions for the government, while humans merely monitor the technology deployment and manage other functions.

The technological progress is moderate and the technology-supported optimization potential for decision-making and other activities is rather limited. Overall, intensive digitization leads to moderate system changes and requires centralized control within the government. While these first two phases of the digital development process can be described as digital-incremental evolution, the next two phases directly refer to digital transformation.

Digital Transformation

The third phase of digital transformation is characterized by changes in the existing value creation constellations as well as new digital interaction paths and user interfaces in business models as a result of increasing digitization. In addition, digital technologies are integrated in almost all system applications and government activities.

The decision-making and activities of governments are technology-driven and, to a large extent, highly automated under human control. Thus, the technology can undertake all functions of a specific application. In this regard, human beings and technologies monitor and control each other's activities. Overall, this phase is characterized by a substantial system change.

Radical Digital Transformation

The final phase of digital development consists of a radical digital transformation that is associated with a fundamental system change. This leads to a complete digital upheaval of the previous system and the establishment of an entirely digital value constellation.

Moreover, this phase is characterized by fully optimized, technology, and machine-controlled knowledge acquisition, evaluation, decision-making, and governance. Machines and their underlying technologies are fully automated without the need of human supervision. Thus, the machines can manage all functions in all situations without relying on human beings.

In particular, between the third phase of digital transformation and the fourth phase of radical digital transformation, there occur substantial upheavals of organizational structures and systems, as digital transformation dissolves the traditional analog structures and processes.

These technological changes call for a new type of leadership that not only corresponds to digital technologies, but also to the potential associated with these technological advancements. This new form of leadership is also known as digital leadership and is described in the following section.

4.2 Digital Leadership

The increasing digitization and the associated digital transformation of economy and society pose a variety of new complex demands on the management of governments. In order to successfully manage digital transformation and to navigate the organization in accordance with their goals, managers and leaders require specific skills and competencies.

On the one hand, these competencies and abilities comprise technical and technological skills to understand and apply digital technologies. On the other hand, digital transformation particularly requires a strategic digital management mindset in order to recognize and successfully address potential and challenges associated with digital technologies, as well as to adapt the design of government structures and human resources management accordingly.

Definitions of Digital Leadership

Against this background, the approach of digital leadership is becoming increasingly important in research and management practice. Yet, there is no generally accepted definition of the term "digital leadership" in the literature. The numerous previous definitional approaches are characterized by a heterogeneous understanding of the term. This is illustrated by the exemplary outline of definitions in Table 4.2.

Table 4.2 Definitions of digital leadership

Author(s)	Definition
Buhse (2012)	Digital Leadership as a form of management that not only masters the old management basics, but is also able to abstract old leadership concepts and recipes for success, compare them with the new values and success models from the digital world and then use them (two-handed leadership). In addition to their traditional role, digital leaders are also required to act as moderators, bridge builders and organizers of networks.
El Sawy et al. (2016)	We define digital leadership as doing the right things for the strategic success of digitalization for the enterprise and its business ecosystem.
Petry (2018)	The five characteristics of network, openness, participation, agility plus trust form the so called NOPA+ model of digital leadership.
Hensellek (2020)	Digital leadership is a reciprocal concept that is not only tied to top management positions in the sense of a top-down approach, but also refers to the active involvement of employees at lower hierarchical levels
Doyé (2018)	Digital leadership means using the collective intelligence of employees and peers (swarm intelligence) with decentralized leadership.

Source: Wirtz (2020, 2021)

Similar to the digital transformation, the derivation of a systematic definition of the term digital leadership requires a differentiation of the listed definitional approaches according to subject-related, functional, and teleological aspects, as well as the identification of content-related commonalities on the respective level.

On a subject-related level, the definitional approaches agree that digital leadership characterizes a certain form of leadership. However, the further subject-related description by the different definitions is quite heterogeneous and generic. In this regard, digital leadership is described as a contemporary, holistic, decentralized, or reciprocal form of leadership.

Aspects of Digital Leadership
Regarding the functional aspects, the integrative effect of digital leadership is emphasized, both in terms of digital challenges and with respect to the employees of the respective organization. A special emphasis is given to the ability to connect and involve employees in a participatory way.

Moreover, teleological aspects are barely considered among the various definitional approaches. The only objectives, purposes, and intentions mentioned in the definitions refer to the strategic digitization success of companies and the exploitation of the collective intelligence of the employees.

In terms of content and scope, the overview illustrates the different emphases and commonalities of the explanations. It is evident that many of the definitions are specific in nature and none of the definitional approaches comprehensively integrates the subject-related, functional, and teleological aspects. In order to overcome the deficit of this narrow and incomplete understanding, a comprehensive, integrated definition of digital leadership is suggested based on existing definitions.

Definition of Digital Leadership (Wirtz 2020, 2021)
Digital leadership characterizes the leadership of organizational systems and actors based on the comprehensive application of digital technologies. Specific features of digital leadership are high agility, networking, participation, flexibility, and responsiveness to external environmental and internal organizational changes. The objective of digital leadership is to achieve greater effectiveness and efficiency in activities.

Traditional Leadership Versus Digital Leadership

Based on this definition, the following section distinguishes digital leadership from traditional forms of leadership and describes its core aspects and competencies. In this way, a fundamental understanding of digital leadership and its implications for companies can be conveyed. Figure 4.3 compares traditional leadership with the innovative concept of digital leadership.

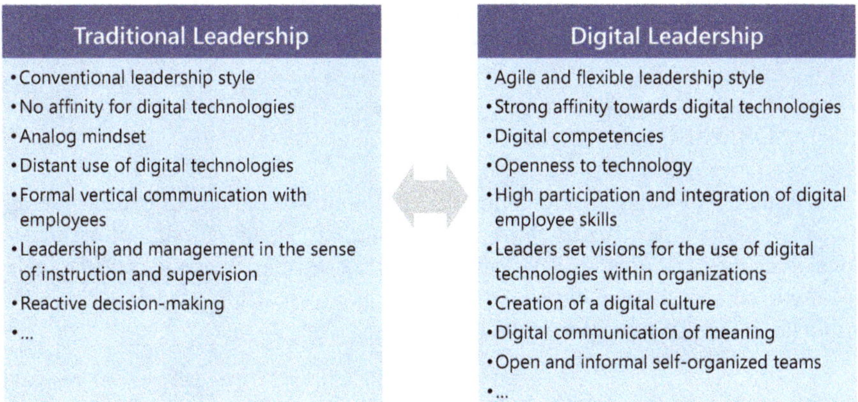

Fig. 4.3 Traditional leadership vs. digital leadership. Source: Wirtz (2020, 2021)

In traditional leadership, digital technologies play no or only a secondary role. Accordingly, traditional leadership is characterized by a distant use of digital technologies and a largely analog mindset. Digital leadership, in contrast, involves not only a high affinity for digital technologies and a fundamental openness to technology, but also comprehensive digital skills and competencies.

Characteristics of Digital Leadership

In this respect, technological and engineering skills are of central importance to understand digital technologies and employ them for the effective pursuit of the organization's objectives. Moreover, digital-specific strategic management skills play a vital role to identify, evaluate, and exploit the potential and challenges of digitization and adapt organizational structures and processes as well as leadership structures accordingly. In addition to this focus on digital technologies, digital leadership also differs from traditional leadership in terms of organizational style and culture. While traditional leadership is characterized by a conventional leadership style, digital leadership emphasizes an agile and flexible leadership approach. Agility and flexibility are essential qualities to keep up with the dynamic development of digitization and its demands on governments. On the interaction level, these two characteristics become apparent by the formation of open and informally self-organized teams.

In contrast to traditional leadership, which is characterized by formal vertical communication with employees and perceives leadership in terms of guidance and supervision, digital leadership is based on a visionary, participative, and integrative leadership approach. Accordingly, managers convey visions for the use of digital technologies within the organization and advocate a high level of participation and integration of digital employee skills. While the authoritarian traditional leadership approach advocates a reactive culture within the government, digital leadership aims to establish a digital leadership culture and achieve digital conveyance of meaning.

Overall, digital transformation requires and entails digital leadership in governments. This has significant effects on the organization and leads to a fundamental digital-based restructuring of the organization. Against this background, the following section presents the central aspects of digital organizations.

4.3 Digital Organization

The substantial dynamics of technological developments and digital transformation not only require a new digital form of leadership, but also a redesign of organizational structures and processes. Organizations must be more dynamic and adaptable in order to address the challenges of digitization and successfully exploit its potential for the achievement of organizational goals.

Definitions of Digital Organization

Against this background, the digital organization of companies becomes increasingly important in research and practice. Digital organizations can look back on a long history of development reaching back to the early 1990s, which was initially shaped by the term virtual organization. In the literature, there is still no uniform understanding of digital or virtual organizations. This lack of definitional consistency is illustrated by the heterogeneity of the definitions provided in Table 4.3.

Table 4.3 Selected definitions of digital/virtual organization

Author(s)	Definition
Wirtz (1995)	A virtual organization can be understood as a temporary network of independent companies (suppliers, co-producers, distributors, but also customers or competitors), which is linked via modern information and communication technologies in order to transfer knowledge (know-how), supplement skills and share costs to open up new product areas and markets.
Mertens and Faisst (1996)	A virtual organization is based on a network of companies that quickly join forces (dynamic configuration and reconfiguration) to take advantage of a competitive opportunity.
Picot et al. (1998)	The virtual enterprise presents itself as a dynamic network. [...] Virtual enterprises are created through the networking of location-distributed organizational units that are involved in a coordinated value-added process based on the division of labor.
Tucci (2011)	A digital enterprise is an organization that uses technology as a competitive advantage in its internal and external operations.
Accenture Consulting (2017)	A digital enterprise is connected and dynamic, flexible enough to embrace continuous change. It uses connected platforms, analytic insights, collaboration and modular operating models to increase productivity, speed and responsiveness while putting customers at the center of whatever it does.
Snow et al. (2017)	A fully digital enterprise is a powerful combination of people, technology, and organizing ability that is well suited to today's economic and social environment.

Source: Wirtz (2020, 2021)

Virtual organizations represent the precursor of digital organizations and were—against the background of the early development phase of information and communication technologies—primarily focused on inter-organization cooperation and organization by means of innovative information and communication technologies. The term virtual organization thus refers in particular to dynamic organizational networks based on the division of labor and partnership-based cooperation processes through new information and communication technologies.

In the course of the ongoing digitization and digital transformation, the technological aspect has become increasingly important. As a consequence, the term digital organization was developed and has been increasingly used in research and practice. The overview of definitional approaches illustrates the different emphases and commonalities of the terms with regard to content and scope.

In essence, the different approaches of defining digital organization refer to the use of technological networking in companies. Based on these different explanations, an integrative definition of digital organization can be derived. This constitutes the foundation of a comprehensive understanding of digital organizations and serves as a starting point for further analysis.

Definition of Digital Organization (Wirtz 2020, 2021)
The digital organization is an organization that is supported by digital information technologies in all essential areas of activities and digitizes all core processes. It thus has a digital-organizational end-to-end structure (value-added organization from the supplier interface to the customer interface). The digital organization uses digital technologies to achieve a sustainable, technology-based competitive advantage.

Development Stages of the Digital Organization

This definition is closely linked to different development stages of the digital organization. In this regard, four central stages can be distinguished: traditional analog organization, initial digital organization, partially integrated digital organization, and fully integrated digital organization. Thereby, the degree of digital automation and the degree of innovation increases with each development stage. Figure 4.4 shows the development stages of digital organizations.

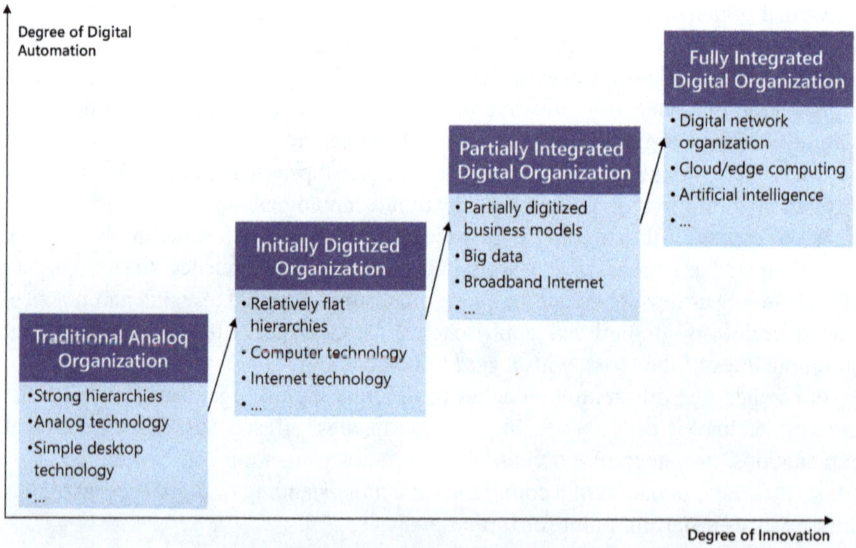

Fig. 4.4 Development stages of digital organizations. Source: Wirtz (2020, 2021)

The various development stages of digital organizations not only differ in their degree of digital automation and innovation, but also in terms of organizational and technological features.

Traditional Analog Organization

The first stage of development is the traditional analog organization. From an organizational point of view, this form of organization essentially corresponds to a primary organization and is characterized by a strongly hierarchical basic structure with a single-line or multi-line system. The management styles and business models associated with these organizations are largely analog and follow the approach of traditional leadership.

The technological characteristics of the traditional analog organization, such as technical equipment, data, and signal transmission, are also analog in nature. Accordingly, only simple desktop technology and analog devices such as fax and telephone are employed. Thus, the traditional analog organization is characterized by the lowest degree of automation and innovation.

Initially Digitized Organization

The second development stage of digital organization refers to initially digitized organizations. From an organizational point of view, this development stage represents a supplementary-hierarchical or cross-hierarchical secondary organization with a line-and-staff system.

Initially digitized organizations have relatively flat hierarchies and focus on aspects such as electronically supported process standardization and organizational stability. They are also characterized by a modified form of management that focuses on the maturity of employees and aims to establish a culture of cooperation within the organization including brief and frequent communication cycles.

In initially digitized organizations, the management adopts the role of a moderator between analog and digital technologies. Although initial digital organizations break up the analog structures of traditional analog organizations, they only achieve a low digital speed of action, reaction, and interaction. This is particularly evident in its technological features, including the use of electronic data processing, data processing service centers, computers, Internet, and email.

Partially Integrated Digital Organization

The third stage of development refers to the partially integrated digital organization. Characteristic features of this stage are flat organizational structures and flat hierarchies.

In this context, digital technologies start playing a central role with regard to organizational structures and processes and have a significant impact on management and intra-organizational cooperation. This stage of development is particularly characterized by features such as partially digitized business models, the use of Scrum, digital collaboration, and data-supported decision-making.

The focus is primarily on process optimization within the organization. In addition, partially integrated digital organizations feature management concepts that are characterized by a proactive organizational culture with decentralized responsibilities. Against this background, the supervisor acts as a digital facilitator and enabler. The collaboration among employees is open, informal, and self-organized.

Overall, companies with a partially integrated digital organization possess moderate digital action, reaction, and interaction capabilities. From a technological perspective, these organizations are characterized by the application of big data, predictive analytics, in-memory computing, broadband Internet, videotelephony, etc.

Fully Integrated Digital Organization

The fourth and final development stage is the fully integrated digital organization. In this stage, there is a comprehensive integration of digital technologies across all areas of the organization. The organization becomes a digital network organization characterized by a digital management mindset, a digital organizational culture, and a digital business model.

The primary focus of fully integrated digital organizations is on digital process automation within companies. In this context, organizational characteristics such as big data-based activities and processes, digital value chains, and a digital-based user orientation are of particular importance.

The management of fully integrated digital organizations primarily follows the principles of digital flexibility and agility and promotes digital collaboration in autonomous digital teams in the sense of self-learning entities.

Accordingly, digital action, reaction, and interaction capabilities in fully integrated digital organizations are highly developed. Technically speaking, the most advanced and highly developed digital technologies are applied at this development stage.

This particularly includes cloud/edge computing, machine learning, Internet of Things, blockchain technology, artificial intelligence, and robotics. Thus, fully integrated digital organization also exhibits the highest degree of digital automation and innovation of all development stages of the digital organization. Figure 4.5 summarizes the essential organizational and technological characteristics of the different development stages.

	Traditional Analog Organization	Initially Digitized Organization	Partially Integrated Digital Organization	Fully Integrated Digital Organization
Organizational Characteristics	• Primary organization • Single-line or multi-line system • Strong hierarchy • Analog mindset • Analog business model • Central responsibility • Process orientation • Low integration or participation of users/customers • Concentration of specialists • Silo thinking • Formal vertical communication • Superior as sole directional control • Leadership and management in the sense of instruction and supervision • Reactive culture • ...	• Secondary organization that completes/ transcends hierarchies • Rod line system • Focus on process standardization • Development culture • Establishment of intensive feedback loops • Relatively flat hierarchies • Focus on organizational stability • Low digital action, reaction and interaction capability • Responsible employees • Short and frequent communication cycles • Culture of cooperation • Manager as moderator between analogue and digital technologies • ...	• Flat organizational structure • Flat hierarchies • Partially digitized business model • Digital integration and participation of users/customers • Focus on process optimization • Data based decision making • Moderate digital action, reaction and interaction ability • Electronic/digital collaboration • Decentralized responsibility • Supervisor as digital conveyor and enabler • Proactive organizational culture • Open informal and self-organized teams • ...	• Digital network organization • Digital mindset/digital organizational culture • Digital business model/digital twin • Big data-based business activities and processes • Digital value chains • Digital interfaces • Digital cross-functional connections • High digital action, reaction and interaction capability • Digital transparency • Digitally based user/customer orientation • Focus on digital process automation • Digital collaboration • Use of agile methods • Digital flexibility and agility • Self-learning organization • Autonomous digital teams • ...
Technological Characteristics	• Analog data • Analog technology • Analog signal transmission • Simple desktop technology • Fax • Telephone • Printer • ...	• Electronic data processing • Data centers • Computer • Internet • Email • Floppy disks • CDs • ...	• Big data • Predictive analytics • Computer-computer connection/cross communication (peer-to-peer-architecture) • In-memory-computing • Electronic collaboration Tools (Cisco Webex) • Videotelephony • Broadband Internet • ...	• Cloud/edge computing • Machine learning • Internet of things • Blockchain technology • Virtual, augmented and mixed reality • Artificial intelligence/ augmented intelligence • Hyper automation • Robotics • Neuromorphic hardware • Brain-computer interfaces • ...

Fig. 4.5 Organizational and technological characteristics of the different development stages of digital organizations. Source: Wirtz (2020, 2021)

The development and design as well as the success of the digital organizations largely depend on the use of digital technologies, instruments, and methods by the organization. In this context, companies have a multitude of technological options at hand. Table 4.4 provides an overview of central digital technologies, instruments, and methods in digital organizations (content adapted from McKinsey & Organization 2018).

Table 4.4 Digital technologies, instruments, and methods in digital organizations

Digital technologies, instruments and methods	Description	Percentage of use in successful digital organizations
 Conventional Web Technologies	• Active use of websites or online applications • Provision of websites and online applications • HTML • JavaScript • ...	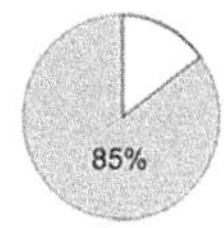
 Cloud-based Services	• Use of external storage capacities • Use of external computing power • Use of external software • Flexible and location-independent access to data, software and computing power • ...	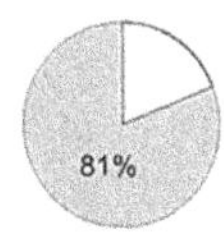
 Mobile Internet Technologies	• Location-independent access to nearly all contents of the Internet • High data transfer rates through 5G technology (10 Gigabit per second) • ...	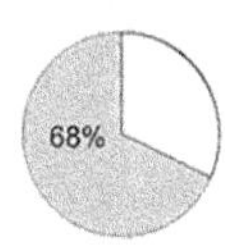

(continued)

Table 4.4 (continued)

 Big Data and Big Data Architecture	• Effective and efficient analysis and processing of large, complex and partly unstructured data sets • Data-based decision making • …	
 Internet of Things	• Interconnectedness of different physical and virtual objects via the Internet • The objects can communicate and interact autonomously via the Internet • …	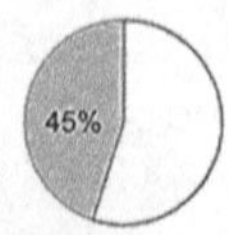
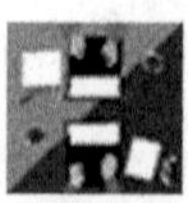 Design Thinking	• Method for solving complex problems • Application of creative techniques and technological tools • …	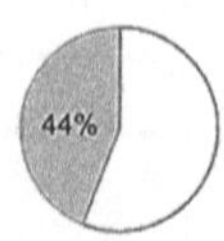
 AI Applications	• Automation of intelligence • Based on a variety of inputs the system learns to find the expected solutions to problems • E.g., in the form of language translation • …	

(continued)

Table 4.4 (continued)

 Robotics	• Use of information technology, mechanical elements and electrical engineering to create a physical connection between a technical unit and the real environment • Interaction between electronics and mechanics • ...	
 Advanced Neural Machine Learning (Deep Learning)	• Artificial neural networks as information-technological replication of the human brain • Machine learning is the artificial generation of knowledge by machines • Subfield of artificial intelligence • ...	
 Augmented Reality	• Virtual extension of human perception • Fictional extension of the environment through digital information and symbols • ...	
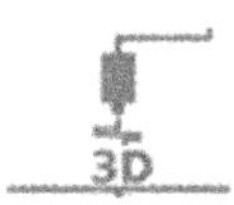 Additive Manufacturing (3D Printing)	• Computer-controlled successive generation of three-dimensional products • E.g., 3D printing • ...	

Source: Wirtz (2020, 2021)

Conventional Web Technologies
The most important technologies listed in this table are conventional web technologies, cloud-based services, mobile Internet technologies, as well as big data and big data architecture. Conventional web technologies refer to the active use or provision of websites and online applications based on the HTML markup language and the scripting language JavaScript, for instance. Conventional web technologies are used by about 85% of successful digital organizations and are thus the most widespread form of technology in the context of digital organizations.

Cloud-Based Services
With a slightly lower usage rate of 81%, cloud-based services are also frequently deployed in successful digital organizations. Cloud-based services refer to the use of external storage capacity, computing power, and software. They allow companies flexible and location-independent access to data, software, and computing power.

Mobile Internet
Another increasingly important technology is the mobile Internet, which is employed by about two-thirds (68%) of successful digital organizations. Mobile Internet technologies offer location-independent access to almost all content and services on the Internet (Kurtz et al. 2021). In this context, the 5G technology represents the latest standard in mobile Internet, which is characterized by high data rates of 10 gigabits per second.

Big Data Architecture
In addition, big data or a big data architecture is one of the most important digital technologies in the context of digital organization. Big data and big data architectures are used by more than half (56%) of successful digital organizations. They enable the effective and efficient analysis and processing of large, complex, and sometimes unstructured volumes of data. This enables companies to make data-based decisions.

In summary, conventional web technologies, cloud-based services, mobile Internet technologies, and big data and big data architecture are the most widespread digital technologies in the context of digital organizations as they are already deployed by most of them.

Technological Trends
In addition, there are a number of other significant digital technologies, instruments, and methods whose potential for digital organization is largely untapped as they are characterized by very low to moderate adoption rates so far. Besides the Internet of Things (45%), design thinking (44%), and AI applications (31%), this includes robotics (21%), advanced neural machine learning (deep learning) (17%),

augmented reality (15%), and additive manufacturing (3D printing) (13%). In particular, the latter technologies have the potential to significantly influence and shape the further development of digital organizations.

The digital-based alterations on the management and organizational level in the course of digital transformation have a substantial effect on the interaction level and especially on the design of interpersonal collaborations within companies. This modified or rather new form of digital-based collaboration primarily happens within digital teams, which are described in the following section.

4.4 Digital Teams

In order to address the complex demands associated with the dynamic development of the digital transformation, companies must implement adjustments on the interaction and cooperation level.

The main guiding principles for collaboration are agility and flexibility in a digitized working environment. They are an integral part of digital leadership and are transferred top-down from the management level to the interaction level through adjusted organizational forms.

However, increasing digitization not only demands adjustments, but also enables new forms of cooperation and working models.

Against this background, digital teams are becoming increasingly important in digital organizations. Similar to the digital organization, digital teams also look back on a longer history of development, which already began in the early 1990s and was initially dominated by the term virtual teams.

Definitions of Digital Teams

The literature still lacks a comprehensive understanding of the concept of digital or virtual teams. This is illustrated by the exemplary definitions in Table 4.5.

Table 4.5 Selected definitions of digital/virtual teams

Author(s)	Definition
Jarvenpaa and Leidner (1999)	A virtual team is an evolutionary form of a network organization (Miles and Snow 1986) enabled by advances in information and communication technology.
Zaccaro and Bader (2003)	The "virtual" team is another phrase that has recently entered prominently into our leadership lexicon. The term "virtual" is misleading because it suggests a degree of unreality, as if such teams exist only in the nether world of electrons. These are real teams having all of the characteristics, demands, and challenges of more traditional organizational teams. The differences reside in two key features. First, members of these new forms of organizational teams either work in geographically separated work places, or they may work in the same space but at different times. Still other teams have members working in different spaces and time zones, as is the case with many multinational teams. The second feature is that most, if not all, of the interactions among team members occur through electronic communication channels.
Hertel et al. (2004)	[. . .] virtual teams consist of two or more persons who collaborate to achieve common goals, while (at least) some of the team members work at different locations (or times) so that communication and coordination is predominantly based on electronic communication media (email, fax, phone, video conference, etc.).
Malhotra et al. (2007)	Virtual teams are teams whose members are geographically distributed, requiring them to work together through electronic means with minimal face-to-face interaction.
Hewitt (2013)	Digital teams are responsible for developing, testing, and implementing a strategy to reach and engage target audiences through digital channels like web, mobile, and social.

Source: Wirtz (2020, 2021)

As a preliminary concept of digital teams, virtual teams have emerged in the course of the early development phase of information and communication technologies and the increasing diffusion of computer-based work processes. The focus primarily is on collaboration among several employees irrespective of location and time by means of conventional information and communication technologies, such as email, fax, and telephone. Thus, the term virtual teams in particular refers to a dynamic and decentralized information and interaction network characterized by the use of information and communication technologies.

Due to the ongoing digitization and the development of digital-based innovative agile working methods (e.g., Scrum) and digital collaboration platforms (e.g., Microsoft Teams) during the last decade, the term digital teams has emerged.

The concept of digital teams refers to the importance and ubiquity of highly developed digital information and communication technologies in cooperation and the corresponding opportunities with regard to networking, speed of action, agility, and flexibility. Against this background, an integrative definition of digital teams can be derived that contributes to a comprehensive understanding of the term and serves as a starting point for the further analysis.

Definition of Digital Teams (Wirtz 2020, 2021)
A digital team is a working group of employees supported by digital information technologies in all essential areas of work, and in which all essential work processes are digitized. At the core of the digital team are digital working environments and platforms that enable agile and flexible collaboration regardless of time, location, or people. Employees can work together interactively, simultaneously, and in real time to complete tasks by means of digital technologies. Digital teams aim at achieving sustainable technology-based efficiency and effectiveness at the work level.

Development Stages of Digital Teams

This definition is based on the different development stages of digital teams. There are three main stages of development including traditional teams, partially digital teams, and digital teams. Analogous to the development stages of the digital organization, the degree of digital automation and the degree of innovation also increase with each development stage. Figure 4.6 shows the development stages of digital teams.

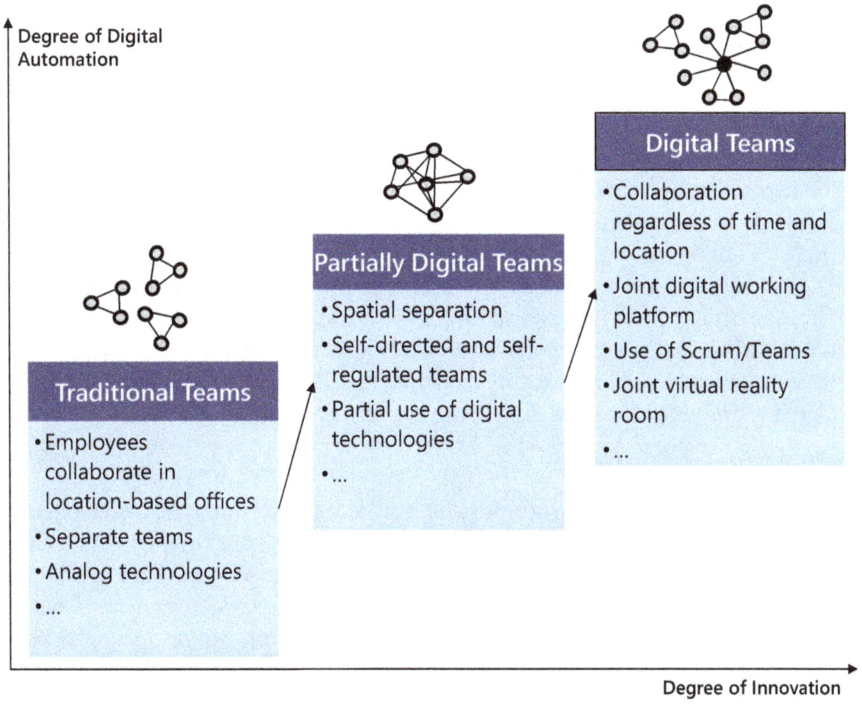

Fig. 4.6 Development stages of digital teams. Source: Wirtz (2020, 2021)

Traditional Teams

The first development stage refers to traditional teams, characterized by the lowest degree of automation and innovation. Several employees work together in location-based offices in separate teams. Traditional teams represent a concentration of specialists whose work is typically characterized by silo thinking.

The collaboration in digital teams mainly relies on analog technologies, such as telephone and fax machines or simple desktop technology. The technological, organizational, and managerial background of this development stage corresponds to the first development stage of digital organization, i.e., traditional analog organization.

Partially Digital Teams

Partially digital teams represent the second development stage of digital teams and come quite close to the initial understanding of virtual teams. The technological as well as organizational and managerial background of partially digital teams reflects the development stage of the partially integrated digital organization.

Partially digital teams are open informal groups that organize and control themselves. They consist of several employees who can act and work spatially separated from each other. In this context, they make partial use of digital information and communication technologies such as broadband Internet, email, videotelephony, and computer–computer connection (peer-to-peer architecture). Thus, partially digital teams form a dynamic decentralized digital collaboration network of employees who can work together regardless of location and time. They have a moderate digital action, reaction, and interaction ability.

Digital Teams

Finally, the last stage of development is represented by the digital teams, which exhibit the highest degree of digital automation and innovation of all stages. The technological, organizational, and managerial background of this development stage corresponds to the last development stage of digital organizations, i.e., the fully integrated digital organization.

Digital teams work autonomously and self-controlled. Collaboration in key areas, activities, and processes is supported by highly developed digital information and communication technologies such as blockchain technology, AI technologies, as well as virtual and augmented reality technologies. Thus, all collaborative activities of digital teams take place in a digital working environment.

Digital Work Environment

At the center of this digital work environment are digital work and collaboration platforms such as Microsoft Teams. These are often referred to as digital workplaces. Such cooperation platforms include useful functions and services for information (e.g., wikis, push notification function), communication (e.g., messenger and email programs), and coordination (e.g., calendar function, process, and resource planning tools).

By using these digital collaboration platforms, digital teams can work on complex projects and tasks regardless of time, location, and people. The members of digital teams can work and complete tasks interactively, simultaneously, and in real time. Thus, digital teams have a high digital action, reaction, and interaction capability. Moreover, the degree of digital transparency, digital networking, and digital collaboration is particularly high in digital teams.

Agile Working Methods

In addition to digital collaboration, digital teams can distinguish themselves by using agile working methods such as Scrum or Kanban. These methods are characterized by a portioned and frequently iterative work process and enable flexible adjustments as well as continuous process improvements even during a project. Digital teams can draw on a variety of different agile techniques.

These include the planning or scrum poker, a dynamic agile technique for estimating the workload. In addition, task or storyboards, which summarize current activities and tasks in an overview, and burn-down charts, which visualize the project and work status, serve as agile techniques. Communication in digital teams is very efficiency-oriented and often characterized by short interactions or conversations. It is largely informal and typically takes place in short daily status meetings (so-called daily stand-up or scrum meetings).

The combination of agile working methods and digital information and communication technologies gives digital teams a high degree of digital flexibility and agility and enables them to meet the complex and constantly changing demands of digital public services. Against this background, the main objective of digital teams at the work level is to generate sustainable technology-based efficiency and effectiveness gains for public services. Table 4.6 presents established agile methods and describes their respective core components.

Table 4.6 Selection of agile methods for digital teams

Method	Concept	Core aspects
Design thinking	Design thinking is based on the assumption that problems can be solved better by interdisciplinary teams. The design thinking process can be divided into six phases, which are processed by interdisciplinary and most of the time in digital teams: understanding, observing, defining, ideating, prototyping, testing. These phases can be processed linearly or iteratively. The visualization is mostly done in digital form and enables working in digital teams	• Interdisciplinary approach • Promotion of collaborative creativity • User/customer centricity • Digital visualization of the phases • Digital collaboration of the team • . . .
Scrum	Scrum is an iterative method of product development. Within defined time periods (sprints), a team develops solutions to requirements specified by a product owner with the support of a scrum master. At the end of the sprint, the team, the product owner, and the scrum master evaluate which solutions have been fully developed and which solutions need further development. Subsequently the next sprint starts. Scrum is often used in a digital context	• Iterative method of product development • Within a defined period of time (sprint), a team develops solutions to requirements specified by the product owner • After evaluation of the result, the next sprint starts • Scrum enables digital planning and implementation of digital teams • . . .
Kanban	Kanban is based on the assumption that tasks should be broken down into manageable subtasks. These subtasks are processed in a planned schedule. Often, the number of subtasks that can be processed simultaneously is limited. This planning process is often visualized in digital formats and enables the working in virtual teams	• Decomposition of tasks into subtasks • Limitation of the tasks that can be processed at the same time • Digital visualization of the subtasks • Digital collaboration of the team • . . .
Business Model Canvas	The basic idea of Business Model Canvas is that a business model can be efficiently developed based on nine fields: customer segments, value proposition, channels, customer relationships, revenue streams, key resources, key activities, key partners, and cost structure. The most important aspects are assigned to these fields in bullet points. This approach allows an easy comparison of different variants and identification of overlaps. Ideas can be visualized, discussed, developed, and evaluated in digital teams using this approach	• Decomposition of central aspects of a business idea into nine areas • Visualization of the aspects within the nine fields • Evaluation and further development of ideas based on visualization • Digital visualization • Digital collaboration • . . .

(continued)

Table 4.6 (continued)

Method	Concept	Core aspects
Rapid prototyping	Within the rapid prototyping process, a minimum valuable product is developed first. This minimum valuable product is made available to selected customers. The feedback received is used directly in further product development. The advantage of this method is faster product development. Rapid prototyping is used in particular in a digital context	• Development of a minimum valuable product • Use of feedback for further development • Reduced development time • . . .
Hackathons	Fast development of a prototype (usually within a period of a few days). This method is used in particular in the ICT sector. Meetings often take place in digital form	• Development of a prototype within a short period of time • Usage of ICT for digital collaboration • . . .

Design Thinking

The first method listed describes design thinking. It basically has the approach of developing all projects from the perspective of the target group. It is based on the assumption that challenges can usually be solved better in interdisciplinary teams through a multi-perspective approach than in homogeneous and hierarchically organized teams. The design thinking process can be divided into six phases, which are worked on interdisciplinarily and frequently in digital teams: understanding, observing, defining, ideating, prototyping, and testing. These phases can be worked through linearly or iteratively. An important aspect is the visualization of the solutions, which often takes place in digital form and thus enables working in digital teams.

Scrum

Another widely used method is the Scrum approach. It describes an iterative method of product development. Within clearly defined periods of time (so-called sprints), a team develops solutions to requirements that are specified by a product owner with the support of a scrum master. At the end of the sprint, the team, owner, and master evaluate which solutions are fully developed and which solutions need further development. The next sprint then begins. Scrum is also frequently used in the digital context. The Scrum method and its various steps and repetition loops are described in detail in Figure 4.7.

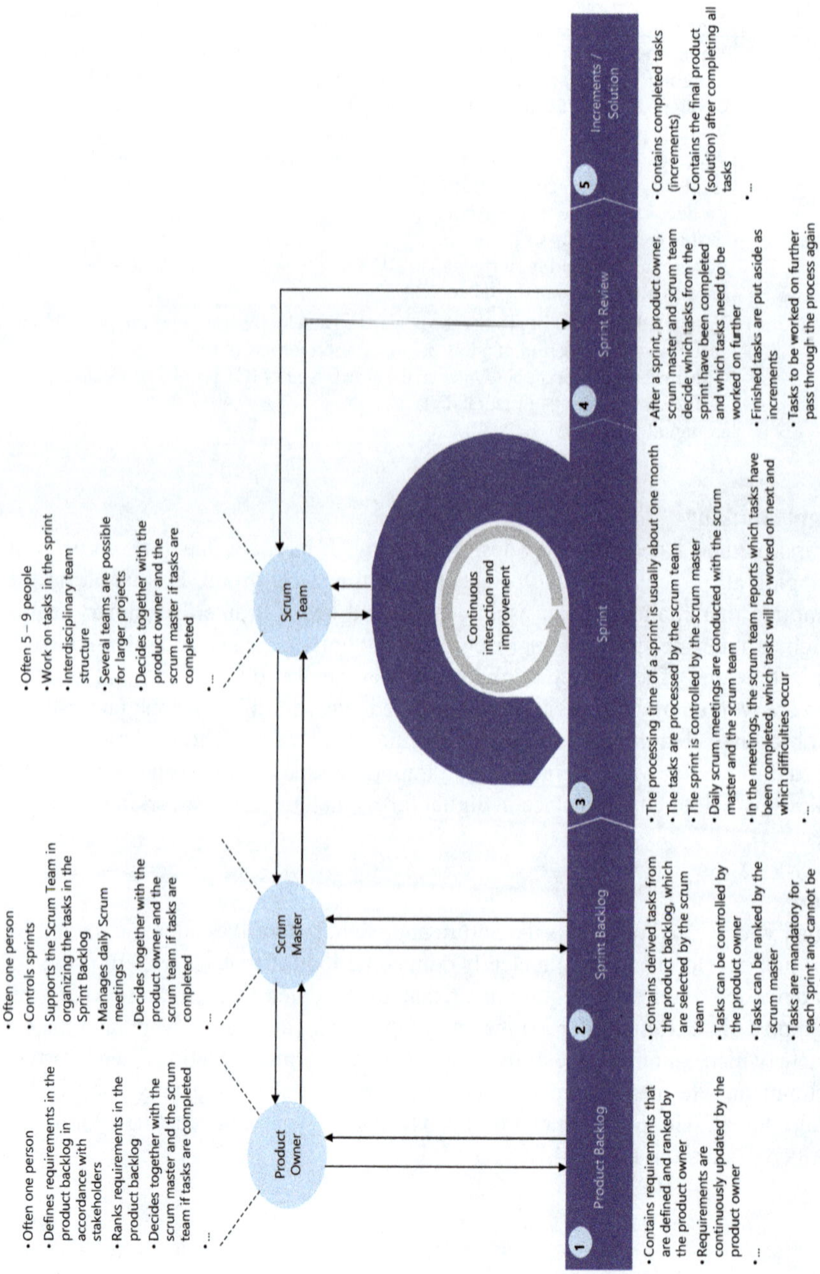

Fig. 4.7 Structure and process of the Scrum method

Kanban

Kanban is also a well-established method. It is based on the assumption that tasks must be broken down into manageable subtasks in order to process them optimally. The subtasks can thus be processed in a clearly planned schedule. This provides a better overview and makes it easier to plan the processing. Frequently, the number of subtasks that can be processed simultaneously is limited. This planning process is often visualized in digital formats and enables work in digital teams.

Business Model Canvas

The Business Model Canvas (BMC) method is also well established in project management. The basic idea of the BMC is based on the assumption that a business model can be efficiently developed using nine fields: customer segments, value propositions, channels, customer relationships, revenue streams, key resources, key activities, key partners, and cost structure. The most important aspects are assigned to these fields in bullet points. This approach makes it easy to compare different variants and identify overlaps. Ideas can be visualized, discussed, developed, and evaluated in digital teams with this approach.

Rapid Prototyping

The methodological approach of rapid prototyping is another agile method that should also be mentioned. In this process, a minimal product is first developed. This simple product is made available to selected customers. The feedback received flows directly into further product development. The advantage of this method is faster product development. Rapid prototyping is also used in a digital context in particular.

Hackathons

Finally, hackathons are another effective method of solving problems using a partly public scene of computer experts. In the context of a competition format, the focus is on the rapid development of a prototype, usually within a period of a few days. This method is strongly rooted in the ICT sector, which is why digital teams are also part of everyday practice here.

4.5 Summary, Review Questions, Topics for Discussion, and Online Exercises

- Digital transformation can be defined as the fundamental change and transformation of economy and society toward a digital-based economic and social system. In this process, all economic and social structures and processes are significantly supported and shaped by digital technologies with the aim of improving efficiency and effectiveness at a higher level of welfare.
- The phases of digital development and transformation are digital evolution and adaption, digital extension and migration, digital transformation, as well as radical digital transformation.

- Digital leadership can be defined as the leadership of organizational systems and actors based on the comprehensive application of digital technologies. Specific features of digital leadership are high agility, networking, participation, flexibility, and responsiveness to external environmental and internal organizational changes. The objective of digital leadership is to achieve greater effectiveness and efficiency in government activities.
- Compared to traditional leadership, digital leadership is characterized by a more agile and flexible leadership style, a strong affinity to digital technologies, digital skills, openness to technology, and a digital culture lived by leaders.
- The digital organizations can be defined as an organization that is supported by digital information technologies in all essential areas of activities and digitizes all core processes. It thus has a digital organizational end-to-end structure (value-added organization from the supplier interface to the customer interface). The digital organization uses digital technologies to achieve a sustainable, technology-based competitive advantage.
- Digital organizations can be divided into traditional analog, initially digitized, partially integrated, and fully integrated digital organizations. These different forms of digital organizations are distinguished by the degree of innovation and the degree of digital automation.
- A digital team can be defined as a working group of employees supported by digital information technologies in all essential areas of work and activity and in which all essential work processes are digitized. At the core of the digital team are digital working environments and platforms that enable agile and flexible collaboration regardless of time, location, or people. Employees can work together interactively, simultaneously, and in real time to complete tasks by means of digital technologies. Digital teams aim at achieving sustainable technology-based efficiency and effectiveness at the work level.
- Digital teams can be divided into traditional, partially digital teams, and digital teams. These different forms of digital teams are distinguished by the degree of innovation and the degree of digital automation.
- Digital teams often draw on agile working methods, which are characterized by a portioned and frequently iterative work process and enable flexible adjustments as well as continuous process improvements even during a project.
- Often used agile methods are design thinking, Scrum, Kanban, the Business Model Canvas, rapid prototyping, and hackathons.

Chapter 4
Review questions, topics for discussion and online exercises

Review questions

1. Describe the digital transformation pyramid.
2. Explain the phases of digital development and transformation.
3. Distinguish digital leadership from traditional leadership.
4. What are the development stages of digital organizations? Name the technological and organizational characteristics of each stage.
5. Describe and explain the Scrum process.

Topics for classroom discussion and team debates

1. Discuss the socio-economic effects of digital transformation for your city.
2. Discuss the advantages and disadvantages of digital leadership in an open and democratic society against the background of traditional leadership.
3. Debate: Will the development towards digital organizations fundamentally change our understanding with regard to social systems and structures? Will digital development lead to the dissolution of traditional forms of organization?

Online Exercises

1. Enter https://www.mckinsey.com/industries/public-and-social-sector/our-insights/digital-public-services-how-to-achieve-fast-transformation-at-scale and explore the site. What are the key lessons learned about the transformation of digital public services from the perspective of a consulting firm?
2. Visit https://www.oecd.org/governance/digital-government/toolkit/12principles/. Explore the Key Issues and Overview for each principle. What are the main points?
3. Access https://www.oecd.org/governance/digital-government/toolkit/self-assessment/. Explore the self-assessments. What are the key lessons learned?

References

Accenture Consulting (2017): Be the new digital enterprise. With assistance of Don Schulman, Shiv Iyer, Gerarda E. van Kirk, Mohammed Hajibashi. Available online at https://www.accenture.com/t20171024T083850Z__w__/us-en/_acnmedia/Accenture/cchange/digital-enterprise/docs/Accenture-Digital-Enterprise-POV.pdf, checked on 7/3/2020.

Berghaus, S.; Back, A. (2016): Stages in digital business transformation: Results of an empirical maturity study. In MCIS 2016 Proceedings (22), pp. 1–17.

Bouée, C.-E.; Schaible, S. (2011): Die digitale Transformation der Industrie. Berlin. Available online at https://bdi.eu/media/presse/publikationen/information-und-telekommunikation/Digitale_Transformation.pdf, checked on 5/18/2021.

Buhse, Willms (2012): Changing the Mindset: Die Bedeutung des Digital Leadership für die Enterprise 2.0-Strategieentwicklung. In Gerald Lembke, Nadine Soyez (Eds.): Digitale Medien im Unternehmen. Berlin, Heidelberg: Springer Berlin Heidelberg, pp. 237–252.

Capgemini Consulting (2011): Digital Transformation: A Road-Map for Billion-Dollar Organizations. Cambridge. Available online at https://www.capgemini.com/resources/digital-transformation-a-roadmap-for-billiondollar-organizations/, checked on 5/18/2021.

Doyé, Thomas (2018): Digital Leadership. In Lars Fend, Jürgen Hofmann (Eds.): Digitalisierung in Industrie-, Handels- und Dienstleistungsunternehmen. Wiesbaden: Springer Fachmedien Wiesbaden, pp. 197–210.

El Sawy, Omar; Amsinck, Henrik; Kraemmergaard, Pernille; Vinther, Anders Lerbech (2016): How LEGO Built the Foundations and Enterprise Capabilities for Digital Leadership. In MIS Quarterly Executive 15 (2). Available online at https://aisel.aisnet.org/misqe/vol15/iss2/5.

Hensellek, Simon (2020): Digital Leadership – Ein Rahmenwerk zur erfolgreichen Führung im digitalen Zeitalter. In Tobias Kollmann (Ed.): Handbuch Digitale Wirtschaft. Wiesbaden: Springer Fachmedien Wiesbaden, pp. 1189–1207.

Hertel, Guido; Konradt, Udo; Orlikowski, Borris (2004): Managing distance by interdependence: Goal setting, task interdependence, and team-based rewards in virtual teams. In European Journal of Work and Organizational Psychology 13 (1), pp. 1–28. DOI: https://doi.org/10.1080/13594320344000228.

Hewitt, Perry (2013): How to build a high-performing team. Edited by Harvard Business Review. Available online at https://hbr.org/2013/08/how-to-build-a-high-performing.html, checked on 5/25/2021.

Jarvenpaa, Sirkka L.; Leidner, Dorothy E. (1999): Communication and Trust in Global Virtual Teams. In Organization Science 10 (6), pp. 791–815. DOI: https://doi.org/10.1287/orsc.10.6.791.

Kofler, Thomas (2018): Digitale Transformation in Unternehmen. Einflusskräfte und organisatorische Rahmenbedingungen. Available online at https://zentrum-digitalisierung.bayern/wp-content/uploads/Dig-Dial_Kofler-Thomas_Digit-Transf-v12-1.pdf, checked on 5/18/2021.

Kurtz, Oliver T.; Wirtz, Bernd W.; Langer, Paul F. (2021): An empirical analysis of location-based mobile advertising—Determinants, success factors, and moderating effects. In Journal of Interactive Marketing 54, pp. 69–85. DOI: https://doi.org/10.1016/j.intmar.2020.08.001.

Malhotra, Arvind; Majchrzak, Ann; Rosen, Benson (2007): Leading Virtual Teams. In Academy of Management Perspectives 21 (1), pp. 60–70. DOI: https://doi.org/10.5465/amp.2007.24286164.

McKinsey & Organization (2018): Smart Cities: Digital solutions for a more livable future. Available online at https://www.mckinsey.com/~/media/McKinsey/Business%20Functions/Operations/Our%20Insights/Smart%20cities%20Digital%20solutions%20for%20a%20more%20livable%20future/MGI-Smart-Cities-Executive-summary.pdf, checked on 5/19/2021.

Mertens, P.; Faisst, W. (1996): Virtuelle Unternehmen - Eine Organisationsstruktur für die Zukunft? In Wirtschaftswissenschaftliches Studium (WiSt) 25 (6), pp. 280–285.

Miles, R. E.; Snow, C. C. (1986): Organizations: New concepts for new forms. In California Management Review 28 (3), pp. 62–73.

Petry, Thorsten (2018): Digital Leadership. In Klaus North, Ronald Maier, Oliver Haas (Eds.): Knowledge Management in Digital Change. Cham: Springer International Publishing, pp. 209–218.

Picot, Arnold; Reichwald, Ralf; Wigand, Rolf T. (1998): Die grenzenlose Unternehmung: Information, Organisation und Management. 3rd ed. Wiesbaden: Gabler.

Snow, Charles C.; Fjeldstad, Øystein Devik; Langer, Arthur M. (2017): Designing the digital organization. In Journal of Organization Design 6 (1). DOI: https://doi.org/10.1186/s41469-017-0017-y.

Tucci, Linda (2011): Digital Enterprise. Available online at https://searchcio.techtarget.com/definition/Digital-enterprise, checked on 5/25/2021.

Wirtz, Bernd W. (1995): Transaktionales Marketingmanagement und Virtualisierung. In Der Betriebswirt 36 (4), pp. 15–20.

Wirtz, Bernd W. (2020): Electronic Business. 7th ed. Wiesbaden: Springer Gabler.

Wirtz, Bernd W. (2021): Digital Business and Electronic Commerce. Cham: Springer International Publishing.

Wirtz, Bernd W. (2022): E-Government. Wiesbaden: Springer Gabler.

Zaccaro, Stephen J.; Bader, Paige (2003): E-Leadership and the Challenges of Leading E-Teams. In Organizational Dynamics 31 (4), pp. 377–387. DOI: https://doi.org/10.1016/S0090-2616(02)00129-8.

Part II

Technology, Smart City and Digital Government Models

Digital Government Technology

5

Contents

Learning Objectives
By working through this chapter, you will be able to:

1. Describe and explain the five phases model of digital transformation.
2. Explain the different client–server interactions such as the distribution of tasks between the client and the server or the Internet addressing with DNS.
3. Describe the HMI model of human–machine interaction and its success factors.
4. List the basic principles and applications of cybersecurity threats in computer networks.
5. Describe the transaction phases and contents of blockchain technology.

The innovation in modern information and communication technologies and the parallel introduction of the Internet have changed many aspects of networking and global communication and have set the basis for innovations like digital government. Against this background, this chapter presents the key technological aspects and IT security issues of digital government.[1]

[1] See for Chapter 5 Digital Government Technology also Wirtz (2020, 2021, 2022).

B. W. Wirtz, *Digital Government*, Springer Texts in Business and Economics,
https://doi.org/10.1007/978-3-031-13086-1_5

In doing so, this chapter first addresses the basics of digital technology by presenting the most important technologies for web development and giving an outlook on specific digital government architectures. Subsequently, the chapter deals with technology at the human–machine interface and describes security concepts and fundamental dangers to computer networks.

Five Phases Model of Digital Transformation

The development of digital transformation began around 1985 and has accelerated significantly since then. It can be divided into five phases, whereby the last phase is open and the development of artificial intelligence and biotechnology cannot be foreseen. Figure 5.1 shows the different phases and lists important technological developments and product innovations.

Fig. 5.1 Five phases model of digital transformation

First Development Phase
The first phase lasted roughly from 1985 to the year 2000, and focused on the technological development of digital technology and the provision of basic digital service innovations—such as the most important one, the World Wide Web.

Second Development Phase
The second phase has seen the emergence of mobile technology and the social component of digital transformation. It shaped the first decade after the turn of the millennium. In particular, it was about the establishment of Web 2.0—i.e., the possibility for users of the Internet to provide information themselves and thus to network socially with each other. In addition, there was the increasing availability of mobile devices that could provide digital services beyond telephony. The introduction of the iPhone and the establishment of Facebook as a global social network particularly characterize this phase of digital transformation.

Third Development Phase
The third phase is to be understood in particular as a deepening phase in which all devices are increasingly connected to the global information network. It lasts from 2010 to around 2015 and creates the basis for the triumph of the mobile Internet and IoT concepts.

Fourth Development Phase
The fourth phase is the phase of structural adaptation and the use of the possibilities of the given infrastructure and computing capacity. It begins in 2015 and will most likely last about 10 years. This phase is characterized by advanced and automated data analysis approaches implemented in decentralized server centers. In this phase, digital transformation is increasingly implementing autonomous processes.

Fifth Development Phase
The final phase of digital transformation is estimated to start in 2025 and will mark the establishment of artificial intelligence. Artificial intelligence will fundamentally challenge many existing framework conditions and place humans in a new role. It remains to be seen exactly how this development will unfold. It is relatively likely that quantum computing and biotechnology will also become heavily involved in digital transformation during this phase.

5.1 Basics of Digital Technology

The Internet has become a standard for supporting, executing, and maintaining data exchange processes between two or more actors via modern information and communication technologies (see for the following Chaffey 2009; Laudon et al. 2010; Wirtz 2013). In principle, the Internet is a global networking and communication system that consists of computer networks, which in turn contain different subnetworks. The fundamental structure of this network rests upon the client–server principle, which—simply speaking—means that server computer provides files and applications that client computers can use (Srinivasan et al. 2002).

A tight network of national, international, and intercontinental data lines forms the physical connection of this structure. The transmission of data via these networks rests on specific protocols and standards, which represent a set of basic rules and requirements, that structure and arrange the data exchange workflow in the networks.

Client–Server Interaction

Since the Internet is a rather loose network with constantly changing participants, each participant has to be uniquely identified in order to allow accurate exchange of digital data (Beynon-Davies 2013). For this reason, each participant receives an exclusive identifier from the TCP/IP when accessing the Internet, the so-called IP address, which is an Internet address written as numbers and separated by periods (e.g., 192.124.238.252). Since accessing websites by using long sequences of numbers is bulky, domain names have been introduced that allow us to identify servers by means of unique character strings (e.g., uni-speyer.de).

DNS Routing
The underlying domain name system (DNS) required is a database that allocates each domain name to the respective IP address. If a user tries to access a website through a domain name, the client sends a request to a DNS server that transmits the associated IP address (Baltzan 2014).

Due to the high number of IP addresses and requests, there are also a considerable number of DNS servers, which map a specific part of the address directory. Therefore, the DNS routing follows a particular cycle. First, the client contacts the DNS server of the respective Internet service provider (e.g., AT&T, Comcast), which checks if the IP address is available in its database or its cache from a previous user query.

If the IP address requested cannot be located, the DNS server of the Internet service provider takes over the role of the requester, contacting 1 of 13 root DNS servers that represent the supreme authority of the DNS directory. The root DNS server identifies the target DNS server, where the initially requested IP address is located and sends it to the requester (Papazoglou and Ribbers 2011). Next, the requester sends the initial IP address request to the target DNS server. After the target DNS server has answered the IP address request to the requesting server, it sends the IP address to the client. After receiving the IP address that is associated with the domain name, the client can access the desired website. Figure 5.2 illustrates the client–server principle and the DNS routing.

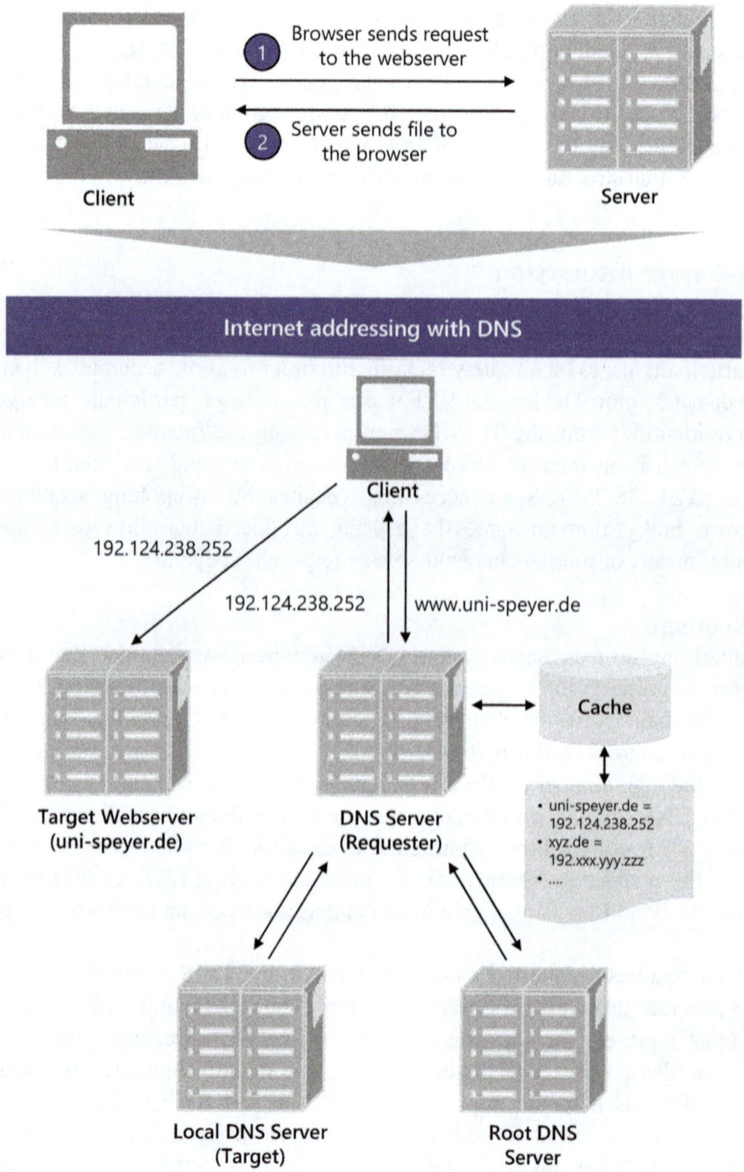

Fig. 5.2 Client–server principle and Internet addressing with DNS. Source: Wirtz (2013, 2020, 2021)

Task Allocation between Client and Server

The types and range of services that a server provides to a client may strongly differ in practice. In principle, a server can supply a client with central services such as storage or processing of data. While the client is normally a common personal computer or mobile Internet device with restricted capability, a server is usually a powerful personal computer or a specific server computer with a very high memory and computing capacity. The type of application and the performance of the clients are essential criteria for the distribution of tasks between the client and the server (Papazoglou and Ribbers 2011). Figure 5.3 illustrates five possibilities of task allocation between client and server (content based on Krcmar 2005; Abts and Mülder 2017).

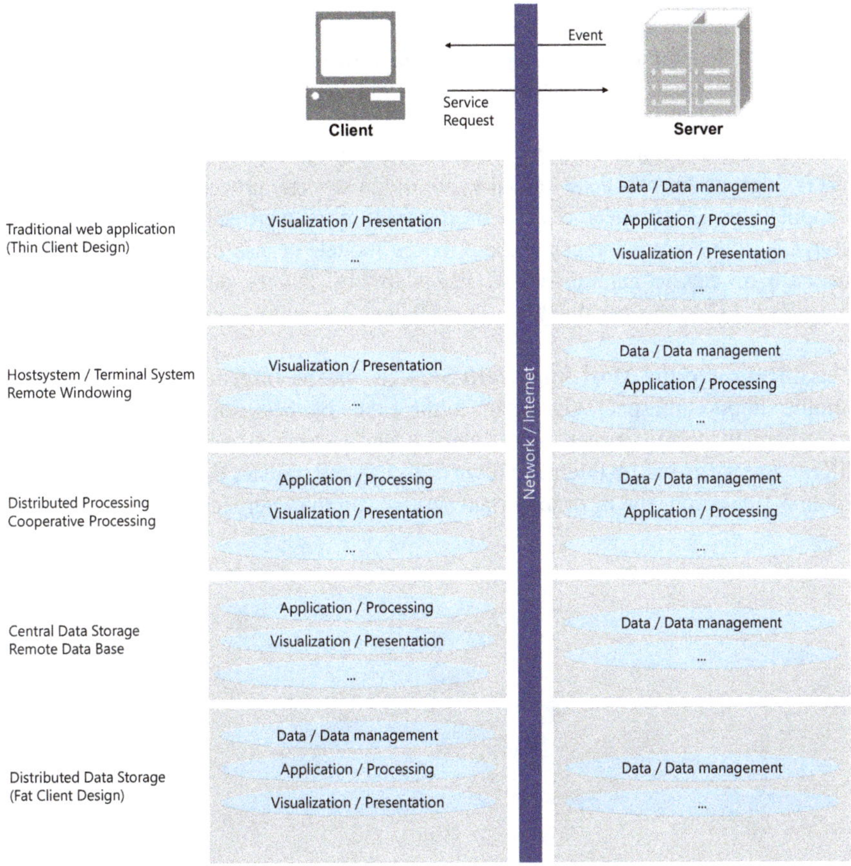

Fig. 5.3 Distribution of tasks between client and server. Source: Wirtz (2021)

The distribution of tasks between client and server may differ with regard to presentation, logic, and data management. The presentation layer describes the visual output to a user or a user interface with the possibility to interact. The respective logic focuses on the processing of user input and application data. Here, the actual data processing takes place. The data management describes the administration and storage of data that are required in the context of the application.

Thin Clients and Fat Clients

The more tasks a client undertakes, the more performant it needs to be. In this connection, a thin client refers to a client that only performs the task of presentation and has a low performance. By contrast, a client with a performant hardware that not only carries out the task of presentation but also processes and manages data is the so-called fat client.

The choice between thin and fat client as well as the type of distribution of tasks between client and server each implies advantages and disadvantages that need to be weighed up in a given case. In some cases, another selection of distribution of tasks may appear reasonable due to new technologies (Gelinas et al. 2004).

While in the past a fat client and the model of distributed database or remote data management used to be mandatory, e.g., for sophisticated (online) games, today such sophisticated (online) games may even run on thin clients.

While the client only displays a video stream and passes on the user input to the server, high-performance servers take care of the storage, processing, and graphical computations. This specific case of application is well suited to explain the advantages and disadvantages of the different models of task distribution. While in the case of classic gaming a user needs to buy a very performant (and thus expensive) PC, a cheaper thin client is sufficient for online cloud gaming.

Classification of the Most Important Services on the Internet

Another important aspect with regard to the exchange between client and server or the communication between users refers to the technical realization. The use of different services on the Internet allows us to use and transfer data and information. Table 5.1 describes the most important services on the Internet.

Table 5.1 Classification of the most important services on the Internet

Services	Protocol	Description	Application
Word Wide Web	HTTP/ HTTPS	Transfer of websites	Web browser (Google Chrome, Internet Explorer, Firefox, Opera, etc.)
Email	SMTP/POP3/ IMAP	Exchange of electronic messages (with data attachments)	Email program (Outlook, Thunderbird, etc.) or web-based interface
Data transfer	FTP/FTPS	Data transfer to Internet server	FTP clients (WS-FTP, FileZilla, etc.)
Encrypted network connections	SSH	Encrypted access to other computers	PuTTY, WinSCP, etc.
Virtual private network (VPN)	IPSec/TSL/ SSL/ViPNet/ PPTP/PPPD	Secure partial networks with restricted access on the Internet	Different clients (OpenVPN, Cisco VPN, etc.)
Remote control	Telnet	Use of remote computers	Functionality provided by operating system
Distributed data exchange (peer-to-peer procedure)	BitTorrent/ Gnutella	Sharing site for decentral exchange of files	BitTorrent, Soulseek, WinMX, etc.
Usenet	NNTP	Discussion forum	News clients, mostly integrated in email programs
Voice over IP (VoIP)	SIP/SIPS/ H.323/IAX/ MGCP/Jingle	Phone via the Internet	Skype, etc.
Instant messaging	OSCAR/ Simple/ Tencent QQ/XMPP	Instant transmission of text messages; type of chat	WhatsApp Web, Facebook Messenger, Skype, etc.

Source: Wirtz (2013, 2020, 2021)

Web Services

The most important and well-known services of the Internet are the World Wide Web (WWW) and email. The WWW led to the breakthrough of the Internet by enabling a graphical user interface and thus a simple and convenient navigation. As a result, the navigation and the provision of information became much easier.

This easy navigation is realized by means of so-called hyperlinks that represent inter-connections to other documents on the Internet, for example, search queries to search engines such as Google.com or Bing.com that present their search results in the form of hyperlinks. Advancements in the WWW technology have facilitated the provision or retrieval of various multimedia content, such as images, sounds, animations, and videos. Email enables individuals and institutions to exchange messages. On the one hand, this allows for transferring pure text messages and, on the other hand, to exchange files, such as image, video, and audio files.

Secure Communication and Data Exchange

Furthermore, there are different formats or opportunities of secure communication and data exchange. While an SSH connection enables encrypted access to another computer, a VPN makes it possible to configure a secure partial network within the Internet with restricted access. An FTP is usually applied to transmit files to a server (host). In the context of private decentral data exchange, the peer-to-peer procedure, email, and instant messaging have become prevalent as the most important Internet services. Telnet is another Internet service through which a user can access remote programs or data and telecontrol computers.

Finally, Internet communication services are becoming more and more popular. Earlier communication offers, such as the Usenet through which users take part in discussion forums, are increasingly replaced by new technologies and applications. Especially instant messaging has become a popular communication service through which several users can communicate with each other by instantly transmitting text messages (Turban et al. 2013). Apart from that, voice over IP has developed to a popular form of communication since conversations on the Internet are free of charge or can be made at low cost into telephone and mobile networks.

World Wide Web Technologies

The Internet provides users with a substantial amount of information content. This content consists of static content and dynamic content. Static content refers to web content that is exactly delivered to the user as stored on the web server (e.g., static presentation of the opening hours). A dynamic website in contrast is processing data and provides the user with customized content (e.g., online creation of address labels for return delivery). This processing can take place on the client (client-side dynamic) or the server (server-side dynamic). Figure 5.4 illustrates the way of functioning of static and dynamic WWW documents.

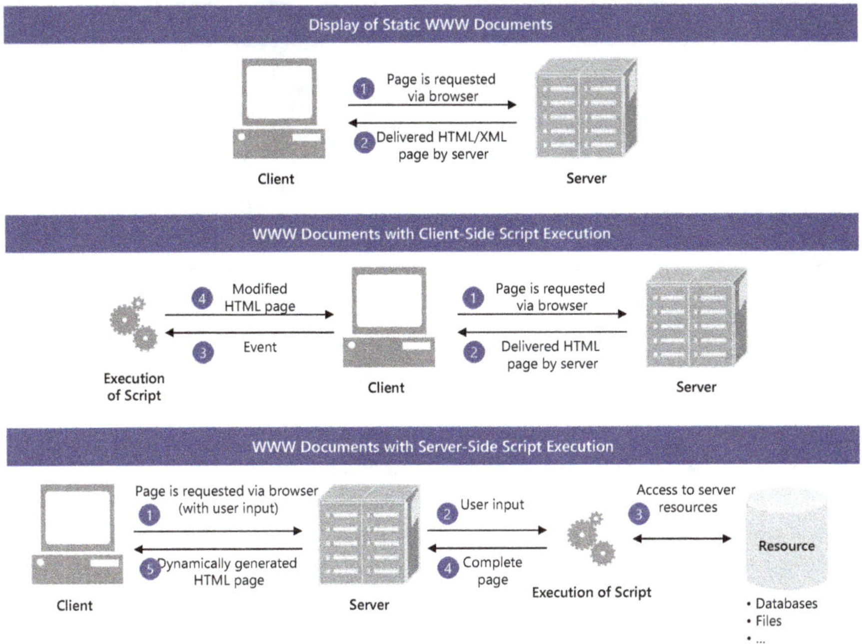

Fig. 5.4 Static vs. dynamic WWW documents. Source: Wirtz (2013, 2021)

From a service provider's point of view, a server-side execution of a script should be preferred, if technically feasible. A client-side execution of a script is subject to the risk that the user has deactivated the execution of the scripting language or the latter is technically not possible. This means that the website does not include the range of functionality planned by the provider. The verification of form checkboxes may serve as an example here.

By means of form checkboxes, a user can communicate with a service provider and transfer data. The service provider can check the data, for instance, for validity (valid email address) or completeness before storing them. This verification may take place through both client-side and server-side script execution. However, in the case of the client-side option, a user can avoid this verification by deactivating the scripting language. The server-side implementation has also certain disadvantages.

The service provider needs to provide appropriate server capacity to supply the service, using server-side processing that performs sufficiently well. A service provider that uses a client-side dynamic can save expenses by employing smaller-dimensioned servers.

Web Development Languages

There are various web development languages to create static and dynamic WWW documents, which differ with regard to syntax, origin, and intended use. Figure 5.5 presents the currently prevalent static and dynamic languages of web development.

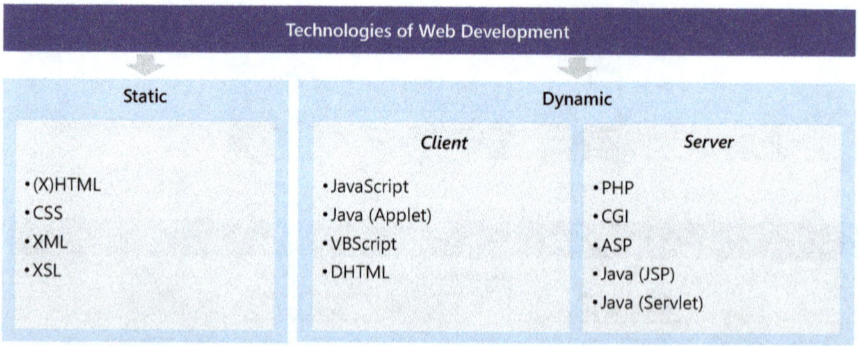

Fig. 5.5 Static and dynamic languages of web development. Source: Wirtz (2013, 2021)

Static Languages of Web Development

Languages for developing static WWW documents are the HyperText Markup Language (HTML), Cascading Style Sheets (CSS), Extensible Markup Language (XML), and Extensible Stylesheet Language (XSL). While (X) HTML and XML are text-based markup languages to structure content, CSS and XSL are formatting languages. This means that HTML/XML can describe the content of a document without requiring a specification of the representation.

In a second step, the graphical representation of the data is specified in respective CSS/XSL files and subsequently integrated into or referred to by the HTML/XML documents. The strict separation between structure and layout has increasingly gained importance lately, since a user can access WWW documents from many different web-enabled devices, such as desktop PCs or smartphones. In this connection, the display formats of the different device classes differ considerably; for instance, the display of a smartphone is much smaller than that of a usual desktop PC. The separation between format and layout takes account of this circumstance and enables us to create a specific layout for each device without having to repeatedly edit content. All of the formatting or markup languages discussed have an own syntax, which is a system of rules that helps to create well-formed expressions for formal representation. The basic setup of the HTML and XML syntax is very similar. Both languages use different elements to structure the content.

Client-Side Dynamic Languages of Web Development

Languages for developing client-side dynamic WWW documents are, for instance, JavaScript, Visual Basic Script, or Dynamic HTML (DHTML). However, with regard to client-side scripting languages only JavaScript has been widely accepted as de facto standard. JavaScript offers the opportunity to create user interaction within a website and to generate or reload content. The syntax is similar to those of the programming languages C or Java, although the critical programming concepts such as the object orientation of JavaScript have a different design.

Server-Side Dynamic Languages of Web Development

The most common languages with regard to server-side dynamic WWW documents are Hypertext Preprocessor (PHP), Common Gateway Interface (CGI), Active Server Pages (ASP), as well as Java Server Pages (JSP). Here, PHP has become most prevalent as de facto standard. Accordingly, about 79.2% of all websites use PHP as server-side programming language (W3Techs 2021). In addition to the abovementioned basic technologies, there are several extensions or combinations of these technologies. An example of such a combined technology that has increasingly gained in importance in the context of Web 2.0 or social media is the Asynchronous JavaScript and XML, or abbreviated AJAX, which is a combination of JavaScript and XML that asynchronously transfers data between the server and client (browser).

AJAX

This asynchronous data transfer or application of AJAX allows for creating the "look and feel" of a classic desktop application for a website. In this connection, the website does not completely reload but only changes at relevant positions. After the website has completely loaded for the first time, the AJAX engine takes over the client-side processing and enables further access to the server. Figure 5.6 depicts the operating principle and schedule of an AJAX application.

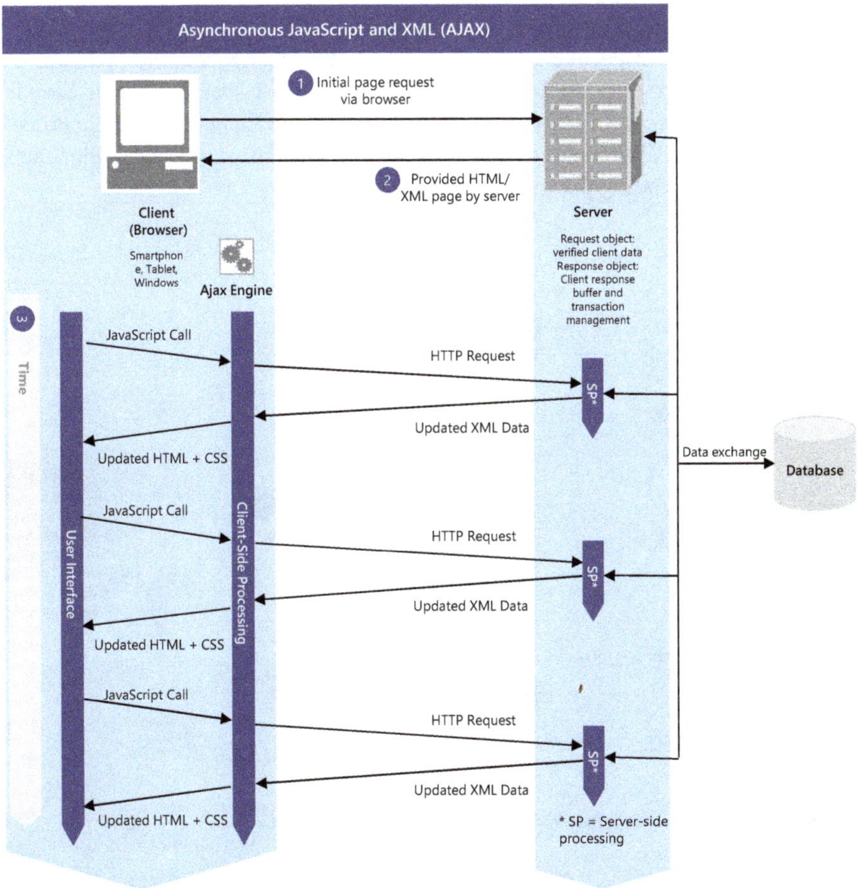

Fig. 5.6 Operating principle and schedule of an AJAX application. Source: Wirtz (2013, 2021)

Besides AJAX, another frequently used technology in the context of Web 2.0 and social media are web services (see for the following Cao et al. 2013). Users can access web services via well-defined interfaces.

Web Service

To access a web service requires that a service provider has made it public in advance. For this reason, the service provider makes a description after building the actual web service by using the Web Services Description Language (WSDL) and defining the interface of the service. WSDL is a meta language that expresses the offered data, types of data, functions, and exchange protocols (Yue et al. 2004).

Following this, the service provider registers the interface or description of the web service at a so-called service broker, which is a standardized directory service, also called Universal Description, Discovery, and Integration Registry (UDDI Registry) in the context of a web service. The directory service contains information about the identity of the service provider, the categorization, as well as a detailed description of the interface of the service. If a user needs a specific service, he or she sends a request to the service broker, searches the directory, and selects a service that fits the respective demands.

After having found an appropriate service through the service broker, the service directly turns to the respective service provider. In this connection, the exchange of data also takes place through standardized protocols. More specifically, the Simple Object Access Protocol (SOAP) or the Extensible Markup Language Remote Procedure Call (XML-RPC) initiates or performs the data exchange. Figure 5.7 illustrates the process and operating principle of a web service.

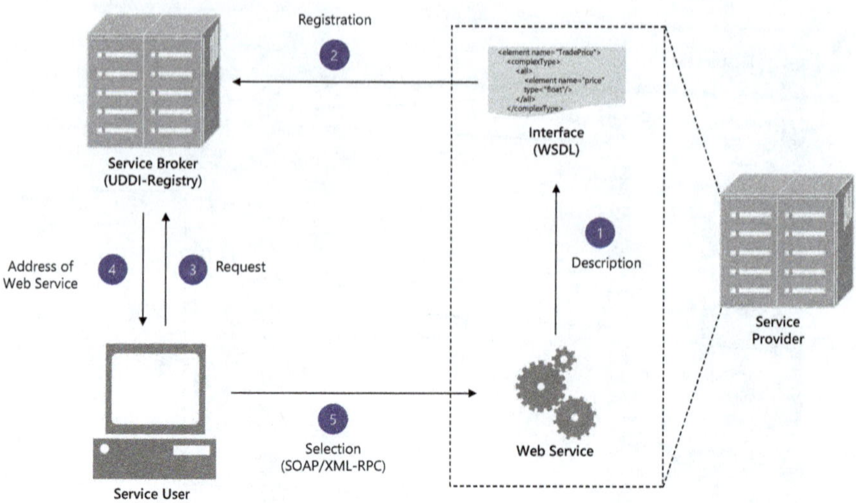

Fig. 5.7 Operating principle of a web service. Source: Wirtz (2021)

Digital Government Architectures

Modern digital government architectures are composed of many different application systems. Depending on the type of user relation, many different technologies may be applied. In the digital government context, usually traditional Internet technologies are used. A user connects to the Internet via an Internet service provider, searches for information or services, and thus makes contact with an organization.

These organizations are also connected to the Internet via an Internet service provider and supply information usually by means of their own web server. Modern organizations that focus on digital government services not only provide static information but also enable a dynamic interaction and a possibility to make use of services via the Internet. In addition to a web server, the internal IT infrastructure therefore often comprises further application servers, database servers, and other back-end systems. These systems are connected to an organization's internal production of goods and services or value chain. The abovementioned web services are often used as interfaces to transfer data beyond organizational boundaries.

Moreover, organizations use electronic data interchange (EDI) to integrate processes and data across organization boundaries. Within this standard, the data are usually transferred by means of XML or a special EDIFACT (electronic data interchange for administration, commerce, and transport) message. In addition to the mere transfer of data, an organization can also get complete IT services from a provider.

In order to electronically exchange data and information, as well as to electronically describe the flow of goods between organizations, the latter often apply technology of radio-frequency identification (RFID). Along the entire logistic supply chain, RFID can capture the movement of goods without contact. The goods are equipped with small transponders (tags) that contain a microchip and antenna. These tags can be read without contact by means of electromagnetic waves and be captured in the companies' information systems. Figure 5.8 presents a cross-organizational digital government architecture by way of example.

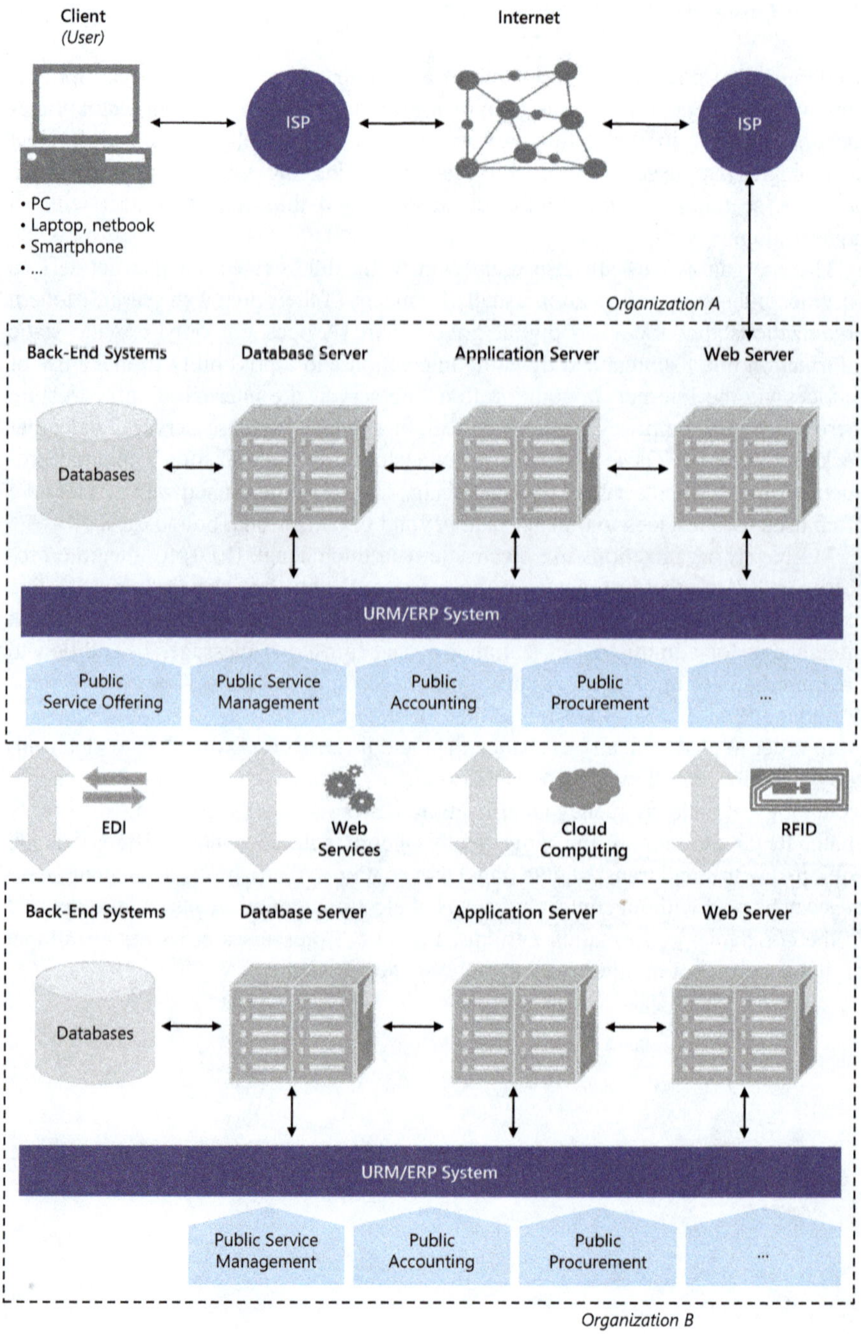

Fig. 5.8 Example of a digital government architecture. Source: Wirtz (2013, 2021)

5.2 Technology at the Human–Machine Interface

The ongoing digitization of all areas of government and life is leading to an omnipresent confrontation with modern information and communication technologies and computer-based machines and systems. This merging of human and machine or technology leads to a special emphasis on interaction at the human–machine interface in the context of digital government.

This chapter deals with essential basics in connection with information technology applications at the human–machine interface in digital government. At first, the chapter illustrates important historical events of the human–machine interface of the last 20 years. It then describes essential dimensions and aspects of the human–machine interaction before presenting central success factors with regard to the design and configuration of the human–machine interface.

Recent Developments of the Human–Machine Interface

The turn of the millennium was the starting point for the increasing introduction of natural user interfaces (NUI), focusing on the interpretation of human body language.

2000 to 2010

In 2002, for instance, the US organization VeriChip Corporation launches the first RFID microchip for humans. In 2003, Sony introduces a camera with microphone called EyeToy for PlayStation 2, which records the body movements of PlayStation players and integrates them into the game.

In 2005, the organization Nintendo launches Wii Remote, a remote control for its eponymous game console Wii, which enables more intuitive game control based on the arm movements of the player. In the same year, scientists at the University of Michigan develop an artificial inner ear on a microchip for deaf people. In 2007, electronically controlled orthoses for paralyzed limbs such as knee joints were introduced. With the introduction of the iPhone by Apple in 2007, the concept of multi-touch operation is also widely used for the first time.

In 2009, Microsoft introduces its Kinect hardware for controlling the Xbox 360 game console, which combines a variety of innovative user interfaces and enables motion-based game control in addition to visual and auditory/verbal interaction mechanisms.

2010 to 2020

In 2010, Apple's iPad becomes the first tablet PC with multi-touch control. In 2011, Apple launches Siri, the first widely used intelligent voice assistant, which becomes an integral part of the iPhone and iPad within their device control system. In the same year, the organization Second Sight Medical Products introduces the Argus II retinal prosthesis, the first electronic visual prosthesis.

In 2012, Google releases its augmented reality glasses Google Glass, which can be operated via motion, speech, and eye control by providing several innovative user interfaces. In 2015, the Defense Advanced Research Projects Agency (DARPA), a research center of the US Department of Defense, develops an artificial hand with a sense of touch and feel.

In 2016, Sony presents the Sony Concept N, a smart collar that is considered a potential successor technology to the smartphone. The collar has Internet access and a digital assistant and can be controlled via an intelligent auditory–verbal user interface. In 2018, the US research initiative BrainGate Research transplants brain implants into a human being for the first time. These implants allow an individual to operate apps, surf the Internet, and send text messages via thought control.

Trends in Human–Machine Interaction

Given the recent developments in the field of human–machine interaction, it can be stated that the trend in recent years has tended to move away from graphical or visual user interfaces toward text- and language-based control elements (conversational user interface—CUI). At the same time, the next development phase in the very dynamic field of human–computer interaction with the expected focus on virtual and augmented reality and the brain–computer interface is already imminent.

Figure 5.9 shows central aspects and milestones with regard to the development of the human–machine interface since the year 2000.

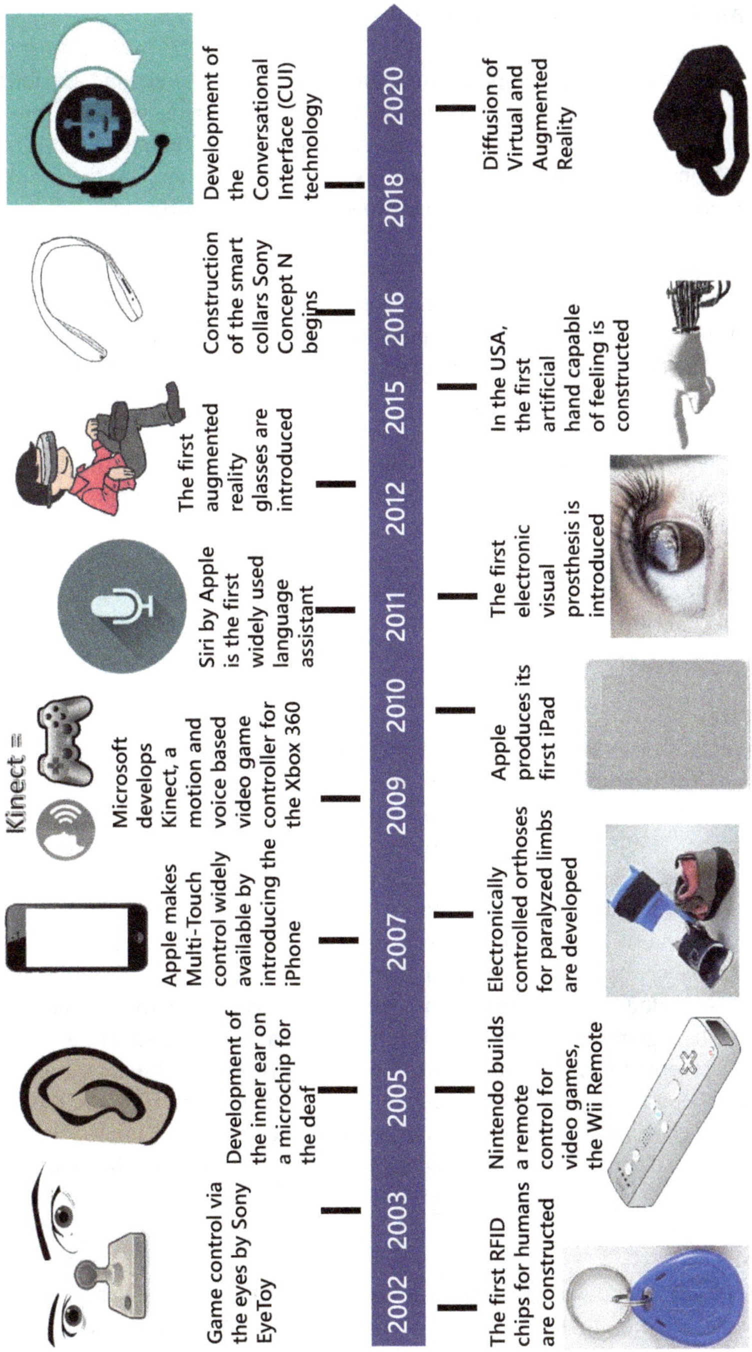

Fig. 5.9 Development of the human–machine interface (since 2000). Source: Wirtz (2020, 2021)

Human–Machine Interaction and Configuration

After illustrating the development of human–machine interaction, the following section describes its main dimensions and aspects. The human–machine interaction can be explained by means of the human–machine interaction model (HMI model). The HMI model comprises five central layers: (1) the human, (2) the input level, (3) the interfaces, (4) the machine (hardware), and (5) the software.

The Human

The starting point of human–machine interaction is the human being. The human brain and sensory organs enable humans to interact not only with humans but also with machines. The sensory organs can function both as sensors and as actuators.

Input Level

The sensors primarily relate to the human senses of seeing, feeling, and hearing and enable the perception and sensing of impulses and information emanating from the machine. At the same time, the sensory organs also serve humans as an actuator to send impulses and information to the machine in the form of sight, touch, and speech. The transmitted impulses and information represent the input of the interaction, which is transformed into a different output in order to achieve a desired outcome.

Interfaces

However, this process always requires an interface that mediates between human and machine. For example, a human can interact with a computer using his sense of touch and physical strength (input) by pressing buttons and keys (interface). These input actions result in the provision of the desired information or in the execution of actions (output). The interface represents the vehicle of interaction between human and machine and requires human control.

The interfaces themselves can be divided into three main categories based on human sensory functions: visual, haptic, and auditory–verbal interfaces. Visual interfaces include smartphones and tablet displays, monitors, head-mounted displays, holograms, and cameras. The haptic interfaces are, for instance, knobs, buttons, levers, touchpads and touchscreens, keyboard and mouse, gamepads, joysticks, remote controls, as well as sensors and electrodes. The auditory–verbal interfaces especially comprise loudspeakers, headphones, microphones, and antennas. By means of these interfaces, humans can control machines and ensure the mutual exchange of impulses and information.

The Machine

The machine or hardware (in the case of data processing systems) has a processor or central processing unit (CPU) and a control unit (CU) that control the sequence of instruction processing within the machine.

Software

In principle, the processor together with potentially applied software takes over the function of the brain in machines. The software also includes aspects relating to the interfaces and the input level. For instance, there is facial recognition software, graphics and monitor drivers, and specific audio and video software.

Against this background, the M2M (machine-to-machine) interaction, which is also controlled by processor and software via the respective IT interfaces, represents an important aspect. Here, sensory or electronic impulses and data are exchanged between two or more machines. Figure 5.10 summarizes the HMI model of human–machine interaction.

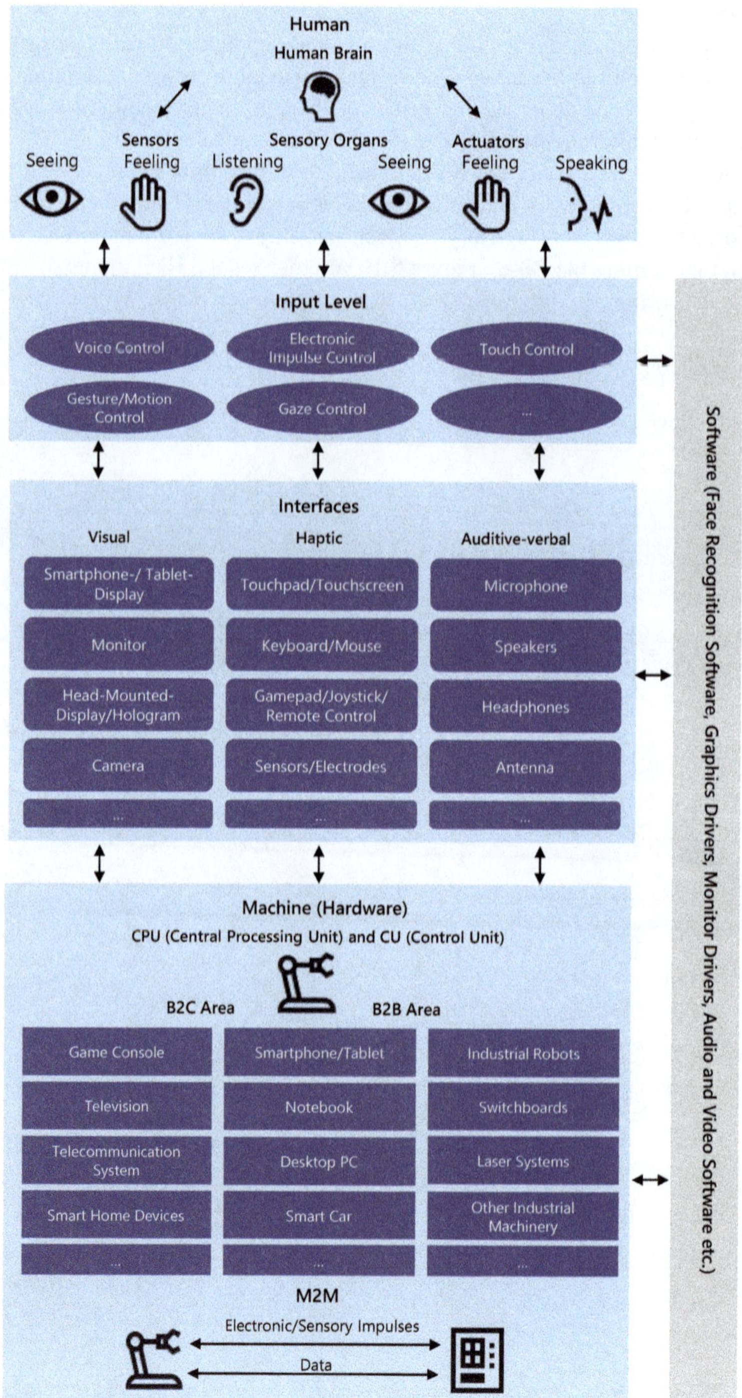

Fig. 5.10 HMI model of human–machine interaction. Source: Wirtz (2020, 2021)

Success Factors of Human–Machine Interaction

Within the framework of human–machine interaction, four essential success factors can be specified with regard to the design and configuration of the interface. These success factors are shown in Figure 5.11.

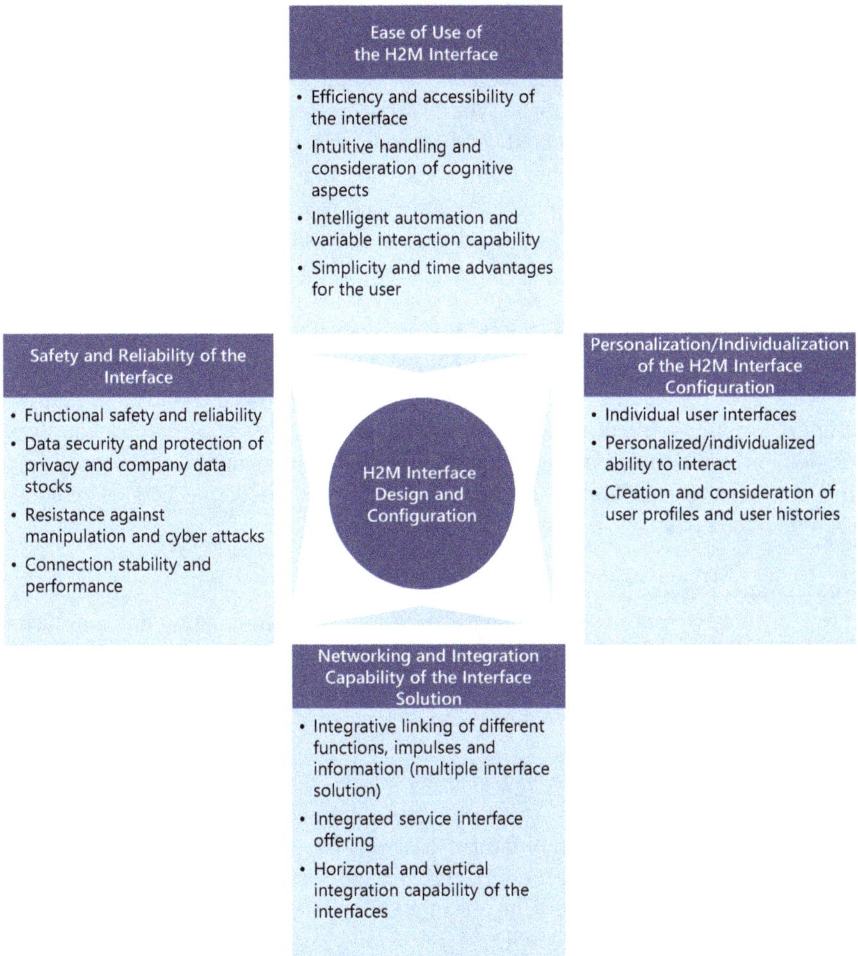

Fig. 5.11 Success factors of H2M interface design and configuration. Source: Wirtz (2020, 2021)

Ease of Use

The user-friendliness of the H2M interface constitutes the first central success factor. In this context, the efficiency and accessibility of the interface is important in order to achieve the best possible adaptation to humans. The user-friendliness is also characterized by an intuitive handling of the interface as well as by the integration of cognitive aspects throughout the design of the interface.

Another important aspect in this context is intelligent automation, especially in combination with a variable interaction capability of the machine and its interfaces. The interaction capability of the machine and its interfaces should not only interact uniformly but should also adapt their interaction to different conditions. After all, ease of use means simplicity and time advantages for users.

Personalization/Individualization

Another success factor in the context of human–machine interaction is the personalization/individualization of the H2M interface. In addition to individual user interfaces, which are geared to the needs and preferences of the user, the personalized/individualized interaction capability of machines and their interfaces are core aspects in this context. Another important aspect relates to the creation and consideration of user profiles and user histories through machines and their interfaces.

Networking and Integration Capability

In addition, the networking and interaction capability of the interface solution is also a central success factor. This is primarily reflected in the integrative linking of different functions, impulses, and information in the sense of a multiple interface solution. In addition, an integrated service interface offer and the horizontal and vertical integration capability are also crucial factors for the success of human–machine interactions.

Security and Reliability

The final success factor of H2M interface design and configuration is the security and reliability of the interface. In addition to functional security and reliability, data security and the protection of privacy or organization data are of special importance for success. In order to achieve this, a certain degree of robustness against manipulation or cyberattacks is required.

After all, the performance and stability of the connection between humans, interfaces, and machines is a key success factor, in particular with regard to functional reliability. The example of human–machine interaction is a particularly good illustration of the outstanding importance that the topic of security has gained in digital government and society in recent years. The following section therefore describes this aspect in more detail.

5.3 Security in Digital Government

The ongoing penetration of modern information and communication technologies in all areas of the economy and everyday life together with the growing network complexity of the associated systems and data increases the importance of cybersecurity.[2] Potential security threats increasingly endanger economically and socially critical infrastructures, thereby affecting people and their personal privacy.

This chapter describes the fundamental principles of security in digital government. First, a cybersecurity framework is presented, which maps the central risks and resources regarding security in digital government. In addition, the main security objectives and digital government security tools are discussed, with a special focus on cryptography and blockchain technology.

Cybersecurity

The security and reliability of electronic transactions has steadily gained in importance in the literature and practice in recent years (Wirtz 2021; Wirtz and Weyerer 2017b). Besides the increasing network complexity of IT applications and systems and the associated data, the main reasons for this development are the growing number of cyberattacks and data scandals in recent years.

It is particularly noteworthy that cyberattacks have both increased in frequency and become more complex, professional, and focused (Wirtz and Weyerer 2017a). Especially in the context of digital government, security is an important determinant for users' trust. In this regard, information technology in general and computer networks in particular are subject to a variety of dangers or threats (Schneider 2017).

Risk-Resource Cybersecurity Framework

The condition of cybersecurity can be described by means of the risk-resource cybersecurity framework that compares risks and resources as two opposing components essential to cybersecurity (Wirtz and Weyerer 2017b). In the context of risks, cyberattacks and their relevance as a key indicator of the current state of cybersecurity represent a central threat to cybersecurity. Another significant risk factor relates to organization-related activities such as the granting of system authorizations or the outsourcing of activities to private providers.

Since organizations are characterized by different requirements for cybersecurity, the degree of potential danger also plays a central role in describing the condition of cybersecurity. Another important factor with regard to cybersecurity risks comprises the concerns of IT experts, customers, and citizens. Furthermore, the lack of risk awareness by superordinate organizational units also represents a risk factor for cybersecurity.

Cybersecurity Resources

In terms of resources, protective measures constitute a central factor of cybersecurity. These can be seen as a counterpart to cyberattacks. Protective measures against cyberattacks include technological tools such as encryption

[2] See for the following Section Security in Digital Government also Wirtz (2021); Wirtz and Weyerer (2017b).

technologies or antivirus software as well as non-technological measures such as access controls or security-related staff training.

Emergency management is another important resource factor in the case of failure of the corresponding safety measures. Emergency management involves the development and application of action plans to reduce vulnerability to threats and to manage the consequences of cyberattacks and potentially resulting disasters. In addition, the professional experience and expertise of an organization's IT staff is an important resource in the context of cybersecurity. After all, successfully managing complex cyberattacks and maintaining cybersecurity require a high level of IT expertise.

Moreover, resource support from upper-level organizational units also represents a significant resource in terms of cybersecurity and the security of information systems. Figure 5.12 illustrates the public risk-resource cybersecurity framework including the central factors of cybersecurity (content based on Wirtz and Weyerer 2017b).

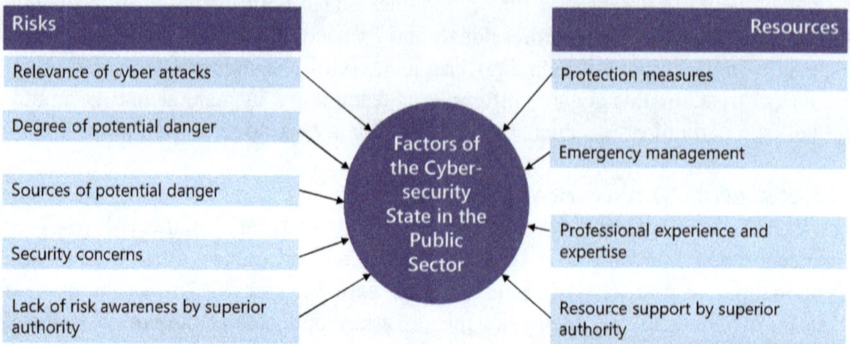

Fig. 5.12 Public risk-resource cybersecurity framework. Source: Wirtz (2020, 2021)

Typical Threats in Digital Government

A number of cybersecurity risks are of particular relevance for the digital government context.[3] An important factor is the relevance of cyberattacks assessed by public administration IT officers. Furthermore, the sources and degree of potential danger that may arise from the combination of vulnerabilities, threats, and/or potential cyberattacks have to be considered in the risk analysis. Figure 5.13 shows an overview of online activities and their potential danger to security as perceived by public administration IT officers.

[3] See for the following Section Typical Threats in Digital Government also Wirtz and Daiser (2017), Wirtz and Weyerer (2017b).

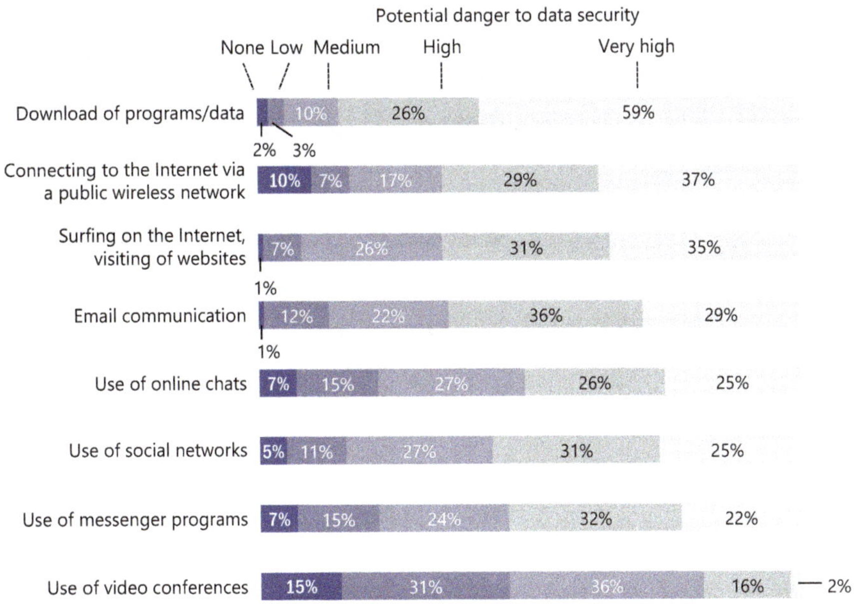

Fig. 5.13 Online activities as potential sources of danger to data security. Data source: Wirtz and Weyerer (2017b)

The vast majority of the respondents of a recent study on cyber-terrorism and cyberattacks in the public sector see a serious potential danger to data security concerning online activities. These activities include aspects such as download of programs or data, surfing on the Internet, connecting to the Internet via a public wireless network, email communication, use of social networks, online chats, messenger programs, and video conferences.[4] With the exception of video conferences, all other online activities showed a clear tendency toward a high or very high potential danger to data security. Apart from online activities, there are also other activities that provide potential sources of danger to data security. Figure 5.14 shows an overview of further important activities.

[4]For further details on the study on cybersecurity in the public sector, please see Wirtz and Weyerer (2017b).

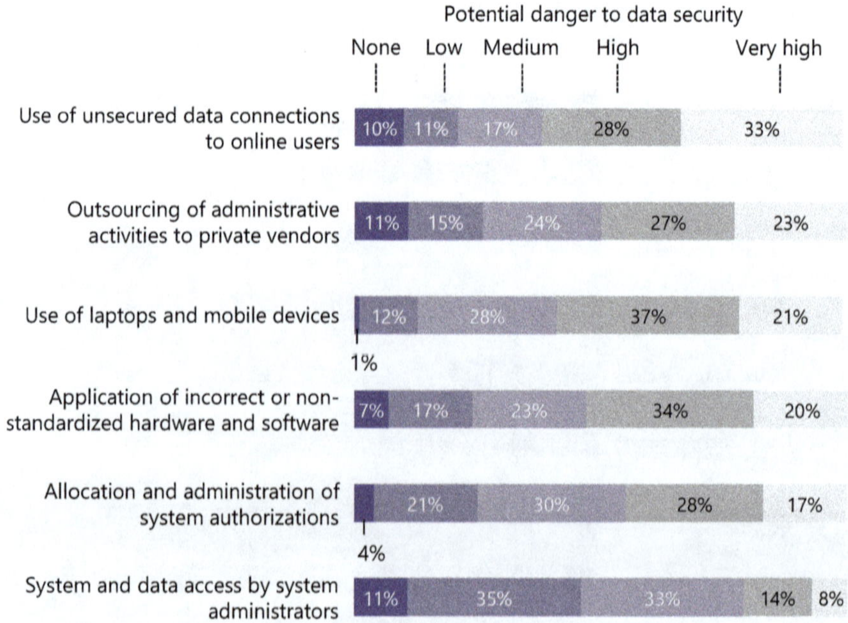

Fig. 5.14 Other activities as potential sources of danger to data security. Data source: Wirtz and Weyerer (2017b)

The activities that are summarized in Figure 5.14 comprise the use of laptops and mobile devices, unsecured data connections to online users, application of incorrect or non-standardized hardware and software, outsourcing of administrative activities to private vendors, allocation and administration of system authorizations, as well as system and data access by system administrators. In summary, all of these activities show a relatively high potential danger to data security.

Apart from the relevance, degree, and sources of potential danger, the security concerns of public administration IT officers as well as citizens are another risk-related factor that characterizes the state of cybersecurity. Against this background, the concerns of both public administration IT officers and citizens should be considered when preparing and managing digital government initiatives.

Security concerns comprise aspects such as fear of data theft, lack of information of data processing, and lack of security of data transfer. Finally, the lack of risk awareness on the part of the superior authority is a further factor that needs to be taken into account since superior levels and authorities have shown to play an important role in the context of cybersecurity in the public sector. The following section outlines typical threats in computer networks in more detail.

Typical Threats in Computer Networks

This section describes the dangers illustrated in the risk-resource cybersecurity framework, before presenting security objectives and measures.

The main threats in computer networks or in the Internet include unauthorized access, data loss and manipulation, as well as data and identity theft. User or internal organization data must be protected and not publicly available (Turban and Sipior 2015). However, often unauthorized persons such as hackers try to obtain confidential organization or user data via the Internet by illegally gaining access to the servers of organizations.

Once a hacker has gained access to an organization's server, he or she can steal or manipulate the data. If a hacker only wants to draw attention to security vulnerabilities, he or she can send the data to the affected organization or the press or may publish them directly on the Internet. If a hacker pursues financial goals, then he or she may sell the data obtained or modify it in a way that benefits him or her.

In addition to data theft, identity theft may also occur in the context of digital government. Here, a hacker takes over another person's identity or pretends to be this person in order to gain access to data or to benefit financially.

Another danger on the Internet or in computer networks is data loss, which may be caused intentionally by a hacker or occur through hardware damage. All these risks need to be considered in digital government application systems (Chaffey 2015). Table 5.2 presents the most important threats that may occur in computer networks (content based on Wirtz 2013, 2021; Chaffey 2015).

Table 5.2 Threats in computer networks

Type of attack	Threat	Description
Malware	Virus	A virus is an integrated code in a (host) program that can reproduce itself and can manipulate system environments or data unnoticed.
	Worm	A worm is an independent program that can spread and reproduce itself. In contrast to a virus it does not require a host program.
	Spyware/adware	Spyware/adware is a spy program that sends user data to the programmer/producer without the users' notice and consent or unwantedly offers them products.
	Scareware	Scareware leads the user to believe that his or her computer is broken or was compromised. Subsequently, it offers the user to eliminate the danger by asking for a payment.
	Dialer	A dialer establishes a dial-up connection to the Internet (via modem/ISDN) and is a form of malware if it establishes a connection to a very expensive fee-based number.
	Trojan	Trojans or Trojan horses are computer programs that give the impression of being useful applications but actually fulfill another or malicious function.

(continued)

Table 5.2 (continued)

Type of attack	Threat	Description
Attacks on IT infrastructures	DoS attack/ DDoS attack	A denial of service attack intentionally causes an overload of a system or a network in order to temporarily limit the availability of one or multiple services. If the attack comes from different systems, it is a called a distributed DoS attack.
	Scanner	A scanner systematically screens systems for security vulnerabilities (such as unsecured network ports) in order to attack them through the detected loophole.
Interception, reading, and manipulation of data	Sniffer	A sniffer not only allows us to intercept and record data packets in networks but also to analyze them subsequently. Sniffers are applied in the context of network analyses but can also be used for abuse purposes and for unauthorized data reading.
	Keylogger	Keyloggers record all user inputs (keyboard) and save them or send them to third parties. In this way, for instance, hackers can gain access to passwords or pin numbers.
	Password cracker	Password crackers are programs that allow us to bypass access barriers. In this connection, they differ with regard to the selected method; often the so-called dictionary or brute force attack (testing all possible combinations) is applied.
	Man-in-the-middle attack (snarfing)	In the case of the man-in-the-middle attack, an attacker logically interposes himself or herself between two communication partners. Here, the attacker can control and arbitrarily look at or manipulate the data traffic between the communication partners.
	Phishing	In the case of phishing, a hacker tries to imitate a trustworthy website (e.g., online banking) and to prompt a user by means of a faked message to reveal sensitive or access data.
Identity theft/deception	Spoofing	Spoofing generally refers to disguising one's own identity. There are many different types of spoofing. In the case of IP spoofing, for instance, a hacker modifies all IP packets with a faked sender IP and creates the impression that the packets are sent from another computer. Moreover, DNS, mail, mac, and DHCP spoofing, etc., are commonly used.
	Social engineering/ social hacking	Social engineering refers to spying out a user's personal environment and faking an identity through this information. This personal identity is used in the context of social hacking to look at private data.

Source: Wirtz (2013, 2020, 2021)

When planning a digital government application system, these potential threats need to be adequately considered. In order to design a basically "safe" application system, the following six fundamental security objectives need to be accomplished: confidentiality, integrity, availability, non-repudiation, authenticity, and reliability (Solms and van Niekerk 2013).

Fundamental Security Objectives

An application system is considered to be confidential, if information cannot be viewed by unauthorized persons, entities, or processes. One can realize confidentiality, for example, by means of an encryption or allocation of special access rights.

Integrity prevails as long as no unauthorized person changes data (data integrity) and application systems are available with the desired performance or intended range of functions (system integrity). A system is available in terms of security if neither its function nor its accessibility has been affected in an unauthorized manner. In addition to availability, liability is an essential part of Internet security. If a communication link can be verified without any doubt and cannot be denied, one speaks of a binding communication. Particularly relevant here is that the entities (systems/user) involved can be clearly identified or assigned to individual actions or processes (Chaffey 2015). Authenticity is present if one can ensure without any doubt not only the entity in terms of a user name or computer but also a person's actual identity. Implicitly, authenticity represents the prerequisite for binding communication. The last security objective of reliability requires that all data and systems provide consistent and desired functions. In the context of digital government and electronic transactions, one can derive four basic determinants from these security objectives.

A reliable transaction requires ensuring mutual identification in order to guarantee the commitment of the transactions. Moreover, one has to ensure the integrity of a transferred message, for instance, of a service request so that the intended service request matches the actual one. Furthermore, the communication or transaction should only be visible for the transaction partners involved in order to guarantee confidentiality. Finally, the issue of non-repudiation is highly relevant since it is the only real way to ensure commitment. All transaction partners not only need to be completely sure about the identities of the others but also the content of the contract in order to assert legal claims, if necessary.

Cryptography

Within the scope of information technology, there are different procedures and methods to implement the abovementioned security objectives in the application systems. From the large spectrum of security instruments, the following section takes the two instruments encryption and the use of a firewall as examples and presents them in more detail (Papazoglou and Ribbers 2006). In practice, one uses encryption methods to ensure the confidentiality of the communication. In the context of information systems and with regard to cryptography, i.e., the encryption of information, one can distinguish between two basic methods: a symmetric and an asymmetric procedure.

Symmetric Encryption

In the case of the symmetric procedure, the sender encodes a message by means of a certain key. With the aid of an algorithm and the corresponding key, a plain text message turns into an incomprehensible encrypted message. If the receiver of the message knows the secret key, he or she can decode the message by means of the algorithm and key. In the case of the symmetric procedure, both communication partners need to know the secret key and the algorithm used.

Asymmetric Encryption

In contrast to symmetric encryption, asymmetric encryption uses two keys. In addition to the secret key, anyone can download a public key via the Internet that is clearly associated with a certain person. In other words, if somebody wants to make sure that only a specific person can read the message, he or she has to use the asymmetric encryption and encode the message by means of the public key of the communication partner. A person can then only decode the message with a secret key that only the sender knows. One can also use the asymmetric procedure in a modified way for digital signatures. Here, however, the order of the applied keys has changed. First, one uses a secret key for encoding and then decodes the message by means of a public key. The digital signature assures the receiver of the message that the electronic message really comes from the respective communication partner, who is the only person that has access to the secret key. Figure 5.15 depicts the functional principle of symmetric and asymmetric encryption.

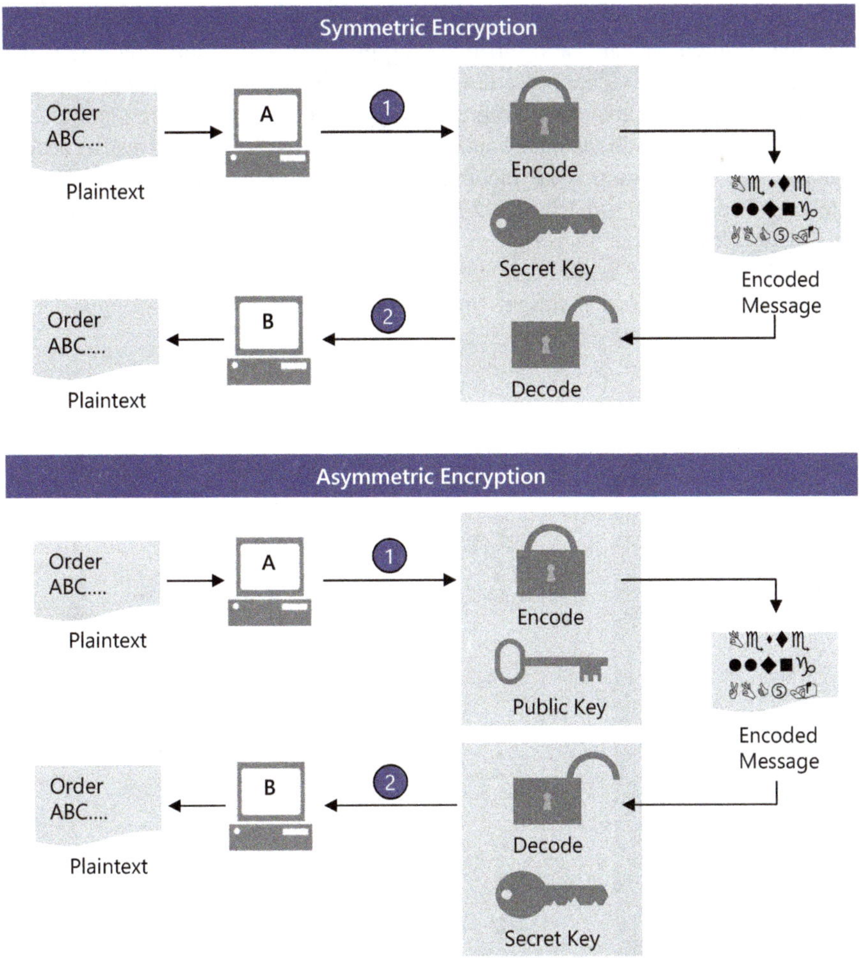

Fig. 5.15 Functional principle of symmetric and asymmetric encryption. Source: Wirtz (2013, 2020, 2021)

Both the symmetric and the asymmetric procedures show some weaknesses or dangers. If communication, for instance, only takes place via the Internet, the key exchange between the communication partners is difficult under the symmetric procedure. Since one can record and intercept plain text messages on the Internet, exchanging the key is not reasonable in this way. The only way to securely transmit a key in the context of symmetric communication would be by means of a media disruption.

In the case of asymmetric communication, the public key is used for encryption. Here, it is problematic that anybody could have sent the message and the identity of the sender is not guaranteed. Moreover, the identity of the receiver could also be fake. Thus, the sender needs to trust that the key, freely accessible on the Internet, really belongs to the respective person. Practitioners increasingly proceed to combine the symmetric and asymmetric encryption method, thus reducing the weaknesses of the individual procedures and increasing security, respectively.

While the application of these different encryption procedures ensures confidentiality, the use of a firewall maintains data integrity. A firewall serves to restrict access to a network and monitors the incoming and outgoing data traffic (see for the following Papazoglou and Ribbers 2006). Based on predefined or set rules, the firewall decides whether to permit or to reject data traffic and thus can prevent undesired access to the network. In addition to these predefined rules, a firewall is basically guided by the addresses of the communication partners. Figure 5.16 presents the functions of a firewall.

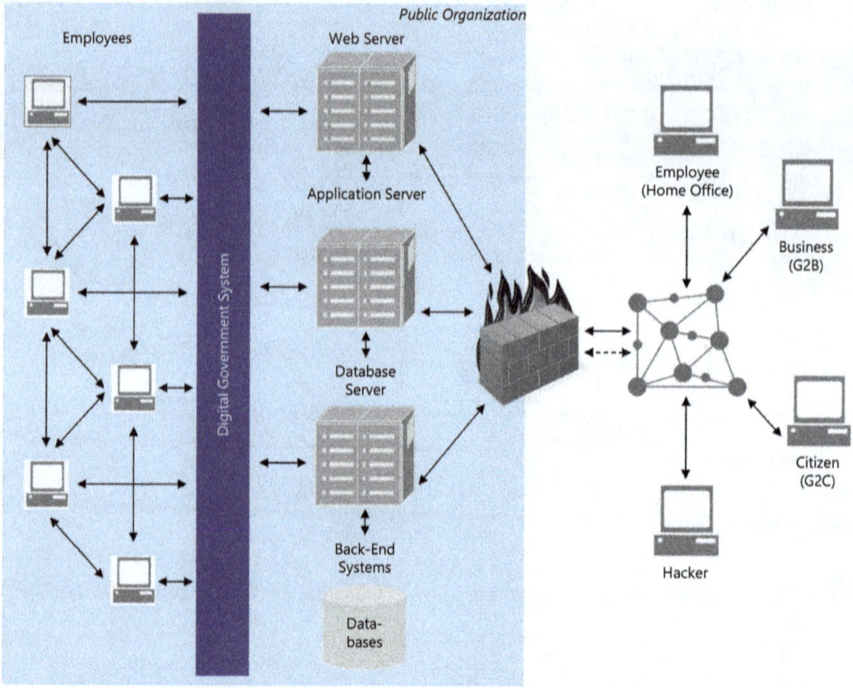

Fig. 5.16 Functions of a firewall. Source: Wirtz (2016, 2020, 2021)

Digital Government Cybersecurity Resources

Also for digital government, after analyzing the potential risks, threats, and vulnerabilities, the next step is to select adequate cybersecurity resources that reduce the impact and risk of potential cyberattacks.[5] In this context, protection measures is

[5]See for the following Section Digital Government Cybersecurity Resources also Wirtz and Daiser (2017).

a vital factor. It covers a broad spectrum of measures, such as access controls, staff training, firewalls, antivirus software, or encryption technologies. These protection measures can be divided into two groups according to their respective form, which can be either dichotomous or polytomous. Figure 5.17 shows an overview of dichotomous in-house protection measures against cyberattacks.

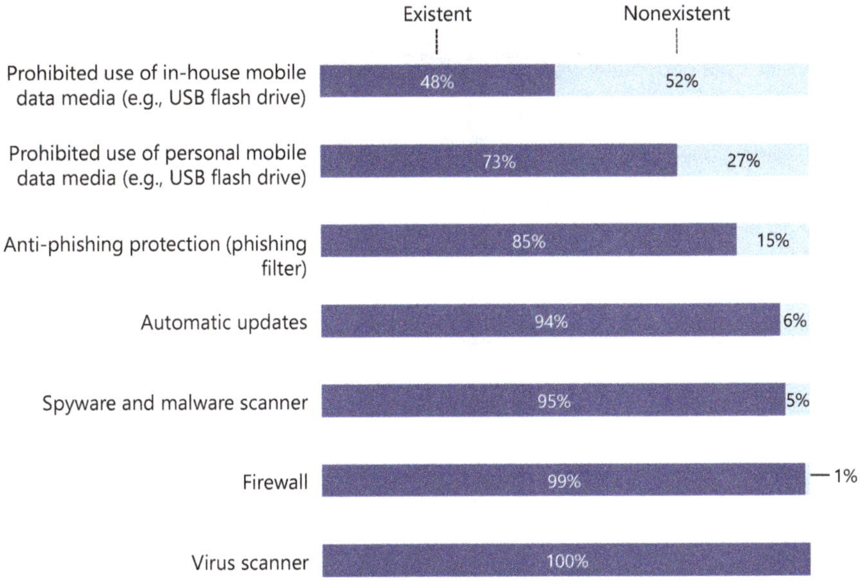

Fig. 5.17 Dichotomous in-house protection measures against cyberattacks. Data source: Wirtz and Weyerer (2017b)

Dichotomous Protection Measures

With regard to dichotomously inquired protection measures, PC security software and automatic updates are most widely existent as all respondents report that they use a virus scanner, 99% declare that they have installed a firewall, 95% report that they have installed common security software, and 94% confirm that they use automatic updates. Moreover, about three out of four respondents report that the use of personal mobile data media is prohibited and about half the respondents state that the use of in-house mobile data media is prohibited.

Polytomous Protection Measures

In addition to the dichotomous protection measures, there are also polytomous in-house protection measures against cyberattacks. Figure 5.18 summarizes the polytomously inquired protection measures that comprise data encryption, access controls, as well as stand-alone networks and staff training. The study shows that public administrators particularly apply encryption technologies with regard to data transfer. Furthermore, access controls are more likely reported to be in place, regardless of whether they are physical or electronic. The same holds true for security-related training of staff.

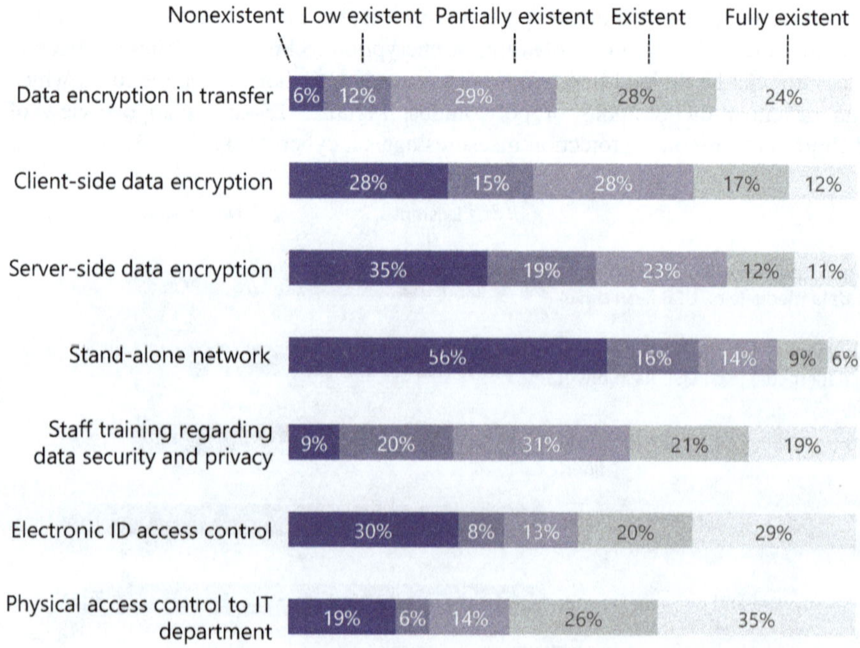

Fig. 5.18 Polytomous in-house protection measures against cyberattacks. Data source: Wirtz and Weyerer (2017b)

If the protection measures fail to prevent a cyberattack, public authorities need to be able to draw on emergency measures to reduce the impact of the attack. Thus, emergency management is also an important factor. Further vital factors concerning public cybersecurity are the professional experience and expertise of the responsible public managers as well as resource support by the superior authority. In particular, the support and commitment of higher authorities and management are seen as key drivers for successful IT system implementation and cybersecurity in the public sector.

Blockchain

Blockchain technology is an encryption approach (cryptography) for the secure transmission of data. A blockchain is a growing list of data records, which are called blocks and linked by cryptography. Each block contains a cryptographic hash of the previous block, a timestamp, and transaction data. The blockchain approach was developed by a person (or group of persons) under the name Satoshi Nakamoto invented in 2008, whereby the identity of Satoshi Nakamoto remains unknown (Nakamoto 2008).

A blockchain database is managed autonomously via a peer-to-peer network and a distributed timestamp server. Once recorded, the data in a particular block cannot be changed retroactively without changing the subsequent blocks. Changing the subsequent blocks would require the consent of the network majority, which is highly unlikely. Although blockchain records are in principle not unalterable, blockchains can be considered very secure, since a widely distributed computer system can hardly be manipulated undetected by all users at the same time. The decentralized consensus on the correctness of the transactions is represented by a blockchain that is continuously expanded with each transaction (Herbert and Litchfield 2015).

Transaction in the Blockchain

In principle, the first step is to initialize a specific transaction. In the second step, this transaction is mapped within a block. This block is then distributed to the network and the network participants. In the fourth step, the participants confirm the transaction, which serves as the basis for including the transaction in the blockchain.

Accordingly, the fifth step integrates the transaction into the blockchain by appending the new block to the existing blockchain in a chain-like manner. In the last step, the respective transactions are executed and confirmed. Figure 5.19 shows the six steps of a transaction in the blockchain.

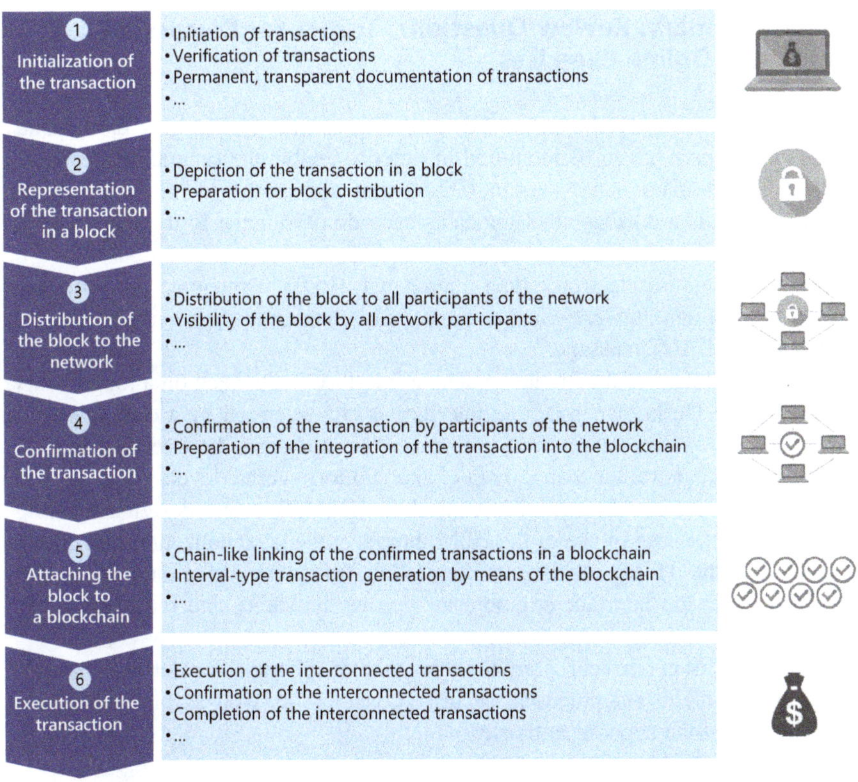

Fig. 5.19 Transactions in the blockchain. Source: Wirtz (2020, 2021)

This procedure enables participants to verify the correctness of transactions independently and relatively inexpensively. The use of a blockchain removes the property of infinite reproducibility from a digital asset. It confirms that each unit of value was transferred only once, which solves the long-standing problem of inexpensive duplication of digital products. Against this background, a blockchain is described as a value exchange protocol that can be used to transfer title rights such as securities or money. This feature made the blockchain the underlying technology of the cryptocurrency bitcoin, which became the first digital currency to solve the problem of reproduction without a trusted authority or a central server.

Smart Contracts

In addition to its utilization as a payment instrument, the blockchain technology serves as the technological basis for smart contracts. Blockchain-based smart contracts are executed or enforced entirely or partially without human interaction.

One of the main advantages of smart contracts is the deposit of automated instructions for concrete executions. For example, it can be used to create invoices that are automatically paid by the customer when a shipment arrives. Alternatively, it is possible to create securities that automatically pay dividends to their owners when profits reach a certain level (Franco 2015).

5.4 Summary, Review Questions, Topics for Discussion, and Online Exercises

- As the Internet is a rather loose network with constantly changing participants, each participant has to be identified in order to enable the accurate exchange of data. The domain name system (DNS) that allows the identification of the participants is a database that allocates each domain name to the respective IP address.
- Organizations use electronic data interchange (EDI) to integrate processes and data. Within this standard, the data are usually transferred by means of XML or a special EDIFACT message.
- The development of the human–machine interface looks back on a long history. Meanwhile, the human–machine interface is characterized by a high degree of automatization and self-learning elements. The interaction between humans and machines occurs on the visual, haptic, and auditory–verbal level.
- The success factors of the human-to-machine (H2M) interface design and configuration are the ease of use of the H2M interface, the personalization/individualization of the H2M interface configuration, the networking and integration capability of the interface solution, as well as the safety and reliability of the interface.
- Risk factors of cybersecurity are the relevance of cyberattacks, potential hazards, the degree of hazard potential, security concerns, as well as the lack of risk awareness of the superior authority.

- In contrast, resource factors to prevent these risks are security measures, emergency management, professional experience and expertise, as well as resource support by the upper-level organizational unit.
- Main threats in computer networks include unauthorized access, data loss, and manipulation.
- Data and identity theft are further typical threats in computer networks and of special relevance in the digital government context.
- Therefore, it is vital that digital governments implement protection measures, such as access controls, staff training, firewalls, antivirus software, or encryption technologies.
- Blockchain technology is an encryption approach for the secure transmission of data. A transaction in the blockchain involves the initialization of the interaction, the representation of the transaction in a block, the distribution of the block to the network, the confirmation of the transaction, the attaching of the block to the blockchain, as well as the final execution of the transaction.

Chapter 5
Review questions, topics for discussion and online exercises

Review questions

1. Describe the five phases model of digital transformation.
2. Present the client-server principle as well as the Internet addressing in an illustration and explain their interrelation.
3. Describe the HMI model of human-machine interaction.
4. Illustrate the risk-resources cybersecurity framework.
5. What is blockchain? Describe transaction phases and contents of blockchains

Topics for classroom discussion and team debates

1. Using the phases of the five phases model of digital transformation, discuss the impact of the fifth phase on public administration and society, particularly with regard to the automation of human labor and mass unemployment.
2. Discuss the future developments of human-machine interaction and configuration against the background of the increasing automation of human work through digital programs and interfaces. What are the risks for a democratic society and a free labor market?
3. Discuss the advantages and disadvantages of comprehensive cybersecurity measures to protect state infrastructure against the background of hacker attacks. Are these protection mechanisms also necessary for the consumer and business sector? In this context, discuss also the possibility of cyber wars between different states.

Online Exercises

1. Visit https://www.publicsafety.gc.ca/cnt/ntnl-scrt/cbr-scrt/index-en.aspx. Using the Canadian example, explore possible cyber threats and security measures at the national level.
2. Enter https://www.cisa.gov/about-cisa. Explore the page and work out the vision and mission of CISA.
3. Access https://read.oecd-ilibrary.org/governance/state-of-the-art-in-the-use-of-emerging-technologies-in-the-public-sector_932780bc-en#page1. Look at emergent technologies in the public sector using the OECD Working Paper on Public Governance No. 31 and define future core technologies.

References

Abts, Dietmar; Mülder, Wilhelm (2017): Anwendungsarchitekturen. In Dietmar Abts, Wilhelm Mülder (Eds.): Grundkurs Wirtschaftsinformatik. Wiesbaden: Springer Fachmedien Wiesbaden, pp. 139–158.

Baltzan, P. (2014): Business driven information systems. 4th ed. New York: McGraw-Hill/Irwin.

Beynon-Davies, Paul (2013): eBusiness. 2nd ed. Houndmills, Basingstoke, New York: Palgrave Macmillan.

Cao, Buqing; Liu, Jianxun; Tang, Mingdong; Zheng, Zibin; Wang, Guangrong (2013): Mashup Service Recommendation Based on Usage History and Service Network. In International Journal of Web Services Research 10 (4), pp. 82–101. DOI: https://doi.org/10.4018/ijwsr.2013100104.

Chaffey, Dave (2009): E-Business and E-Commerce Management. Strategy, Implementation and Practice. 4th ed. Harlow, New York: FT Prentice Hall.

Chaffey, Dave (2015): Digital business and e-commerce management. Strategy, implementation and practice. 6th ed. Harlow u.a.: Pearson.

Franco, Pedro (2015): Understanding Bitcoin. Cryptography, engineering, and economics. Chichester, UK: John Wiley & Sons, Ltd.

Gelinas, Ulric J.; Sutton, Steve G.; Fedorowicz, Jane (2004): Business processes and information technology. Mason, Ohio: Thomson/South-Western.

Herbert, Jeff; Litchfield, Alan (2015): A novel method for decentralised peer-to-peer software license validation using cryptocurrency blockchain technology. In Proceedings of the 38th Australasian Computer Science Conference, pp. 27–35. Available online at openrepository.aut.ac.nz/bitstream/handle/10292/10328/CRPITV159Herbert.pdf?sequence=6&isAllowed=y, checked on 5/27/2021.

Krcmar, H. (2005): Informationsmanagement. 4th ed. Berlin: Springer.

Laudon, Kenneth C.; Laudon, Jane Price; Schoder, Detlef (2010): Wirtschaftsinformatik. Eine Einführung. 2nd ed. München, Boston: Pearson Studium (Wirtschaft).

Nakamoto, Satoshi (2008): Bitcoin: A Peer-to-Peer Electronic Cash System. Available online at https://bitcoin.org/bitcoin.pdf, checked on 5/27/2021.

Papazoglou, M.; Ribbers, P. (2011): E-business. Organizational and technical foundations. 2nd ed. Chichester: Wiley.

Papazoglou, Michael P.; Ribbers, Piet M. A. (2006): E-business. Organizational and technical foundations. Chichester: Wiley. Available online at http://www.loc.gov/catdir/enhancements/fy0622/2005019358-d.html.

Schneider, Gary P. (2017): Electronic commerce. Twelth edition. Boston MA: Cengage Learning.

Solms, Rossouw von; van Niekerk, Johan (2013): From information security to cyber security. In Computers & Security 38, pp. 97–102. DOI: https://doi.org/10.1016/j.cose.2013.04.004.

Srinivasan, Raji; Lilien, Gary L.; Rangaswamy, Arvind (2002): Technological Opportunism and Radical Technology Adoption: An Application to E-Business. In Journal of Marketing 66 (3), pp. 47–60. DOI: https://doi.org/10.1509/jmkg.66.3.47.18508.

Turban, E.; Sipior, Janice C. (2015): Information technology for management. Digital strategies for insight, action, and sustainable performance. 10th ed. Hoboken, New Jersey: Wiley.

Turban, Efraim; Volonino, Linda; Wood, Gregory R.; Sipior, Janice C. (2013): Information technology for management. Advancing sustainable, profitable business growth. 9th ed. Hoboken, N.J.: Wiley.

W3Techs (2021): Usage statistics of server-side programming languages for websites. Available online at https://w3techs.com/technologies/overview/programming_language, checked on 5/26/2021.

Wirtz, Bernd W. (2013): Electronic Business. 4th ed. Wiesbaden: Gabler.

Wirtz, Bernd W. (2016): Electronic Business. 5th ed. Wiesbaden: Springer Gabler.

Wirtz, Bernd W. (2020): Electronic Business. 7th ed. Wiesbaden: Springer Gabler.

Wirtz, Bernd W. (2021): Digital Business and Electronic Commerce. Cham: Springer International Publishing.

Wirtz, Bernd W. (2022): E-Government. Wiesbaden: Springer Gabler.

Wirtz, Bernd W.; Daiser, Peter (2017): E-government. Strategy, process, instruments. 2nd ed. Speyer.

Wirtz, Bernd W.; Weyerer, Jan C. (2017a): Cyberangriffe und Datensicherheit in öffentlichen Netzwerken und Dateninfrastrukturen in Deutschland. In Verwaltung & Management - Zeitschrift für moderne Verwaltung 23 (3), pp. 154–159. Available online at https://www.nomos-elibrary.de/10.5771/0947-9856-2017-3-154/cyberangriffe-und-datensicherheit-in-oeffentlichen-netzwerken-und-dateninfrastrukturen-in-deutschland-jahrgang-23-2017-heft-3, checked on 5/26/2021.

Wirtz, Bernd W.; Weyerer, Jan C. (2017b): Cyberterrorism and cyber attacks in the public sector. How public administration copes with digital threats. Online first 07 November 2016. In International Journal of Public Administration 40 (13), pp. 1085–1100. DOI: https://doi.org/10.1080/01900692.2016.1242614.

Yue, Kun; Wang, Xiao-ling; Zhou, Ao-ying (2004): Underlying Techniques for Web Services: A Survey. In Journal of Software 15 (3), pp. 428–442. Available online at http://citeseerx.ist.psu.edu/viewdoc/summary?doi=10.1.1.85.5423.

Artificial Intelligence, Big Data, Cloud Computing, and Internet of Things

6

Contents

Learning Objectives
By working through this chapter, you will be able to:

1. Define artificial intelligence (AI) and describe aspects of AI.
2. Describe the strategic four AI governance model.
3. Explain the seven layers of the big data architecture.
4. Describe the different types of provision and service models of cloud computing and to what extent these differ in terms of the organizational IT infrastructure.
5. Explain the basic technological concepts of the Internet of Things (IoT) and the IoT-specific IT infrastructure model.

Artificial intelligence (AI), cloud computing, and big data are relevant concepts for IoT technology and considered key technological aspects of the 21st century.[1] Due to their outstanding innovation and opportunity potential, they are increasingly finding their way into digital governance.

As a cross-sectional technological concept, AI is finding its way into all branches and areas of digital government and society and will change related structures and processes significantly and sustainably. The first section describes basic applications and governance issues in the context of AI. First, the meaning and functioning of AI

[1] See for Chapter 6 Artificial Intelligence, Big Data, Cloud Computing and Internet of Things also Wirtz (2020, 2021, 2022).

B. W. Wirtz, *Digital Government*, Springer Texts in Business and Economics,
https://doi.org/10.1007/978-3-031-13086-1_6

are described. In addition, the most important applications and the central opportunities and risks of AI are explained. Finally, the concept of AI governance is addressed. In this context, the different levels of AI-based governance and a strategic governance model are presented. For this purpose, a framework is presented that describes the four strategic components in AI governance.

In Section 6.2, the concept of big data is introduced. This includes a general understanding of the big data architecture. The following section (Section 6.3) addresses aspects of cloud services as well as the provision and service models of cloud computing. Three types of cloud service models are outlined. Section 6.4 presents basics, applications, and user behavior regarding the Internet of Things (IoT). The combined use of IoT technology and robotics is outlined.

6.1 Artificial Intelligence Services and Applications

Artificial intelligence (AI) is a field of application that has already been subject to discussion and development since the 1950s. At this time, intelligent hardware and software capable of technologically reproducing and automating human thought and behavior are central to development. The aim is to solve problems and support humans by means of intelligent analysis and interaction between human and computer systems (Wirtz and Weyerer 2019a, b). Almost all leading IT companies today are strongly engaged in the development or implementation of AI approaches.

Voice-Controlled Applications

AI is not only important to search engines such as Google or Bing but in fact represents a crossover technology that takes almost all applications in the human–machine interaction to a new level. Especially, voice-controlled applications such as Apple's Siri, Microsoft's Cortana, Amazon's Alexa, or Google Assistant provide great potential in the context of AI implementation into everyday life. In light of the so far dominating text-based input in the context of the human–computer interaction, it becomes apparent that voice-based interaction has clear advantages in many application areas, as it allows multitasking approaches and is a natural form of expression that requires no further training or constitutes little cognitive load. In addition, AI will play an important role in the context of decentralized processing and storage of data by cloud applications but also in practical fields such as self-driving cars, medical robots, and industrial production.

AI and Big Data

In addition, big data applications require AI in order to intelligently utilize large datasets. Microsoft, for instance, has been working on AI that uses large datasets since the early 1990s. Another example is Facebook with its huge and still growing pool of information on individuals. Facebook has two large AI-related departments, the Applied Machine Learning and the Artificial Intelligence Research Unit, which intensively explore and implement AI in Facebook applications. The same applies to Google, which has more than 1000 separate AI projects. Its CEO Sundar Pichai sees Google as an "AI-first organization" (Wired 2017) and states: "Over time, the computer itself—whatever its form factor—will be an intelligent assistant helping you through your day. We will move from mobile first to an AI first world" (Eadicicco 2016). He further states: "In an AI-first world we are rethinking all our products" (Waters 2017).

Definition of Artificial Intelligence

In order to fully understand the development and functioning of AI, it is important to create a common understanding of the terminology. The idea of AI is also coined by the work of Alan Turing. In 1950, he formulated an idea of how to determine whether a computer had a capacity for thinking equivalent to a human being (Turing 2009). This test was initially only a theoretical sketch and was only formulated more precisely after Turing's suicide in 1954 after AI had become an academic subject as a subarea of computer science. Since then, this test has been very present in the discussion about AI and has repeatedly served to revive the idea of the thinking machine for the computer age.

Turing Test

In the course of this test, a human interrogator, using a keyboard and a screen without visual or auditory contact, conducts a conversation with two people unknown to him. Thereby, one is represented by a human and the other is represented by a machine. If, after the intensive questioning, the questioner cannot say which of the two the machine is, the machine has passed the Turing test. Thus it can be assumed that the machine has a thinking ability equal to that of a human being. Against this background, an AI must be able to sense, reason, engage, and learn at least to some extent.

Despite the exceptional and far-reaching significance of AI, the literature is largely characterized by a heterogeneous understanding of the concept of AI. Table 6.1 lists various definitions of AI in academic research.

Table 6.1 Selected definitions of AI

Author(s)	Definition
McCarthy et al. (2006)	The study is to proceed on the basis of the conjecture that every aspect of learning or any other feature of intelligence can in principle be so precisely described that a machine can be made to simulate it.
Rich et al. (2009)	[. . .] the study of how to make computers do things which, at the moment, people do better.
Adams et al. (2012)	[. . .] a system that could learn, replicate, and possibly exceed human-level performance in the full breadth of cognitive and intellectual abilities.
Russell and Norvig (2016)	AI may be organized into four categories: Systems that think like humans. Systems that act like humans. Systems that think rationally. Systems that act rationally.
Rosa and Feyereisl (2016)	[. . .] programs that are able to learn, adapt, be creative and solve problems.
Thierer et al. (2017)	The exhibition of intelligence by a machine. An AI system is capable of undertaking high-level operations; AI can perform near, at, or beyond the abilities of a human. This concept is further divided into weak and strong AI.
Wirtz et al. (2019a)	[. . .] AI refers to the capability of a computer system to show humanlike intelligent behavior characterized by certain core competencies, including perception, understanding, action, and learning.

Source: Wirtz (2020, 2021)

In essence, all definitions presented refer to the characteristic of machine-based systems and human-like intelligent behavior. The AI tries to reproduce human thinking and learning and specially to imitate human problem-solving abilities to increase performance in a more efficient way. However, most definitions fall short of covering the full scope of the term. The definition by Wirtz et al. (2019a) integrates many components of the other definitions, which is why it will be used as a foundational definition of AI in the following.

Definition of Artificial Intelligence (Wirtz et al. 2019a, p. 599)
AI refers to the capability of a computer system to show human-like intelligent behavior characterized by certain core competencies, including perception, understanding, action, and learning, in order to support human and systemic behavior in the best possible way.

Besides the integrated general definition of AI, it is important to recognize and understand the complexity of AI. The concept of AI is highly sophisticated and can be differentiated according to various criteria. With regard to the fact that the development of AI is still in an initial stage of progress, one of the first and most meaningful differentiation refers to the stage of development of AI.

Development Stages of AI

These stages are largely associated with the independence of technology from human activity. This means that the more technology acts autonomously, the more independent it is and the less specific its field of application. Kaplan and Haenlein (2019) distinguish three subareas of AI according to the levels of independence: the super artificial intelligence, the general AI, and the narrow artificial intelligence. It is clear that the least independent and yet most specific approach to AI is a form that is less complex than other forms and more available. However, all AI is distinguishable from conventional processing as described in more detail later in this section. Figure 6.1 illustrates the three stages of AI development.

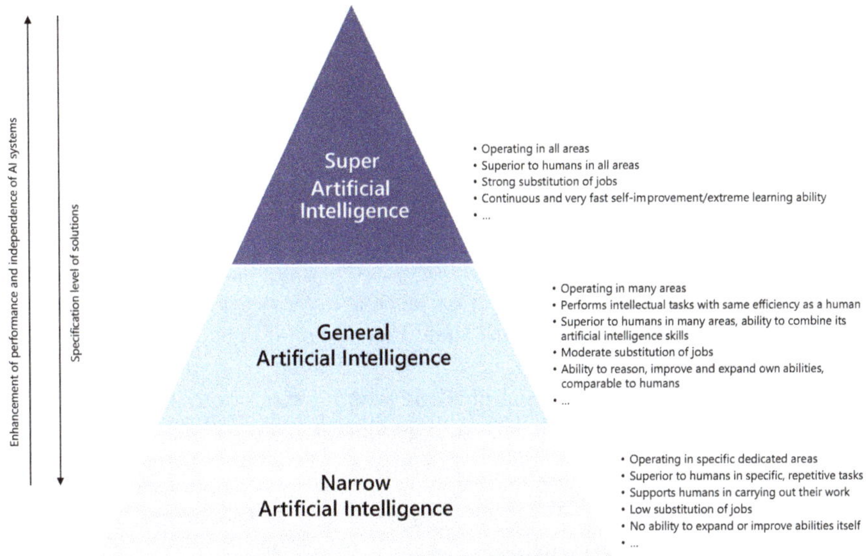

Fig. 6.1 Development stages of artificial intelligence. Source: Wirtz (2021)

Narrow Artificial Intelligence

The part that is called narrow AI refers to sophisticated artificial decision algorithms that are already applied in various IT companies. This part represents the least enhanced performance and independence of AI systems. Therefore, narrow AI is mostly applied in specified fields that have a clear scope of activity and require specific decision solutions. However, the decision algorithms incorporating a large pool of data usually lead to a superior performance than those of ordinary computer processes and humans that are occupied with similar tasks. Therefore, those AI approaches are operating in specific dedicated areas mostly in repetitive tasks, in which humans tend to take more biased decisions or become less reliable or concentrated over time. Moreover, such AI applications can also be used to support humans in carrying out their work. In this context, it is likely that one of the major fears associated with the application of AI, the substitution of jobs, does not apply as strongly with narrow AI as with more sophisticated AI approaches. This is also related to the fact that narrow AI is not able to expand or improve its own capabilities. Therefore, it is limited to very basic learning and not as much to self-improvement.

General Artificial Intelligence

General AI is an AI area that describes a more autonomous technology. It represents a more enhanced performance and independence of AI systems than the above-described narrow AI. Therefore, general AI is applied in various fields with a large scope of activity that require automated decision solutions. General AI can perform intellectual tasks with the same efficiency as a human but in a more efficient and reliable way. Thus, it is seen to be superior to humans due to its ability to combine various intelligence factors. It has the ability to reason, improve, and expand own abilities, which is comparable to human being. Due to their outperformance of humans in terms of efficiency and reliability, they are expected to substitute conventional jobs.

Super Artificial Intelligence

The so-called Super AI is the most sophisticated form of artificial thinking. This part represents the strongest increase in performance and the strongest independence of AI systems from human intervention. Therefore, Super AI is believed to be able to do whatever task given by analyzing from large data and carrying out respective learning. Super AI can be operating in all areas and is superior to humans in every aspect. Such AI technologies have the strongest effect on the job market as they are able to substitute all tasks of today's employees. This is due to their ability to continuous self-improvement.

Learning Approaches of Artificial Intelligence

Another approach of differentiation is based on the learning approach. In this context, it is not an exclusive separation of terminology but rather a further specialization of the concept of AI, which refers to an automated repetitive learning that is usually based on natural language processing.

Machine Learning

The concept of machine learning can be understood as a part of AI. It refers to the idea of human-independent learning from a dataset of an AI technology. In the AI context, a basic approach to learning is to create the ability of reproducing regularities. The results are known through laws of nature or expert knowledge and are used to teach the system. A learning algorithm attempts to find a hypothesis that makes predictions that are as accurate as possible. A hypothesis is a figure that assigns the assumed output value to each input value.

The method is therefore based on a predefined output, which is to be learned by analyzing data. The results of the learning process can be compared with the known, correct results, i.e., supervised. If the results of the output are available in a continuous distribution, whose results can assume any quantitative values of a given range of values, one usually speaks of a regression problem. An example of such a regression problem is to predict the price development of houses based on certain variables or to determine the age of a person from other information about the person. Therefore, it is mostly about predictions. If, by contrast, the results are available in discrete form or the values are qualitative, this is referred to as a classification problem. An example here is to determine whether an email is spam or not.

Unsupervised Learning
Unsupervised learning refers to machine learning without known targets and without environmental rewards. The learning machine tries to detect patterns in the input data that deviate from structureless noise. An artificial neural network orients itself by the similarity to the input values and adapts the weights accordingly. Different things can be learned. Popular is the automatic segmentation (clustering) or the compression of data for dimension reduction.

Semi-supervised and Reinforcement Learning
There are also some approaches that are called semi-supervised learning, which incorporates methodologies of both supervised and unsupervised. Similarly, reinforcement learning refers to a set of machine learning methods in which an agent independently learns a strategy to maximize received rewards. The agent is not shown which action is the best in which situation but rather receives a reward at certain points in time, which can also be negative. Using these rewards, the agent approximates a utility function that describes the value of a certain state or action. The term is borrowed from psychology and has been used since the beginnings of cybernetics.

Deep Learning
Deep learning is a method of machine learning that uses artificial neural networks with hidden layers between the input and output layers, thereby forming an extensive internal structure. The concept is inspired by the biological understanding of brains, which is considered a special method of information processing. The problems solved in the early days of AI were intellectually difficult for humans but easy for computers to process. These problems could be described by formal mathematical rules.

The real challenge to AI, however, was to solve tasks that were easy for humans to perform but whose solution was difficult to formulate through mathematical rules. These are tasks that humans solve intuitively, such as speech or face recognition. A computer-based solution for this type of task involves the ability of computers to learn from experience and to understand the world in terms of a hierarchy of concepts. Each concept is defined by its relationship to simpler concepts. By gathering knowledge from experience, this approach avoids the need for human operators to formally specify all the knowledge that the computer needs for its work.

The hierarchy of concepts allows the computer to learn complicated concepts by assembling them from simpler ones. This is why this approach is called "deep learning." It is difficult for a computer to understand the meaning of raw sensory input data, such as in handwriting recognition, where a text initially exists only as a collection of pixels. The transformation of a set of pixels into a chain of numbers and letters is complex. Multifaceted patterns must be extracted from raw data. Learning or evaluating this association seems insurmountably difficult if it had been programmed manually.

Use of Hierarchical Layers

Deep learning, a subset of machine learning, uses a series of hierarchical layers or a hierarchy of concepts to perform the process of machine learning. The artificial neural networks used in this process are built like the human brain, with neurons inter-connected like a network. The first layer of the neural network, the visible input layer, processes raw data input, such as the individual pixels of an image. The data input contains variables that are accessible to observation and hence constitute a "visible layer." This first layer forwards its outputs to the next layer. This second layer processes the information from the previous layer and passes the result on as well. The next layer receives the information from the second layer and further processes it. These layers are called hidden layers. The characteristics contained in them become increasingly abstract. Their values are not specified in the original data. Instead, the model must determine which concepts are useful for explaining the relationships in the observed data. This continues at all levels of the artificial neural network. The result is the output in the visible last layer. This divides the desired complicated data processing into a series of nested simple mappings, each described by a different layer of the model. Against this background, deep learning is based on huge neural networks to learn complex patterns in large amounts of data.

Despite the detailed understanding of the concepts and the functionality of deep learning, machine learning, and AI in general, it is important to have a broad understanding of the concepts, from a managerial perspective. Each concept is relevant to digital government and thus should be considered in its respective field. Figure 6.2 outlines the different concepts (content based on Copeland 2016; Wittpahl 2019).

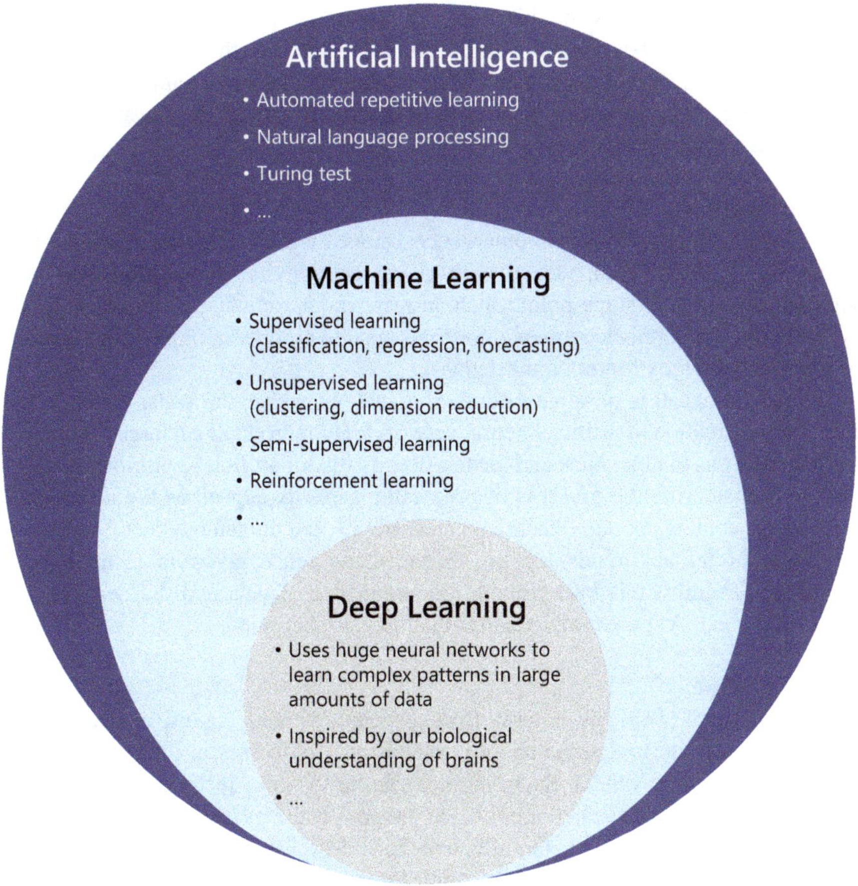

Fig. 6.2 Methods of artificial intelligence. Source: Wirtz (2021)

Cognitive and Memory Levels of Technology

Despite the description by differentiation according to stages and methods, AI technology can also be described along specific criteria that refer to the cognitive and memory levels of the technology. According to Joshi (2019), there are four functionality concepts that separate AI from conventional digital analytics and data processing: (1) self-awareness, (2) theory of mind, (3) limited memory, and (4) reactive machines.

Self-Awareness

Self-awareness of an AI describes the ability of an artificial subject, which "can be literally said to understand and have cognitive states" (Searle 1980, p. 417). Therefore, it is assumed to think similar to a human or at least as a sophisticated living creature. Awareness in living creatures refers to a person or animal's current situational consciousness of his, her, or its environment and the resulting implications. By considering the implications, awareness thus touches not only perceptual psychological phenomena (e.g., attention), but also social psychological processes (e.g., decision-making behavior of others). However, the question remains what status defines self-awareness.

Consciousness

The concept of consciousness emergence refers to the idea that it arises with increasing cognitive competence: with rising complexity, a consciousness will automatically arise at some point. Such an increase in complexity can be achieved by increasing the sophistication of algorithms and the number of processing memory cells and the degree of inter-connectedness.

In this context, it is possible to draw the analogy with brain cells, which is the basis for the creation of artificial neural networks. By reproducing a large number of artificial neurons that fire back and forth, a new quality of artificial consciousness can emerge. Considering the progress of processing capacity as well as the increase of data storage centers, modern machines can easily exceed human intellect. Moreover, the limits of human minds are not in the same sense given in technological approaches. Against this background, the abundance of data and the new way of processing make AI potentially smarter than any human mind.

Theory of Mind

Theory of mind (ToM) is a term from psychology and cognitive sciences. It describes the ability to assume about consciousness processes in other people and to recognize these in others. Such abilities can be to sense feelings, needs, ideas, intentions, expectations, and opinions in others. There is a difference between affective and cognitive ToM: the affective ToM describes the ability to recognize and understand the emotions of others, while the cognitive ToM is the ability to draw conclusions about the intentions of others.

Alan M. Leslie sees the ToM as a mechanism of selective attention (Leslie 2000). Here, the existence of mental concepts is the basis for focusing attention on corresponding mental states of actors. In this way, these qualities can be tapped. There is also the concept of mentalization by Peter Fonagy. He defines the term mentalization as the ability to interpret one's own behavior or the behavior of other people by attributing mental states (Fonagy et al. 2018). Through targeted processing of the data generated during the interaction with the user, an attempt is made to obtain information about the user's thoughts and feelings and to use this information to predict the user's future behavior.

Mental Artificial Intelligence

A mental AI is the next level of AI systems that is currently subject to research. An AI that lives up to the concept of ToM will be able to better understand the entities with which it interacts by recognizing their needs, emotions, beliefs, and thought processes. Artificial emotional intelligence is already an emerging industry and a field of interest for leading AI researchers. However, achieving AI that includes development in others at the level of the mind goes a step further. To truly understand human needs, AI machines must perceive people as individuals whose minds are shaped by a variety of social and emotional factors that can only be recognized by an empathic capacity.

Limited Memory of Machines

Another relevant concept in this context is the limited memory of machines. Such a limit is thus by nature the same for human and machine. Dealing with it is not a skill that has to be reserved for humans but can also be solved technologically. Reactive machines, similar to humans, can learn from historical data in order to make decisions. Today all existing AI applications fall into this category. Today's AI systems that use deep learning, for example, are trained by large amounts of data that they store in their memory to form a reference model for solving future problems. For example, an image recognition AI is trained using thousands of images and their descriptions to teach it to name objects that it scans. When an image is scanned by such an AI, it uses the training images as references to understand the content of the image presented to it. Based on this learning experience, it is possible to describe new images with increasing accuracy. The recourse to previous computing power is thus a core concept of the AI and can be traced back to the limited memory. Figure 6.3 illustrates the four cognitive and memory levels of AI (content partially based on Joshi 2019).

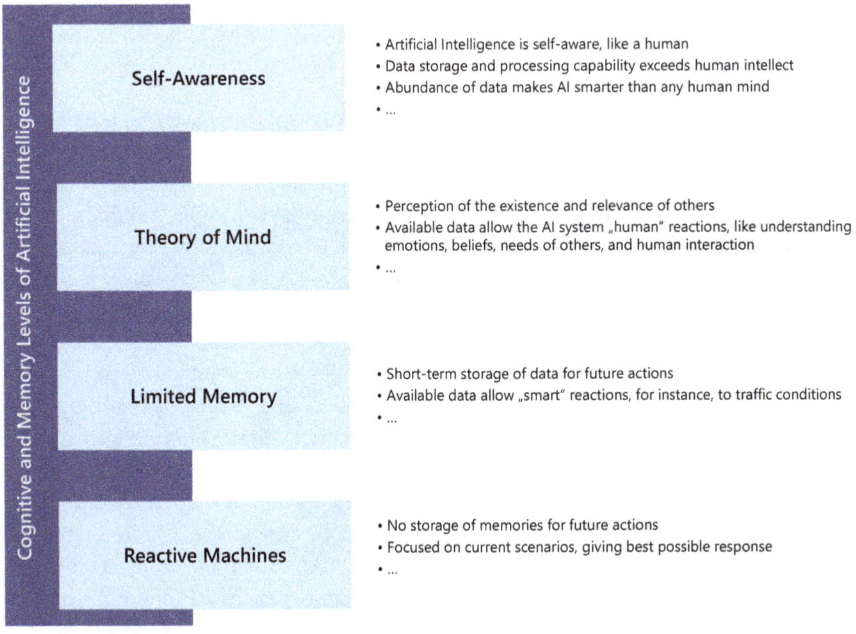

Fig. 6.3 Cognitive and memory levels of artificial intelligence. Source: Wirtz (2021)

Analytical Activity of Artificial Intelligence

Despite the cognitive and memory levels of AI, there is an additional approach to distinguish the use of AI by the type of analytical activity. From a digital business perspective, respective analytical methods are traditionally covered by data mining and business intelligence. However, AI, which can, to some extent, be understood as an autonomous form of big data analytics, draws on respective analytic concepts.

Descriptive and Diagnostic Analytics

The basis of any analytical activity is to understand what happens through historical information. This is covered by descriptive analytics, which helps to understand what happened, and by diagnostic analytics, which tries to understand why it happened. In this context, diagnostic analytics is a key concept of AI as it does not only describe information but also has the ability to interpret historical data and reasons for what has happened.

The next level is covered by three disciplines called advanced analytics. They try to use and add knowledge in order to make better decisions in the future, and they also provide additional insights.

Predictive Analytics

Predictive analytics uses historical data to predict future events, including those in the financial, security, economic, or mobility sectors. Historical data is used to derive a mathematical model that captures key trends. This predictive model is then applied to current data to predict what will happen next. Predictive analytics has received much attention in recent years as supporting technologies have made great strides, especially in the areas of big data and machine learning.

Prescriptive Analytics

Prescriptive analytics uses machine learning to make decisions based on predictions made by an algorithm. Prescriptive analytics works with predictive analytics, which uses data to determine short-term outcomes. In this context, it is created to help to make better decisions on any time horizon. Therefore, it can be regarded as an approach of advanced analytics, which uses machine learning to enhance decision-making processes mostly in a commercial context.

Cognitive Analytics

Cognitive analytics is a field of analytics that attempts to imitate the human brain by drawing conclusions based on existing information and then reintegrating this information into the knowledge base for future conclusions. This creates a self-learning feedback loop. It mostly refers to the ability to apply a human-like intelligence for specific tasks. The idea is to reproduce the process of human reasoning for signal processing. In this context, deep learning can be considered a reproduction of human-like thinking as it uses artificial neural networks of artificial neurons that fire back and forth. Figure 6.4 illustrates the five analytical types of AI (content partially based on Decide Soluciones 2017; Ulster University 2020).

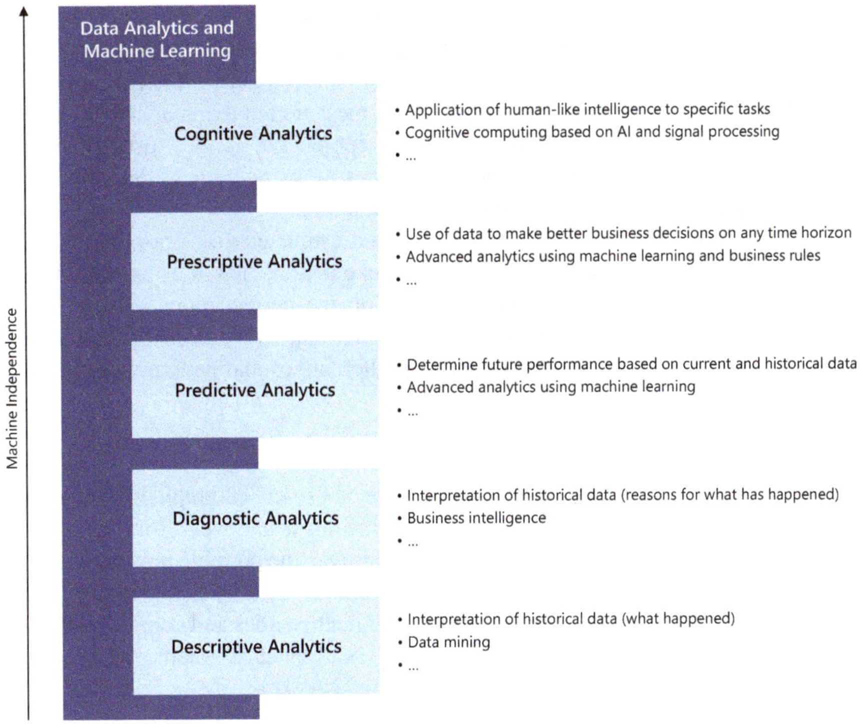

Fig. 6.4 AI analytics approaches. Source: Wirtz (2021)

Each of these disciplines uses statistical and mathematical techniques to achieve the proposed goals. They help to understand what and why something happens, what could happen, and what someone could do to make something specific happen. In addition, these techniques also focus on how to make human-like decisions. AI technologies can automate decision-making by guaranteeing the quality of those decisions and their contribution. To make this possible, they all require large amounts of data.

Logical Representation

However, despite the availability of data and the general concepts of different aspects of AI, it is important to understand the basic approaches of AI functioning. The first approaches of AI were based on classical principles of mathematical logic. In propositional logic, simple logical operations such as AND, OR, and NOT can be combined and statements can be assigned a truth content (TRUE, FALSE), whereas in predicate logic, arguments can be formulated and checked for their truth content.

The first systems of AI were such logical representation systems that help to trace and prove simple conclusions. For instance, from the two statements (1) "Yesterday was Tuesday" and (2) "We received the letter yesterday" it can be concluded that: "The letter arrived on Tuesday." AI systems based on logic are used for much more complex mathematical proofs and theorems and are still used today in modern AI applications such as IBM's Watson (Lally and Fodor 2011) with the help of logical programming languages like Prolog (Colmerauer and Roussel 1996). This approach is sensible, because the capabilities of AI can be measured in terms of how well they play against humans. The advantage of these approaches is their usually simple system of rules and easily describable possibilities of action with, at the same time, almost unlimited variations depending on the situation.

Chess, for example, has very simple rules but estimated 10^{120} possible moves. This very large number is beyond human imagination, and it is impossible to calculate all the possibilities in order to develop the perfect game strategy. This high number of possible moves is due to the fact that every decision, i.e., every possible move in chess, creates new decision alternatives and new moves but with different starting situations and so on.

Decision Trees

These decision variants can be described as a tree or a so-called graph, in which each hand or node represents a possibility—in the game this is a move—from which new and different ones arise to infinity. Just as a tree grows, the possible moves unfold in ever new branches and ramifications to the quasi infinity of all possible moves. Such a tree is called a decision tree, and whole areas of mathematics and computer science are concerned with the most efficient search in such branched graphs.

Heuristics

A very effective way to search in decision trees is to use the so-called heuristics. A heuristic is a procedure that determines the usefulness of a further in-depth search for every point in such a graph and thus prevents the best strategy from being searched for a long time—in the worst case infinitely long. In chess, this means that the possible moves are evaluated according to certain criteria and the possibilities resulting from obviously bad moves are no longer considered. Accordingly, heuristics lead to a decision tree being searched very specifically until a satisfactory result is obtained, which does not necessarily have to be the best possible result.

In AI, decision trees and the associated heuristics are a very effective method for problems that can be described by a clear and unchangeable rule system. The first successes of AI in the field of logic and games were followed by attempts to extend the procedures to more general applications. In the 1970s, expert systems were developed which, via "if-then relationships," attempt to transform a human knowledge base into information readable by computers. With the possibilities for logical conclusions and effective searching in these knowledge bases by means of heuristics, the systems initially had some success and raised great expectations for the possibilities of AI in the 1980s. A major disadvantage of these systems, however, is the great effort involved in capturing human knowledge and transforming it into the knowledge base required for the expert system.

AI Winter

At the beginning of the 1990s, the great expectations of AI were disappointed: many companies that had previously bought expert systems for a lot of money abolished them. A large number of companies that had offered such systems disappeared from the market. These failures, together with a significant reduction of research funds in the field of AI from the late 1970s onward, led to the first and second phase of the so-called AI winter (Crevier 1993).

Foundations for Machine Learning

Notwithstanding the aforementioned setbacks for research, in the 1980s the foundations were laid for the machine learning approach, which is so central today. The basic idea is simple: How do you get a computer program that has a specific task to learn from experience and use this experience to better fulfill the task in the future (Mitchell 2008)? The difference to a static program is that the decision rules adapt to what has been learned via feedback. Figure 6.5 illustrates the difference between conventional software programming and unsupervised machine learning (content based on Kirste and Schürholz 2019; Wittpahl 2019; Damron 2019; DataRobot 2020).

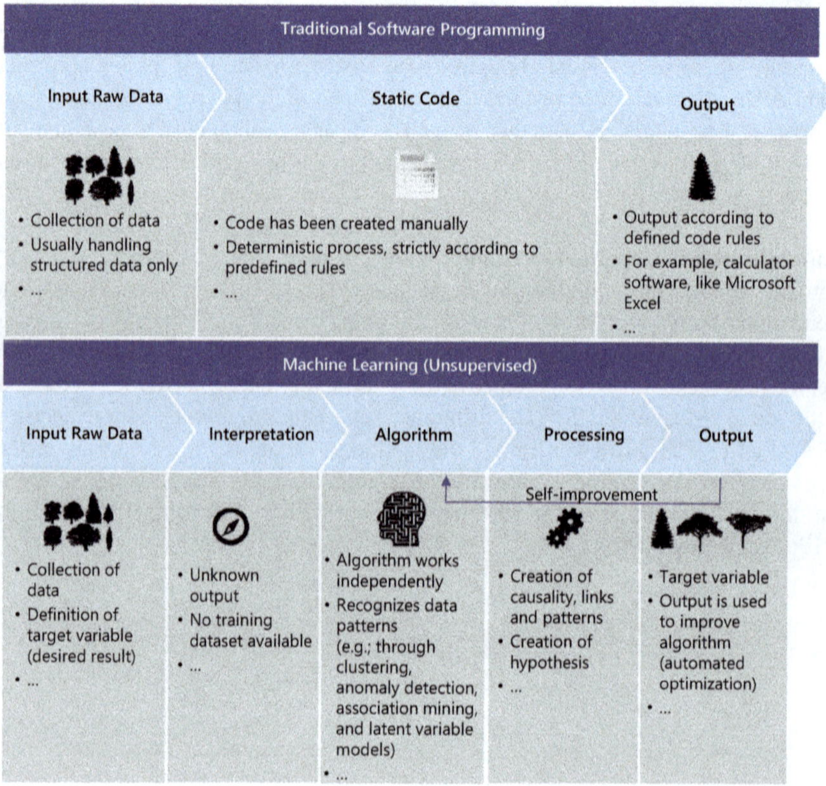

Fig. 6.5 Machine learning process vs. traditional software programming. Source: Wirtz (2021)

Artificial Intelligence Framework

AI has a broad range of applications due to its function as crossover technology. The consultancy Accenture has developed an AI framework that combines three core capabilities (sense, comprehend, act) with six technological forms of AI. Figure 6.6 illustrates this framework (content based on Accenture 2016).[2]

[2]See for the following Section Artificial Intelligence Framework also Accenture (2016).

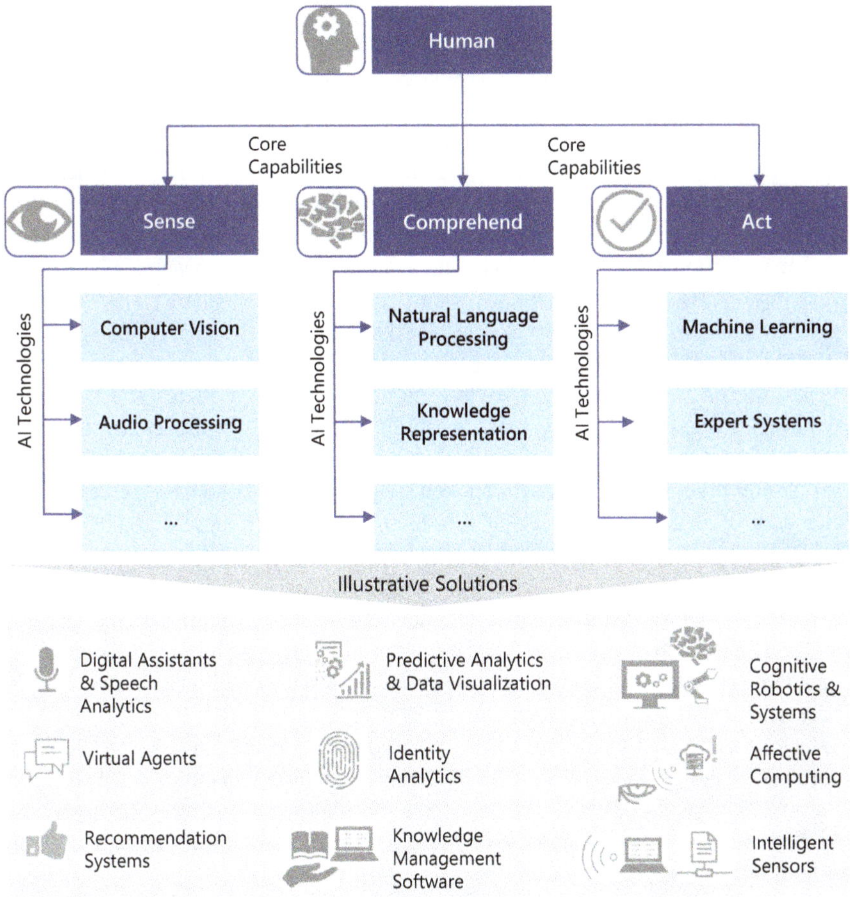

Fig. 6.6 AI framework. Source: Wirtz (2018, 2020, 2021)

AI comprises three core capabilities, (1) sense, (2) comprehend, and (3) act, which are characterized by an experiential learning ability and adaptability. The first core capability refers to the sensing or perception of the environment.

Sense
AI-based technologies such as computer vision and audio processing are able to perceive certain aspects of the environment by capturing and processing images and sounds. A good example in this connection is the use of intelligent facial recognition at self-serving terminals (smart border kiosks) in the context of border controls.

Comprehend
The second core capability pertains to the comprehension of the information acquired from the environment. Technologies such as natural language processing and inference engines, which are developed by including procedures of knowledge

representation, allow AI systems to analyze and understand the information collected. These technologies are used, for instance, in the context of language translation for search engines and smart speakers (e.g., Amazon Echo or Google Home).

Act

The third core capability refers to the action in terms of a physical activity. Technologies like machine learning, expert systems, or inference engines enable AI systems to take actions in a physical environment. Examples in this connection are, for instance, autopilot functions and intelligent braking systems of vehicles (Accenture 2016).

Applications of AI

Against the background of the abovementioned core competencies and AI-based technologies, there is a diverse range of applications of AI. In this connection, the field of digital assistants and speech analytics refers to software that is able to intelligently recognize and process spoken language. Here, one can use the digital voice control as a personal assistant. Common examples of these digital assistants are the software Siri by Apple, Cortana by Microsoft, Amazon Alexa, or Google Now.

Virtual agents are animated graphical chatbots with human appearance that are usually displayed on websites and programmed to interact with people. Companies often deploy them particularly as virtual customer service employees in the context of customer relationship management.

Recommendation systems are software-based recommendation services that filter information and seek to predict the preferences of users in order to give them recommendations on this basis. A good example in this connection is the organization Amazon and its recommendation system with regard to book titles and other products.

Predictive Analytics and Data Visualization

Predictive analytics and data visualization is another specific application area of AI and refers to the processing of large data volumes to make forecasts and create meaningful visualizations. Here, for instance, machine learning as a subarea of AI plays an important role. The use of AI in the context of predictive analytics supersedes the selection of the right mathematical algorithm because the machine provides the correct solution based on its AI algorithms. IBM's Watson Analytics platform serves as a good example in this connection since it offers intelligent automated predictive analytics and data visualization.

Identity Analytics

Identity analytics is another application area of AI and represents a combination of big data, advanced analytics, and identity access management (IAM) to manage access of IT systems and automate risk-based identity controls. In this area, AI-based machine learning technologies are also applied to better protect IT systems and identities. The application of identity analytics by credit card companies (e.g., VISA) in the context of fraud detection is a particularly relevant example in this connection. Knowledge management software serves companies to generate and systematize knowledge and addresses the way in which companies collect, store, access, and share information. In doing so, it applies AI-based methods such as natural language processing, machine learning, or expert systems, for instance, for automating recognition and comprehension of information or words, as well as in the context of intelligent search. Examples of knowledge management software are Bloomfire, Intelligence Bank, or Oxcyon.

Cognitive Robotics and Systems

Cognitive robotics and systems refer to adaptive robots or systems with cognitive intelligence. AI-based techniques help robots and systems to analyze information in order to generate a knowledge map. An example in this context is the service robot Relay by Savioke, which is used in hotels as room service, for instance.

Affective Computing

Affective computing pertains to learning systems that have emotional intelligence and can automatically recognize and understand human expressions of emotion. AI-based techniques assist, for example, in the recognition of facial expressions and speech. In this context, the organization Affectiva, for instance, is developing AI-based technology products for the detection of emotions.

Intelligent Sensor Technology

Intelligent sensor technology describes the intelligent acquisition and processing of measured values by means of sensors. AI-based techniques such as expert systems or neural networks support the sensors in their learning ability and adaptability. Intelligent sensor technology is applied in almost all areas of IoT and particularly plays a prominent role in the context of industrial Internet of Things (IIoT) (for more information on IIoT, see also Section 6.4). An example in this context represents the intelligent sensors that are attached to components of industrial machinery and are able to automatically identify wear patterns as well as preventively initiate a maintenance and repair process.

AI Applications and Use Cases

Based on the abovementioned illustrative AI solutions, a classification of AI applications can be derived and merged into a superordinate concept in terms of an overview of AI applications. Table 6.2 presents such an overview, describing the different AI applications with their value creation and functional proposition as well as respective use cases in practice (content based on Wirtz and Weyerer 2019d; Wirtz et al. 2019a).

Table 6.2 Potential AI applications and use cases

AI application	AI value creation and functional proposition	Use cases
AI-based knowledge management software	• Generation and systematization of knowledge—gather, sort, transform, record, and share knowledge • Natural language processing, machine learning, and expert systems can support the codification of knowledge • Use of neural networks enables to analyze, distribute, and share knowledge with others • . . .	• Decision support for management in the context of big data analyses • Clinical documentation powered by AI • Knowledge transfer during induction of employees • Preservation and management of knowledge during generational change of employees • . . .
AI-based process automation systems	• Automation of standard tasks; perform formal logical tasks with unpredictable conditions in consistent quality • Complex human action processes (formal logical or dangerous tasks) can be transferred to automation systems, which can support humans in performing tasks • May include rule-based assessment, workflow processing, schema-based suggestions, data mining, case-based reasoning, intelligent sensor technology • Robotic process automation has emerged as a subarea through further technology innovations. This leverages the ability of software robots or AI-driven workers to mimic human interaction with user interfaces of software systems • . . .	• Automated image diagnostics in medicine • Automation and optimization of product development and production • Optimization of environmental plants • Faster and higher quality request processing for immigration application forms • Human–computer interaction for repetitive tasks like data entry, etc. • . . .
Virtual agents	• Computer-based system that interacts with the user by means of speech analytics, computer vision, and written data input • May also include real-time universal translation and natural language processing systems and affective computing • Software that can perform tasks for humans • Subareas are chatbots and avatars • . . .	• Recruiting chatbot • Virtual nursing assistant • Automated user correspondence • A chatbot helping refugees that seek asylum to fill out and search documents • Purchasing and consulting assistants • . . .

(continued)

Table 6.2 (continued)

AI application	AI value creation and functional proposition	Use cases
Predictive analytics & data visualization	• Analytics are based on the quantitative and statistical analysis and meaningful visualization of large amounts of data for forecasting purposes • Processing of big data for reporting, prescriptive analysis, and predictive analysis • Machine learning as a technical subarea based on algorithms that can learn from data • . . .	• Medical diagnostics • Control and performance monitoring in public areas for police departments to determine terror threats and crime hotspots for preventive action • Determine high crime-risk situations to secure public transport • Forecast model to predict water levels • Predictive maintenance in production • Financial forecasting, price optimization, and sales forecasting • . . .
Identity analytics	• Software combined with big data, advanced analytics, and identity access management to control access to IT systems and automate risk-based identity checks • May include deep learning and machine learning, affective computing, and artificial immune systems • . . .	• Face recognition for identification of persons • Security robot for monitoring airports • AI fraud detection to secure governmental data • Customer recognition in shops • . . .
Cognitive robotics & autonomous systems	• Systems with higher-level cognitive functions that involve knowledge representation and are able to learn and respond • Sometimes in connection with affective computing to determine and adapt human behavior as well as respond to respective emotions • . . .	• Automated driving • Electric-powered autonomous vehicles for public transport • Robot-assisted surgery • Care robots • . . .
Recommendation systems	• An information filtering system • Software-based systems that screen personalized information to predict preferences of individuals • . . .	• Personalized marketing • Product and service recommendations • E-service for government offices to provide personalized information for employees • . . .
Intelligent digital assistants	• Software based on speech analytics • Digital voice control enables functionality of a personal digital assistant • Providing an intuitive interface between a user and a system/device to search for information or complete simple tasks • . . .	• Smart procurement assistants • Driving assistance • Assistants for visually impaired people • Connection of federal programs to intelligent digital assistants to make public service information available for users • . . .

(continued)

Table 6.2 (continued)

AI application	AI value creation and functional proposition	Use cases
Speech analytics	• Software for intelligent recognition and processing of language • Understand or respond to natural language • Translate from spoken to written language or from one to another natural language • May include real-time universal translation and natural language processing systems • …	• Universal real-time translation of language and text in public service settings • Administrative workflow support by translating speech into text • Bot for the care of refugees • …
Cognitive security analytics & threat intelligence	• Additional application for cognitive technologies to analyze security information through natural language processing and machine learning • Interpret and organize information and provide reasoning • …	• Behavior pattern recognition for higher IT security • Monitoring of financial transactions • Sample diagnoses for better fraud detection • Applications like Watson for cybersecurity to support human security analysis in the public sector • …

Source: Wirtz (2020, 2021)

AI has a wide range of applications due to its function as cross-sectional technology (Wirtz et al. 2019a). The AI applications shown in Table 6.2 are used by companies in all economic sectors.

Industry-Specific Effects of AI

The use of these AI applications is characterized by considerable economic potential and effects that differ across the various economic sectors. Against this background, Table 6.3 shows the AI-related automation potential, potential productivity, and demand effects from AI and AI use cases with high potential for selected industries (content based on Wirtz and Weyerer 2019d).

Table 6.3 Industry-specific potential and effects of AI

Industry	Automation potential	Effect on productivity[a]	Effect on demand[b]	Use cases with high potential benefit
Production	60%	8.3%	2.2	• Improved monitoring and automatic adjustment of production processes • Optimization of production and supply chain • On-demand production
Transportation & logistics	60%	7.0%	3.2	• Autonomous deliveries and transportation by trucks • Better traffic control and congestion reduction • Increased road safety
Retail trade	53%	13.2%	3.0	• Better personalization and customization in design and production • Improved forecasting of product demand • Optimization of inventory and delivery management
Energy & supply	44%	6.8%	2.2	• Intelligent meters and measuring systems (smart metering) • Higher efficiency of network operation and storage • Predictive maintenance of the infrastructure
Finance	43%	8.4%	3.3	• Better personalization of financial planning • Optimizing the prevention and detection of money laundering and fraud • Automated customer business
Technology, media & communication	41%	9.9%	3.1	• Improved archiving, search, and media recommendations • Generation of custom content • Better personalization and customizing for advertising and marketing
Health & social affairs	36%	27.9%	3.7	• Better diagnostic support • Improved early detection of potential pandemics • Improved image diagnosis

Data source: PwC (2017, 2018a, b), McKinsey (2017), Wirtz (2020, 2021)
[a]Growth of gross domestic product (GDP) through AI in Germany
[b]Values are based on the AI impact index valuation of PwC. The scale ranges from "1" to "5," with "1" being the lowest potential impact of AI on demand and "5" the highest

Automation Potential

Of particular economic importance is the AI-related automation potential, which describes the proportion of work activities that can be automated using AI. The production and transportation and logistics sectors each have the highest automation potential with 60% each and, together with retail trade (53%), form the top group.

The sectors energy and supply, finance as well as technology, media and communication each form a homogeneous middle field with just over 40%. This is followed by the health and social affairs sector with 36% (McKinsey 2017).

Furthermore, the potential productivity effect and demand represent central aspects with regard to the economic contribution of AI. The productivity effect results primarily from the automation of routine tasks and the AI-based skills enhancement of the staff, which can therefore concentrate more on value-adding activities (PwC 2017).

AI-based growth of GDP

The productivity effect can be represented by the AI-based growth of the gross domestic product (GDP) in the respective industries. The greatest productivity effect is achieved with 27.9% in the health and social sector. The retail industry follows clearly behind with 13.2%. The sectors technology, media and communication, finance, production, transport and logistics, as well as energy and supply showed similar productivity effects, all of which ranging between 7 and 10% (PwC 2018a).

Demand Effect

The demand effect describes the demand and consumption effects of AI. The AI-based increases in productivity, time savings, and improvements in the quality and personalization of products and services lead to an increase in demand and changes in consumer behavior (PwC 2017).

The AI-based demand effect can be illustrated by means of the AI impact index assessment of PwC. The strongest demand effect is seen in the area of health and social affairs (3.7). The areas of finance, transport and logistics, technology, media and communication, and retail trade are each characterized by a similar demand effect with a value between 3.0 and 3.3. The areas of production and energy and supply have the lowest demand effect with a value of 2.2 (PwC 2017).

Use Cases

Based on the automation potential as well as the productivity and demand effect, particularly promising use cases with high benefit potential can be derived for the individual industries. In the area of production, improved monitoring, automatic adjustment of production processes, optimization of the production and supply chain, and on-demand production are particularly noteworthy. In the field of logistics and transport, autonomous deliveries and truck transports, better traffic control and congestion reduction, as well as increased traffic safety are applications with high potential benefits. The use cases with particularly high potential benefits in retail relate to better options for personalization and customizing in design and production, improved forecasting of product demand, and the optimization of inventory and delivery management.

In the field of energy and supply, intelligent meters and measuring systems (smart metering), the higher efficiency of network operation and storage, as well as predictive maintenance of the infrastructure (predictive maintenance) are associated with a high benefit potential.

The financial industry benefits in particular from improved personalization options for financial planning, the prevention and detection of money laundering and fraud, and automated customer business.

In technology, media and communication, the improved archiving, search and recommendations of media, the generation of custom content, and the better possibilities of personalization and customizing in advertising and marketing are characterized by high potential benefits.

Finally, promising use cases in the health and social affairs sector relate in particular to better diagnostic support, improved early detection of potential pandemics, and improved image diagnosis (PwC 2018b).

Against the background of this industry-specific potential and effects of AI, it can be seen that AI opens up considerable opportunities for both companies and society. At the same time, however, the use of AI is associated with considerable risks that can endanger the success of AI projects.

Opportunities and Risks

Accordingly, a comprehensive understanding of AI-related opportunities and risks is essential, especially for companies, in order to ensure successful and beneficial use of AI. Table 6.4 therefore compares key opportunities and risks of AI (content based on Wirtz and Weyerer 2019c).

Table 6.4 Opportunities and risks of AI

Dimensions	Opportunities	Risks
Social & ethical	• Increased road safety and time savings for people through self-driving vehicles based on AI (e.g., Waymo) • Improved medical diagnostics and early detection of pandemics through AI systems (e.g., IBM Watson) • Increased public security by means of AI-based video surveillance and pattern recognition (e.g., ivisX) • . . .	• Moral dilemmas of autonomous AI applications • Discrimination of people by AI algorithms • Lack of compatibility between mechanical and human value judgment • AI-based rule-setting for human behavior without a normative-ethical basis • Global technological arms race, especially in the military sector (e.g., AI-based autonomous weapons) • . . .
Legal & regulatory	• Improved legal case analysis through AI-based e-discovery software (e.g., Exterro) • Prediction of judgments with high accuracy by AI systems (e.g., case crunch) • Improved risk assessment of the likelihood of recidivism of offenders through AI systems and reduction of the prison population • . . .	• Technology obedience and loss of control due to lack of governance of autonomous intelligent systems • Threat to cybersecurity and data protection through AI cyberattacks • Unclear responsibility and liability for decisions and actions of AI systems • . . .
Technological & implementation-oriented	• Improved AI-based data and information processing enables efficient and sustainable resource allocation • Higher IT security through improved AI-based behavior pattern recognition • Faster and easier access to the Internet and digital services using AI-based personal assistants (e.g., Amazon Alexa, Google Assistant and Duplex, Siri from Apple, or Microsoft's Cortana) • . . .	• Loss of control over technologically autonomous AI systems • Security problems and failure of the AI system in mission-critical and life-critical situations due to immaturity of the AI-technology and lack of experience • Lack of specialization and expertise as well as a lack of skilled workers • High entry, transition, and implementation costs • . . .
Economic	• Free up work capacity and increase productivity by automating repetitive tasks using AI-based process automation systems and virtual agents • Rationalization and process optimization through AI systems • Considerable efficiency advantages through AI-based IoT applications • Improved AI-based data analysis and improved financial and sales	• Social resistance of workers to the introduction of AI systems • Loss of management and control of processes due to transformation of human–machine and machine–machine interaction and increased autonomous AI automation • Lack of social and customer-related acceptance and low trust into AI systems and manufacturer through AI failures

(continued)

Table 6.4 (continued)

Dimensions	Opportunities	Risks
	forecasting creates significant efficiencies and better management decisions • . . .	• Substitution and transformation of the labor market and unemployment, especially in production and manufacturing industry • . . .

Source: Wirtz (2020, 2021)

Social and Ethical

Here, it is evident that the AI-related opportunities in the social and ethical area relate primarily to the increase of traffic safety and public safety, as well as improved medical diagnostics and early detection of pandemics, while the AI-related risks refer in particular to moral dilemmas of autonomous AI applications or the discrimination of people by AI algorithms (Wirtz et al. 2020).

Legal and Regulatory

The opportunities in the legal and regulatory area lie primarily in improved legal case analysis and forecasting of court decisions.

The main risks in this context are the loss of control due to a lack of governance of AI systems, the threat to cybersecurity, and data protection posed by AI cyberattacks, as well as unclear responsibility and liability for AI-based decisions and actions (Wirtz and Müller 2019).

Technological and Implementation-Oriented

In addition, technological and implementation-oriented opportunities relate in particular to improved AI-based data and information processing and the resulting more efficient allocation of resources. They also relate to higher IT security through improved AI-based behavior pattern recognition, as well as enhanced access to the Internet and digital services by means of AI-based personal assistants.

Key technological and implementation-oriented risks include the loss of control over technologically autonomous AI systems, security problems and the failure of the AI system in mission-critical and life-critical situations, the lack of specialization and expertise associated with the shortage of AI specialists, and the high entry, transition, and implementation costs.

Economic

Finally, the opportunities of AI refer in particular to the release of labor capacity and increased productivity through the automation of repetitive activities as well as rationalization and process optimization. The efficiency gains through AI-based IoT applications as well as the efficiency advantages and better management decisions resulting from the improved data analysis and forecasting options are also of central economic importance.

The economic risks posed by AI relate in particular to the social resistance of employees to the introduction of AI systems and the loss of management and control of processes as a result of increasingly autonomous AI automation. In addition, the lack of social and customer-related acceptance and the low level of trust in AI systems and their manufacturers must also be mentioned in this context, just as the substitution and transformation of the labor market and the associated threat to jobs.

Due to the diverse and serious risks posed by AI to companies and society, the regulation or strategic governance of AI is of particular relevance to companies to ensure the success of their AI projects. In the following section, the governance aspect of AI is examined in more detail.

Artificial Intelligence Governance

A central consideration in this context is the increasing automation and independence of AI from humans, which also means an increase in AI-based governance. Figure 6.7 illustrates different levels of AI-based governance.

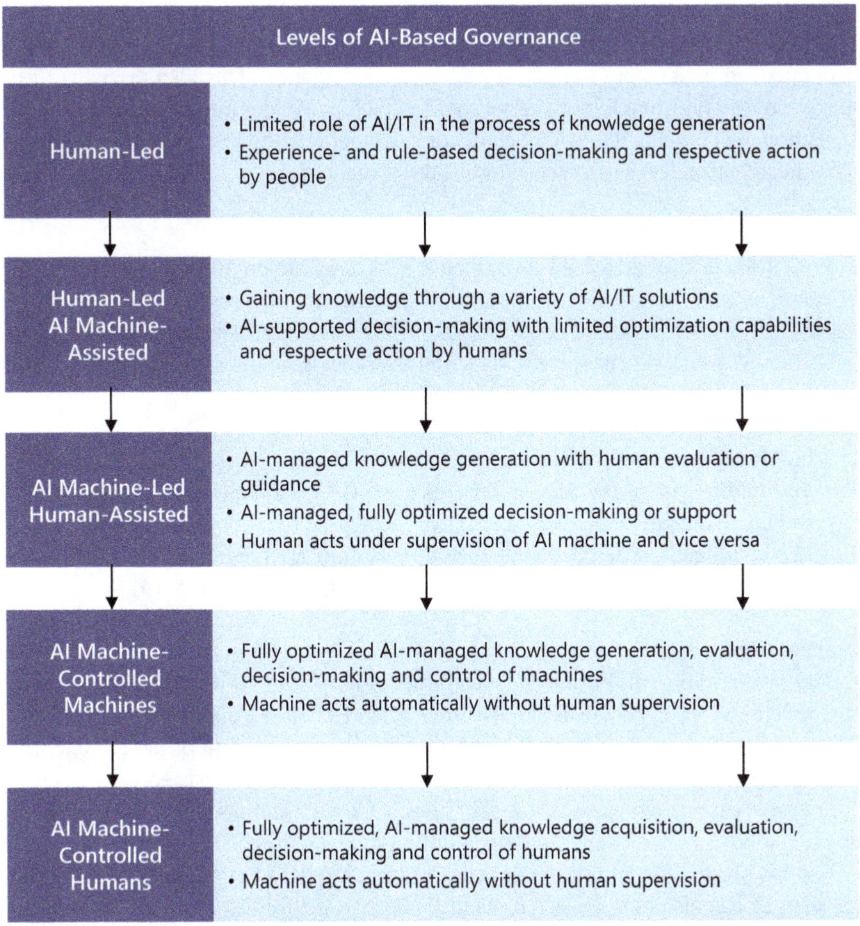

Fig. 6.7 Levels of AI-based governance. Source: Wirtz (2020, 2021)

Human-Led

Five main levels can be distinguished (Miller 2019). At the first level, "human-led," AI, or IT plays a subordinate role and is only used partially in the context of gaining knowledge. The decision-making and the resulting actions are taken exclusively by humans on the basis of experience and rules (Miller 2019).

Human-Led AI Machine-Assisted

In the second stage, "human-led AI machine-assisted," a variety of AI/IT solutions are used in the context of knowledge generation. Humans are supported in decision-making by AI machines, which are, however, still characterized by a limited capacity for optimization. The execution of the resulting actions is still exclusively in human hands.

AI Machine-Led Human-Assisted
At the third level, "AI machine-led human-assisted," knowledge is gained by AI machines and is subject to human evaluation or guidance. This also involves fully optimized decision-making or support by AI machines under human supervision. At the action level, both the AI machine can act under human supervision and the human can act under the supervision of the AI machine.

AI Machine-Controlled Machines
In the fourth stage of AI-based governance, "AI machine-controlled machines," the AI machine acts completely autonomously, ensuring fully optimized knowledge acquisition as well as associated evaluation and decision-making. On the action level, the AI machine independently controls other machines and thus acts fully automatically without human influence and supervision.

AI Machine-Controlled Humans
The fifth level of AI-based governance, "AI machine-controlled humans," corresponds to the previous level in terms of the degree of autonomy and automation with the significant difference that the AI machine no longer only controls and manages other machines but also the humans themselves (Miller 2019).

Current State
A clear classification of the current state of development of AI proves to be difficult. The development of AI is still in its infancy, and most AI applications are at the "human-led AI machine-assisted" level, so that the current state of development is more likely to be at the second level "human-led AI machine-assisted."

In some cases, however, AI applications such as chatbots are already in use, which can be assigned to the "AI machine-led human-assisted" level.

For this reason, the current AI development with regard to the stages of AI-based governance can also be seen as a transition phase to the third stage "AI machine-led human-assisted."

Development of AI-Based Governance
However, given the considerable and very rapid technological progress in the field of AI, it can be assumed that the level of development of AI will establish itself at the third stage in the coming years and that even the achievement of the subsequent stages seems to be only a matter of time.

In view of this development and the associated risks presented by AI for companies and society, the topic of strategic governance of AI is increasingly coming to the fore from an organization perspective, in order to ensure the security and success of AI-based activities (Wirtz and Weyerer 2018; Bullock 2022).

For companies, strategic AI governance represents a kind of management tool in the form of a higher-level framework for managing and controlling AI-related activities, systems, and processes as well as their effects.

Strategic Four AI Governance Model

Against this background, the strategic four AI governance model in Figure 6.8 summarizes the risks described above and presents four specific governance countermeasures and the strategic AI governance agenda (content based on Wirtz and Weyerer 2019c).

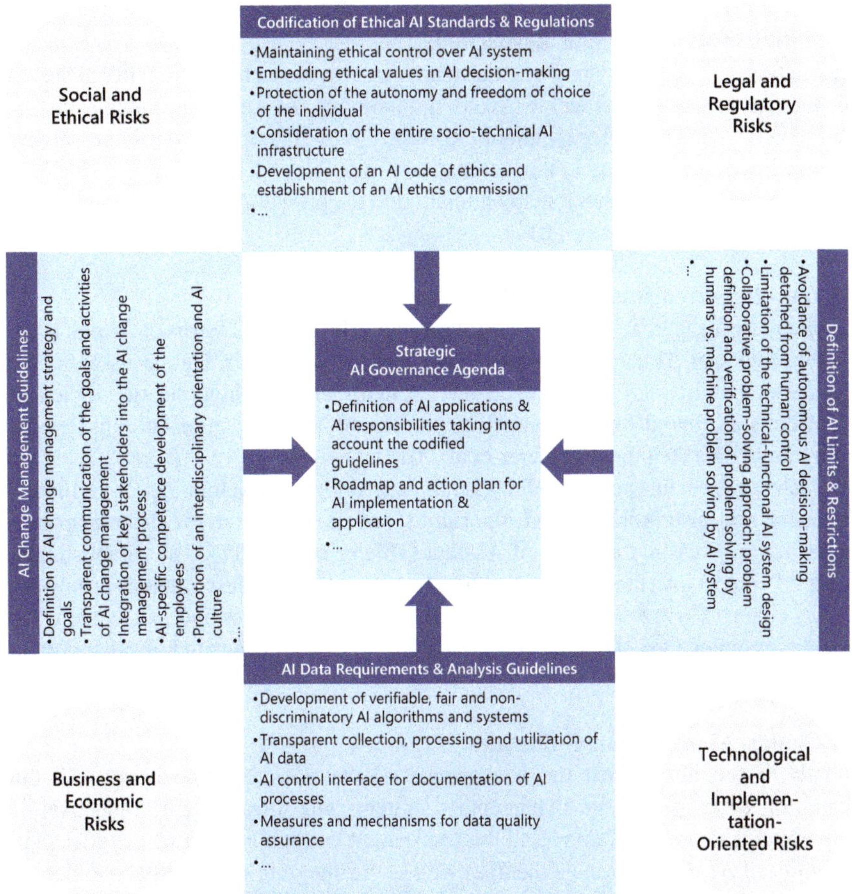

Fig. 6.8 Strategic four AI governance model. Source: Wirtz (2020, 2021)

Codification of Ethical AI Standards and Regulations

First, the social and ethical risks associated with AI require a codification of ethical AI standards and rules. Maintaining human control over ethical aspects related to the AI system, embedding ethical values in AI decision-making, and protecting the autonomy and freedom of the individual are of particular importance (Wirtz and Müller 2019). It is also important that companies consider the entire socio-technical infrastructure and value chain in the context of AI, as this is also characterized by social and ethical aspects.

Other key AI governance tools in the social and ethical field are an AI code of ethics and an AI ethics committee, which ensure that ethical principles are adhered to in the context of AI activities (Thierer et al. 2017). In addition, the setting of AI restrictions and limits is another important governance tool in the context of all types of AI risks (Wirtz and Müller 2019).

Definition of AI Limits and Restrictions

Restrictions are necessary in particular with regard to the technical-functional design of the AI system in order to avoid autonomous AI decision-making that is completely detached from human control. A collaborative problem-solving approach seems promising in this context, where problem definition and verification of the problem solution are done by humans and the problem solution is provided by the AI system (Eggers et al. 2017).

AI Data Requirements and Analysis Guidelines

Another key measure in strategic AI governance relevant to all forms of AI risk is the establishment of AI data requirements and analysis guidelines. Data is essential for the learning ability and performance of AI systems, since their application logic and algorithms are based on the collection, processing, and utilization of considerable amounts of data (big data) (Thierer et al. 2017).

Such requirements and guidelines shall be used for the development of verifiable, fair, and non-discriminatory AI algorithms and systems and for the transparent collection, processing, and use of AI data (Thierer et al. 2017). The establishment of an AI control interface for the documentation of all AI processes seems promising in this context (Wirtz and Müller 2019). In addition, measures and mechanisms for quality assurance of the data are necessary to avoid undesired results due to incorrect data.

AI Change Management Guidelines

Finally, especially against the background of the risks associated with AI, the definition of an AI change management strategy and corresponding objectives is important. This involves above all the transparent communication of the goals and activities of AI change management, as well as the integration of key stakeholders in the AI change management process.

In addition, AI-specific competence development of employees and the promotion of an interdisciplinary orientation and AI culture are important governance aspects in this context. Taken together, these four specific governance countermeasures form the basic framework for action in the strategic AI governance agenda. This agenda determines the AI-related applications, activities, and responsibilities and provides a roadmap and action plan for the implementation and application of AI systems for companies.

In summary, it can be stated that the importance of AI for enterprises and their competitiveness will continue to increase. As a cross-sectional technology, AI is characterized by a particularly broad range of applications and a very large potential for opportunities. At the same time, however, there are also considerable risks and challenges associated with AI, which require systematic and effective governance and regulation. Due to the human-like intelligent behavior of AI in terms of the reproduction of human thought and learning as well as corresponding problem-solving abilities, AI has a particular influence on the development of information technology applications at the human–machine interface.

6.2 Big Data

The development of AI approaches is based on a sophistication of data analysis itself. With the digital revolution and the ever-increasing processing capacities, there is also a revolution in data analysis approaches. The application of these big data analysis methods is becoming more and more important for organizations to survive in competitive digital markets. The following section provides information about the increasing relevance and introduces the application of these big data analysis methods.

Relevance and Growth of Big Data

The concept of big data has gained increasing importance in recent years. Big data represents an essential technological foundation of IoT since an intelligent and systematic analysis and evaluation of the data provided by IoT is relevant to success. Big data is one of the fastest growing information technology sectors worldwide. For example, global big data market sales for software, hardware, and services are expected to increase from USD42 billion in 2018 to USD103 billion in 2027, representing an annual growth rate of just over 10% (Kobielus 2018). Big data refers to the processing of large and often complex data volumes in real time.

The increasing digital transformation of all life and government areas and the associated exponential growth of data worldwide are the starting point for this development and the establishment of the big data concept. According to expert estimates, the global volume of data will more than quintuple in the next few years, rising from 33 zettabytes in 2018 to 175 zettabytes (1 zettabyte equals 1 billion gigabytes) in 2025 (Reinsel et al. 2018). The analysis of these very large amounts of data (big data) gives companies considerable potential for added value and has become a decisive competitive factor for them.

Traditional relational database systems are not able to process these considerable amounts of data in a meaningful way, which can only be handled by specific big data applications. Big data applications are far superior to traditional relational database systems in terms of data velocity, data volume, and data variety. In this context, data velocity describes the speed at which data is generated, processed, and transferred, whereas data volume represents the quantity or size of the data. Data variety refers to the diversity of the collected data and data formats.

Applications and Use Cases of Big Data Analyses

Against this background, big data represents an essential technological basis for digital government, as an intelligent and systematic analysis and evaluation of data information is relevant to the success of digital government. For this reason, a large number of companies now use big data analyses. In this context, Figure 6.9 shows the use of big data analyses in companies.

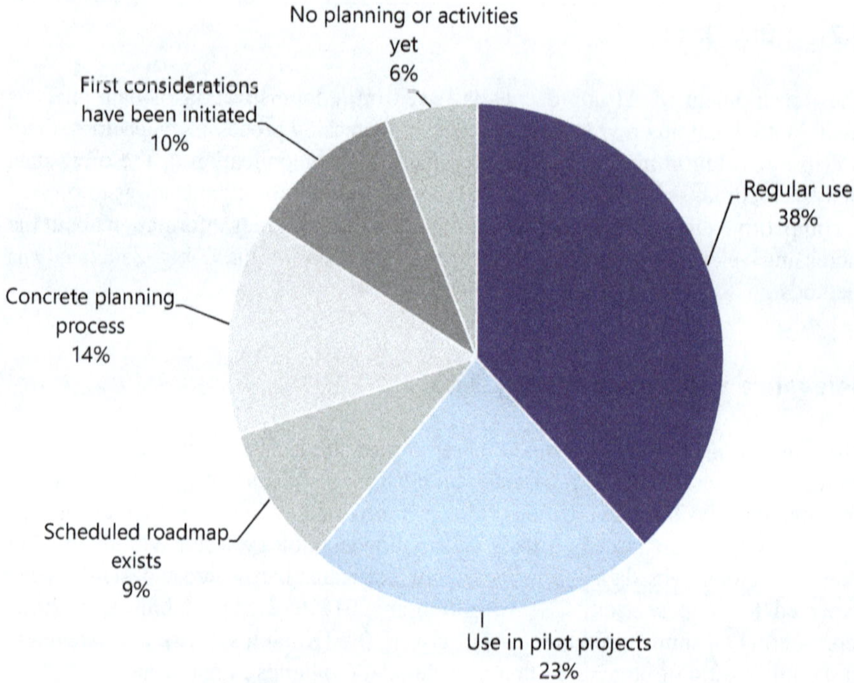

Fig. 6.9 Application of big data analytics in practice. Data source: techconsult (2018), Wirtz (2021)

More than half of the companies use big data analysis. This is already regularly the case in 38% of the companies, and in 23% the application is still carried out in the context of pilot projects. About one-third of the companies are in the planning and reflection process, and a small minority of 6% do not have any planning or activity related to big data analysis (techconsult 2018).

These figures on the application or distribution of big data analyses in companies show that big data is still in an early development phase in practice.

Data Processed in Big Data Analyses

Digital government provides a variety of data (e.g., data from transactions or social media, sensor and log data, RFID-supported movement data, or traffic data), which are processed by means of big data analyses into important decision-relevant findings, for example, on processes. In this context, Figure 6.10 summarizes the most important data that are processed by companies in big data analyses.

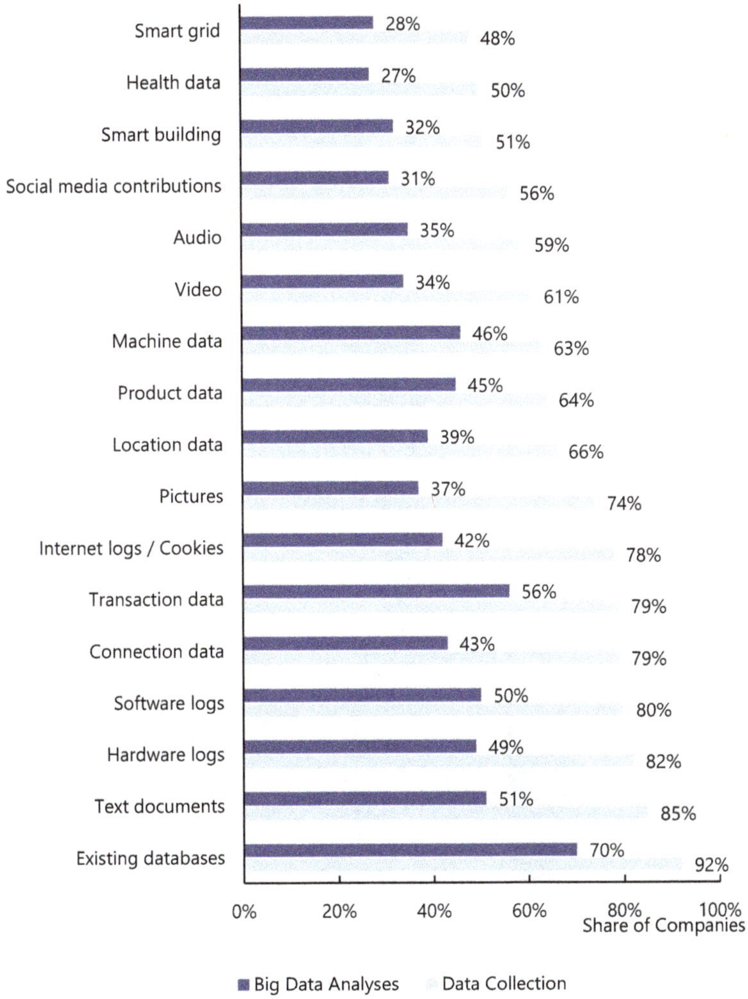

Fig. 6.10 Data processed by companies in big data analyses. Data source: techconsult (2018), Wirtz (2021)

Big Data Architecture

In order to capture and analyze the diverse and large amounts of data characteristic of big data and to generate the aforementioned benefits from it, a powerful big data platform is necessary that is capable of handling the requirements in terms of data volume, data velocity, and data variety. For the architecture of big data platforms, different applications such as the open-source framework Hadoop or Cloudera are employed. A typical big data architecture is shown in Figure 6.11 and is described below (content based on Singh 2013; Mezghani et al. 2015; Wang et al. 2015).

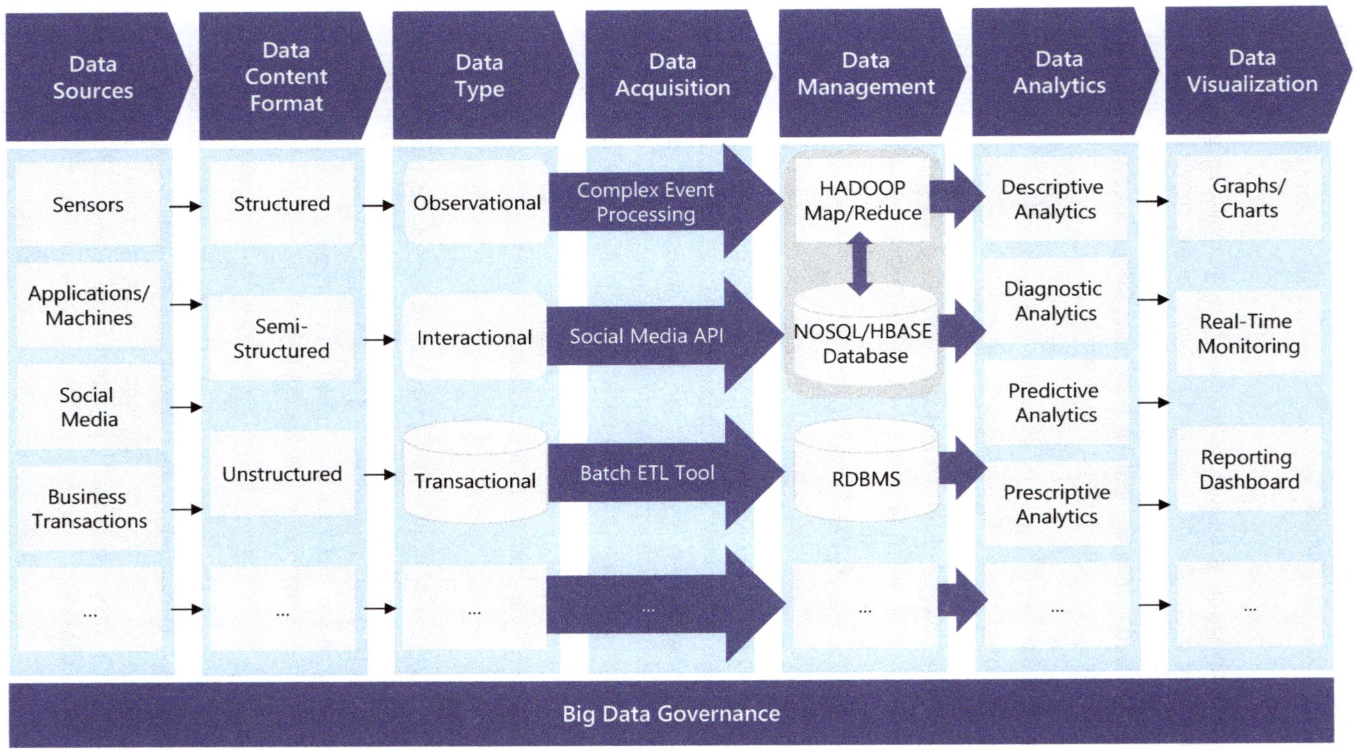

Fig. 6.11 Exemplary illustration of a big data architecture. Source: Wirtz (2018, 2020, 2021)

The big data architecture consists of seven layers: (1) data sources, (2) data content format, (3) data type, (4) data acquisition, (5) data management, (6) data analytics, and (7) data visualization.

Data Sources

The first layer includes all data sources necessary to generate insights that are required to improve operations or to solve a problem. In the context of big data, the sources, content formats, and types of data distinguish themselves through a particular variety. Data can arise and be collected, for instance, from sensors, applications/machines, social media, and transactions.

Data Content Format

The second layer refers to the content format in which data may occur. Data can be present in structured, unstructured, and semi-structured form. While structured data is characterized by a predefined format and can be easily processed, unstructured data does not have a formalized structure, and their processing is difficult. Semi-structured form lies between these two extremes and only shows a formalized structure to a certain extent (Phillips-Wren 2014).

Data Type

The third layer refers to the data type that is determined by the origin of the data. In principle, data can arise from transactions (transactional data), interactions (interactional data), and observations (observational data). Transactional data are, for instance, historical structured data from important application systems. Interactional data are, for instance, data collected from social media platforms (e.g., Facebook, LinkedIn, and Twitter) or web content such as images, videos, blogs, and clickstreams. Observational data are IoT-based data such as streaming data or machine-generated data captured by means of sensors, RFID, or GPS technology.

Data Acquisition

The fourth layer refers to data acquisition and represents the starting point of the big data administration process. Here, the focus is on reading the data that comes in from various data channels at different speed and in different frequencies, sizes, and formats. Depending on the data source, different processing methods are deployed (e.g., batch processing or complex event processing).

Data Management

In the fifth layer, the actual big data management takes place by means of respective big data technologies. Depending on the type of data and data sources, different technologies are applied, for instance, the open source framework Hadoop, the non-relational NoSQL database HBASE, or a traditional relational database management system (RDBMS).

Data Analytics

The sixth layer of the big data architecture refers to the analysis of data. Here, there are also different forms of analytics that one can choose, depending on the data type, data sources, and processing mode. In this connection, the field of predictive and prescriptive analytics has particularly gained in importance in the context of big data that focus on making forecasts and providing guidance on how to act with regard to a future event, respectively.

Data Visualization

Data visualization represents the last step of the data administration process and the big data architecture. Depending on the source, type, and processing mode of data, one can choose among different forms and tools of visualization, such as graphs/charts, real-time monitoring, or a reporting dashboard. Finally, an important element within a big data architecture is the governance of big data that pertains to all layers or stages in the architecture and refers to the overall management of big data, regulating aspects such as accessibility, availability, and security of data.

Big Data and AI

In summary, big data is one of the most important and promising technologies and serves companies to analyze their data and to gain valuable insights that contribute to maintaining their competitiveness. AI is closely linked to big data, as both stand for key technologies. On the one hand, AI supports the preparation, processing, and analysis of datasets within the framework of big data and can thus contribute to uncovering fundamental structures in the data. On the other hand, AI itself requires technologies that are capable of processing very large amounts of data and is therefore relying on big data analytics.

Accordingly, big data plays an essential role in the learning and performance of AI and has contributed significantly to the great breakthrough of AI in recent years. The more data AI has at its disposal, the better its analysis and learning progress. Due to the outstanding importance of new technologies in the context of big data, new and modified digital strategies are emerging. Therefore, the increasingly important approach of cloud computing will be addressed in the following.

6.3 Cloud Computing

Cloud computing has experienced a significant increase in importance in recent years. It allows a decentralization of computing and storage capacities and a far-reaching application and networking of smart devices. Cloud computing thus plays a central role in digital government and society. Therefore, this section addresses the topic of cloud computing. Besides the infrastructural basis, analytical progress is also of considerable importance in this context.

Location Independency, Scalability, and Elasticity

Cloud computing refers to the provision of servers, databases, software, network components, and storage via the Internet. Cloud computing represents an essential technological basis for digital government and society, since the decentralized and demand-oriented provision of servers, databases, or software is often crucial in terms of success in this context. The various components of cloud computing are usually provided by external cloud service providers such as Amazon Web Services (AWS), IBM, SAP, or Microsoft but also smaller companies. Microsoft, for example, offers with its cloud platform Windows Azure a variety of different products and services in the cloud segment (Microsoft 2020).

Lower Barriers to Entry

A cloud delivery model transforms investment (such as server purchases) into operational expenses, thereby lowering barriers to entry. This is due to the fact that the infrastructure is typically provided by a third party and does not need to be purchased for one-time or infrequent, intensive computing tasks. The pricing of utility computing is often based on usage-based billing options. The implementation of projects with cloud computing also requires less internal IT knowledge, since the organization's own server infrastructure can be partially replaced by external server services.

Device and Location Independency

Device and location independency allow users to access systems via a web browser, regardless of their location and the device they use (e.g., PC or mobile phone). As the off-site infrastructure (typically provided by a third party) is accessible via the Internet, users can connect to it from any location.

Maintenance of cloud computing applications is more convenient because there is no need to install them on each user's computer, and they can be accessed from different locations (e.g., from different workstations, while traveling, etc.). Off-premises software is generally referred to as "software as a service" ("SaaS") or "cloud software." This is different from on-premises software (sometimes referred to as "shrink-wrap" software), which runs on computers on a person's or organization's premises and is therefore managed locally (Godse and Mulik 2009; Boillat and Legner 2013; Winkler and Brown 2013).

Increased Resource Utilization

Off-premises software enables the sharing of resources and costs across a large pool of users through multi-client capability. The centralization of the infrastructure at locations with low costs plays a relevant role here. In this way, for example, electricity or building costs for necessary infrastructure elements can be minimized. In addition, the aim is to increase peak load capacity. As a result, users do not have to plan and provide their own resources and equipment. This aspect also leads to increased resource utilization and lower costs for users, since they do not have to invest in materials and equipment. Thus, especially the utilization and the increase of efficiency of systems are seen as relevant points (Metzger et al. 2011).

Increased System Reliability
The performance of the clouds is monitored by the service provider's IT experts, so consistent and loosely coupled architectures are set up using web services as a system interface. Productivity can be increased by having multiple users working on the same data at the same time, instead of spending time storing data and sending it via email.

This saves time, as the cloud no longer requires information to be re-entered into fields or synchronized. Similarly, users do not need to install additional application software upgrades on their computers. Multiple redundant sites ensure increased system reliability. This speaks for well thought-out cloud computing for continuity and disaster recovery. Accordingly, the extent of a local disaster can be minimized.

Scalability and Elasticity
Scalability and elasticity through dynamic ("on-demand") provision of resources is possible almost in real time without users having to schedule for peak loads, considering that the server startup time varies depending on server type, location, operating system, and cloud provider. This provides the ability to scale as usage needs increase or decrease when resources are unused. New approaches to elasticity management include the use of machine learning techniques that propose efficient elasticity models.

Security and Vendor Lock-In

Security in cloud computing can be increased, for instance, through the centralization of data and strict security-oriented resources. While concerns remain about potential loss of control over sensitive data and the lack of security for stored kernels, security is as good as or even better than other traditional systems. Partly, this is due to the resources of service providers that are allocated to address security issues that many customers could not otherwise afford.

However, some users lack the technical knowledge to cope with complex security requirements. This is due to the fact that data is usually distributed over several devices or used in multi-tenant systems to which different users have access. In addition, user access to security audit logs can be difficult or even impossible. Private cloud deployment is therefore partly motivated by users' desire to remain in control of the infrastructure and avoid losing control of saved information.

Increased Dependence
Besides the aspects of operational control, however, there is also the risk of increased dependence with regard to the freely selectable relationship between provider and user. In this context, the vendor lock-in problem in cloud computing describes the situation in which customers are dependent (i.e., locked in) on a single technology

implementation of a cloud provider and cannot switch to another provider in the future without incurring significant costs, legal restrictions, or technical incompatibilities (Sitaram et al. 2012).

To further substantiate this from a software developer's point of view, the lock-in situation is that applications developed for certain cloud platforms (e.g., Amazon EC2, Microsoft Azure) cannot easily be migrated to other cloud platforms, and users become vulnerable to changes by their providers. In fact, the lock-in problem arises when, for example, a government decides to change cloud providers (or perhaps integrate services from different providers) but is unable to move applications or data across different cloud services because the semantics of cloud provider resources and services do not match.

This heterogeneity of cloud semantics and cloud application program interfaces (APIs) creates technical incompatibility, which in turn leads to interoperability and portability problems. This makes interoperation, collaboration, portability, and manageability of data and services a very complex and elusive task. For these reasons, it becomes important to maintain flexibility, change providers according to needs, or even keep internally some of the components that are less critical due to security risks. Interoperability and portability between cloud vendors can avoid the problem of vendor lock-in and would significantly impact the competitiveness of the market. For example, cost savings, greater flexibility, a (local) distributor, and also mobile access to IT services or greater speed and scalability of IT services are cited.

Provision and Service Models of Cloud Computing

Basically, cloud computing distinguishes between four different forms of provision and three types of services. These delivery and service models are shown in Figure 6.12 (content based on Chou 2010; Ghosh 2013; Digital Technology 2017).

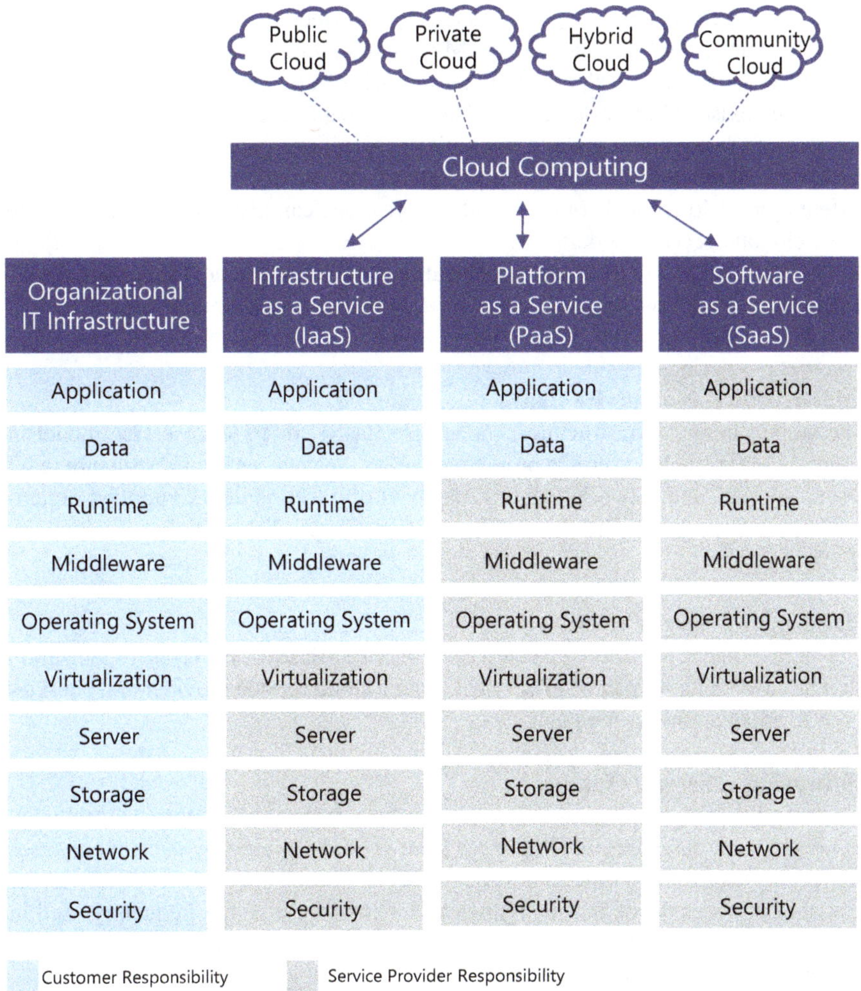

Fig. 6.12 Provision and service models of cloud computing. Source: Wirtz (2016, 2020, 2021)

Three Types of Cloud Service Models

In the case of the public cloud, a cloud service provider, such as Amazon or Microsoft, makes services and infrastructure available to the public against payment of a fee. An example is the public cloud Azure by Microsoft or Amazon's AWS (Amazon Web Services). Here, the services and infrastructure are owned and managed by the cloud service provider (Perry and Hendrick 2013).

Private cloud refers to a model of cloud computing in which IT services and infrastructure reside mostly in the own organization and are only used by the latter. Here, one can particularly customize important aspects of cybersecurity to the specific requirements of an organization. A hybrid cloud usually represents a mixed form of public and private cloud. Most commonly, sensitive data reside in enterprises in the private cloud and other resources in the public cloud. As a result, there often exists a higher degree of IT flexibility with additional service options. In the case of the community cloud, multiple organizations operate and use the cloud resources. Here, only the community partners can access the cloud. Besides the different provision models of the cloud services, one can distinguish between three types of cloud service models.

In Figure 6.12 the left pillar "organizational IT infrastructure" describes the IT functions ranging from applications to security on premise, within an organization's own data center.

Infrastructure as a Service (IaaS)

The second pillar "infrastructure as a service (IaaS)" refers to a service model in which an external cloud service provider supplies the data center infrastructure (e.g., server, storage, and networks) against payment of a fee, while the supplied organization manages the applications (Chou 2010; Ghosh 2013; Digital Technology 2017).

Platform as a Service (PaaS)

The third pillar represents "platform as a service (PaaS)." Here, an organization obtains an even larger part of IT services from a cloud service provider and confines itself to application development.

Software as a Service (SaaS)

The last pillar in Figure 6.12 is "software as a service (SaaS)." In this service model, an organization purchases all IT services from a cloud service provider and only uses them. This brings along the highest degree of outsourcing and dependence, as the fewest IT services reside in the organization. Cloud services are frequently used in combination with AI in the context of IoT. In this connection, AI will become particularly important in the future.

6.4 Internet of Things

Within the last two decades, digital government and society have been particularly shaped by innovation in information technology. Invention and innovation are at the center of attention in this context, more so than in any other area. Innovation in this context is understood as the successful market penetration of invention. The so-called Internet of Things (IoT) has been one of the most essential and innovation-based developments of digital transformation in recent years. IoT is often associated with various aspects and issues like big data, artificial intelligence, cloud computing, smart home, or industry 4.0.[3]

Increasing IT Networking
The foundation of IoT is the increasing information technology networking of products, services, machines, or sensors via an IP network: "IoT will increase the ubiquity of the Internet by integrating every object for interaction via embedded systems, which leads to a highly distributed network of devices communicating with human beings as well as other devices" (Xia et al. 2012, p. 1101).

The following section outlines basics, applications, and success factors of IoT. It first presents the basics of IoT by providing a general understanding and definitions, as well as depicting an explanatory model of IoT. Afterwards, it deals with the applications of IoT, illustrating their relevance and market potential as well as giving practical examples. It then takes a closer look at the combined use of IoT technology and robotics in an industrial context. Afterwards it focuses on the users of IoT technology and their behaviors. Finally, the last section discusses success factors of IoT, indicating important starting points for in the IoT market.

Basics of Internet of Things

The vision of IoT is often credited to Mark Weiser and his essay "The Computer for the 21st Century" (Weiser 1991). At the end of the 1990s, Kevin Ashton further developed the vision of Mark Weiser. Ashton had a determining influence on the development of the radio-frequency identification (RFID) approach at the Auto-ID Center at the Massachusetts Institute of Technology (now MIT Auto-ID Labs) and coined the term Internet of Things (Weiser 1991). RFID enables the Internet-based networking of products, services, machines, or sensors and is an information technology for sender–receiver systems to identify and localize them based on radio waves, thus playing a crucial role in the context of IoT.

Especially in recent years, IoT has gained great importance. Its basic networking character with regard to products, services, machines, or sensors is associated with a very wide base of application for various application contexts and industries. Market forecasts expect a significant increase of IoT within the next years, assuming that the global market volume of IoT will decuple from USD151 billion in 2018 to USD1.567 trillion by 2025 (IoT Analytics 2018). In addition, experts assume that within the same period the number of connected devices worldwide will increase nearly threefold from 7 billion to more than 21.5 billion (IoT Analytics 2018). The focus of this growth development especially refers to the areas smart machine to machine (M2M), smart electronics, and smart mobility (Statista 2013). The three major IoT markets worldwide are China, the USA, and Japan (Statista 2014).

[3] See for the following Section 6.4 also Wirtz (2020, 2021).

Definition of IoT

The market potential and the related possibility to introduce new applications and business models make IoT a huge market.

A closer look at the concept shows that the essential core is the feature of Internet-based networking of various factors within a network. Against this background, the following definition is proposed and referred to throughout the book.

> **Definition of Internet of Things (Wirtz 2018)**
> Internet of Things refers to the Internet-based networking of physical and digital products, services, machines, sensors, and humans.

IoT IT Infrastructure

Smart IoT products and services require an innovative IT infrastructure that enables to meet the challenges and exploit the advantages associated with IoT (Porter and Heppelmann 2014).

It becomes apparent that particularly basic information technology enables IoT. In this context, the concepts and technologies of big data, cloud computing, and artificial intelligence are particularly relevant, which have been explained in more detail in Sections 6.1–6.3. In addition, the information technology infrastructure is important (see Figure 6.14). Therefore, the following explains these concepts and corresponding technologies in detail. Figure 6.13 provides a general overview of the basic technological concepts of IoT.

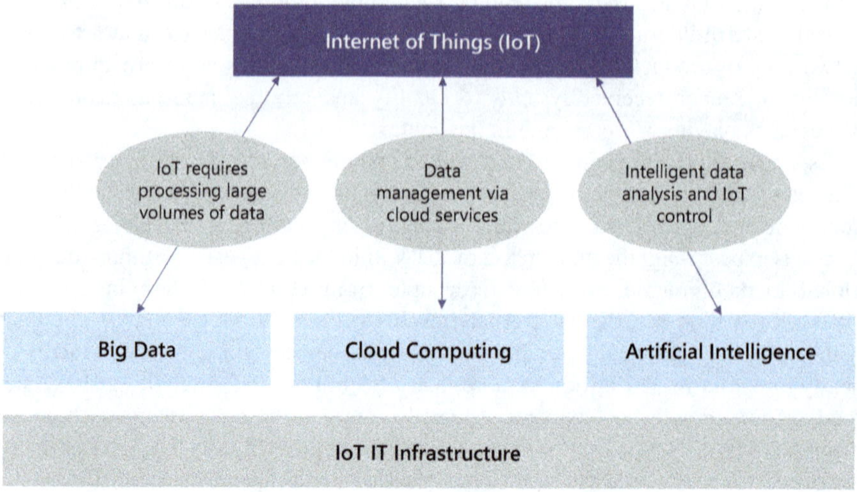

Fig. 6.13 Basic technological concepts of IoT. Source: Wirtz (2018, 2020, 2021)

The Internet of Things has a comprehensive application spectrum. The integration of big data, cloud computing, and artificial intelligence in the context of IoT significantly increases the complexity and available data. An efficient IT infrastructure is therefore essential for effective and efficient data exchange within the framework of IoT. Figure 6.14 illustrates how IoT technology generally works by means of the IoT IT infrastructure.

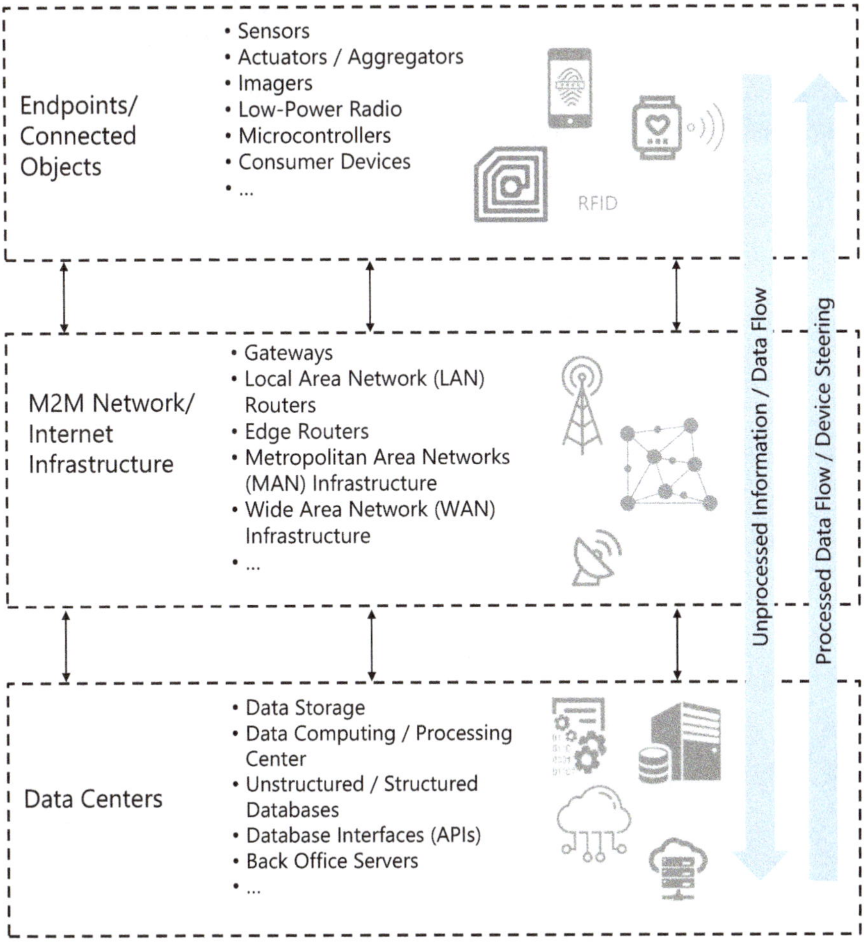

Fig. 6.14 IoT IT infrastructure. Source: Wirtz (2018, 2020, 2021)

At the detection level of the endpoints/connected objects, the necessary information and data is collected by means of sensors, RFID tags, actuators, or consumer devices. This information and data is then forwarded to the network level (M2M networks, Internet infrastructure). Due to the large number of sensors and transmitting devices as well as the associated very large and complex amount of data, a high-performance network infrastructure is necessary. In particular, the high number of mobile devices requires a highly developed mobile network in the 5G technology spectrum in the medium term. From the network level, the information and data is sent to servers in data centers. There, the very complex and large amount of data is processed by means of appropriate intelligent software such as AI software or big data analytics and redirected to the connected objects in the form of a "controlling" data flow. In summary, it can be stated that IoT is not only characterized by a broad and heterogeneous application spectrum but also by various basic technologies that are often used in conjunction with one another.

In this connection, Figure 6.15 depicts an exemplary IoT-specific IT architecture that contains the essential aspects of information technology with regard to IoT (content based on Porter and Heppelmann 2014; Wirtz et al. 2019b).

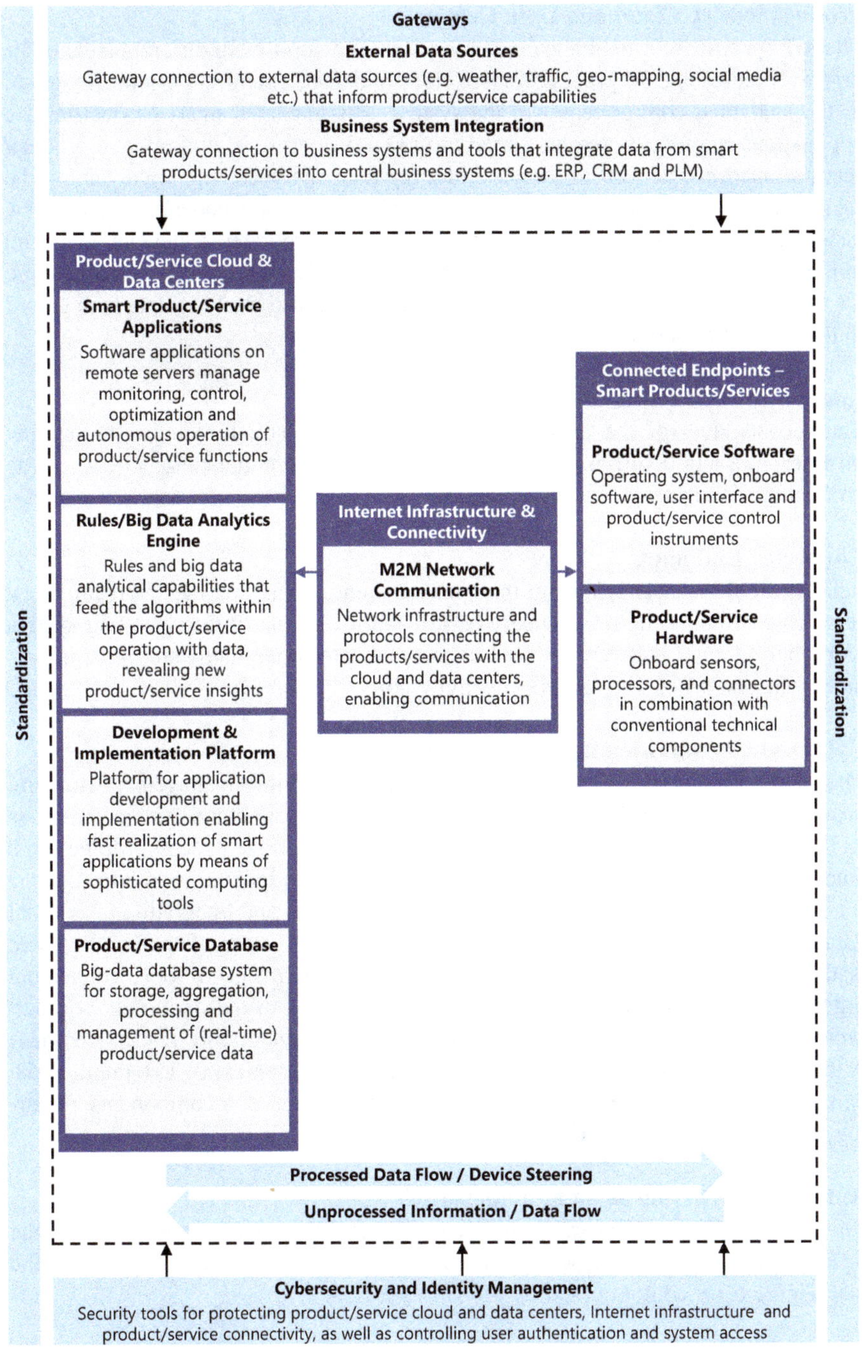

Fig. 6.15 Exemplary IoT-specific IT architecture. Source: Wirtz (2020, 2021)

Product/Service Cloud and Data Centers
The IoT-specific information technology system is composed of different layers. The first layer represents the product/service cloud and data centers and can be thought of as the analytical control center of the system. This includes smart product/service applications running on remote servers to monitor, optimize, and operate product/service functions, as well as a rules and a big data analytics engine containing the logics and big data analytical capabilities (algorithms and codes) to reveal new insights. In addition, the product/service cloud incorporates a development and implementation platform for building software as well as a product/service database for the aggregation and management of real-time and historical big data with regard to the product or service.

Internet Infrastructure and Connectivity
The second layer of the information technology infrastructure refers to Internet infrastructure and connectivity and thus the network communications between the product/service and product/service cloud.

Connected Endpoints
Finally, the third layer relates to the connected endpoints, i.e., the smart products/services containing the product/service software, particularly the operating system and other onboard software, as well as the product/service hardware, most importantly sensors, processors, and connectivity ports.

Cybersecurity and Identity Management
These layers are surrounded by a cybersecurity and identity management structure providing a set of security tools to control user authentication and system access, as well as to protect each layer against attacks and unauthorized access. Moreover, a gateway links external data sources to the connected endpoints or smart products/services and product/service cloud, enabling the retrieval and integration of external data (e.g., weather and traffic data, geo-mapping, or social media data). Finally, there is also a gateway to government or business systems by means of tools, connecting organization systems (e.g., ERP and URM) to the connected endpoints or smart product/service and product/service cloud as well as integrating respective smart data from both systems. An important challenge in the context of IoT refers to the compatibility of the different information technology tools and components, requiring respective standardization.

Autonomous Driving as an Example of IoT
The following section illustrates the interaction and the areas of application of the different enabling technologies by means of an IoT example from the area of traffic (see Figure 6.16, content based on McKinsey 2017).

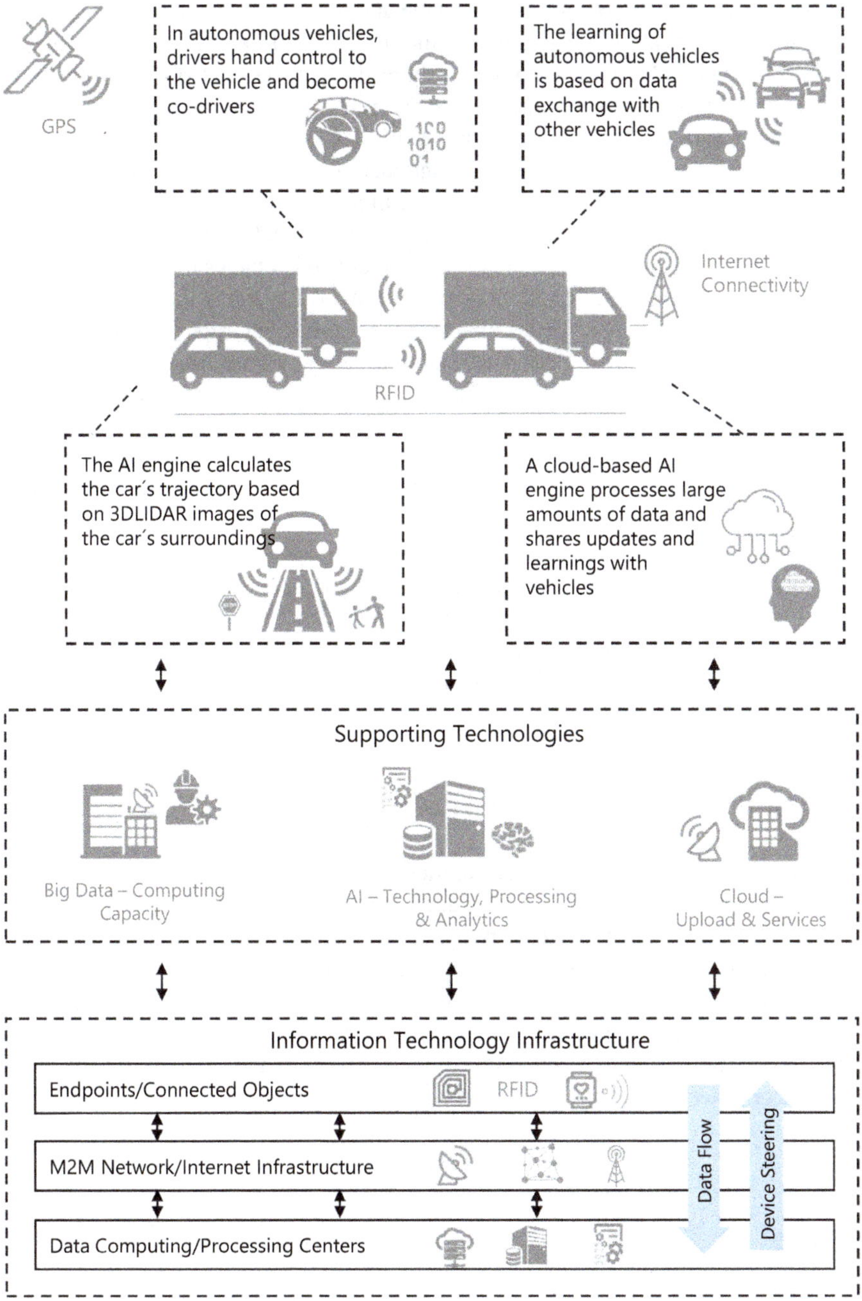

Fig. 6.16 Illustrative example of IoT with application areas of enabling technologies. Source: Wirtz (2018, 2020, 2021)

The example of autonomous driving in the automotive context is particularly well suited as it involves all IoT enabling technologies and is of importance to society as a whole. The basic idea of autonomous driving is that the controls are left to the vehicle itself and drivers become riders. In principle, autonomous vehicles are supposed to learn by exchanging information with other vehicles and in the long run share what they have learned through interaction or via a centralized platform. In this context, AI-based techniques such as machine learning approaches (e.g., neural networks) are particularly important and already used in advanced driver assistance systems. Although the introduction of highly automated vehicles into the road traffic is expected in 2025, there are already the first hybrid systems that integrate self-learning elements (such as Tesla) and numerous other automobile manufacturers seeking to expand the use of AI. The goal is to develop fully integrated, learning-based systems that are optimized by AI algorithms. An AI engine calculates the route based on 3D images that are created by means of the so-called LIDAR systems, i.e., laser scanners for optical distance and speed measurement. The formation of such AI systems requires large amounts of sensor data, as well as considerable computing power and capacity. A cloud-based AI engine serves to process large amounts of data as well as to pass on updates and learned information to vehicles.

In addition to basic technologies such as GPS, RFID, and Internet connectivity, as well as the above-mentioned AI technologies, the technological infrastructure needs to have both respective big data resources and a respective cloud platform.

After having presented the basics of IoT, the next section addresses application areas of IoT technology.

Application Areas of the Internet of Things

Based on a superior IoT infrastructure, there are various applications of IoT. The field of application is particularly wide due to the universal character of application in terms of the Internet-based networking, information, and management. The scope of application ranges from smart home, smart factory, and smart health to smart mobility or smart cities. In this connection, the McKinsey Global Institute (2015) has identified nine basic application areas of IoT in their study. Figure 6.17 illustrates these applications sorted according to their revenue and market potential in descending order (content adapted from McKinsey Global Institute 2015).

Setting	Description	Examples	Size in 2025*
Factories	Standardized production areas	Locations with repetitive workflows, such as farms and hospitals; operational efficiencies, asset utilization optimization and inventory	1,210 - 3,700
Cities	Urban areas	Public spaces and infrastructure in urban environments; resource management, environmental monitoring, smart meters, adaptive traffic control system	930 - 1,660
Human	Portable devices attached to or inside the human body	Devices (wearables and ingestibles) for monitoring and preserving human health and well-being; improved fitness, disease management, increased productivity	170 - 1,590
Retail	Places where consumers engage in commerce	Shops, malls, restaurants, banks, self-service checkout	410 - 1,160
Worksites	Custom production areas	Construction, mining, oil and gas; operating efficiency, safety and health, predictive maintenance	160 - 930
Outside	Outside of urban and other areas	Autonomous vehicles outside of urban environments, railroad tracks, shipment tracking, flight navigation; real-time routing	560 - 850
Vehicles	Inside of vehicles	Cars, trucks, trains, ships, airplanes, helicopters, condition-based maintenance, usage-based design,	210 - 740
Home	Inhabited buildings	Security and home automation control systems	200 - 350
Offices	Places where knowledge workers operate	Security and energy management in office buildings; increased productivity	70 - 150

○ Low Potential ● High Potential

*Potential economic impact of IoT in 2025 [in billion USD]

Fig. 6.17 Application areas of IoT. Data source: McKinsey Global Institute (2015), Wirtz (2020, 2021)

Against this background, it becomes apparent that the use of IoT applications shows the highest value potential in the areas smart factories (factories), smart cities (cities), and smart human devices (human).

Operational Logic of IoT Applications

According to the McKinsey Global Institute (2013, p. 52), the operational logic of IoT applications comprises three steps:

- "capturing data from the object (for example, simple location data or more complex information),
- aggregating that information across a data network,
- and acting on that information—taking immediate action or collecting data over time to design process improvements."

The first step pertains to the initial collection of data and the measuring technology by means of which it is captured. The latter particularly refers to sensor technology, which includes simple identification tags, such as RFID tags, as well as more sophisticated sensors and actuators, such as micro-electromechanical systems (MEMS) that go beyond the scope of location tracking and communicate more complex data (e.g., performance, condition, etc.). The second step describes the processing, aggregation, and storage of data, as well as their integration with an organization's core systems. This particularly requires a rules and analytics engine as well as big data database system. The third step refers to the utilization of the information gained by means of IoT-technology and deriving benefit therefrom. The creation of value can take many forms, such as improved efficiency and operational improvements, strongly depending on the field of application.

Internet of Robotic Things: IoT, Robotics, and Industrial Automation

In recent years, the Internet of robotic things has gained significant importance in the field of IoT. In the context of IoT application in the industrial sector or in production, the terms industrial Internet of things (IIoT) and industry 4.0 are used frequently. They are essentially characterized by intelligent networking, automation, collaborative control, and real-time monitoring. IoT offers various advantages to industrial companies, for instance, through the development of more efficient technological solutions for problems in production, improved workflows and operating procedures, and a rise in productivity. Especially in the automation industry and the related areas of industrial control, measuring technology and process automation, IoT is important and represents a significant success factor.

Opportunities and Challenges of Industry 4.0

Meanwhile, many companies in the industrial sector have implemented organization-internal, proprietary IoT networks for the automation in production. In doing so, IIoT or industry 4.0 provides a wide range of challenges and opportunities for companies. The greatest opportunities of industry 4.0 from a business perspective are improved planning and controlling in production and logistics, higher customer satisfaction, increased flexibility in production, faster time to market, improved quality, and the possibility of individualization of products

(PricewaterhouseCoopers 2014). The greatest challenges of industry 4.0 from a business perspective are the uncertain economic benefits and excessive investments, insufficient qualifications of employees, and the lack of regulations, standards, and forms of certification.

Moreover, there are challenges due to the uncertain legal situation regarding the use of external data, the low maturity level of required technologies, and unresolved questions concerning data security (PricewaterhouseCoopers 2014). Figure 6.18 shows the most important opportunities and challenges of industry 4.0 from a business perspective (content based on PricewaterhouseCoopers 2014).

IoT Opportunities	IoT Challenges
•Improved planning and controlling •Higher customer satisfaction •Increased flexibility in production •Faster time to market •Improved quality •Individualization of products •...	•Uncertain economic benefits and exceeding investments •Insufficient qualifications of employees •Lack of regulations, standards and forms of certification •Uncertain legal situation regarding the use of external data •Low maturity level of required technologies •Unresolved questions concerning data security •...

Fig. 6.18 Key opportunities and challenges of industry 4.0 from a business perspective. Source: Wirtz (2020, 2021)

In IIoT or industry 4.0, the field of robotics is gaining significant importance with regard to automation of production. The Internet of robotic things (IoRT) is a new concept that combines IoT technologies with robotic and autonomous systems, thus improving the capabilities of current IoT and robotic systems, and enabling the creation of new, revolutionary applications and services in the context of industrial automation (Simoens et al. 2018).

Stages of Industrial Automation

With regard to industrial automation, various stages of development can be distinguished, whereby the level of automation generally increases in line with technological progress. Previously documented levels of automated driving can serve as a point of reference and be transferred to a more general machine application context (SAE 2018; NHTSA 2017; United Nations 2018).

Against this background, Figure 6.19 shows the development stages of industrial automation that is increasing according to progress in IoT technologies and robotics.

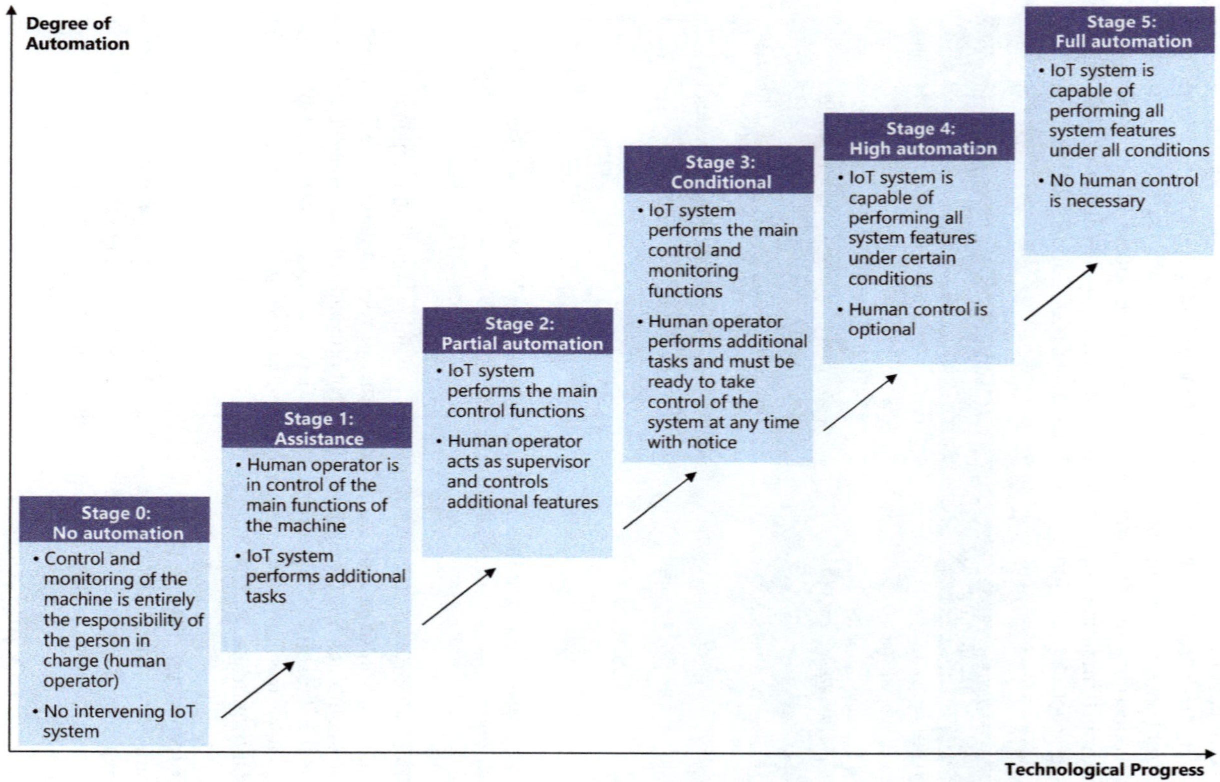

Fig. 6.19 Stages of industrial automation. Source: Wirtz (2020, 2021)

Stage 0: No Automation

Starting point (Stage 0) is the non-automated state, where controlling and monitoring of the system is the responsibility of the person in charge (human operator) and no intervening IoT/AI system is active.

Building upon this, five further stages of development can be distinguished: assistance (Stage 1), partial automation (Stage 2), conditional automation (Stage 3), high automation (Stage 4), and full automation (Stage 5).

Stage 1: Assistance

In Stage 1, an IoT/AI system assists the human operator in controlling a machine or system. The human operator is responsible for controlling the main functions of the machine, while the IoT/AI system controls additional features.

Stage 2: Partial Automation

Stage 2 is characterized by a semi-automated level of automation. Here, the IoT/AI system controls the main functions of the machine, while the human operator acts as a supervisor and controls additional machine features.

Stage 3: Conditional

In Stage 3, industrial machines are conditionally automated. This involves the IoT/AI system controlling the main functions of the machine, while the human operator controls additional features and needs to be ready to take control of the system at any time when the IoT/AI system gives notice.

Stage 4: High Automation

Stage 4 implies a high degree of automation. This means the IoT/AI system is capable of controlling all machine functions under certain conditions, while the human operator has the option to take control.

Stage 5: Full Automation

Stage 5 is the last stage of automation development and describes the state of full automation, according to which the IoT/AI system is capable of controlling all machine features under all conditions and human control is unnecessary.

5G Network

The increasing implementation and application of advanced IoT technology and robotic solutions in order to automate production in many companies will generate an immense volume of data. The way this data is processed and analyzed will play a decisive role in the development progress and quality of automation. However, current communication technologies, such as 3G and 4G mobile networks, cannot meet the requirements of IIoT or IoRT, particularly in terms of low latency, high data rate, coverage, and reliability, thus hindering automation development. Against this background, especially 5G network is expected to have a high value creation potential to further advance the development of IIoT and industrial automation (Cheng et al. 2018).

In summary, it can be stated that within the broad spectrum of application fields of IoT, most notably the industrial sector is of particular importance, characterized by a variety of opportunities and challenges. Especially the combination of IoT technology and robotics is advancing progress in automation in the industrial sector, leading to more efficient problem solutions, workflows, and operational processes, as well as increased levels of productivity.

IoT, Big Data, Cloud Computing and AI

Against the background of its various fields of application and modes of action, it becomes apparent that particularly basic information technology enables IoT. Above all, IoT requires the processing of large amounts of data. The large amounts of data and information available in the context of IoT are increasingly transferred and processed via cloud computing technologies, i.e., data management is essentially carried out via cloud services. In the context of IoT, cloud services are increasingly used in combination with artificial intelligence services. In this matter, artificial intelligence will play a particularly important role in the future, especially for intelligent data analysis and IoT control. Thus, the concepts and technologies of big data, cloud computing, and artificial intelligence are particularly relevant. After having discussed the technological infrastructure of IoT and fields of application, the next section focuses on user behavior concerning the Internet of things.

IoT User Behavior

The use of IoT has increased considerably in recent years and is about to increase even more in the years to come. Regarding the use of IoT, two essential groups of users can be distinguished: industry and consumers. In the following, central aspects of IoT user behavior of these two user groups will be described.

Industry

First and foremost, especially in the industrial context IoT is considered to be of special importance. In a survey among 3000 decision-makers from six countries, Microsoft has examined adoption as well as the most important benefits of IoT for businesses. A majority of 85% of the interviewed decision-makers are using IoT technology and another 5% have used IoT in the past. Industry use cases of IoT range from the areas of retail/wholesale (90% IoT use) or transportation (86% IoT use) to government (83% IoT use) and healthcare (82% IoT use). Manufacturing (87% IoT use) is of course another major area of IoT application in an industrial context.

In organizations that have adopted IoT, experienced benefits include increased efficiency (91%), increased yield (91%), and improved quality (85%; (Microsoft 2019). Figure 6.20 exemplifies the IoT benefit increased efficiency.

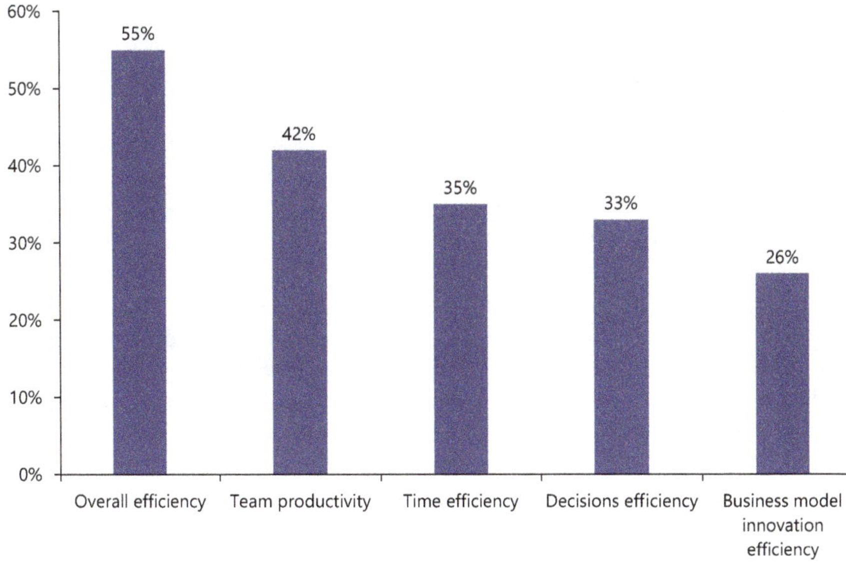

Fig. 6.20 IoT benefit increased efficiency. Data source: Microsoft (2019), Wirtz (2021)

The most often mentioned benefit of IoT implementation in organizations is increased overall efficiency, which is appreciated as an IoT top benefit by 55% of decision-makers. In the cluster of increased efficiency, it is followed by the aspects improved team productivity and time efficiency. IoT also facilitates the efficiency of decisions and can lead to more efficiency in business model innovation, thus contributing to various efficiency aspects in an organization.

Besides industry, consumers are another essential user group of IoT. The IoT usage behavior of industry and consumers differs greatly. The spectrum of IoT use is much smaller and more homogeneous on the consumer side than in industry or business. In addition, the share of IoT use is also much smaller among consumers than in industry.

Consumers

Two important main areas of consumer IoT use are smart homes and smart cities. The term smart home refers to the use of IoT technology at home to monitor, control, and regulate electronic devices in the household such as refrigerator, air conditioning, and lighting, as well as other household appliances such as heating, electricity, door lock, or a security camera (Kim et al. 2017).

A relatively high proportion of smart home households is found particularly in the USA (33%), but also in Great Britain (25%). Germany and Japan have similar shares of 20% and 19%, respectively. China, by contrast, is far behind the other leading industrial nations with a share of 8% (Statista 2019). In this context, Table 6.5 shows the distribution of smart home users by age in the USA.

Table 6.5 Smart home users by age

	Average	18–25	26–35	36–45	46–60	61+
Overall	24%	33%	46%	29%	14%	15%
Smart appliance	16%	18%	33%	18%	6%	6%
Smart thermostat	14%	14%	22%	16%	9%	9%
Smart lights	13%	25%	25%	15%	6%	6%
Other	7%	6%	14%	8%	3%	3%

Data source: Walker Sands (2017), Wirtz (2021)

First of all, it can be seen that smart home solutions are especially accepted in the younger to middle-age segments. The 26- to 35-year-olds are the top group with a usage share of 46%, followed by the 18- to 25-year-olds with a usage share of 33% and the 36- to 45-years olds with a share of 29%. Among the older age groups, however, smart home use is not as pronounced, with 14% usage share among 46- to 60-year-olds and a slightly higher share of 15% among people who are 61 years and older (Walker Sands 2017).

Perceived benefits of smart home solutions for consumers are an improved quality of life, safety provision, and the perception that smart home solutions make things more effortless and provide comfort. However, the main drawbacks for most consumers are the increased dependence on technology and the monitoring of private activities (Singh et al. 2018).

The IoT solutions for consumers presented so far are IoT applications for private use. Another area of application of IoT that is extremely important for consumers is smart city, which essentially refers to IoT applications for public use in cities and urban areas.

Against this background, a user survey in Germany shows that 34% of citizens are interested in smart city solutions (Wyman 2020). Figure 6.21 presents their interest with regard to different solution clusters.

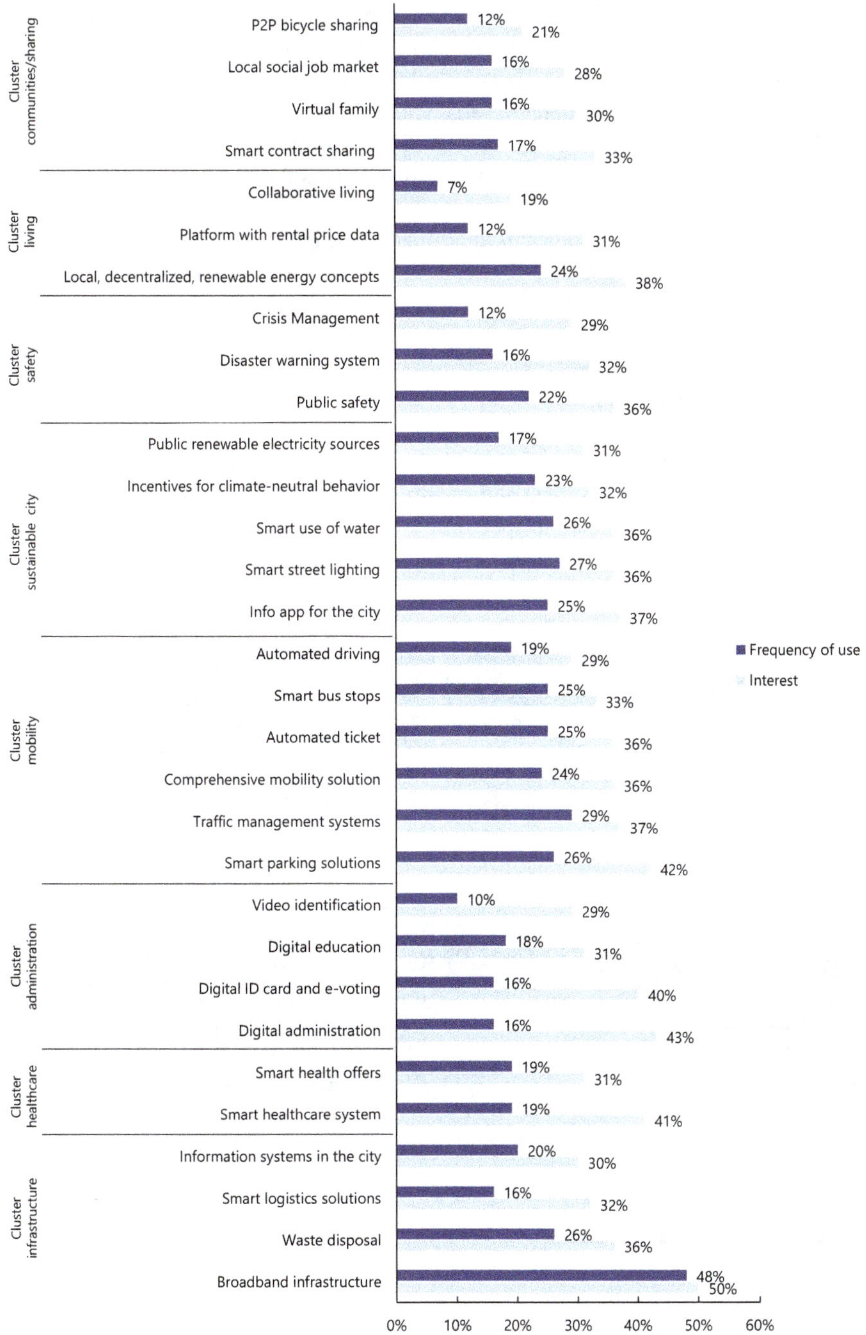

Fig. 6.21 Interest in smart city solutions and frequency of use. Data source: Wyman (2020), Wirtz (2021)

Citizens show most interest in the clusters infrastructure (37%), healthcare (36%), administration (36%), and mobility (35%). Particularly young people under the age of 38 demonstrated interest in smart city solutions.

Overall, the spectrum of potential IoT applications is smaller than for industrial use. However, there is an increase in use in this area as well. In addition to the private use context, the public use context with smart city solutions is also relevant for consumers in urban areas.

It is apparent that smart solutions are of particular interest to younger consumers. For the acceptance and use of IoT solutions by both consumers and the industry, certain success factors are important, which are described in the following section.

Success Factors of IoT

The Internet of Things has been one of the most important and most promising innovations in digital government and society in recent years. In particular, its broad and comprehensive application spectrum is crucial for further development. In connection with IoT, there are four key success factors shown in Figure 6.22.

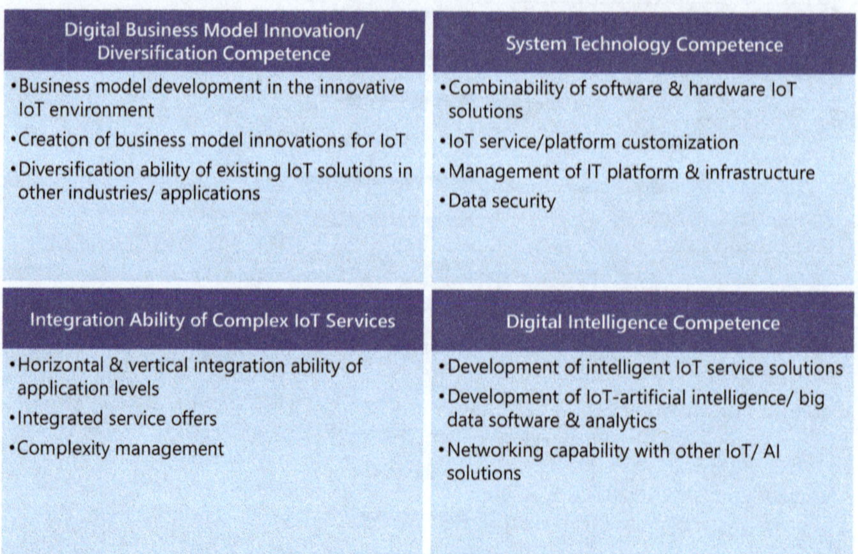

Fig. 6.22 Success factors of IoT. Source: Wirtz (2018, 2020, 2021)

IoT Key Competencies

Digital Business Model Innovation and Diversification Competence

The first success factor is digital business model innovation and diversification competence. Here, the systematic development of the business model in the innovative IoT environment is important. This area is characterized by a high dynamic and innovation rate, which has special requirements for the design of the business model (Wirtz et al. 2007). In this connection, the emergence of business model innovations for customized IoT solutions is particularly important. In addition, the ability of existing IoT solutions in the business model to diversify into other industries and applications is essential to realize economies of scale and scope in the business model.

System Technology Competence

The second success factor is system technology competence. Here, the technological combinability of software and hardware IoT solutions is of importance. This capability is particularly relevant to align and customize the IoT services and platform according to different customer needs (customization). An essential aspect of the competence system technology refers to the management of the IT platform and infrastructure. The IoT places special demands on the IT platform and IT services due to the variety and density of interaction with devices, connected objects, M2M interaction, or complex data computing. In connection with the system technology competence, data security plays a significant role. Since sensitive and proprietary data—for instance, organization or personal data—are often used and subject to analysis, IoT customers demand a special level of security. This high level of data security must be ensured, especially against the background of potential cyberattacks and manipulations.

Integration Ability of Complex IoT Services

The third success factor is the ability to integrate complex IoT services. Here, the horizontal and vertical integration ability at the application levels is particularly important. In the case of the horizontal integration ability, the above-mentioned technological combinability is relevant in order to combine the IoT core services with other services and technologies important to the customer into an overall IoT package and thus to provide an integrated service offering. It is also important to integrate the IoT solutions precisely into the existing ecosystem at the customer's site.

The vertical integration ability characterizes the compatible and functional interaction among the three different levels of the IoT IT infrastructure, which are depicted in Figure 6.14. Furthermore, the complexity management of the integrated service offering is of importance due to the above-mentioned variety and density of interaction with devices, connected objects, the M2M interaction, or complex data computing in the context of IoT.

Digital Intelligence Competence

The fourth success factor is the digital intelligence competence. Here, the development of intelligent IoT service solutions is particularly important. In this connection, artificial intelligence also plays a significant role. The accelerated development and application of AI-based software and analytics programs will enable high automation and control of the entire IoT process environment. Furthermore, the networking capability of developed IoT-based artificial intelligence and big data software and analytics is important, not only in connection with other customer IoT/AI solutions, but also with those of other providers in the general process environment.

6.5 Summary, Review Questions, Topics for Discussion, and Online Exercises

- Artificial intelligence refers to the capability of a computer system to show human-like intelligent behavior. This behavior is characterized by core competencies like perception, understanding, action, and learning.
- Three stages of artificial intelligence can be distinguished: narrow AI that is operating only in dedicated areas and specialized in repetitive tasks, general AI that can perform intellectual tasks with the same efficiency as humans and is thus operating in many areas, and super AI that is characterized by very fast self-improvement and is superior to humans in all areas.
- Besides its high economic potential, AI also involves social and ethical advantages, such as improved medical diagnostics and early detection of pandemics.
- However, there are also economic and social risks associated with AI, such as impending job losses and a loss of control over technologically autonomous AI systems, as well as the threat of cyberattacks and insufficient data protection.
- Against this background, governance of AI is essential. A helpful tool in this regard is the strategic four AI governance model, which takes into account social and ethical, legal and regulatory, business and economic, and technological and implementation-oriented risks. Based on this, a strategic AI governance agenda can be developed.
- Big data represents an essential basis for digital government as it allows for intelligent and systematic analysis and evaluation of data information.
- The big data architecture consists of seven layers: (1) data sources, (2) data content format, (3) data type, (4) data acquisition, (5) data management, (6) data analytics, and (7) data visualization. Another important element is the governance of big data, which relates to all seven layers of the architecture and covers general management and regulatory aspects such as accessibility, availability, and security of data.
- Cloud computing refers to the provision of servers, databases, software, network components, and storage via the Internet and represents another essential technological basis for digital government. Advantages of cloud computing are, for

example, device and location independency, greater speed and scalability of IT services, as well as cost savings.

- The term Internet of Things refers to the Internet-based networking of physical and digital products, services, machines, sensors, and humans. Essential for the IoT is an efficient IT infrastructure, as well as the integration of big data, cloud computing, and artificial intelligence.
- For a successful integration of IoT technology in the government context, it is important to have diversification competence, system technology competence, integration ability of complex IoT systems, and digital intelligence competence.

Chapter 6
Review questions, topics for discussion and online exercises

Review questions

1. Present the different stages and functionalities of AI.
2. Explain the AI framework.
3. Describe the different types of provision and service models of cloud computing and explain differences in terms of the organizational IT infrastructure.
4. Describe the concept of the Internet of Things.
5. Explain the development stages of industrial automation in the field of IoT.

Topics for classroom discussion and team debates

1. In a not too distant future, there will be AI machines that are superior to human work in many areas and will replace it to a large extent. Discuss the ethical aspects of such a situation and in particular the impact on the labor market and possible mass unemployment.
2. Discuss on the basis of the levels of AI-based governance how socially desirable it is to have AI machines control humans.
3. The IoT has considerable potential for change in our economy. Discuss the advantages and disadvantages of the technological development of IoT for the society and the economy.

Online Exercises

1. Enter https://digital-strategy.ec.europa.eu/en/policies/european-approach-artificial-intelligence. Explore the site. Derive the AI goals of the European Commission and elaborate the new rules and actions for excellence in AI.
2. Visit https://trumpwhitehouse.archives.gov/briefings-statements/white-house-launches-national-artificial-intelligence-initiative-office/ and compare the objectives and contents with those of the European Commission.
3. Enter https://www.cisa.gov/sites/default/files/publications/CISA%20IoT%20White%20Paper_3.6.19%20-%20FINAL.pdf. Explore the site and work out important aspects of the Internet of Things for Public Safety.

References

Accenture (2016): Why artificial intelligence is the future of growth. Available online at http://s3.amazonaws.com/medias.ccei.quebec/ouvrage/Accenture-Why-AI-is-the-Future-of-Growth.PDF, checked on 5/31/2021.

Adams, Sam; Arel, Itmar; Bach, Joscha; Coop, Robert; Furlan, Rod; Goertzel, Ben et al. (2012): Mapping the Landscape of Human-Level Artificial General Intelligence. In AI Magazine 33 (1), pp. 25–42. DOI: https://doi.org/10.1609/aimag.v33i1.2322.

Boillat, Thomas; Legner, Christine (2013): From On-Premise Software to Cloud Services: The Impact of Cloud Computing on Enterprise Software Vendors´ Business Models. In J. theor. appl. electron. commer. res. 8 (3), pp. 7–8. DOI: https://doi.org/10.4067/S0718-18762013000300004.

Bullock, J. (Ed.) (2022): Oxford Handbook on AI Governance. Oxford: Oxford University Press.

Cheng, Jiangfeng; Chen, Weihai; Tao, Fei; Lin, Chun-Liang (2018): Industrial IoT in 5G environment towards smart manufacturing. In Journal of Industrial Information Integration 10, pp. 10–19. DOI: https://doi.org/10.1016/j.jii.2018.04.001.

Chou, Yung (2010): Cloud Computing for IT Pros (2/6): What Is Cloud. Microsoft. Available online at https://docs.microsoft.com/de-de/archive/blogs/yungchou/cloud-computing-for-it-pros-26-what-is-cloud, checked on 6/2/2021.

Colmerauer, Alain; Roussel, Philippe (1996): The birth of Prolog. In Thomas J. Bergin, Richard G. Gibson (Eds.): History of programming languages---II. New York, NY, USA: ACM, pp. 331–367.

Copeland, Michael (2016): What's the difference between artificial intelligence, machine learning and deep learning? Edited by NVIDIA Blog. Available online at https://blogs.nvidia.com/blog/2016/07/29/whats-difference-artificial-intelligence-machine-learning-deep-learning-ai/, checked on 5/31/2021.

Crevier, Daniel (1993): AI. The tumultuous history of the search for artificial intelligence. New York, NY: Basic Books.

Damron, Stacia (2019): AI Academy: What is Machine Learning? Available online at https://www.onemodel.co/blog/ai-academy-what-is-machine-learning, checked on 5/31/2021.

DataRobot (2020): Unsupervised machine learning. Available online at https://www.datarobot.com/wiki/unsupervised-machine-learning/, checked on 5/31/2021.

Decide Soluciones (2017): Let's talk about Advanced Analytics: A brief look at Artificial Intelligence. Available online at https://becominghuman.ai/lets-talk-about-advanced-analytics-a-brief-look-at-artificial-intelligence-bf1c7a7d3f96, checked on 5/31/2021.

Digital Technology (2017): Cloud computing: Roles and responsibilities. Available online at http://digitaltechnology4u.com/2017/07/18/cloud-computing-roles-and-responsibilities/, checked on 6/2/2021.

Eadicicco, Lisa (2016): Read the Google CEO's New Letter on the Organization's Future. In Time, 4/28/2016. Available online at https://time.com/4311233/google-ceo-sundar-pichai-letter/, checked on 5/28/2021.

Eggers, William D.; Fishman, Tiffany; Kishnani, Pankaj (2017): AI-augmented human services: Using cognitive technologies to transform program delivery. Deloitte Insights. Available online at https://www2.deloitte.com/content/dam/insights/us/articles/4152_AI-human-services/4152_AI-human-services.pdf, checked on 5/31/2021.

Fonagy, Peter; Gergely, Guörgy; Jurist, Elliot L.; Target, Mary (2018): Affect Regulation, Mentalization, and the Development of the Self. London: Routledge.

Ghosh, Abhishek (2013): Security in the Cloud : The Divided Responsibilities. Available online at https://thecustomizewindows.com/2013/01/security-in-the-cloud-the-divided-responsibilities/, checked on 6/2/2021.

Godse, Manish; Mulik, Shrikant (2009): An Approach for Selecting Software-as-a-Service (SaaS) Product. In : IEEE International Conference on Cloud Computing, 2009 (CLOUD '09). Second part] ; 21 - 25 Sept. 2009, Bangalore, India ; [including workshops papers. IEEE Computer

Society; IEEE International Conference on Cloud Computing 2009, Part 2. Piscataway, NJ: IEEE.

IoT Analytics (2018): State of the IoT 2018: Number of IoT devices now at 7B – Market accelerating. Available online at https://iot-analytics.com/state-of-the-iot-update-q1-q2-2018-number-of-iot-devices-now-7b/, checked on 6/2/2021.

Joshi, Naveen (2019): 7 types of artificial intelligence. With assistance of COGNITIVE WORLD. Edited by Forbes. Available online at https://www.forbes.com/sites/cognitiveworld/2019/06/19/7-types-of-artificial-intelligence/?sh=276c395b233e, checked on 5/31/2021.

Kaplan, Andreas; Haenlein, Michael (2019): Siri, Siri, in my hand: Who's the fairest in the land? On the interpretations, illustrations, and implications of artificial intelligence. In Business Horizons 62 (1), pp. 15–25. DOI: https://doi.org/10.1016/j.bushor.2018.08.004.

Kim, Yonghee; Park, Youngju; Choi, Jeongil (2017): A study on the adoption of IoT smart home service: using Value-based Adoption Model. In Total Quality Management & Business Excellence 28 (9-10), pp. 1149–1165. DOI: https://doi.org/10.1080/14783363.2017.1310708.

Kirste, Moritz; Schürholz, Markus (2019): Einleitung: Entwicklungswege zur KI. In Volker Wittpahl (Ed.): Künstliche Intelligenz. Technologie. Anwendung. Gesellschaft. Berlin, Heidelberg: Springer Berlin Heidelberg, pp. 21–35.

Kobielus, James (2018): Wikibon's 2018 Big Data Analytics Trends and Forecast. Available online at https://wikibon.com/wikibons-2018-big-data-analytics-trends-forecast/, checked on 5/31/2021.

Lally, Adam; Fodor, P. (2011): Natural Language Processing With Prolog in the IBM Watson System. In The Association for Logic Programming (ALP) (Newsletter 9).

Leslie, Alan M. (2000): "Theory of Mind" as a Mechanism of Selective Attention. In Michael S. Gazzaniga (Ed.): The new cognitive neurosciences. 2nd ed. Cambridge, MA, London: MIT Press, pp. 1235–1247.

McCarthy, John; Minsky, Marvin L.; Rochester, Nathaniel; Shannon, Claude E. (2006): A Proposal for the Dartmouth Summer Research Project on Artificial Intelligence, August 31, 1955. In AI Magazine 27 (4), pp. 12–14.

McKinsey (2017): Smartening up with Artificial Intelligence (AI). What's in it for Germany and its Industrial Sector? Available online at https://www.mckinsey.com/~/media/McKinsey/Industries/Semiconductors/Our%20Insights/Smartening%20up%20with%20artificial%20intelligence/Smartening-up-with-artificial-intelligence.pdf, checked on 5/31/2021.

McKinsey Global Institute (2013): Disruptive technologies: Advances that will transform life, business, and the global economy. Available online at https://www.mckinsey.com/business-functions/mckinsey-digital/our-insights/disruptive-technologies, checked on 6/2/2021.

McKinsey Global Institute (2015): The internet of things. Mapping the value beyond the hype. Available online at https://www.mckinsey.com/~/media/McKinsey/Industries/Technology%20Media%20and%20Telecommunications/High%20Tech/Our%20Insights/The%20Internet%20of%20Things%20The%20value%20of%20digitizing%20the%20physical%20world/The-Internet-of-things-Mapping-the-value-beyond-the-hype.pdf, checked on 6/2/2021.

Metzger, Christian; Reitz, Thorsten; Villar, Juan (2011): Cloud Computing. München: Carl Hanser Verlag GmbH & Co. KG.

Mezghani, Emna; Exposito, Ernesto; Drira, Khalil; Da Silveira, Marcos; Pruski, Cédric (2015): A Semantic Big Data Platform for Integrating Heterogeneous Wearable Data in Healthcare. In Journal of medical systems 39 (12), pp. 185–192. DOI: https://doi.org/10.1007/s10916-015-0344-x.

Microsoft (2019): IoT signals. Summary of research learnings 2019. Available online at https://azure.microsoft.com/de-de/resources/iot-signals/, checked on 7/7/2020.

Microsoft (2020): Storage limits in Outlook.com. Available online at https://support.microsoft.com/en-us/office/storage-limits-in-outlook-com-7ac99134-69e5-4619-ac0b-2d313bba5e9e, checked on 6/1/2021.

Miller, Michael J. (2019): AI: A slow-motion explosion. Available online at https://www.pcmag.com/news/ai-a-slow-motion-explosion, checked on 5/31/2021.

Mitchell, Tom Michael (2008): Machine learning. International ed. New York, NY: McGraw-Hill (McGraw-Hill series in computer science).

NHTSA (2017): Automated driving systems 2.0. A vision for safety. Available online at https://www.nhtsa.gov/sites/nhtsa.gov/files/documents/13069a-ads2.0_090617_v9a_tag.pdf, checked on 6/2/2021.

Perry, Randy; Hendrick, Stephen D. (2013): The business value of Amazon web services accelerates over time. Available online at https://media.amazonwebservices.com/IDC_Business_Value_of_AWS_Accelerates_Over_time.pdf, checked on 6/2/2021.

Phillips-Wren, Gloria (2014): Intelligent Systems to Support Human Decision Making. In John Wang (Ed.): Encyclopedia of Business Analytics and Optimization: IGI Global, pp. 1297–1309.

Porter, Michael E.; Heppelmann, James E. (2014): Spotlight on managing the Internet of Things. In Harvard Business Review (92), pp. 65–88.

PricewaterhouseCoopers (2014): Industry 4.0 – Opportunities and Challenges of the Industrial Internet. Available online at https://www.pwc.nl/en/assets/documents/pwc-industrie-4-0.pdf, checked on 6/2/2021.

PwC (2017): Sizing the prize. What's the real value of AI for your business and how can you capitalise? Available online at https://www.pwc.com/gx/en/issues/analytics/assets/pwc-ai-analysis-sizing-the-prize-report.pdf, checked on 5/31/2021.

PwC (2018a): Auswirkungen der Nutzung von künstlicher Intelligenz in Deutschland. Available online at https://www.pwc.de/de/business-analytics/sizing-the-price-final-juni-2018.pdf, checked on 5/31/2021.

PwC (2018b): Künstliche Intelligenz als Innovationsbeschleuniger in Unternehmen. Zuversicht und Vertrauen in Künstliche Intelligenz. Available online at https://www.pwc.de/de/digitale-transformation/ki-als-innovationsbeschleuniger-in-unternehmen-whitepaper.pdf, checked on 5/31/2021.

Reinsel, David; Gantz, John; Rydning, John (2018): The digitization of the world. From edge to core. IDC. Available online at https://www.seagate.com/files/www-content/our-story/trends/files/idcseagate-, checked on 7/16/2020.

Rich, Elaine; Knight, Kevin; Nair, Shivashankar B. (2009): Artificial Intelligence. 3rd ed. New Delhi: Tata/McGraw-Hill.

Rosa, Marek; Feyereisl, Jan (2016): A Framework for Searching for General Artificial Intelligence, pp. 1–54. Available online at https://arxiv.org/pdf/1611.00685, checked on 5/28/2021.

Russell, Stuart J.; Norvig, Peter (2016): Artificial intelligence. A modern approach. With assistance of Ernest Davis, Douglas Edwards. Third edition, Global edition. Boston, Columbus, Indianapolis: Pearson (Always learning).

SAE (2018): SAE International Releases Updated Visual Chart for Its "Levels of Driving Automation" Standard for Self-Driving Vehicles. Available online at https://www.sae.org/news/press-room/2018/12/sae-international-releases-updated-visual-chart-for-its-%E2%80%9Clevels-of-driving-automation%E2%80%9D-standard-for-self-driving-vehicles, checked on 6/2/2021.

Searle, John R. (1980): Minds, brains, and programs. In Behav Brain Sci 3 (3), pp. 417–424. DOI: https://doi.org/10.1017/S0140525X00005756.

Simoens, Pieter; Dragone, Mauro; Saffiotti, Alessandro (2018): The Internet of Robotic Things. In International Journal of Advanced Robotic Systems 15 (1), 172988141875942. DOI: https://doi.org/10.1177/1729881418759424.

Singh, Deepika; Psychoula, Ismini; Kropf, Johannes; Hanke, Sten; Holzinger, Andreas (2018): Users' Perceptions and Attitudes Towards Smart Home Technologies. In. International Conference on Smart Homes and Health Telematics: Springer, Cham, pp. 203–214. Available online at https://link.springer.com/chapter/10.1007/978-3-319-94523-1_18.

Singh, Pramod (2013): Big Data: What on earth is it? Fujitsu. Available online at https://blog.au.fujitsu.com/?p=441, checked on 6/1/2021.

Sitaram, D.; Manjunath, G.; Deily, D. R. (2012): Moving to the cloud. Developing apps in the new world of cloud computing. Amsterdam: Syngress/Elsevier.

Statista (2013): Prognose zum weltweiten Umsatz mit vernetzten Geräten nach Sektor im Jahr 2020. Available online at https://de.statista.com/statistik/daten/studie/295253/umfrage/umsatzprognose-auf-dem-weltmarkt-fuer-vernetzte-geraete-nach-sektor/, checked on 6/2/2021.

Statista (2014): Leading M2M markets worldwide by number of connections in 2013. Available online at https://www.statista.com/statistics/376708/leading-m2m-markets-worldwide/, checked on 6/1/2021.

Statista (2019): Smart home - global comparison - household penetration, 2019. Available online at https://www.statista.com/outlook/279/137/smart-home/germany, checked on 5/14/2019.

techconsult (2018): Das hochintelligente Unternehmen: Sind deutsche Enterprise-Rechenzentren in der Lage über Big-Data-Analytics den Unternehmenserfolg zu sichern? Available online at https://www.intel.de/content/dam/www/public/emea/de/de/documents/pdf/techconsult-studie-das-hochintelligente-unternehmen.pdf, checked on 5/31/2021.

Thierer, Adam D.; Castillo, Andrea; Russell, Raymond (2017): Artificial Intelligence and Public Policy.

Turing, Alan M. (2009): Computing Machinery and Intelligence. In Robert Epstein, Gary Roberts, Grace Beber (Eds.): Parsing the Turing Test. Dordrecht: Springer Netherlands, pp. 23–65.

Ulster University (2020): Cognitive Analytics - combining Artificial Intelligence (AI) and Data Analytics. Available online at https://www.ulster.ac.uk/cognitive-analytics-research/cognitive-analytics, checked on 5/31/2020.

United Nations (2018): Frontier technologies for sustainable development. With assistance of H. Rashid, H. Wai Cheng, N. Hunt, S. Nazrul Islam, K. Iversen, A. Julca. New York: United Nations.

Walker Sands (2017): Future of retail 2017. The connected consumer and the changing face of commerce. Available online at https://www.walkersands.com/resources/the-future-of-retail-2017/, checked on 6/2/2021.

Wang, Yichuan; Kung, Leeann; Ting, Chaochi; Byrd, Terry Anthony (2015): Beyond a Technical Perspective: Understanding Big Data Capabilities in Health Care. In : 2015 48th Hawaii International Conference on System Sciences. 2015 48th Hawaii International Conference on System Sciences (HICSS). HI, USA, 05.01.2015 - 08.01.2015: IEEE, pp. 3044–3053.

Waters, R. (2017): Google says it is 'rethinking all our products' for the AI age. In Financial Times, 5/18/2017. Available online at https://www.ft.com/content/8ec09bea-3b38-11e7-821a-6027b8a20f23, checked on 7/14/2020.

Weiser, Mark (1991): The computer for the 21st century. In Scientific American 265 (3), pp. 94–104.

Winkler, Till J.; Brown, Carol V. (2013): Horizontal Allocation of Decision Rights for On-Premise Applications and Software-as-a-Service. In Journal of Management Information Systems 30 (3), pp. 13–48. DOI: https://doi.org/10.2753/MIS0742-1222300302.

Wired (2017): Sundar Pichai Sees Google's Future in the Smartest Cloud. Available online at https://www.wired.com/2017/05/sundar-pichai-sees-googles-future-smartest-cloud/, checked on 5/28/2021.

Wirtz, Bernd W. (2016): Electronic Business. 5th ed. Wiesbaden: Springer Gabler.

Wirtz, Bernd W. (2018): Electronic Business. 6th ed. Wiesbaden: Springer Gabler.

Wirtz, Bernd W. (2020): Electronic Business. 7th ed. Wiesbaden: Springer Gabler.

Wirtz, Bernd W. (2021): Digital Business and Electronic Commerce. Cham: Springer International Publishing.

Wirtz, Bernd W. (2022): E-Government. Wiesbaden: Springer Gabler.

Wirtz, Bernd W.; Mathieu, A.; Schilke, Oliver (2007): Strategy in Information Technology Markets. In Long Range Planning 40 (6).

Wirtz, Bernd W.; Müller, Wilhelm M. (2019): An integrated artificial intelligence framework for public management. In Public Management Review 21 (7), pp. 1076–1100. DOI: https://doi.org/10.1080/14719037.2018.1549268.

Wirtz, Bernd W.; Weyerer, Jan C. (2018): Artificial intelligence in the public sector. Edited by A. Farazmand. Springer International Publishing. Cham (Global Encyclopedia of Public Administration, Public Policy, and Governance).

Wirtz, Bernd W.; Weyerer, Jan C. (2019a): Ein integratives KI-Leitlinienmodell für die öffentliche Verwaltung. In Verwaltung & Management 25 (2), pp. 90–95.

Wirtz, Bernd W.; Weyerer, Jan C. (2019b): Künstliche Intelligenz im öffentlichen Sektor: Anwendungen und Herausforderungen. In Verwaltung & Management 25 (1), pp. 37–44.

Wirtz, Bernd W.; Weyerer, Jan C. (2019c): Künstliche Intelligenz: Chancen, Risiken und strategische Governance. In WIST 48 (11), pp. 4–9. DOI: https://doi.org/10.15358/0340-1650-2019-11-4.

Wirtz, Bernd W.; Weyerer, Jan C. (2019d): Künstliche Intelligenz: Erscheinungsformen, Nutzungspotenziale und Anwendungsbereiche. In Wirtschaftswissenschaftliches Studium (WiSt) 48 (10), pp. 4–10. DOI: 10.15358/0340-1650-2019-10-4.

Wirtz, Bernd W.; Weyerer, Jan C.; Geyer, Carolin (2019a): Artificial intelligence and the public sector. Applications and challenges. In International Journal of Public Administration 42 (7), pp. 596–615. DOI: https://doi.org/10.1080/01900692.2018.1498103.

Wirtz, Bernd W.; Weyerer, Jan C.; Schichtel, Franziska T. (2019b): An integrative public IoT framework for smart government. In Government Information Quarterly 36 (2), pp. 333–345. DOI: https://doi.org/10.1016/j.giq.2018.07.001.

Wirtz, Bernd W.; Weyerer, Jan C.; Sturm, Benjamin J. (2020): The dark sides of artificial intelligence: An integrated AI governance framework for public administration. In International Journal of Public Administration 43 (9), pp. 818–829. DOI: https://doi.org/10.1080/01900692.2020.1749851.

Wittpahl, Volker (Ed.) (2019): Künstliche Intelligenz. Technologie. Anwendung. Gesellschaft. Berlin, Heidelberg: Springer Berlin Heidelberg.

Wyman, Oliver (2020): Smart City: Schalter umlegen für den Kunden. Technische Universität München. Available online at https://www.oliverwyman.de/content/dam/oliver-wyman/v2-de/publications/2020/Smart%20City_Schalter%20umlegen%20f%C3%BCr%20den%20Kunden_Oliver%20Wyman.pdf%20Kunden_Oliver%20Wyman.pdf, checked on 7/8/2021.

Xia, Feng; Yang, Laurence T.; Wang, Lizhe; Vinel, Alexey (2012): Internet of Things. In International Journal of Communication Systems 25 (9), pp. 1101–1102. DOI: https://doi.org/10.1002/dac.2417.

Social Media and Public Disinformation

7

Contents

Learning Objectives
By working through this chapter, you will be able to:

1. Define and distinguish social media and Web 2.0.
2. Explain the components of the Social Media Four-Factor Model.
3. Describe types of social media applications, as well as the different groups of social media users and their activities.
4. Explain the issue of digital disinformation and potential governance mechanisms.
5. Describe the success factors of social media.

Due to the increasing acceptance and growing commercial use and dissemination of the Internet, online marketing has become a key success factor for companies and organizations. Social media plays an important role in this context (Aral et al. 2013; Wirtz and Ullrich 2008), consisting of innovative platforms and applications with high potential to shape the future of the Internet.[1] Users and providers collectively define and shape the content through collaborative participation and thus determine the development of social networks (Turban and Sipior 2015). The purpose of social media applications is the distribution of content and the networking among users (Xiang and Gretzel 2010). This chapter outlines the opportunities for governments to use Web 2.0 or social media technologies. Section 7.1 explains the basics of social

[1] See for Chapter 7 Social Media and Public Disinformation also Wirtz (2020, 2021, 2022).

B. W. Wirtz, *Digital Government*, Springer Texts in Business and Economics,
https://doi.org/10.1007/978-3-031-13086-1_7

media by providing a general understanding and definitions, as well as presenting an explanatory model of social media (Social Media Four-Factor Model). Subsequently, Section 7.2 outlines the current setup of the social media world including a differentiation of user groups and applications. Moreover, it presents the use of these applications for the private sector. In Section 7.3 news consumption on social media and the issue of digital disinformation are explained, as well as possible governance measures. Finally, Section 7.4 discusses success factors in social media.

7.1 Basics of Social Media

The increasing importance of social media is determined by a fundamental increase in users of social media and Web 2.0 applications. In this context, particularly the increasing amount of advertising financing with regard to popular social networks such as Facebook is a reliable indicator for the rising significance of social media.

Social media advertising revenues in the USA have grown steadily from 2.8 billion USD in 2012 to 35.6 billion USD in 2019. This increase is characterized by a compound annual growth rate of 37.42%. While social media accounted for approximately 14% of total Internet advertising revenues in 2014, their respective share already increased to 28.6% in 2019 (IAB/PWC 2020). The trend of rising social media advertising revenues is assumed to continue, reaching a market volume of about 66.2 billion USD by 2023 in the USA (Statista 2019). In terms of revenue, the most preferred social media platforms by marketers in 2020 were Facebook (94%), Instagram (76%), LinkedIn (59%), Twitter (53%), and YouTube (53%) (Social Media Examiner 2020).

Most Frequently Used Social Media Services

This is also reflected in Table 7.1 that presents the most frequently used social media services in the world.

Table 7.1 Most frequently used social media services in the world

Platform	Activity in %
Facebook	17.2
YouTube	13.8
WhatsApp	13.8
FB Messenger	9.0
Weixin/WeChat	8.0
Instagram	6.9
Douyin/TikTok	5.5
QQ	5.0
Qzone	3.6
Sina Weibo	3.6
Reddit	3.0
Kuaishou	2.8
Snapchat	2.7
Twitter	2.7
Pinterest	2.5

Data source: We Are Social (2020), Wirtz et al. (2021)

As shown in Table 7.1, particularly social networking websites have gained popularity. In 2019, the number of social media users worldwide amounted to 2.95 billion, which is assumed to reach 3.43 billion by 2023, thus representing one third of the world population (Statista 2020d). Given the widespread dissemination of social media, it has also become increasingly relevant in the context of digital government. The following section presents the essential features of social media.

Web 2.0 vs. Social Media

When investigating social media, one often comes across the term Web 2.0. Since both social media and Web 2.0 are relatively young fields of research, there is no clear demarcation between these two terms. In the academic literature, both terms are frequently used with similar meaning. Most definitions of social media and Web 2.0 combine characteristics such as interaction, dialogue, networking, and user-generated content.

The focus of interest within social media and Web 2.0 is the exchange of information, experience, and perspectives in online communities (Wirtz and Elsäßer 2012a). Against this background, this section first discusses the differences between Web 2.0 and social media. The heart of Web 2.0 is the communication or interaction between Internet users (O'Reilly 2005; Little 2007). It uses basic functions that allow the user to continuously contribute and modify web content. Web 2.0 technologies are, for example, (Kaplan and Haenlein 2010):

- Adobe Flash: common method for programming and displaying multimedia and interactive content, such as animations, audio and video streams

- RSS (Really Simple Syndication): a web feed format for simple and structured publication of consecutive changes on websites
- AJAX (Asynchronous Java Script): a technique for obtaining data on web servers to update web content without altering the layout and operation of the website

Social media, by contrast, is a group of Internet applications, technically and ideologically based on Web 2.0. They allow to post and exchange user-generated content. Attributes of user-generated content are as follows:

- It is published on social media platforms
- It contains a degree of creative personal contribution
- It is created outside of professional routines and practices (Kaplan and Haenlein 2010).

Figure 7.1 compares the characteristics used in the literature and gives respective examples (content based on Kaplan and Haenlein 2010).

	Web 2.0	Social Media
Characteristics	• Users can continuously contribute and modify web content • Diverse basic functions allow the use of the Web 2.0 (see examples) • Ideological and technological basis for social media	• Group of Internet applications based on Web 2.0 • Allows creating and exchanging user-generated content
Examples	• Adobe Flash • RSS (Really Simple Syndication) • AJAX (Asynchronous Java Script)	• Social networking (e.g., Facebook) • Video sharing platforms (e.g., YouTube) • Wikis (e.g., Wikipedia)

Fig. 7.1 Web 2.0 vs. social media. Source: Wirtz (2016, 2021)

Definition of Social Media and Social Media Management

Against this background, the term social media comprises different features and aspects and is thus defined as follows.

Definition of Social Media (Wirtz and Ullrich 2008; Wirtz 2016, 2020)
Social media are applications, services, and platforms on the Internet with high, mostly interactive and personalizable creative potential. They are characterized by the active generation and creation of diverse content through the cooperative participation of users. User-generated content in conjunction with platform services forms social networks that enable users to network in a communicative and content-related way.

Based on the definition of social media, a definition of social media management can be formulated.

Definition of Social Media Management (Wirtz 2013, 2018)
The term social media management describes the initiation as well as the support, management, and maintenance of transactions between economic partners via social media tools.

Social Media Four-Factor Model

A suitable approach to explain the characteristics and the opportunities in digital government through social media is the Four-Factor Model (Wirtz et al. 2010). This is one of the few integrated models of social media, which is empirically validated (Wirtz et al. 2013). The four dimensions of the model are:

- "Social networking": networking of groups and individuals via Internet platforms and applications.
- "Interaction orientation": interactions between organizations and users on social media applications.
- "Customization and personalization": segment-specific alignment and adjustment of the market offers to the needs of users or user groups.
- "User-added value": value created for and by users on social media platforms.

The four dimensions of the Social Media Four-Factor Model are each composed of several components. Figure 7.2 illustrates these dimensions and their components (content based on Wirtz et al. 2010).

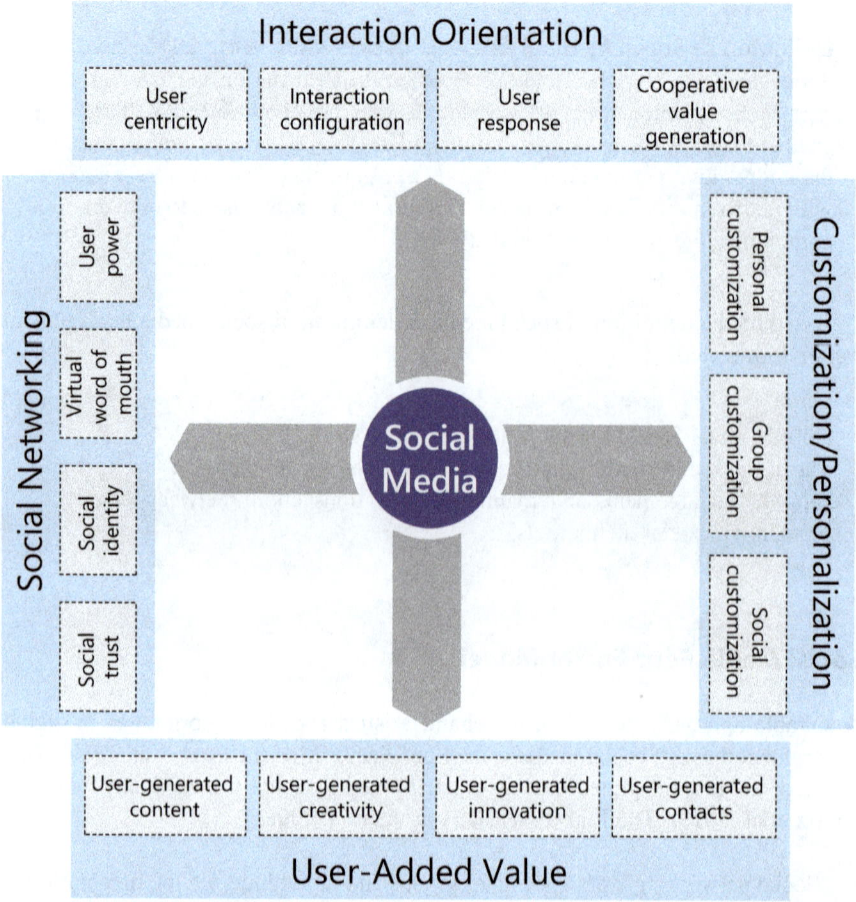

Fig. 7.2 Social Media Four-Factor Model. Source: Wirtz (2013, 2021), Wirtz and Daiser (2017)

Interaction Orientation

Interaction orientation represents the ability to effectively manage the demand of the general public for more intense and more authentic two-way communication organizations (Rayport et al. 2005). This factor manifests itself in four important subfactors: user centricity, interaction configuration, user response, and cooperative value generation. User centricity puts users at the center of attention and orients organizational activities toward the users. This brings along a major paradigm shift for many organizations, which requires a strategic and operative reorientation toward users. Interaction configuration particularly refers to the structure of the interaction process, focusing on the content of the information exchanged and the interaction partners involved, as well as the reasons and motives underlying the interaction. User response describes an organization's capacity to manage the dialogue with the user, especially referring to its ability to react appropriately to user requests or feedback in order to establish sustainable relationships to users and thus to achieve user loyalty in the long run. Cooperative value generation is closely connected to this component and reflects an organization's ability to integrate users into the respective processes in order to cooperatively create value. For instance, the organization may improve products or services according to the respective user feedback (Hettler 2010; Wirtz et al. 2010).

Customization and Personalization

The factor customization and personalization refers to the possibility for users to customize websites, applications, and online offers to their needs and preferences. It is composed of the subfactors personal customization, group customization, and social customization. Personal customization gives users the opportunity to reconfigure a portal or website to their particular needs and preferences. For instance, Facebook users can select whether they would like to receive email notification when there is a status change or a new post on a Facebook fan page. Group customization enables a group of individuals connected through the Internet to design, build, or reconfigure platforms, products, services, and so on. Organizations may, for example, consult customers when naming new products. Suggestions are subject to ratings by other users and an official jury that finally decides. Social customization refers to customized products or services that are primarily offered to distinct social layers.

User-Added Value

User-added value describes value creation through the involvement of users that contribute content, creativity, innovation, and contacts, which thus adds value through new information and innovation. Accordingly, this concept comprises various phenomena, including user-generated content, user-generated creativity, as well as user-generated innovation and user-generated revenue/contacts. User-generated content covers various content types including profiles, video or audio files, as well as other website contents (e.g., recommendations or reviews). In the same way, users can participate through user-generated creativity, contributing a completely new perspective and bringing in innovative ideas for the further development of organizations. In the context of user-generated innovation, this is how they become a critical part of product and process innovations. This kind of user involvement has been strongly facilitated through open-source programs and APIs (application programming interfaces (Wirtz et al. 2010). User-generated revenue/contacts describes the possibility of expanding the range of service offers through new user contacts and the resulting added value (Goh et al. 2013). Organizations can benefit from active users in various ways, for instance, through user recommendations of interesting fan pages on Facebook. This kind of ability to attract and benefit from new users has become an important value driver for organizations in the digital context.

Social Networking

Social networking describes structures of online interactions among individuals and consists of the four subfactors: social identity, social trust, digital word of mouth, and increasing user power. Its underlying concept is the connection of individuals and social groups via online applications and platforms that are often based on certain topics (Beynon-Davies 2013). User participation in social networks is mainly driven by the search for social approval and the desire for group membership. Social networks are of vital importance since the information put online in these networks becomes a trusted source of knowledge for various personal decisions. The subfactor social identity refers to the users' desire to belong to specific social groups and to manage their image in particular online environments. This can be addressed, for instance, by means of specific organization channels on YouTube or fan pages on Facebook. Social trust is similar to social identity as it builds upon the behavior of people, who believe that beneficial behavior in their interactions with others will conversely lead to beneficial behavior toward them. This underlying belief creates confidence in the information provided by other users. Examples are wiki projects and collaboration projects. Digital word of mouth is also closely related to the two above-mentioned subfactors but rather refers to informal information exchange between users through email, blogs, review websites, and so on. Increasing user power is a result of rising interaction through social media, since it creates transparency and user opinions become ubiquitously available. In this connection, users act as multipliers, for instance, by sharing and linking an organization's fan page on Facebook they have liked (Wirtz et al. 2014).

To sum up, the Social Media Four-Factor Model provides a clear conceptual guidance as well as the key characteristics for using and adapting suitable social media applications. These applications enable the fulfillment of the respective challenges regarding the factors of the different dimensions of the Social Media Four-Factor Model to meet the requirements of the users involved. Therefore, the following chapter presents the relevant applications and the involved user groups.

7.2 Applications and User Groups in Social Media Management

Social media has become a fundamental part of modern information society. This development has massively changed individuals' everyday life and thus significantly changed the entire economy (Richards 2014). Against this background, this chapter first presents different social media applications to give an overview of various social media applications. Next, user groups in social media management are presented and analyzed.

Social Media Applications

Social media offers organizations a variety of applications to communicate with users and other stakeholders (Dahnil et al. 2014). From a channel perspective, there are several social media applications that have to be taken into account (Scott 2015). These are presented in Table 7.2 (content based on Enderle and Wirtz 2008), showing the respective application's business model, service offer, and user value.

Table 7.2 Overview of social media applications

Application	Business model	Service offer	User value
Social networking e.g., facebook.com	- Compilation and provision of user-generated content on a single platform - Revenues through ad sales/data mining	- Self-presentation of the user - Networking among users - Connection between users and content	- Mediation of social contacts through digital interaction - High suitability for use in the mobile context (mobile networking)
Blogs & RSS feeds e.g., blogger.com	- Systematization and compilation of online diaries - Revenues through ad sales/usage or subscription fees/data mining	- Provision of an authoring tool for the creation of blogs - Hosting of blogs - Categorization of blogs	- Unfiltered personal publishing for "everyone" - Visual presentation of content
Microblogs, e.g., twitter.com	- Compilation and provision of user-generated content on a single platform - Revenues through ad sales/data mining	- Special type of blogging to quickly publish short messages	- Fast and convenient opportunity to publish - High suitability for use in the mobile context
File exchange & sharing, e.g., youtube.com	- Archiving and systematization of user-generated content (e.g., videos) - Revenues through ad sales/data mining	- Provision of online storage - Systematization of content, e.g., through categorization and ratings	- Broadcasting for "everyone" - Access to a large number of users/audience
Rating Portals e.g.,, yelp.com	- Aggregation and systematization of product- and service-related information - Revenues from agency commissions and through ad sales/data mining	- Aggregation of product and service information - User-generated reviews of products and services - Price comparisons with links to online stores	- Independent product/service reviews from users - Simplifying and supporting decision-making and the buying process
Instant messengers, e.g., whatsapp.com	- Exchange of text, audio, and video messages and content - Revenues through subscription fees, cooperation with companies, and data mining	- Instant exchange of push messages - Support of data, audio and video streams	- Fast and convenient exchange of messages - High suitability for use in the mobile context
Podcasts e.g., podcasts.com	- Provision of audio or video content - Revenues through pay-per-use, subscription, and ad sales	- Topic-specific audio and video content - Possibility of subscription	- Location and time-independent use of content
Wikis e.g.,	- Collection, systematization, and	- Tools for creating and editing content by	- Aggregation of subject-specific

(continued)

Table 7.2 (continued)

Application	Business model	Service offer	User value
wikipedia.com	further development of information - Revenues from donations	users - Provision of a platform for searching and presenting information/knowledge	information - Freedom concerning content/authors - Users as a collective editorial
Tagging/social bookmarking e.g., delicious.com	- Classification and systematization of Internet offers - Revenues, e.g., from the sale of click streams for data mining purposes	- Central archiving and ubiquitous availability of bookmarks - Tagging of bookmarks - Access to link collections of other users	- Individual editorial workup of the Internet
Online forums e.g., topix.com	- Compilation, classification, and provision of user-generated content on a single platform - Revenues through ad sales/data mining	- Exchange and archiving of thoughts, opinions, and experiences	- Increase in knowledge - Problem-solving through community - Structured documentation of topics and opinions
Mashups e.g., parkingcarma.com	- Combination of multiple online software products/API services - Revenues through ad sales and/or membership fees	- Creation of new media content by recombining already existing content	- Exploitation of synergies between different social media applications - Time savings

Source: Enderle and Wirtz (2008), Wirtz (2011, 2021)

Social Networking

Social networking refers to platforms that use computer-mediated communication to link individuals in groups or communities, so-called social networks (Laudon and Traver 2017). Examples of social networking sites are Facebook, Twitter, or Instagram. The business model of social networking includes the compilation and provision of user-generated content on a single platform, generating revenue based on ad sales and data mining. The service offer provides the opportunity of self-presentation for the users, as well as networking among users and between users and content. Thus, users can basically present their profiles on the web and interact or network with other users. In particular, the mediation of social contacts through digital interaction and the high suitability for use in the mobile environment provides value to the user. These social media applications can be quickly and easily set up to start interaction and thus are highly relevant (Scott 2015). Due to their scope and growth in recent years, social networks are among the most popular applications in the social media management (Beynon-Davies 2013; Wamba and Carter 2014). One of the world's most popular social media applications is WhatsApp with around two billion users in April 2020. With approximately 2.5 billion users, Facebook, the organization that owns WhatsApp, has even a larger user group on its original network (Statista 2020b). Instagram, also owned by Facebook, has about one billion active users (Statista 2020b). The business network LinkedIn has 690 million active users (LinkedIn 2020).

Blogs and RSS Feeds

Blogs and RSS feeds provide online publishing opportunities for businesses and organizations and enable visual presentation of content (Laudon and Traver 2017). These technologies reside more or less between traditional print and broadcast media and mainly serve information purposes. The business model of blogs and RSS feeds involves the systematization and compilation of online diaries and generates revenue based on ad sales, usage or subscription fees, and data mining. Its service offer entails the provision of an authoring tool for creating blogs, as well as the hosting and categorization of blogs. The opportunity of publishing and visually presenting unfiltered and personal content represents the core user value. Overall, these applications are quickly and easily set up and thus reflect helpful tools to keep users informed.

Microblogs

Microblogs represent a more specific type of blogging through which users can publish short messages that often have less than 140 characters and that can be made accessible to the public or a selected group of people. Twitter is the world's leading and by far most frequently used microblogging service. The business model of microblogs includes the compilation and provision of user-generated content on a single platform and generates revenue based on ad sales and data mining. Its service offer is a special type of blogging for quickly publishing short messages. In particular, the fast and convenient opportunity to publish and the high suitability for the mobile context provide value to the user. For organizations such a service may be an important means to approach the general public, bind users and advertise their services.

File Exchange and Sharing

In addition to blogs and social networks, file exchange and sharing is another type of social media. Among the most popular file exchange and sharing websites on the Internet are YouTube, Flickr, and SlideShare. These platforms allow to spread multimedia content like photos or videos usually uploaded by users. File exchange and sharing applications allow users to share media content, which here refers primarily to file transfer and content distribution. Accordingly, the business model of file exchange and sharing contains the archiving and systematization of user-generated content (e.g., videos), generating revenue based on ad sales and data mining. The service offer entails the provision of online storage and the systematization of content, for instance, through categorization and ratings. The opportunity of broadcasting for "everyone" and the access to a large number of users or audience represent the core user value. These services also offer social features to their members. For instance, users can watch, rate, and comment on videos published by organizations on YouTube. The comment feature also allows organizations to communicate with users. However, many users of these websites do not have a membership but only visit them to look at photos and videos. If organizations have their own channel on YouTube, users can subscribe to this channel to obtain information on a regular basis and to be able to directly access further video posts of the organization. These posts, for instance, may also contain service offers, as well as information with regard to special campaigns or new services. Overall, these applications can provide a lot of potential for organizations by informing users through additional media channels. Unfortunately, professional and sustainable file exchange or sharing communication usually requires expensive and complex preparation, like video shootings, photographers, etc. (Sheldon 2015).

Rating Portals

Rating portals such as yelp.com are further important social media applications that foster independent product and service reviews. This creates market transparency, supporting, and influencing decision-making processes of users. Especially this characteristic makes rating portals a double-edged sword. Digital word-of-mouth recommendations enjoy considerable trust among users, and negative impressions may hinder service provision. Hence, organizations have to care for objective online feedback and actively manage associated web content (Yoo et al. 2015). The business model of rating portals involves the aggregation and systematization of product- and service-related information, generating revenue based on agency commissions, ad sales, and data mining. The service offer comprises the aggregation of product and service information, the provision of user-generated reviews of products and services, as well as price comparisons with links to online stores. In particular, the independency of reviews from other users, as well as the simplification and support in the decision-making and buying process, provides value to the user.

Instant Messengers

Instant messengers such as WhatsApp or Viber are social media applications that allow users to exchange messages quickly and conveniently. More specifically, their business model includes the exchange of text, audio, and video messages and content, generating revenue based on subscription fees, cooperation with companies, and data mining. The service offer accordingly includes the instant exchange of push messages, as well as support of data, audio and video streams. The value for the user lies particularly in the speed and convenience of exchange and the high suitability for use in the mobile context. The most famous example of an instant messenger is the mobile messaging app WhatsApp that has pretty much replaced the function of SMS use on mobile devices. Beyond normal text messaging as well as audio and video calls, WhatsApp users can create groups and send each other images and video and audio files without limit. Organizations are increasingly using WhatsApp to communicate directly with users and to inform them about news from the organization.

Podcasts

Podcasts are helpful tools that enable users to consume online content at any place and at any time. Popular podcast providers are, for instance, Libsyn or podcast.com. Similar to blogs and RSS feeds, podcasts allow a quick and easy setup of an additional online information application. Users can subscribe to these podcasts and stay informed about the respective content. The business model of podcasts contains the provision of audio or video content, generating revenue through pay-per-use and subscription fees, as well as ad sales. The service offer not only comprises topic-specific audio and video content but also the possibility to subscribe to respective offers. In particular, the location- and time-independent use of content provides value to the user.

Wikis

Wikis are collaborative platforms that serve as community-based knowledge creation and sharing exchange stations. Users aggregate subject-specific information and participate as a collective editorial team, creating extensive knowledge encyclopedias. Thus, wikis provide an excellent opportunity for collaborative knowledge creation between users and organizations in a digital setting. The business model of wikis entails the collection, systematization, and further development of information, generating revenue from donations. The service offer comprises tools for creating and editing content, as well as the provision of a platform for searching and presenting information or knowledge. The value for the user lies particularly in the aggregation of subject-specific information, the freedom with regard to content and authors, as well as the collective creation process among users with regard to editorial work.

Tagging and Social Bookmarking

Tagging and social bookmarking applications such as delicious.com classify and systematize Internet offers through the individual editorial workup of bookmarks. Accordingly, the business model of tagging and social bookmarking services consists of the classification and systematization of Internet offers, generating revenue based on the sale of click streams for data mining purposes. The service offer comprises the central archiving and ubiquitous availability of bookmarks, as well as the tagging of bookmarks and the access to link collections of other users. Thus, users can also share their links with other users and create common collections. While the individual editorial workup of the Internet provides value to the user, service providers can market their portal by creating the possibility to tag their service offer. Apart from that, organizations should seek to be present on tagging platforms to create user awareness and actively market their own bookmarks.

Online Forums

Online forums such as topix.com are technology-based and topic-oriented discussion platforms on the Internet, where users can publish content and share their thoughts, opinions, and experiences with other users. The exchange of information follows the principle of a bulletin board or starts with an initial user post to which other users respond. The resulting thread is mostly presented in chronological order. Moreover, moderators or administrators usually monitor online forums. The business model of online forums includes the compilation, classification, and provision of user-generated content on a single platform, generating revenue based on ad sales and data mining. The service offer refers to the exchange of archiving of thoughts, opinions, and experiences. In particular, the increase in knowledge, the problem-solving through the community, and the structured documentation of topics and opinions provide value to the user.

Mashups

Mashups such as parkingcarma.com describe the creation of new content based on combinations of already existing content. In the context of digital government, the business model involves the combination of different online software products or API services, generating revenue through ad sales and membership fees. The service offer contains the creation of new media content by recombining already existing content. The value for the user particularly results from the synergies between the diverse social media applications and the associated time saving.

Given these social media application characteristics, social media can be generally expected to become more and more important for B2C and G2C communication and interaction (Huang and Benyoucef 2013). Against this background, social media adoption will constantly increase, making it a top priority on every digital government and organization agenda (Wirtz and Göttel 2016).

Social Media Microtargeting and Social Media Multiplier Effects

Social media offers the possibility of optimizing advertising and digital communication by using targeting. Especially microtargeting plays an increasingly significant role in the context of social media. In this context, microtargeting refers to gathering data or information about individuals via social media and using it to target and approach specific target groups with personalized messages. For example, microtargeting is regarded a crucial driver of President Trump's success in the 2016 US presidential election. More specifically, Trump's election campaign was supported by an organization that created personal profiles of potential voters based on their Likes on Facebook and then targeted them with personalized marketing messages (Forbes 2016).

However, it is essential to consider carefully the desired social media purposes with their respective benefit potential. Against this background, blogs and content communities should be mainly used for information purposes, while social networking sites are rather suitable for B2C or G2C interaction. Apart from that, wikis and podcasts are helpful tools to build up knowledge-creation platforms, as well as file exchange and sharing platforms that support information diffusion through respective applications (Sheldon 2015).

Another characteristic of social media is that almost all tools can be linked to each other or integrated. This represents an important feature of social media, since most members of a particular social network are often active on other platforms as well. Examples of integration (or mashups) are as follows:

- The Facebook page of an organization can be linked to its Twitter account to present tweets outside of Twitter.
- YouTube videos can be embedded in the organization's blog or Facebook page.
- If an organization links bookmarks on delicious.com, other blogs can automatically publish their posts.

Social media have specific characteristics that distinguish them from other media. Not every tool is equally suitable for different entrepreneurial objectives. In principle, however, social media management companies take advantage of the multiplier effect that can be achieved in social media applications with high user numbers. Figure 7.3 describes this effect.

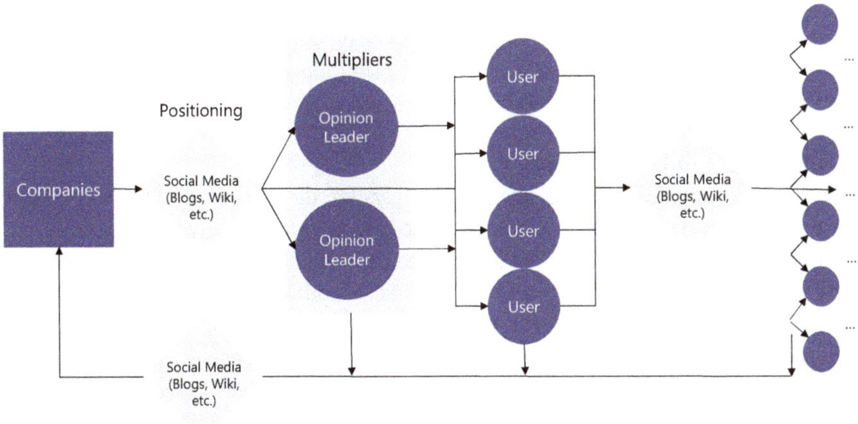

Fig. 7.3 Multiplier effect of social media. Source: Wirtz (2012, 2021)

In a digital context, organizations are especially active on major communities, platforms, and portals to pursue their respective activities. In order to reach a high number of potential users, organizations should try to target opinion leaders. These are main influencers in many forums or other social networks, as they act as experts and thus have high influence within social communities.

Social Media Convergence and Integration

Recently, the social media landscape has been undergoing two major developments. On the one hand, social media services are becoming increasingly concentrated within a few companies through strategic acquisitions. Facebook, for example, has acquired more than 50 companies since its formation in 2004. Among its most famous takeovers are the photo-sharing application Instagram for 1 billion USD in 2012 and the mobile instant messenger WhatsApp for 19 billion USD in 2014. Moreover, Facebook also tried to buy the image messaging service Snapchat in 2013, but the 3 billion USD acquisition offer was turned down by Snap Inc. On the other hand, social media offers are increasingly assimilating or converging in terms of their set of features. Facebook and Twitter, for instance, have repeatedly imitated certain features of each other in the past. While Facebook adopted the so-called hashtag feature from Twitter, the latter introduced a title picture in addition to the profile picture, shortly after Facebook had launched this feature. Other social media providers pursue a similar strategy. Snapchat, for example, was originally a messenger app through which users could send each other pictures that were automatically deleted after a short period. In the meantime, it has developed more and more into a service like WhatsApp, which is more suitable for the mass. Just like with WhatsApp, Snapchat users can now also send each other videos as well as text and audio messages or make phone and video calls. This convergence of social media offers or emergence of me-too products especially results if an acquisition is not possible. If an organization cannot take over its competitors, it needs to imitate their products or create similar ones in order to cannibalize their success and prevent them from maximizing their market shares.

Keeping Users in Own Product World

Moreover, companies seek to keep their users in their own product world and prevent user churn particularly to those competitors with similar value propositions. From a strategic point of view, a main reason why Facebook acquired Instagram and tried to take over Snapchat was not only because both companies were innovative start-up players with similar value propositions but also in response to user churn with regard to younger users who increasingly prefer to use Instagram and Snapchat (iTech Post 2016).

User Growth

Another significant reason for such strategic acquisitions is user growth. For instance, when Facebook took over WhatsApp, it acquired about 500 million active WhatsApp users. From a strategic perspective, companies aim to achieve a high user base to use it as a strategic barrier to market entry and thus to increase their market power.

Finally, the above-mentioned acquisition and convergence strategies also represent measures for companies to achieve their goal of an integrated product or service portfolio. If companies accomplish to cover and satisfy the full range of user needs, the user is likely to have no reason or desire to leave. In this connection, Figure 7.4 illustrates the development of Facebook's integrated product and service offering, showing the organic functional enhancements and acquisitions over time (content based on Meta 2022).

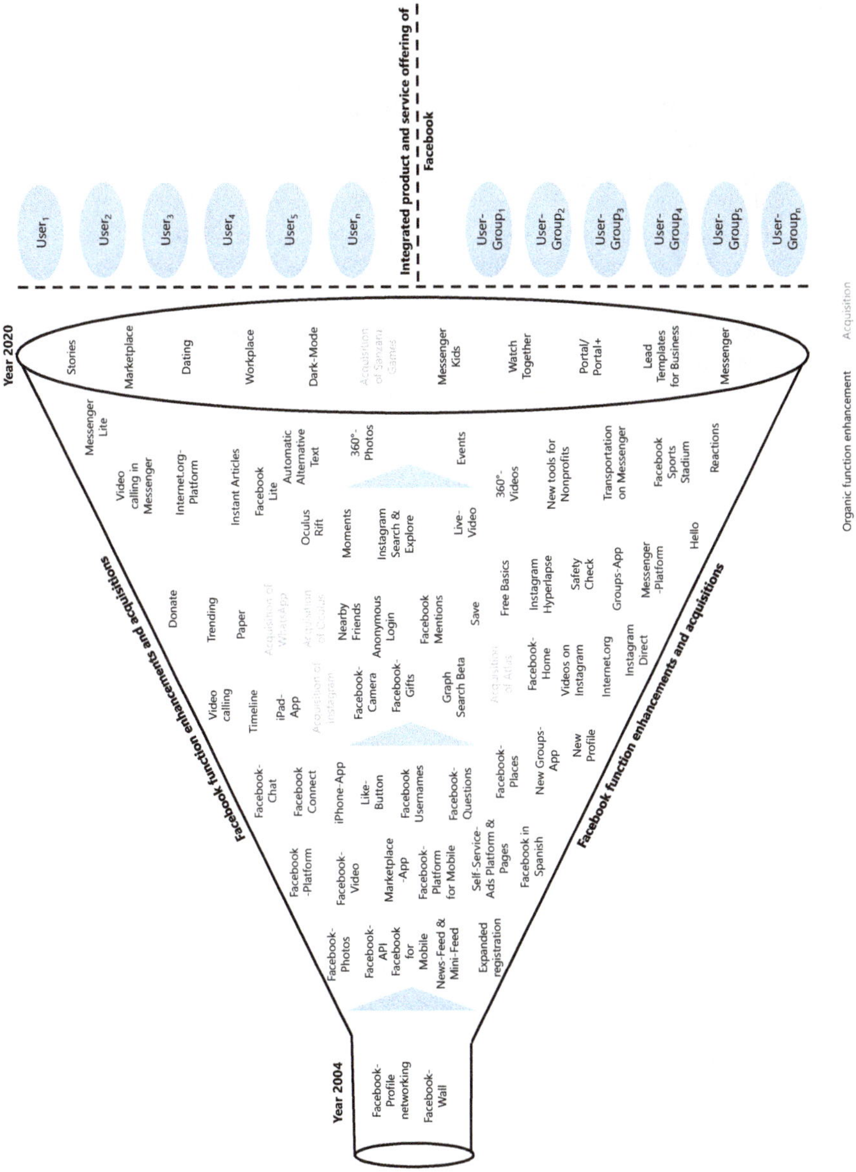

Fig. 7.4 Development of the integrated product and service offering of Facebook. Source: Wirtz (2019, 2021)

User Groups in Social Media Management

Moreover, the availability of knowledge represents an important criterion for selecting an appropriate instrument for social media management. The respective organization should have an understanding of the target recipient and thus shape the activities in social media according to the targeted groups. These groups differ by means of their involvement. Organizations can therefore make a distinction between inactive users, spectators, newcomers, collectors, critics, and creatives. The level of activity is the decisive criterion in this definition. While the "inactive" deny the use of social media, the "spectators" are passive and only consume social media content that requires no registration. "Newcomers" have their own profiles on social platforms and are active in developing their profiles. "Collectors" and "critics," by contrast, have increased activity and contribute actively with reviews or by modifying content. "Creatives" eventually run their own platforms and significantly define the content of social media. Table 7.3 outlines the different user groups (content based on Li and Bernoff 2011).

Table 7.3 Social media users and their activities

User groups with different involvement	Social media activities
Inactive users	• No interest in a social media presence • No sign of any activity on social media applications
Spectators	• Consume content on different social media platforms such as product review sites, blogs, streaming platforms • No contribution of own content
Newcomers	• Regular maintenance of the profiles on social media platforms • Open to other social networking sites
Collectors	• Use of RSS feeds • Use of bookmarking services
Critics	• Active participation in product rating portals • Modification of articles on wikis • Commenting on blog posts
Creatives	• Release own publications on blogs and other sites • Customize design of own websites • Upload of videos, music, or other media contents • Publication of own articles

Source: Wirtz (2013, 2021)

An important decision criterion for organizations on which social media channel they ought to show presence is the usage intensity of different user groups (Wirtz et al. 2017). In this regard, significant differences for the various social media instruments can be noticed.

Against this background, it is useful to take a look at the development of social media use in recent years. Figure 7.5 illustrates the development of monthly user numbers for a variety of social media services.

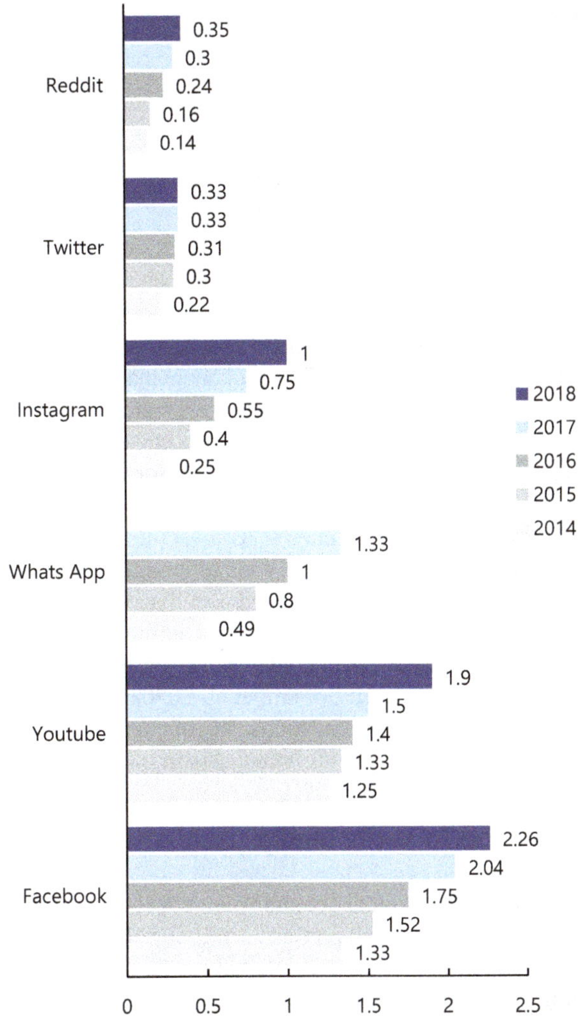

Fig. 7.5 Development of monthly social media users in billions. Data source: OurWorldinData (2019), Wirtz (2021)

Consequently, organizations worldwide use very different social media channels, dependent on their purposes and target groups.

US Facebook User Profile

At present, the social networking site Facebook is the most important platform as it is the most popular site for users and thus also for companies and advertisers. Therefore, the following Table 7.4 depicts the profile of Facebook users in the USA according to gender and age.

Table 7.4 US Facebook user profile

Age	Male	Female
13–17	1.1%	1.3%
18–24	7.0%	7.5%
25–34	13.6%	13.6%
35–44	8.8%	10.1%
45–54	6.6%	7.9%
55–64	4.8%	7.0%
65+	4.1%	6.6%

Data source: NapoleonCat (2020), Wirtz (2021)

The above table shows that usage is distributed across all age groups. In general, female persons tend to use Facebook more than males. The groups of the 25- to 34- and 35- to 44-year-olds represent the highest number of Facebook users. The age group of 13- to 17-year-olds shows the lowest Facebook use in this analysis. Overall, the social networking site is an important platform for digital government, especially due to its different user groups, as it unifies various target groups for companies and advertisers.

Facebook is also of interest as a useful social media tool for governments and public authorities worldwide. Motivational factors for the use of public authorities' Facebook pages are the perceived usefulness and ease of use, social motivation, and most importantly the quality of public administration content on the Facebook page. The intention to use public authorities' Facebook pages is positively related to the intention to recommend (Wirtz et al. 2020a, b). Due to the interactive character of social media, recommendations are of particular interest. The following section explains the importance of influencers in this context.

Influencer in Social Media

In the context of digital communication and social media activities, influencers have become particularly important in recent years. Organizations integrate influencers (opinion leaders) in their brand and marketing communication. Influencers such as bloggers or vloggers (video bloggers) are regarded as trustworthy, influential, and wide-reaching multipliers in social media such as YouTube and Instagram.

They present products and services of organizations in a promotional way and describe them in their postings or videos. The remuneration for their advertising activities is usually based on their reach, for example, in the form of the number of subscribers and followers, or on their positive sales contribution measured in terms of linked sales revenues. Influencers are a familiar term to almost all Internet users. The term is increasingly associated with specifically created and paid advertising (Wavemaker 2019). Numerous organizations already use influencer marketing or intend to do so in the future. This is also explained by the advantages commonly attributed to influencer marketing.

Influencer Marketing

Influencer marketing is considered to be more authentic than classical marketing. Already 70% of the young people trust a product recommendation of an influencer more than those of usual prominent advertising partners. Influencer marketing also improves communication with target groups and thus represents for 22% of the marketers the preferred and most economically priced method of acquiring new customers (Digital Marketing Institute 2020). In addition, 67% of marketers use the high reach of influencers to spread their own content. Social media contribute significantly to consumers' purchase decisions. Accordingly, 74% of consumers trust product reviews presented by influencers and about 40% decide to buy as a result of influencer marketing (Digital Marketing Institute 2020).

Especially the young user group trusts the recommendations of influencers who are particularly convincing with their product knowledge and authenticity. Six out of ten young people follow an influencer rather than reacting to traditional marketing methods. In many cases, followers can benefit from a discount that is granted to them for their activity as followers of a particular influencer (Digital Marketing Institute 2020).

Influencer-Communication-Follower (ICF) Model

Figure 7.6 depicts the influencer-communication-follower (ICF) model that illustrates the basic communication structure between influencers and users by means of five levels.

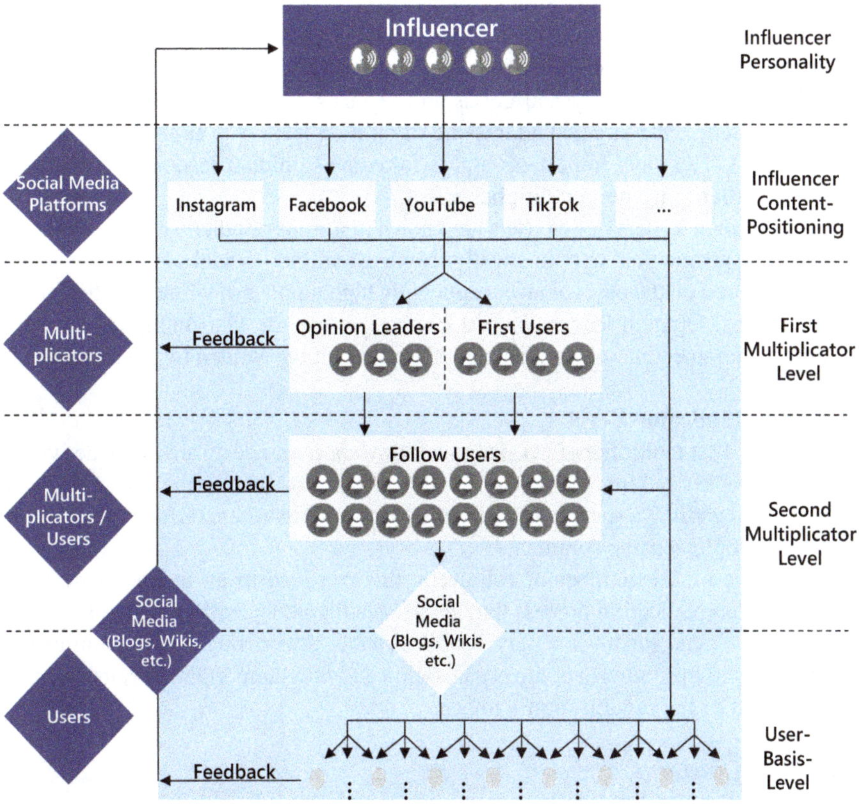

Fig. 7.6 Influencer-communication-follower (ICF) model. Source: Wirtz (2020, 2021)

On the first level are the influencers. They use various channels like YouTube, Instagram, or Tik Tok to reach their followers. A distinction is made between niche influencers, micro influencers, and macro influencers. The former use several channels, but each of them has only a small reach. They address specific topics such as a particular sport or a special diet. A micro influencer uses one or more channels and can reach up to 50,000 followers. Macro influencers, by contrast, have more than 50,000 followers and usually deal with different topics on different channels (BVDW 2018).

Influencer Content-Positioning

In this context, influencer content positioning is a decisive factor for the success of an influencer's contribution. The influencer must provide a suitable social media platform with a correspondingly large number of followers in order to be considered for a marketing campaign of an organization.

At this point, the influencer generates a viral message that is as attractive as possible and tailored to the respective followers in order to achieve the greatest possible attention for the product or service presented. In doing so, the influencer emphasizes the positive characteristics for the target groups and underlines them with personal experience reports. In this way, an influencer builds an emotional relationship with his or her followers and can thus communicate the practical and advantageous contents of the product or service.

First Multiplicator Level

Especially when selling physical goods and services while avoiding the costs of a physical presence, the targeted addressing of opinion leaders is an important aspect (Wirtz 2016). The most important goal is to address opinion leaders in a targeted manner in order to trigger a multiplier effect.

These opinion leaders or first users are known in forums or other social networks as experts in a specific field and thus well-recognized within a social community. They can be identified on the basis of an exceptionally high number of written contributions or evaluations. Opinion leaders or first users represent the first multiplier level by picking up, commenting on, or evaluating the contributions written by the influencers.

Second Multiplicator Level

Based on the first multiplier effect, various followers are made aware of the activities of opinion leaders and first users. These followers, in turn, take up their feedback and evaluations regarding a specific product or service and pass them on, sometimes with their own supplementary comments.

Depending on the number of followers, this can lead to an independent, self-sustaining communication process that grows steadily and generates a high reach. In this context, social media not only enable product advertising but also influence target groups in the interests of the organization and thus support the development or improvement of the organization's image.

User-Basis-Level

The user base is not necessarily represented directly by subscribers or followers of the influencers, but is also addressed indirectly via created communication channels. Thus, there is both a direct and indirect way from the influencer to the users with regard to the product or service communication. The users can learn about products or services, for instance, via blogs, wikis, or any other channels.

Due to the multiplier effect, this can lead to end customers encountering the same product several times in social media, even though the influencer has addressed it only once. The right positioning of influencer content in connection with the various multipliers can result in a successful and widespread marketing campaign.

PCRI Model of Influencer Management

A successful integration of influencers is determined by several factors. In addition, the impact or success of an influencer's contribution can be measured by performance measures. The personality content reach impact (PCRI) model in Figure 7.7 describes these aspects of social media influencer marketing.

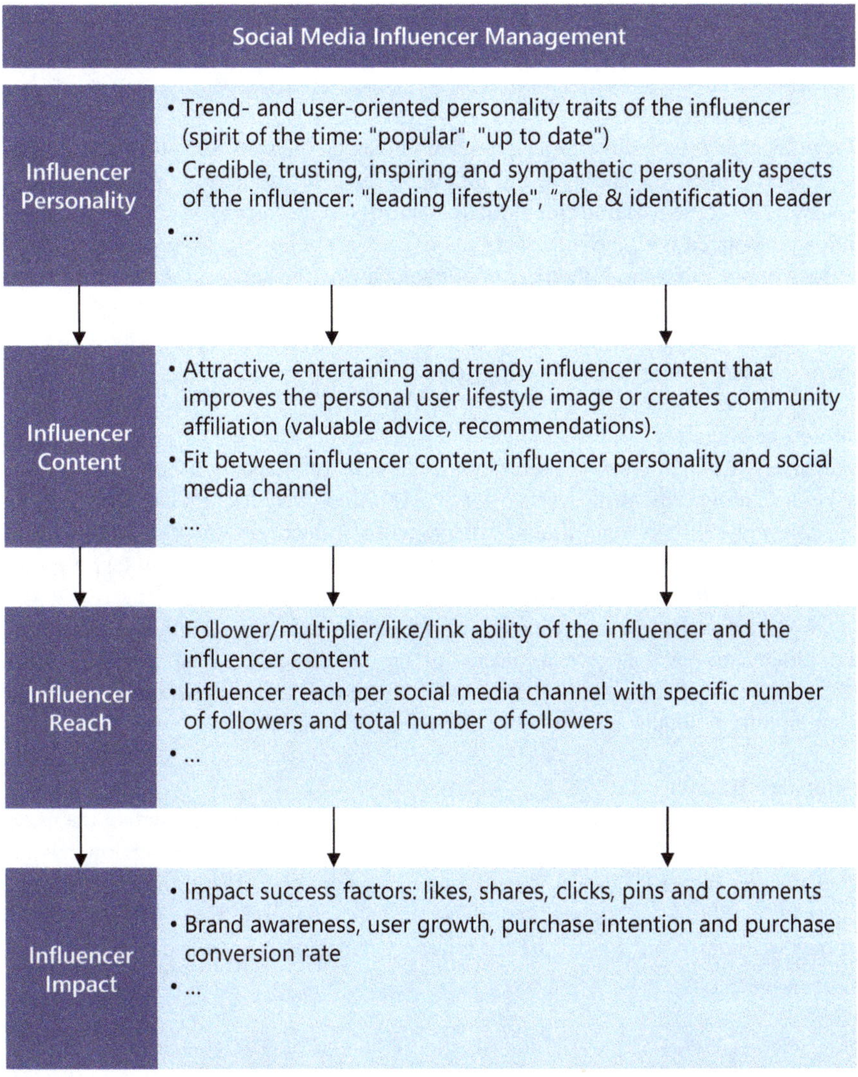

Fig. 7.7 PCRI model of influencer management. Source: Wirtz (2020, 2021)

Influencer Personality

The PCRI model has four levels. In the first level of influencer personality, important personality traits of the influencer are located. The influencer personality is of considerable importance for influencer marketing as a whole. This is due to the fact that the selected channels of influencers have to be accessed in a targeted manner in most cases and are not, as with the classic, linear television program, broadcasted on a regular and repeated basis. Trend and user-oriented personality traits are decisive criteria for followers to spread an influencer's message.

This also includes the credible, trustworthy, and sympathetic performance of the influencer, which is particularly important in connection with the principle of social trust. This refers to the high level of credibility that users grant other users with regard to the information and content they provide. Due to the usually very personal form of presentation regarding the experience with the selected product/service, influencers present themselves to their followers as "one of them" and thus benefit from the social trust principle.

Influencer Content

The influencer personality has a significant impact on the selection and marketing of influencer content. In addition, the influencer content influences the success of a posting. The content should be attractive and trendy according to the target group and be associated with the influencer.

This implies that the influencer communicates his or her message on a suitable social media platform with the appropriate content in a credible and likeable way. The influencer content is especially relevant in terms of user identification and the improvement of the user lifestyle image.

Influencer Reach

Influencers are particularly successful if their recommendations contribute to a perceived improvement in the user's lifestyle. Moreover, it is crucial that there is an appropriate fit between influencer personality, influencer content, and the social media channel. This is particularly important for ensuring that the right target group is addressed with low scatter loss and high impact.

Only the harmonious combination of influencer personality, influencer content, and influencer reach allows a successful digital campaign. The success of the campaign is usually measured in terms of likes, shares, clicks, pins, and comments regarding the products and services advertised by an influencer.

Influencer Impact

In addition, the achieved brand awareness in the target group, the growth of the users in the target group, the purchase intention, and the final purchase conversion rate are of particular importance for the advertising companies. Finally, non-monetary variables such as likes, shares, and clicks must be converted into an effective and efficient purchase conversion rate for influencer marketing to be successful.

7.3 Digital Disinformation on Social Media

Over the past two decades, the Internet and social media have become important sources of information and news stories. Reading and sharing information and news content via social media has become a common habit within our societies.

News Consumption on Social Media

The high distribution of social media has significantly changed online communication structures. Internet users are no longer only recipients of news and information but have also become important transmitters. Since mobile Internet has become widely available, exchange of news and information is possible almost at anytime and anywhere for anyone.

In these circumstances, the Internet is not only a main source of information on shopping, health issues, and career options, but it has increasingly grown to be a key source of news about world affairs. Thus, the Internet and especially social media have turned into a tool of political opinion formation. Given the high relevance of the Internet and social media as opinion-forming news media, the phenomenon of digital disinformation is gaining increasing importance. Figure 7.8 illustrates this development, showing that in 2018 social media outpaced print newspapers in the USA as a news source.

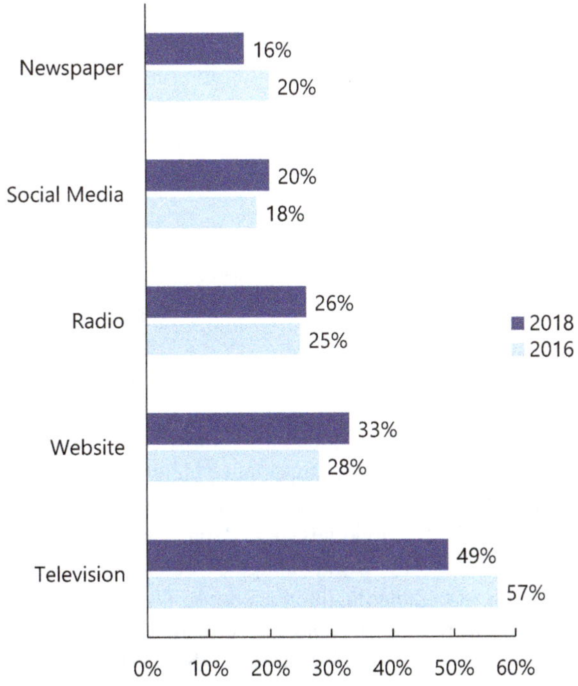

Fig. 7.8 Regularly used news sources in the USA. Data source: Pew Research Center (2018), Wirtz (2021)

In 2018, 20% of US Americans reported to have often used social media as a news source (Pew Research Center 2018). In November 2019, 18% of adults in the USA used social media even as their main source to receive political and election news, exceeded only by news websites and apps, which are used as the main source of political news by 25% of adult US Americans (Statista 2020c). In a survey among millennials in the USA in April 2019, 47% declared to use social media as a news source on a daily basis, making it the most popular source to consume news on a daily basis among millennials (Statista 2020a). Figure 7.9 illustrates that this trend is dependent on users' age. Younger users are more often consuming news on social media, while people at the age of 65 years and older get news most often from television and print newspapers.

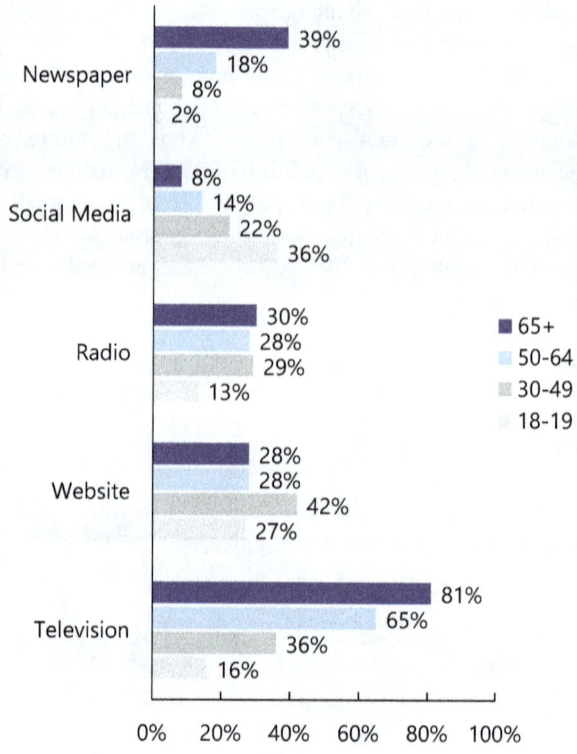

Fig. 7.9 Most often used news sources by age in the USA. Data source: Pew Research Center (2018), Wirtz (2021)

Given these developments in news consumption, digital disinformation has become an increasingly important challenge. Digital disinformation describes the systematic and intentional faking of online news and information. Organized groups or independent individuals spread false and misleading information to their own advantage or to the disadvantage of other individuals or groups. The Internet and especially social media, like Facebook, Twitter, or WhatsApp, are playing a key role and work as a catalyst in the dissemination of false news and misleading content. As news consumption and information sharing have shifted to the digital context, they are now in a hardly regulated field that has already been plagued by several large-scale disinformation campaigns.

Integrated Model of Digital Disinformation

The process of digital disinformation can be depicted in an integrated model of digital disinformation (see Figure 7.10) comprising five interdependent layers: (1) actors and their underlying motives, (2) types of disinformation, (3) distribution channels, (4) dissemination mechanisms, and (5) target groups of disinformation.

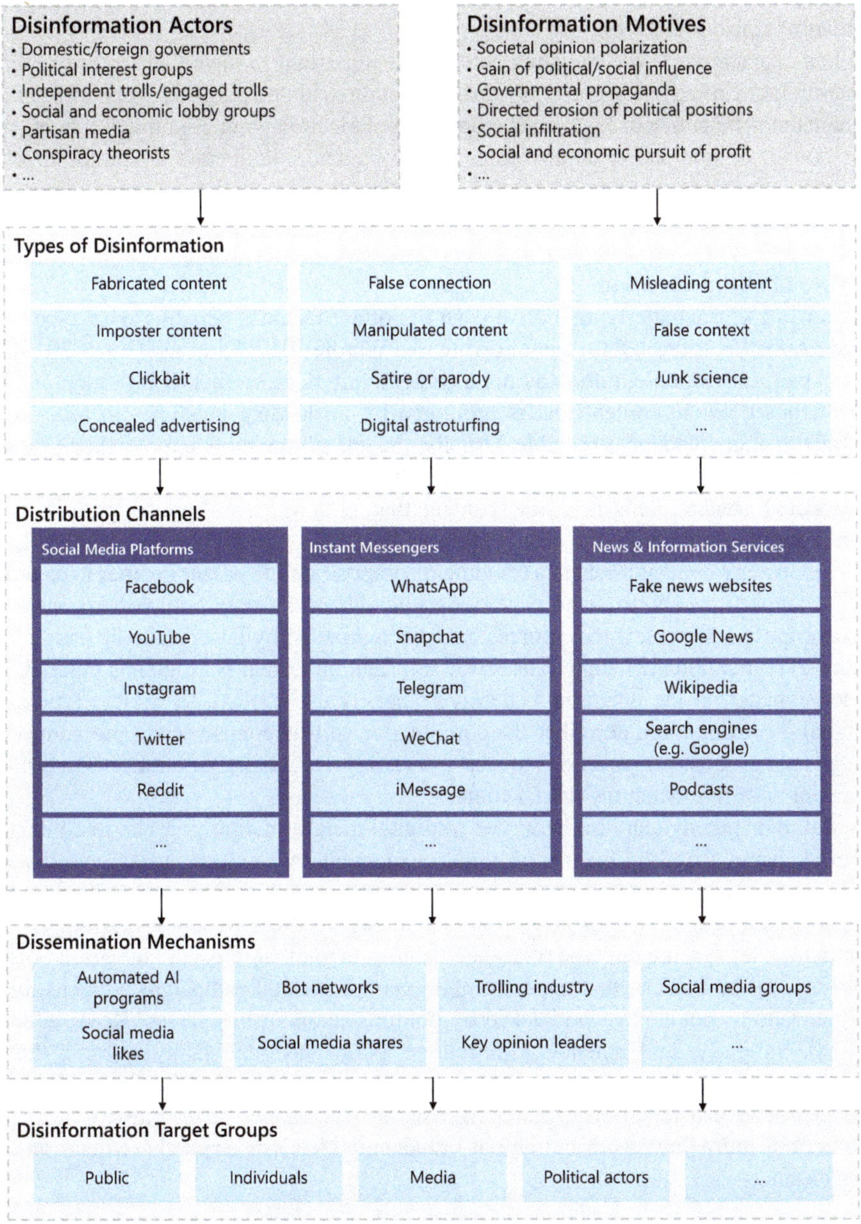

Fig. 7.10 Integrated model of digital disinformation. Source: Wirtz (2020, 2021)

Disinformation Actors

Disinformation actors are the individuals or institutions that initiate the disinformation process in the first place. Among the most important digital disinformation actors are domestic and foreign governments, political parties, minor interest groups, companies and individuals, as well as trolls engaged by third parties. Trolls are people who deliberately provoke and spread misinformation on social networks and forums in order to harm other people, groups, or companies.

Disinformation Motives

When characterizing the initiating actors, it is important to have their motives and intentions in mind, as there is no disinformation without purpose. Very different intents may be pursued, e.g., societal opinion polarization, gain of political influence or power, dissemination of governmental propaganda, deliberate undermining of political positions, change of opinion, social infiltration, and social or economic pursuit of profit.

Types of Disinformation

Accordingly, the underlying motive is an important factor in deciding what type of disinformation is created (in the following, see Wardle 2017; Farte and Obada 2018). Clickbait, for example, refers to online content with dubious factual information or erroneous political content that is promoted by misleading headlines in order to attract as many readers as possible. Usually, the underlying motive for clickbait is to gain advertising revenues per click. Another type of digital disinformation is fabricated content. This is a new content that is untrue and has the purpose to harm and deceive others.

Misleading content refers to a fraudulent composition of content in order to create false connections and to manipulate or deceive others. False information is considered imposter content, if true sources have been imitated by false, made-up sources. Moreover, manipulated content uses true information or real photographs that have been edited with the intention to deceive others. False context, as another type of digital disinformation, describes the combination of true content with false context information. False connections occur if headings, captions, subtitles, or visual content does not match the linked content.

Satire or parody can also be a type of digital disinformation. It refers to content that is characterized by the use of humor, exaggeration, mockery, irony, and false information to comment on certain events, however, not with the intent to harm but to entertain people (Rubin et al. 2015; Zimdars 2016). Digital astroturfing is a particular, less prominent type of digital disinformation that refers to fake grassroots activity on the Internet that appear in the guise of societal campaigns, citizens, or organizations, but are instead backed by political actors or businesses (Kovic et al. 2018). Similarly, junk science is inaccurate, poor, and often faulty research that might be published to push an agenda. As another example of digital disinformation, concealed advertising refers to paid advertisements that appear in the guise of factual content or journalism work but aim at influencing elections or purchase decisions, for instance.

Distribution Channels

Social media platforms differ in terms of user groups and purpose, representing unique social contexts. On Facebook, users typically share content with an assigned list of friends, while posts on Twitter and Instagram are mostly public. Due to its limitations on characters per post, Twitter is a popular tool for short and immediate commentary on real-time happening, while Instagram is a platform intended for sharing pictures, thus containing mainly self-promotional content. YouTube focuses on video content and is as such, second to Facebook, an important channel for news consumption in many countries. There are no strict boundaries between dissemination channels as it is common, for instance, to read news content on Facebook and share it via the messaging platform WhatsApp (Reuters Institute 2018).

Within the category news and information services, first to be mentioned are fake news websites (e.g., NYTimes.com.co, ABCnews.com.co, American News) that are deliberately spreading false information and in some cases are trying to masquerade as established news media (e.g., The New York Times, ABC News, etc. (Bump 2016; Murtha 2016; Weissmann 2015)). Moreover, websites like Wikipedia that depend on voluntary user participation can be intentionally corrupted by false information. Even algorithms of trusted search engines like Google or online news services like Google News can be duped to push fake news and make them seem more credible than they actually are. Eventually, any kind of information stream, be it news articles and audio or video podcasts, etc., may contain disinformation.

The companies providing these new digital distribution channels specify which actions are possible (e.g., on a specific social network) and what kind of behavior is rewarded, be it gratifications by attention or even commercial revenues, also depending on their own business models (Unver 2017). This contributes significantly to the diffusion of disinformation and makes the role of social media companies an important one.

Dissemination Mechanisms

Certain dissemination mechanisms define how disinformation diffuses online (Wardle 2017). Characteristics of the different channels, such as the so-called filter bubbles on Facebook and Twitter, are particularly suited to increase dissemination. Cognitive drivers, i.e., psychological effects like truth bias, confirmation bias and in-group favoritism, play an important role for liking and sharing content on social media and bring about social multiplier effects. Moreover, AI-based algorithms and automated AI programs that autonomously operate complex disinformation campaigns are of special importance in the digital context.

Bots

Due to the rapid technological progress and the very dynamic development in the field of AI, these advanced systems become more and more effective and efficient and thus will gain even more importance in the area of digital disinformation in the future. AI-based automation tools are currently particularly popular in the form of the so-called bots, which are becoming increasingly prevalent in the social media disinformation context. Social media bots are automated identities that are used to support disinformation campaigns. They are especially capable of completing simple, repetitive tasks like collecting information or providing information in an automated and fast way. At the same time, they are capable of communicating with other people and systems or interacting with other users' content while masquerading as real human users by means of fake user profiles (Woolley and Howard 2017).

Trolling

Apart from bots, the trolling industry constitutes another important dissemination mechanism of disinformation. In the context of digital disinformation, trolls are individuals that deliberately provoke and spread false information online in order to harm others. Troll factories or troll armies are hidden units of trolls that are engaged by governments, intelligence agencies, parties, or political movements to operate targeted disinformation campaigns on the Internet or in social media, trying to influence public opinion in favor of their clients.

This phenomenon has gained particular awareness in connection with Russian disinformation policy. For example, there are hundreds of people working in troll factories in St. Petersburg, sitting in a common building from where they are deliberately spreading fabricated or false information on the West and the Russian opposition on social media, in order to strengthen the Russian government in public perception and to weaken its opponents (Berger 2016).

Social Media Groups

Another mechanism of digital disinformation dissemination are social media groups that are purposefully and systematically mobilizing and organizing themselves online. By means of certain tools, such groups can arrange their campaigns and activities in a fast and easy way and spread their uniform messages coordinately and constantly (Broderick 2017). Likewise, key opinion leaders or influencers may serve as multipliers in disseminating disinformation. Opinion leaders have great public influence, since many people follow their opinions and advice.

Disinformation Targets

Finally, the fifth layer refers to the targets of disinformation action. Digital disinformation is often aimed at individuals (e.g., via microtargeting), politicians, media, or the public at large.

In summary, the Internet and especially social media have become an established information medium, and particularly the younger generation uses them as a main source of information. Against this background, Internet and social media platforms are increasingly used for digital disinformation purposes in order to manipulate public opinion formation. The focus is not only on the multitude of actors and motives of digital disinformation but also on the different types, distribution channels, and dissemination mechanisms of digital disinformation.

Governance of Digital Disinformation

Since information is a mainstay for decision-making, governance of digital disinformation has become an important subject for online companies, governments, and societies. A variety of possible countermeasures against digital disinformation are shown in Table 7.5. They range from using the deterrent effect of monitoring disinformation to education on media literacy, self-regulation of social-media platforms, and governmental data protection laws (which can, e.g., impede harmful microtargeting).

Table 7.5 Governance of digital disinformation

	Social Measures	Organizational & Technological Measures	Public & Legal Measures
Disinformation Actors and Motives	• Monitoring Disinformation	• (Crowd-based) source ratings	• State sanctions
Disinformation Types	• Independent fact-checking organizations and websites	• Human-curated algorithmic fact-checking • (Crowd-based) reporting tools • Inverse image search	• Gatekeeping • Certifications • Indexing
Distribution Channels	Self-regulation: • Standards and Guidelines • Voluntary self-regulation authorities	• Internal standards and guidelines • Digital Disinformation Officer (DDO) • Rethinking business models • Revised technological infrastructure	• Fact-checking requirements • Requirement of verified standards and guidelines
Dissemination Mechanisms	Education: • Source criticism • Media literacy • Media effects	• Social media alerts	• Ban of trolling industry and dissemination bots • Ban of purchased social media interaction
Disinformation Targets	Communication: • Agenda-setting • Corrections • Framing	• Clearing • Fact-checking app • Reactive public relation strategies	• Data protection and data security laws

Source: Wirtz (2021)

7.4 Success Factors in Social Media

Social media management is a challenge for organizations. An early adaption of activities in social media can be an important competitive advantage. Organizations have the opportunity to gain a competitive advantage if they use the cross-linked structures of the target groups and the resulting potential for their own purposes at an early stage (Broderick 2017).

Appropriate Handling of Data Protection

A major challenge of social networks is data protection. Users, who publish a lot of personal information, offer organizations the chance to identify their target groups and give them the opportunity to address users individually. However, persistent problems with both copyright infringement and data protection can result in legal disputes with social network sites or other communities. Due to these problems, users often use false information in the registration and creation of their user profiles. However, it is important for organizations to detect truthful information about the users, in order to match the respective social media management campaign to the adequate target groups. This is only possible if the data is based on true demographic information (Conrad 2009).

If this issue can be resolved for the users of social media, a wide range of opportunities for governments will arise through the use of social media, also in connection with other forms of digital government. For example, social media management has already strong links to m-government. Powerful smartphones together with mobile Internet access provide favorable conditions for the growth of mobile social media management. The owners of smartphones use multiple social platforms in a much higher frequency than people without mobile devices (Universal McCann 2013). As the technological development is advancing and smartphones become increasingly cheaper, the mobile use of social media will continue to grow and open up further opportunities for social media management.

Four-Factor Model and Social Media Success

Further success factors of social media management from an organization perspective mainly rest upon the Social Media Four-Factor Model that provides an appropriate categorization in this respect. It distinguishes between four characteristic social media dimensions: social networking, interaction orientation, customization and personalization, and user-added value. With regard to the success factor of social networking, weblogs, microblogs, file-sharing and streaming platforms, rating portals, podcasts, mashups, wikis, social tagging and bookmarking services, as well as online forums facilitate the dialogue with customers or users. It also offers the opportunity to address multipliers and thus to achieve critical mass for success (Wirtz and Kurtz 2016).

Social Networking

Social networks, instant messengers, and online forums are particularly suitable with regard to the success factor of social networking because they enable organizations to systematically monitor customers/users and offer them greater possibilities for participation. Moreover, social networks, instant messengers, and online forums also offer organizations a wide range of opportunities within the scope of interaction orientation, as they support a strong interaction with customers/users. While interacting via weblogs, microblogs, and rating portals may also be promising, this is much less likely with regard to social media management tools such as file-sharing and streaming platforms, podcasts, mashups, wikis, or social tagging and bookmarking services.

Personalization

While social networks also offer manifold opportunities for personalization or reconfiguration and thus highly take account of individual user preferences, the majority of social media applications—including weblogs, microblogs, file-sharing and streaming platforms, rating portals, instant messengers, podcasts, mashups, wikis, as well as online forums—show medium potential with regard to individual adjustments. Social tagging and bookmarking services have only low potential for customization and personalization.

User-Added Value

Regarding the success factor user-added value, especially social networks, rating portals, mashups, wikis, social tagging and bookmarking services, as well as online forums show very high potential. While other social media tools such as weblogs, microblogs, as well as file-sharing and streaming platforms mainly focus on generating user-generated content or user know-how and thus have medium potential with regard to user-added value, instant messengers and podcasts show low potential with regard to this dimension.

Digital Government Potential of Various Social Media Tools

Table 7.6 illustrates the suitability of the various social media instruments with regard to the dimensions of the Social Media Four-Factor Model and concludes with an assessment of their aggregate social media management potential (content based on Wirtz and Elsäßer 2012b).

Table 7.6 Communication and interaction potential of social media tools (organization perspective)

	Social Networking	Interaction Orientation	Customization/ Personalization	User- Added Value	Business Potential
Social Networks e.g., facebook.com	●	●	◕	●	●
Weblogs e.g., blogger.com	◔	◑	◑	◑	◑
Microblogs e.g., twitter.com	◔	◕	◑	◑	◑
File Exchange & Sharing e.g., youtube.com	◔	◔	◑	◑	◔
Rating Portals e.g., yelp.com	◔	◑	◑	◔	◑
Instant Messengers e.g., whatsapp.com	●	●	◑	◔	◑
Podcasts e.g., podcasts.com	◔	◔	◑	◔	◔
Mashups e.g., parkingcarma.com	◔	◔	◑	◕	◑
Wikis e.g., wikipedia.com	◔	◔	◑	●	◑
Social Tagging & Bookmarking e.g. delicious.com	◔	◔	◔	●	◔
Online Forums e.g., topix.com	●	●	◑	●	◕

Legend: ○ = No Potential ● = Very High Potential

Source: Wirtz (2020, 2021)

Altogether, social networks and online forums are best suited for the social media management of most organizations. While weblogs, microblogs, rating portals, instant messengers, mashups, and wikis can also be promising instruments, file-sharing and streaming platforms, podcasts, as well as social tagging and bookmarking services have a comparatively low social media management potential. Considering the growth development of social media, there are many indications that this is not a short-term hype. This projection particularly rests on the stringent development of the information society with its high degree of information and participation among users.

7.5 Summary, Review Questions, Topics for Discussion, and Online Exercises

- Social media are a group of Internet applications that are based on Web 2.0 technology and allow the creation and exchange of user-generated content. Social media management describes the initiation, support, management, and maintenance of transactions between economic partners via social media tools.
- The Social Media Four-Factor Model consists of the four dimensions: social networking, interaction orientation, customization and personalization, and user-added value. It provides conceptual guidance and the key characteristics for using and adapting suitable social media applications.
- Social networking describes structures of online interactions and consists of the subfactors social identity, social trust, digital word of mouth, and increasing user power. Drivers for user participation in social networks are especially the search for social approval and the desire for group membership.
- Interaction orientation refers to the ability to effectively manage the demand of the general public for intense and authentic two-way communication organizations and consists of the factors user centricity, interaction configuration, user response, and cooperative value generation.
- The possibility for users to customize online offers to their needs and preferences is reflected by the factor customization and personalization. Its subfactors are personal customization, group customization, and social customization.
- User-added value refers to the value creation through the involvement of users and comprises various phenomena, like user-generated content, user-generated creativity, user-generated innovations, and user-generated revenue and contacts.
- There is a great variety of social media applications that differ in terms of business model, service offer, and user value. These include, e.g., social networking that allows self-presentation and connection with other users, blogs and RSS feeds, file exchange, rating portals and instant messengers, as well as mashups.
- User groups on social media can be characterized by their distinct levels of involvement. Inactive users show the lowest involvement as they don't show any sign of activity on social media applications. In contrast, creatives represent the most involved user group on social media, as they release own publications on, e.g., blogs, customize their websites' design or upload media content.
- As the Internet and social media have become important sources for news and information, digital disinformation poses an increasing challenge in this regard. The process of digital disinformation can be presented in an integrated model of digital disinformation, consisting of actors and their motives, types of disinformation, distribution channels, dissemination mechanisms, and targets of disinformation.
- Countermeasures against digital disinformation can take all of these layers into account. Conceivable are social countermeasures, and organizational and technological countermeasures, but also public and legal countermeasures.

Chapter 7
Review questions, topics for discussion and online exercises

Review questions

1. What is social media? Describe the difference between social media and Web 2.0.
2. Describe the Social Media Four Factors Model.
3. Explain the applications of social media with their respective service offerings and user benefits.
4. Describe the Digital Disinformation Model.
5. Describe the different governance mechanisms for the integrated Digital Disinformation Model.

Topics for classroom discussion and team debates

1. Discuss the effects of social media on the democratic understanding of open societies.
2. Discuss the advantages and disadvantages of social media for your personal use of the Internet and their effects on your social and leisure time behavior. Are social media really making the world a better place?
3. Discuss the dangers of fake news in social media. What social dangers arise from fake news and how can they be countered?

Online Exercises

1. Visit https://digital-strategy.ec.europa.eu/en/policies/online-disinformation and work out from this and the following pages how the European Commission is dealing with fake news.
2. Enter https://assets.publishing.service.gov.uk/government/uploads/system/uploads/attachment_data/file/930167/Social_Media_Acceptable_Use_Policy.pdf and elaborate on key elements of the social media acceptable use policy of the British government.
3. Visit https://www.commerce.gov/about/policies/social-media and identify the key cornerstones of the U.S. Department of Commerce's social media and web 2.0 policy.

References

Aral, Sinan; Dellarocas, Chrysanthos; Godes, David (2013): Introduction to the Special Issue — Social Media and Business Transformation: A Framework for Research. In Information Systems Research 24 (1), pp. 3–13. DOI: https://doi.org/10.1287/isre.1120.0470.

Berger, A. (2016): Die Arbeit eines russischen Trolls. Available online at https://www.deutschlandfunk.de/russlands-desinformationspolitik-die-arbeit-eines.795.de.html?dram:article_id=347314, checked on 11/17/2021.

Beynon-Davies, Paul (2013): eBusiness. 2nd ed. Houndmills, Basingstoke, New York: Palgrave Macmillan.

Broderick, Ryan (2017): Trump supporters online are pretending to be french to manipulate France's election. Available online at https://www.buzzfeednews.com/article/ryanhatesthis/inside-the-private-chat-rooms-trump-supporters-are-using-to, checked on 6/8/2021.

Bump, P. (2016): Denzel Washington endorsed Trump, according to AmericaNews, Breitbartt, USANewsHome - and Facebook. Available online at https://www.washingtonpost.com/news/the-fix/wp/2016/11/14/denzel-washington-endorsed-trump-according-to-americanews-breitbartt-usanewshome-and-facebook/?utm_term=.a9462682cf68, checked on 11/17/2021.

BVDW (2018): Umfrage zur Nutzung von Inluencer Marketing. Available online at https://www.bvdw.org/fileadmin/user_upload/BVDW_Umfrage_Influencer_Marketing__112018.pdf, checked on 6/8/2021.

Conrad, R. (2009): Friends with benefits-Networking in a new economy. Penryn.

Dahnil, Mohd Irwan; Marzuki, Kamarul Mizal; Langgat, Juliana; Fabeil, Noor Fzlinda (2014): Factors Influencing SMEs Adoption of Social Media Marketing. In Procedia - Social and Behavioral Sciences 148, pp. 119–126. DOI: https://doi.org/10.1016/j.sbspro.2014.07.025.

Digital Marketing Institute (2020): 20 influencer marketing statistics that will surprise you. Available online at https://digitalmarketinginstitute.com/blog/20-influencer-marketing-statistics-that-will-surprise-you, checked on 6/8/2021.

Enderle, Martin; Wirtz, Bernd W. (2008): Weitreichende Veränderungen - Marketing im Web 2.0. In Absatzwirtschaft - Zeitschrift für Marketing 51 (1), pp. 36–39.

Farte, Gheorge Ilie; Obada, Daniel Rares (2018): Reactive Public Relations Strategies for Managing Fake News in the Online Environment. In Postmodern Openings 9 (2), pp. 26–44. DOI: https://doi.org/10.18662/po/16.

Forbes (2016): Exclusive Interview: How Jared Kushner Won Trump The White House. With assistance of Steven Bertoni. Available online at https://www.forbes.com/sites/stevenbertoni/2016/11/22/exclusive-interview-how-jared-kushner-won-trump-the-white-house/?sh=1663f0d33af6, checked on 6/7/2021.

Goh, Khim-Yong; Heng, Cheng-Suang; Lin, Zhijie (2013): Social Media Brand Community and Consumer Behavior: Quantifying the Relative Impact of User- and Marketer-Generated Content. In Information Systems Research 24 (1), pp. 88–107. DOI: https://doi.org/10.1287/isre.1120.0469.

Hettler, U. (Ed.) (2010): Social Media Marketing - Marketing mit Blogs, Sozialen Netzwerken und weiteren Anwendungen des Web 2.0. München.

Huang, Zhao; Benyoucef, Morad (2013): From e-commerce to social commerce: A close look at design features. In Electronic Commerce Research & Applications 12 (4), pp. 246–259. DOI: https://doi.org/10.1016/j.elerap.2012.12.003.

IAB/PWC (2020): Internet advertising revenue report. Full year 2019 results and Q1 2020 revenues. Available online at https://www.iab.com/wp-content/uploads/2020/05/FY19-IAB-Internet-Ad-Revenue-Report_Final.pdf, checked on 6/7/2021.

iTech Post (2016): Facebook loses more grip of its younger users, falls behind Snapchat and Instagram. Available online at https://www.itechpost.com/articles/43252/20161019/facebook-loses-more-grip-of-its-younger-users-falls-behind-snapchat-and-instagram.htm, checked on 6/7/2021.

Kaplan, Andreas M.; Haenlein, Michael (2010): Users of the world, unite! The challenges and opportunities of Social Media. In Business Horizons 53 (1), pp. 59–68.

Kovic, Marko; Rauchfleisch, Adrian; Sele, Marc; Caspar, Christian (2018): Digital astroturfing in politics: Definition, typology, and countermeasures. In Studies in Communication Sciences 18 (1). DOI: https://doi.org/10.24434/J.SCOMS.2018.01.005.

Laudon, Kenneth C.; Traver, Carol Guercio (2017): E-commerce. Business, technology, society. 12th ed. New Jersey: Pearson.

Li, Charlene; Bernoff, Josh (2011): Groundswell. Winning in a world transformed by social technologies. Expanded and rev. ed. Boston, Massachusetts: Harvard Business Review Press.

LinkedIn (2020): About Us. Available online at https://news.linkedin.com/about-us#1, checked on 7/30/2020.

Little, Arthur D. (2007): Web-reloaded? - Driving convergence in the real world. Available online at https://www.adlittle.com/sites/default/files/viewpoints/ADL_Web_2_0.pdf, checked on 6/7/2021.

Meta (2022): Our history. Available online at https://about.facebook.com/organization-info/, checked on 2/15/2022.

Murtha, J. (2016): How fake news sites frequently trick big-time journalists. Available online at https://www.cjr.org/analysis/how_fake_news_sites_frequently_trick_big-time_journalists.php, checked on 11/17/2021.

NapoleonCat (2020): Facebook users in United States of America. Available online at https://napoleoncat.com/stats/facebook-users-in-united_states_of_america/2020/02, checked on 6/8/2021.

O'Reilly, Tim (2005): What is Web 2.0. Available online at https://www.oreilly.com/pub/a/web2/archive/what-is-web-20.html, checked on 6/7/2021.

OurWorldinData (2019): The rise of Social Media. With assistance of Esteban Ortiz-Ospina. Available online at https://ourworldindata.org/rise-of-social-media, checked on 6/8/2021.

Pew Research Center (2018): Social media outpaces print newspapers in the U.S. as a news source. Available online at https://www.pewresearch.org/fact-tank/2018/12/10/social-media-outpaces-print-newspapers-in-the-u-s-as-a-news-source/, checked on 6/8/2021.

Rayport, Jeffrey F.; Jaworski, Bernard J.; Kyung, Ellie J. (2005): Best face forward: improving companies' service interfaces with customers. In Journal of Interactive Marketing 19 (4), pp. 67–80.

Reuters Institute (2018): Reuters Institute digital news report 2018. Available online at http://media.digitalnewsreport.org/wp-content/uploads/2018/06/digital-news-report-2018.pdf, checked on 6/8/2021.

Richards, Michael (2014): Social media. Dominating strategies for social media marketing with Twitter, Facebook, YouTube, LinkedIn and Instagram. California: CreateSpace Independent Publishing Platform.

Rubin, Victoria L.; Chen, Yimin; Conroy, Nadia K. (2015): Deception detection for news: Three types of fakes. In Proceedings of the Association for Information Science and Technology 52 (1), pp. 1–4. DOI: https://doi.org/10.1002/pra2.2015.145052010083.

Scott, D. M. (2015): The new rules of marketing & PR. How to use social media, online video, mobile applications, blogs, news releases, and viral marketing to reach buyers directly. Hoboken, N.J.: Wiley.

Sheldon, Pavica (2015): Social media. Principles and applications. Lanham: Lexington Books.

Social Media Examiner (2020): 2020 social media marketing industry report. How marketers are using social media to grow their businesses. With assistance of Michael A. Stelzner.

Statista (2019): Social Media Advertising. Available online at https://www.statista.com/outlook/dmo/digital-advertising/social-media-advertising/united-states, checked on 2/6/2019.

Statista (2020a): Frequency of using selected news sources among millennials in the United States as of April 2019. Available online at https://www.statista.com/statistics/1010456/united-states-millennials-news-consumption/, checked on 6/2/2020.

Statista (2020b): Most popular social networks worldwide as of April 2020, ranked by number of active users. Available online at https://www.statista.com/statistics/272014/global-social-networks-ranked-by-number-of-users/, checked on 6/2/2020.

Statista (2020c): Most popular sources of news for political and government issues among adults in the United States as of November 2019. Available online at https://www.statista.com/statistics/330295/distribution-of-sources-of-government-and-politics-news-usa/, checked on 6/8/2021.

Statista (2020d): Number of social network users worldwide from 2010 to 2023. Available online at https://www.statista.com/statistics/278414/number-of-worldwide-social-network-users/, checked on 6/2/2020.

Turban, E.; Sipior, Janice C. (2015): Information technology for management. Digital strategies for insight, action, and sustainable performance. 10th ed. Hoboken, New Jersey: Wiley.

Universal McCann (2013): Wave 7 - Cracking The Social Code- The Story of Why. Available online at http://wave.umww.com/assets/pdf/wave_7-cracking-the-socialcode.

Unver, H. Akin (2017): Digital challenges to democracy: Politics of automation, attention, and engagement. In Journal of International Affairs 71 (1), pp. 127–146.

Wamba, Samuel Fosso; Carter, Lemuria (2014): Social Media Tools Adoption and Use by SMES. In Journal of Organizational & End User Computing 26 (2), pp. 1–17. DOI: https://doi.org/10.4018/joeuc.2014040101.

Wardle, Claire (2017): Fake news. It's complicated. Available online at https://firstdraftnews.org/articles/fake-news-complicated/, checked on 6/8/2021.

Wavemaker (2019): Spotlight influencer 4.0. Wavemaker. Available online at https://www.schau-hin.info/fileadmin/content/Downloads/Sonstiges/_m_SCIENCE_Spotlight_Influencer_4.0.pdf, checked on 6/8/2021.

We Are Social (2020): Digital 2020 April global statshot report. Available online at https://www.slideshare.net/DataReportal/digital-2020-april-global-statshot-report-april-2020-v01, checked on 6/7/2021.

Weissmann, C. G. (2015): Watch out for this fake news website masquerading as The New York Times. Available online at https://www.businessinsider.com/nytimescomco-posts-fake-news-articles-pretending-to-be-the-new-york-times-2015-6?IR=T, checked on 11/17/2021.

Wirtz, Bernd W. (2011): Media and Internet Management. 1st ed. Wiesbaden: Gabler.

Wirtz, Bernd W. (2012): Direktmarketing-Management. Grundlagen - Instrumente - Prozesse. 3rd ed. Wiesbaden: Gabler.

Wirtz, Bernd W. (2013): Electronic Business. 4th ed. Wiesbaden: Gabler.

Wirtz, Bernd W. (2016): Electronic Business. 5th ed. Wiesbaden: Springer Gabler.

Wirtz, Bernd W. (2018): Electronic Business. 6th ed. Wiesbaden: Springer Gabler.

Wirtz, Bernd W. (2019): Medien- und Internetmanagement. 10th ed. Wiesbaden: Springer Gabler.

Wirtz, Bernd W. (2020): Electronic Business. 7th ed. Wiesbaden: Springer Gabler.

Wirtz, Bernd W. (2021): Digital Business and Electronic Commerce. Cham: Springer International Publishing.

Wirtz, Bernd W. (2022): E-Government. Wiesbaden: Springer Gabler.

Wirtz, Bernd W.; Daiser, Peter (2017): E-government. Strategy, process, instruments. 2nd ed. Speyer.

Wirtz, Bernd W.; Elsäßer, Marc (2012a): Instrumente im social media marketing. In Wirtschaftswissenschaftliches Studium (WiSt) 41 (10), pp. 512–518.

Wirtz, Bernd W.; Elsäßer, Marc (2012b): Prozess im social media marketing. In Wirtschaftswissenschaftliches Studium (WiSt) 41 (11), pp. 572–576.

Wirtz, Bernd W.; Falke, I.; Schmitt, Daniel (2021): Mobile government: Research, development and research perspectives. In International Journal of Public Administration. DOI: https://doi.org/10.1080/01900692.2021.1993910.

Wirtz, Bernd W.; Göttel, Vincent (2016): Technology acceptance in social media: Review, synthesis and directions for future empirical research. In Journal of Electronic Commerce Research 17 (2), pp. 97–115.

Wirtz, Bernd W.; Göttel, Vincent; Daiser, Peter (2017): Social networks: Usage intensity and effects on personalized advertising. In Journal of Electronic Commerce Research 18 (2), pp. 103–123.

Wirtz, Bernd W.; Göttel, Vincent; Langer, Paul F.; Thomas, Marc-Julian (2020a): Antecedents and consequences of public administration's social media website attractiveness. In International Review of Administrative Sciences 86 (1), pp. 38–61. DOI: https://doi.org/10.1177/0020852318762310.

Wirtz, Bernd W.; Kurtz, Oliver Tuna (2016): Citizen preferences toward e-government city portals - An empirical analysis of full online mobile and social media services. In International Public Management Review 17 (1), pp. 1–20. Available online at https://core.ac.uk/download/pdf/234704965.pdf.

Wirtz, Bernd W.; Langer, Paul F.; Göttel, Vincent; Thomas, Marc-Julian (2020b): Public social media services: A citizen's perspective. In Public Performance & Management Review 43 (6), pp. 1342–1358. DOI: https://doi.org/10.1080/15309576.2020.1760112.

Wirtz, Bernd W.; Nitzsche, Phillip T.; Ullrich, Sebastian (2014): User integration in social media: an empirical analysis. In International Journal of Electronic Business 11 (1), pp. 63–84.

Wirtz, Bernd W.; Piehler, Robert; Ullrich, Sebastian (2013): Determinants of social media website attractiveness. In Journal of Electronic Commerce Research 14 (1), pp. 11–33.

Wirtz, Bernd W.; Schilke, Oliver; Ullrich, Sebastian (2010): Strategic development of business models: implications of the Web 2.0 for creating value on the internet. In Long Range Planning 43 (2), pp. 272–290.

Wirtz, Bernd W.; Ullrich, Sebastian (2008): Geschäftsmodelle im Web 2.0 — Erscheinungsformen, Ausgestaltung und Erfolgsfaktoren. In HMD Praxis der Wirtschaftsinformatik 45 (3), pp. 20–31. DOI: https://doi.org/10.1007/BF03341209.

Wirtz, Bernd W.; Ullrich, Sebastian; Mory, Linda (2012): EHealth in the public sector: An empirical analysis of the acceptance of Germany's electronic health card. In Public Administration 90 (3), pp. 642–663.

Woolley, Samuel C.; Howard, Philip N. (2017): Computational Propaganda Worldwide. Executive Summary (Working Paper No. 2017.11). University of Oxford. Available online at https://demtech.oii.ox.ac.uk/wp-content/uploads/sites/89/2017/06/Casestudies-ExecutiveSummary.pdf, checked on 6/8/2021.

Xiang, Zheng; Gretzel, Ulrike (2010): Role of social media in online travel information search. In Tourism Management 31 (2), pp. 179–188. DOI: https://doi.org/10.1016/j.tourman.2009.02.016.

Yoo, Chul Woo; Kim, Yong Jin; Sanders, G. Lawrence (2015): The impact of interactivity of electronic word of mouth systems and E-Quality on decision support in the context of the e-marketplace. In Information & Management 52 (4), pp. 496–505. DOI: https://doi.org/10.1016/j.im.2015.03.001.

Zimdars, M. (2016): False, misleading, clickbait-y, and/or satirical "news" sources. Available online at https://21stcenturywire.com/wp-content/uploads/2017/02/2017-DR-ZIMDARS-False-Misleading-Clickbait-y-and-Satirical-%E2%80%9CNews%E2%80%9D-Sources-Google-Docs.pdf, checked on 11/17/2021.

Smart City

8

Contents

Learning Objectives
By working through this chapter, you will be able to:

1. Explain the concept of a smart city.
2. Describe the main changes with regard to urban development dynamics up to the year 2050 according to the United Nations.
3. State essential smart city targets in the three areas: social smart city targets, economic smart city targets, and ecological smart city targets.
4. Describe the smart city service provision framework and demand preferences.
5. Describe and explain the smart city ecosystem.

With increasing digital transformation in all areas of life, municipal institutions are also increasingly digitizing their processes and services.[1] In this context, and especially against the backdrop of the massive urbanization of recent years, the topic is becoming increasingly relevant: 70% of the world's population will live in cities by 2050, according to a United Nations study (United Nations 2019). Against this background, the following chapter is dedicated to the concept of the smart city. The first section explains the concept and its relevance. Then the structures and processes are discussed in more detail and the concept of smart city ecosystems is presented comprehensively.

[1] See for Chapter 8 Smart City also Wirtz (2021, 2022); Wirtz et al. (2020, 2021c); Wirtz/Müller (2021, 2022a, b).

B. W. Wirtz, *Digital Government*, Springer Texts in Business and Economics,
https://doi.org/10.1007/978-3-031-13086-1_8

8.1 Development of Smart Cities

Smart city development is a comparatively new, innovative phenomenon.[2] In the last 100 years, there has been a considerable migration of the population to urban agglomerations. According to analyses of the United Nations, this development will continue in the future. Against this background, the next section will first present conceptual aspects of smart cities and their relevance. Section Smart City Service Conception will then deal specifically with the migration development in urban agglomerations.

Smart City Definition

In order to obtain a comprehensive understanding of a smart city, the underlying concepts must first be understood and a uniform understanding must be given. This is, however, a difficult matter in view of the fact that the concept of smart city has grown historically and has therefore never been defined uniformly.

The Smart City Concept

In the academic literature, the concept of the smart city is a comparatively young one (Winkowska et al. 2019), but it is receiving a lot of attention both in academia and in practice (Eremia et al. 2017; Wirtz and Müller 2021). The main challenge is the lack of a common understanding of the term. This lack of consensus on the content of the term and on the basic concept of smart cities is also to thank for many sometimes contradictory statements (Anthopoulos 2015).

What exactly is meant by "smart" seems to be the biggest challenge. Some see in the term "smart" only a strong digital anchoring of the city, others go much further and also consider ecological and social components. Basically, the term seems to indicate an understanding of the concept of smart city as an (urban) area with an agglomeration of people where ICT is used to generate benefits for these people (Dameri 2013). The following Table 8.1 lists some further definitions.

[2] See for the following Section Development of Smart Cities also Wirtz (2022); Wirtz et al. (2020, 2021c); Wirtz/Müller (2021, 2022a, b).

Table 8.1 Smart city definitions

Author(s)	Definition
Dameri (2013)	A smart city is a well-defined geographical area, in which high technologies such as ICT, logistic, energy production, and so on, cooperate to create benefits for citizens in terms of wellbeing, inclusion and participation, environmental quality, intelligent development; it is governed by a well-defined pool of subjects, able to state the rules and policy for the city government and development.
Caragliu et al. (2009)	We believe a city to be smart when investments in human and social capital and traditional (transport) and modern (ICT) communication infrastructure fuel sustainable economic growth and a high quality of life, with a wise management of natural resources, through participatory governance.
Anthopoulos (2017c)	[. . .] the utilization of ICT and innovation by cities (new, existing or districts), as a means to sustain in economic, social, and environmental terms and to address several challenges dealing with six (6) dimensions (people, economy, governance, mobility, environment, and living).
Monzon (2015)	A Smart City is an integrated system in which human and social capital interact, using technology-based solutions. It aims to efficiently achieve sustainable and resilient development and a high quality of life on the basis of a multistakeholder, municipality based partnership.

The definitions presented differ in particular with regard to their focus. What they have in common is that there must always be a reference to ICT in order to describe a city as smart. However, the use of these ICTs and especially the objectives are usually very broad. Dameri (2013) sees the goal as generating fundamental benefits for the city's citizens in terms of well-being, inclusion and participation, and environmental quality. It is clear that an exclusive citizen orientation is chosen and the interests of companies and organizations are not included.

The definition of Caragliu et al. (2009) is much more comprehensive, since not only ICT investments but also investments in traditional communication infrastructure and the promotion of human and social capital are considered as a basis. Their primary goal is to enable sustainable economic growth and a high quality of life.

The definition by Anthopoulos (2017c) identifies six concrete dimensions as target parameters for smart cities: people, economy, governance, mobility, environment, and housing. These are to be sustainably improved in economic, social, and environmental terms.

The definition by Monzon (2015) specifically addresses the integration of different factors and thus refers to a kind of ecosystem that allows human and social capital to interact through the use of technology. Monzon (2015) also sees the goal as improving sustainability, resilience, and quality of life while promoting collaboration and cooperation between stakeholders and communities.

Smart City Definition

In view of the different definitions and focal points, it is important to derive a uniform understanding for a clear grasp of the following discussion. Consequently, a precise definition of a smart city is provided below.

Definition of Smart City
A smart city is an integrated system based on digital information technologies that focuses on improving the well-being of society through efficient and effective use of resources in an urban context. In particular, it is about meeting key stakeholder requirements through transparency, participation, and collaboration.

Relevance of Smart Cities

The relevance of smart cities can be considered from different perspectives. It is worthwhile to use proven concepts such as the Quadruple Helix for clear differentiation. The aim of the Quadruple Helix classification is to show that the four spheres—society, business, academia, and government—are closely integrated to create a network of relationships that can generate innovations and contribute to social prosperity (Selada 2017). Figure 8.1 shows the four spheres of the quadruple helix.

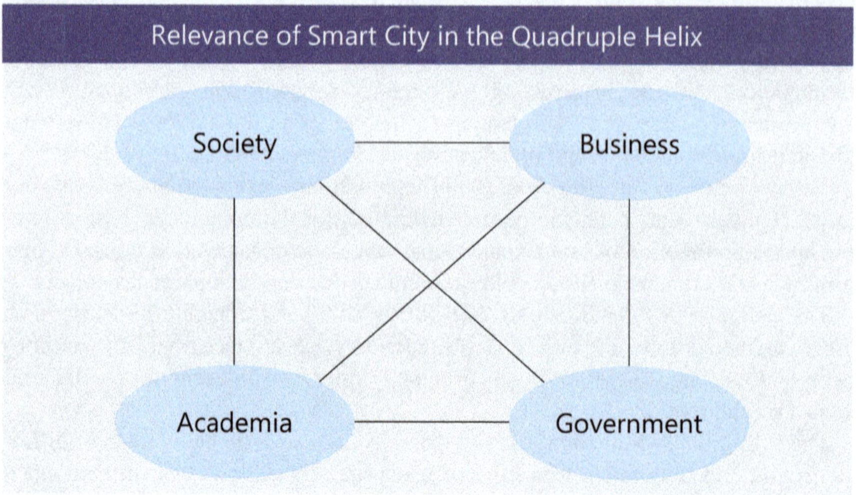

Fig. 8.1 The four spheres of the quadruple helix

Society
To start with the individual level, it makes sense to first look at the relevance for citizens (Society). For many, citizens are also the central point of reference for why smart cities are important (Dameri 2013). The central focus is on improving the quality of life of a city's citizens (Yeh 2017). This includes not only improving

services and the environment through the targeted use of ICT. It is also centrally about the component of citizen participation that can take place much more directly and efficiently (Berntzen and Johannessen 2015).

Business

Another sphere to be considered is the local economic structure and its actors. There is a high relevance for all types of companies. This applies in particular to the perspective of the providers of smart city solutions. In addition, it is also of great importance for SMEs that a city offers the corresponding digital infrastructure in order to connect their own value creation to it and, if necessary, to participate.

In particular, leading global technology companies such as IBM, Siemens, and Cisco recognized the market at an early stage and have since become important players in the development of smart city systems through smart city innovations (Selada 2017). Investment in smart infrastructure and other similar services and products has been growing strongly for years. A study by PwC (2019) shows that this area is not only characterized by high growth figures but already represents a significant economic factor. In 2020, the 1000 billion USD mark was surpassed and annual growth of over 15% is expected over the coming years. Table 8.2 presents the figures from the PwC study.

Table 8.2 Market value smart city investments

Year	Global smart city market in billion USD
2018	737
2019	858
2020	1.007
2021	1.194
2022	1.428
2023	1.721
2024	2.094
2025	2.577

Data source: PwC (2019)

Academia

Academia in general plays a significant role in the context of innovation. Besides basic education and research into the fundamentals of innovation, economics, systems, etc., academia is also a driving force in shaping the fundamentals of a society. In the smart city context, its research and its role as an experimental domain is a crucial criterion for smart city success. Universities, colleges, and research institutions are of course highly relevant when it comes to basic and application-oriented smart city solutions. In particular, the view of science in various research areas (ICT, digital government, urban planning, etc.) is of considerable importance (Meijer and Bolívar 2016).

Government

The final sphere relates to the public sector (government). Given the primary responsibility of providing digital infrastructure and at the same time ensuring political participation, there is always a high relevance from the perspective of the city administration. In this context, the smart city refers to a wealth of different urban house demands. The potential solutions are closely linked to technical approaches combined with intelligent strategies for introduction and implementation (Müller-Seitz et al. 2016). Areas of application include concepts of smart governance and e-governance, smart social services, smart resources and smart environment, and smart mobility and smart infrastructure (Wirtz et al. 2020).

Smart City Development in the Global Context

The intensity of urban problems will continue to increase as a result of progressive urbanization (United Nations 2019). Figure 8.2 shows how the proportion of the world's population is shifting significantly over the years and how, in addition to the already growing world population, the urban share of population is increasing significantly and will account for over 70% in 2050.

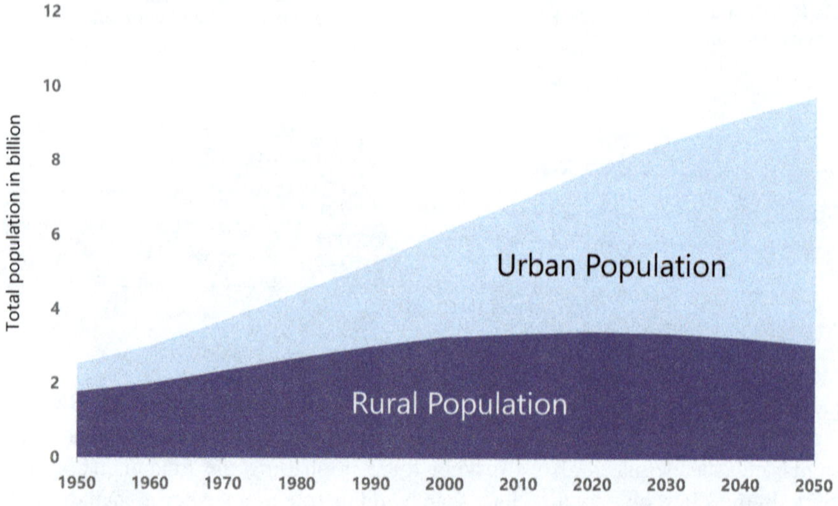

Fig. 8.2 Growth and ratio of urban to rural population. Data source: United Nations (2019)

Due to the strong increase of urban population until 2050, a proportion of more than 90% of the townspeople is expected across various countries. Figure 8.3 shows this development visually.

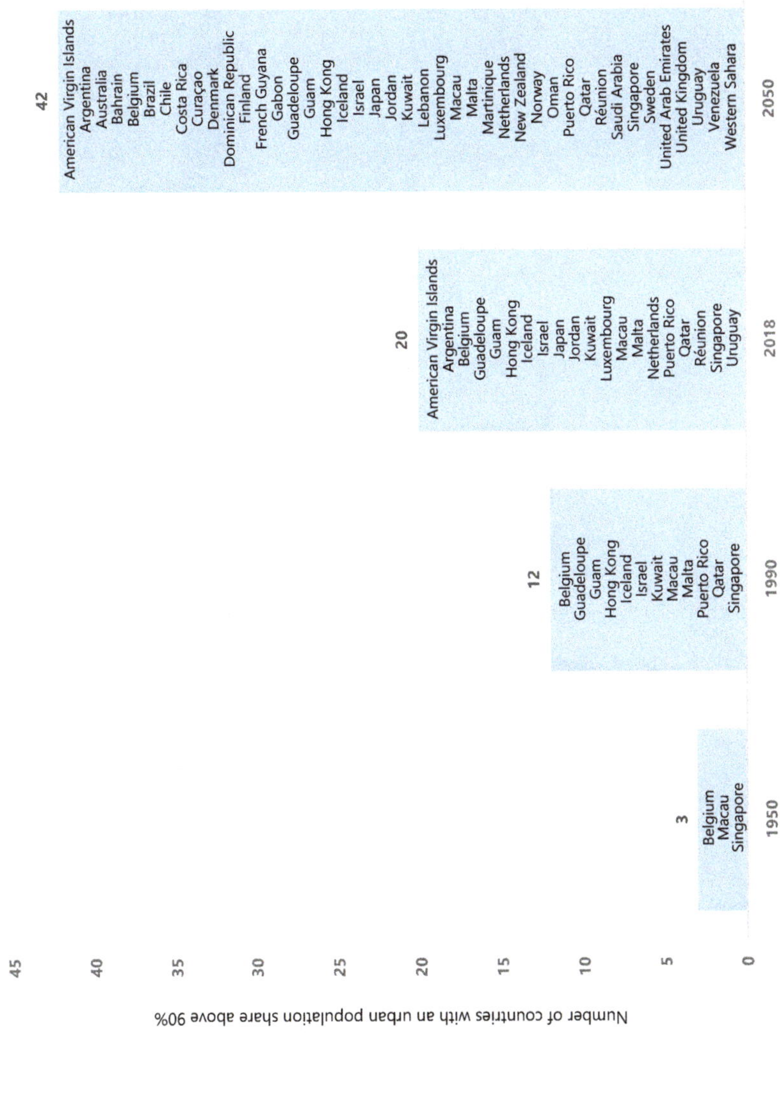

Fig. 8.3 Development of the number of countries with an urban population above 90%. Data source: United Nations (2019)

If we look at the future development, we notice that most people will not live in the so-called megacities—i.e., cities with more than 10 million inhabitants—but the majority will live in cities with less than 5 million inhabitants. Figure 8.4 shows this development of the global urban population.

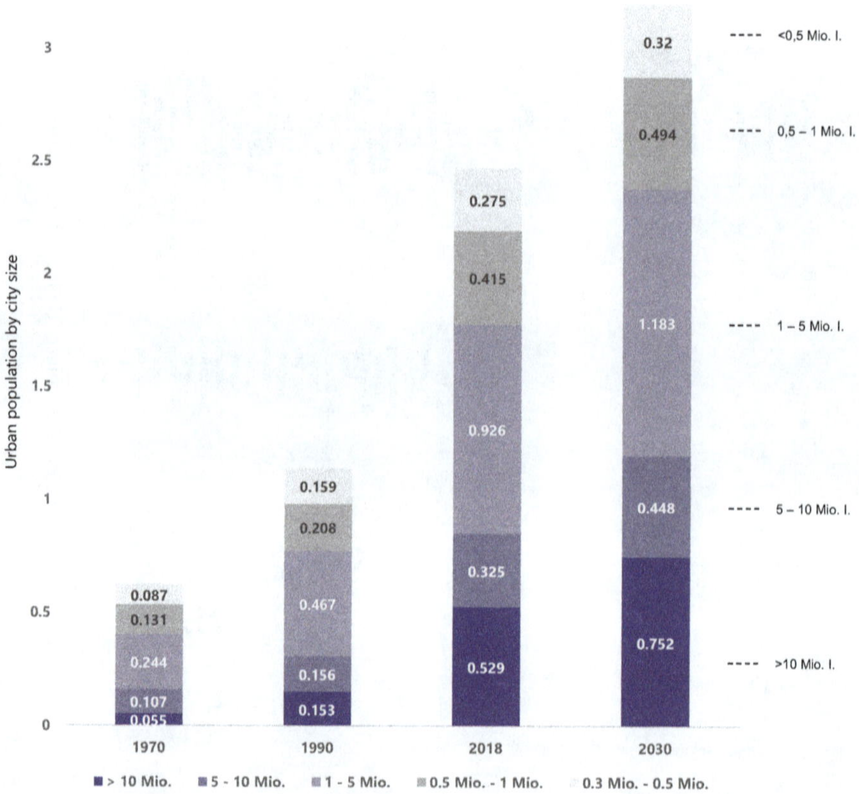

Fig. 8.4 Development of the global urban population based on respective size clusters. Data source: United Nations (2019)

Smart City Development

The history of the smart city concept is noteworthy. The first approach to an open data concept was in London and dates back to 1986 (Shields 2014). In 1994, there was a first digital city concept in Amsterdam (Anthopoulos 2017b), which already presented a digital overall system for the city. In 1999, the city of Dubai presented its first integrated smart city concept (Anthopoulos 2017b). In 2007, the first European Smart City Group was established and in 2011 the first US Smart City Group (Anthopoulos 2017b). In the context of the various launches of smart city concepts, a standard for smart cities was presented in 2014 (Anthopoulos 2017b). In 2016, a global smart city association was established at the initiative of the IEEE (Institute of Electrical and Electronics Engineers; (Anthopoulos 2017b).

Public Funding

With these fundamental developments came, of course, an increase in political relevance and public interest. Many governments published special funding programs that allowed for increased investment in cities. For example, the funding programs "Urban Innovative Actions" or URBACT from the EU Commission are important vehicles for urban innovation investments (European Commission 2021). National programs such as the German-based funding program "Smart Cities Made in Germany" also contribute significantly to an increased effort on the part of cities to accelerate their activities (Bundesministerium für Wohnen, Stadtentwicklung und Bauwesen 2021). In this context, it is not surprising that there is a significant increase in investment in the smart city services market, which is expected to exceed 2000 billion USD by 2024 (PwC 2019). Figure 8.5 presents the historical development of the smart city concept.

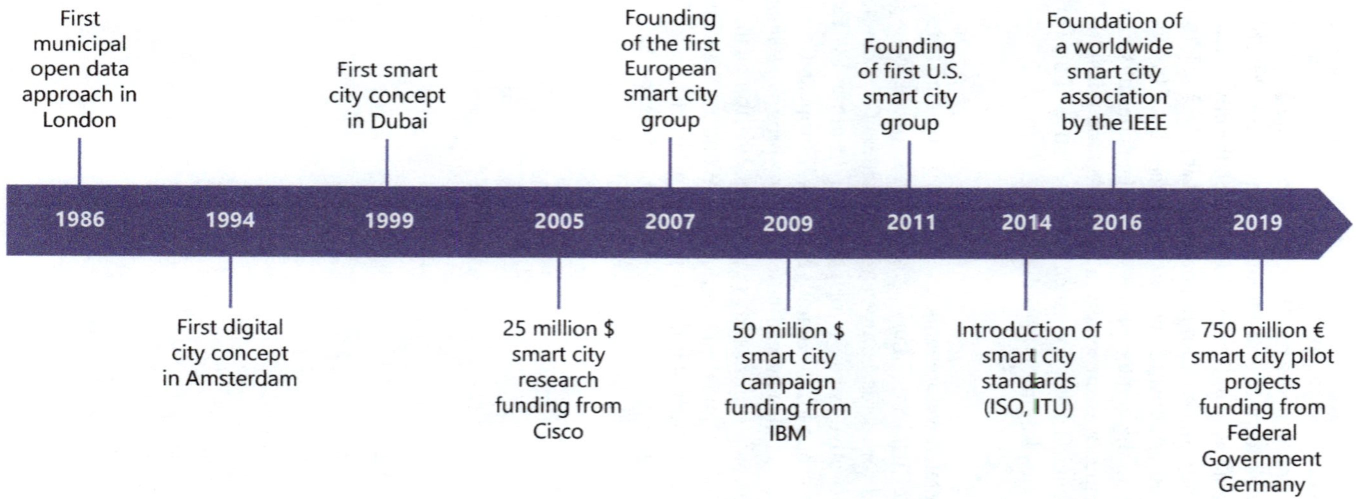

Fig. 8.5 Development of the smart city concept. Data source: Shields (2016), Anthopoulos (2017a), Bundesministerium des Innern und für Heimat (2019), GlobalData Thematic Research (2020)

Smart City Targets

The targets of a smart city are diverse. Basically, the goals can be assigned to three dimensions. First, there is the social dimension, which considers the positive impact on society, its social and cooperative interaction and basic well-being. Secondly, there is the economic dimension, which measures economic development and thus looks at the success of businesses and the associated income situation of citizens. And thirdly, there is the ecological dimension, which looks at how nature and its resources are treated and, in the context of global climate change, how emissions are reduced (Dameri and Rosenthal-Sabroux 2014). Figure 8.6 presents selected smart city targets.

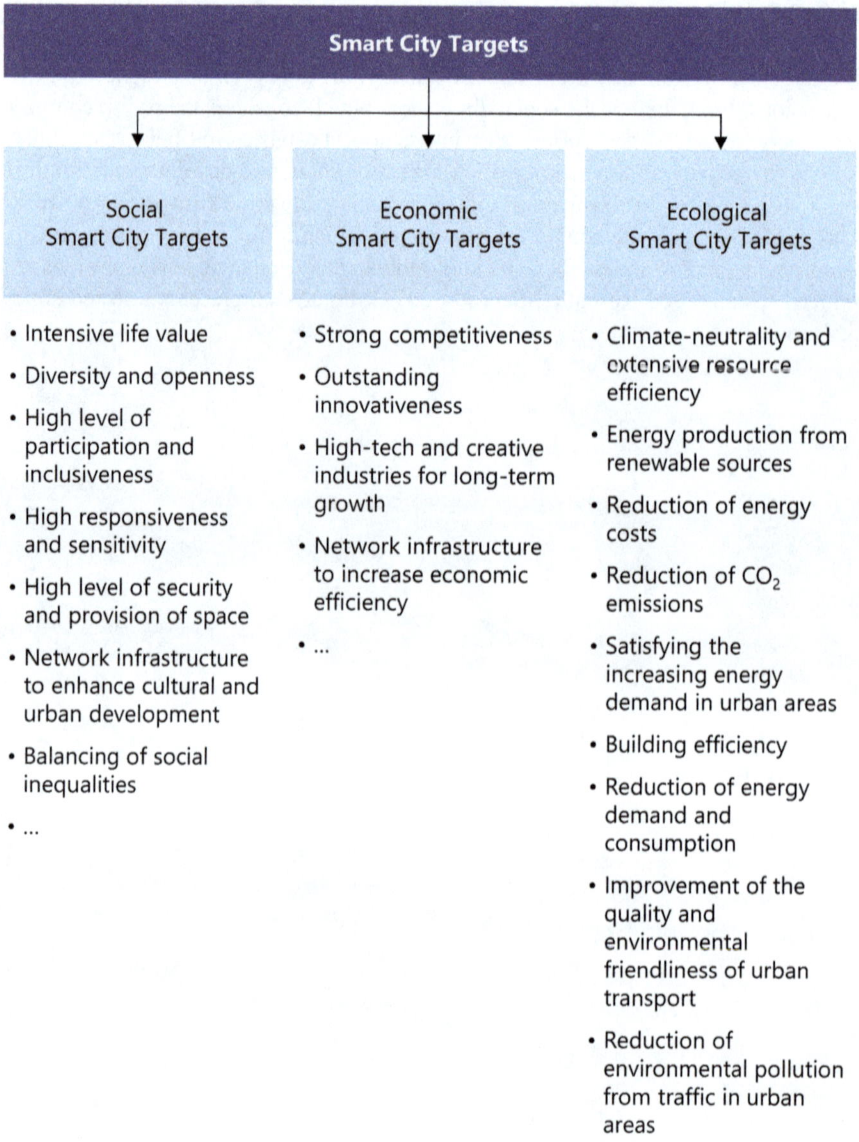

Fig. 8.6 Three target dimensions of a smart city

Improvements Through Smart Measures

According to a study by McKinsey, there are four areas in which smart city measures can bring about a significant improvement in terms of welfare optimization in the urban context (McKinsey and Organization 2018). These four are (1) Smart

Governance and E-Governance, (2) Smart Social Services, (3) Smart Resources and Smart Environment, and (4) Smart Mobility and Smart Infrastructure.

Improvements in Smart Governance

In the area of Smart Governance, which refers in particular to management aspects of the public sector and citizen participation, four concrete potentials for improvement were defined. According to estimates by the McKinsey Global Institute, smart cities can increase the sense of connection between the inhabitants and their city by up to 15%. The increase in the residents' sense of connection to their city administration is expected to be even higher, estimated at 25%. With smart cities, unemployment rates can be reduced by 1–3% and communication time with administrations can be reduced by 45–65%.

Improvements in Smart Social Services

In the area of Smart Social Services, the following improvement potentials can be expected. The burden of disease can be reduced by up to 15%, the crime rate by up to 40%, deaths due to accidents by up to 10%, and the expenditure of citizens can be reduced by up to 3%. At the same time, emergency response time can be decreased by up to 35%.

Improvements in Smart Resources and Smart Environment

In the area of Smart Resources and Smart Environment, it is expected that there will be a significant reduction in environmental damage. Greenhouse gases can be reduced by up to 15%, water consumption by up to 30%, and non-recyclable waste by up to 20% through appropriate Smart City measures.

Improvements in Smart Mobility and Smart Infrastructure

Finally, in the area of Smart Mobility and Smart Infrastructure, a reduction in travel times of up to 20% can be expected. Table 8.3 provides an overview of the most important results of the McKinsey study.

Table 8.3 Potential for improvements through smart public services

Domain	Improvement through smart services
Smart Governance & E-Governance	• Increase of the residents' sense of connection to their city by up to 15% • Increase of the residents' sense of connection to their city administration by up to 25% • Reduce the unemployment rate by 1–3% • Reduce the communication time with administrations by 45–65% • ...
Smart Social Services	• Reduction of the disease burden by 8–15% • Reduce citizen spending by 1–3% • Decrease in emergency response time by 20–35% • Reduce crime rate by 30–40% • Reduce deaths by 8–10% • Reduce health care communication time by 45–65% • ...
Smart Resources & Smart Environment	• Reduce greenhouse gas emissions by 10–15% • Reduce water consumption by 20–30% • Reduce non-recyclable waste by 10–20% • ...
Smart Mobility & Smart Infrastructure	• Reduce travel times by 15–20% • . . .

Data source: McKinsey and Organization (2018)

It is therefore evident that smart cities have a decisive influence on the welfare of citizens and the fundamental upgrading of services in cities. Several rankings elicit in their best practices this development towards more Smart City activities in the urban context.

Smart City Ranking

This can also be seen in the Smart City Ranking of the Institute for Management Development. The study shows which cities have excelled in their smart city strategies valued by respective experts. They are listed in Table 8.4.

Table 8.4 Smart city ranking

Rank	City
1	Singapore
2	Helsinki
3	Zurich
4	Auckland
5	Oslo
6	Copenhagen
7	Geneva
8	Taipei
9	Amsterdam
10	New York

Data source: Institute for Management Development (2020)

This ranking shows that the topic of smart cities is receiving special attention in Europe. Of the 10 highest-ranked smart city metropolises, six are located in Europe, two in Asia, and two in America. This can also be explained by the fact that the establishment of smart cities is seen as a means of coping with climate change, an issue that is politically more discussed in Europe than in many other regions. Especially the Green Deal initiative of the European Commission will strongly support future Smart City activities (European Commission 2022).

8.2 Smart City Concept and Services

Smart cities will be of paramount importance for social development in the future.[3] It is therefore particularly important to understand which conceptual aspects and, in particular, which services are associated with the smart city. For this reason, the basic conceptual factors and, building on them, a differentiated smart city service structure are presented below.

Smart City Service Conception

Smart cities are characterized in particular by their digital service offerings for citizens and other stakeholders. In principle, the service offerings can be mapped by a comprehensive smart city service concept. Figure 8.7 shows this integrated service concept (content based on Wirtz et al. 2021c; Wirtz and Müller 2022a).

Appropriate smart city technologies are essential for smart city services. For example, data servers, Internet/network infrastructure, and the respective end points or connected objects can be mentioned here. For connected objects in particular, Internet of Things (IoT) technology in conjunction with 5G will be of paramount importance for the development of smart cities in the future.

Based on the technology, four smart city service areas can be identified: Smart Governance and E-Government, Smart Social Services, Smart Resources and Smart Environment, and Smart Mobility and Smart Infrastructure. The smart city service portfolio can be defined within the four smart city service areas. The Smart Governance and E-Government service area includes, for example, Smart Services such as Smart Economy and Social Welfare or Smart Law and Order. The Smart Healthcare and Smart Education services, for example, can be assigned to the Smart Social Services area. The Smart Resources and Smart Environment service area includes Energy Monitoring and Smart Waste and Recycling services. The Smart Mobility and Smart Infrastructure service area includes in particular the Smart Transportation and Freight and Smart Mobility and Traffic services.

[3] See for the following Section Smart City Concept and Services also Wirtz (2022); Wirtz et al. (2021c); Wirtz/Müller (2022a, b).

Smart City services are delivered to users through various Smart City distribution channels. E-mails, official websites, and social media are exemplary distribution channels. Basically, three different interfaces can be distinguished between smart cities and users: Function-oriented interfaces emphasize aspects such as the functionality of the interaction environment. Service-oriented interfaces emphasize aspects of the offer, such as the offer of a complaint management system. User-oriented interfaces focus on user-relevant aspects such as IT security and privacy.

Building on the smart city distribution channels, the smart city user level is the final stage in smart city service construction. Here, the three user groups citizens, private organizations, and public organizations may be differentiated.

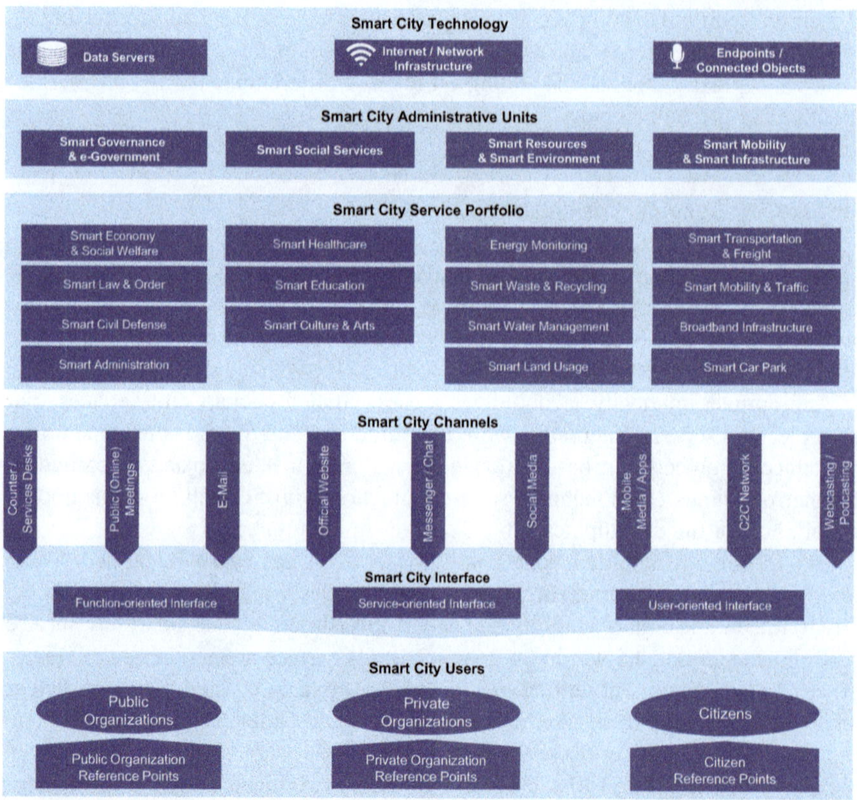

Fig. 8.7 Smart City Service Provision Framework

The Smart City Service Provision Framework shows that the Smart City is based on a network of actors. The actors have different meanings and a variety of interactions. Figure 8.8 shows this stakeholder network.

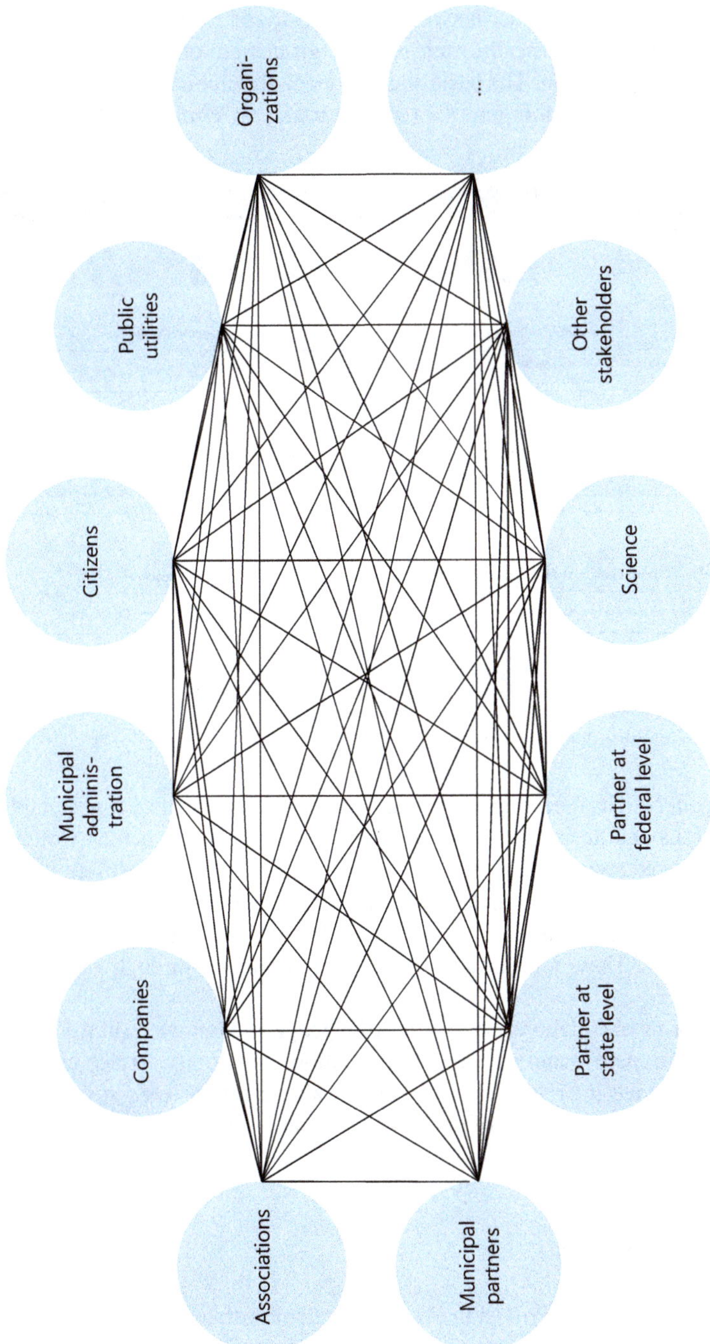

Fig. 8.8 Smart city stakeholder network

The smart city stakeholder network is characterized by a high level of collaboration and co-creation. Basically, four primary groups are of particular relevance for collaborative co-creation. The basic smart city collaboration model for these primary actor groups is shown in Figure 8.9 (content based on Wirtz and Müller 2022b).

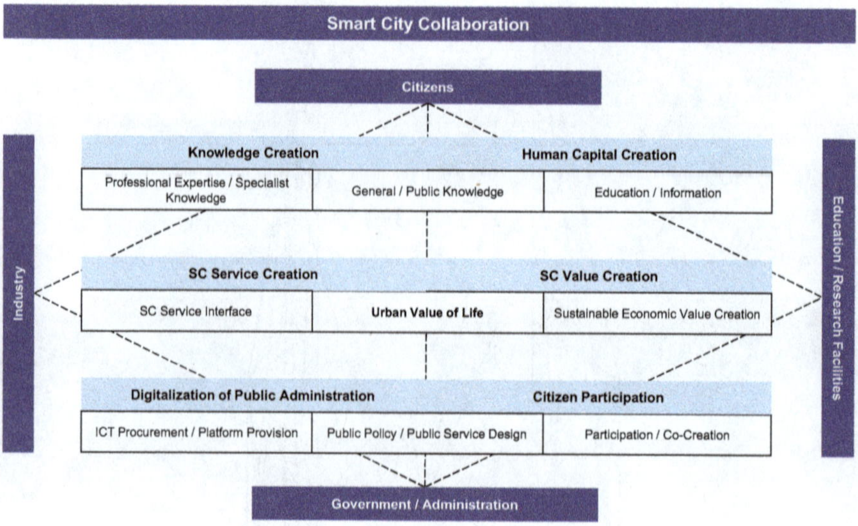

Fig. 8.9 Smart city collaboration model

The model elicits the complex structure and the difficulty of finding suitable smart city solutions and decisions in co-creation among the various actors. Collaboration basically characterizes the cooperation and joint development of different smart city services and values. The Smart City Collaboration model consists of four primary groups of actors: Citizens, education/research institutions, administration, and industry/other actors. These four groups of actors are connected through various forms of collaboration.

These forms of collaboration include knowledge and human capital creation (e.g., professional expertise and education/information), smart city service creation (e.g., smart city service interface) and smart city value creation (e.g., sustainable urban value creation), digitalization of public administration (e.g., platform provision), and citizen participation (e.g. participation).

Smart City Services

The Smart City Service Provision Framework demonstrates that there are four basic service areas: Smart Governance and E-Government, Smart Social Services, Smart Resources and Smart Environment, and Smart Mobility and Smart Infrastructure. Figure 8.10 shows these service areas with their subcategories.

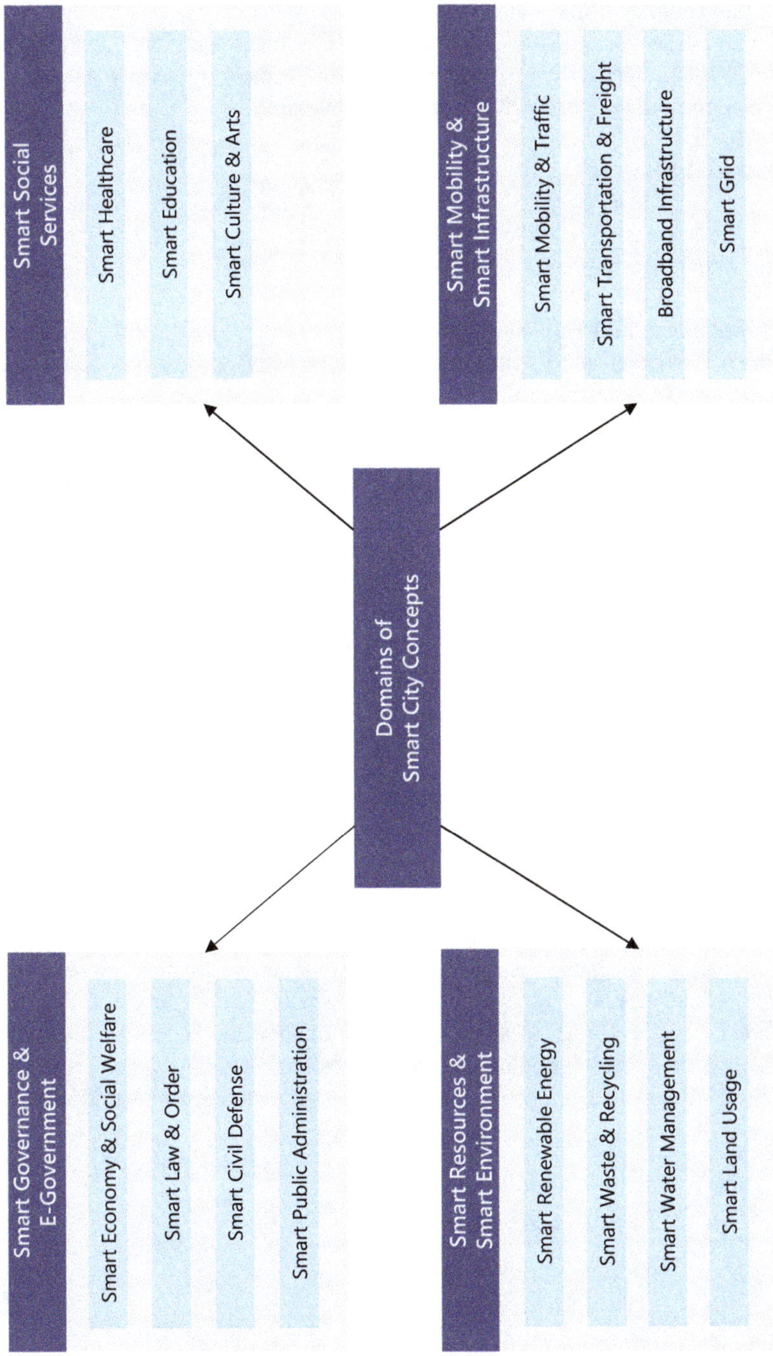

Fig. 8.10 Stakeholder domains of smart city concepts

Smart Governance and E-Governance

The Smart Governance and E-Government area includes traditional administrative services at the municipal level. These include, for example, smart city services such as the electronic ID card or an app for disaster warning.

Smart Social Services

The Smart Social Services area includes health, education, and cultural services. These include smart city services such as telemedicine, public online libraries, and apps for interactive city tours.

Smart Resources and Environment

The Smart Resources and Environment area includes offerings from the municipal utilities. These include smart city services such as energy supply or a smart electricity meter.

Smart Mobility and Smart Infrastructure

The Smart Mobility and Smart Infrastructure segment includes public transport and infrastructure services. These contain smart city services such as bike-sharing systems, cab apps, and public Wi-Fi infrastructure.

In principle, the smart service areas can be further differentiated, resulting in a service portfolio with individual services. Figure 8.11 demonstrates a differentiated smart city portfolio that reveals a large number of individual services (content based on Wirtz and Müller 2022a). The smart city portfolio illustrates in particular that the smart city is characterized by a high level of complexity and a large number of services.

Smart City Demand Structure

The success of smart city services is centrally related to the demand structure (Wirtz et al. 2012, 2016; Piehler et al. 2016). The demand structure represents the preferences and needs of the "smart city customers." Smart city activities must therefore always be fundamentally aligned with the demand needs and preferences. This section therefore highlights the preferences of smart city users. To this end, study results based on a comprehensive lead user survey in Germany are presented.[4]

[4] See for the following sections also Wirtz et al. (2021c).

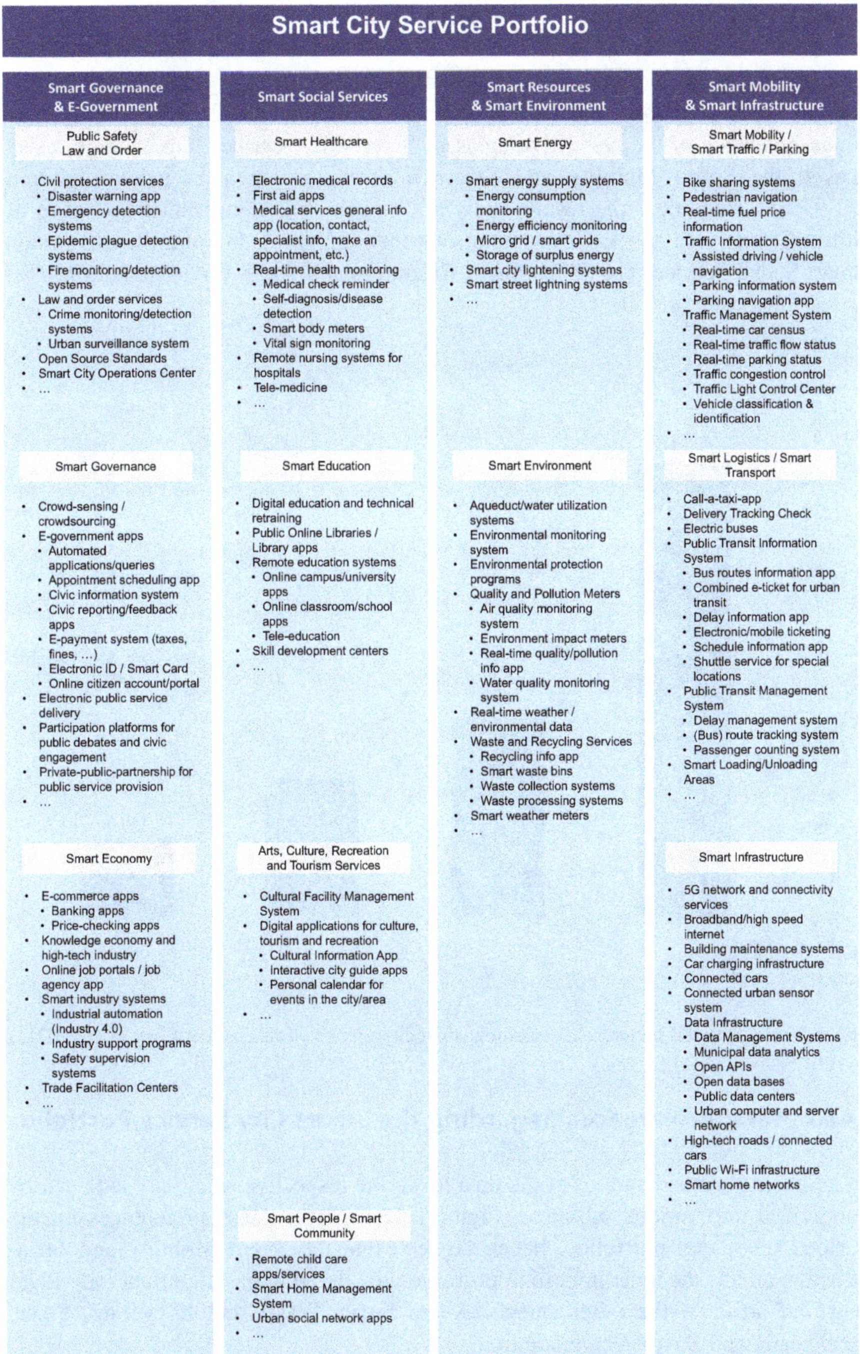

Fig. 8.11 Smart city service portfolio

Lead Users' Preferences Regarding Smart City Services

Smart city service preferences of users differ fundamentally with respect to the various smart city portfolios (Wirtz et al. 2021a). Figure 8.12 shows the average usage relevance of the respective areas of Smart City services. On average, users ranked the Smart Mobility and Smart Infrastructure area as most important (51.97%). In addition, the results show a lower but still significant importance of Smart Governance and E-Government Services (22.93%). In contrast, users rated Smart Social Services (16.08%), Smart Resources and Smart Environment (9.01%) as less important.

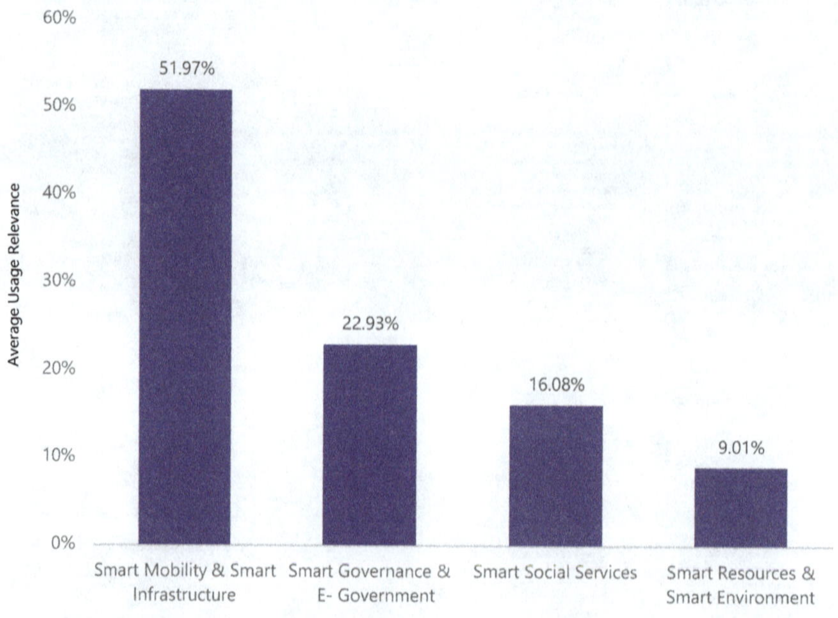

Fig. 8.12 Lead users' preferences regarding smart city services. Data source: Wirtz et al. (2021c)

Lead Users' Preferences Regarding the Smart City Service Portfolio

In addition to considerations at the area level, the respective smart city area can be subdivided into various sub-areas. Figure 8.13 shows the user preferences for the various smart city portfolios. It can be seen that the Smart Mobility and Infrastructure area is the most important portfolio area. In addition, important individual portfolio areas in the other categories are Smart Waste and Recycling, Smart Healthcare, and Smart Administration.

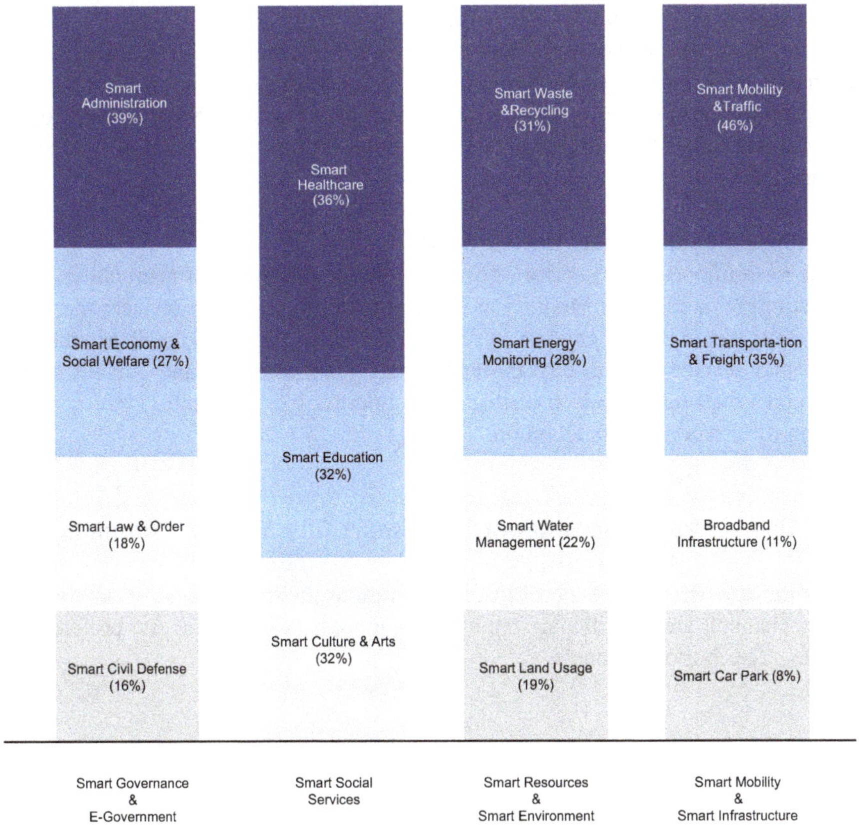

Fig. 8.13 Participants' preferences for different smart city service domains. Data source: Wirtz et al. (2021c)

Smart Governance and E-Government

Smart governance and e-government show a high relevance of supplementing municipal administration with ICT-supported smart service solutions (39%) and providing "smart solutions" for the economy and institutions entrusted with maintaining social standards (27%). By contrast, users rate the future smart services of the judicial authorities as less important (18%) and indicate a rather low level of interest in the Civil Defense providing smart services for the urban public (16%).

Smart Social Services

In the area of Smart Social Services, the sub-areas are of roughly equal importance to users. Smart Art and Culture (32%), Smart Education (32%), and Smart Health Care (36%) can therefore be regarded as equally important.

Smart Resources and Smart Environment

With regard to the Smart Resources and Smart Environment service area, users emphasize the importance of smart solutions for waste disposal and recycling (31%) and for monitoring energy consumption and distribution (28%). Smart Social Services and Smart Environmental Services, however, appear to be of only secondary interest.

Smart Mobility and Smart Infrastructure

As the most important sub-sector of Smart Mobility and Smart Infrastructure, users most strongly rated Smart Mobility and Transportation, i.e., those services that help users cover distances in a city (46%). In addition, users also rated the distribution of goods and services in the city through Smart Transportation and Freight as an important urban task, while broadband and internet infrastructure (11%) and car parking (8%) received less attention.

Lead Users' Preferences Regarding Smart City Service Channels

In addition to the service portfolio considerations in the demand structure, the service channels are of particular importance. Figure 8.14 shows the user preferences for these distribution channels.

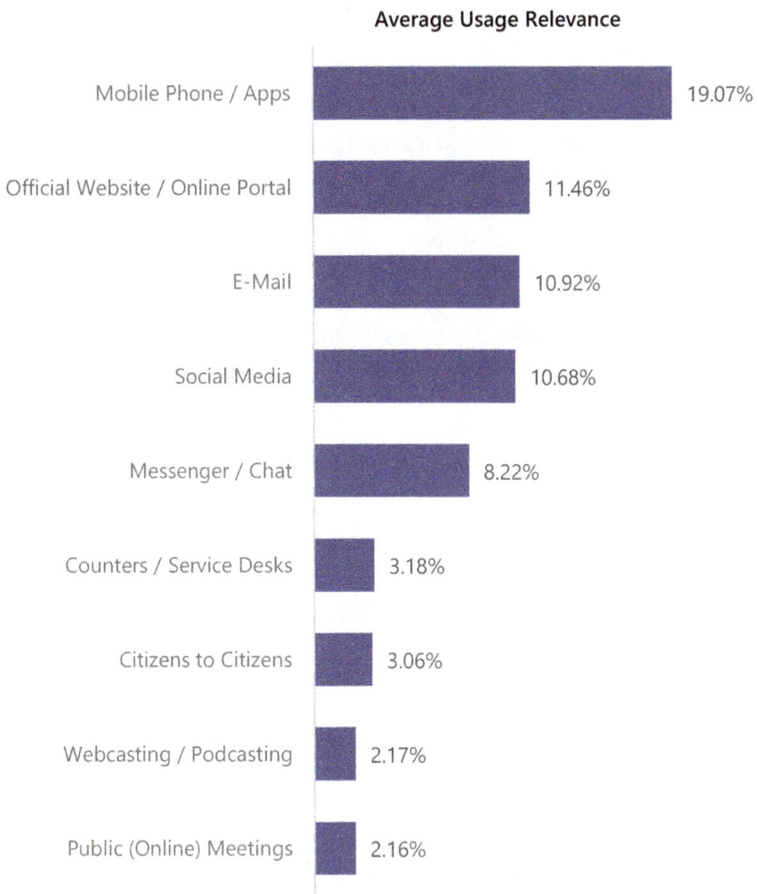

Fig. 8.14 Preferences of smart city service channels. Data source: Wirtz et al. (2021c)

The most important channel for smart city users is by far the cell phone with corresponding app solutions (19.02%). In addition, access to online services via official websites and online portals (11.46%) or via e-mail accounts (10.92%) is still of great importance to users. Furthermore, forms of online interaction and communication via social media (10.68%) or via messenger/chat rooms (8.22%) are equally moderately preferred, while users predominantly reject traditional forms of service interaction via counters/service desks (3.18%) and public meetings (2.16%), thus showing a significantly lower relevance.

Characteristics of Successful Smart Cities

In principle, the identification of characteristics of successful smart cities in the form of effective, efficient, and user-centered service provision is highly relevant. Three success dimensions of smart city services can be distinguished: functional, service-oriented, and technological success.

Function-Oriented Success Factors

With regard to the function-oriented success factors, user-friendliness and user orientation are decisive for successful smart services (12.23%). In addition, quality of information and service (9.08%) and responsiveness to citizen concerns (7.99%) also represent important function-oriented success factors for smart city services. In addition, success factors related to the implementation of mobile applications (4.93%) and social media (3.32%) as intermediaries of smart city services are minor in contrast to the results of a previous survey (Wirtz et al. 2021b, c). The results are presented in Figure 8.15.

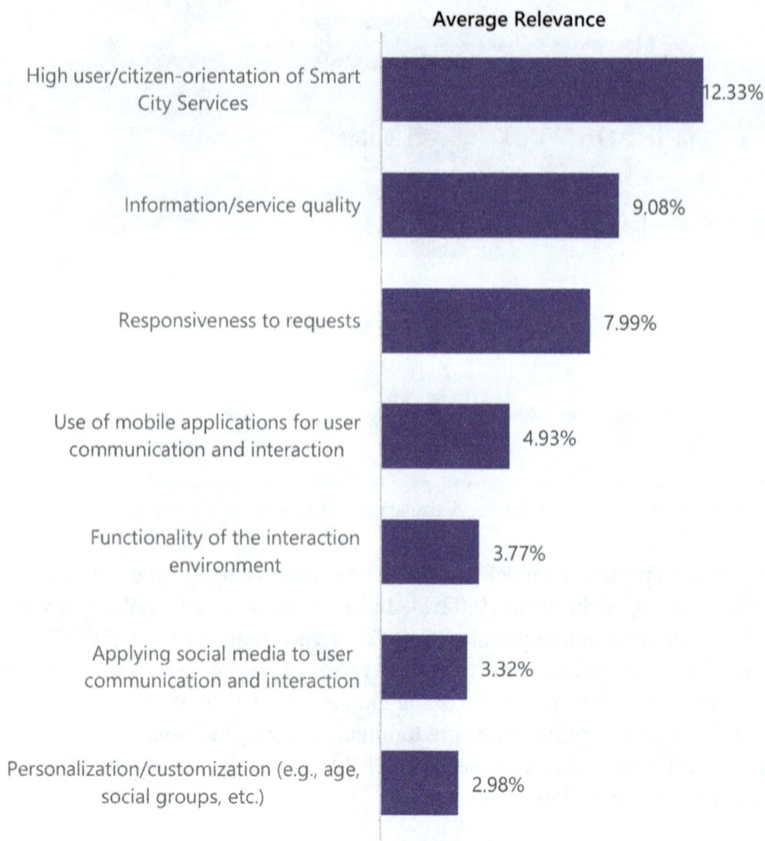

Fig. 8.15 Functional user demands of smart cities. Data source: Wirtz et al. (2021c)

Service-Oriented Success Factors

In terms of service-oriented success factors, a comprehensive range of complete online services of a smart city (11.40%) with a broad spectrum of smart city services (7.15%) is particularly important to users. The ability for users to track the processing status of their requests online and thus make public administration processes more transparent and comprehensible is also cited by users as an important feature of smart city service systems (6.83%). Participatory smart city services (2.97%) and open access to urban data (2.52%) are given a rather low relevance. Figure 8.16 illustrates these results.

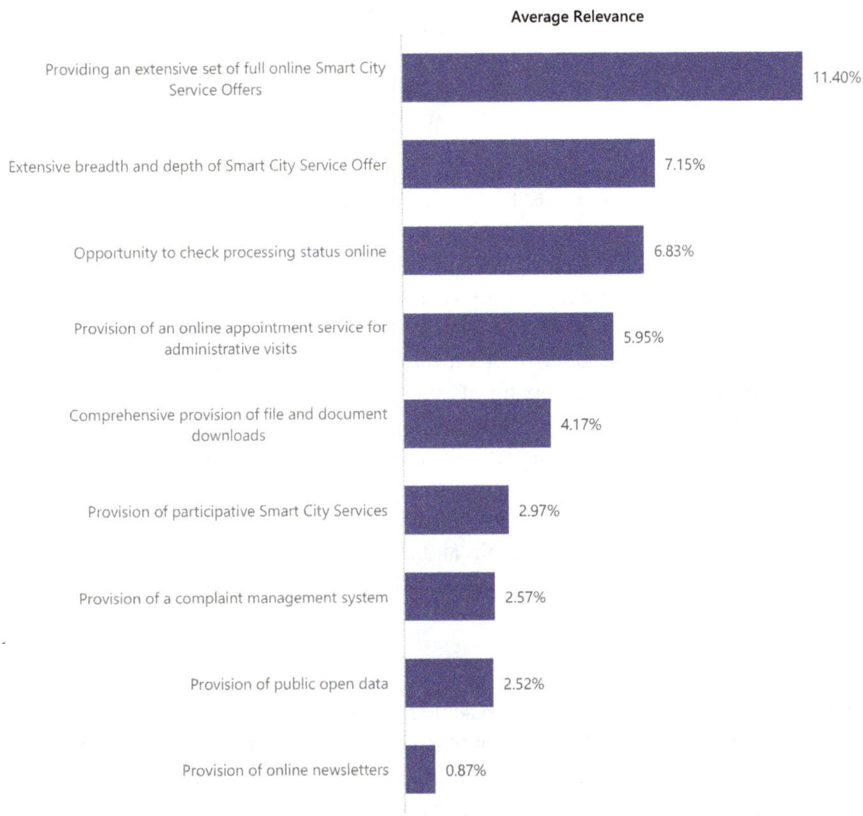

Fig. 8.16 Smart city performance user demands. Data source: Wirtz et al. (2021c)

Technological Success Factors

In addition to the function and service-oriented success factors of smart city services, the technological characteristics of the system are an essential prerequisite for the successful use of smart services. The success factors associated with IT technology are important for building a citywide data system. The most relevant technological IT characteristics of smart city implementation are shown in Figure 8.17.

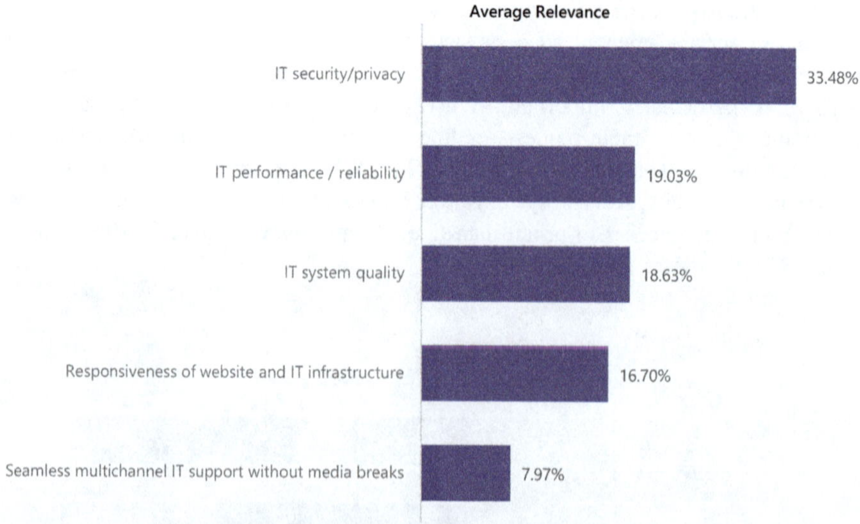

Fig. 8.17 Smart city IT user demands. Data source: Wirtz et al. (2021c)

According to users, IT security and privacy are the most important factors for smart services (33.4%). In addition, users also rated the reliability, robustness, and performance of the system as relevant factors for the success of smart urban services (19.03%). In addition, the quality of the IT system, which includes accessibility, system interoperability, and compatibility with users' devices, is cited as a somewhat important aspect for the success of the smart city system (18.63%), along with the responsiveness of related software and websites (16.70%). In contrast, the presence and accessibility of smart services across a variety of channels appears to be of low importance to the success of smart city services (7.97%). This suggests that users are more interested in establishing reliable and secure online and mobile city services than in seamless delivery of services across all channels available through technical capabilities.

Lead User Preferences

Basically, the results of the study presented show a clear preference of users for smart mobility services and for smart public administration. In addition, users show a high preference for digital channels, i.e. mobile applications, online platforms or websites, compared to traditional analog channels such as public meetings or service counters. Analog channels are expected to become increasingly less important for accessing smart city services. Furthermore, usability is a key primacy for smart urban services offered in smart cities and the provision of a wide range of services with versatile service features while ensuring the reliability, robustness, and security of the underlying IT system.

In smart cities, a large number of services can be found in the various smart city service areas. However, the service areas and individual services do not exist as isolated phenomena in the smart city, but are part of a system of offerings and uses, which is also referred to as the smart city ecosystem. The Smart City Ecosystem is presented in the following section.

8.3 Smart City Ecosystem and Implementation

Smart cities are characterized by a multitude of actors, interactions, and services.[5] In principle, this complex urban system can be represented in the form of an ecosystem. An ecosystem basically represents a network of several actors that are characterized by a common value creation. In biology, an ecosystem is originally understood as a habitat of organisms of several species. In the smart city context, the smart city ecosystem can be described as a network of different actors and interactions in a common system that has several functional or object areas. The Smart City Ecosystem as a central concept for representing the urban value creation process is presented in more detail in the following sections.

Smart City Ecosystem

The term digital ecosystems describes the idea of an environment based on digital means.[6] It is related to the concept of ecosystems, which is a concept inspired by biology and ecology (Scaringella and Radziwon 2018) and outlines the accord of numerous organizations that "coevolve capabilities around a new innovation: they work cooperatively and competitively to support new products, satisfy [...] needs, and eventually incorporate the next round of innovations" (Moore 1993, p. 76).

Smart City Ecosystem Definition
Accordingly, in contrast to the traditional view of value chains, an ecosystem contains all actors affecting processes even those outside of the linear value creation process (Clarysse et al. 2014; Iansiti and Levien 2004). Thus, value creation loses its linearity (Moore 1996) and spreads in a network of interrelated organizations, which contribute their specific mechanisms to the realization of an overall purpose (Christensen and Rosenbloom 1995). The merging in an ecosystem therefore enables value creation that none of the actors involved would achieve individually (Adner 2006).

Cooperation and Competition
According to Moore (1993), participants of a digital ecosystem cooperate by collaboratively providing value to the user. Consequently, there is exchange between the participants, which is of a collaborative and of competitive nature. Therefore, the various models might incorporate market structures and value chain components. An

[5] See for the following Section Smart City Ecosystem and Implementation also Wirtz (2021, 2022); Wirtz/Müller (2022a, b).

[6] See for the following Section Smart City Ecosystem also Wirtz et al. (2020); Wirtz (2021); Wirtz and Müller (2022b).

interaction layer assigns specific roles to the various parties, and ultimately, determines the activities of each stakeholder in terms of value creation and capture within a specific ecosystem.

Ecosystem Perspective

Participation in urban ecosystems brings actors more innovation and access to new users. However, many actors find it difficult to define the strategic approach and goals for their specific role in an ecosystem, as these require, for example, new ways of thinking and a better distribution of resources. Such steps help to quickly develop and successfully merge products and services. For successful collaboration within the ecosystem, leaders need to fundamentally change their mindset and add the ecosystem perspective to their business perspective. They need to allow their ecosystem partners to play to their strengths.

Smart and Urban Ecosystems

There are different understandings of smart urban ecosystems. They can be seen as a proprietary platform environment with a high degree of compatibility that attracts a variety of actors who build their activities on the platform environment.

The other understanding refers to a macro perspective that includes various actors who build their activities largely on digital means. It also includes different stakeholders with different backgrounds, such as businesses, consumers, NGOs, and the state/city authorities. Such an inclusive understanding requires a unified definition of smart ecosystems. It refers to an interconnected context of multiple digital actors, value chains, and business relationships that form a dynamic, complex, and relational structure representing all digital transactions that are more productive and effective together than individually.

> **Definition of Smart City Ecosystem (Wirtz 2021)**
> A smart city ecosystem is an integrated framework of different actors, value chains, and organizational relationships that represent all smart city activities leading to a dynamic and complex relationship network that collaboratively creates value.

In order to postulate and govern the essentials and their interrelationships, a complex ecosystem needs to be subdivided into "a number of related groups of organizations" (Iansiti and Levien 2004). The main socioeconomic interest groups, i.e. stakeholders, represent an essential subdivision of the ecosystem's actors. In this sense, it is important to differentiate the activity and influence of stakeholders and create a structure without neglecting the overlapping nature of many of these spheres.

Sub-models of a Digital Ecosystem

Figure 8.18 presents the respective sub-models within an entire digital ecosystem (content based on Wirtz 2021; Wirtz and Müller 2022b). The integrative consideration of the various elements of an ecosystem shows that a comprehensive approach includes the digital ecosystem structure (governance model, collaboration model, interaction and services model) and the digital ecosystem technical operations (software infrastructure model, physical infrastructure model).

In order to structure the complex setup of a smart urban ecosystem, it is important to model its characteristics and interdependencies. Such ecosystems can be simplified and differentiated according to their technical basis, which enables all processes, "the technical processes of the digital infrastructure," and the organizational levels, "the structure of the ecosystem."

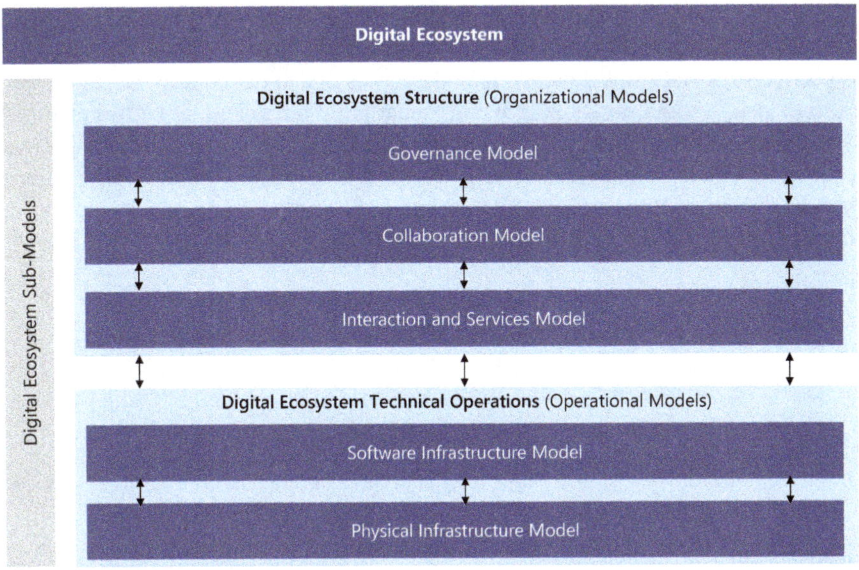

Fig. 8.18 Sub-models of a digital ecosystem. Source: Wirtz et al. (2021b)

Organizational Models

Organizational models determine the generation of knowledge assets, the function of collective learning mechanisms, and the efficiency and reliability of information transactions between research institutions, agencies, industry, and the users. Combining the sub-models into a sound conceptual model requires a detailed insight into scientific progress compared to the findings of previous ecosystem approaches.

Three levels define the structure of the smart ecosystem and thus address the area of organizational models. The governance model describes the regulatory context with laws, conventions, subsidies and incentive systems, etc. The collaboration model describes the cooperation between important stakeholder groups. The interaction and service model describes the complex process of value creation within a specific smart ecosystem.

Operational Models

The technical basis of smart ecosystems, the "technical operation of the digital infrastructure," consists of two layers, the software infrastructure, which refers to all software-related aspects, and the physical infrastructure, which refers to all hardware aspects.

Integrated Framework of a Smart City

The sub-models of a smart city ecosystem are a rather abstract representation of different layers that can be further explained with an interlocking framework of the different layers. In addition to the question of what should be made available to the respective smart city stakeholders, it is also necessary to define how these services are provided, i.e. the functioning of the underlying hardware and software (infrastructure model) as well as the design of the interactions between the different actors involved in smart city service delivery (business model).[7] Figure 8.19 represents a detailed flowchart of the various components and layers of the smart city ecosystem framework (content based on Wirtz 2021; Wirtz and Müller 2022a, b).

[7]See for the following Section Integrated Framework of a Smart City also Wirtz and Müller (2022b).

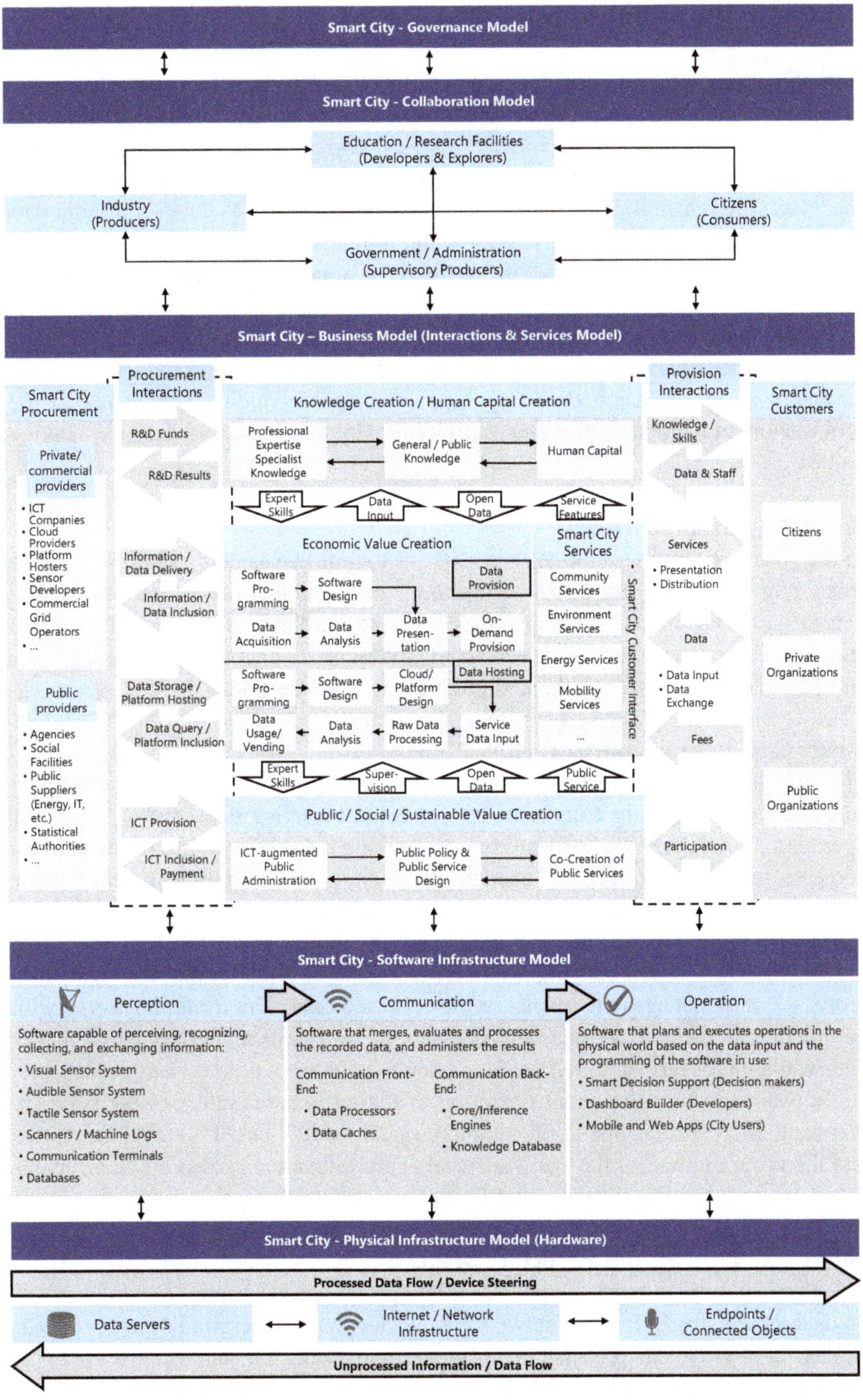

Fig. 8.19 Integrated smart city ecosystem framework

Smart City Governance and Collaboration

Both the strategic content orientation and the technical design of a smart city are part of the guidelines of a specific smart city policy. Such a policy provides the direction for the development and implementation of the corresponding (building) measures and sets a reference point for the review of the development progress by means of a roadmap. The transmission of large amounts of data as well as the use of large data servers with built-in machine evaluation algorithms also requires the establishment of a backup and control component for the entire smart city system (Chauhan et al. 2016).

In the first step of the regulatory process, both the policy and the strategic direction of the smart city system are set by policy makers and subsequently defined in the decision-making bodies (e.g., the municipal council). This leads to the formulation and adoption of a smart city policy by the respective decision-making bodies.

Smart City Business Model

In the smart city business model, the input factors of private and public actors of a smart city are displayed. These contribute to the public value creation (service generation). The various smart city services represent the result of the public value creation. These are made available to smart city users (in the form of citizens, private and public organizations) as the end product of value creation.

Smart City Software Infrastructure Model

The software infrastructure model illustrates a data logistics process consisting of software for recognizing data, software for communicating data, and software for operating digital systems. Software for recognizing data refers to programs that can perceive, recognize, collect, and exchange data about the environment. This is done on the basis of visual sensor systems, acoustic sensor systems, tactile sensor systems, scanners or machine protocols, communication terminals and databases.

Software for communicating data refers to software that combines, evaluates, processes, and manages the results of the collected data. The front end works with the previously recognized data by processing or storing data. The back-end makes data available for further activities, for example in the form of knowledge databases.

Software for the subsequent operation of digital systems refers to the software that plans and executes operations in the physical world—based on the data entered and the programming of the software used. This software can also be described as user-specific operating software that forms the user interface.

Smart City Physical Infrastructure Model

The physical infrastructure model basically represents a hardware fundament based on data servers, the Internet or network architecture, and corresponding endpoints or connected objects. The physical infrastructure represents the data usage cycle. This consists, on the one hand, of a download stream, which accesses the stored data in databases through the network and, on the other hand, of an upload stream, which uploads the data from the end devices of the users to the respective databases.

The success of the entire smart city ecosystem is generated by efficient and effective management with appropriate governance specifications. Therefore, the smart city governance model is crucial for the creation of public value.

Smart City Ecosystem Governance Model

As the smart city ecosystem is a complex and regulation-intensive structure, the control or management aspect is of particular importance. Control or governance in the smart city context is of particular importance in order to ensure a user-oriented contribution to success across all groups of actors and interactions. Figure 8.20 presents a governance model showing the steps involved in bringing about an appropriate smart city strategy (content based on Wirtz and Müller 2022b).

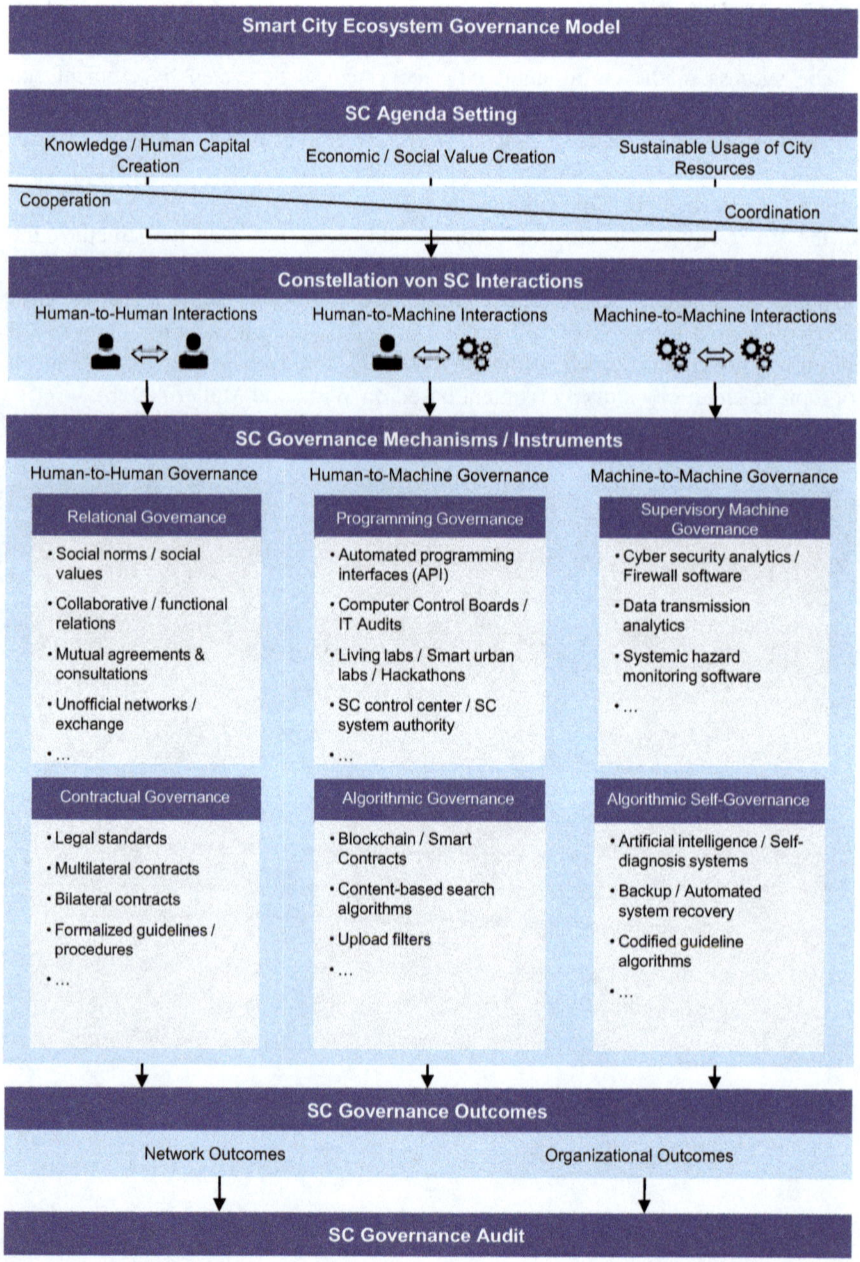

Fig. 8.20 Smart city ecosystem governance model

In principle, there is a need to define a smart city agenda with regard to knowledge/human capital creation, economic/social value creation, and the sustainable use of city resources. In this context, it is important to define target-oriented rules for cooperation and coordination between the actors.

Based on the SC agenda with the corresponding objectives and the distribution of cooperative/coordinative tasks, three constellations of smart city interactions can be distinguished: Human-to-Human interactions, Human-to-Machine interactions, and Machine-to-Machine interactions. These interactions in turn have specific smart city governance mechanisms or instruments.

In human-to-human governance interaction, a distinction can be made between the mechanisms of relational governance and contractual governance. Relational governance instruments include, for example, social norms/social values and collaborative/functional relationships. Contractual governance instruments include legal standards and multilateral agreements.

In human-to-machine governance, a distinction can be made between programming governance and algorithmic governance mechanisms. Programming governance instruments include, for example, automated programming interfaces (APIs) and computer control boards/IT audits. Algorithmic governance instruments include blockchain/smart contracts and content-based search algorithms.

In machine-to-machine governance, a distinction can be made between the mechanisms of supervisory machine governance and algorithmic self-governance. Instruments of supervisory machine governance include, for example, cyber security analytics/firewall software and data transmission analytics. Algorithmic self-governance tools include artificial intelligence/self-diagnostic systems and backup/automated system recovery.

It can be seen that there are different control and governance options depending on the interaction structure with regard to the human and machine recipients. These are essentially based on the fact that human and machine actor structures are subject to different personnel, organizational and technological characteristics. The effective and efficient control of these different forms of interaction ultimately leads to a value creation contribution. This can also be divided into a network and organizational value result. The result and the governance mechanisms that build on it should be subjected to an audit in a final step, which checks the effectiveness and efficiency of the governance and identifies potential for improvement.

Smart City Ecosystem Implementation

In addition to the governance of a smart city, its organizational implementation is of particular importance. This requires organizational implementation of the smart city concept and the ecosystem. Figure 8.21 shows an example of smart city organizational implementation.

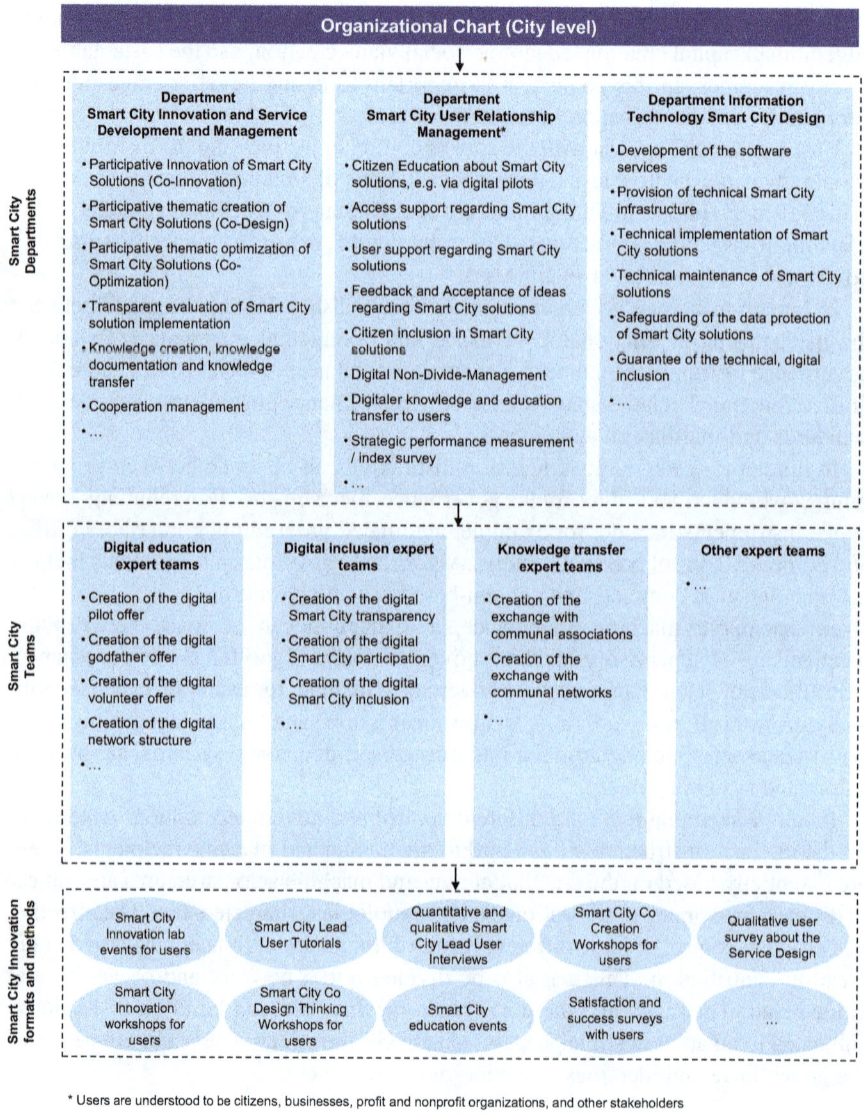

Fig. 8.21 Organizational design within Smart Cities

Figure 8.21 shows that the establishment of three organizational departments for the development, cooperation, and interaction of smart city services is particularly useful for the organizational implementation of a smart city. The first department relates to smart city innovation and service development/management. The second department refers to smart city user relationship management and the third department is related to smart city design based on information technology. The respective departments focus on different tasks, which enable the goal-oriented fulfillment of Smart Cities activities.

Based on the departments, various smart city teams can be formed. These teams can take on specific, particularly relevant tasks within a smart city on a temporary or permanent basis. These project work teams reflect the dynamic task character of the smart city and ensure optimal adaptation of all organizational activities. For the organizational design, the selection and organizational consideration of appropriate innovation formats and methods is also useful, which the smart city departments and project teams can use. In the context of cooperative and participative smart city development, design thinking workshops, qualitative user surveys, or innovation platform forums can be cited as promising methods of joint value creation.

On the basis of the implementation of the smart city service concept and organization, measuring the success of a city's smart city activities is of paramount importance, since all activities must be measured against the value contributions generated for the various stakeholders.

Basically, four different index success measurement areas can be identified here. Figure 8.22 shows a strategic smart city success measurement of the external stakeholders.

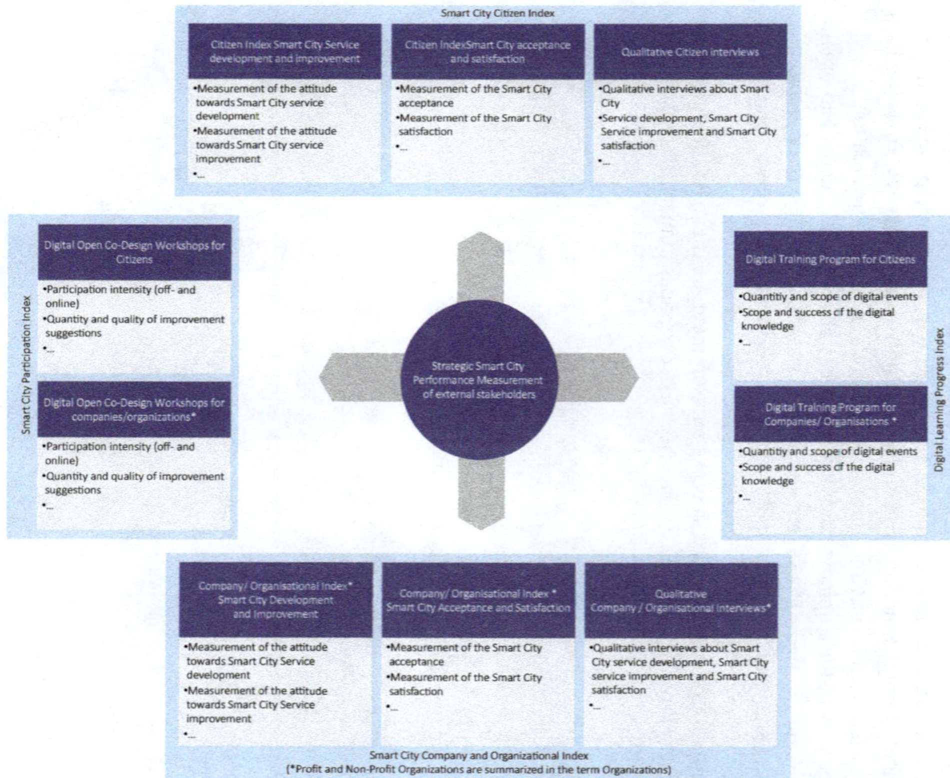

Fig. 8.22 Strategic smart city performance measurement of the external stakeholders

The first area, the Smart City Citizen Index, can be divided into the three sub-areas: Citizen Index Smart City Service Development and Improvement (e.g., measuring attitudes toward Smart City Service Development), Citizen Index Smart City Acceptance and Satisfaction (e.g., measuring Smart City Acceptance), and Qualitative Citizen Interviews (e.g., on Smart City Service Development, Smart City Service Improvement, and Smart City Satisfaction).

The second domain, the Digital Learning Progress Index, can be divided into Digital Training Programs for Citizens (e.g., number and scope of digital events) and Digital Training Programs for Businesses/Organizations (e.g., number and scope of digital events). The third area, the Smart City Organization and Organization Index, includes the three sub-areas Organization/Organization Index Smart City Service Development and Improvement (e.g., measuring attitudes toward Smart City Service Development), Organization/Organization Index Smart City Acceptance and Satisfaction (e.g., measuring Smart City Acceptance), and Qualitative Organization/Organization Interviews (e.g., Qualitative Interviews on Smart City Service Development, Smart City Service Improvement, and Smart City Satisfaction).

The fourth area, the Smart City Participation Index, can be divided into the areas of digital open co-design workshops for citizens (e.g., participation intensity—offline and online) and digital open co-design workshops for companies/organizations (e.g., participation intensity—offline and online).

In principle, the indices listed here can be collected from stakeholders through quantitative surveys, workshops, or interviews. It is important that the survey results are consistently aligned with the future design of the smart city service. This means that the customers of the smart city services represent the central focus and orientation point of all smart city activities.

Building on the measurement of success, an integrated strategic smart city success audit/evaluation system is useful for the successful implementation and continuation of a smart city. This is illustrated in Figure 8.23 (content based on Wirtz 2021; Wirtz and Daiser 2017).

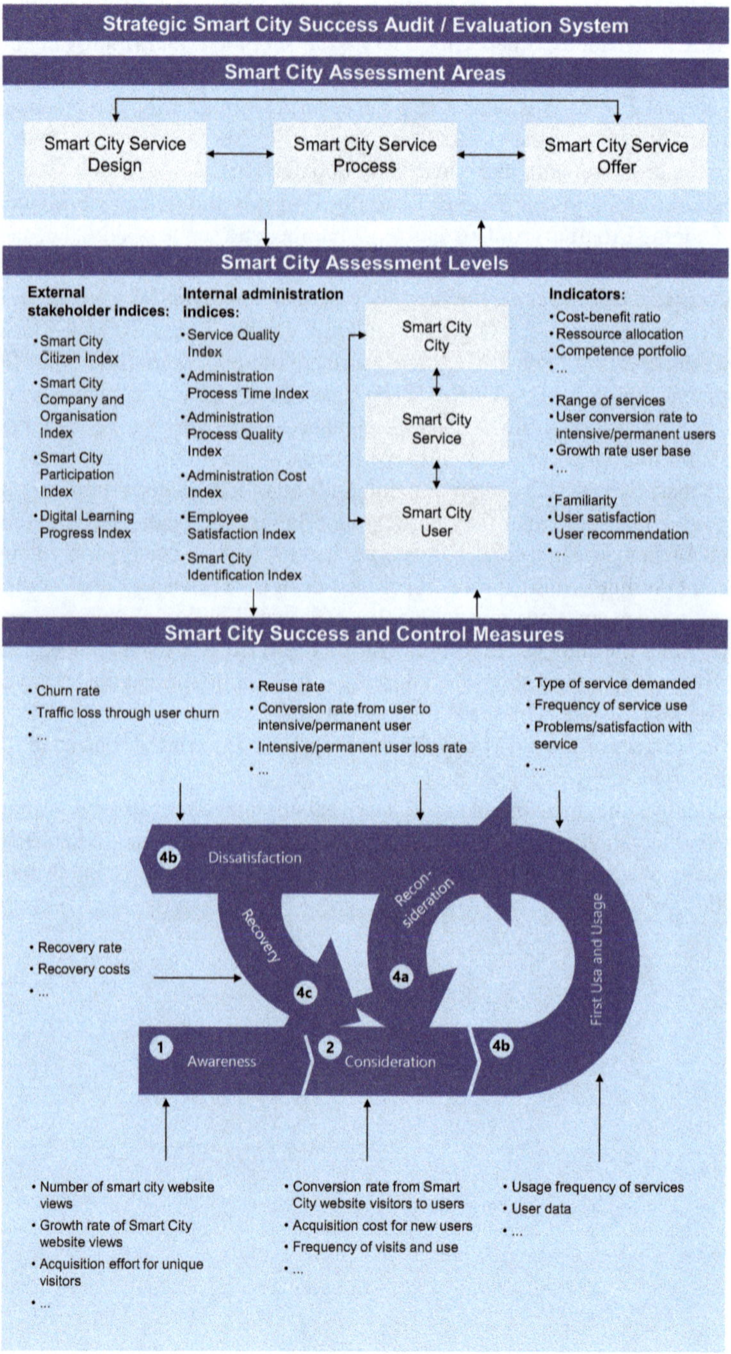

Fig. 8.23 Strategic smart city success audit/evaluation system

On this basis, the three assessment areas of smart city service design, smart city service process, and smart city service offering can be differentiated. In the next field, smart city evaluation level, smart city, smart city service, and smart city user are to be differentiated. On the aggregated smart city level as well as on the smart city service level, the internal management indices (e.g., service quality index) and level-specific indices (e.g., cost–benefit ratio on city level) are used to measure success. At the smart city user level, external stakeholder indices (e.g., smart city citizen index) and user-specific indicators (e.g., awareness) are particularly relevant for measuring success. At the user level, the success variables can be further differentiated. These smart city success and control variables vary depending on the process status (see also Chapter 10).

Contact Process

As part of the contact process, it is particularly important to identify and analyze potential users and their demand requirements and to position the organization's smart city services accordingly with promising potential users. Typical success and control variables in the awareness phase are the number of smart city page impressions, the growth rate in the number of visitors of the smart city portal, and the acquisition costs for an individual user.

Consideration

The core task of the Consideration phase, on the other hand, is to communicate the benefits of the smart city service offering. This is associated with the establishment of preferences on the part of the user with regard to the smart city services. Marketing messages must be adapted to the relevant interests of the individual in order to achieve the intended effect on the recipient. This requires the most detailed knowledge possible about the interests and preferences of the interested parties.

In order to measure the success of the consideration phase, the conversion rate of visitors into users, the acquisition costs for a new user, and the absolute and relative user frequencies are helpful performance indicators.

Utilization Decision and Utilization Process

The central task of the usage decision and usage process is to support the utilization of services by users. Appropriate information about the core smart city services and superior services are intended to improve the satisfaction of users and, consequently, the loyalty of users.

In addition, contact with users should be used to examine the degree of user satisfaction through user feedback, complaint and monitoring systems. This supports continuous monitoring and further development of the smart city service offering and its provision. The usual performance indicators for these two phases are the frequency with which the services are used, feedback from users on complaints and satisfaction with the services offered, and the type of service requested.

Reconsideration

During the reconsideration process, it is particularly important to maintain or intensify the perceived advantages of the smart city service offering and the existing user preferences with regard to smart city services. The goal is to turn a first-time visitor into a loyal user.

The most important measures for achieving this goal are informing users about new smart city services and optimizations as well as providing easy smart city access and useful content for repeated use of information and services. The rate of change of users into regular users and the loss rate of regular users are typical performance indicators in the reconsideration phase.

Dissatisfaction

If the user is not satisfied with the smart city service or some aspects of it, there is a risk that the user will leave. In this phase, the potential for dissatisfaction on the part of the user is usually so high that the user stops using the service altogether or migrates to competing offerings.

In this context, it is important to identify user dissatisfaction and to prevent the final migration of users. To prevent user churn, it is essential to monitor the satisfaction or dissatisfaction of users with appropriate feedback systems as early as the usage phase. Complaint management, which must be used in a targeted manner especially in the late usage phase and in the early churn phase, is of particular importance here. Important performance indicators in the dissatisfaction phase are the churn rate and the loss due to users turning away.

Reclamation Process

An important success factor in the smart city user relationship management process is the recovery management. In the event of churn, extensive win-back measures can be initiated to keep the user in the smart city user relationship after all or to prepare the user to enter the smart city user relationship again.

In win-back management, for example, price discounts, improved smart city service, or extended warranty commitments can help to successfully win back the user. Recovery management should be based on the meaningful results of a corresponding analysis of demand and user value, as only users who are attractive in terms of revenue should be recovered (Stauss and Friege 2017). The recovery rate and the cost of winning back users are common performance indicators for measuring the success of activities in the recovery phase.

8.4 Summary, Review Questions, Topics for Discussion, and Online Exercises

- The term smart city is found in various forms in the literature. Important core aspects of an integrated definition include the construction of smart city on digital information and communication technologies with the aim of developing resources in an urban environment. In this context, special importance is attached to the stakeholder groups, whose requirements for transparency, participation, and collaboration must be met in the smart city context.

- The relevance of smart cities becomes particularly clear when looking at the quadruple helix, which, among other things, represents the area of participation of a smart city. These consist of the four spheres of society, business, science, and government. In addition, the trend toward a growing urban population highlights the need to prepare urban administrations for the future by developing them into smart cities.
- The development of Smart City can be traced back to the first Open Data concept in London in 1986. In the last decade in particular, the smart city sector has experienced a significant increase in importance. In 2019, for example, the German Federal Ministry of the Interior, for Building and the Homeland provided €750 million in Smart City funding.
- The central goals of a smart city can be divided into three groups: Social smart city goals (e.g., diversity and openness), economic smart city goals (e.g., strong competitiveness), and environmental smart city goals (e.g., climate-neutral and comprehensive resource efficiency).
- Smart City services can be mapped in the integrated Smart City Service Provision Framework. This highlights the importance and interaction of smart city technologies, smart city service areas, smart city service portfolio, smart city distribution channels, and smart city users.
- The smart city actor network illustrates the multitude of interactions. Based on this, the Smart City Co-Creation Model depicts four primary groups in collaborative co-creation. These consist of citizens, education/research institutions, administration, and industry/other actors.
- In principle, four basic service areas can be distinguished from one another: Smart Government and E-Government, Smart Social Services, Smart Resources and Smart Environment, and Smart Mobility and Smart Infrastructure. The Smart City Service Portfolio differentiates further sub-categories within these service areas.
- Smart mobility and infrastructure are the most important areas of a smart city from the user's perspective. Users generally prefer apps and their cell phones to access smart city services, followed by official websites and online portals.
- The complex urban system with a multitude of actors, interactions, and services can be represented in the form of an ecosystem. The integrated collaborative smart city ecosystem framework illustrates a detailed flowchart of the different components and layers of a smart city model. These consist of the smart city governance model, smart city collaboration model, smart city business model, smart city software infrastructure model, and smart city physical infrastructure model (hardware).
- The Smart City Ecosystem Governance Model describes the steering or governance in the Smart City context. The aspects of SC agenda setting, constellation of SC interactors, SC governance mechanisms/instruments, SC governance outcomes, and SC governance audit are combined.
- Of particular relevance to the success of smart city concepts is the way in which they are implemented. In particular, the stakeholders Smart City departments and Smart City teams play an important role in the implementation. Smart City innovation forms and methods serve as common tools in the implementation.
- To measure the success of the Smart City implementation, the external stakeholders are to be analyzed in particular. The overall strategic Smart City success audit/evaluation system consists of the Smart City assessment areas, the Smart City assessment level, and the Smart City success and control measures.

Chapter 8
Review questions, topics for discussion and online exercises

Review questions

1. Define the concept of a smart city.
2. Outline the development of the world population on the basis of the United Nations analysis up to the year 2050. What are the main changes with regard to urban development dynamics?
3. List essential smart city targets in the three areas social, economic and ecological.
4. Describe the smart city ecosystem.
5. Outline the main smart city user demand factors and their assessment.

Topics for classroom discussion and team debates

1. Discuss why smart cities are a central task for the global society against the background of the development of the world population.
2. In light of the increasing deterioration of resource quality (resource scarcity) and drastic climate change in the coming decades, the successful development and implementation of the smart city concept will be of crucial importance for the prosperity of the world's population. Discuss this statement in the context of the contribution of smart cities to resource conservation and climate improvement.
3. Smart city ecosystems are complex systems in terms of management and governance. Based on the model of stakeholder domains of smart city concepts, discuss how the governance of such systems can best be designed.

Online Exercises

1. Visit https://unece.org/housing/sustainable-smart-cities. Explore the main areas and opportunities of sustainable smart cities. What are the key lessons learned?
2. Enter https://smart-cities-marketplace.ec.europa.eu/. Use the map on smart city project sites as a starting point to explore the smart city projects of the European Commission.
3. Visit https://smartamerica.org/teams/smart-cities-usa/ and explore the public-private partnership between San Jose and Intel using this website. Describe the challenges that are presented.

References

Adner, Ron (2006): Match your innovation strategy to your innovation ecosystem. In Harvard Business Review 84 (4), pp. 1–11.
Anthopoulos, Leo (2017a): Smart utopia VS smart reality: Learning by experience from 10 smart city cases. In Cities (63), pp. 128–148. DOI: https://doi.org/10.1016/j.cities.2016.10.005.
Anthopoulos, Leonidas G. (2015): Understanding the Smart City Domain: A Literature Review. In Rodríguez Bolívar, Manuel Pedro (Ed.): Transforming city governments for successful smart cities. Cham: Springer (Public Administration and Information Technology, 8), pp. 9–22.
Anthopoulos, Leonidas G. (2017b): The Rise of the Smart City. In Leonidas G. Anthopoulos (Ed.): Understanding Smart Cities: A Tool for Smart Government or an Industrial Trick?, vol. 22. Cham: Springer International Publishing (Public Administration and Information Technology), pp. 5–45.
Anthopoulos, Leonidas G. (2017c): Understanding Smart Cities. Cham: Springer International Publishing (Public Administration and Information Technology, v.22). Available online at https://ebookcentral.proquest.com/lib/gbv/detail.action?docID=4841627.
Berntzen, Lasse; Johannessen, Marius Rohde (2015): The Role of Citizen Participation in Municipal Smart City Projects: Lessons Learned from Norway. In José Ramón Gil García, Theresa Pardo, Taewoo Nam (Eds.): Smarter as the new urban agenda. A comprehensive view of the 21st Century city. Cham: Springer (Public Administration and Information Technology, volume 11), pp. 299–314.
Bundesministerium des Innern und für Heimat (2019): Auftakt für erste Staffel Modellprojekte Smart Cities - Wissenstransfer soll in die Breite wirken. Available online at https://www.bmi.bund.de/SharedDocs/pressemitteilungen/DE/2019/09/smart-cities-modellprojekte.html, checked on 1/14/2022.
Bundesministerium für Wohnen, Stadtentwicklung und Bauwesen (2021): Smart Cities. Stadtentwicklung im digitalen Zeitalter. Available online at https://www.bmi.bund.de/DE/themen/bauen-wohnen/stadt-wohnen/stadtentwicklung/smart-cities/smart-cities-node.html, checked on 1.6.21.
Caragliu, Andrea; Del Bo, Chiara; Nijkamp, Peter (2009): Smart Cities in Europe. In Journal of Urban Technology 18, pp. 65–82. DOI: https://doi.org/10.1080/10630732.2011.601117.
Chauhan, Sumedha; Agarwal, Neetima; Kar, Arpan Kumar (2016): Addressing big data challenges in smart cities: a systematic literature review. In Info 18 (4), pp. 73–90. DOI: https://doi.org/10.1108/info-03-2016-0012.
Christensen, Clayton M.; Rosenbloom, Richard S. (1995): Explaining the attacker's advantage: Technological paradigms, organizational dynamics, and the value network. In Research Policy 24 (2), pp. 233–257. DOI: https://doi.org/10.1016/0048-7333(93)00764-K.
Clarysse, Bart; Wright, Mike; Bruneel, Johan; Mahajan, Aarti (2014): Creating value in ecosystems: Crossing the chasm between knowledge and business ecosystems. In Research Policy 43 (7), pp. 1164–1176. DOI: https://doi.org/10.1016/j.respol.2014.04.014.
Dameri, Renata Paola (2013): Searching for smart city definition: a comprehensive proposal. In International Journal of computers & technology 11 (5), pp. 2544–2551.
Dameri, Renata Paola; Rosenthal-Sabroux, Camille (2014): Smart city and value creation. In: Smart city: Springer, pp. 1–12.
Eremia, Mircea; Toma, Lucian; Sanduleac, Mihai (2017): The smart city concept in the 21st century. In Procedia Engineering 181, pp. 12–19.
European Commission (2021): Funding for Cities. Funding Opportunities. Edited by European Commission. European Union. Available online at https://ec.europa.eu/info/eu-regional-and-urban-development/topics/cities-and-urban-development/funding-cities_en, updated on 6/1/2021, checked on 6/1/2021.
European Commission (2022): A European Green Deal. Available online at https://ec.europa.eu/info/strategy/priorities-2019-2024/european-green-deal_en, checked on 2/16/2022.

GlobalData Thematic Research (2020): History of smart cities: Timeline. Available online at https://www.verdict.co.uk/smart-cities-timeline, checked on 1/14/2022.
Iansiti, Marco; Levien, Roy (2004): Strategy as ecology. In Harvard Business Review 82 (3), pp. 68–78.
Institute for Management Development (2020): Smart City Index 2020. Available online at https://www.imd.org/globalassets/wcc/docs/smart_city/smartcityindex_2020.pdf, checked on 5/20/2021.
McKinsey & Organization (2018): Smart Cities: Digital solutions for a more livable future. Available online at https://www.mckinsey.com/~/media/McKinsey/Business%20Functions/Operations/Our%20Insights/Smart%20cities%20Digital%20solutions%20for%20a%20more%20livable%20future/MGI-Smart-Cities-Executive-summary.pdf, checked on 5/19/2021.
Meijer, Albert; Bolívar, Manuel Pedro Rodríguez (2016): Governing the smart city: a review of the literature on smart urban governance. In International Review of Administrative Sciences 82 (2), pp. 392–408.
Monzon, Andres (2015): Smart Cities Concept and Challenges. Bases for the Assessment of Smart City Projects. In : 2015 international conference on smart cities and green ICT systems (SMARTGREENS): IEEE. Available online at https://ieeexplore.ieee.org/stamp/stamp.jsp?tp=&arnumber=7297938.
Moore, James F. (1993): Predators and prey: a new ecology of competition. In Harvard Business Review 71 (3), pp. 75–86.
Moore, James F. (1996): The death of competition. Leadership and strategy in the age of business ecosystems. Chichester: Wiley.
Müller-Seitz, Gordon; Seiter, Mischa; Wenz, Patrick (2016): Was ist eine Smart City? Betriebswirtschaftliche Zugänge aus Wissenschaft und Praxis. Wiesbaden: Springer Gabler.
Piehler, Robert; Wirtz, Bernd W.; Daiser, Peter (2016): An analysis of continuity intentions of egovernment portal users. In Public Management Review 18 (2), pp. 163–198.
PwC (2019): Creating the smart cities of the future. A three-tier development model for digital transformation of citizen services. Available online at https://www.pwc.com/gx/en/sustainability/assets/creating-the-smart-cities-of-the-future.pdf, checked on 5/19/2021.
Scaringella, Laurent; Radziwon, Agnieszka (2018): Innovation, entrepreneurial, knowledge, and business ecosystems: Old wine in new bottles? In Technological Forecasting and Social Change 136, pp. 59–87. DOI: https://doi.org/10.1016/j.techfore.2017.09.023.
Selada, Catarina (2017): Smart Cities and the Quadruple Helix Innovation SystemsConceptual Framework: The Case of Portugal. In Sara Paulina de Oliveira Monteiro, Elias G. Carayannis (Eds.): The Quadruple Innovation Helix nexus. A smart growth model, quantitative empirical validation and operationalization for OECD countries. London: Palgrave Macmillan US (Palgrave studies in democracy, innovation, and entrepreneurship for growth), pp. 211–244.
Shields, R. (2016): SMART Cities Timeline. Available online at https://era.library.ualberta.ca/items/d6765e57-9909-4d2f-8e67-1ba0530c4f97/view/556a48cc-3b0d-4b8a-b8eb-58bb4fff12cc/SMARTcitiestimeline.pdf, checked on 1/14/2022.
Shields, Rob (2014): Smart Cities Timeline. Available online at https://www.spaceandculture.com/2014/12/22/smart-cities-timeline/, checked on 5/21/2021.
Stauss, B.; Friege, C. (Eds.) (2017): Kundenwertorientiertes Rückgewinnungsmanagement. Kundenwert- Grundlagen - Innovatiove Konzepte - Praktische Umsetzungen. With assistance of S. Helm, B. Günter, B. Eggers. 4th ed. Wiesbaden.
United Nations (2019): World urbanization prospects. The 2018 revision. New York: United Nations.
Winkowska, Justyna; Szpilko, Danuta; Pejić, Sonja (2019): Smart city concept in the light of the literature review. In Engineering Management in Production and Services 11 (2), pp. 70–86. DOI: https://doi.org/10.2478/emj-2019-0012.
Wirtz, Bernd W. (2021): Digital Business and Electronic Commerce. Cham: Springer International Publishing.
Wirtz, Bernd W. (2022): E-Government. Wiesbaden: Springer Gabler.

Wirtz, Bernd W.; Becker, Marcel; Schmidt, Florian W. (2021a): Smart city services: an empirical analysis of citizen preferences. In Public Organization Review. DOI: https://doi.org/10.1007/s11115-021-00562-0.

Wirtz, Bernd W.; Daiser, Peter (2017): E-government. Strategy, process, instruments. 2nd ed. Speyer.

Wirtz, Bernd W.; Falke, I.; Schmitt, Daniel (2021b): Mobile government: Research, development and research perspectives. In International Journal of Public Administration. DOI: https://doi.org/10.1080/01900692.2021.1993910.

Wirtz, Bernd W.; Müller, Wilhelm M. (2021): A meta-analysis of smart city research and its future research implications. In International Public Management Review 21 (2), pp. 18–39.

Wirtz, Bernd W.; Müller, Wilhelm M. (2022a): An integrated framework for public service provision in smart cities. In International Journal of Public Sector Performance Management, Forthcoming.

Wirtz, Bernd W.; Müller, Wilhelm M. (2022b): An integrative collaborative ecosystem for smart cities. A framework for organizational governance. In International Journal of Public Administration. DOI: https://doi.org/10.1080/01900692.2021.2001014.

Wirtz, Bernd W.; Müller, Wilhelm M.; Schmidt, Florian (2020): Public smart service provision in smart cities: A case-study-based approach. In International Journal of Public Administration 43 (6), pp. 499–516. DOI: https://doi.org/10.1080/01900692.2019.1636395.

Wirtz, Bernd W.; Müller, Wilhelm M.; Schmidt, Florian W. (2021c): Digital public services in smart cities – An empirical analysis of lead user preferences. In Public Organization Review 21 (2), pp. 299–315. DOI: https://doi.org/10.1007/s11115-020-00492-3.

Wirtz, Bernd W.; Piehler, Robert; Rieger, Vanessa; Daiser, Peter (2016): eGovernment Portal Information Performance and the Role of Local Community Interest. Empirical Support for a Model of Citizen Perceptions. In Public Administration Quarterly 40 (1), pp. 48–83.

Wirtz, Bernd W.; Ullrich, Sebastian; Mory, Linda (2012): EHealth in the public sector: An empirical analysis of the acceptance of Germany's electronic health card. In Public Administration 90 (3), pp. 642–663.

Yeh, Hsiaoping (2017): The effects of successful ICT-based smart city services: From citizens' perspectives. In Government Information Quarterly 34 (3), pp. 556–565. DOI: https://doi.org/10.1016/j.giq.2017.05.001.

Digital Government Business Models 9

Contents

Learning Objectives
By working through this chapter, you will be able to:

1. Explain the concept of public business models.
2. Describe the partial models of the integrated public business model.
3. Describe the ICTI digital government business models.
4. Illustrate the advantages of hybrid public business models and outline their drivers.
5. Explain the public business model innovation process.

Business models are an important topic in the management and business environment.[1] In these fields, the term business model is closely related to creating competitive advantage. Moreover, management of business models and organization success are frequently mentioned in one breath.

Changes in Market Conditions and Competition
This important role that has become attached to business models is in particular associated with the significant changes in market conditions and competition. Digitalization, globalization, deregulations, economic integration—to name a few—have led to more dynamic, more competitive, and more complex markets.

[1] See for Chapter 9 Digital Government Business Models also Wirtz (2011, 2019, 2021, 2022), Wirtz and Daiser (2015, 2017b).

B. W. Wirtz, *Digital Government*, Springer Texts in Business and Economics,
https://doi.org/10.1007/978-3-031-13086-1_9

This situation forces companies to constantly adapt to the steadily changing market conditions in a quick, effective, and efficient manner.

Leadership and Management Tool

Here, business models become an important leadership and management tool by simplifying the complexity of reality and shifting the focus from habitual to game-changing organizational activities. Moreover, the process of designing and developing business models supports the generation of new business ideas as well as the assessment of existing strategies, structures, and business activities. Thus, the business model concept supports organizations in systematically analyzing their success factors and adapting their business activities in a target-oriented way (Wirtz et al. 2016b, 2022b; Wirtz 2020).

Business Models in the Public Sector

Transferred to the public sector, a business model represents the service systems of a public sector organization and illustrates in a simplified, aggregated form which resources are used and how these are transformed into the service offering of the public sector organization (Wirtz et al. 2021b).

In this context, a business model contains information about the strategy of the public sector organization, the production factors, and the functions the actors involved have. Thus, the business model approach can be considered as a public management instrument that supports the systematic creation of better, superior service offerings and provides public services for society with higher value for the public, supporting the public sector's service remit.

Moreover, business models are considered especially suitable for digital government endeavors since they assist and encourage the continuous adaption and re-engineering of organizational practices to new circumstances. These are key reason why the business model concept is regarded as appealing and useful in the public sector and why governments worldwide are increasingly applying business models to enhance their digital government related service delivery (Janssen et al. 2008).

9.1 Business Model Concept

When talking about business models, one has to keep in mind that there is a general superordinate orientation reflecting the general demand. In business, for instance, this refers to a specific market that demands a particular product or service, such as the market for smartphones or fashion. Here, global trends set the overall direction for the respective business models, though leaving niche markets on different levels.

In terms of digital government, this superordinate orientation refers to the general agreement of the nations that establish and promote digital government, to set up electronic systems for handling administration and democracy processes in the context of governmental activities by means of information and communication technologies to support public duties efficiently and effectively.

Business Model Levels

Although this superordinate orientation on the supranational level provides a strategic and operative direction for setting up a digital government business model, it leaves plenty of room for interpretation and allows ample individual scope for realization. From an integrative perspective, several interdependent business model levels can be distinguished: supranational, national, regional, and local.

While the supranational level reflects the superordinate orientation of digital government in an international or global context (so to speak the overall digital government environment), the national level is the first degree of abstraction. This level is of particular importance since a nation usually shows the following attributes that favor a consistent and systematic digital government implementation within its territory: uniform legal framework, common history, culture, and language, as well as homogeneous public administration (see Figure 9.1).

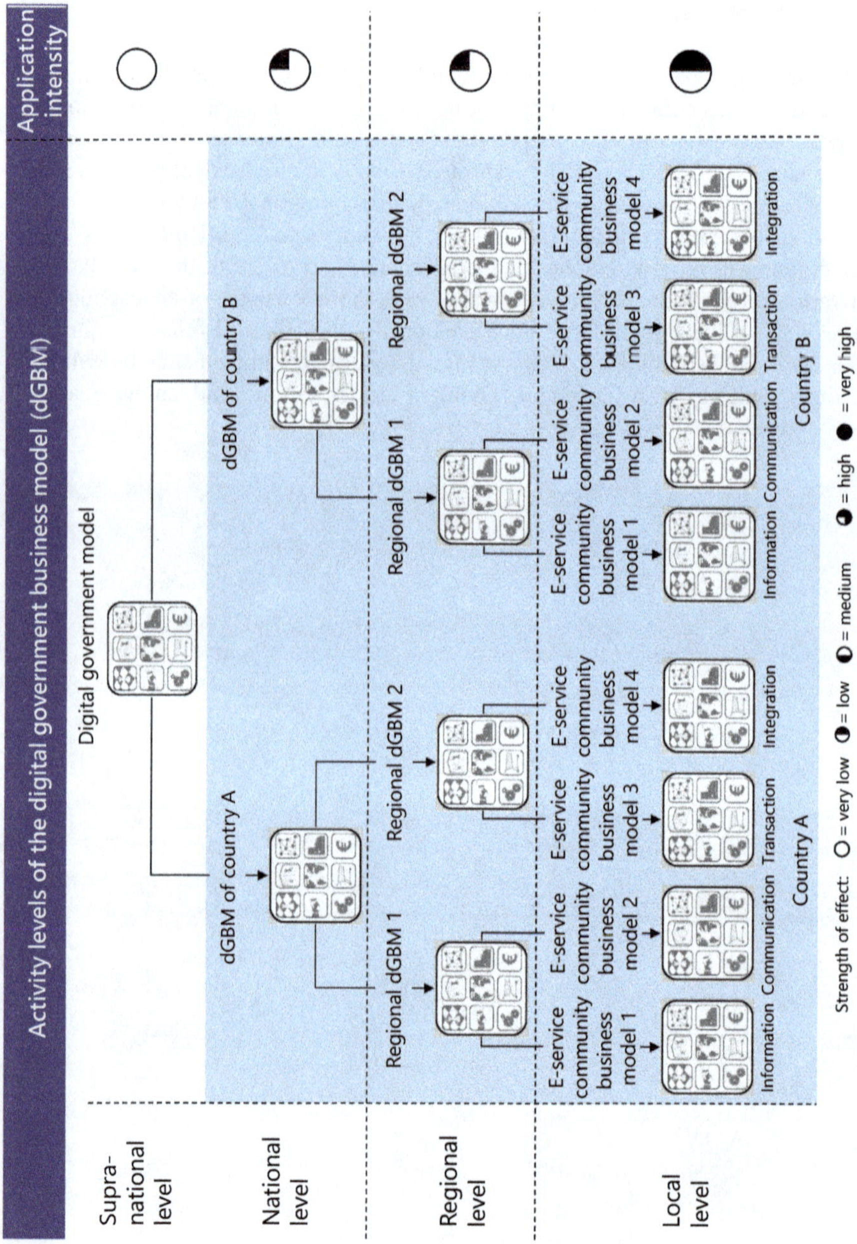

Fig. 9.1 Digital government business model levels. Source: Wirtz (2011, 2021), Wirtz and Daiser (2015)

Centralized or Decentralized Character of a Country

An important factor for the design, functionality, and management of the national, regional, and local levels is the nation's political imprint concerning its centralized (e.g., France) or decentralized (e.g., Germany) character. While countries with a decentralized character rather possess powerful public authorities on a regional and local level, countries showing a centralized character focus on expertise and competencies at a central or supreme authority level. Against this background, public business models from politically centralized and decentralized nations tend to show differences with regard to service orientation and responsibility.

Business models for the local level, which primarily aim at providing the community with digital government services, show a stronger user orientation than the levels above and provide the main platform interfaces for user access. For this reason, the local level should demonstrate the highest usage intensity. This relationship could be observed in a digital government user survey. The study showed that local digital government portals are the main Internet interface between the government and the citizens. Nearly half of the participants (43%) demonstrate high and very high usage of city portals, while these figures are 15% and 8% for regional and national portals, respectively. Figure 9.2 presents the usage-related results of the study.

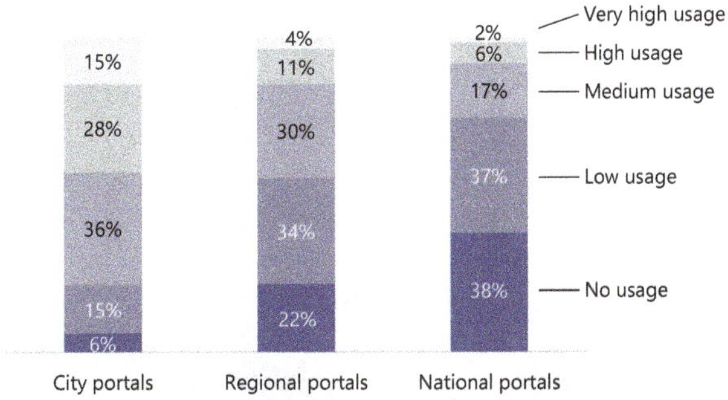

Fig. 9.2 Digital government portal use (Germany). Data source: Wirtz (2015)

In the scientific literature, various business model concepts can be found. The three main directions are the technology-oriented, the organization-oriented, and the strategy-oriented approach.

Technology-Oriented Business Model Approach

The technology-oriented business model approach is heavily influenced by the concepts of business modeling and electronic business. Many electronic business concepts are explained by this approach.

Organization-Oriented Business Model Approach

Creating superior organizational design is at the heart of organization-oriented approaches. Here, size and composition of units, responsibilities, roles, organizational culture, organizational learning, etc. within an organization are defined to create a more efficient and more effective organization and thus a competitive advantage.

Strategy-Oriented Business Model Approach
The third direction is the strategy-oriented approach, which creates a close connection between an organization's business model and its strategy, taking into account the internal and external view on the organization, as well as its core assets and core competencies.

Business Model Processes
Although these three main directions show clear differences concerning their orientations, all approaches share the assumption that business model processes are an important aspect: technology-oriented approaches regard process modeling as a vital factor, organization-oriented approaches consider process optimization to be crucial, and in strategy-oriented approaches business model processes are a medium for operationalizing strategy. For this reason, also processes are a fundamental part of business models.

Definition of Public Business Models
Against the background of the different directions and large number of academic publications concerning business models, scientific literature shows various definitions for this subject.[2] Considering the existing research streams and taking into account the relevance of business processes, we propose a rather general definition for the public business model:

> **Definition of Public Business Model (Wirtz 2011; Wirtz and Daiser 2015, 2017b)**
> A public business model is a simplified and aggregated representation of the relevant services, processes, and activities of a public sector organization that describes how information, products, and services that create additional value for society are developed and managed, while also considering strategic and processual as well as user and public demand components to support sustainable public value creation for society and the public service remit.

Business models can be found in various fields with differing scopes. A business model for a start-up of a local digital government platform, being built on initial data and assumptions and aiming to get the digital services running, as well as quickly acquiring a decent user base, is significantly different from a business model that is, for instance, applied to a change management process of a well-established, traditional cross-departmental administrative procedure.

[2]For an extensive overview of business model definitions, please refer to Wirtz (2020, 2021).

Organizational Advantage

Irrespective of these potential deviations, the primary objective of the business model is always connected to developing, implementing, and maintaining a sustainable, successful organizational advantage. Furthermore, a business model should always integrate the relevant internal and external aspects and present an aggregated conceptual framework of the underlying components.

This way, the business model illustrates the approach of creating better, superior service offerings and increasing value for the organization as well as public value for society in form of a transparent conceptual framework. This framework consists of partial models that provide the basic input for the integrated public business model, which is made up of three component layers: the public strategic component, the customer/user and public demand component, as well as the public value creation component.

These three components consolidate the strategy, user, public demand, and public value creation perspective to finally lead to an overarching business model that is set up on the necessary level of detail, while providing the advantage of reduced complexity required for effective and efficient management.

Partial Models of the Integrated Public Business Model

The level of detail comes from the partial models, which possess a crucial role within an integrated business model approach since these are all closely intertwined, creating interdependent relationships. Figure 9.3 presents the partial models of the integrated public business model, which are described in the following.

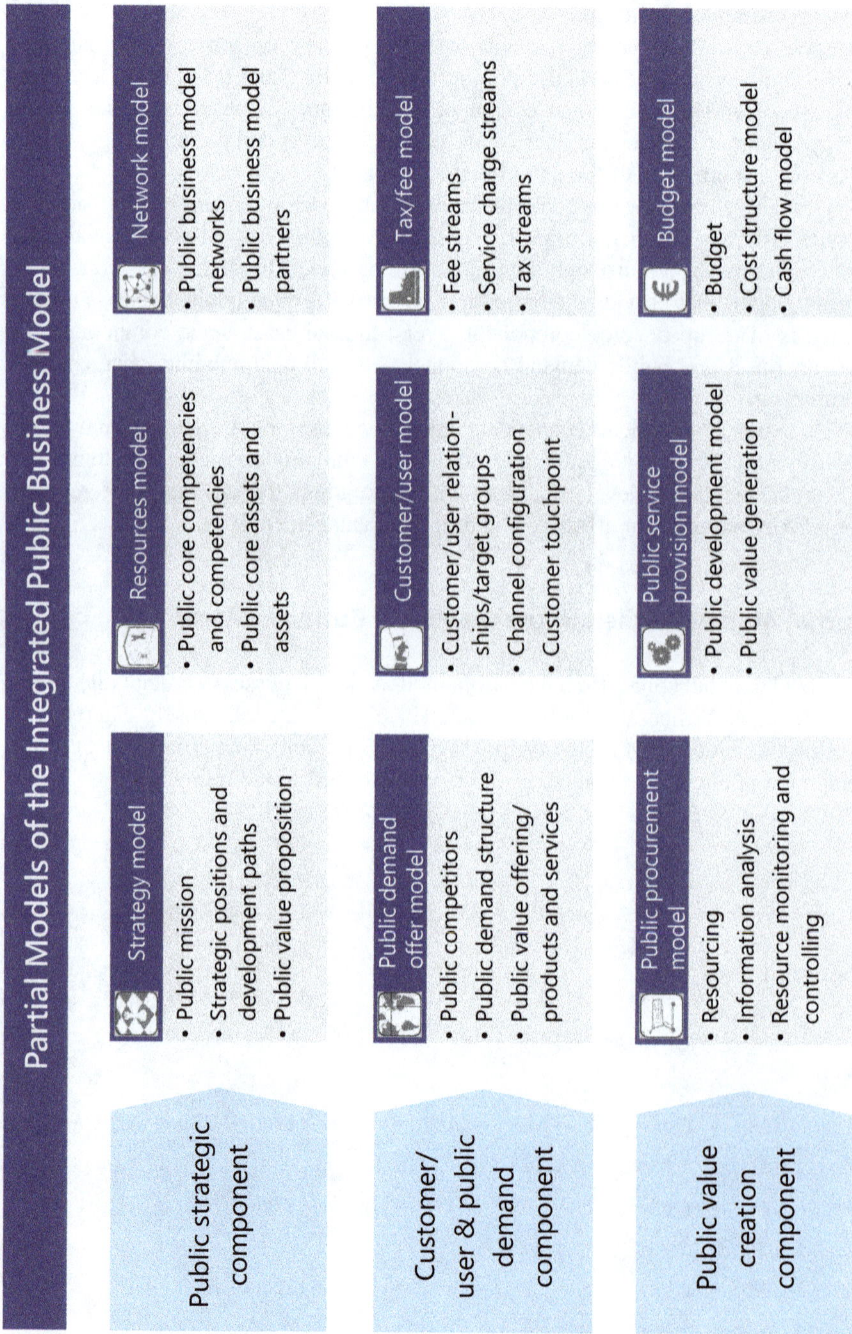

Fig. 9.3 Partial models of the integrated public business model. Source: Wirtz (2011, 2021), Wirtz and Daiser (2015)

Strategy Model
In the strategy model, the digital government leader determines the long-term targets of the digital government system.[3] Thus, this partial model contains the public mission, the strategic positions and development paths, as well as the public value proposition of the digital government system.

Resources Model
The resources model serves the integration of the public assets and core assets as well as the public competencies and core competencies that are relevant for public value creation. Therefore, the resources model represents a summary of all relevant value-creating input factors of the business model.

Network Model
The network model provides an overview of vital public business model partners that have a significant impact on the public value creation process as well as of important connections between the different public business models. This model can be regarded as a management instrument to control and manage different network partners, processes, and services.

Public Demand Offer Model
The public demand offer model is concerned with the external demand analysis, which primarily assesses public stakeholder needs, demands, and behaviors. Here, further relevant external aspects like legal or political changes as well as future developments of information and communication technology are important since these may influence public online service provision.

Customer/User Model
The customer/user model identifies the customers/users that are relevant for the public business model. Since it is not reasonable to manage customers/users on an individual basis, specific target groups need to be determined. These target groups are usually defined on the basis of distinctive demographic criterions and according to the respective fields of application.

Tax/Fee Model
The tax/fee model determines the public sectors organization's cash inflows, such as fee streams, service charge streams, and tax streams. These cash inflows can be classified into direct and indirect as well as transaction-dependent or independent forms. Whereas direct streams are generated through the service provided and the related fee itself, indirect streams are generated through additional activities, such as

[3] The analytical and methodical steps required for gathering the relevant information to develop the partial business models are laid out in Section 3.3 Strategic Management of Digital Government. For further details on the partial business models, please see Wirtz (2020a).

sponsorship or marketing of advertising space on the portal.[4] Cash streams that are directly linked to a specific transaction are called transaction-dependent, while transaction-independent streams are already generated through the service provision itself and are thus independent from the actual usage of the service.

Public Procurement Model

The public procurement model describes the structure and sourcing of the input factors as well as the related analysis, monitoring, and controlling activities. For this purpose, the public procurement model contains the goals and measures for systematically procuring the relevant input factors for the service offering as well as managing and optimizing the related processes.

Public Service Provision Model

The public service provision model defines the key parameters for the customer/user-oriented service provision business model by determining the services that are offered to the customer/user target groups and its related processes. Thus, the public service provision model gives an overview of the internal conversion process that shows the transformation of the input factors into superior services that increase public value.

Budget Model

The budget model combines the budget, cost structure, and cash flow perspective into an integrated partial business model, which reflects the monetary impact of the other partial models. Thus, it presents the cost, revenue, and cash flow streams of the public sector organization.

These partial models add up to the overall public business model that provides a compressed overview of the organizational activities, which supports management and coordination of the public sector organization. Thus, it promotes public value enabling governments to reach their professional ideal regarding, e.g., accountability, equity, and legality. It allows reaching their efficiency ideal, regarding, e.g., performance, productivity, and effectiveness. Furthermore it helps reaching their service ideal and engagement ideal, manifested in, e.g., trust and reliance, citizen centricity, democracy, transparency, and participation (Wirtz et al. 2022a).

In the next step, this rather abstract meta-description of a public business model is adapted to the offering and the requirements of digital government systems.

[4]Advertising space on public sector portals is still rare. However, individual examples exist on municipal level.

9.2 ICTI Digital Government Business Model Approach

Concerning classification criteria for systematizing digital government business models, there exist various possible approaches. For the following classification, we decided to choose the primary service offering as the critical element. On the one hand, because the diversity and complexity of digital government service provision has increased over time, which has also had a considerable impact on the development of the associated business models.

On the other hand, because a service offer classification can be directly transferred to the related utilization requirements, giving users and providers the chance to directly distinguish between usage-oriented categories. Summing up, the classification of digital government business models according to their primary service offering is regarded as particularly useful here.

Information, Communication, Transaction, and Integration (ICTI)
The relevant public business models in a digital government context can therefore be classified into four basic stand-alone business models: Information, Communication, Transaction, and Integration (ICTI). As laid out before, this ICTI Digital Government Business Model Approach, which is illustrated in Figure 9.4, is based on an abstraction of digital government service provision characteristics.

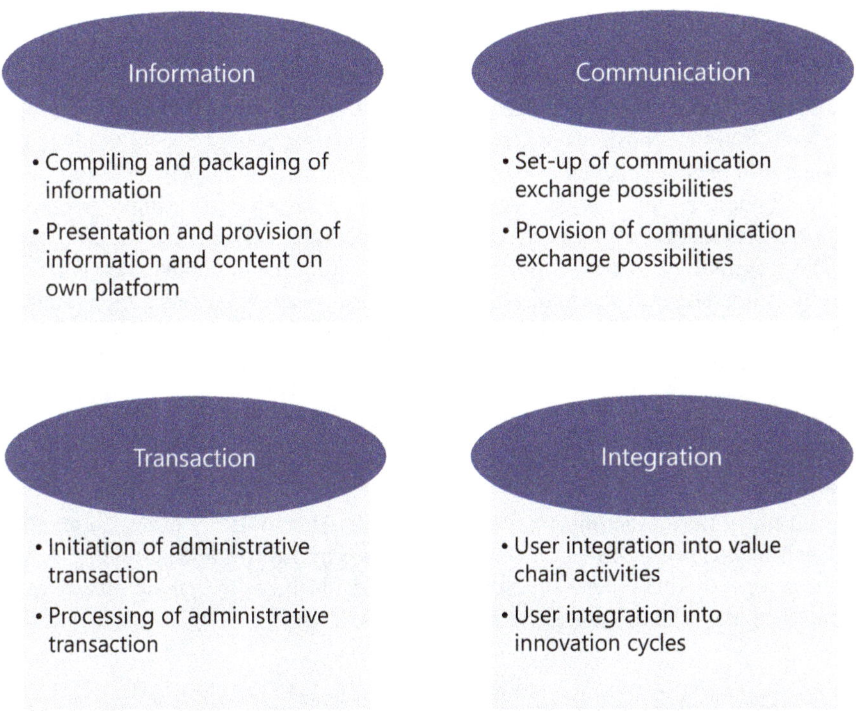

Fig. 9.4 ICTI digital government business models. Source: Wirtz and Daiser (2015, 2017b)

Against the background that all four digital government business models can be regarded as independent, separate public business models, which could be applied and operated individually, these fulfill the prerequisites of being stand-alone digital government models. Nevertheless, most digital government portals today are hybrid business models that apply a combination of the four basic stand-alone models.

The development of public business models paralleled the advancement of modern information and communication technologies. For this reason, the first one was the Information Business Model, presenting static information to the users. With increasing data transmission capacities and more sophisticated software and programming languages, the technological environment allowed the design of new business models, such as the Communication or Transaction Business Model.

The ICTI Business Models

The Information Business Model builds upon the strategy to provide users with information in a simple, convenient, and appealing way. Thus, key processes of this business model are collecting, selecting, systemizing, structuring, compiling, and packaging information as well as presenting and providing the respective content on an online platform.

The Communication Business Model follows the approach to provide the users with a comfortable online communication platform. For this reason, setting up, maintaining, and developing of online communication exchange possibilities, which support and foster interaction between public administration and its stakeholders, are key activities.

The Transaction Business Model targets at the initiation, handling, and processing of administrative procedures through the digital government platform. The core aim of this business model is to complement or partially or fully substitute existing offline government services. Therefore, automatization and data processing, service bundling, and service development are, for example, important core competencies that are required for realizing the digital government platform.

The Integration Business Model aims at integrating public stakeholders directly into the value chain of the public sector organization as well as its administrative procedures. This means that the user has the possibility to influence governmental activities through participative and collaborative action.

Information Business Model

The subcategories of the Information Business Model, mandatory information offer and non-mandatory information offer, serve the purpose to illustrate the range of services provided in an ideal structure. Figure 9.5 illustrates the public information business model with the respective subcategories.

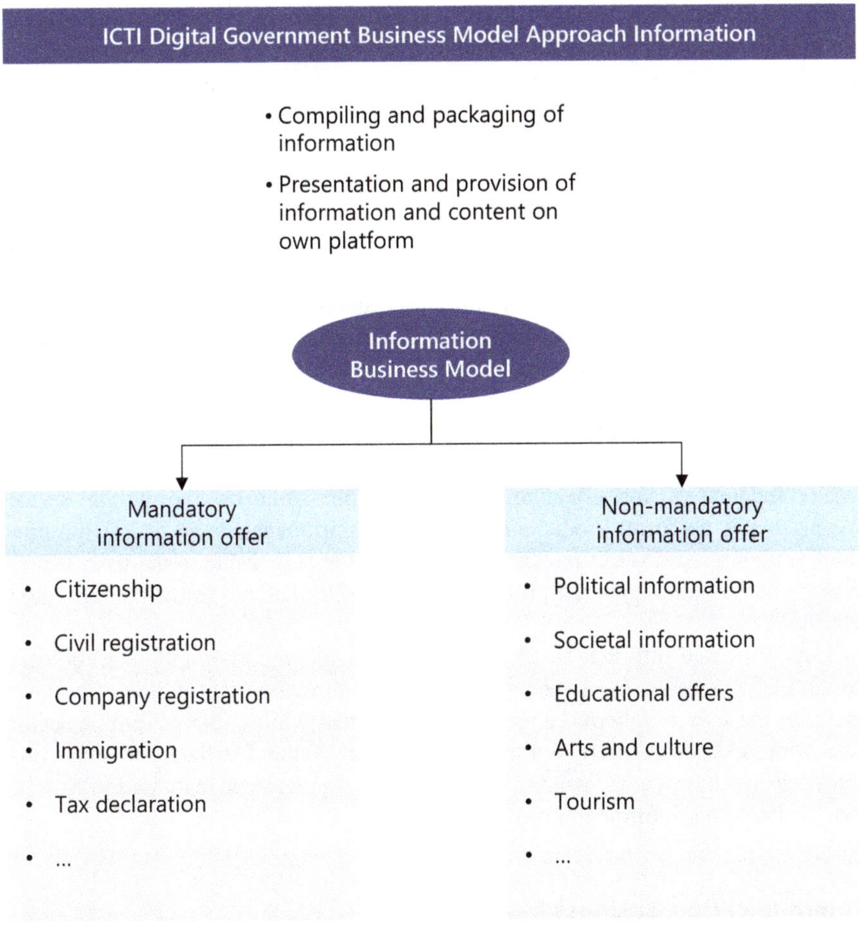

Fig. 9.5 Digital government business model for information. Source: Wirtz and Daiser (2015, 2017b)

Mandatory Information Offer

Mandatory information offers refer to information that needs to be supplied to public stakeholders in connection with services that have to be provided in accordance with laws or regulations. Examples are information concerning citizenship, civil registration, organization registration, immigration, or tax declaration.

Non-Mandatory Information Offer

The term non-mandatory information offer describes information services that are neither required by law nor associated with any obligatory government service. These may cover various subjects, such as political, societal, educational, arts and culture, tourism, etc.

The most important aspect of the information presented is that it shows a clear informative value-add to the user. Therefore, it should either provide a solution to a specific user problem or increase user convenience by delivering a relevant set of different information from one digital government portal.

Core Assets of the Information Business Model

From this point of view, especially existing and obtained public sector data are core assets since these are initially not available to other information providers. Another important aspect for mandatory information offers is the public sector organization's knowledge concerning its administrative procedures and internal processes. This enables the information providing institution to particularly create value-added information for its users with regard to its service offering.

Core Competencies of the Information Business Model

User relationship management and information and service bundling are important core competencies for effective information provision on the public sector organization's platform. Productive user relationship management allows the provider to identify and select relevant information that is of value to the user. Moreover, the information creation process can be directly tailored to their information requirements.

Target-oriented information and service bundling supports public stakeholders through a clear and convenient presentation of information that is interesting and useful to the user. Furthermore, combining and intertwining internal public sector data with additional external information creates value for the user since this approach generates new insights or supplementary aspects that hardly can be provided by other information providers.

Communication Business Model

The core target of the Communication Business Model is the provision of online communication possibilities for government-to-user interaction. These can be divided into two subcategories: interactive communication offers and automated communication offers. Figure 9.6 shows the Communication Business Model.

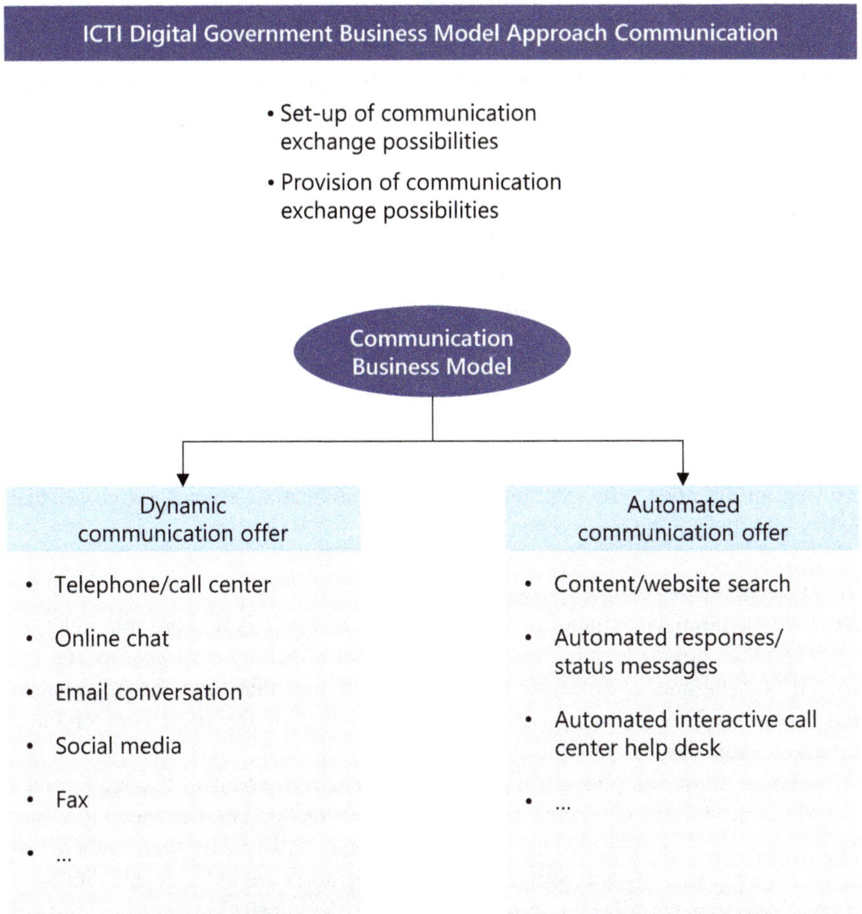

Fig. 9.6 Digital government business model for communication. Source: Wirtz and Daiser (2015, 2017b)

Dynamic Communication Offer

Interactive communication offers, such as telephone, call centers, online chats, communication via email or social media, foster information exchange between two active participants that have an impact on each other. Therefore, interactive communication refers to a dynamic two-way flow of information.

Automated Communication Offer

Automated communication offers may show a one-way or two-way flow of information, but the sender–recipient effect is not dynamic. Therefore, the information exchange does not have a considerable impact from an information content perspective. A content or website search, for example, is based on an automated search algorithm. If the user changes the search terms, the results will vary in accordance with these search modifications.

At first glance, these results seem to be dynamic, but the searched content is static. Moreover, the user does not have a direct impact on this underlying static content. Considering this as well as the automated search procedure makes a content of website search an automated communication offer.

Further examples are automated responses and status messages, such as automated out-of-office messages or notifications about received user requests, or automated interactive call center help desks, which, for instance, guide the user through a question and answer menu by selecting predefined options with the phone keypad.

Core Assets of the Communication Business Model

Core assets of the Communication Business Model are employees, the IT platform, as well as the technological infrastructure. These resources form the basis for ensuring an effective, efficient, and stable communication service provision that creates a lasting digital government advantage.

Core Competencies of the Communication Business Model

User relationship management, experience design, technology and programming, as well as service development are core competencies necessary for transforming the previously mentioned core assets into superior services that have the potential to create user preferences and to increase public value of the digital government communication services provided.

Here, user relationship management and experience design are vital competencies since the communication process needs to be established and implemented in a way that not only satisfies the actual users' requirements, but also makes them want to use the service. Technology and programming competencies are indispensable abilities for the Communication Business Model since they are needed to set up, maintain, and develop the relevant communication services and integrate them into the IT infrastructure.

Transaction Business Model

The Transaction Business Model focuses on the initiation, handling, and processing of administrative procedures through the digital government platform with the aim to complement or substitute existing offline government services. This online service offering can either be partial or full. Figure 9.7 illustrates the Transaction Business Model setting.

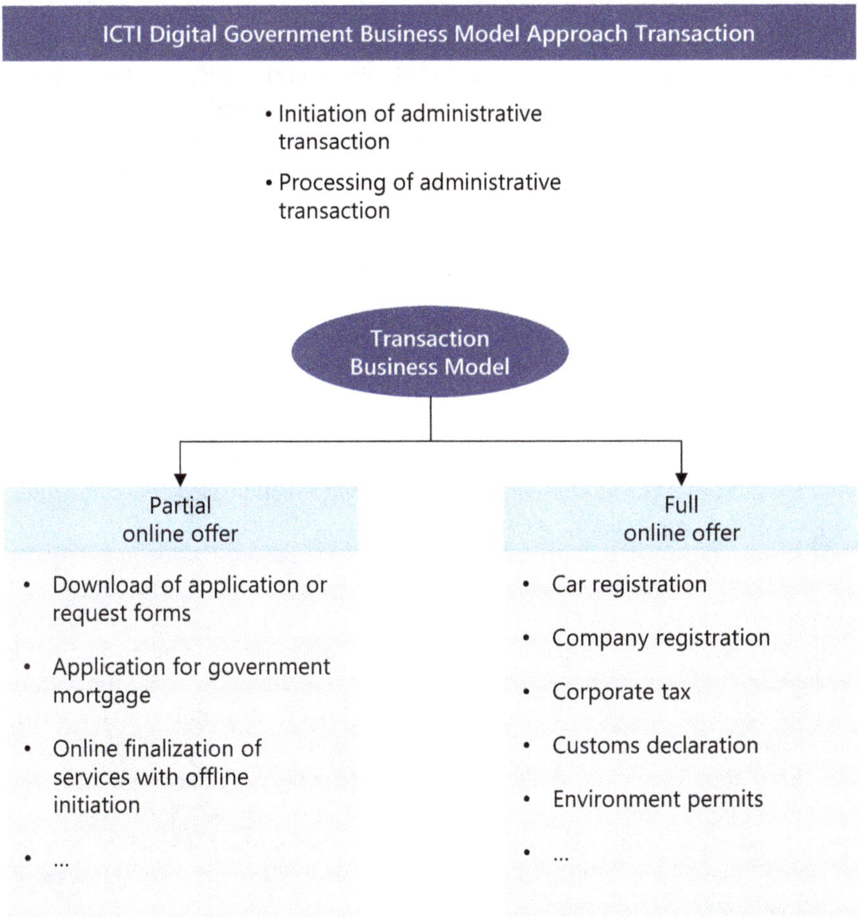

Fig. 9.7 Digital government business model for transaction. Source: Wirtz and Daiser (2015, 2017b)

Partial Online Offer

Partial online offers refer to services that cannot be completed without at least one further media break. Examples are the download of application or request forms, an application for a government mortgage, or an online finalization of services that have been initiated offline. Concerning, for instance, the download of an application form, the respective document is provided on a digital government platform for the user, who prints out and fills in the form and then sends it back to the public sector organization in question.

Although this kind of service provision brings an improvement compared to offline service provision, because the administrative procedure may be initiated without visiting the public sector organization in person, it does not harness the full digital government potential.

Full Online Offer

The full potential can only be generated through fully automated procedures. A well-known example of a comparable undertaking is electronic banking. While the clients usually needed to visit a branch in person to conduct a manual transaction, people nowadays can settle nearly all banking transactions at any time from home. This form of automatization and outsourcing of activities to the client has, for example, led to a significant cost reduction of 70–90% in e-banking service delivery.

Core Assets of the Transaction Business Model

Core assets of the Transaction Business Model are exclusive alliances and networks, the IT platform, as well as the technological infrastructure. These resources form the basis for a comprehensive full online service provision.

Core Competencies of the Transaction Business Model

The realization of this business model requires the following core competencies: automatization and data processing, collaboration, information and service bundling, technology and programming, as well as service development.

Automatization and data processing skills are mandatory since the services provided need to be entirely computerized for realizing the full digital government potential. Collaboration competency is a prerequisite for the Transaction Business Model because different participants of the public sector organization's value chain usually have to cooperate to enable a comprehensive full online service provision.

Moreover, since the establishment of a comprehensive full online service provision demands automated use and interaction of various systems and databases, this also places high demands on the technology and programming abilities of the respective digital government service provider. Apart from that, information and service bundling as well as service development are indispensable skills to develop individual value-adding services and integrate or bundle them into service packages that are attractive for the user.

Integration Business Model

The Integration Business Model handles the integration of public stakeholders into the value chain of the public sector organization. This integration may take the form of participative, collaborative, or cooperative action. The subcategories of the Integration Business Model are public innovation, public participation, as well as public collaboration and coproduction.

Public Innovation

In public innovation undertakings, the user becomes part of the governmental or public sector innovation process. This requires, for example, access to shared developer suites, open interface systems, open innovation systems, and open government data to allow user access to relevant information and systems. This way, external experts and other interested parties can engage in the innovation process of the public sector to combine public and private sector knowledge and experience with the key aim of enhancing public value and public sector performance.

Public Participation

Public participation is about integrating public stakeholder preference, feedback, and opinion into public policy-making, administrative procedures, and public management. The concept aims at collecting ideas and expertise from the public, information that is widely dispersed in society, aggregating this input into applicable knowledge and thus allowing incorporation into governmental action. Well-known examples of electronic public participation are digital petitions, electronic voting, as well as feedback, reputation, and complaint management systems.

Public Collaboration and Coproduction

Public collaboration and coproduction takes this one step further. While public participation takes into account public stakeholder preference, feedback, and opinion, the user takes a proactive role in this subcategory. This means that the effectiveness and efficiency of the public sector is improved through active collaboration and coproduction between public sector organizations and individuals as well as private organizations. The Integration Business Model is shown in the following Figure 9.8.

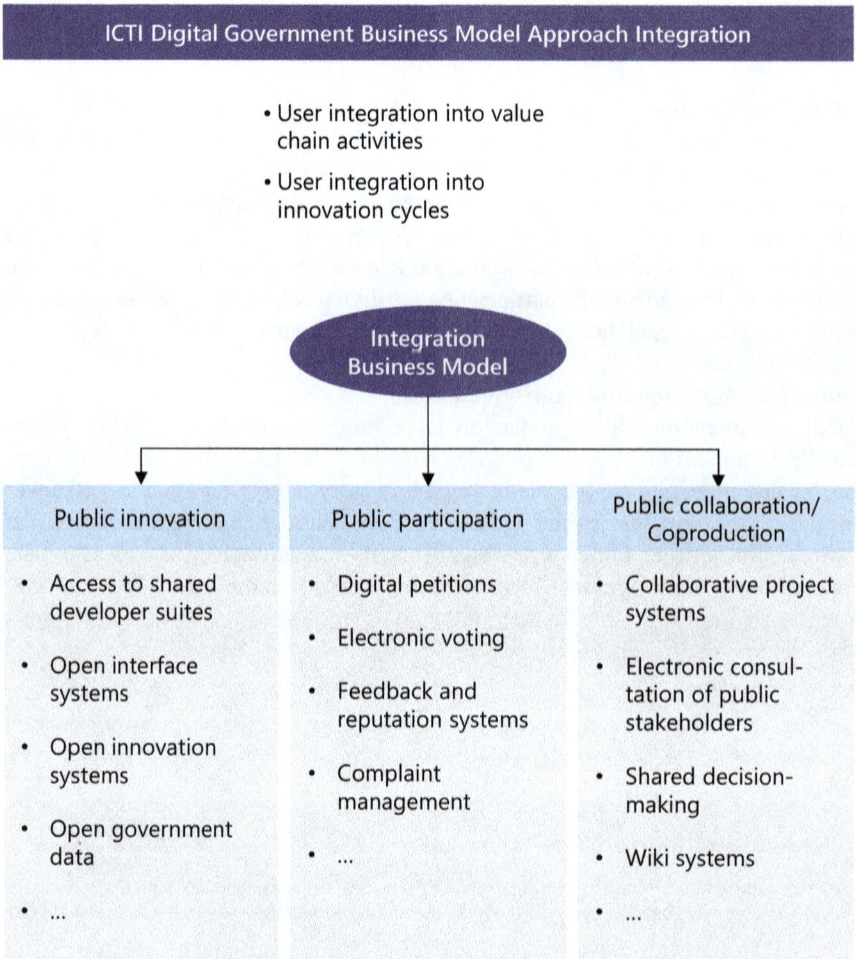

Fig. 9.8 Digital government business model for integration. Source: Wirtz and Daiser (2015, 2017b)

Examples of public collaboration and coproduction are collaborative project systems, electronic consultation of public stakeholders, shared decision-making, or digital government wiki systems. In collaborative project systems, citizens, for instance, help other citizens by providing information on administrative procedures in an online forum.

Alternatively, if individuals or private organizations are, for example, selected as consultants that collaborate electronically, they play an active role in the modification of the respective activity. The same holds true for public stakeholders that take an active role in a shared decision-making process or help elaborating a wiki system that supports users in handling digital government matters.

Core Assets of the Integration Business Model

Core assets of the Integration Business Model are employees, the IT platform, as well as the technological infrastructure. These resources are prerequisites for an effective integration of the user into governmental and administrative procedures.

Core Competencies of the Integration Business Model

User relationship management, experience design, technology and programming, as well as service development are core competencies necessary for transforming the previously mentioned core assets into superior services that have the potential to create user preferences and to increase public value of the communication services provided. The associated core competencies that are necessary to take advantage of the benefits that are connected with this business model are collaboration, content creation, user relationship management, and experience design.

ICTI Digital Government Models in Practice

In the initial phase of the digital government development, public sector service providers mainly offered informational services online. With the advancement of modern information and communication technologies and the increasing number of best practice examples from private sector e-commerce, the public sector started to develop new digital government business models, each with a specific service range.

Although these individual unifunctional business models may be run stand-alone, overall digital government systems have gradually become multifunctional. For this reason, most digital government portals today are hybrid forms of the ICTI Digital Government Business Model, providing services from more than one business model.

In 2014, for instance, it was the first time that all 193 United Nations member states had a national website, running at least an Information Business Model. Even though the majority of these countries does not yet provide complex Integration Business Model digital government services, many already offer communication and transaction digital government services (United Nations 2014).

Hybrid Public Business Models

The three key drivers for the development and rise of hybrid public business models are integrated transaction benefits, multiple user retention, and network effects. Integrated transaction benefits bring several advantages to the user and the digital government service provider. The development of hybrid business models is illustrated in the following Figure 9.9.

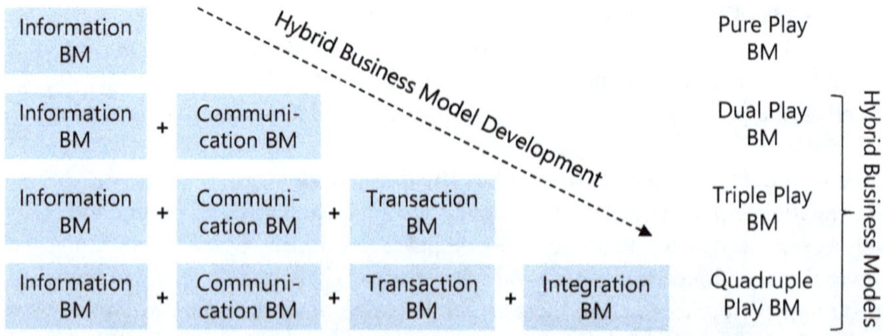

Fig. 9.9 Hybrid business model development. Source: Wirtz and Daiser (2015, 2017b)

Given a digital government platform that solely offers information as part of their business model, this would refer to a pure play business model. Starting with applying two business models, one can speak of a hybrid business model. In this particular case, a dual play business model. A triple play or quadruple play business model applies three or four different business models, respectively.

Advantages of Hybrid Public Business Models

From a user perspective, having a single point of access to various information and service offerings is convenient and reduces the user's search effort. From a provider perspective, the shift from offline to online costs through automatization of public services is a major benefit. The cost structure of digitized services is characterized by high fixed costs and low variable costs. This setting carries a vital advantage, because the higher the proportion of the fixed costs, the higher the benefits from economies of scale.

Economies of Scale

Economies of scale denominate the cost advantages that an organization obtains with increasing output. The underlying principle is that the cost per output unit decreases incrementally as the fixed costs are distributed over more output units. Transferred to digital government, this means that the service unit costs decrease with increasing scale if the number of service units provided increases.

As the major part of the fix costs arises with the initial installment of the basic digital government system, which provides the general digital government functionality, each additional service implementation is generally less expensive. Thus, the bigger the digital government service range offered and the more service units are provided, the higher the potential benefit of online service provision.

Multiple User Retention

Multiple user retention is a further aspect of hybrid public business models. The concept refers to user retention on several business model levels (Wirtz and Lihotzky 2001, 2003). Thus, acquiring and retaining users take place on the basis of more than one business model, which increases the number of digital government relations to the user. The resulting multiple user retention on different levels fosters user loyalty.

Creating intertwined user connections by conveniently providing multiple digital government business model services through a one-stop interface generates lock-in effects through high system change costs. This means that the exit barrier for the user is higher for multiple user relationships than for a singular user relationship. Thus, multiple user retention increases the switching cost for the user to change to an alternative system.

Network Effects

The network effects of hybrid public business models mainly result from economies of scale to expand digital government service provision, and from network effects to strengthen the digital government user base. On the one hand, the economies of scale related expansion of digital government service provision is achieved through extending the service range of existing users (e.g., a user that so far has only used the online tax declaration service starts using other digital government services, such as civil or organization registration). This way, existing user traffic can be transferred to other service offerings.

On the other hand, network value increases for both digital government service provider and user with growing network size. For the provider, any additional user potentially reduces the service unit cost and further justifies the means of the digital government system. For the user, a bigger network finally leads to more information through an increased user base and better digital government service provision through economies of scales that demand efficient automated service provision.

The growing value of the network also increases the incentive to participate for new users since people tend to follow strong groups or networks. However, there is also a drawback to the generally positive network effects. If a network loses users and thus, the value of network becomes smaller, leaving a network becomes a viable option for the users, too. The drivers for hybrid digital government business models are presented in the following Figure 9.10.

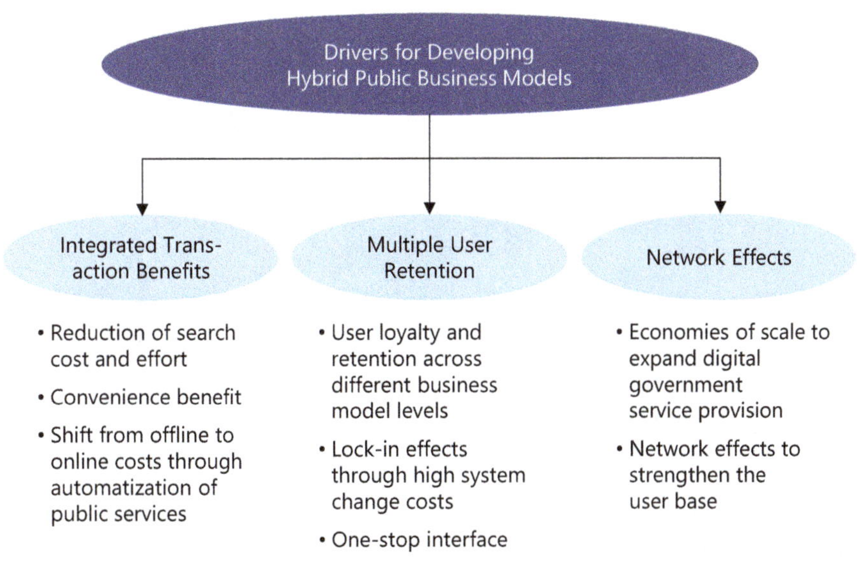

Fig. 9.10 Drivers of hybrid digital government business models. Source: Wirtz (2001, 2020b), Wirtz and Daiser (2015)

Exemplary Business Model of NYC 311

The digital government portal of the City of New York, called 311, is an example of a hybrid public business model that combines all four individual digital government business models.[5] This portal shows a very high development stage of their digital government service offering and belongs to the most advanced digital government portals worldwide (Holzer et al. 2014).

The City of New York provides a large quantity of content and various digital government services by using numerous technologies and different applications, such as Facebook, Twitter, or YouTube. A media channel refers to a specific service offer on the digital government platform, e.g., NYC Mayor's Office on Flickr, New York City Department of Cultural Affairs Facebook site, Twitter earthquake information community. Figure 9.11 illustrates the public business model of New York City.

[5]The 311 portal is New York City's main source of government information and services. For further information on the portal, please see www.nyc.gov

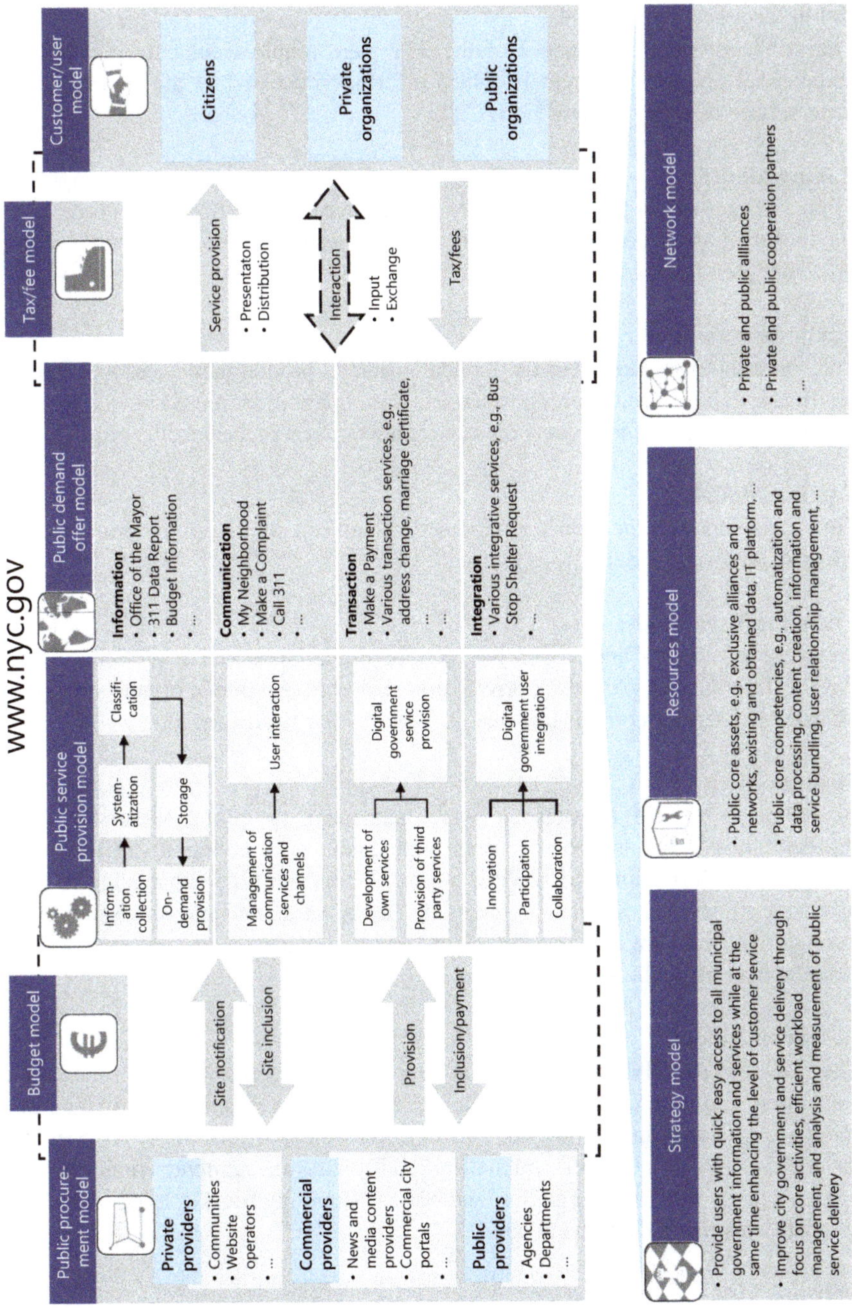

Fig. 9.11 New York City digital government business model (illustrative example). Source: Wirtz (2010), Wirtz and Daiser (2015, 2017b)

Public Procurement Model
The public procurement model of the 311 page requires content from private, commercial, and public providers, which is further processed for the digital government service offering of New York City.

Budget Model
From a budget model perspective, this service offering interaction (site notification, site inclusion, provision, and inclusion/payment) leads to information and payment flows between the respective parties.

Public Demand Offer Model
The portal shows a clear focus on public demand by providing services that address information, communication, transaction, and integration requirements and the underlying public service provision models are tailored to the specific requisitions.

Tax/Fee Model
The tax/fee model is the monetary connection between public service provision and the customer/user model.

Customer/User Model
Service provision and interaction between the digital government service provider and the different users (citizens, private organizations, and public organizations) are fundamental service components that cause particular payments.

Strategy Model
According to the 311 mission and vision statement, the portal pursues two key strategic aims: First, to provide users with quick, easy access to all municipal government information and services while at the same time enhancing the level of customer service. Second, to improve city government and service delivery through focus on core activities, efficient workload management, and analysis and measurement of public service delivery.

Resources Model
The resources model of the 311 digital government offering deals with the public core assets and core competencies that are required for effective information and service provision. Considering the extensive provision of full online services, for instance, exclusive alliances and network, IT platform, automatization and data processing, as well as information and service bundling are key core assets and competencies that have to be at hand.

Network Model
This is also reflected in the network model since private and public alliances as well as collaboration with cooperation partners are important aspects for providing such a comprehensive set of public information and services. From this point of view,

effective supervision of network partners is an essential part of New York City's digital government management.

9.3 Digital Government Business Model Innovation

During the past years, business model innovation has experienced considerable attention within science and management.[6] Especially the requirements, the structure, and the implementation aspects of business model innovations are of great interest for academics and practitioners.

Business Model Innovation

The concept of business model innovation is closely linked to the emergence of business models. After the burst of the new economy bubble, many organizations were forced to rethink and often radically change their business model since in many cases the survival of the organization largely depended on the new strategic and operative orientation (Wirtz et al. 2021a, c). It was in this phase that the concept of business model innovation appeared as a term for radical business model change or transformation.

Today, innovating business models is an essential part of management, strategy, and organization theory and a vital leadership approach in the private as well as the public sector (Wirtz et al. 2016a; Wirtz and Daiser 2018). The business model innovation concept has been applied by a myriad of organizations in various situations. Thus, its relevance and originality are only scarcely questioned anymore, as both practice and literature emphasize the importance of successful business model innovation for lasting success.

In 2008, for instance, 98% of 1130 interviewed CEOs and Public Sector Leaders reported in a worldwide survey that they had already taken advantage of business model innovation and thus also applied changes to their business models. Moreover, approximately 70% of the respondents planned to fundamentally implement business model innovation procedures (IBM 2008).

Integrated Concept of Public Business Model Innovation

The success of business model innovations depends on various factors. The most important aspects to business model innovation are consolidated into an integrated model in the following section.[7]

Figure 9.12 illustrates this integrated concept of public business model innovation (content based on Wirtz and Daiser (2017a)). The integrated concept of public

[6] See for the following Section 9.3 also Wirtz (2021).

[7] See for the following Section Integrated Concept of Public Business Model Innovation also Wirtz and Daiser (2017a) and Wirtz (2020a).

business model innovation comprises environmental dimensions and central dimension. The environmental dimensions include aspects on the macro- and micro-level. The macro-level contains factors, such as globalization, technology, industry, and market changes as well as regulatory and economic issues. The microlevel comprises changing user needs, product and service innovations, competitors, and organization dynamics that have a clear impact on an organization's business model innovations and thus significantly influence the central dimensions of business model innovation.

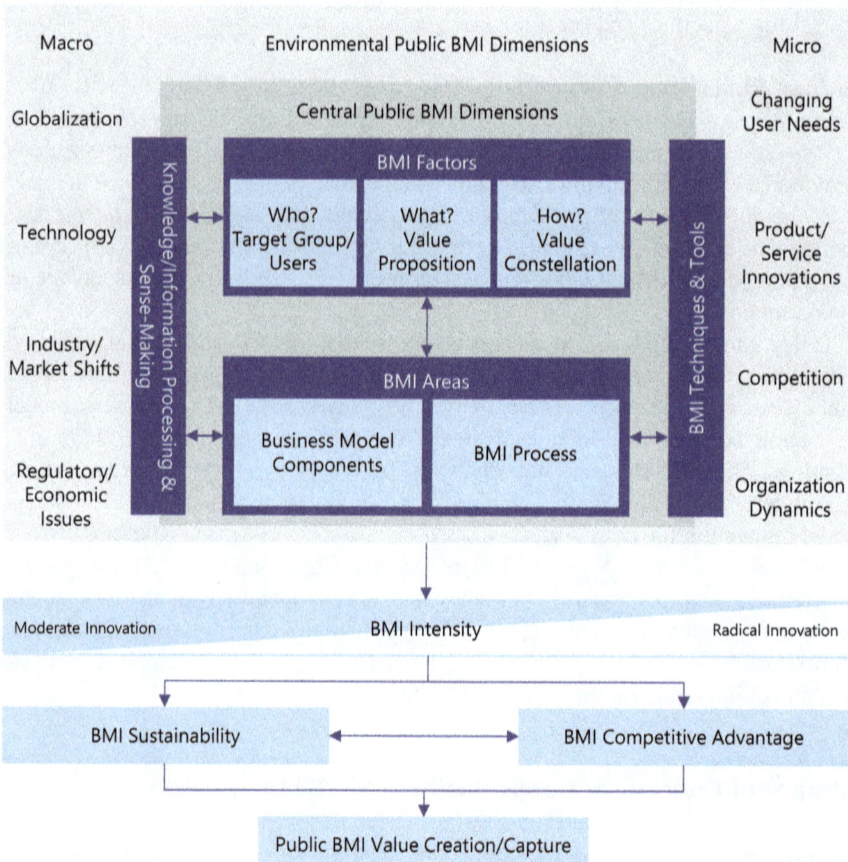

Fig. 9.12 Integrated concept of public business model innovation. Source: Wirtz and Daiser (2017a), Wirtz (2020a)

Central Public BMI Dimensions

The central dimensions consist of the business model innovation factors (BMI Factors) and the business model innovation areas (BMI areas). The BMI factors are the "who" (target user), "what" (value proposition), and "how" (value constellation) (Mahadevan 2004; Yang et al. 2014; Deloitte 2002). These factors determine the character of the business model innovation (e.g., business model innovation through changing user needs, value proposition, and/or the value constellation that transforms the value chain and thus represents an important element of the central dimensions of the concept of business model innovation).

The changes of the business model components and the business model innovation process are two important options for innovating existing business models, because both, collectively or individually, can have a significant impact on the efficiency and effectiveness of the business model innovation. This is why both options need to be carefully examined and assessed in the framework of public business model innovation.

The aspects of the environmental and central dimensions are closely connected to one another and create an interactive dynamic, because innovation-related changes lead to mutual adjustments (Mahadevan 2004). An organization or organization that revolutionizes an existing industry or technology, for instance, significantly influences the linked environment aspects, which in turn also influence the central dimensions of business model innovation.

This relationship indicates the great importance of a fundamental understanding of the internal and external aspects and factors that influence business model innovations. Against this background, the creation of knowledge and information (knowledge/information processing and sense-making) and the business model innovation tools and technics play an outstanding role (Eppler and Hoffmann 2012; Denicolai et al. 2014; Yang et al. 2014).

Knowledge/Information Processing and Sense-Making

The objective of generating knowledge and information is mostly to identify relevant information within the environmental dimensions and to evaluate them with regard to the existing business model and business model innovation.

BMI Techniques and Tools

This process should be carried out by means of structured tools and techniques to make the process understandable and repeatable (Eppler and Hoffmann 2012). This enables a systematic knowledge generation at the interface between the environmental dimension and central dimension. The basis of this method is, first, to generate knowledge/information and, second, to analyze and use this knowledge/information base in the own context for a business model innovation (Malhotra 2000; Denicolai et al. 2014).

In connection with the goals and the information from the central business model innovation dimensions, it is possible to derive certain business model adjustments.

BMI Intensity

These can differ in their intensity of change (Markides 2006; Bucherer et al. 2012; Hargadon 2015). The change intensity is an important aspect of the concept of business model innovation, since a high change intensity is also associated with a high risk and substantial effort with regard to the implementation of the business model innovation.

Most business model innovations are rather simple and only require moderate adjustments of the existing business model (Hargadon 2015). Major adjustments of existing business models result from radical business model innovations that substantially change existing business models (Demil and Lecocq 2010).

Moreover, there are various constellations of business model innovation that lie in between moderate and radical business model innovations and that also differ with regard to their intensity of business model innovation. Generally, it can be concluded that a higher level of business model innovation leads to a higher level of change intensity.

Public BMI Value Creation/Capture

A successful business model innovation leads to a sustainable business model innovation and also to competitive advantages (Teece 2010; Günzel and Holm 2013). Both aspects are closely linked to the general organization success or the success of the business model innovation.

A successful business model innovation allows organizations to create great value. In particular, the aspects of sustainability and competitive advantage that result from a business model innovation contribute to creating great value. The BMI literature considers value creation as the main objective of business model innovation. Therefore, value creation is the last aspect of the concept of business model innovation (Chesbrough 2010; Amit and Zott 2001).

The business model innovation process, which has already been referred to in the integrated concept of public business model innovation, will be discussed in more detail in the following section.

Public Business Model Innovation Process

Like in classical innovation management, public business model innovation shows a linear processual structure. This structure consists of a series of seven consecutive innovation steps, which finally sum up to an overall public business model innovation process presented in Figure 9.13.

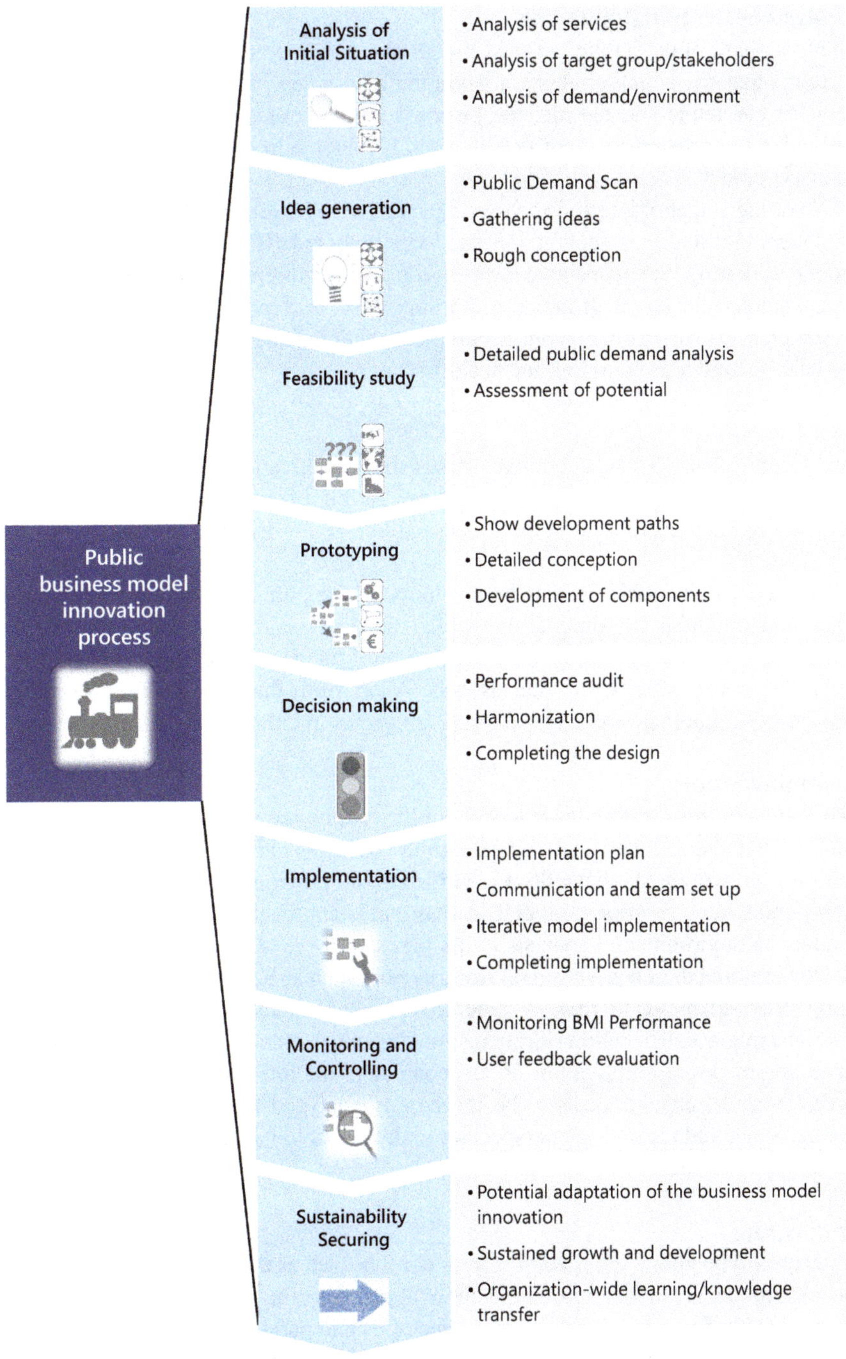

Fig. 9.13 Public business model innovation process. Source: Wirtz (2011, 2021), Wirtz and Daiser (2015)

Analysis of the Initial Situation

The first phase of the public business model innovation process is the analysis of the current situation, which contains a deviation assessment, showing the discrepancy between the actual and the planned business model course. To begin with, it is of particular importance to identify substantial vulnerabilities of the current public business model.

Next, the stakeholders and the user needs have to be identified and the coverage of stakeholder and user satisfaction has to be assessed. This is an essential step in order to identify the respective user needs and requirements. For public sector organizations the target group is often very diverse if not the entire community (Wirtz et al. 2021b). This first phase completes with the analysis of citizen needs and the current digital government service offering.

Idea Generation

The second phase, idea generation, serves the identification of potential business model innovations and the systematic generation of ideas. Starting points for innovations can occur within both the public sector organization itself and its environment.

The task for the public leaders here is to recognize public demand and to identify ideas and potential for innovation, which need to be transformed into suitable concepts. In this context, especially the design of the associated value propositions and value constellations are vital aspects. Apart from that, regular brainstorming sessions with internal or external experts are useful to collect ideas for innovation.

Feasibility Study

The main activities of the third step, feasibility study, are a detailed analysis of the public demand and the estimated impact of the business model innovation. Thus, the ideas for innovation that have been identified in the previous step are scrutinized for their public value creation potential. A reasonable approach for this procedure is to conduct an environmental analysis in the first step.

Often, global digital government frontrunners, such as Seoul, New York, or Hong Kong, or companies from the e-commerce sector have already similar or comparable solutions in place. This allows drawing conclusions for the development and implementation of desired innovation. In a second step, the intended digital government business model change needs to be thoroughly analyzed from a demand, content, management, and technology perspective with respect to its feasibility and expected public value impact.

Prototyping

In the prototype phase, the specific components as well as the prototype of the future business model are elaborated. In this innovation stage, the leadership team may still choose between various development trajectories and paths that need to be balanced before finally determining the dominating alternative. During this process, several detailed or fine-tuned concepts are usually established, which represent the relevant set of possible alternatives.

Decision Making

The selection and finalization of the definite alternative is made in the decision-making phase. For this purpose, the previously elaborated business model prototypes are detailed in a business plan to analyze and evaluate the cost–benefit ratio. Furthermore, the alternatives are harmonized with regard to their business model structure and design. At this level, final weaknesses and vulnerabilities of the alternatives should be uncovered and weak alternatives discarded.

Implementation

The implementation phase of business model innovation process covers the planning and integration of activities that are associated with the implementation of the modified business model. Implementation, however, is not a linear process. It rather requires constant revisions and change loops to apply necessary adjustments to the planning or implementation deviations.

The required change management capabilities usually parallel the extent of the model change. Changing, for instance, a detail in a recently added business model component will cause less resistance and demand less change management effort and experience than an entire change of a business model component with a long-lasting organizational tradition.

Since a business model implementation possesses a clear project character, it is reasonable to handle the implementation within a project organization framework. A project refers to an activity that is of novel, risky, and complex nature, finished within a specific period of time, and planned to achieve a particular aim.

The implementation project requires a detailed implementation plan that is prepared on the basis of a stepwise realization of the business model. Furthermore, the project communication and the team setup for the implementation phase are of paramount importance. The selected members of the project team need to have the motivation, the skills, the knowledge, and the empowerment that are necessary to conduct and complete the implementation project.

Monitoring and Controlling

Having implemented the public business model, the project performance needs to be monitored and controlled. For this purpose, the leadership team has to develop relevant project milestones and performance indicators in advance of the project launch. These key figures have to be constantly monitored and evaluated to be able to intervene and make further adjustments if deviations from the planned performance occur.

Sustainability Securing

In the final stage of the public business model innovation process, the responsible public managers have to secure the sustainability of the business model innovation. This means that they have to assure that necessary adaptations of the business model innovation are applied in order to support the business model innovation's long-term development. Furthermore, they have to ensure a continual knowledge transfer and organization-wide learning.

The success of an implemented public business model largely depends on the fulfillment of the user's needs and requirements. Against this background, many demand factors and user service preferences have been identified in science and public management. These are presented in the following chapter.

9.4 Summary, Review Questions, Topics for Discussion, and Online Exercises

- A business model represents the service systems of a public sector organization and illustrates in a simplified, aggregated form what resources are used and how they are transformed into the public sector organization's service offering.
- Several interdependent business model levels can be distinguished: the supranational business model level, the national business model level, the regional business model level, and the local business model level.
- The three main directions of business model concepts are the technology-oriented business model approach, the organization-oriented business model approach, and the strategy-oriented business model approach.
- Within an integrated business model approach nine partial business models can be distinguished. These are the strategy model, the resources model, the network model, the public demand offer model, the customer/user model, the tax/fee model, the public procurement model, the public service provision model, and the budget model. The partial business models are all closely intertwined, creating interdependent relationships.
- The ICTI digital government business model approach focuses on the primary service offering as the critical element for classification. The relevant public business models in a digital government context can thus be classified into four basic stand-alone business models: Information, Communication, Transaction, and Integration (ICTI).
- The Information Business Model focuses on the compiling and packaging of information, as well as the presentation and provision of content on the own platform. Subcategories of the information business model are the mandatory information offer and the non-mandatory information offer.
- The core target of the Communication Business Model is the successful setup and provision of communication exchange possibilities. Subcategories of the communication business model are the dynamic communication offer and the automated communication offer.
- Focus of the Transaction Business Model are the initiation and processing of administrative transaction with the aim to complement or substitute existing offline government services. There can be either a partial online offer or a full online offer.
- The Integration Business Model handles the user integration into value chain activities and the innovation cycles. Subcategories are public innovation, public participation, and public collaboration/coproduction.

- Although the ICTI business models may be run stand-alone, overall digital government systems have gradually become multifunctional. The three key drivers for the development and rise of hybrid public business models are integrated transaction benefits, multiple user retention, and network effects.

Chapter 9
Review questions, topics for discussion and online exercises

Review questions

1. Define public business models. On which levels of digital government can business models be set up?
2. Describe and explain the partial models of the integrated public business model.
3. Explain the ICTI digital government business model approach.
4. Elaborate on why there are usually no pure play business models anymore. Present the development from pure play business models to quadruple play business models.
5. Explain the public business model innovation process.

Topics for classroom discussion and team debates

1. The business model concept originates from business practice. Discuss within the class why it is useful and necessary to apply the business model concept also in the public sector (reduction of bureaucracy, stronger citizen orientation, public value).
2. Discuss which of the four ICTI business models are most important for the creation of public value and to what extent each of these business model forms can be found in the digital government context of your city.
3. Debate why there is so little innovation in digital government and why a structured public business model innovation process is necessary.

Online Exercises

1. Visit https://www.nyc.gov/ and identify the underlying ICTI digital government business models based on the services presented. Classify the provided services accordingly.
2. Go to https://oecd-opsi.org/toolkits/digital-policy-model-canvas and work through the toolkit. Use it exemplary for your own city.
3. Enter https://govcrate.org/2019/05/05/why-business-models-are-important-for-your-e-government-initiative/ and explore the website. Discuss why business models are important for the public sector.

References

Amit, Raphael; Zott, Christoph (2001): Value creation in E-business. In Strategic Management Journal 22 (6-7), pp. 493–520. DOI: https://doi.org/10.1002/smj.187.

Bucherer, Eva; Eisert, Uli; Gassmann, Oliver (2012): Towards Systematic Business Model Innovation: Lessons from Product Innovation Management. In Creativity and Innovation Management 21 (2), pp. 183–198. DOI: https://doi.org/10.1111/j.1467-8691.2012.00637.x.

Chesbrough, Henry (2010): Business Model Innovation: Opportunities and Barriers. In Long Range Planning 43 (2-3), pp. 354–363. DOI: https://doi.org/10.1016/j.lrp.2009.07.010.

Deloitte (2002): Business model innovation. New York: Deloitte.

Demil, Benoît; Lecocq, Xavier (2010): Business Model Evolution: In Search of Dynamic Consistency. In Long Range Planning 43 (2-3), pp. 227–246. DOI: https://doi.org/10.1016/j.lrp.2010.02.004.

Denicolai, Stefano; Ramirez, Matias; Tidd, Joe (2014): Creating and capturing value from external knowledge: the moderating role of knowledge intensity. In R&D Management 44 (3), pp. 248–264. DOI: https://doi.org/10.1111/radm.12065.

Eppler, Martin J.; Hoffmann, Friederike (2012): Does method matter? An experiment on collaborative business model idea generation in teams. In Innovation 14 (3), pp. 388–403. DOI: https://doi.org/10.5172/impp.2012.14.3.388.

Günzel, Franziska; Holm, Anna B. (2013): One size does not fit all: Understanding the front-end and backend of business model innovation. In International Journal of Innovation Management 17 (1), pp. 1–34. DOI: https://doi.org/10.1142/S1363919613400021.

Hargadon, Andrew (2015): How to discover and assess opportunities for business model innovation. In Strategy & Leadership 43 (6), pp. 33–37. DOI: https://doi.org/10.1108/SL-08-2015-0069.

Holzer, Marc; Zheng, Yueping; Manoharan, Aroon; Shark, Alan (2014): Digital Governance in Municipalities Worldwide (2013-2014). Sixth Global E-Governance Survey: A Longitudianl Assessment of Municipal Websites Throughout the World. Edited by Rutgers School of Public Affairs and Administration. Newark. Available online at https://spaa.newark.rutgers.edu/sites/default/files/files/EGov/Publications/Digital-Governance-Municipalities-Worldwide-2014.pdf, checked on 6/30/2015.

IBM (2008): The Enterprise of the Future. Global CEO Study. Edited by IBM Corporation. Available online at https://www-03.ibm.com/industries/ca/en/healthcare/files/2008_ibm_global_ceo_study.pdf, checked on 6/30/2015.

Janssen, Marijn; Kuk, George; Wagenaar, René W. (2008): A survey of Web-based business models for e-government in the Netherlands. In Government Information Quarterly 25 (2), pp. 202–220.

Mahadevan, B. (2004): A framework for business model innovation. In IMRC (Ed.): IMRC Conference: Bangalore, pp. 16–18.

Malhotra, Yogesh (2000): Knowledge management and new organization forms: A framework for business model innovation. In Information Resources Management Journal 13 (1), pp. 5–14.

Markides, Constantinos (2006): Disruptive Innovation: In Need of Better Theory. In Journal of Product Innovation Management 23 (1), pp. 19–25. DOI: https://doi.org/10.1111/j.1540-5885.2005.00177.x.

Teece, David J. (2010): Business Models, Business Strategy and Innovation. In Long Range Planning 43 (2-3), pp. 172–194. DOI: https://doi.org/10.1016/j.lrp.2009.07.003.

United Nations (2014): United Nations E-Government Survey 2014. E-Government for the Future We Want. With assistance of Department of Economic and Social Affairs. New York. Available online at http://unpan3.un.org/egovkb/Portals/egovkb/Documents/un/2014-Survey/E-Gov_Complete_Survey-2014.pdf, checked on 12/1/2014.

Wirtz, Bernd W. (2010): Business model management. Design - Instrumente - Erfolgsfaktoren von Geschäftsmodellen. 1st ed. Wiesbaden: Gabler.

Wirtz, Bernd W. (2011): Business Model Management. Design - Instruments - Success Factors. 1st ed. Wiesbaden: Gabler.
Wirtz, Bernd W. (2015): E-Government. Perspektiven des kommunalen E-Government. E-Government Studie. Mainz: Ministerium des Innern, für Sport und Infrastruktur. Edited by Land Rheinland-Pfalz. Ministerium des Innern, für Sport und Infrastruktur.
Wirtz, Bernd W. (2019): Digital Business Models. Concepts, Models, and the Alphabet Case Study. Heidelberg.
Wirtz, Bernd W. (2020a): Business Model Management. Design - Process - Instruments. 2nd ed. Cham: Springer International Publishing.
Wirtz, Bernd W. (2020b): Electronic Business. 7th ed. Wiesbaden: Springer Gabler.
Wirtz, Bernd W. (2021): Business Model Management. Design - Instrumente - Erfolgsfaktoren von Geschäftsmodellen. 5th ed. Wiesbaden: Springer Gabler.
Wirtz, Bernd W. (2022): E-Government. Wiesbaden: Springer Gabler.
Wirtz, Bernd W.; Daiser, Peter (2015): E-Government. Strategy, process, instruments. 1st ed. Speyer.
Wirtz, Bernd W.; Daiser, Peter (2017a): Business model innovation: An integrative conceptual framework. In Journal of Business Models 5 (1), pp. 14–34.
Wirtz, Bernd W.; Daiser, Peter (2017b): E-government. Strategy, process, instruments. 2nd ed. Speyer.
Wirtz, Bernd W.; Daiser, Peter (2018): Business model innovation processes: A systematic literature review. In Journal of Business Models (6), pp. 40–58. DOI: https://doi.org/10.5278/ojs.jbm.v6i1.2397.
Wirtz, Bernd W.; Göttel, Vincent; Daiser, Peter (2016a): Business model innovation: Development, concept and future research directions. In Journal of Business Models 4 (1), pp. 1–28.
Wirtz, Bernd W.; Kohler, Julia; Weyerer, Jan C. (2022a): Public business model management: A literature review-based integrated framework. In International Journal of Public Sector Performance Management. DOI: https://doi.org/10.1080/01900692.2021.1947319.
Wirtz, Bernd W.; Kubin, Pascal R. M.; Weyerer, Jan C. (2021a): Business model innovation in the public sector: an integrative framework. In Public Management Review. DOI: https://doi.org/10.1080/14719037.2021.1972703.
Wirtz, Bernd W.; Langer, Paul F.; Schmidt, Florian W. (2021b): Digital government: Business model development for public value creation. A dynamic capabilities based framework. In Public Administration Quarterly 45 (3), pp. 232–255.
Wirtz, Bernd W.; Lihotzky, Nikolai (2001): Internetökonomie, Kundenbindung und Portalstrategien. In Die Betriebswirtschaft 61 (3), pp. 285–305.
Wirtz, Bernd W.; Lihotzky, Nikolai (2003): Customer retention management in the B2C electronic business. In Long Range Planning 36 (6), pp. 517–532. DOI: https://doi.org/10.1016/j.lrp.2003.08.010.
Wirtz, Bernd W.; Müller, Wilhelm M.; Langer, Paul F. (2022b): Quo vadis business model innovation? BMI status, development and research implications. In International Journal of Innovation Management, Forthcoming.
Wirtz, Bernd W.; Müller, Wilhelm M.; Weyerer, Jan C. (2021c): Digital pandemic response systems: A strategic management framework against covid-19. In International Journal of Public Administration 44 (11-12), pp. 896–906. DOI: https://doi.org/10.1080/01900692.2020.1858316.
Wirtz, Bernd W.; Pistoia, Adriano; Ullrich, Sebastian; Göttel, Vincent (2016b): Business models: Origin, development and future research perspectives. In Long Range Planning 49 (1), pp. 36–54.
Wirtz, Bernd W.; Vogt, Patrick; Denger, Katharina S. (2001): Electronic Business in der Versicherungswirtschaft. In Zeitschrift für die gesamte Versicherungswirtschaft 90 (1), pp. 161–190.
Yang, D.-H.; You, Y.-Y.; Kwon, H.-J. (2014): A framework for business model innovation using market, component and innovation tool. In Journal of Applied Engineering Research 9 (21), pp. 9235–9248.

Part III

Digital Government Services, Channels and Implementation

User-Driven Digital Government 10

Contents

Learning Objectives
By working through this chapter, you will be able to:

1. Describe the USS e-demand factor system and the aspects of its three quality functions.
2. Outline the structure of a schematic digital government portal network.
3. Divide the digital government service preference categories into top, middle, and low priority areas with regard to their importance to users.
4. Explain the different methods of targeting.
5. Describe and explain the digital government user relationship management process.

Creating a common interface for various public stakeholders that possess distinctive information and service needs as well as different educational and technical backgrounds inevitably leads to demanding issues.[1] Thus, designing, implementing, and maintaining a digital government system that adds public value to society is a challenging task.

[1] See for Chapter 10 User-driven Digital Government also Wirtz (2015, 2020, 2021, 2022); Wirtz and Daiser (2015, 2017).

B. W. Wirtz, *Digital Government*, Springer Texts in Business and Economics,
https://doi.org/10.1007/978-3-031-13086-1_10

Digital Government Portal Layout Perspective
In the early digital government stages, there were diverse discussions on how this should be tackled from a digital government portal layout perspective. Basically two mainstreams were present at that time: a provider and a user perspective. One of the first suggestions how to evaluate digital government portals—therefore, indirectly setting the design targets—was to assess their overall compliance with laws and regulations (Eschenfelder et al. 1997).

Elaboration of User-Centered Designs
Another approach was to elaborate user-centered designs that were supposed to be useful to the users (Huang and Chao 2001) and allowed easy interaction (Bertot and Jaeger 2006). The idea was that only a shift from the traditional provider orientation to a clear user focus in digital government development and implementation would lead to a transformation of government (Jaeger and Bertot 2010).

Today, providing services that are tailored to the users' needs is the dominating digital government approach. For the provider of digital government portals this means that they have to consider numerous essential elements when designing, implementing, and maintaining digital government systems. For this purpose, vital functional aspects and user preferences are presented in the following.

10.1 Functional Digital Government Demand Factors

By shifting the focus from provider-oriented to user-oriented aspects, digital government is regarded to have the potential to enhance the interaction between the government and its stakeholders (Wirtz and Kurtz 2017). To achieve this, governments need to be aware of the service and resource requirements of their users. Therefore, the major questions that need to be answered are: What do users want and what do they expect from digital government?

Perceived Digital Government Factors
There exists an extensive collection of studies in the scientific literature on this topic, which provides various relevant user-oriented digital government factors. These range from elementary factors, such as technology readiness, to complex factors, like trust in the government. It is important to understand that these factors are perceived factors. This means that there is usually not a definite, objective criteria, but only the perception of the individual user who evaluates the respective issue based on personal reflection of reality, knowledge, prior biases, and experiences.

USS E-Demand Factor System

The functional e-demand factors can be organized in three quality packages: Use quality, System quality, and Service quality (USS). Use quality refers to user-related factors before, during, and after usage of the digital government system. System and service quality handle factors that are associated with the overall system quality or the quality of the service provided, respectively. Figure 10.1 presents the USS E-Demand Factor System.

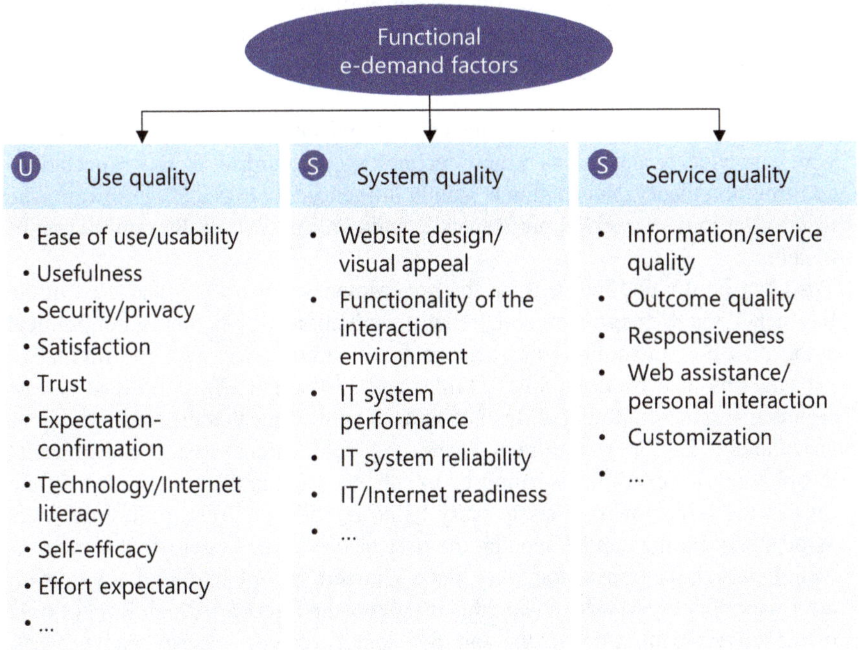

Fig. 10.1 USS e-demand factor system. Source: Wirtz and Daiser (2015, 2017)

Use Quality Factors

The e-demand factors that are illustrated in the use quality category in Figure 10.1 are presented in chronological sequence (before, during, and after use). These factors rather show a user-orientation, while system quality and service quality instead are more provider-oriented.

- Ease of use/usability measures the perceived user effort to become acquainted with and learn to use a new technology. It is a factor of the Technology Acceptance Model (Davis 1986), according to which the attitude of a user towards using a new technology is mainly determined through the two factors ease of use and usefulness. These two factors are one of the most important factors for predicting the use of new technologies.
- Usefulness measures a user's subjective perception or impression concerning if the use of a specific technology facilitates tasks or enhances performance. If, for instance, a new technology is not perceived as a value-adding or performance-

enhancing tool, then why take the effort and bear the risk of changing the status quo?

- Security/privacy: Security and privacy are important prerequisites for the acceptance of digital government. Here, security and privacy are understood as the perceived safety, secrecy, and confidentiality of individual user data as well as network-based information processing. These factors influence the likeliness of users to perform digital government transactions online. Apart from that, they are closely related to trust.
- Satisfaction: Satisfaction refers to the extent to which a user is satisfied or pleased with a service or the use of a new technology. According to the expectation-confirmation theory, satisfaction is mainly influenced by expectations towards the new technology, perceived performance, and confirmation or disconfirmation of beliefs.
- Trust can be divided into trust in the government or institution and trust in the Internet: Trust in the government "reflects evaluations of whether or not political authorities and institutions are performing in accordance with the normative expectations held by the public" (Miller and Listhaug 1990, p. 358). It can be regarded as a measurement of the faith and the confidence that the public has in its government. Digital government, increasing public transparency and citizens' information, for example, is supposed to enhance trust in the government. While trust in the government refers to party-based confidence, trust in the Internet is associated with the confidence that the user places in the system or the environment in which the transaction takes place. Concerning online digital government information and service provision this usually is the Internet. A high level of trust in the government, trust in the Internet, and perceived security and privacy, increases the likelihood that public stakeholders use a digital government system.
- The expectation-confirmation concept aims to explain post-adoption satisfaction through expectation, perceived performance, and confirmation or disconfirmation of beliefs (Oliver 1977, 1980). Simply speaking, a high expectation of a new technology that shows a low perceived performance would lead to a disconfirmation of beliefs and thus would cause a decrease in user satisfaction. Therefore, the active management of expectations is an important activity as raising excessive user expectations can be counterproductive.
- Technology/Internet literacy: A key factor for using digital government portals is the users' ability to successfully use the services provided. This requires two perspectives: a user and a provider perspective. Computer and Internet skill discrepancies, language differences, or disparities in reading literacy are just a few examples that governments have to consider in their online information and service provision. Furthermore, effective interaction requires public stakeholders to understand the procedures and the structure of public administration. Therefore, digital government providers have to provide the content and the services in an informative and constructive way for the users.
- Self-efficacy: Self-efficacy is the extent or strength of a person's belief that he or she is capable of performing a particular action or reaching a specific goal. In connection with digital government, this factor measures, for example, a citizen's

belief about his capability to apply for an ID card or to make a tax declaration online.

- Effort expectancy: Apart from being able to use a new technology and believing in one's abilities to do so, the user's expectation about the effort to use a new technology is an important factor. If users, for instance, believe that it takes high effort to use the digital government system, they are more reluctant to use it.

System Quality Factors

The system quality-related e-demand factors are important aspects from an overall system perspective that should be considered when designing, implementing, and maintaining a digital government system:

- Website design/visual appeal: The appearance of the website and its content are vital factors for the use of digital government portals. Key aspects of this factor are the content's presentation as well as the website layout, which mainly refer to graphical elements such as color, typeface, or illustrations. Together with performance and reliability, this factor forms a group of elements that is of paramount importance from a system quality perspective.
- Functionality of the interaction environment is also seen as an important factor for attracting users and increasing digital government portal use. Examples of the functionalities of the interaction environment are automated completion of forms or electronic contact recommendations.
- Perceived IT system performance is a vital factor for the use of a digital government system. If the user believes that service delivery performance is weak, this may reduce the user's intention to reuse a new technology since he is not satisfied with its input-output ratio.
- The impact of perceived IT system reliability is more or less the same as the effect of perceived performance. If a system is perceived to be unreliable, in other words, it also shows a rather low performance, this leads to a reduction of the intention to use or to reuse a new technology.
- IT/Internet readiness: This factor measures the maturity of the technology used. The origin of technology readiness lies in the method to systematically analyze the current development stage of a new technology. This so-called technology readiness level was first used by the NASA for rating technology developments on a 1 (observation and description of the operating principle) to 9 (qualified system with proof of successful use) scale. Transferred to digital government, a higher degree of readiness will increase the likelihood of using a digital government system.

Service Quality Factors

The service quality-related e-demand factors show a strong connection with the provision of digital government information or services. Like the system quality factors, these are also rather provider-oriented:

- Information/service quality refers to the quality of the services and the information provided. Concerning perceived information quality, for instance, timeliness, completeness, accuracy, and relevance of the information provided, as well as an adequate amount of content are valued aspects. A high degree of, for example, reliability, functionality, and ease of use are crucial elements for high perceived service quality (Wirtz and Birkmeyer 2017; Wirtz and Kurtz 2018).
- While perceived information/service quality refers to the process of using the digital government portal, perceived outcome quality is concerned with the result of the service delivery, and thus with the person's satisfaction and experience with the outcome of the services provided. If the user is satisfied and looks back to a positive experience concerning the service offering, this positively influences future behavioral intentions to revisit the digital government portal.
- Responsiveness refers to two aspects: first, the degree to which employees or digital government portals provide information and services (e.g., information, communication, transaction, or integration services) and second, the time between inquiry and service provision (e.g., appointment request and confirmation). High responsiveness fosters user satisfaction, which in turn increases the likelihood of using a digital government system.
- Although digital government service provision tends to be of automated technology-based nature that increases the self-serving character of public service offering, the possibility of web assistance or personal interaction makes the digital government system more convenient to the user. Moreover, the opportunity for personal interaction fosters user trust and confidence in using digital government services.
- Customization refers to the possibility of tailoring websites, applications, or other online offers to the personal preferences of the user. A high level of customization, for example, satisfies the desire of users to personalize online offers, which in turn should increase the likelihood of using or reusing a digital government portal.

Multitude of Important Factors

Summing up, when designing, implementing, and maintaining a user-oriented digital government portal, various important factors must be taken into account. Essential elements are that information needs to be up-to-date, comprehensive, accurate, and relevant, and services require easy, transparent, and performant handling.

In a nutshell, information and service provision demands convenient, appealing, and reliable administration from a user's perspective. Furthermore, especially security, privacy, risk, and trust-related factors are crucial. In addition, expectation management takes a significant role since unfulfilled user expectation may lead to dissatisfaction and thus a decreasing likelihood of sustainable digital government service use. In addition, user abilities, such as Internet literacy and skills, as well as user self-efficacy need to be considered when developing digital government solutions.

The above-mentioned functional e-demand factors represent fundamental digital government elements that provide the underlying cornerstones for the development and maintenance of a digital government portal. A digital government portal can provide a single point of access to meet user demands. Its network structure is illustrated in the following section.

Schematic Digital Government Portal Network

Although multiple systems are in use and connect the data from various providers, the digital government platform is the single point of access for the user, and the transactions can be conducted via the Internet since modern information and communication technologies as well as increasing interconnectedness of participants provide the necessary environment for adequate online data transmission.[2] In this context, digital government portals serve as service bundling platforms that combine the service offering of the respective public sector organizations and allow comfortable service provision.

One-stop-digital-government Portal
In this way, a one-stop-digital-government portal can be generated that centrally provides the formerly analog public services to its stakeholders online. This single point of access reduces the search effort for the user and allows more efficient administrative processes, resulting in cost and time savings. Figure 10.2 illustrates a schematic digital government portal network.

[2] See for the following Section Schematic Digital Government Portal Network also Wirtz (2021).

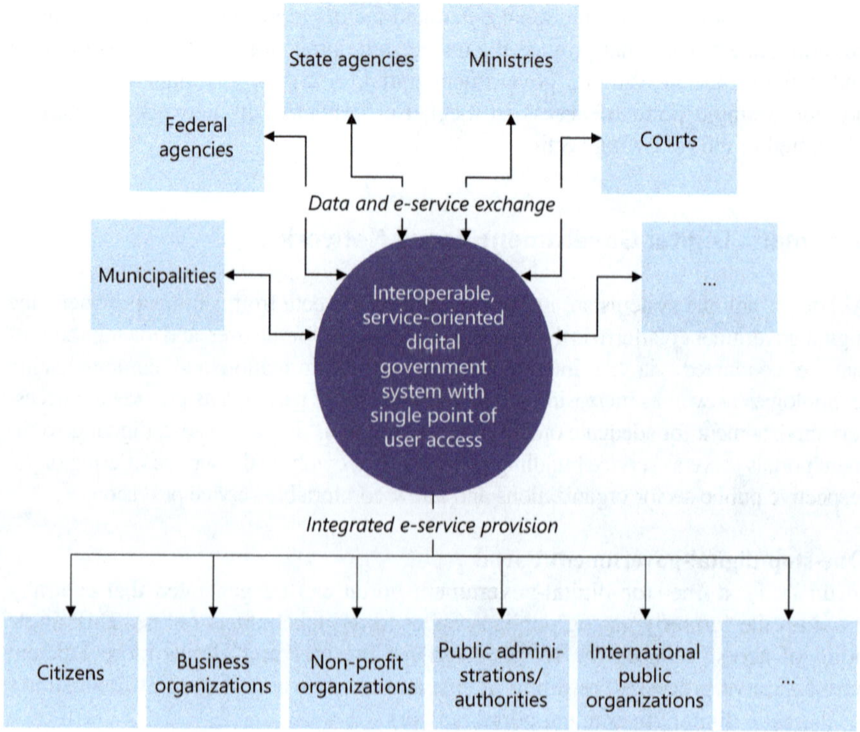

Fig. 10.2 Schematic digital government portal network. Source: Wirtz and Daiser (2015), Wirtz (2021)

In order to appropriately address the public stakeholders, the functional e-demand factors have to be merged with public demand aspects to derive an adequate reflection of their digital service preferences. These are explained in the following section.

10.2 Digital Government Service Preferences

An effective digital government portal interaction requires that users find their way around the digital government portal easily and get to the desired services quickly. For this reason, the individual services offered are grouped and usually organized in specific digital government service preference categories. This way, the digital government services are provided in a thematic classification that is built on a multi-level design.

These subject categories should be defined in a logical structure and as mutually exclusive as possible to avoid inconsistencies in their composition. On the first level, these preference categories have to give the user a clear picture of the subject, and thus on the digital government information and services that the user will find in the category. Therefore, the preference categories need to be determined from a public stakeholder perspective, clearly reflecting user needs and user demand.

Digital Government Service Preference Categories

In the course of a digital government user preference survey, the digital government service preference categories of several digital government portals were analyzed.[3] The services provided and their groupings were compared and filtered in various runs to derive the following generic classifications, which are illustrated in Table 10.1.

Table 10.1 Digital government service preference categories

Digital government service preferences	Information and service examples
Civic and immigration services	ID card, residence permit, and driver license application, divorce information, voter assistance
Health and medical services	Insurance services, facility information, nutrition information, vaccines information
Business and employment services	License application, financial services, legal assistance, job portal, job hunting information
Taxes and duties services	Tax declaration service, tax payment service, property tax information
Car, transport, and road services	Vehicle registration, public transport information, parking license service, accident information
Housing and property services	Affordable housing information, construction permit services, utility information
Social and volunteering services	Social security information, community program information, donation service
Family services	Child care information, adoption information, day care center information
Government, law, and order services	Electoral matters, consumer protection, crime and government reports, coast guard information
Arts, culture, and tourism services	Locations, activities, funding and support, visitor information
Recreation and sport services	Park and nature information, sport locations, sport activities, youth event information
Libraries and education services	Enrollment, e-book services, student support, rules and policies, adult education
Environment and recycling services	Garbage and recycling information, animal control, air and water quality information

Source: Wirtz (2015, 2021)

Since the scope of the study was on municipal digital government service offerings, the resulting service preference classifications are geared to local and regional digital government requirements, which tend to show a stronger user

[3]See for the following Section 10.2 also Wirtz (2015).

orientation than digital government portals on national level. Furthermore, digital government on a local and a regional level provides the main platform interfaces for user access.

Civic and Immigration Services
The civic and immigration services preference category summarizes topics that provide public stakeholders with information on and services of responsible agencies and officials (e.g., contact information, communication provision), public record management (e.g., ID card, passport, address), immigration services (e.g., foreign government and embassy information, residence permit), and related statistics (e.g., population data, city management report, city council information). Full online availability for renewal of ID cards or passports ranks first in terms of importance among citizens as a single public e-service in this category (Wirtz and Kurtz 2016).

Health and Medical Services
The health and medical services preference category covers information and services that are associated with the health care system, healthy nutrition, living, and environment. In the employment services preference category, information and services concerning the topics job search, recruitment, labor legislation, employee protection, occupational safety and health, etc. are summarized.

Business and Employment Services
The business and employment services preference category contains information and services that are associated with starting and managing a business as well as employment-related consumer information. In the taxes and duties services preference category, information and services concerning all forms of tax declaration and payment (e.g., income tax, property tax, value-added tax) are provided.

Car, Transport, and Road Services
The car, transport, and road services preference category covers information and services for getting around, either by car or by public transport. Thus, this category supports public stakeholders in topics like vehicle registration, parking, tickets, towing, accidents, buses, trains, taxis, bicycles, etc.

Housing and Property Services
In the housing and property services preference category, relevant information and services concerning buildings, construction, properties, property management, land, etc. are summarized.

Social and Volunteering Services
In the social and volunteering services preference category, public stakeholders get information and services that are related to public provision of benefits (e.g., assistance, food, utilities, benefits for disabled people), donations, community groups and programs, and provision of voluntary community services.

Family Services
The preference category family services covers family-related topics, such as child adoption, child abuse, day care center, domestic violence, home care.

Government, Law, and Order Services
In the government, law, and order services preference category, users have the possibility to inform themselves and use services with regard to government structure, government reports and publications, payment of government bills, election-related topics, law and the legal system, crime, emergencies, etc.

Arts, Culture, and Tourism Services
The preference category arts, culture, and tourism services summarizes information and services concerning arts venues, arts organizations, cultural programs, monuments, museums, sightseeing, travelling, and so forth.

Recreation and Sport Services
The preference category recreation and sport services offers its users information and services that closely relate to topics such as leisure activities, beaches, country parks, sport events, as well as sports organizations and facilities.

Libraries and Education Services
The libraries and education services preference category provides public stakeholders with information and services on libraries (e.g., library facilities, rules and regulations, library cards application, reading groups, and activities), on schools, colleges, and universities (e.g., enrollment, eligibility information, college preparation information), as well as adult education (e.g., literacy information, vocational services).

Environment and Recycling Services
In the preference category environment and recycling services, public information and services concerning, for instance, garbage, recycling, air and water quality, environmental protection, noise protection, and animal control are provided.

This exemplary digital government service preference category structure provides a clear and transparent service offer that supports the user in finding the desired services. Furthermore, by aggregating the information and service offers into 13 categories on the first level, the user is not confronted with an information overload and can access the respective information and services step by step. This way, the user may also discover further relevant information or additional services.

Importance of Digital Government Service Preference Categories
However, the presented digital government service preference categories differ in their importance concerning public demand. According to the digital government citizen preference study by Wirtz (2015), the service preference categories can be divided into three priority areas: top, middle, and low priority.

Top Priority Areas

The four categories (1) taxes and duties services, (2) civic and immigration services, (3) car, transport, and road services, as well as (4) arts, culture, and tourism services were evaluated as important or very important by clearly more than half of the participants. Especially the services of the categories taxes and duties services (64%) as well as civic and immigration services (63%) were regarded as vital online service offers, being rated as important or very important by six out of ten respondents.

Middle Priority Areas

The middle priority areas were made up of seven preference categories: (1) libraries and education services, (2) housing and property services, (3) environment and recycling services, (4) government, law, and order services, (5) social and volunteering services, (6) recreation and sport services, and (7) business and employment services. Approximately four to five out of ten respondents see these categories as important or very important for digital government service provision.

Low Priority Areas

Family services as well as health and medical services brought up the rear with 42% and 38%, respectively. Although these two categories were considered less important than the other service categories, it needs to be taken into account that still four out of ten respondents rated them as either important or very important.

Further details concerning the importance of digital government service categories are summarized in the following Figure 10.3, which is based on a digital government study of Wirtz (2015) with 717 participants.

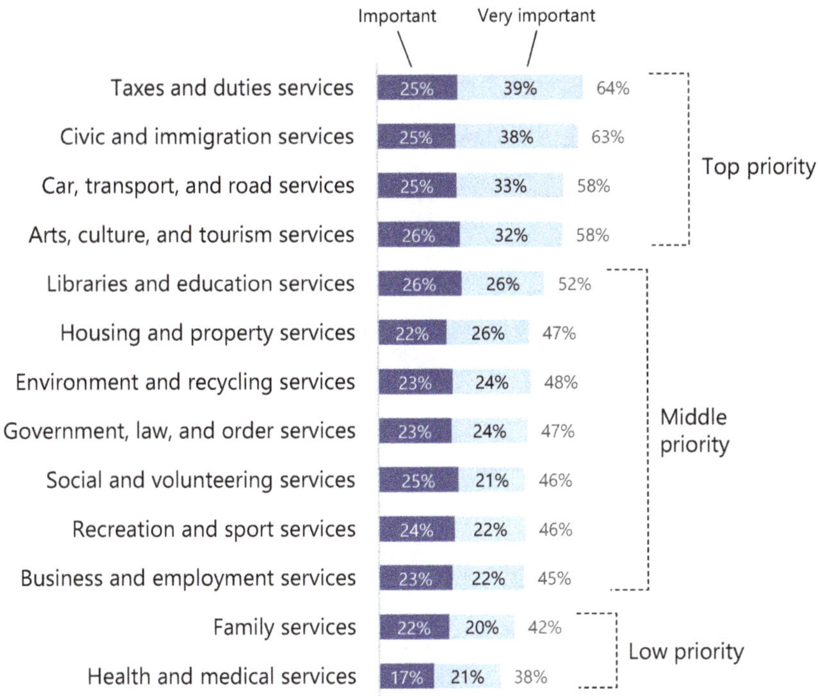

Fig. 10.3 Importance of digital government service preference categories. Data source: Wirtz (2015)

With regard to the user-centered digital government focus and the resulting importance of the user relation, this relationship requires systematic customer care. Thus, apart from tailoring the digital government service offering to the needs of the user, the relationship between user and digital government provider demands a professional relationship management that puts the user into the center of attention. Therefore, after having explained the digital government service preference categories the next sections present the identification of potential users and the design of the user relationship.

10.3 Targeting of Users

The central starting point for successfully addressing potential users is (online) targeting. Online targeting refers to the use of digital and automated advertising measures tailored to specific target groups.

Targeting Process

The corresponding targeting process can generally be divided into five successive phases: Scan/actual analysis, target/area definition, targeting instruments, implementation, and evaluation. Figure 10.4 shows the basic targeting process.

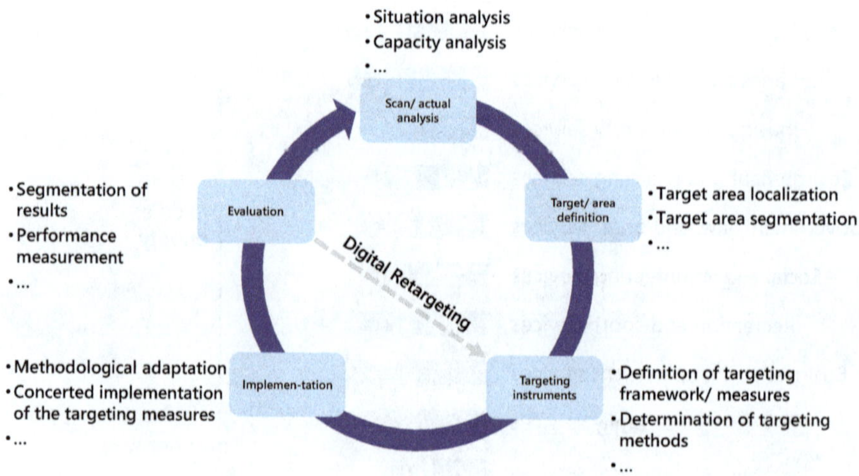

Fig. 10.4 Targeting process. Source: Wirtz (2020, 2021)

Scan/Actual Analysis

The targeting process starts with a scan/actual analysis, in which the current situation is analyzed and evaluated. In particular, a deviation evaluation between current and planned organization and marketing goals is carried out. In this context, it is essential to detect significant weaknesses in current marketing activities with regard to the achievement of organizational goals and the capacities and resources available for marketing.

Target/Area Definition

In the next phase of target or area definition, the target area is localized and segmented. Based on the findings of the scan/actual analysis, relevant target areas are identified first. The overall area is then segmented into the desired target areas by means of certain criteria, also known as targeting variables. One can distinguish between six main types of targeting variables for segmentation: Relationship to the organization, demographics, psychographics and attitudes, value for the organization, phase in the life cycle and behavior (Chaffey et al. 2019; Meffert et al. 2019).

Targeting Instruments

The third phase of the targeting process deals with the determination and selection of adequate targeting instruments. Based on the localization and segmentation of the target area, the targeting framework and the associated targeting measures are defined, before deriving and specifying adequate targeting methods.

Implementation

The fourth phase refers to the implementation of the targeting by means of the previously defined targeting methods. Here, the business requirements and management specifications are technically implemented. This means that the technically relevant instruments for targeting as well as the processing, delivery, and display of the advertising media, in particular the ad server, are adapted or programmed according to the respective requirements. As soon as this technical and methodological adaptation is completed, a concerted implementation of the targeting measures can take place.

Evaluation

In the final phase of the targeting process, the targeting measures are evaluated by means of the ad server. This facilitates a segmentation of results and a measurement of the performance of the targeting activities and the associated advertising media. If the targeting and related advertising objectives have not been achieved, digital retargeting can be initiated. In this case, users who were not reached with the first targeting attempt are marked and are found and addressed again in the retargeting process.

Retargeting

The associated targeting instruments and advertising media can be modified beforehand to increase the chances of success of the retargeting activities. Retargeting starts again in the third process phase and can be repeated as many times as required until the desired target group has been successfully reached. Regarding the available targeting instruments, the increasing development of digital government has led to the development of more and more targeting methods that can be used to address a desired target group.

Targeting Methods

A total of 16 different targeting methods can be distinguished. Figure 10.5 provides an overview of the multitude of different targeting methods in digital government.

The targeting methods shown in Figure 10.5 can be divided into six main categories: technical-based targeting, language-based targeting, sociodemographic-based targeting, attitude- and behavior-based targeting, enterprise-based targeting, and integrated targeting.

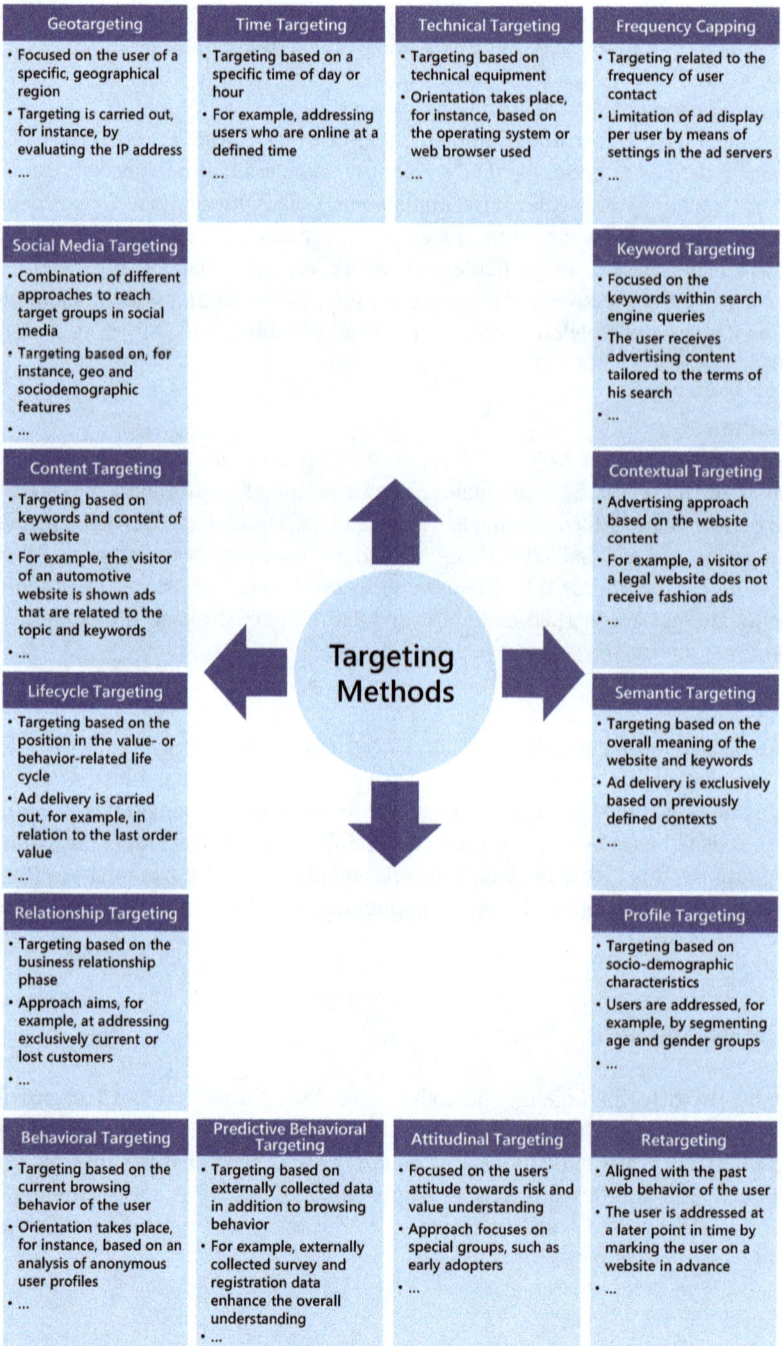

Fig. 10.5 Targeting methods. Source: Wirtz (2020, 2021)

Technically-Based Targeting

Technically-based targeting addresses users based on technical parameters and includes geo targeting, time targeting, technical targeting, and frequency capping. Geotargeting is the process of targeting the delivery of advertisements to the user in a specific geographic region. This is done, for example, by evaluating the IP address that contains information about the user's location.

Time targeting directs the advertising to a specific time of day or hour. For example, only users who are online at a specified time are addressed. Technical targeting is an alignment of the advertising media based on the technical equipment. The orientation depends, for example, on the operating system or web browser used. Frequency capping is the last targeting method within the framework of technical targeting and describes an orientation related to the frequency with which users are addressed. This targeting method is characterized by a limitation of the ad display per user by means of settings in the ad servers.

Language-Based Targeting

Language-based targeting is realized by means of linguistic aspects and includes the targeting methods: keyword targeting, contextual targeting, and semantic targeting. Keyword targeting is aimed at the keywords of users in the context of search engine queries. The user receives advertising content that is tailored to the terms of his search. In contextual targeting, the delivery of an advertisement is based on previously defined keywords and the context of the website. The visitor of a website is only shown advertisements if the keywords defined in advance are contained in the text of the website and match its context.

Semantic targeting represents an advancement of this targeting method. Here, the delivery of an advertisement is not based on individual keywords, but on the overall semantic meaning of the website content and its fit to a previously defined topic. The user is thus shown a topic-specific advertisement when visiting a website and dealing with a certain topic.

Sociodemographic-Based Targeting

Sociodemographic-based targeting addresses users based on their sociodemographic characteristics and refers to the targeting method of profile targeting. For instance, the delivery of the advertisement is based on gender, education level, and age.

The targeting of a user when visiting a website is usually based on a predefined sociodemographic user profile, which represents a combination of such characteristics.

Attitude- and Behavior-Based Targeting

Attitudinal and behavioral targeting includes the targeting methods: attitudinal targeting, behavioral targeting, predictive behavioral targeting, and retargeting. In the case of attitudinal targeting, the delivery of an advertisement is based on the user's psychographic criteria, such as motives and attitudes. When visiting a website, the user is thus shown advertisements that match his or her personality and attitudes, for example, in connection with his or her price awareness or brand loyalty.

Behavioral targeting is based on the user's surfing behavior, which is identified and analyzed by means of web analytics. When visiting a website, the user only receives advertisements that match his or her interests derived from his or her surfing behavior. Predictive behavioral targeting is an advancement of this targeting method. Here, the delivery of an advertisement is based on a combination of the user's surfing behavior and other additionally gained knowledge, such as user surveys or other data sources.

Retargeting is the last attitude- and behavior-based targeting method and aligns the placement of advertising with the user's past surfing behavior and related actions. Usually, the user has not completed an action desired by the advertiser and is therefore retargeted at a later point in time with the respective advertisement and motivated to carry out the action desired by the advertiser.

Enterprise-Based Targeting

Enterprise-based targeting addresses users in terms of organization-related characteristics and includes the targeting methods: relationship targeting and lifecycle targeting. Relationship targeting refers to aligning the delivery of an advertisement with the business relationship of a user to the corresponding organization. For example, the user is addressed with the aim of reaching potential customers, existing customers, or lost customers.

Lifecycle targeting is based on the position of a user in the value and behavior-related life cycle. For instance, the delivery of an advertisement is based on the user's last order value or the time passed since registration.

Integrated Targeting

Integrated targeting is performed by means of a combination of different targeting methods and includes content targeting and social media targeting. Content targeting is a hybrid targeting method that consists of various language-based targeting methods. The delivery of the advertisement is therefore based on keywords as well as topics and content on a website. Social media targeting is a hybrid form as well. It is a combination of different approaches to reach specific target groups in social media, particularly including language-based, sociodemographic-based as well as attitude- and behavior-based targeting methods.

Overall, targeting is of great importance in order to identify and address potential users. The considerable technological advances in the field of big data analytics and artificial intelligence are opening up increasingly intelligent and differentiated targeting opportunities for organizations. These targeting opportunities enable organizations to address target groups more effectively and efficiently, thus making a significant contribution to their communication success. After dealing with how to identify and address users, the next section focuses on user relationship management.

10.4 User-Driven Relationship Management

User-driven relationship management has become an important topic over the past decades.[4] Especially its relevance for systematically fostering user loyalty is seen as a vital factor for enhancing organizational success. The connection of relationship management and user loyalty is supported by Kotler (1994, p. 48), who states that "the task of creating strong customer loyalty is called relationship marketing."[5]

Importance of Relationship Management
Since user loyalty is regarded to have diverse positive effects on quantitative organizational targets, the general importance of successful relationship management becomes clear. This connection formed the basis for the advancement of a target-oriented, systematic relationship management (Wirtz and Lihotzky 2003; Wirtz et al. 2017; Wirtz and Schmitt 2018).

This development was complemented by the rise of modern information and communication technologies at the end of the 1990s. While the resulting potential for managing user relations was overhyped in the beginning, especially during the Internet bubble, its chances and risks are seen more realistically today.

ICT and Relationship Management
On the one hand, modern information and communication technologies allow to manage user relations more effectively and more efficiently than ever before. Despite the Internet's mass media nature, its inherent possibilities for interaction allow efficient one-to-one or one-to-many communication.

Apart from that, strategic use of network effects, cost structure advantages of information services, and personalization of websites or services foster user loyalty. On the other hand, the massive increase in transparency concerning information, services, and product offers lowers change barriers, which can cause a decrease in user loyalty.

Although the concepts of relationship management and user loyalty bare risks, their important role for organizational success is now generally considered beyond dispute. However, since the topic looks back to continuous advancements, there are still differences concerning the understanding of relationship management.

Definition of Relationship Marketing

Apart from that, the term relationship marketing is often used interchangeably with relationship management (Parvatiyar and Sheth 2001; Payne and Frow 2005).

[4] See for the following Section 10.4 also Wirtz (2020).

[5] Since it is not common to describe public stakeholders as customers, we refer to user relationship management instead of using the term customer relationship management in the following.

Against this background, several definitions from the scientific literature are presented in the following Table 10.2.

Table 10.2 Selected definitions of relationship marketing

Author(s)	Definition
Copulsky and Wolf (1990)	Relationship marketing combines elements of general advertising, sales promotion, public relations, and direct marketing to create more effective and more efficient ways of reaching consumers. It centers on developing a continuous relationship with consumers across a family of related products and services
Morgan and Hunt (1994)	Relationship marketing refers to all marketing activities directed toward establishing, developing, and maintaining successful relational exchanges
Sheth and Parvatiyar (1995)	Relationship marketing attempts to involve and integrate customers, suppliers, and other infrastructural partners into a firm's developmental and marketing activities
Heller Baird and Parasnis (2011)	Customer relationship management strategy, enabled by processes and technologies, is designed to manage customer relationships as a means for extracting the greatest value from customers over the lifetime of the relationship. These strategies typically concentrate on the operational responses required to manage the customer

Source: Wirtz (2013, 2020, 2021)

While early definitions focus on the establishment of a continuous relationship and successful relational exchanges, the last definition moves on to a management perspective that puts value creation into the center of attention. This shall be achieved through process and technology-enabled activities that are conducted to respond to the needs and requirements of the customer/user. Transferred to the digital government context, we therefore derive the following definition:

Definition of Digital Government-related User Relationship Management (Wirtz 2003)

Digital government user relationship management includes the information and communication technology-based planning, organizing, steering, and controlling of user relationships, with the aim to make a successful contribution to public value.

Target Dimensions of User Relationship Management

User relationship management contains three essential target dimensions: sustainable user loyalty, usage frequency, and length of stay.

Sustainable User Loyalty
Thereof, sustainable user loyalty forms the core target dimension, as it always needs to be considered when taking user relationship actions.

Usage Frequency
The second target dimension refers to the usage frequency of a digital government offer within a certain period of time. Thus, the more often a user uses a particular service, the higher the usage frequency. This target dimension can be divided into an absolute and a relative perspective.

The absolute perspective is determined by the number of page impressions per user. The relative perspective takes this number and builds a ratio by relating the absolute perspective to the overall user page impressions in similar service offerings, therefore, showing the ratio between the portal visits of one provider and other providers with a similar service offering.

Length of Stay
The third target dimension covers all actions carried out by the provider to maximize the length of stay per digital government portal visit. The intention is that incrementing the length a user stays on the digital government service portal leads to an increase in service usage. In e-commerce, the technical term for the potential that a user stays on a website is called stickiness.

Thus, a sticky website increases the likelihood that users will stay longer and will use more services on this website than on others that are not or less sticky. This is of particular importance to reduce the rush at the expensive physical counters by shifting transactions from the personal offline to the automated online environment.

Target Dimensions of User Loyalty
The three target dimensions, however, are neither substitutes for each other nor competing elements. Thus, user loyalty actions may aim at individual target dimensions or at any combination of them. Many user relationship management initiatives, for instance, pursue all three of them. Figure 10.6 provides an overview of the three target dimensions of user loyalty.

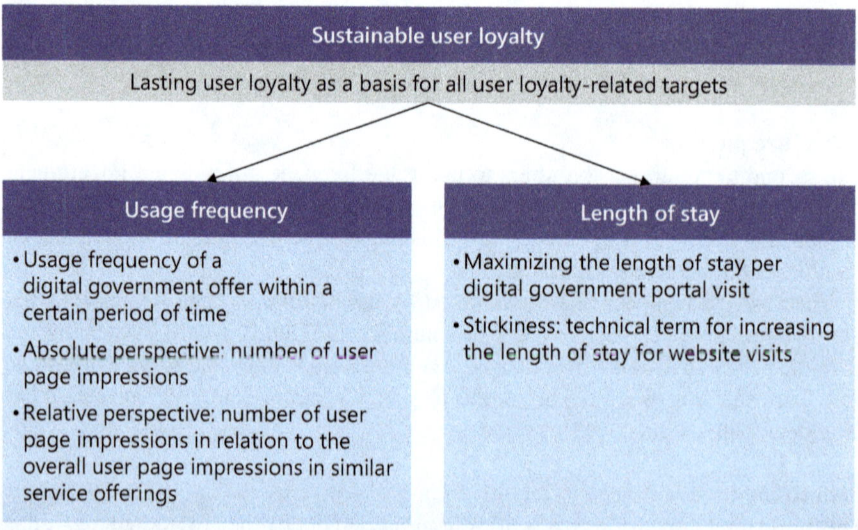

Fig. 10.6 Target dimensions of user loyalty. Source: Wirtz (2003, 2020, 2021)

User Relationship Management Process

Establishing a successful user relationship usually is a complex process. The goal of digital government-related user relationship management is the maintenance of user relations to induce users that have already used a service, to use this service again or to use another service of the service offering. This management process consists of a sequence of phases: awareness, consideration, usage, reconsideration, dissatisfaction, and recovery.

Following the management principle set by Peter F. Drucker "If you can't measure it, you can't improve it," the planning and steering of the individual phases should be accompanied by appropriate performance indicators that support impartial measurement of the success of the particular activities. The phases as well as selected performance indicators are outlined in the following Figure 10.7.

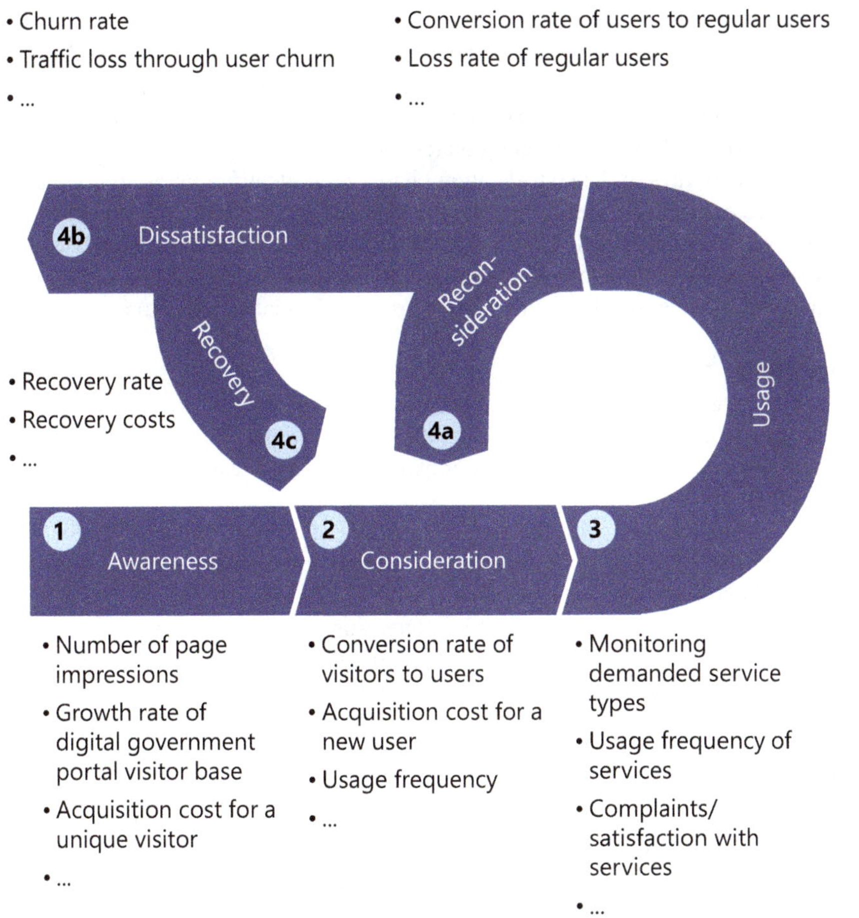

Fig. 10.7 Digital government user relationship management process. Source: Wirtz (2003, 2020, 2021)

Awareness Phase

The initial key tasks of the awareness phase are to identify the general public demand for digital government services, potential user groups, as well as the needs and the requirements of the individual users. Based on this information, the digital government information and service offering have to be marketed and popularized among the potential user groups.

The overall target is that the user recognizes the availability of the service offering, which suits his needs. Based on this awareness creation, an initial user contact is established via information and communication technologies (e.g., visiting the website). Typical performance indicators of the awareness phase are the number of page impressions, the growth rate of the digital government portal visitor base, and the acquisition cost for a unique visitor.

Consideration Phase

In the next phase, consideration, the potential user is confronted with the service offerings from the digital government system, which are tailored to the expected user needs. This requires a profound knowledge of public digital government demand as well as the potential user needs and preferences.

The core activities in the consideration phase are to identify interested users and to create preference by underscoring the benefits and the superior characteristics of the service offering provided. To measure the success of the consideration phase, the conversion rate of visitors to users, the acquisition cost for a new user, as well as the absolute and relative user frequencies are helpful performance indicators.

Usage Phase

The overall target of the usage phase is to create user satisfaction with information or service provision. For this purpose, information and service consumption needs to be easy to use and useful to the user: the user expectation has at least to be met or better surpassed.

If the user is satisfied with the service handling and the outcome of the online interaction, the likelihood for reusing the digital government service offering increases. Therefore, the services offered need to be designed and provided in a way that satisfy the users' needs. Furthermore, this point of interaction should be used to examine the level of user satisfaction through user feedback, complaint, and controlling systems that support constant monitoring and evolution of the service offering and its provision.

This is of particular importance since a dissatisfied user may not use the service again, may discourage others from using the service, or may even leave the entire platform. Usual performance indicators of the usage phase are the monitoring of the types of service demanded, the usage frequency of services used, as well as complaint and satisfaction user feedbacks concerning the services provided.

Reconsideration Phase

The aim of the reconsideration phase is to turn first users into loyal regular users. Key activities to achieve this aim are to maintain and intensify user preference, inform users about new services and optimizations, and provide easy access and useful content for repeated information and service usage. The conversion rate of users to regular users and the loss rate of regular users are typical performance indicators in the reconsideration phase.

Dissatisfaction Phase

If users are not convinced of the service provision and enter the dissatisfaction phase, actions to prevent upcoming user churn have to be initiated. First, the reasons for the users' lack of satisfaction and thus the rationale for the potential user churn have to be analyzed. Here, user surveys are helpful tools to identify performance discrepancies.

In parallel, the complaint management should be improved and extended to gather additional information on potential hazards. Second, the identified issues and performance gaps have to be solved. Important performance metrics of the dissatisfaction phase are the churn rate as well as the traffic loss through user churn.

Recovery Phase

In the next step, the user relationship management process enters the recovery phase. This means that dissatisfied users should be approached with the objectives of regaining user confidence and making the digital government service offering attractive again for the user.

Key activities of this stage are the selection of recovery target groups, presenting optimized performance outcomes and benefits, and illustrating recovery incentives to the user. The recovery rate and the user recovery costs are common performance indicators to measure the success of the activities in the recovery phase.

Integrated Digital Government User Relationship Management

For a successful management of the user relationships all phases of the process have to be managed actively. For this purpose, adequate user interfaces must be set up and maintained that support the establishment of integrated user relationships. In the case of digital government, this particularly concerns the usage of Web 2.0 technologies and applications that are applied according to the inherent business model-related user demand. Since the technologies show differing characteristics, these are suitable for different purposes.

Examples on Local, Regional, and National Level

Figure 10.8 on the following page illustrates the application of Web 2.0 technologies using the examples of a local (the digital government portal of New York City), a regional (the digital government portal of Hong Kong), and a national digital government portal (Germany) for an integrated digital government user relationship management.

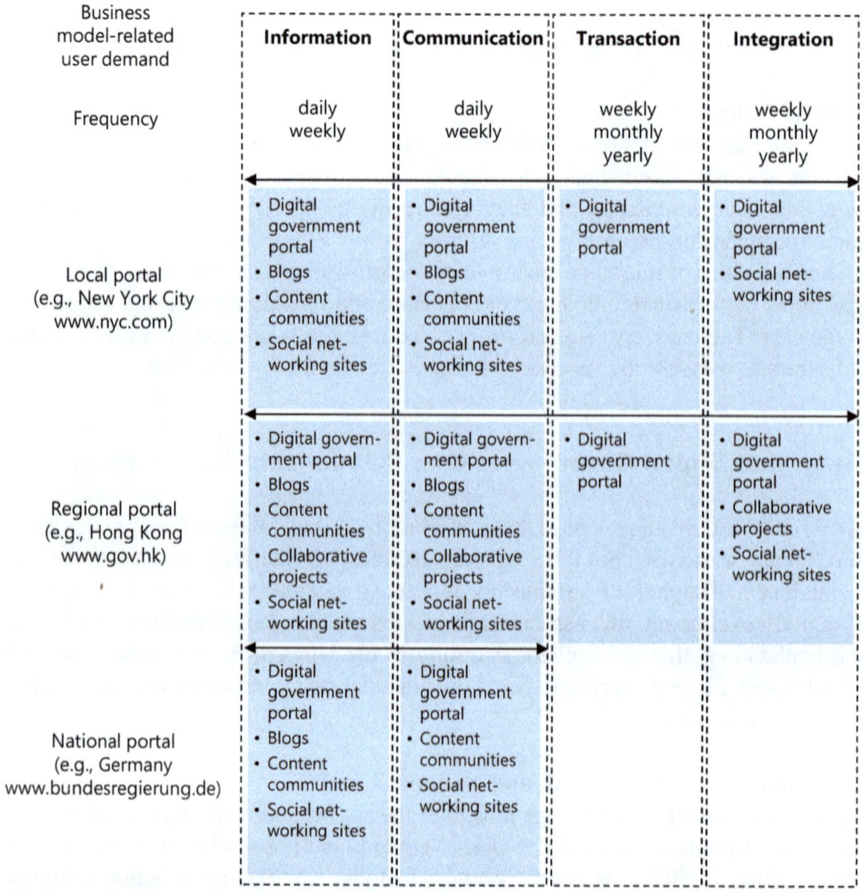

Fig. 10.8 Integrated digital government user relationship management. Source: Wirtz (2013, 2020, 2021); Wirtz and Daiser (2015, 2017)

While all levels in the example apply multiple technologies with the information and communication business model, the transaction model is built on the own digital government portal. Concerning the use of further applications, blogs, content communities, and social networking sites are frequently applied.

Blogs

A blog resides between traditional print and broadcast media and mainly serves information purposes. Although blogs usually—compared to traditional media like newspapers—only have a little number of readers, they significantly contribute to public opinion formation (Woodly 2008).

Content Communities

The primary purpose of content communities (e.g., YouTube, Flickr) is to facilitate the sharing of media content (John 2014). Collaborative projects, such as online forums and wikis, enable the users to jointly and simultaneously create content. Concerning their subject-related structure, they, for instance, provide the possibility to create sustainable applicable knowledge (Coffey and Woolworth 2004; Meijer et al. 2012).

Social Networking Sites

Social networking sites like Facebook offer computer-mediated communication that allows individuals to connect and interact with other users (Kietzmann et al. 2011; Song 2010). Apart from that, modern information and communication technologies provide the technological basis that allows to set up and maintain digital government portals that are accessed via the Internet. Thus, a digital government portal is another example of applying Web 2.0 technologies, which shows specific characteristics that are suitable to manage particular user relationships.

Considering the four different digital government business models information, communication, transaction, and integration, a smart combination of Web 2.0 technologies with the respective business model purpose fosters effective and efficient user relationship management. Since the creation of a user-oriented digital government service portfolio that adds public value is of paramount importance for a successful digital government portal, it is essential to look at digital government services, which are outlined in the following chapter.

10.5 Summary, Review Questions, Topics for Discussion, and Online Exercises

- The functional e-demand factors consist of three quality packages: Use quality, System quality, and Service quality (USS). Use quality refers to factors before, during, and after usage of the digital government system. These factors are rather user-oriented, while system quality and service quality instead are more provider-oriented.
- According to a digital government citizen preference study top priority areas of digital government are the four categories: (1) taxes and duties services, (2) civic and immigration services, (3) car, transport, and road services, as well as (4) arts, culture, and tourism services, which were evaluated as important or very important by clearly more than half of the participants.
- The central starting point of successfully addressing potential users is (online) targeting, meaning the use of digital and automated, target group-specific advertising measures. The associated targeting process can be divided into five phases: scan/actual analysis, target/area definition, targeting instruments, implementation, and evaluation.
- There are 16 different targeting methods, which can be divided into 6 main categories: technically-based targeting, language-based targeting,

sociodemographic-based targeting, attitude- and behavior-based targeting, enterprise-based targeting, and integrated targeting.
- User-driven relationship management has become an important topic, especially to promote user loyalty and thus enhance organizational success.
- Digital government-related user relationship management aims at maintaining user relationships in order to encourage citizen who have already used a service to reuse this or another service. This management process consists of a sequence of phases including awareness, consideration, usage, reconsideration, dissatisfaction, and recovery.
- User relationship management encompasses three key target dimensions: sustainable user loyalty, usage frequency, and length of stay.
- Digital government user relationship management entails the information and communication technology-based planning, organizing, steering, and controlling of user relationships, with the aim to make a successful contribution to public value.

Chapter 10
Review questions, topics for discussion and online exercises

Review questions

1. Outline the USS e-demand factor system and describe all aspects of the three quality functions.
2. Describe the schematic digital government portal network structure.
3. Divide the digital government service preference categories into top, middle, and low priority areas based on their importance to users.
4. Name the 16 targeting methods and briefly explain them.
5. Describe the digital government user relationship management process with performance and target parameters.

Topics for classroom discussion and team debates

1. Debate why digital government use is low in many countries. Focus in particular on the aspect of whether public administration successfully implements the user success factors according to the USS e-demand factor system.
2. Discuss the most important service groups and individual services for the success of digital government in terms of the different service categories (taxes, arts, etc.). Should all these service categories be offered in one portal or in different portals at local/regional/national level?
3. Against the background of the digital government user relationship management process, discuss the success factors that the design of the user relationship must have in order to create a successful city user portal. In your discussion, consider the integrated relationship management of information, communication, transaction, and integration.

Online Exercises

1. Go to https://www.cityoflondon.gov.uk/ and identify the service categories offered.
2. Visit https://www.lacity.org, https://www.ca.gov/ and https://www.usa.gov/. Compare the websites in terms of service aspects.
3. Keeping in mind the three levels (local, regional, and national) determine if these pages are specifically targeted to the digital government user relationship process. Identify relevant points of the USS e-demand factor system for each page.

References

Bertot, John Carlo; Jaeger, Paul T. (2006): User-centered e-government: Challenges and benefits for government Web sites. In Government Information Quarterly 23 (2), pp. 163–168.

Chaffey, Dave; Edmundson-Bird, David; Hemphill, Tanya (2019): Digital business and e-commerce management. Strategy, implementation and practice. Seventh edition. Harlow England, New York: Pearson.

Coffey, Brian; Woolworth, Stephen (2004): "Destroy the scum, and then neuter their families:" the web forum as a vehicle for community discourse? In The Social Science Journal 41 (1), pp. 1–14.

Copulsky, Jonathan R.; Wolf, Michael J. (1990): Relationship marketing: positioning for the future. In Journal of Business Strategy 11 (4), pp. 16–20.

Davis, Fred D. (1986): A Technology Acceptance Model for Empirically Testing New End User Information Systems: Theory and Results. Doctoral dissertation. Massachusetts Institute of Technology, Boston.

Eschenfelder, Kristin R.; Beachboard, John C.; McClure, Charles R.; Wyman, Steven K. (1997): Assessing US federal government websites. In Government Information Quarterly 14 (2), pp. 173–189.

Heller Baird, Carolyn; Parasnis, Gautam (2011): From social media to social customer relationship management. In Strategy & Leadership 39 (5), pp. 30–37.

Huang, Chaomeng James; Chao, Mei-Hui (2001): Managing WWW in public administration: Uses and misuses. In Government Information Quarterly 18 (4), pp. 357–373.

Jaeger, Paul T.; Bertot, John Carlo (2010): Designing, implementing, and evaluating user-centered and citizen-centered e-government. In Christopher G. Reddick (Ed.): Citizens and E-Government. Evaluating Policy and Management. Hershey: Information Science Reference, pp. 1–19.

John, Nicholas A. (2014): File Sharing and the History of Computing: Or, Why File Sharing is Called "File Sharing". In Critical Studies in Media Communication 31 (3), pp. 198–211.

Kietzmann, Jan H.; Hermkens, Kristopher; McCarthy, Ian P.; Silvestre, Bruno S. (2011): Social media? Get serious! Understanding the functional building blocks of social media. In Special Issue: Social Media 54 (3), pp. 241–251.

Kotler, Philip (1994): Marketing Management. Analysis, Planning, Implementation, and Control. 8th ed. Englewood Cliffs: Prentice Hall (Prentice-Hall series in marketing).

Meffert, Heribert; Burmann, Christoph; Kirchgeorg, Manfred; Eisenbeiß, Maik (2019): Marketing. Grundlagen marktorientierter Unternehmensführung Konzepte - Instrumente - Praxisbeispiele. 13th ed. Wiesbaden: Springer Gabler.

Meijer, A. J.; Curtin, D.; Hillebrandt, M. (2012): Open government: connecting vision and voice. In International Review of Administrative Sciences 78 (1), pp. 10–29.

Miller, Arthur H.; Listhaug, Ola (1990): Political Parties and Confidence in Government: A Comparison of Norway, Sweden and the United States. In British Journal of Political Science 20 (3), pp. 357–386.

Morgan, Robert M.; Hunt, Shelby D. (1994): The Commitment-Trust Theory of Relationship Marketing. In Journal of Marketing 58 (7), pp. 20–38.

Oliver, Richard L. (1977): Effect of expectation and disconfirmation on postexposure product evaluations: An alternative interpretation. In Journal of Applied Psychology 62 (4), pp. 480–486.

Oliver, Richard L. (1980): A cognitive model of the antecedents and consequences of satisfaction decisions. In Journal of Marketing Research, pp. 460–469.

Parvatiyar, Atul; Sheth, Jagdish N. (2001): Conceptual Framework of Customer Relationship Management. New Delhi: Tata/McGraw-Hill.

Payne, Adrian; Frow, Pennie (2005): A Strategic Framework for Customer Relationship Management. In Journal of Marketing 69 (4), pp. 167–176.

Sheth, Jagdish N.; Parvatiyar, Atul (1995): The Evolution of Relationship Marketing. In International Business Review 4 (4), pp. 397–418.

Song, Felicia Wu (2010): Theorizing Web 2.0: A Cultural Perspective. In Information, Communication & Society 13 (2), pp. 249–275.

Wirtz, Bernd W. (2003): Kundenbindung durch E-CRM. In Manfred Bruhn (Ed.): Handbuch Kundenbindungsmanagement. Strategien und Instrumente für ein erfolgreiches CRM. 4., überarb. und erw. Aufl. Wiesbaden: Gabler, pp. 371–387.

Wirtz, Bernd W. (2013): Electronic Business. 4th ed. Wiesbaden: Gabler.

Wirtz, Bernd W. (2015): E-Government. Perspektiven des kommunalen E-Government. E-Government Studie. Mainz: Ministerium des Innern, für Sport und Infrastruktur. Edited by Land Rheinland-Pfalz. Ministerium des Innern, für Sport und Infrastruktur.

Wirtz, Bernd W. (2020): Electronic Business. 7th ed. Wiesbaden: Springer Gabler.

Wirtz, Bernd W. (2021): Digital Business and Electronic Commerce. Cham: Springer International Publishing.

Wirtz, Bernd W. (2022): E-Government. Wiesbaden: Springer Gabler.

Wirtz, Bernd W.; Birkmeyer, Steven (2017): Mobile government services: An empirical analysis of mobile government attractiveness. In International Journal of Public Administration 41 (16), pp. 1385–1395. DOI: https://doi.org/10.1080/01900692.2017.1390583.

Wirtz, Bernd W.; Daiser, Peter (2015): E-Government. Strategy, process, instruments. 1st ed. Speyer.

Wirtz, Bernd W.; Daiser, Peter (2017): E-government. Strategy, process, instruments. 2nd ed. Speyer.

Wirtz, Bernd W.; Kurtz, Oliver Tuna (2016): Citizen preferences toward e-government city portals - An empirical analysis of full online mobile and social media services. In International Public Management Review 17 (1), pp. 1–20.

Wirtz, Bernd W.; Kurtz, Oliver Tuna (2017): Determinants of citizen usage intentions in e-government. An empirical analysis. In Public Organization Review 17 (3), pp. 353–372.

Wirtz, Bernd W.; Kurtz, Oliver Tuna (2018): Local e-government services: quality aspects and citizen usage preferences. In Electronic Government, an International Journal 14 (2), pp. 160–176. DOI: https://doi.org/10.1504/EG.2018.090928.

Wirtz, Bernd W.; Lihotzky, Nikolai (2003): Customer retention management in the B2C electronic business. In Long Range Planning 36 (6), pp. 517–532. DOI: https://doi.org/10.1016/j.lrp.2003.08.010.

Wirtz, Bernd W.; Mory, Linda; Piehler, Robert; Daiser, Peter (2017): E-government: A citizen relationship marketing analysis. In International Review on Public and Nonprofit Marketing 14, pp. 149–178. DOI: https://doi.org/10.1007/s12208-016-0164-9.

Wirtz, Bernd W.; Schmitt, Daniel (2018): Mobile Government: Umsetzung und Entwicklungsperspektiven. In Verwaltung & Management 24 (1), pp. 33–41. DOI: https://doi.org/10.5771/0947-9856-2018-1-33.

Woodly, Deva (2008): New competencies in democratic communication? Blogs, agenda setting and political participation. In Public Choice 134 (1-2), pp. 109–123.

Digital Government Services

11

Contents

Learning Objectives
By working through this chapter, you will be able to:

1. Describe the digital government development stage model and its five stages.
2. Outline the digital government interaction matrix.
3. Describe and explain the schematic digital government actors and interaction structure.
4. Describe the ICTI digital government business models and their subcategories in a government to citizen context, as well as in a government to business context.
5. Explain in detail the main transaction services for citizen and companies within the ICTI digital government business model.

Digital government services have become an important instrument of public administration. The main drivers for their evolution during the past two decades have been the development of modern information and communication technologies and the public demand for more convenient public service provision.[1]

This has led to the advancement of existing digital government services and prepared the way for new innovative digital government information and service provision. Moreover, it triggers radical process changes in public administration organizations. For example, the introduction of electronic tax declarations, which

[1] See for Chapter 11 Digital Government Services also Wirtz (2022); Wirtz and Daiser (2015, 2017).

B. W. Wirtz, *Digital Government*, Springer Texts in Business and Economics,
https://doi.org/10.1007/978-3-031-13086-1_11

significantly reduced transmission efforts and processing times since direct electronic data processing substituted former workflows (e.g., mail delivery, digitization of information or documents) and electronic completion of forms drastically limited incorrectly filled out declarations.

This digital government service evolution, however, was not a digital process that only required to flip the switch and all public service offers would automatically be available to the public stakeholders. It rather has been a long and cumbersome way of sequential service development and technology steps to reach the level of today's digital government service provision.

11.1 Digital Government Development Stages

Following the chronological course of digital government service evolution, various practitioners and scientists divided this process into specific development stages. These development stages represent a categorization that determines particular digital government portal maturity levels.

Therefore, maturity models are used, for example, to compare the development status of different digital government portals, to support public service development, and to serve as a guide for evaluating and improving digital government portal quality.

Digital Government Development Stage Model

Taking into account the findings of previous digital government maturity level studies, five key digital government development stages can be identified: (1) presentation/information, (2) communication, (3) transaction, (4) participation, and (5) open integration.[2] With each stage, the digital government application reaches a higher degree of interaction, which in turn is also connected to an increase in complexity. Figure 11.1 schematically illustrates this relationship.

[2] See for the following Section 11.1 also Wirtz (2020).

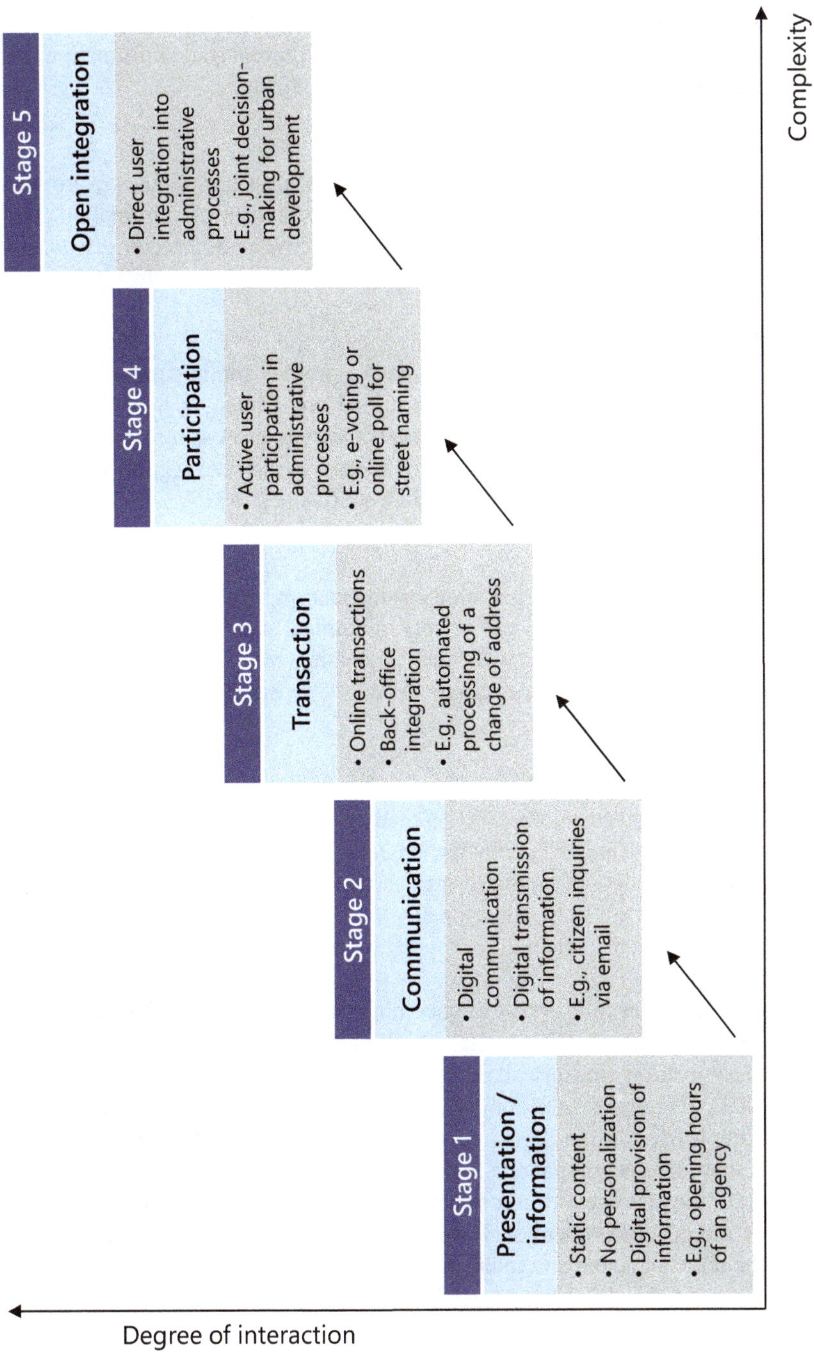

Fig. 11.1 Digital government development stage model. Source: Wirtz (2010, 2021), Wirtz and Daiser (2015)

Presentation/Information

First-stage digital government systems are limited to present static information, such as opening hours and contact information, online to the user.

Communication

In the communication stage, digital government systems are amplified by providing the possibility for communication and digital transmission of information. Here, users can, for instance, communicate with the respective public sector organization via email.

Transaction

In the transaction stage, users can initiate and/or process administrative procedures and services online. For this purpose, the digital government system is integrated into the back-office system, which allows automated processing of the initiated administrative procedure. Thus, a change of address in the civil register is automatically updated in related databases, e.g., address of vehicle owner.

Participation

The participation stage permits participatory interaction between the digital government provider and its users. Instead of only initiating a standardized digital government transaction, users can actively play a shaping role in the process through feedback, opinion surveys, or electronic voting. An example of this stage is an online poll for naming a street.

Open Integration

In the open integration stage, the user is directly integrated into public processes and value creation and manages interconnected administrative procedures that support an automated execution of multiple transactions. Thus, the user is ubiquitously engaged with public administration, openly sharing data and public input through various devices and channels while cooperating and collaborating with the respective public entities.

Although the stages differ greatly concerning the related degree of interaction and the level of complexity that is associated with the respective stage, favoring one of them does not make sense since all play a vital role in digital government. According to the digital government development stages and the associated degrees of interaction and complexity, various digital government interaction patterns are conceivable.

Within these interaction patterns, several public digital government stakeholders form a part of the government-user structure. Against this background and the target to provide digital government services in a user-oriented way, it is important to identify the relevant actors and interaction patterns.

11.2 Actors and Interaction Patterns of Digital Government

All recipients and providers of digital government information and services within the digital government interaction procedures form the group of actors. This group can be divided into people (citizens), private sector organizations (organization), and public sector organizations (administration), which interact with each other and thus build the basis for the interaction patterns. Figure 11.2 presents these relationships.

The providers of digital government information and services establish the basis for service provision within the underlying electronic networks. They supply services that can be used by the recipients. For digital government, public administration (administration) is the prevalent information and service provider.

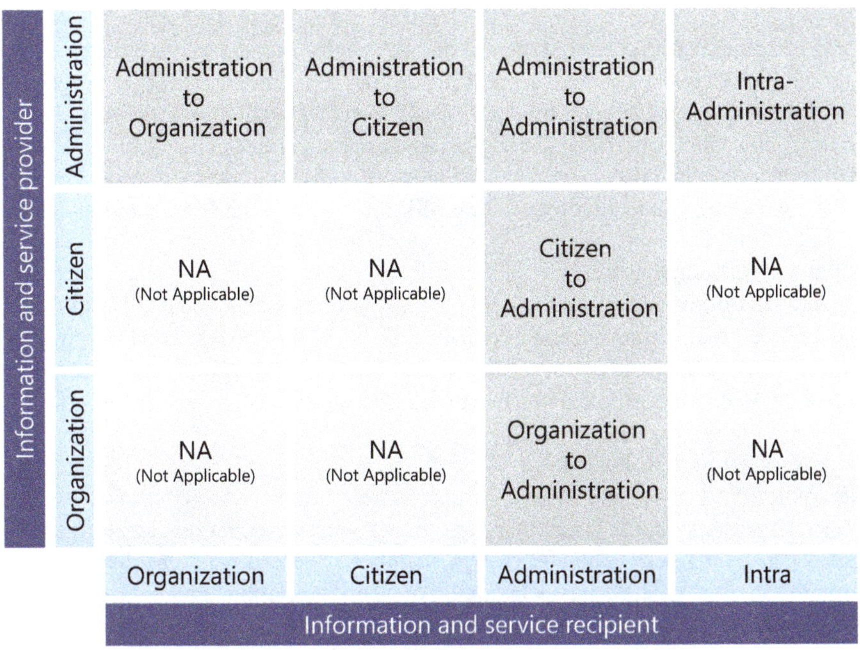

Fig. 11.2 Digital government interaction matrix. Source: Wirtz (2013a, 2021), Wirtz and Daiser (2015)

Administration to Organization

Administration to organization: This interaction pattern belongs to the most relevant ones since it includes important administrative procedures to handle the interaction between private organizations, such as small, medium, and large companies, as well as non-profit organizations, and public administration (e.g., transactions related to income tax, value-added tax, social security).

Administration to Citizen
Administration to citizen: This interaction pattern mainly serves public administration in providing information and services to citizens. Most of these offers are provided free of charge, such as an online job portal of the employment agency. However, there are also fee-based interactions that require payment to complete the transaction (e.g., auctions of confiscated goods, visa application).

Administration to Administration
Administration to administration: With growing data and service exchange as well as increasing collaboration between public sector entities on a national and international level, this interaction pattern becomes more and more important. Here, vivid examples are the Federal Administration Office, which provides services for other public sector organizations, or the improved cooperation between judicial authorities and police forces with particular emphasis on the central role of Europol.

Intra-Administration
Intra-administration: Automated one-stop digital government portals also require well-functioning exchange of information and services within the respective public sector organization providing the digital government service. Therefore, this interaction pattern is mainly concerned with network-based, intra-organizational online procedures (e.g., connecting registration office data with vehicle registration data).

Citizen to Administration
Citizen to administration: Here, public administration is the recipient of information and services that are provided by citizens. Thus, in the citizen to administration interaction pattern, citizens, for instance, send information to public institutions via online devices. An example is the electronic transmission of income tax returns.

Organization to Administration
Organization to administration: This interaction pattern is the equivalent to the citizen to administration interaction pattern, but with organizations as information and service providers. Therefore, it is mainly concerned with the handling of administrative tasks (e.g., tax declarations) or business relation tasks (e.g., electronic procurement) of private organizations.

Schematic Digital Government Actors and Interactions Structure
The interconnection among the digital government actors and the associated interaction patterns can lead to complex structures.[3] In the following, a schematic digital government actors and interactions structure is presented to better illustrate potential relationships that need to be established and managed.

[3]See for the following Section Schematic Digital Government Actors and Interactions Structure also Wirtz (2020).

Internet Service Provider and Infrastructure Provider

The Internet service provider maintains the system between the user and the Internet, supplying the technological prerequisites for accessing the digital government platform. This access may take place via stationary or mobile devices. The Internet service provider works closely with the infrastructure providers, who connect the various Internet service providers with fast backbone networks across different countries and continents.

Digital Government Information and Service Provider

The digital government information and service provider develops, designs, and manages the digital government portal as well as the associated content and service offering. While service transactions are still mainly executed under their own direction, content creation is partly outsourced to content providers. In addition, other public sector organizations regularly take an expert role and provide content concerning digital government transactions within their scope of functions. Moreover, user-generated content plays an increasingly important role.

In combination, Internet service providers as well as infrastructure providers offer digital government service providers to host their system and/or the technological infrastructure for digital information and service provision. Usually depending on their size, the digital government service provider either possesses the necessary know-how internally or buys it on the market from external technology providers or software developers and programmers.

Another essential aspect is the digital government service provider's focus on the user since increasing user acceptance leads to a wider dissemination of the services provided. This in turn leads to a release of public administration because services that have previously been provided face-to-face are then processed automatically. Figure 11.3 illustrates a schematic structure of digital government actors and interactions.

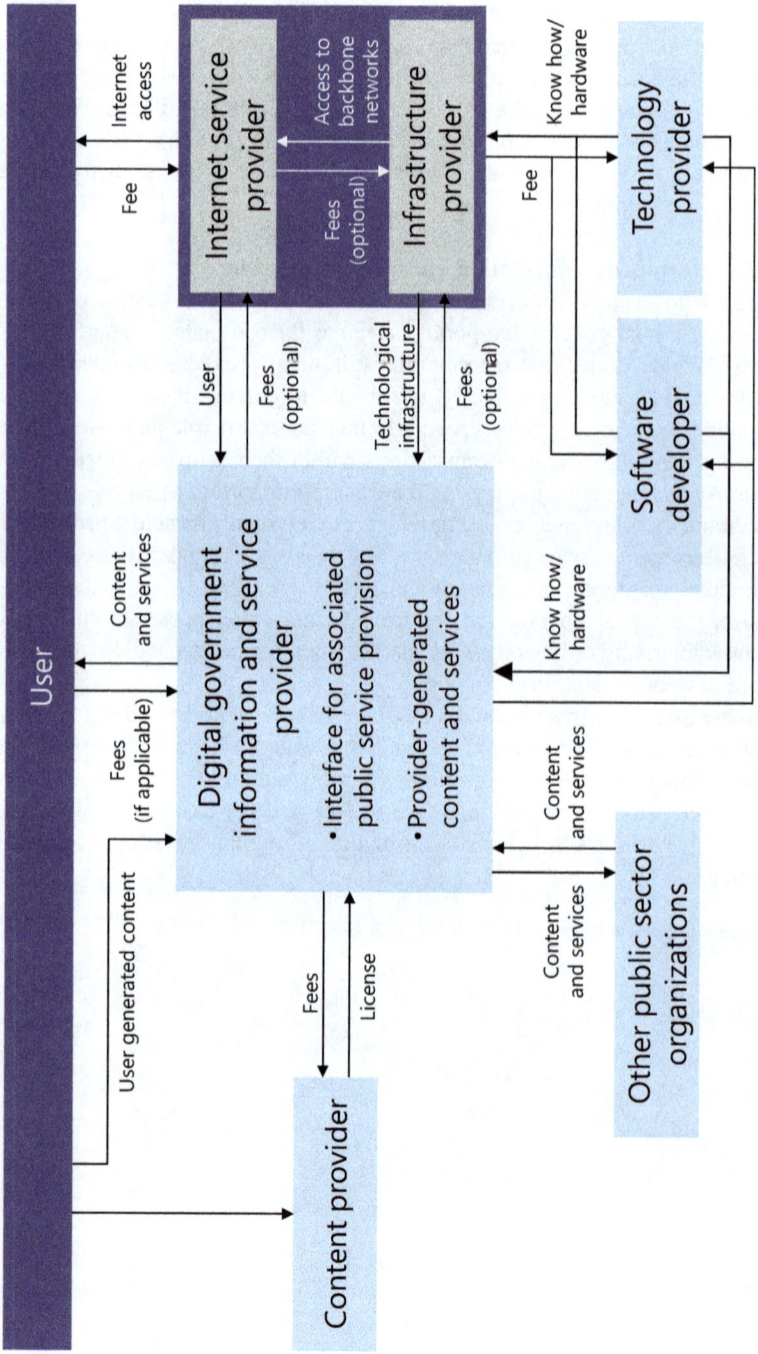

Fig. 11.3 Schematic digital government actors and interactions structure. Source: Wirtz (2013b, 2021), Wirtz and Daiser (2015)

Having defined the relevant digital government actors, interaction patterns, and interaction structure leads to determining the information and service offering. Thus, a broad set of digital government services that has been identified in the scientific literature is presented in the following two sections.

11.3 Government-to-Citizen Services (G2C)

Digital government services have become an important part of public service provision. For this reason, this topic is a frequently discussed subject within science as well as public management and administration. Against this background, there exist a large number of scientific publications that study digital government services.

These studies either investigate a particular service, look at a specific service cluster, or analyze digital government service provision in general. Since a comprehensive overview of digital government services that also provides a systematic taxonomy for this field could not be found, it is developed in the following.

Development of a Comprehensive Overview of Digital Government Services

To derive an exemplary set of available digital government services, the investigation was conducted by means of the peer-reviewed scientific literature since this source represents state-of-the-art research (Arduini and Zanfei 2014). Moreover, this approach ensures that an adequate and comparable level of service cluster detail is maintained without running the risks of introducing too much detail or being too generic—issues that easily occur if services are directly collected from various digital government platforms.

The collected services were classified according to their service offering since this gives users and providers the possibility to distinguish between the respective categories in accordance with their desired utilization requirements. Furthermore, considering the historical development of digital government services, digital government service diversity has grown significantly in recent years. This growth was accompanied by an increase in digital government service complexity, which also suggests a classification of service offers.

ICTI Digital Government Business Models with Subcategories

Since a business model represents an abstracted, simplified system behind an organization's service offer and service provision, the ICTI Digital Government Business Model is used for service classification and clustering.[4] This approach carries an additional advantage: The ICTI Digital Government Business Model also serves as a management instrument, which allows to directly link digital government services with the digital government business model management. Figure 11.4 again presents the ICTI Digital Government Business Models with the respective subcategories.

[4]For further information on the ICTI Digital Government Business Model Approach, please refer to Section 9.2.

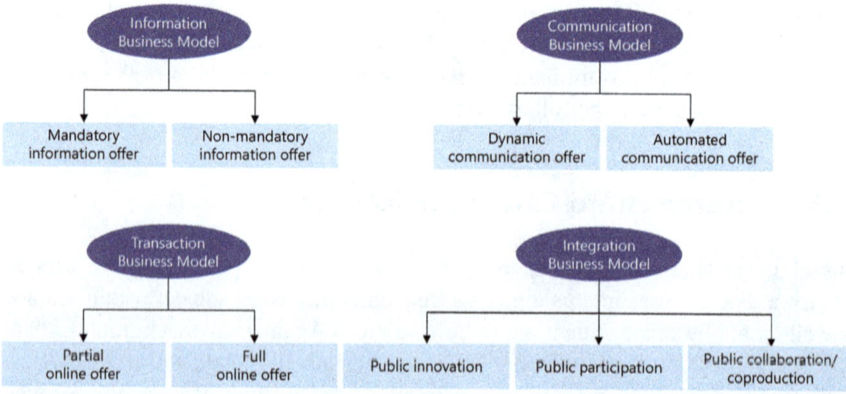

Fig. 11.4 ICTI digital government business models with subcategories. Source: Wirtz and Daiser (2015, 2017)

Information Digital Government Services (G2C)

In the following, the digital government services that were identified in the scientific literature are presented according to their affiliation with the respective digital government business model and the corresponding subcategory. Considering that the overview of digital government service offerings is based on a literature review and the ongoing, dynamic development of digital government services, the list cannot claim to be complete. But in light of the extensive analysis, it is considered more than acceptable to provide a thorough synopsis of digital government services.

Information-related digital government service offers can be divided into mandatory information offers and non-mandatory information offers.

Mandatory Information Offer

Mandatory information offers refer to information that needs to be supplied to public stakeholders in connection with services that have to be provided in accordance with laws or regulations. Examples are online administration information, online citizen identity information, and online information about laws and statistics.

Non-mandatory Information Offer

Non-mandatory information offers describe information services that are neither required by law nor associated with any obligatory government service. Thus, non-mandatory information offers refer to services such as educational resources, online business location information, online cultural agenda, and online information about culture and welfare. Figure 11.5 shows typical information digital government services in a government-to-citizen setting.

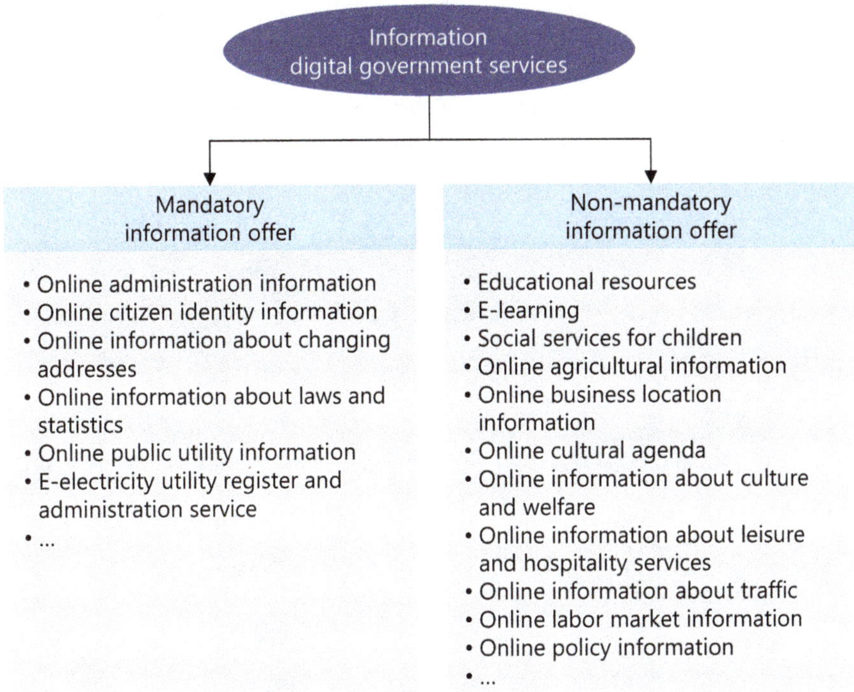

Fig. 11.5 Information digital government services (G2C). Source: Wirtz and Daiser (2015, 2017)

Communication Digital Government Services (G2C)

The target of communication digital government services is the provision of online services that serve as communication possibilities for government-to-user interaction. These are made up of two subcategories: interactive communication offers and automated communication offers.

Dynamic Communication Offer

Interactive communication services, such as call center services, help desk services, mailing services, online courses, or online consulting, require a two-way flow of information. The information exchange takes place between two active participants that have an impact on each other, and thus these communication services are of dynamic nature.

Automated Communication Offer

Automated communication services may show a one-way or two-way flow of information, but at least one participant of the communication is a machine or computer that exchanges information based on predefined algorithms. This means that automated communication takes place human-to-computer or computer-to-computer. Digital government service examples of automated communication services are automated email notifications, information kiosks, mobile SMS-based notifications, online job searching portal, and online map service. Dynamic and automated communication digital government services are presented in Figure 11.6.

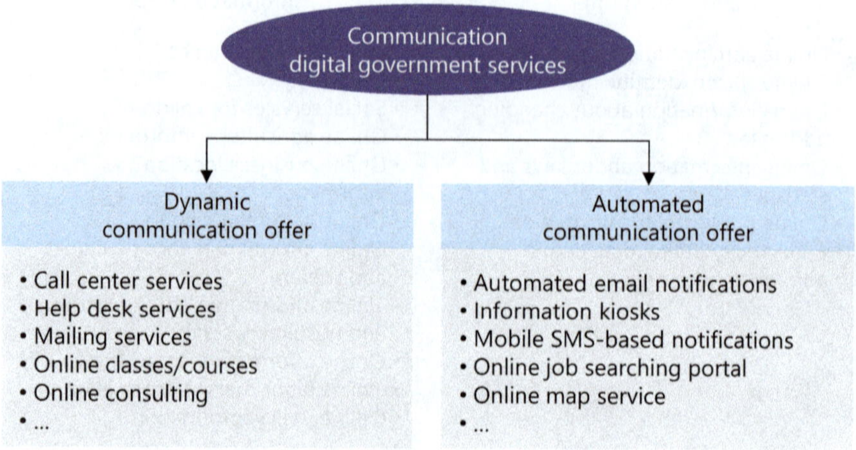

Fig. 11.6 Communication digital government services (G2C). Source: Wirtz and Daiser (2015, 2017)

Transaction Digital Government Services (G2C)

Transaction digital government services serve to initiate, handle, and process administrative procedures online. Their service offering can either be partial or full.

Partial Online Offer

Partial online offers refer to services that cannot be completed without at least one further media break. Examples of partial transaction digital government services are form and document service, online application for welfare benefits, and online visa application. Figure 11.7 presents typical transaction digital government services.

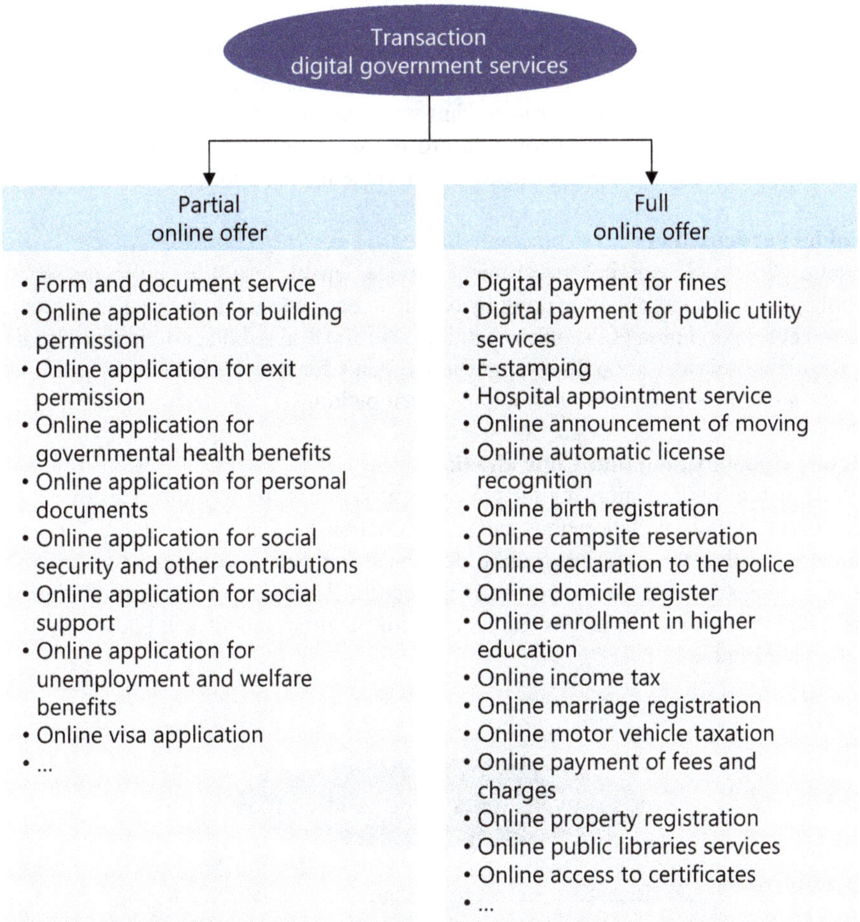

Fig. 11.7 Transaction digital government services (G2C). Source: Wirtz and Daiser (2015, 2017)

Full Online Offer
In contrast, full online offers, such as digital payment for public utility services, online automatic number plate recognition, online enrollment in higher education, and online public libraries services, allow to initiate, process, and complete an administrative procedure entirely online.

Integration Digital Government Services (G2C)

Integration digital government services serve to integrate users into the value chain of the public sector organization via participative, collaborative, or cooperative action. These services can be divided into the following subcategories: public innovation, public participation, as well as public collaboration and coproduction.

Public Innovation
Public innovation digital government services enable the user to become part of the governmental or public sector innovation process. Examples are virtual planning and online complaint submission services. This way, external groups and individuals can engage in the public sector innovation process to complement public with citizen knowledge and experience and create higher value for the public.

Public Participation
Public participation digital government services enable users to indirectly shape public decisions and policy-making by calling attention to their preferences through user feedback, opinion polls, online petitions, etc. Typical public participation digital government services are online suggestion systems for new cycle paths or new bus stops, government auctions, and online citizen petitions.

Public Collaboration and Coproduction
While public participation digital government services allow indirect exertion of influence, public collaboration and coproduction digital government services directly involve the user into public decisions and policy-making by giving the user a proactive role in the respective process. Examples of integration digital government services in a government-to-citizen environment are shown in the following Figure 11.8.

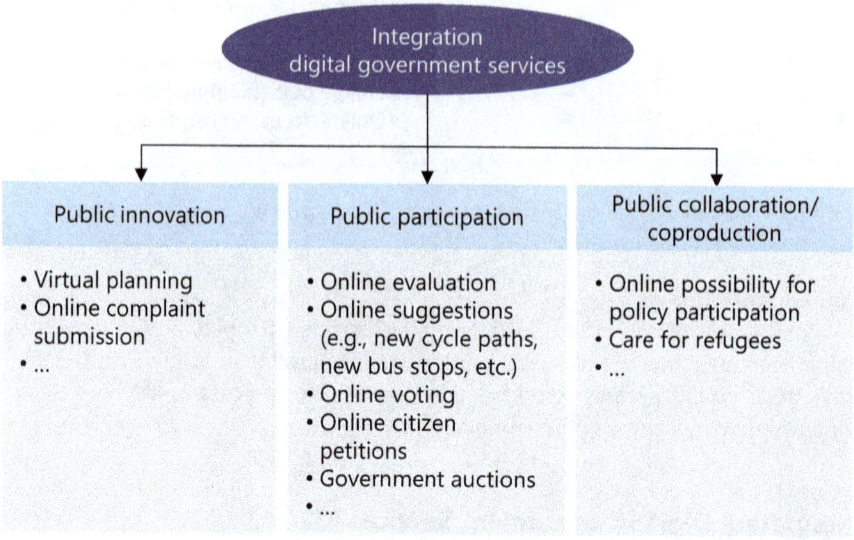

Fig. 11.8 Integration digital government services (G2C). Source: Wirtz and Daiser (2015, 2017)

11.4 Government-to-Business Services (G2B)

Although government-to-citizen and government-to-business digital government services appear similar at first glance, there are significant differences embedded in these two service streams. These differences can be broken down into explicit and tacit dissimilarities.

Differences Between G2C and G2B Services

Explicit dissimilarities are digital government services that de facto can only be used by either citizens or businesses. Examples of services that only apply to individuals are online birth registration, online marriage registration, or election services. Since companies do not fall in love and do not possess the right to vote, these digital government services are not relevant for business entities. Tacit dissimilarities refer to differences in content and trait of the digital government services provided as well as distinct characteristics of the service recipients.

While government-to-citizen digital government services aim at serving a huge number of citizens that are subject to manifold socio-cultural impacts, looking for convenient public service provision, and mainly driven by individual choices, preferences, and decisions, the government-to-business digital government services environment differs considerably from these attributes.

Business organizations represent a considerably lower number of service recipients and rather follow a rational cost–benefit approach. Moreover, their efficiency-oriented actions are usually based on collective, formalized decision-making. Against the background of the explicit and tacit dissimilarities between government-to-citizen and government-to-business digital government service provision, the digital government service provider always has to ensure to cover both perspectives.

Hong Kong's Digital Government Portal as an Example

The digital government portal of Hong Kong is a good example to demonstrate this circumstance. Here, this issue has been solved by entirely separating public online digital government service provision for the two target groups (Hong Kong 2021).[5] When accessing the digital government portal, the user has the possibility to switch between citizen and business service offerings. Even though many services still appear to be similar, the service provision is completely tailored to the needs and requirements of the respective users. This boosts clarity, transparency, and user-orientation of the digital government service offering.

[5] See http://www.gov.hk

Information Digital Government Services (G2B)

Similarly to the government-to-citizen setting, information-related digital government service offers are broken down into mandatory information offers and non-mandatory information offers. Although many services have the same denomination and show similar functionalities like in government-to-citizen service provision, the presentation and the content of the information have to be specified to the needs and requirements of business users. Figure 11.9 shows typical information digital government services in a government-to-business setting.

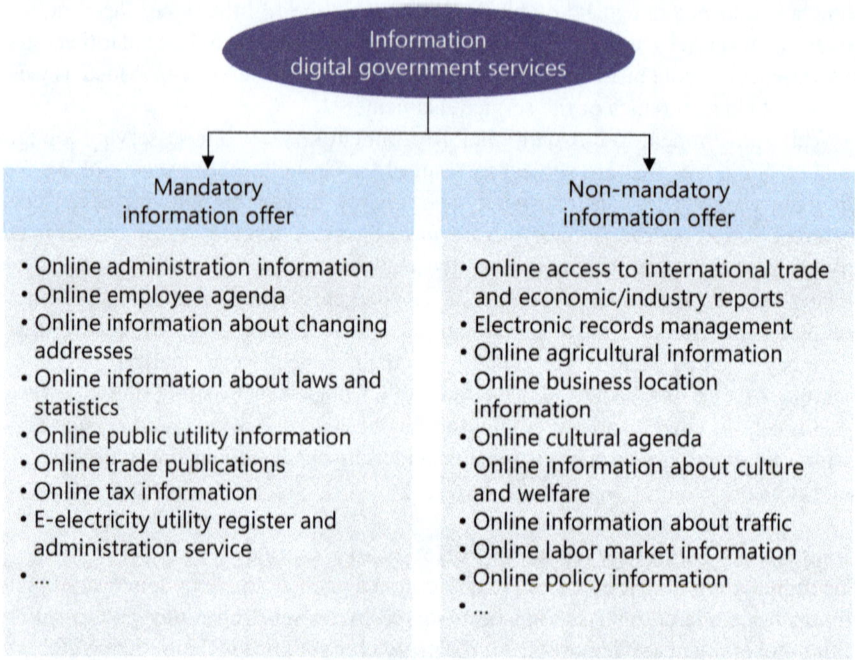

Fig. 11.9 Information digital government services (G2B). Source: Wirtz and Daiser (2015, 2017)

Communication Digital Government Services (G2B)

Concerning communication digital government services, which refer to the provision of online services that serve as communication possibilities for government-to-user interaction, greater differences between the service offerings of the two target groups can be seen.

In the digital government service subcategory dynamic communication offer, for example, particular business services, such as assistance on complying with local, state, and federal regulations, business online network/contractors, and videoconferencing services, are provided. Figure 11.10 outlines common communication digital government services.

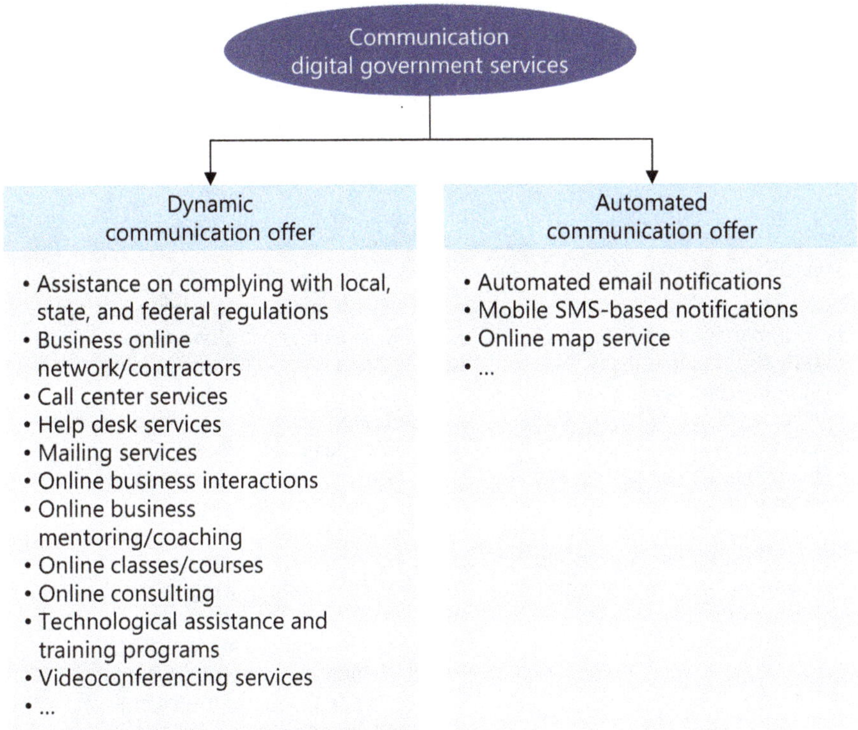

Fig. 11.10 Communication digital government services (G2B). Source: Wirtz and Daiser (2015, 2017)

Transaction Digital Government Services (G2B)

When comparing transaction digital government services of a government-to-citizen and a government-to-business setting, which serve to initiate, handle, and process administrative procedures online, several different services can be identified. In the case of partial online offers, examples of typical transaction digital government services in a government-to-business setting are event management, HR management, as well as online declaration and notification of corporation tax services.

The same holds true for full online offers. Here, e-billing, electronic workflow management, online transaction of social contribution for employees, online public procurement, online document and trademark filing, online submission of data to statistical offices are examples of digital government services that particularly fit the needs of business users. Figure 11.11 presents typical transaction digital government services in a government-to-business setting.

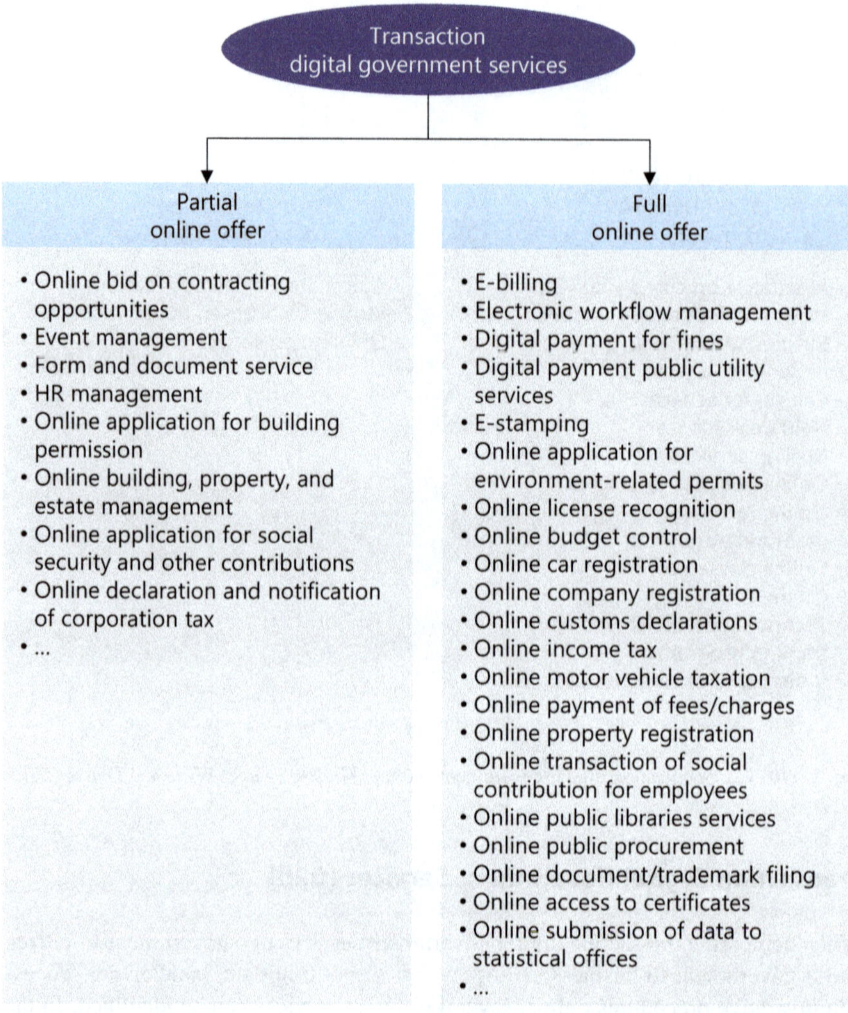

Fig. 11.11 Transaction digital government services (G2B). Source: Wirtz and Daiser (2015, 2017)

Integration Digital Government Services (G2B)

Integration digital government services integrate users into the value chain of the public sector organization via participative, collaborative, or cooperative action. Sticking to the ICTI Digital Government Business Model methodology, these services can be divided into the subcategories public innovation, public participation, as well as public collaboration and coproduction.

For public innovation services, no particular differences regarding digital government services (e.g., virtual planning and online complaint submission) could be identified between the government-to-citizen and the government-to-business digital government service offering. In the public participation service category, the government-to-business setting shows less digital government service offers since daily life services, online voting, or online petitions are pure citizen services.

Concerning the findings of the literature review, which was conducted to identify the set of digital government services that serves as a basis for this digital government service overview, no government-to-business service could be identified that fits the public collaboration and coproduction service subcategory. Figure 11.12 shows typical integration digital government services in a government-to-business setting.

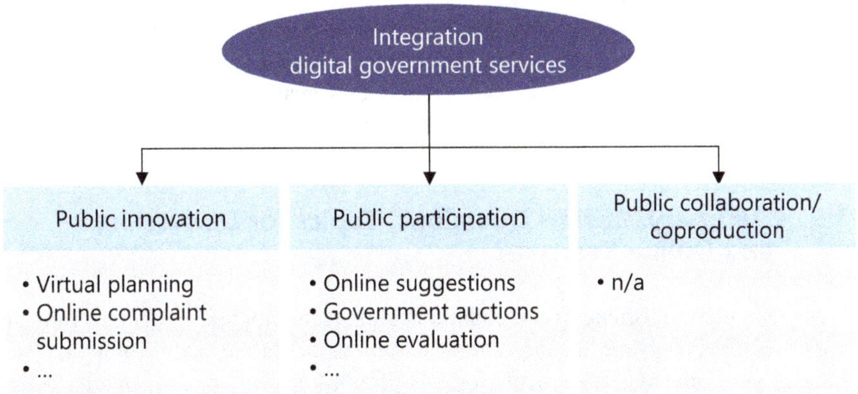

Fig. 11.12 Integration digital government services (G2B). Source: Wirtz and Daiser (2015, 2017)

Summing up, the high number of already available digital government services, ranging from information to integration purposes, demonstrates that digital government has come a long way since the first digital public information provision. Moreover, this shows that digital government service provision has become an important instrument of public governance and administration.

Focus on Target Groups

From a digital government management perspective, digital government service provision needs a clear focus on the target groups that ought to be covered by the digital government portal. When selecting actors and interaction patterns citizens, private sector organizations and public sector organizations have to be taken into account.

Although the digital government service offering can conceptually be built straightaway on the ICT Digital Government Business Model and its respective service subcategories, the dissimilarities of a government-to-citizen and a government-to-business setting have to be kept in mind when designing, developing, and maintaining the digital government portal.

Non-exhaustive Overview of Services

Apart from that, it has to be mentioned that the service overview—despite the extensive underlying literature review—cannot claim to be exhaustive. Even if it could, it would not reflect the services of top-notch digital government portals anymore by the time of publication since information and communication technology is advancing and the digitalization of public sector organizations is increasing.

However, the overview should provide acceptable insights into digital government service provision. Especially, the systematic allocation of digital government services to the ICTI Digital Government Business Models seems useful for managing online public service offers and provides a clear-cut approach to digital government service supervision.

The next step of successful digital government service provision is to develop the ability to interact with existing and potential users on various channels and platforms to make the digital government services ubiquitously available to the stakeholders of the respective public sector organization. This is outlined in the following chapter.

11.5 Summary, Review Questions, Topics for Discussion, and Online Exercises

- Due to modern information and communication technologies, digital government services have become an important instrument of public administration. The digital government service evolution has been a long way of sequential service development and technology steps. Five key digital government development stages can be identified: (1) presentation/information, (2) communication, (3) transaction, (4) participation, and (5) open integration.
- The group of actors of digital government consists of all recipients and providers of digital government information and services. This group can be divided into people (citizens), private sector organizations (organization), and public sector organizations (administration), which interact with each other and thus build the basis for the interaction patterns.
- The ICTI digital government business models can serve as a management instrument and represent an abstracted, simplified system behind an organization's service offer and service provision.
- Information-related digital government service offers in a government to citizen context can be divided into mandatory information offers and non-mandatory information offers.
- Mandatory information offers need to be provided in accordance with laws or regulations. Non-mandatory information offers are not associated with any obligatory government service. They refer, e.g., to educational resources, online business location information, or online information about culture and welfare.
- Communication digital government services in a government to citizen context aim at providing possibilities for government-to-user interaction. They are made up of two subcategories: dynamic communication offers and automated communication offers.

- Dynamic communication offers are interactive in nature, the information exchange takes place between two active participants. Automated communication services may show a one-way or two-way flow of information, but at least one participant of the communication is a machine or computer that exchanges information based on predefined algorithms.
- The service offering of transaction digital government services can either be partial or full. Transaction digital government services are intended for the initiation, handling, and processing of administrative processes online.
- Partial online offers refer to services that cannot be completed without at least one further media break, e.g. form and document services, or online visa application. In contrast, full online offers allow to initiate, process, and complete an administrative procedure entirely online, e.g. digital payment for public utility services, or online enrollment in higher education.
- Integration digital government services aim to integrate users into the value chain of the public sector organization via participative, collaborative, or cooperative action. They can be divided into the subcategories: public innovation, public participation, as well as public collaboration and coproduction. Besides government to citizen services, there are also government to business services, which can also be subdivided according to the ICTI digital government business models.

Chapter 11
Review questions, topics for discussion and online exercises

Review questions

1. Outline the digital government development stage model.
2. Illustrate the digital government interaction matrix.
3. Describe the schematic digital government actors and interaction structure.
4. Explain the ICTI digital government business models and their subcategories.
5. Outline in detail the main transaction services for users within the ICTI digital government business model. Provide an outline of these for the business context as well.

Topics for classroom discussion and team debates

1. Discuss why in many countries the development of digital government often remains in the field of information and communication and transaction and integration services are only offered to a limited extent. Two aspects in particular are relevant here: funding and implementation barriers, especially a bureaucratic administrative culture.
2. There are a variety of stakeholders in the field of digital government. Discuss to what extent they have conflicting objectives and how these can be resolved.
3. Discuss for your city which services are of particular interest to you and other citizens and whether they are associated with a high utility value. When discussing the digital government services of your city, also consider the extent to which the entire spectrum of services is offered in accordance with the ICTI digital government business models.

Online Exercises

1. Visit https://digital-strategy.ec.europa.eu/en/policies/egovernment. Discuss the advantages and disadvantages of cross-border availability of digital public services.
2. Go to https://gds.blog.gov.uk/2021/05/20/government-digital-service-our-strategy-for-2021-2024/?utm_medium=referral&utm_source=gdsorgpage&utm_campaign=gdsstrategy. Look at the UK Government Digital Service mission and discuss whether the path and focus for this mission are effective and efficient.
3. Explore https://www.usa.gov/ and look at the different types of services available.

References

Arduini, Davide; Zanfei, Antonello (2014): An overview of scholarly research on public e-services? A meta-analysis of the literature. In Special issue on: Selected papers from the 10th Conference in Telecommunications, Media and Internet Techno-economics Special issue on : The development of public e-services: Empirical analysis and policy issues 38 (5–6), pp. 476–495.

Hong Kong (2021): GovHK. Available online at https://www.gov.hk/en/residents/, checked on 5/18/2021.

Wirtz, Bernd W. (2010): Electronic business. 3rd ed. Wiesbaden: Gabler.

Wirtz, Bernd W. (2013a): Electronic Business. 4th ed. Wiesbaden: Gabler.

Wirtz, Bernd W. (2013b): Medien- und Internetmanagement. 8th ed. Wiesbaden: Gabler.

Wirtz, Bernd W. (2020): Electronic Business. 7th ed. Wiesbaden: Springer Gabler.

Wirtz, Bernd W. (2021): Digital Business and Electronic Commerce. Cham: Springer International Publishing.

Wirtz, Bernd W. (2022): E-Government. Wiesbaden: Springer Gabler.

Wirtz, Bernd W.; Daiser, Peter (2015): E-Government. Strategy, process, instruments. 1st ed. Speyer.

Wirtz, Bernd W.; Daiser, Peter (2017): E-government. Strategy, process, instruments. 2nd ed. Speyer.

Multichannel E-Service Delivery

12

Contents

Learning Objectives
By working through this chapter, you will be able to:

1. Define multichannel systems and explain their advantages for governments and citizen.
2. Explain the service channel diversification model (SCD model) and its four cases.
3. Describe the channel characteristics of public service delivery according to the public service delivery model.
4. Describe the differences between the Isolated Channel Strategy, Combined Channel Strategy, and Integrated Channel Strategy.
5. Illustrate the strategic multichannel management process.

12.1 Multichannel Digital Government Strategy

As part of the dissemination and commercial use of modern information and communication technologies and the Internet as well as the public acceptance of these media, online-based channels were put in place that have created various new

B. W. Wirtz, *Digital Government*, Springer Texts in Business and Economics,
https://doi.org/10.1007/978-3-031-13086-1_12

e-service delivery possibilities.[1] These stationary or mobile Internet-based interaction channels have become a vital factor for public service provision and user relationship management (Wirtz et al. 2003).

The Internet as a New Channel

In e-commerce, for instance, the Internet and the forms of distribution based on this technology represent up-to-date distribution channels that are used in numerous ways to either replace or complement traditional sales channels (Wirtz 2022a). The particular importance of combining online and offline channels lays in the additional advantages that are related to Internet-based service offering benefits as well as to the specific cost structure of the Internet.

Online banking is a textbook example of multichannel e-commerce service delivery. Today, clients can use several channels to carry out their banking transactions (e.g., via counter, telephone, mail, or Internet). The increasing shift of activities from traditional face-to-face counter interactions to automated modern online transactions brings along tangible benefits for the banking institutions.

Cost Savings

If all factors remain constant, an increase in online banking activities leads to a reduction in offline banking activities because customer traffic is relocated to automated online service provision. Therefore, banks could reduce the size of their expensive branch network, which led to a significant cost reduction of 70–90% in e-banking service delivery.

Concerning digital government service provision, efficiency gains and cost benefits of digital government services compared to traditional public service provision are undisputed (United Nations 2014). In a UK government survey, for instance, the consulting firm PricewaterhouseCoopers (2009) estimated cost benefits of online public service provision at 3.30–12.00 GBP per transaction.

Advantages for Users

In addition to the efficiency and monetary benefits that multichannel digital government service delivery offers providers, there are also various advantages for users, such as 24/7 availability and an overall improved customer service (Teerling and Pieterson 2011; Wirtz and Kurtz 2017; Wirtz et al. 2017). "As a result, the delivery of public services is becoming increasingly multichannel: over the counter, by mail and telephone, over the Internet, via text and television, etc." (Gagnon et al. 2010, p. 213).

But since the reasons to provide online digital government services are mainly driven by rational arguments like cost efficiency and the reasons to utilize them rather depend on personal and situational characteristics, there still exists a strong mismatch between government and citizen channel preferences.

[1] See for Chapter 12 Multichannel E-Service Delivery also Wirtz (2008, 2021b, 2022b), Wirtz and Daiser (2015, 2017).

Since users do not directly have to bear the costs of digital government service provision, the latter have to be tailored to the users' needs and preferences to incentivize them to switch to cost-efficient online services (Gagnon et al. 2010; Teerling and Pieterson 2011). Here, the challenge for public administration is to provide digital government services that are suitable for all citizens and organizations.

Definition of Multichannel Systems

In the literature, the simultaneous use of two or more channels for the provision of the same product is unanimously regarded as the constituent feature of a multichannel system. These channels can, for example, be directed at different user segments. Multichannel systems can thus be defined as follows:

Definition of Multichannel System (Wirtz 2008, 2021b)

A multi-channel system exists when at least two different marketing channels are used to distribute products or services.

Definition of Multichannel Marketing

Against this background, a definition of multichannel marketing can be derived, referring to the overall objective of marketing, the realization of organizational goals through a lasting satisfaction of user needs. Based on this, multi-channel marketing can be defined as follows:

Definition of Multichannel Marketing (Wirtz 2008, 2021b)

Multichannel marketing is the process of planning, implementing, and controlling all marketing activities in a multi-channel system. The aim is to achieve organizational goals by satisfying user needs in the long term.

Since effective multichannel delivery of government services requires a clear multichannel strategy, the following section explores strategic aspects in more detail.

Multichannel digital government management consists of a strategic and an operative component that both aim at harmonizing the different user preferences with the constraints of public administration and the limitations of the channels used. This task is cumbersome since public sector organizations usually do not adapt to pressure from competition or the market. What makes them move is public demand or political will (Lynn 1998).[2] For this reason, multichannel digital government service delivery often lacks user orientation (Reddick and Turner 2012), and thus new service channels sometimes just emerge because of certain add-on trends

[2] See for the following Section 12.1 also Wirtz and Langer (2017).

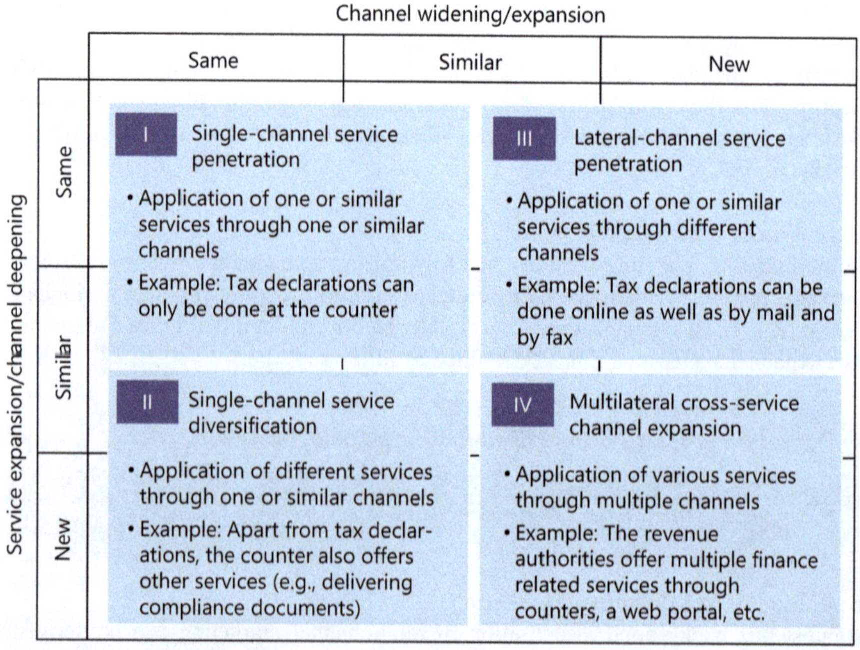

Fig. 12.1 Service-channel diversification model (SCD model). Source: Wirtz (2013a, 2021a), Wirtz and Daiser (2015)

instead of establishing them in a purposeful and target-oriented way. Apart from that, this evolutionary process may carry further essential disadvantages.

Normally, channel structures and the underlying technology follow path dependencies that are not designed for interdependence with other channels (Wilson and Daniel 2007). Moreover, it is often neglected if the channels actually have been proven to be particularly useful or if their complementary use provides additional value (Ebbers et al. 2008).

12.2 Service-Channel Diversification Model (SCD Model)

From a strategic digital government perspective, public sector organizations have the choice to expand their digital government service delivery through new channels or broaden existing channels. Following Ansoff's approach for strategic diversification, the Service-Channel Diversification Model in Figure 12.1 helps to explain whether and how digital government service delivery should be expanded [content based on Wirtz and Langer (2017).[3]

[3]The original Ansoff matrix (1957), which showed product-market strategies for business growth alternatives, differentiated existing and new markets and existing and new products.

The SCD model is based on the two perspectives of channel widening/expansion and service expansion/channel deepening. This leads to a fourfold table providing the following four generic strategies: (1) single-channel service penetration, (2) single-channel service diversification, (3) lateral-channel service penetration, and (4) multilateral cross-service channel expansion.

Single-Channel Service Penetration and Diversification

Single-channel service penetration focuses on a particular service within a particular channel. This can be an effective strategy for digital government services that are already successfully provided to the users. However, this one-channel strategy may also aim at further improving the specific service within the existing channel and thus tailoring it even better to the users' needs and requirements. This digital government service development refers to the single channel service diversification strategy.

Lateral-Channel Service Penetration and Multilateral Cross-Service Channel Expansion

Lateral-channel service penetration strategy refers to taking an existing service but offering it through various channels. In the case of a multilateral cross-service channel expansion strategy, a new digital government service is provided to the users via new channels. Although one could think that a maximum strategy (using as many channels and services as possible) may be the best way to go, this does not necessarily lead to better user orientation or to more effective service provision. Here, a proper multichannel digital government management that suits the particular requirements is the better solution (Gagnon et al. 2010).

12.3 Multichannel Model for E-Services

Before going further into the digital government multichannel strategy subject, we will have a look at the channel characteristics of public service delivery. According to the public multichannel model of Wirtz and Langer (2017), public service provision and customer relationship management can be conducted via several channels in a digital government multichannel context.

Distinction Between Online and Offline Channels

In a first step, they categorized relevant digital government service channels and distinguished between online and offline-based service provision (Wirtz and Kleineicken 2005; Wirtz et al. 2009; Wirtz and Langer 2017). At first glance, it may seem unusual to see telephone and telefax services in the online service category since these were established long before the rise of the Internet. However, telephone and telefax were switched from analogue to digital IP-based technology and thus clearly classify as online channels.

Evaluation According to Communication Capacity, Service Delivery Capacity, and Cost–Benefit Ratio

In a second step, the determined channels (e.g., counter/service desks, postal mail, social media, etc.) were evaluated according to their communication capacity, service delivery capacity, and cost–benefit ratio, which are two important channel characteristics from a provider perspective, describing their particular digital government value. Figure 12.2 shows the characteristics of the available online and offline channels and depicts the different citizen and user touchpoints (content based on Wirtz and Langer (2017)).

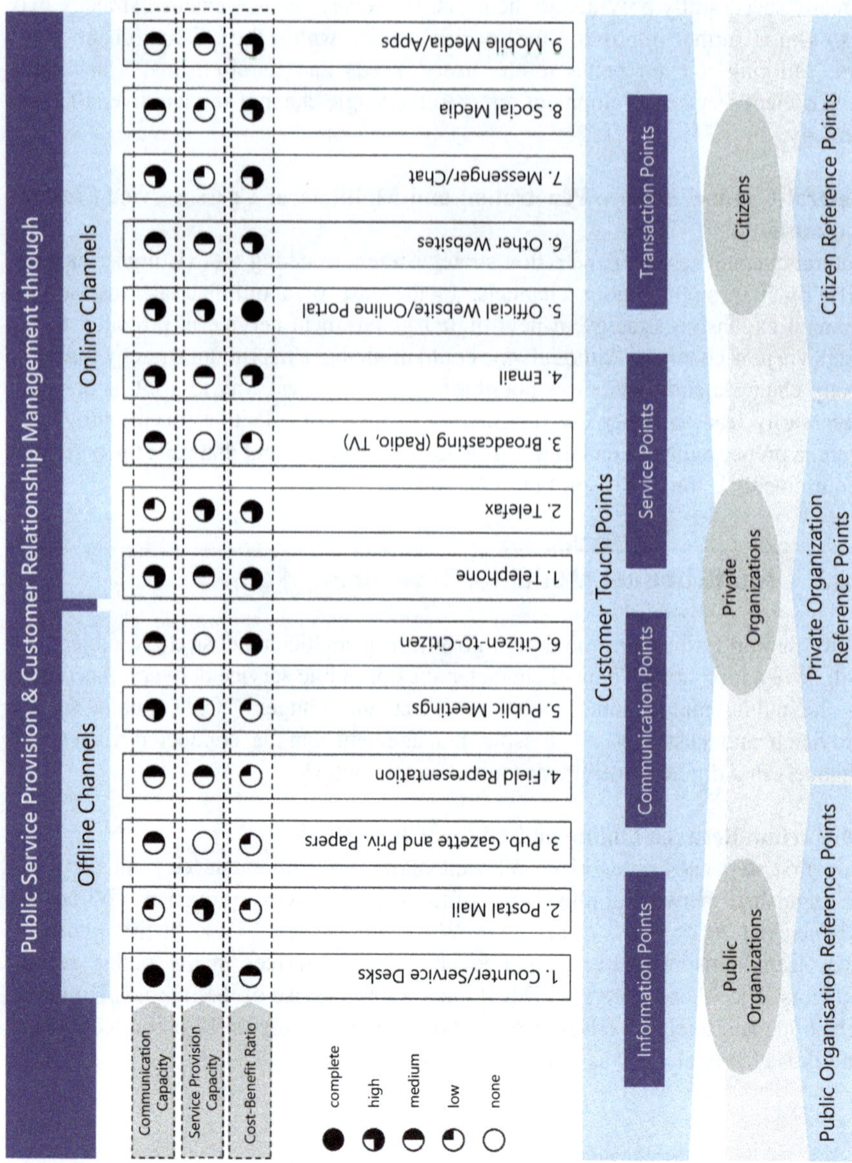

Fig. 12.2 Public service delivery model. Source: Wirtz (2005, 2021a), Wirtz and Daiser (2015)

A channel provides value to the multichannel digital government system if it is useful, effective, and efficient. These dimensions are reflected in the two criteria communication capacity, which refers to communicative characteristics of the channel, and service delivery capacity, which refers to the ability to support financial and legal interaction.

Communication Capacity

Personal service provision through the service desk, for instance, allows immediate personalized interaction. This generally provides the highest possible communication capacity. However, this form of interaction also carries significant inefficiencies: regularly providing repetitive or similar information to individual visitors, including media breaks, expensive to maintain, etc. Therefore, the communication capacity is still seen as high, but not complete.

On the one hand, online channels generally support service provision with lower transaction costs than offline channels, especially when taking into account automated online communication channels. On the other hand, automated service provision is limited with regard to communication interaction.

Service Provision Capacity

Service provision capacity refers to a channel's ability to provide or support financial and legal interaction. Similarly to the former category, usefulness, effectiveness, and efficiency determine a channel's level of service capacity. While public gazettes and private papers, for example, allow communication, they do not support financial or legal interaction. Hence, they are not regarded to possess any relevant service provision capacity.

Considering the service provision capacity of the counter/service desk, all financial and legal services provided by the public sector organization can be used. For this reason, the service provision capacity of this channel is rated as complete, which represents the highest degree of service provision capacity.

Customer Touch Points

The customer touch points, which function as customer interfaces, present the connection between the offline and online service channels and digital government. Similar to the different service channels, customer touch points vary in their communication and service provision capacities. Wirtz and Langer (2017) identified the following constellations: information points, communication points, service points, and transaction points.

Information Points

Information points represent the interface with the lowest level of user–provider interaction since these only allow one-way communication and thus do not provide any feedback or communication option. Examples are static websites that only show information content as well as newspapers or television, which in principle do not support two-way communication.

Communication Points

Communication points enable two-way communication between the digital government provider and its stakeholders. These customer touch points mainly serve personalized consultation purposes. Typical examples are telephone, citizen-to-citizen, social media, and messenger/chat service channels.

Service Points

Service points are customer touch points that allow physical non-legal interaction between the user and the digital government service provider. At the service points, which function as a kind of public service receptions, citizens can collect forms and documents, receive garbage stamps, etc.

Transaction Points

Transaction points represent the most comprehensive interface between the user and the digital government provider. At these customer touch points, public stakeholders can execute legal and financial procedures, such as applying for IDs and passports, birth certificates, marriage certificates, payments, etc. Examples of transaction points are counter/service desks and full online service digital government portals.

Influence on Public Stakeholders

In addition to the service channels and customer touch points that are established and used by the digital government service provider, public stakeholders are also influenced by effects that are much more difficult to control. These influences, which are, for example, caused by word-of-mouth and review information, come from the so-called reference points that are not directly controllable by the service providing organization (Reichheld 2003; Wirtz 2013b).

All public stakeholders—citizens, private organizations, and public organizations—possess certain reference points, which are beyond a digital government provider's direct control but influence their opinion about particular topics. For this reason, digital government providers should try to follow reference point information flows to take appropriate measures in case these become conducive and constraining forces. Figure 12.2 provides an overview of relevant digital government online and offline channels as well as the associated customer touchpoints.

12.4 Multichannel Strategies

Designing and implementing an efficient multichannel management demands a strategic and target-oriented approach. But so far, only little knowledge concerning systematic management of multichannel digital government is available for public managers. Figure 12.3 depicts a strategic multichannel system (content based on Wirtz (2013a) and Wirtz and Langer (2017)). This strategic multichannel system breaks public multichannel management down into three different strategies: Isolated Channel Strategy, Combined Channel Strategy, and Integrated Channel Strategy.

Aspects \ Approach	Isolated Channel Strategy	Combined Channel Strategy	Integrated Channel Strategy
Coordination	• Uncoordinated channels/ channel-inherent management • Closed channel structure • Channel competition	• Partially coordinated channels/channel-inherent management • Loosely linked channel structure • Channel competition	• Completely coordinated channels/comprehensive channel management • Interdependent channel structure • No competition between channels
Formation	• Lead channel structure • Channel-specific management	• Mostly lead channel Structure • Comprehensive channel management	• Multichannel structure • Centralized overall channel management
Organization	• High individual responsibility • Low coordination • High decentralization		• High interdependence • High coordination • High centralization

Fig. 12.3 Strategic multichannel system. Source: Wirtz (2013a, 2021b), Wirtz and Daiser (2015)

Isolated Channel Strategy

An Isolated Channel Strategy refers to the situation that the individual channels of the multichannel system are run independently and are not linked to each other. This means, the individual channels compete with one another since users have to decide which channel to use and stick to their decision.

This structure often is the outcome of an evolutionary multichannel management, where additional channels have been added over time (Kernaghan 2005). In this respect, usually one channel (e.g., counter/service desk) serves as a key channel and the other channels (e.g., postal mail, mobile apps, etc.) are run as a kind of add-on service provision. Summing up, an Isolated Channel Strategy places high responsibility on the individual channels and is characterized by a generally decentralized structure.

Combined Channel Strategy

The Combined Channel Strategy also follows the approach of having a lead channel, but distinguishes itself from the Isolated Channel Strategy through the symbiotic use of additional channels that complement the lead channel. Instead of pursuing individual stand-alone channels, the Combined Channel Strategy requires a comprehensive multichannel approach.

An example of Combined Channel Strategy use is an online scheduling platform that supports visitor management at the counter/service desks. Although the counter is the primary channel, waiting lines can be avoided and digital government providers can enhance their personnel planning.

This way, the advantages of different channels can be combined into the overall service provision. Moreover, a target-oriented, value-creating application of various channels leads to cost and convenience benefits for the user and the provider.

Integrated Channel Strategy

The Integrated Channel Strategy aims at providing digital government services through interconnected and interchangeable service channels. This means that users can conduct administrative procedures in person or remotely and switch to another service channel during the process. For instance, a user begins a service online from a stationary personal computer, continues the service processing by handing in particular documents that he or she does not want to transmit via mail or Internet at the counter, and follows the status of the administrative procedure on a mobile device, such as a tablet or mobile phone.

In this setting, the channels are interdependent, their management demands high coordination efforts, and the multichannel system shows a centralized structure. This is required since the digital government service provider needs to plan, coordinate, and control the entire multichannel service portfolio. This approach allows to tailor the digital government service offer specifically to the needs and preferences of particular user groups and to combine them reasonably for achieving value-adding synergies.

Management Alignment to Strategy

From an organization perspective, the three strategies demand a different handling. While the Isolated Channel Strategy usually requires less coordination effort from a central management view, the Integrated Channel Strategy follows a centralized approach that needs a key responsible person or department that coordinates the digital government service provision. The Combined Channel Strategy lies in between the other strategies. Thus, it is a management process of give and take between central, staff, and decentral departments. It can be stated that an increasing digital government service integration level leads to a rising central coordination effort.

The design and implementation of a public multichannel management system demands a coordinated approach, involving all internal stakeholders of the digital government provider. For this reason, a systematic proceeding is recommended, which is explained in the following section.

12.5 Multichannel Strategy Process

The process of designing the multichannel system consists of four consecutive steps, which illustrate the entire progress of an ideal development of multichannel strategies and systems.[4] These four steps comprise the analysis of the initial strategic situation, a market segmentation, the strategic definition of the multichannel management strategy, and the design of the multichannel management system.

[4] See for the following Section 12.5 also Wirtz (2021).

Analysis of Initial Strategic Situation

Strategic decision-making is long-term oriented. The planning process for strategy development starts with an analysis of the initial strategic situation of the digital-government-providing public sector organization.[5] Thus, in the first step, the external and internal influences need to be analyzed and an analysis of the strengths, weaknesses, opportunities, and threats of the digital government multichannel endeavor has to be conducted.

The overall aim of this step is to get a transparent view on the specific user and market needs as well as requirements. Furthermore, the internal analysis, which focuses on the organization's competencies and resources, should deliver the organization's status concerning personnel and technical readiness for approaching the respective strategies.

Market Segmentation

Based on the results of these analyses, the market segmentation step divides the market into particular target groups. These target groups have to be determined in a way that allows a successful, target group-oriented market cultivation. For this purpose, geographic, sociodemographic, behavioristic, psychographic, and use-oriented market segmentation approaches are frequently applied.

Strategic Definition of Multichannel Management Strategy

The third step of multichannel strategy and system design is the strategic definition of the multichannel management strategy. In this part of the process, the responsible decision-makers determine the thrust of the digital government multichannel system. Thus, the definition of the market cultivation strategy and the user-oriented strategy are key parts of this step.

Design of the Multichannel Management System

The final step, design of the multichannel management system, can be broken down into four substeps: potential channels and user-oriented strategy, multichannel management layout, selection of multichannel system channels, and selection of channel participants. Figure 12.4 shows the schematic overall flow of the strategic multichannel management process.

[5] For further details on strategic management, please refer to Section 3.3.

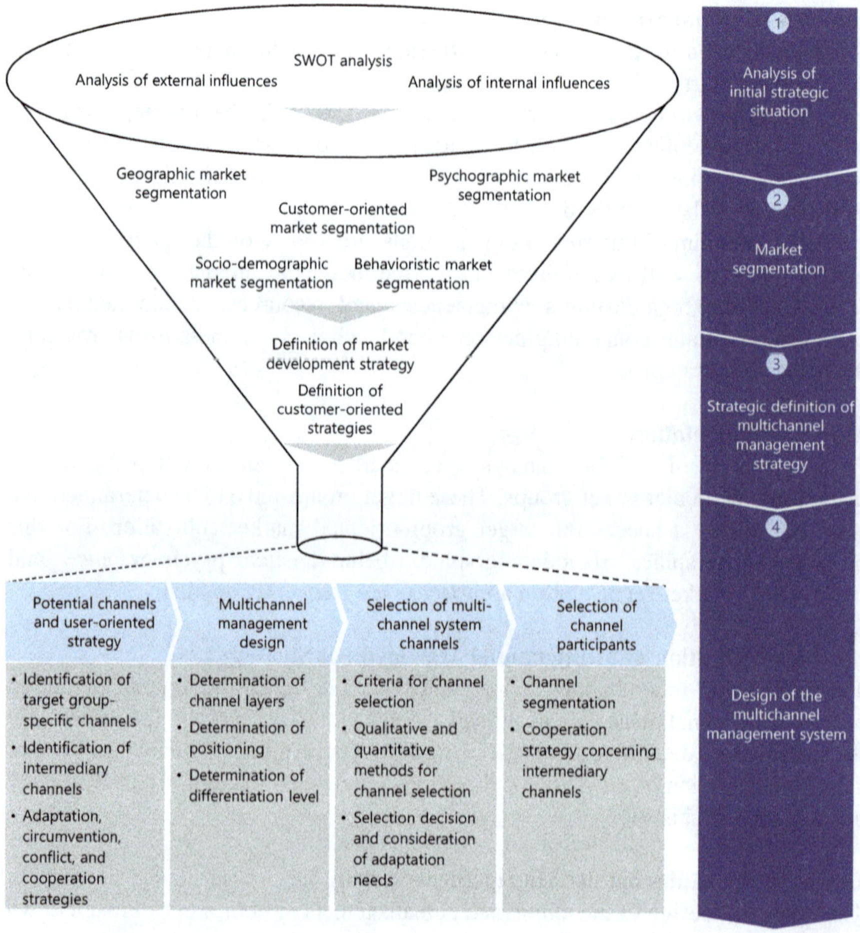

Fig. 12.4 Strategic multichannel management process. Source: Wirtz (2013b, 2021b), Wirtz and Daiser (2015)

Potential Channels and User-oriented Strategy

The process step potential channels and user-oriented strategy covers activities that are associated with the identification of group-specific channels, identification of intermediary channels, as well as the definition of the adaptation, circumvention, conflict, and cooperation strategies. Concerning digital government multichannel management, intermediary channels summarize the channels that are operated by third parties, but used within the digital government service provision (e.g., Facebook, Twitter, TV channels, city portals, etc.).

Multichannel Management Design

The substep multichannel management design refers to the activities that define the number of channel layers, the positioning of the system, and the level of differentiation that the channels shall possess. The number of channel layers determines the number of distribution steps that are necessary from service initiation to service completion. The positioning of the system brings in the marketing perspective by dealing with the positioning activities that are necessary to attract user attention. Concerning the variety of the channels, the level of differentiation determines the distinctiveness of the digital government services.

Selection of Multichannel System Channels

The selection of multichannel system channels begins with the definition of channel selection criteria. The following selection process should be supported by using qualitative and quantitative methods that allow a holistic and rather objective picture to compare the different channel solutions. Based on the result of the selection analysis, a selection decision must be made, which should already take into account the potential management of changes.

Selection of Channel Participants

Having defined the multichannel approach and associated channels, the desired structure of the multichannel system with regard to own and intermediary service channel provision has to be defined. This means that the channels follow a clear segmentation approach that allocates them to the respective process participants and thus determines who operates and who takes responsibility for the channel. This is especially important for service offers that are provided by intermediary channels since the technical handling is not made in-house.

The right mix of multichannel digital government service delivery also strongly depends on the fulfillment of relevant success factors. Important digital government success factors that should be maintained from a provider perspective are outlined in the following chapter.

12.6 Summary, Review Questions, Topics for Discussion, and Online Exercises

- In the past years, Internet-based interaction channels have become an important factor for public service provision and user relationship management.
- The particular importance of combining online and offline channels lies in the additional benefits associated with the advantages of Internet-based service offerings, such as 24/7 availability and an overall improved customer service, as well as in the advantageous cost structure of the Internet.
- The service-channel diversification model (SCD model) is based on the two perspectives of channel widening/expansion and service expansion/channel deepening. It leads to a fourfold table providing the following four generic strategies: (1) single-channel service penetration, (2) single-channel service diversification, (3) lateral-channel service penetration, and (4) multilateral cross-service channel expansion.

- Thus, the SCD model helps to explain whether and how digital government service delivery should be expanded.
- Channel-characteristics of public service delivery can be distinguished into online and offline-based channels, which can be evaluated according to their communication capacity, service delivery capacity, and cost–benefit ratio.
- The public multichannel strategy framework breaks multichannel management down into three different strategies: Isolated Channel Strategy, Combined Channel Strategy, and Integrated Channel Strategy.
- The Isolated Channel Strategy refers to the situation that the individual channels of a multichannel system are run independently and not linked to each other. Instead, the individual channels compete with each other and users have to decide which channel to use.
- In the Combined Channel Strategy, a lead channel is complemented through the symbiotic use of additional channels. Hence, the Combined Channel Strategy requires a comprehensive multichannel approach.
- The Integrated Channel Strategy focuses on providing digital government services through interconnected and interchangeable service channels. Users can switch between channels during the process. The different channels are interdependent, and their management demands high coordination efforts.
- The process of designing a multichannel system consists of four consecutive steps, namely, the analysis of the strategic initial situation, a market segmentation, the strategic definition of the multichannel management strategy, and the design of the multichannel management system.

Chapter 12
Review questions, topics for discussion and online exercises

Review questions

1. Define multichannel systems.
2. Describe the service-channel diversification model (SCD model).
3. Outline the public service delivery model and explain the channel evaluation.
4. Explain the public multichannel strategy framework.
5. Describe the strategic multichannel management process.

Topics for classroom discussion and team debates

1. Discuss the difficulties that public administrations have encountered/are encountering in transferring services from offline to online channels.
2. Discuss the respective advantages and disadvantages of online and offline channels from the citizens' perspective for your city. Consider the perspectives of the different groups of citizens (rich - poor, impaired - non-impaired, ...).
3. Discuss within the class whether a multichannel approach leads to more access fairness for different groups of citizens.

Online Exercises

1. Visit https://about.healthdirect.gov.au/healthcares-future-is-consumer-focused-and-multichannel. Work out the key points of multichannel healthcare in Australia. What trends are emerging?
2. Go to https://digitaldenmark.dk/solutions/ and explore the site. What reasons led to the emergence of numerous public multichannel offerings in Denmark?
3. Enter https://www.bahrain.bh/wps/portal/!ut/p/a0/hcrNCoJAEADgV_Gyx5gxSewoEYYXoYhsL7UJoJvrrD-j1NuHT9Dxgw80lKDZrLYxYj0bt1nH1aXAONwn-zyJ7hGmRXy6Hs8YZniAGzHk_1IJT_seR52Crj0LfQRKavw6-EmMq4gVtr4nheNi6y5wlrtZoXn5RYLt0cQ9sSjsFyd2V7eGmVwwy2SEmi8MXfb4AQ91Ldc!/ and explore the site. How can Bahrain's multichannel strategy be described?

References

Ansoff, H. Igor (1957): Strategies for Diversification. In Harvard Business Review 35 (5), pp. 113–124.

Ebbers, Wolfgang E.; Pieterson, Willem J.; Noordman, H. N. (2008): Electronic government: Rethinking channel management strategies. In Government Information Quarterly 25 (2), pp. 181–201.

Gagnon, Yves-C; Posada, Elizabeth; Bourgault, Mario; Naud, Alain (2010): Multichannel Delivery of Public Services: A New and Complex Management Challenge. In International Journal of Public Administration 33 (5), pp. 213–222.

Kernaghan, Kenneth (2005): Moving towards the virtual state: integrating services and service channels for citizen-centred delivery. In International Review of Administrative Sciences 71 (1), pp. 119–131.

Lynn, Laurence E. (1998): The new public management: How to transform a theme into a legacy. In Public Administration Review 58 (3), pp. 231–237.

PricewaterhouseCoopers (2009): Champion for Digital Inclusion. The Economic Case for Digital Inclusion. Race Online 2012. Available online at http://www.go-on.co.uk/wp-content/uploads/2014/08/pwc_report.pdf, checked on 7/16/2015.

Reddick, Christopher G.; Turner, Michael (2012): Channel choice and public service delivery in Canada: Comparing e-government to traditional service delivery. In Government Information Quarterly 29 (1), pp. 1–11.

Reichheld, Frederick F. (2003): The One Number You Need to Grow. In Harvard Business Review 81 (12), pp. 46–55.

Teerling, Marije L.; Pieterson, Willem (2011): How to improve e-government use: An empirical examination of multichannel marketing instruments. In Information Polity 16 (2), pp. 171–187.

United Nations (2014): United Nations E-Government Survey 2014. E-Government for the Future We Want. With assistance of Department of Economic and Social Affairs. New York. Available online at http://unpan3.un.org/egovkb/Portals/egovkb/Documents/un/2014-Survey/E-Gov_Complete_Survey-2014.pdf, checked on 12/1/2014.

Wilson, Hugh; Daniel, Elizabeth (2007): The multi-channel challenge: A dynamic capability approach. In Industrial Marketing Management 36 (1), pp. 10–20.

Wirtz, Bernd W. (2005): Integriertes Direktmarketing. Grundlagen - Instrumente - Prozesse. Wiesbaden: Gabler (Lehrbuch).

Wirtz, Bernd W. (2008): Multi-Channel-Marketing. Grundlagen, Instrumente, Prozesse. 1st ed. Wiesbaden: Gabler.

Wirtz, Bernd W. (2013a): Medien- und Internetmanagement. 8th ed. Wiesbaden: Gabler.

Wirtz, Bernd W. (2013b): Multi-Channel-Marketing. Grundlagen - Instrumente - Prozesse. 2nd ed. Wiesbaden: Springer Gabler.

Wirtz, Bernd W. (2021a): Digital Business and Electronic Commerce. Cham: Springer International Publishing.

Wirtz, Bernd W. (2021b): Multi-Channel-Marketing. Grundlagen - Instrumente - Prozesse. 3rd ed. Wiesbaden: Springer Fachmedien Wiesbaden GmbH.

Wirtz, Bernd W. (2022a): Digital-Marketing. Grundlagen, Instrumente und Prozesse. 4th ed. Wiesbaden.

Wirtz, Bernd W. (2022b): E-Government. Wiesbaden: Springer Gabler.

Wirtz, Bernd W.; Büttner, Tobias; Schwarz, Joachim (2003): Multi-Channel-Management: eine empirische Analyse zu ausgewählten Aktionsparametern und deren Erfolgsrelevanz. In Jahrbuch der Absatz-und Verbrauchsforschung 49 (1), pp. 65–83.

Wirtz, Bernd W.; Daiser, Peter (2015): E-Government. Strategy, process, instruments. 1st ed. Speyer.

Wirtz, Bernd W.; Daiser, Peter (2017): E-government. Strategy, process, instruments. 2nd ed. Speyer.

Wirtz, Bernd W.; Kleineicken, A. (2005): Electronic Procurement - eine empirische Analyse zu Aktionsparametern und Erfolgswirkungen. In Zeitschrift Führung und Organisation 74 (5), pp. 339–347.

Wirtz, Bernd W.; Kurtz, Oliver Tuna (2017): Determinants of citizen usage intentions in e-government. An empirical analysis. In Public Organization Review 17 (3), pp. 353–372.

Wirtz, Bernd W.; Langer, Paul (2017): Public multichannel management. An integrated framework of off- and online multichannel government services. In Public Organization Review 17 (4), pp. 563–580. DOI: https://doi.org/10.1007/s11115-016-0356-0.

Wirtz, Bernd W.; Lütje, Sebastian; Schierz, Paul Gerhardt (2009): An empirical analysis of the acceptance of e-procurement in the German public sector. In International Journal of Public Administration 33 (1), pp. 26–42.

Wirtz, Bernd W.; Mory, Linda; Piehler, Robert; Daiser, Peter (2017): E-government: A citizen relationship marketing analysis. In International Review on Public and Nonprofit Marketing 14, pp. 149–178. DOI: https://doi.org/10.1007/s12208-016-0164-9.

Success Factors of Digital Government 13

Contents

Learning Objectives
By working through this chapter, you will be able to:

1. Explain the barriers of digital government.
2. Describe the improvement approaches for digital government.
3. Explain the various digital government success factors.
4. Outline user-centered, e-service, and IT success factors.
5. Explain the differences between e-service success factors and IT success factors.

Today's society has come a long way to a modern and efficient digital government. But at the same time, it is also obvious that there are still many challenges that have not been solved yet.[1] The increasing digital transformation of our society demands a further strengthening of digital government systems and service provision.

This calls for a new e-skill profile for public administration. Important components of this profile are consistent citizen orientation, compelling cooperation, participation and transparency, high transaction interactivity with distinctive dialogue and responsiveness of public management, and last but not least a comprehensive multichannel digital government.

[1] See for Chapter 13 Success Factors of Digital Government also Wirtz (2015, 2022), Wirtz and Daiser (2015, 2017), Wirtz and Kubin (2021).

B. W. Wirtz, *Digital Government*, Springer Texts in Business and Economics,
https://doi.org/10.1007/978-3-031-13086-1_13

Focus on Users' Needs and User-friendliness

Since local digital government portals are the main Internet interface between the government and citizens (see Section 9.1), a further expansion and optimization of local online portals is required that clearly focuses on the users' needs as well as on increasing user-friendliness of the digital government services.

This development needs to go hand in hand with broadening the full online digital government service range and increasing service depth. In addition, online communication with the users should be further intensified and the provision of participation and collaboration digital government services expanded.

Digital Government Service Culture

From an organizational point of view, public sector organizations have to carry on with the establishment of a digital government service culture and the stepwise relocation of resources from offline to online digital government service provision. In order to keep track with the pace of the ongoing digital government development, small municipalities that do not possess the necessary resources should aim at creating regional digital government network solutions to benefit from the partner's economies of scales and experience.

Regardless of the size of the municipality or administration, there are a number of barriers to the successful implementation of digital Government, particularly in Germany. These barriers are explained in more detail in the following section.

13.1 Barriers of Digital Government

Although modern information technologies are developing continuously and citizen and user expectations are rising, digital government is still significantly underdeveloped in many countries (Wirtz et al. 2019b). This can be seen in particular with regard to the weak performance of countries such as Germany in the UN rankings on e-government and e-participation.[2] Against this background, Wirtz and Kubin (2021) have divided the barriers to the successful implementation of digital government into four central areas. Figure 13.1 shows the four-barrier model of digital government (content based on Wirtz and Kubin 2021). It distinguishes between (1) political and societal, (2) legal, (3) cultural and organizational, and (4) information technology barriers.

[2] See for the following Section 13.1 also Wirtz and Kubin (2021).

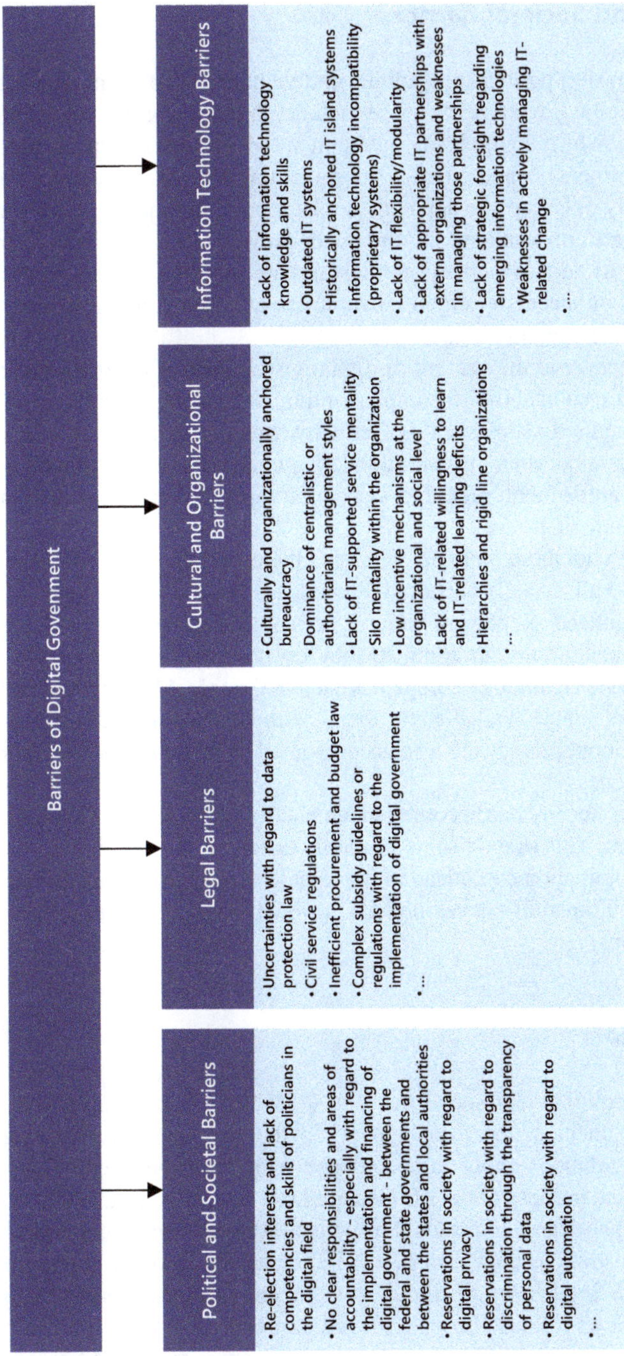

Fig. 13.1 The four-barrier model of digital government

Political and Societal Barriers

In many countries, political and administrative barriers are the main obstacles to the success of digital government. These include, in particular, the re-election interests of politicians, which are typically based on an opportunistic attitude. Since complex digital government change processes often require high investments, whose positive effects usually only become apparent at a later point in time, politicians are inclined to avoid these investments in order to prevent their re-election from being jeopardized. In addition, many politicians lack the digital skills to recognize the requirements of successful digital government and to initiate the associated change processes at the operational level.

Another barrier to the success of digital government is the often unclear lines of authority and responsibility for implementing and financing digital government. In federally structured states such as Germany, this primarily affects communication and cooperation between the central federal government and the state governments. Similar ambiguities with regard to areas of competence and responsibility can also arise at the municipal level.

In addition to these political barriers, there are also societal barriers. These include, above all, socially anchored reservations about digital privacy. Many people have a pronounced skepticism when it comes to sharing their personal data with government institutions. In contrast, they do not have these reservations when it comes to private technology companies such as Google, Meta, or Amazon and make their personal data available to them without any major reservations. The reservations about privacy are also accompanied by a fear of discrimination through data transparency.

In addition, society has become fundamentally skeptical about digital automation in recent years. This skepticism is primarily based on the fear that developments in the field of automation could lead to job losses. Some people transfer this fear to the increasing automation developments through digital government in public administrations.

Legal Barriers

Apart from political and social barriers, legal barriers can hinder the success of digital government at the formal level. In the EU countries, for example, data protection regulations apply in accordance with the EU General Data Protection Regulation. The purpose of the EU General Data Protection Regulation is to give EU citizens a higher degree of personal responsibility with regard to their personal data. Public administrations must also take these formal data protection requirements into account when implementing digital government. Against this backdrop, existing data privacy laws can also be a significant barrier to digital government.

Furthermore, civil servant law represents another significant barrier to digital government. In some countries, such as Germany, civil servants are subject to the so-called lifetime principle. This means that they benefit from special legal advantages such as extensive protection against dismissal. As a result, there is often a lack of legal incentives to encourage civil servants to implement digital government effectively and efficiently.

In addition, in some countries, such as Germany, there are procurement and budgetary regulations that inhibit digital government. Since public administrations are often dependent on the IT capabilities of private IT companies, procurement law can slow down the selection and commissioning of these IT companies.

In addition, many countries have complicated legal requirements for funding. If a public administration needs timely funding for digital government, it must comply with the relevant funding regulations. This can lead to public administrations orienting themselves exclusively to the funding requirements in order not to jeopardize their inflow of funds. As a result, they may make investments that comply with the funding requirements, but which may not serve the sustainable further development of digital government.

Cultural and Organizational Barriers

In addition, cultural and organizational barriers are also of considerable importance in the successful implementation of digital government. Since the socio-technical information systems implemented in the context of digital government affect both cultural aspects and organizational processes, these barriers should not be neglected. In this context, a culturally and organizationally induced understanding of bureaucracy is considered to be a major barrier to digital government.

In addition, it can be stated that centralistic or authoritarian management styles continue to dominate most public organizations. As a result, decisions concerning digital government are primarily made by central managers, without other administrative employees being able to participate in the decision-making process. As a result, creative ideas and innovative approaches by administrative employees often remain unheard. Yet it is precisely these employees who can contribute important implications for successful digital government due to their experience at the operational level. In addition, the successful implementation of digital government requires dynamic change processes. Consequently, centralistic or authoritarian management styles without a minimum of individual responsibility inhibit the efficient management of these dynamic processes. Furthermore, traditional centralistic management styles lead to increasing insecurity among operationally active administrative staff. This in turn can increase their susceptibility to errors when implementing digital government.

Another cultural or organizational barrier to digital government is the lack of an IT-based service mentality. Many administrative employees find it difficult to combine traditional administrative logic with the potential of new information technologies. Against this background, administrative employees often work without supporting technologies, even though their personal work efficiency would increase through the use of these technologies. This clearly shows that culturally anchored mentalities represent a significant resistance to digital government.

Moreover, there is often a silo-mentality at the organizational level. This silo mentality manifests itself, for example, in non-existent or poor collaboration between different teams. In addition, employees may have problems with objective criticism and avoid constructive feedback. Against this background, silo mentality can prevent organizational synergy effects with regard to the implementation of digital government, and in this way impede progress and change.

Parallel to the legal incentives, there is also a lack of social incentive mechanisms within public organizations. Instead of motivating each other and supporting the successful implementation of digital government, administrative employees mostly protect each other from change and at the same time prevent healthy internal competition. Thus, there is a lack of incentive mechanisms that could increase the willingness of administrative employees to change with regard to the successful implementation of digital government.

Another barrier to digital government is a lack of IT-related willingness to learn, which is particularly pronounced in public administrations. This barrier is closely related to the lack of incentive mechanisms explained earlier. A lack of incentives implicitly impairs the willingness to learn new skills. If there is a lack of willingness on the part of administrative employees to learn these skills, this can jeopardize the success of digital government. After all, digital government is built on the IT-related skills of administrative employees. Furthermore, there are IT-related learning deficits that have arisen primarily as a result of the neglect of IT skills in internal and external training courses.

In addition, public administrations are mostly line organizations with pronounced hierarchies. These rigid structures make dynamic changes difficult.

Information Technology Barriers

In addition to cultural and organizational barriers, information technology barriers can also impede digital government. Against the background of the complexity associated with new information technologies, digital government requires information technology knowledge and skills. Since public administrations are often unable to provide this knowledge and capability on their own, they must enter into suitable partnerships with technology companies. Such partnerships always involve risks, which is why a lack of information technology skills is a major barrier to digital government.

In addition, IT systems are often outdated and costly to maintain. All the financial resources that go into maintaining these legacy systems cannot be invested in new IT systems. In addition to these outdated systems, IT island systems that have grown historically due to a lack of strategic foresight impair digital government. As a result of these IT island systems, there is a lack of compatibility between IT systems in many public administrations. This incompatibility impairs both information technology communication within public administrations and between public administrations. Since in many cases there is a lack of coherent IT systems with appropriate interfaces, it is difficult for public administrations to provide a comprehensive digital government system. At the same time, this incompatibility also impairs the flexibility and modularity of digital government systems. Even minor changes mean that existing IT systems have to be redesigned or reprogrammed.

In addition, public administrations often lack experience in managing IT partnerships with private technology companies. However, due to the lack of internal IT capabilities, they are mostly dependent on external partnerships. Against the backdrop of this structural dependency, deficits in the governance of IT partnerships represent significant barriers to digital government.

Furthermore, it can be stated that public administrations often lack strategic vision with regard to information technology innovations. While private companies are directly exposed to information technology innovations due to the dynamics of competition, public administrations reveal a certain inertia in identifying innovative technologies.

In addition, public administrations often have difficulties in independently managing the digital transformation and the associated change processes. Against this backdrop, they are increasingly dependent on external consultants, whose commissioning places an additional burden on the public budget and may cause a lack of understanding among the population.

The barriers identified in the four areas represent considerable resistance to the successful implementation of digital government. Since some of the barriers are mutually dependent, they should not be viewed in isolation. Rather, a holistic perspective is required that takes into account the connections and interactions between the different barriers. For example, the lack of information technology knowledge and skills in public administrations is closely linked to the lack of IT-related learning readiness. In the following section, adequate approaches for improvement will be derived.

13.2 Improvement Approaches for Digital Government

Against the background of the identified barriers and the considerable development lag of digital government in many countries, Figure 13.2 shows potential improvement approaches in the form of the five-dimensional optimization model of digital government (content based on Wirtz and Kubin 2021). The model identifies (1) political-administrative, (2) societal, (3) legal, (4) cultural and organizational, and (5) information technology improvement approaches.[3]

[3] See for the following Section 13.2 also Wirtz and Kubin (2021).

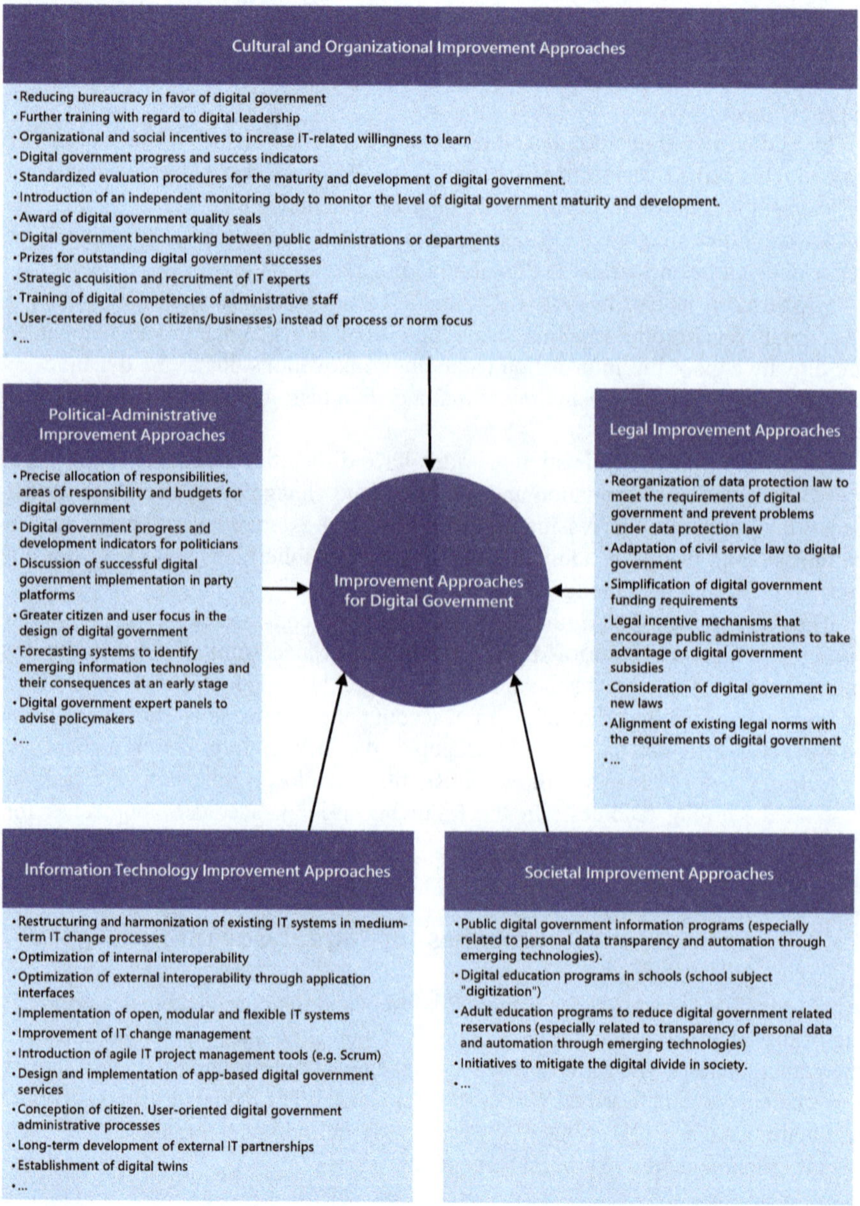

Fig. 13.2 The five-dimensional optimization model of digital government

Political-Administrative Improvement Approaches

In the political-administrative sphere, clear areas of competence, responsibility, and budgets should be determined in order to improve digital government. This clear definition creates a higher degree of political-administrative accountability. This accountability can prevent politicians and public sector executives from shirking their responsibilities with regard to digital government implementation.

In addition, digital government development indicators should be introduced for politicians so that the population has an indication which federal, state, and local politicians are really committed to digital government. Besides these digital development indicators, digital government should be more strongly addressed in party programs so that voters can better understand political strategies with regard to digital government.

Moreover, there is a need at the political level to prioritize citizen or user needs in the design of digital government. In addition, the dynamic nature of technological developments requires adequate forecasting instruments that enable policymakers to identify promising technologies and their potential applications in the area of digital government at an early stage. Such forecasting instruments provide considerable support for political decision-making.

Furthermore, expert committees should advise policymakers and, in particular, federal, state and local governments on the successful implementation of digital government and, if necessary, provide support in the form of progressive digital concepts.

Societal Improvement Approaches

In terms of society, there should be appropriately designed information campaigns to dispel the widespread reservations among the population regarding data transparency and digital automation. After all, digital government systems can only function effectively and efficiently if citizens or users are convinced of the benefits they offer, otherwise investments in digital government systems would not be worthwhile.

Moreover, digital education initiatives should be introduced in schools and adult education. In particular, a school subject on digitization would help young people learn how to use digital technologies responsibly at an early stage and understand the potential of these technologies in terms of public service delivery. With regard to adult education, the focus should also be on eliminating the digital divide that exists in many countries. For this purpose, it is of great importance to teach people with little affinity for technology the basic handling of the necessary hardware as well as the underlying operating systems and user interfaces. Furthermore, adults in particular should be made aware of the potential of data transparency and digital automation so that they can reconsider their personal reservations about these technological developments and adopt a more differentiated perspective. This should also enhance the acceptance of the increasingly automated service processes in digital government.

Legal Improvement Approaches

The legal improvement approaches primarily involve adapting data privacy law to the demands of digital government. In this regard, it is very important to exploit the potential of digital government without excessively restricting individual data sovereignty. In addition, civil service law needs to be adapted to compensate for the lack of legal incentive mechanisms. This improvement approach will be difficult to implement in most states, as civil servants have a special position in the government's service delivery and therefore benefit from legal privileges.

With regard to existing funding regulations, legal simplification is needed in many states. This applies in particular to the requirements that public administrations must fulfill in order to even consider applying for funding for the organizational implementation of digital government. If the legal hurdles are too high, public administrations will refrain from submitting applications and will continue to neglect the implementation of digital government due to a lack of financial support. In addition to simplifying the funding regulations, legal incentives should be introduced to encourage public administrations to actually take advantage of the funding programs.

In addition, both existing and new legal standards relating to digital government should be adapted to the dynamic progress of digitization. This is of considerable importance in order to form a reliable and efficient legal framework for digital government.

Cultural and Organizational Improvement Approaches

At the cultural and organizational level, there is a particular need to cut red tape in administrative structures and processes. This debureaucratization is a basic prerequisite for the smooth implementation of digital government. If bureaucratic structures and processes persist, this can reduce the effectiveness and efficiency of digital government systems that are based on this bureaucracy.

In addition to this debureaucratization, there should be ongoing training for public managers in the area of "digital leadership." This will enable executives to learn the challenges of the digital age and manage the necessary digital transformation processes.

Moreover, there is a need for organizational or social incentive mechanisms in public organizations. These incentive mechanisms should be embedded in an organizational culture that encourages administrative staff to learn the skills required for digital government and, based on the skills learned, to take appropriate action to promote digital government. In a sense, these incentives force the development of digital competencies and can lead to increased acceptance of digital government among administrative employees.

Apart from this, there is a need for specific digital government progress or success indicators that provide a point of reference regarding the maturity or development level of digital government. These digital government progress and success indicators require the introduction of independent monitoring bodies that regularly check the digital government maturity and development of public administrations. On the basis of these audits, digital government quality seals should be awarded, performance comparisons between different administrations and departments should be made, and public administrations or departments with particular success in the area of digital government should receive awards. In this way, a competitive dynamic can be created between public organizations and their departments.

In the field of human resources management, the focus should also be on recruiting IT experts. In view of the shortage of skilled workers and the considerable importance of IT experts in the digital age, public administrations are competing with companies in the private sector. Since these tend to be able to pay higher salaries, the special advantages of the public sector, such as job security or the meaningful purpose of the activity, should be placed in the foreground when designing specific recruiting strategies. In order to compensate for the lack of IT skills, the training and continuing education of administrative employees should also focus on skills that are relevant to the success of digital government.

Moreover, public administrations should move away from the traditional focus on processes and standards when implementing digital government and instead strive for a user-centric focus on results. This change of perspective helps public administrations to align their digital government closely with the requirements and needs of citizens, companies, and other users.

Information Technology Improvement Approaches

In terms of information technology, the main requirement is to realign or harmonize existing IT systems in order to eliminate the insular IT architecture in medium-term IT change processes. This requires both an improvement in internal interoperability and an optimization of interoperability with external IT applications through application interfaces.

Since information technologies evolve dynamically, open, modular, and flexible IT systems should also be implemented. This enables the effective and efficient integration or incorporation of new information technologies into existing IT systems.

In addition, public administrations should improve their IT change management with regard to digital government so that system-related changes do not cause serious interruptions in process flows. Apart from that, the introduction of agile IT project management methods such as the Scrum method is necessary. Using these techniques, IT projects can be continuously adapted to changing external and internal expectations.

It should also be taken into account that users increasingly expect app-based services. Public administrations should ideally combine all services in one app in order to meet user expectations and create app-based services.

In addition, digital administrative processes should be checked for their citizen or user orientation during their development and adapted if necessary. This requires regular citizen and user surveys to support IT experts in the technical design of these processes.

Apart from this, public organizations should establish long-term IT partnerships with IT companies to compensate for the lack of information technology resources and skills. In addition, it is becoming increasingly necessary for successful digital government to use digital twins to map real administrative processes on a digital level and thus improve efficiency and reduce susceptibility to errors.

13.3 Digital Government Success Factors

Against the background of the improvement approaches, central success factors can be derived. These success factors can be divided into user-centered, service-centered, and IT-centered success factors and are presented in the following section.

User-Centered Success Factors

From a provider perspective, there are five key user-centered success factors that a digital government system should provide by all means. These are ease of use/usability, usefulness, website design/visual appeal, assistance/support, and multichannel digital government service usage.

Ease of Use/Usability

Ease of use/usability measures the perceived user effort to become acquainted with and learn to use a new technology. If user effort is perceived to be high, then this reduces the probability that users actually use the technology (Davis 1986). Transferred to the digital government context, this means that the digital government portal needs to be set up in a way that is easy to understand and to use for the users (Wirtz et al. 2015; Wirtz and Kurtz 2016).

Usefulness

Usefulness measures the user's subjective perception or impression that using a specific technology facilitates tasks or enhances performance (Wirtz and Piehler 2016). If, for instance, a new technology is not perceived as a value-adding or performance enhancing tool, then why take the effort and bear the risk of moving on to a new technology or system (Wirtz et al. 2019a). Thus, the digital government system needs to provide a clear value for the user.

Website Design/Visual Appeal

Website design/visual appeal is a further vital factor for the setup of a digital government system (Wirtz et al. 2016). In summary, this refers to a user-friendly, transparent, and clear structure of the digital government portal or website. Key aspects are the presentation of content and the website layout, which mainly refer to graphical elements, such as color, typeface, or illustrations that should be deployed in a way to achieve a professional, harmonious, and appealing design.

Assistance/Support

Although digital government service provision tends to be automated technology-based, web assistance or personal interaction are very important factors for the users (Piehler et al. 2016). Furthermore, it fosters user trust and confidence in using digital government services. Here, digital government providers have to ensure that assistance and support staff are technically well-trained and that they provide help in a polite, convenient, caring, respectful, and friendly way.

Multichannel Digital Government Service Usage

Multichannel digital government service usage has become a vital factor for user relationship management, especially against the background that the key reasons for providing digital government services are mainly driven by rational arguments like cost efficiency.

Digital government providers need to be aware of the persisting mismatch between government and user channel preferences and thus have to adapt their service offering specifically to the users' needs and requirements. The challenge for public administration is to provide digital government services that are suitable for all citizens and organizations. Thus, effective and efficient digital government service delivery requires a clear multichannel focus that aims at reaching all relevant public stakeholders. The following Figure 13.3 illustrates the main user-centered success factors from a provider perspective.

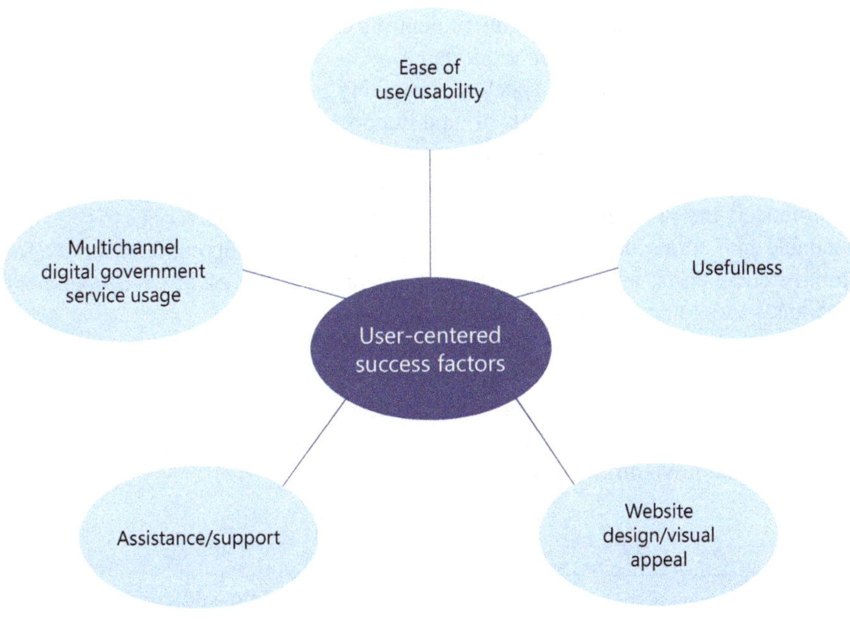

Fig. 13.3 User-centered success factors. Source: Wirtz and Daiser (2015, 2017)

Another set of highly relevant success factors is directly associated with the digital government services and their provision. While user-centered success factors rather present important framework aspects on a meta-level, e-service success factors specifically address vital factors and characteristics of the digital government service portfolio. These are presented in the following section.

E-Service Success Factors

Today's digital government portals provide manifold services, ranging, for example, from comprehensive digital government offerings on citizenship, registration, and traffic to e-health offers or online job portals.[4] In addition, many digital government providers present services for complaint management, for online appointment service, for checking the processing status online, for booking local sport and leisure activities online, and for online newsletters concerning local information.

However, it is not just about providing digital government services to the users. It is also important to tailor the digital government offers to the needs and the requirements of the users. For this reason, there are particular success factors that are specifically associated with digital government service provision. These can be divided into two categories: service-oriented and function-oriented success factors (see Figure 13.4).

Service-oriented Success Factors

While service-oriented success factors are primarily concerned with the question what services should be offered, function-oriented success factors deal with the question how these services should be offered. Thus, the latter also take into account behavioral aspects of the digital government-providing public sector organization, such as responsiveness to citizen requests.

From a service-oriented perspective, providing an extensive set of full online digital government service offers is of vital importance. If users have the possibility to benefit from a far-reaching digital government service offering that can be entirely conducted online, this substantially increases user convenience.

Moreover, the provision of participative digital government services is recommendable and online checks of the processing status, online appointment service for administrative visits, as well as a comprehensive provision of file and document downloads should be available on the portal.

Further important digital government services that should be in place are a complaint management system, public open data provision, and the possibility to subscribe to online newsletters. This way, the user can stay in touch with the digital government provider, can give feedback, and stay informed about system changes and new digital government services.

[4] See for the following Section E-Service Success Factors also Wirtz (2015).

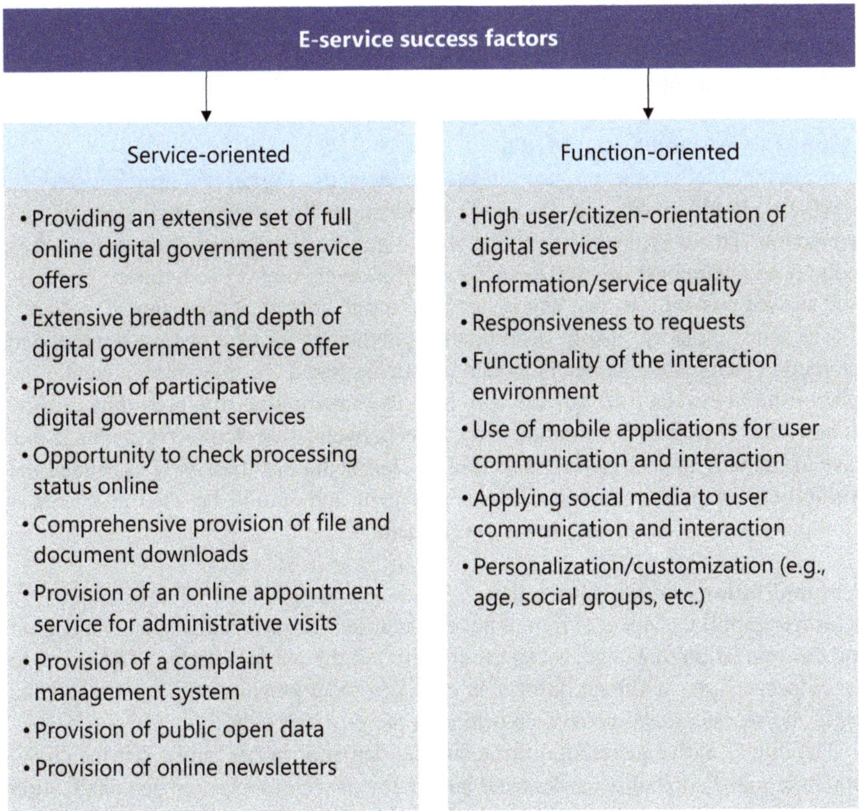

Fig 13.4 E-service success factors. Source: Wirtz and Daiser (2015, 2017)

Function-oriented Success Factors

Considering function-oriented success factors, it is indispensable that digital government service providers align the services provided with the needs and the requirements of the users. Thus, a strong focus on user/citizen-orientation is highly recommendable when designing and implementing digital government services. A further important aspect is information and service quality. This means that the digital government offers—the information and services provided—need to meet high standards. Therefore, all digital government information and services have to be reliable, relevant, credible, helpful, and usable. Responsiveness to requests is another vital success factor for digital government service provision. Here, responsiveness refers to the time needed to respond to user enquiries as well as the perceived quality of the response. Responsible employees should be well-trained to be able to provide helpful support in a competent and emphatic manner.

The functionality of the interaction environment is a further relevant point that digital government service providers should take into account. Since modern information and communication technologies allow automated information exchange with other applications, which clearly facilitates user–government interaction and makes their interplay more convenient, digital government providers should take full advantage of this opportunity.

Mobile Devices and Social Media

Considering the increasing use of mobile devices, digital government service providers should make use of mobile applications for user communication and interaction. This way, users can access digital government information and services without any temporal or local restriction. Moreover, mobile technology provides new service possibilities that can be applied to public service provision.

The same applies to using social media applications for user communication and interaction (compare Chapter 7). Social media has had a considerable impact on the relationship between the government and its stakeholders by providing a new channel for fostering information exchange between two active participants that have an impact on each other. Therefore, social media has massively expanded the possibilities of public multichannel management and should be used as a further significant pillar to leverage digital government.

Personalization and Customization

A further important aspect of digital government service provision is personalization and customization (e.g., age, social groups, etc.) of the online offering. This refers to two aspects: first, modification of web offers to meet personal expectations of the users and second, customized web offers on the provider side.

The digital native generation, for example, demands better public service provision in terms of convenient access and interaction as well as ongoing personalization and customization possibilities. Considering elderly people, specific web offers that are already tailored to the needs of this particular target group are beneficial.

Having outlined user-centered success factors as well as e-service success factors, there remains a third category of relevant digital government success factors: IT success factors. These success factors, which are rather technological, are presented in the following section.

IT Success Factors

Concerning the success of a digital government system, there are a couple of important IT success factors that should be considered when designing, implementing, and maintaining such a system. Since these factors refer to technology-related aspects, it is necessary to possess the respective technical IT skills and competencies—either in-house or out-house. Figure 13.5 summarizes the IT success factors.

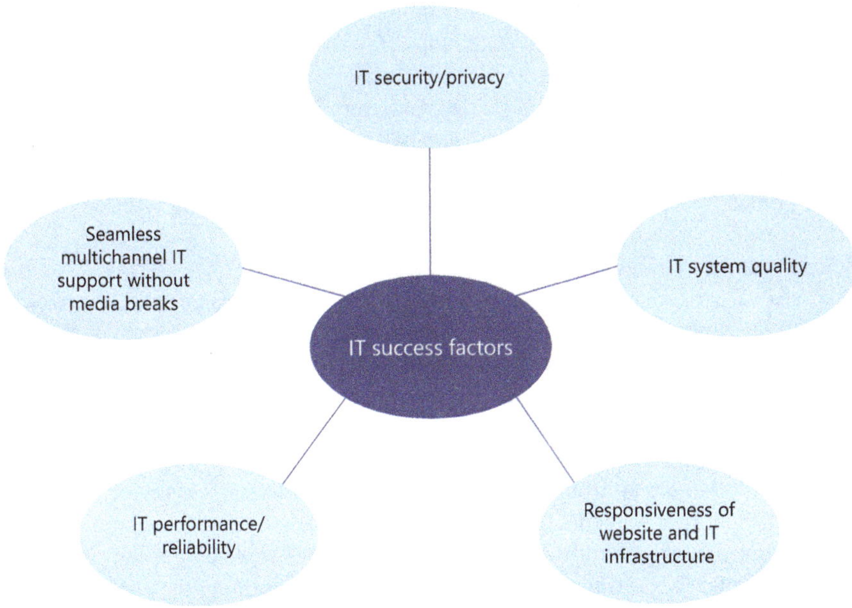

Fig. 13.5 IT success factors. Source: Wirtz and Daiser (2015, 2017)

IT Security/Privacy
Very crucial factors are IT security and privacy, which are two important prerequisites for digital government user trust and user acceptance. In this context, security and privacy are understood as perceived safety, secrecy, and confidentiality of personal user data and network-based information processing. If users believe that their personal information is not safe, they will be more reluctant to perform digital government transactions online or will not conduct them online at all. For this reason, public managers have to take care that adequate security guidelines are in place and that these are communicated to the relevant public stakeholders to establish an adequate IT security and privacy awareness.

IT System Quality
IT system quality is another key success factor for creating a favorable digital government environment. It includes all technological aspects of an information system as well as the associated digital government processes and resources. From a system management point of view, the digital government provider has to take care that a transparent performance monitoring with a clear focus on system quality is in place.

Responsiveness of Website and IT Infrastructure
IT infrastructure fault tolerances, server performance capabilities, as well as inspection and security procedures, for example, are important facets of IT system quality management. In addition, the entire digital government team needs to be aware of the

detrimental effects of portal downtime, unreliable service provision, and so on. In case of a potential IT attack or breakdown, effective contingency plans have to be immediately at hand.

Responsiveness of website and IT infrastructure is closely related to IT system quality. Here, digital government providers have to ensure that the website responds and the data exchange takes place within a reasonable period of time. Today, long waiting times for new pages or data processing are not tolerated by users anymore.

IT Performance/Reliability
Perceived IT performance and reliability is a vital factor for using a digital government system. Like the previous factor, it is also associated with IT system quality. If performance or reliability of the digital government system is perceived to be weak, this finally reduces the user's desire to use the digital government services provided.

Seamless Multichannel IT Support
Another important factor from a technology perspective is seamless multichannel IT support without further media breaks, meaning that users should be technologically enabled to make use of full online digital government services through different online channels. This sets high demands on the interoperability of the applied digital government system and channels.

Taking into account the key digital government success factors from a user, e-service, and IT perspective should provide a solid basis for designing, implementing, and maintaining a successful digital government system. However, there are further important aspects that have to be considered when implementing a digital government system. These are outlined in the following chapter.

13.4 Summary, Review Questions, Topics for Discussion, and Online Exercises

- The increasing digital transformation of our society requires a further strengthening of digital government systems and service provision, demanding a clear understanding of and a target-oriented focus on barriers, improvement approaches, and digital government success factors.
- The success of digital government is affected by political and social, legal, cultural and organizational, and information technology barriers. These barriers can be explained with the four-barrier model of digital government.
- To overcome these barriers to digital government, public organizations should consider political-administrative, legal, social, cultural, organizational, and information technology improvement approaches. Together, these improvement approaches form the five-dimension optimization model.
- For digital government to be successful, the user-centered success factors (ease of use/usability, usefulness, website design/visual appeal, assistance/support, and multichannel digital government service usage) need to be considered.

Additionally, service-oriented and function-oriented digital service success factors should be addressed.

- With regard to the success of a digital government system, there are also a number of important IT success factors that should be considered when designing, implementing, and maintaining such a system. As these factors refer to technology-related aspects, it is necessary to have the appropriate technical IT skills and competencies—either internally or externally.
- IT success factors of digital government can be subdivided into IT security/privacy, IT system quality, responsiveness of website and IT infrastructure, IT performance/reliability, and seamless multichannel IT support without media breaks. They should not be neglected either in order for digital government to be successful.

Chapter 13
Review questions, topics for discussion and online exercises

Review questions

1. Present the four-barrier model of digital government.
2. Explain the five-dimension optimization model of digital government.
3. Describe the user-centric success factors of digital government.
4. Describe the service-centric success factors of digital government.
5. Outline the IT-related success factors of digital government.

Topics for classroom discussion and team debates

1. Discuss which of the digital government barriers are the biggest obstacle to digital government success.
2. Discuss whether we need digital government improvement approaches at all, and if so, why.
3. Discuss the digital government success factors using your city's website as an example. Are all success factors present there?

Online Exercises

1. Go to https://www.cityoflondon.gov.uk/ and find out to what extent IT success factors can be identified. Are all of them present?
2. Visit https://www.nyc.gov/ and work out where service-oriented success factors can be found. Are all of them present?
3. Enter https://www.gov.sg/ and work out where function-oriented success factors can be found. Are all of them present?

References

Davis, Fred D. (1986): A Technology Acceptance Model for Empirically Testing New End-User Information Systems: Theory and Results. Doctoral dissertation. Massachusetts Institute of Technology, Boston.

Piehler, Robert; Wirtz, Bernd W.; Daiser, Peter (2016): An analysis of continuity intentions of egovernment portal users. In Public Management Review 18 (2), pp. 163–198.

Wirtz, Bernd W. (2015): E-Government. Perspektiven des kommunalen E-Government. E-Government Studie. Mainz: Ministerium des Innern, für Sport und Infrastruktur. Edited by Land Rheinland-Pfalz. Ministerium des Innern, für Sport und Infrastruktur.

Wirtz, Bernd W. (2022): E-Government. Wiesbaden: Springer Gabler.

Wirtz, Bernd W.; Birkmeyer, Steven; Langer, Paul F. (2019a): Citizens and mobile government: an empirical analysis of the antecedents and consequences of mobile government usage. In International Review of Administrative Sciences 87 (4), 836-854. DOI: https://doi.org/10.1177/0020852319862349.

Wirtz, Bernd W.; Daiser, Peter (2015): E-Government. Strategy, process, instruments. 1st ed. Speyer.

Wirtz, Bernd W.; Daiser, Peter (2017): E-government. Strategy, process, instruments. 2nd ed. Speyer.

Wirtz, Bernd W.; Kubin, Pascal R. M. (2021): E-Government in Deutschland: Entwicklung, Barrieren und Verbesserungsansätze. In Verwaltung & Management 27 (6), pp. 285–294. DOI: https://doi.org/10.5771/0947-9856-2021-6-285.

Wirtz, Bernd W.; Kurtz, Oliver Tuna (2016): Local e-government and user satisfaction with city portals – The citizens' service preference perspective. In International Review on Public and Nonprofit Marketing 13 (3), pp. 265–287. DOI: https://doi.org/10.1007/s12208-015-0149-0.

Wirtz, Bernd W.; Piehler, Robert (2016): Egovernment applications and public personnel acceptance. An empirical analysis of the public servant perspective. In International Journal of Public Administration 39 (3), pp. 238–247.

Wirtz, Bernd W.; Piehler, Robert; Daiser, Peter (2015): E-government portal characteristics and individual appeal: An examination of E-government and citizen acceptance in the context of local administration portals. In Journal of Nonprofit & Public Sector Marketing 27 (1), pp. 70–98.

Wirtz, Bernd W.; Piehler, Robert; Rieger, Vanessa; Daiser, Peter (2016): eGovernment Portal Information Performance and the Role of Local Community Interest. Empirical Support for a Model of Citizen Perceptions. In Public Administration Quarterly 40 (1), pp. 48–83.

Wirtz, Bernd W.; Weyerer, Jan C.; Schichtel, Franziska T. (2019b): An integrative public IoT framework for smart government. In Government Information Quarterly 36 (2), pp. 333–345. DOI: https://doi.org/10.1016/j.giq.2018.07.001.

Digital Government Implementation 14

Contents

Learning Objectives
By working through this chapter, you will be able to:

1. Describe the pre-implementation analysis phase.
2. Explain the individual phases of the implementation phases.
3. Clarify the three depreciation areas and their mutual influence on each other.
4. Describe the three assessment levels.
5. Identify general target orientations for successful digital government implementation.

The development and design of a high-quality, citizen-centric digital government offering is a demanding challenge.[1] In particular for smaller local authorities, it is often difficult to provide the required resources and competencies. In this case, it usually makes sense to consider cooperation potential with other public sector organizations at an early stage of the digital government implementation design. This way, additional economies of scale and synergy advantages regarding significant cost items and system performance can be developed and achieved.

Despite the size of the digital government-providing public sector organization and the disposable resources and competencies, successful digital government implementation should at least include two major parts: First, a systematically

[1] See for Chapter 14 Digital Government Implementation also Wirtz and Daiser (2015, 2017), Wirtz (2021, 2022).

B. W. Wirtz, *Digital Government*, Springer Texts in Business and Economics,
https://doi.org/10.1007/978-3-031-13086-1_14

developed digital government roadmap that provides a transparent overview of the necessary implementation activities and milestones. Second, a digital government audit and evaluation concept that determines the respective performance indicators as well as the monitoring and controlling processes, and allows early intervention or to take mitigating action in the event of adverse changes.

Therefore, Section 14.1 outlines four steps of the pre-implementation analysis phase that serve as a basis for a systematic and well-prepared implementation process. Section 14.2 presents the following six steps of the implementation phase that ends with the digital government audit and evaluation concept based on respective performance indicators. Section 14.3 deals with the evaluation and controlling of the business model implementation phase as they hold a key role for successful implementation. Against this background, the 3+3 audit and evaluation system is presented as a management approach that helps to carry out a systematic evaluation and controlling approach.

14.1 Pre-implementation Analysis Phase

Launching a digital government implementation requires a solid base of information. Therefore, the pre-implementation analysis phase is essential and serves as a basis for a systematic and well-prepared implementation process. It is the fundamental backbone of each implementation process and also helps to analyze whether the implementation is worth to be carried out. The pre-implementation analysis phase consists of four steps: (1) a SWOT analysis, (2) benchmarking, (3) the analysis of customer demand and preferences, and (4) the development of a digital government strategy concept. Figure 14.1 illustrates the pre-implementation analysis phase.

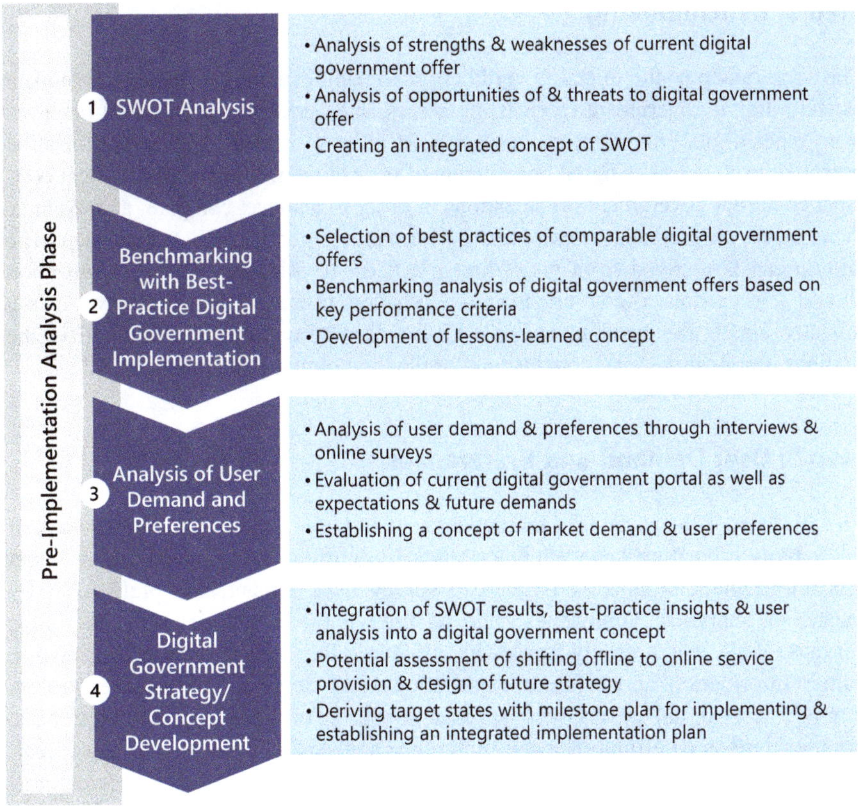

Fig. 14.1 Pre-implementation analysis phase. Source: Wirtz (2021)

Step 1: SWOT Analysis

In the first step, digital government service providers need to develop a clear understanding of the strengths and weaknesses as well as the opportunities and threats (SWOT) with regard to their existing digital government offer or solution.

The general procedure starts with the environmental and organizational analysis, which can be presented in a matrix that contrasts the respective strengths and weaknesses as well as the opportunities and threats of a digital venture. Various strategic consequences can then be derived from the combination of the analyses. For this reason, they need to perform a related analysis from both an internal view and from an external expert perspective that includes the user view. The results of these two angles of analysis are then combined into an integrated concept that includes the strengths and weaknesses as well as the opportunities and threats of digital government.

Step 2: Benchmarking

The second step of the digital government roadmap development serves to compare existing digital government services, processes, and performance with best practices from other digital government approaches in order to identify further optimization potential for the present digital government offer. At first, it is important to select best-practice digital government organizations in order to analyze, compare, and evaluate them based on particular pre-defined performance criteria in the second step. The criteria can be derived from given best practices. In this context, the organization should select similar digital organizations or offers to ensure comparability. At last, this step entails the development of a lessons-learned concept that summarizes the findings, implications, and conclusions for the own digital government offer.

Step 3: User Demand and Preferences

The third step is the analysis of market demand and user preferences. The key task of this activity is creating a concept that summarizes current and expected needs. To get this information, organizations need to survey user demand and preferences by means of analytical approaches such as interviews, benchmarking, and online surveys. Here, it is not only important to explore the current situation but also to gather information about future expectations and demand. To achieve success through new digital government approaches based on specific user preferences, organizations need a multifactorial preference analysis and forecasts in quasi-real-time manner. Only those who correctly assess the market of locally differentiated preferences can satisfy user demand. With the right approaches, organizations are able to adapt their strategy to specific preferences and thus maximize future success by accurately forecasting demand.

Step 4: Digital Government Strategy Concept

Having finished the third step, the organization can start to develop their digital government strategy or concept. The key target of this set of activities is to achieve a target state for the digital government system with a clearly defined implementation concept and action plan. For this purpose, the organization has to integrate the results of the previous steps (strengths and weaknesses analysis, best-practice insights, user needs and requirements) into a basic digital government concept that reflects the future strategy.

14.2 Implementation Phase

The second major phase addresses the implementation process and comprises the following six steps: (5) definition of digital government implementation model master plan, (6) digital government implementation model option selection, (7) digital government implementation model design/development, (8) digital government implementation model pilot testing & training, (9) digital government implementation model deployment, and (10) digital government implementation model monitoring & audit. Figure 14.2 illustrates the implementation phase with its six steps.

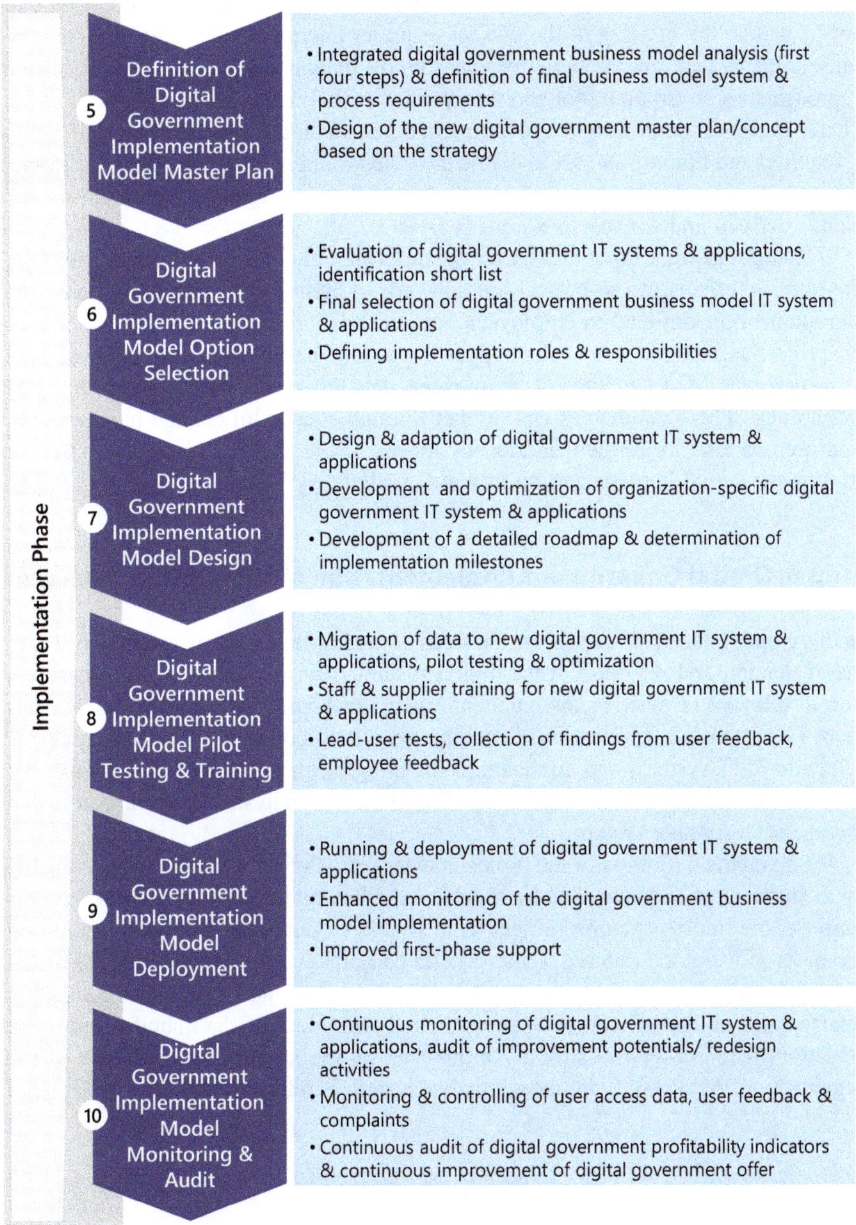

Fig. 14.2 Implementation phase. Source: Wirtz (2021)

Step 5: Definition of Digital Government Implementation Model Master Plan

In the implementation phase, the developed target concept is transferred to the reality of the organization. Various problems can arise in the process, which can lead to the failure of implementation. For example, it can happen that individual managers do not recognize the benefits of the project or prefer alternative concepts. This can be caused by a lack of strategic orientation of management, which uses digital approaches as an isolated tool and thus promotes traditional departmental thinking. Therefore, an integrated digital government business model analysis (first four steps) is required and findings are set to define the final requirements of the business model process. Against this background, the design of the new digital government master plan is derived and a respective strategy is set.

If changes to work flows and employee tasks are only made after implementation, the positive effects of the project are delayed. In addition, poor internal corporate communication can lead to employees not understanding the goals and benefits of the project and therefore not fully supporting it. In extreme cases, this can even lead to a problem of acceptance if employees develop reservations about the new technology. These challenges can be met through successful change management. The preparations for implementation by means of the analysis create the basis for starting the actual implementation of the new digital system.

Step 6: Digital Government Implementation Model Option Selection

In this context, the sixth step of the ten steps of the implementation roadmap refers to the evaluation and selection of the digital system. This step includes the identification of relevant IT systems and applications by evaluating different digital government IT systems & applications. The aim here is to compile a list with a narrow selection of IT systems and applications for the project, which serves as a basis for the analysis and evaluation of the same. Based on this analysis, the organization can then select a suitable system.

Based on the definition of the project master plan, the software products available on the market are to be checked for their fit with the organization's situation. For this purpose, the implementation project team should compare the solutions offered on the basis of weighted criteria. These criteria can include, for example, implementation and maintenance costs, compatibility with internal and external organization interfaces, usability as well as experience and references of the manufacturer. The selection of the criteria is strongly influenced by the specific requirements of the organization. As a result, the most suitable system is selected for use.

Step 7: Digital Government Implementation Model Design/Development

The seventh step relates to the design and development of the digital project. This step includes in particular the design, setup, and optimization of organization-specific IT systems and applications. The focus is on the integration of the required interfaces and data formats. It therefore must be clarified which requirements are already fulfilled by the system or can be acquired as an additional module and which requirements need individual adjustment.

The next task of this step is to derive target states with a milestone plan for implementation. Finally, the organization has to establish an integrated implementation plan. Figure 14.3 presents an exemplary digital government implementation plan.

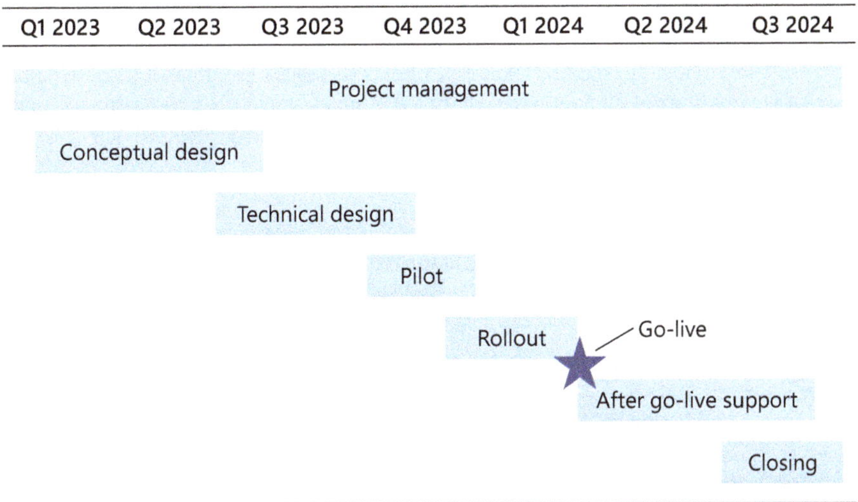

Fig. 14.3 Exemplary digital government implementation plan. Source: Wirtz (2010, 2021)

The presented phases of the exemplary digital government implementation plan are briefly explained in the following. The conceptual design phase covers the activities that are needed for the conception of the digital government organization. The technical design phase aims to establish the technical plan that represents the formerly defined conception. In the pilot phase, the initial prototype of the digital government system is developed.

After successful prototype testing, the pilot is duplicated or transferred to other parts of the organization. The go-live specifies the point in time when the new system becomes activated. The after go-live support is a specific time period during which special support is available to the employees of the organization. The closing phase determines the official end of the project upon project completion.

Step 8: Digital Government Implementation Model Pilot Testing & Training

After the development and optimization of the system, the eighth step is the data migration, pilot testing, and training. Accordingly, the responsible individuals must migrate the data to the new system, which then must be tested and optimized. An important task in this implementation step is the training of the personnel and suppliers with regard to the new IT systems and applications (Wirtz et al. 2016). It is important to incorporate all stakeholders such as the staff and suppliers of the new digital government IT system and applications.

Moreover, the user experience must be evaluated. Thus, lead-user tests can bring valuable insights. It is important to incorporate findings from user feedback and employee feedback on the new digital system. In contrast to step three, it is now possible to see the result of the new approach. In order to be successful the digital government approach is supposed to address specific user preferences. Therefore, it is important to test whether the multifactorial preference analysis and forecasts hold true in a quasi-real-time manner. The pilot helps to assess the market response and allows to check locally differentiated demand. With the testing it is possible to adapt the strategy to specific user preferences and thus maximize future success by accurately forecasting demand.

Step 9: Digital Government Implementation Model Deployment

In the ninth step, the digital government business model and its applications are put into live operation, which means that the system is used in the work environment and can be accessed and used in everyday business. This step is also known as go-live. The advantage of a digital product over an analog system at the go-live is that it is based on existing systems and does not have to be introduced by complete changeover. Instead, organizational departments can be gradually involved in its use. The experience gained from the partial implementations increases the manageability of the overall process and thus the chances of success of introducing the digital approach. Accordingly, it makes sense to first start a pilot project and then to connect further departments to the new system in a phased rollout.

Step 10: Digital Government Implementation Model Monitoring & Audit

The last step of the implementation scheme concerns the monitoring and control of the system. Here, the IT system and its applications are monitored continuously. In addition, regular audits are conducted to identify potential for improvement.

This step allows continuous identification of optimization potential in relation to the implemented system. These activities have to go hand in hand with the continuous improvement of the digital government service.

In this context, the digital government strategy audit indicators represent a decisive monitoring tool that the organization has to apply continuously to improve their digital offer. In particular, they have to calculate and observe digital government probability indicators. Furthermore, the organization also has to examine to what extent the previously defined and implemented strategies have the desired effect. Thus, the digital government strategy audit indicates the effectiveness of the implemented digital government strategies and finds possible weak points or potential for improvement.

The last step is of special importance as it aims at the long-term success of the project. Many projects fail due to their lack of long-term monitoring and controlling. Therefore Section 14.3 presents a robust and systematic digital government audit and evaluation system. The entire ten steps of the digital government business model implementation plan consisting of the two phases pre-implementation and implementation are presented in Figure 14.4.

Fig. 14.4 10-Steps of the digital government implementation roadmap. Source: Wirtz (2021)

Success Factors of Digital Government Implementation

The success of the entire implementation process is based on a variety of different factors and determined by the achievement of various targets. There are eight central success factors, i.e. target orientation, a suitable project team, sensitive culture orientation, top-down management support, a supportive change management strategy, respective training and practice, an inclusive open innovation approach, and finally, an adequate equipment of resources.

Target Orientation

Target orientation refers to the notion of having all implementation approaches in line with a clear digital government target, which is concrete and feasible.

Project Team

A suitable project team incorporates individuals with the right digital government competencies who work together efficiently and effectively.

Culture Orientation

Culture orientation stands for an implementation approach that is well aligned with the organization culture. It is important that all individuals involved respect and care for cultural aspects of the organization.

Top-down Management Support

Top-down management support refers to the notion that the implementation project receives backing from top management, which means that decisions to promote implementation are supported by the senior management.

Change Management

Another success factor is the existence of a substantial change management plan. It is vital that all changes linked to the implementation project are considered and followed up by a change management strategy.

Training and Practice

Another important factor is the training and practice of all employees affected. New projects require well-trained staff as well as sufficient space and time to become acquainted with the new process and technologies.

Open Innovation Approach

Another component is the open innovation approach of the project. The implementation project is supposed to incoporate all stakeholders. This can be achieved by strategic involvement of external and internal creative sources. Such approach will bring advantages to the project as it benefits from new ideas and gains stakeholder support.

Adequate Resources

Finally, it is important that the project has access to an adequate pool of resources. The implementation project must be equipped with a suitable budget and sufficient resources in terms of time and people involved. Figure 14.5 outlines the eigth central success factors of digital government implementation.

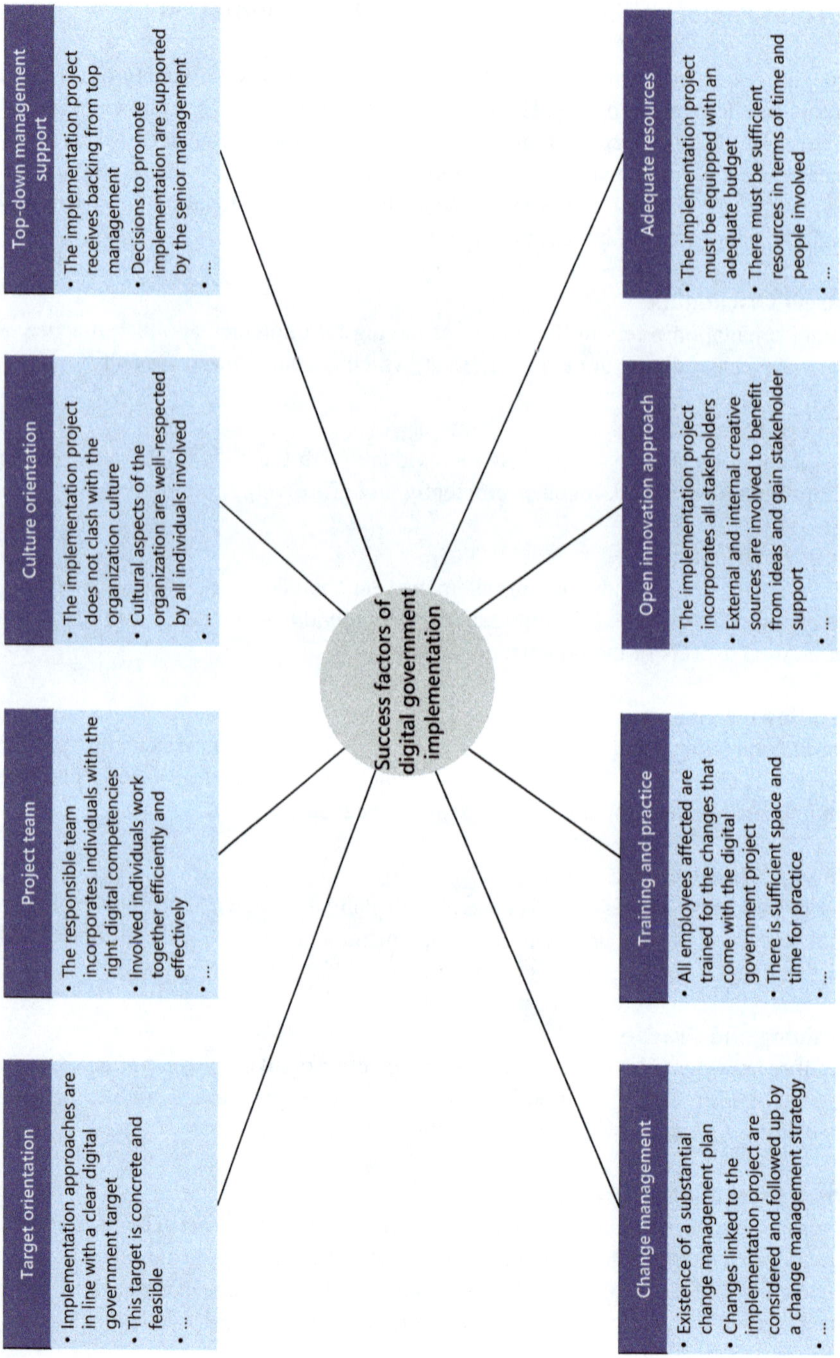

Fig. 14.5 Success factors of digital government implementation. Source: Wirtz (2021)

The implemented digital government system should be subject to regular audits and evaluations to ensure that it constantly meets the needs and requirements of the users as well as the providers. The key aspects of this approach are outlined in the following section.

14.3 Digital Government 3+3 Audit and Evaluation System

The audit and evaluation of a digital government system principally refers to a systematic and transparent way of assessing the performance of all associated digital government activities. This approach is embedded in a continuous improvement circle that focuses on a constant enhancement of the overall digital government system. The umbrella guideline for this activity is the entire value chain workflow of the digital government service creation process—from initial concept to final implementation and operation.

For a comprehensive picture on the digital government situation, the audit approach is divided into two main components: assessment areas and assessment levels evaluation. The assessment areas pursue the aim to control the digital government system from a workflow and performance perspective, while the assessment levels look at the different digital government layers. All assessment areas and levels are consistently examined from both perspectives, which allows a holistic assessment of the entire digital government system and its value chain.

Assessment Areas

There are three digital government assessment areas, which from a continuous improvement view influence each other through systematic feedback circuits: design, process, and outcome. Although the sequence of these three areas generally is linear, identified gaps or discrepancies during the evaluation process may lead to modifications in prior areas (see Figure 14.6).

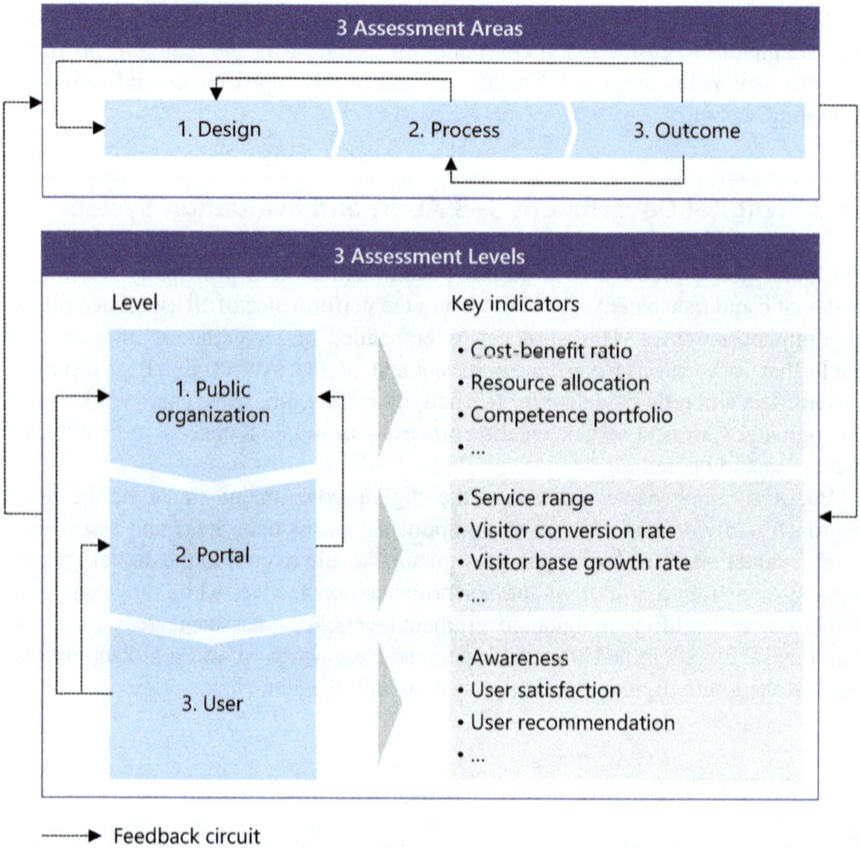

Fig. 14.6 Digital government 3+3 audit and evaluation system. Source: Wirtz and Daiser (2015), Wirtz (2021)

Design

Design deals with the aspects that are related to the development and the intended aims of the digital government system. This means that the auditor has to evaluate if the digital government system pursues the right goals, if the content of the digital government service provision suits the overall digital government targets, if the design of the digital government system supports the achievement of objectives, and so on. In particular, if the digital government system is still up-to-date and maintained in an adequate manner.

Process

The process assessment area covers the technical realization-related and service creation-related aspects of the digital government system in logical continuation of the design assessment area. Here, the auditor evaluates if the technical execution or implementation of the digital government system—usually the portal or website—

and the service creation process fulfill the initially defined conceptual requirements as well as anticipated developments. In the case of discrepancies, the result of the process evaluation may impact the design area if modifications are required.

Outcome
The outcome assessment area deals with the performance of the digital government service provision as well as the fulfillment of supply-driven and demand-driven success factors. For this purpose, the auditor evaluates the actual performance of the provided digital government services from a user-perspective and a provider-perspective, meaning if the corresponding success factors are adequately fulfilled or not. And again, if outcome gaps between the actual and the desired digital government state should be identified, this may lead to modifications within the design or process assessment areas.

Assessment Levels

Following this integrative approach, the three assessment levels—public organization, portal, and user—have to be examined. These are set up in terms of a dependent layer structure, meaning that the public organization level may influence the portal level, which again may influence the user level and vice versa through the respective feedback circuits.

Public Organization Level
The public organizational level serves to evaluate the digital government performance from a public sector organizational view. Therefore, important organizational performance indicators, such as the cost–benefit ratio of the implemented digital government system, the resource allocation between offline and online service provision, and the available competency portfolio, have to be controlled according to the design, process, and outcome logic of this level.

Portal Level
The portal level refers to directly measureable indicators of the portal or website level. Key performance indicators are, for example, the service range, which shows the depth and breadth of the services provided, the conversion rate of visitors to digital government users, or the growth rate of the visitor base.

These indicators are of particular importance since they directly refer to the target of shifting users from the offline to the online environment and thus, to the overall aim of increasing public value. The great thing about measuring these indicators is that the relevant data can be collected straightaway from the digital government portal.

User Level
The evaluation on the user level is more elaborate and complex, and thus it is generally more expensive since the respective performance indicators cannot be

directly captured from the digital government system. Crucial indicators for this layer are, for example, awareness, user satisfaction, and user recommendation. Awareness is the primary step to attract visitors to the digital government portal. If they are satisfied with the information and service provision, they may turn into regular users. In this context, user recommendation is a valuable asset that again fosters awareness.

The collection of this data usually requires additional surveys, such as interviewing users or carrying out user panels, in order to get evaluable information with regard to these indicators. However, this effort is unavoidable since this knowledge forms an elementary part of a user-oriented digital government service provision. The digital government audit and evaluation cycle is illustrated in the following figure.

Summing up, evaluating a digital government system is an ambitious task that demands profound auditing expertise, technical knowledge, and managerial experience, because the procedure requires comprehensive examination of all activities that are associated with digital government service provision.

In addition, some performance indicators may be of tacit nature, which makes measurement sometimes problematic. Irrespective of this difficulty, public management needs to elaborate adequate ex-ante and ex-post comparisons for system evaluation and justification, which makes digital government auditing and evaluation an indispensable activity in digital government management (Homburg 2008).

However, systematically examining the three assessment areas (design, process, and outcome) as well as the three assessment levels (public organization, portal, and user) provides a clear guidance for a digital government audit or evaluation. Apart from that, considering digital government implementation in general, one can learn much by comparing and benchmarking existing digital government platforms. For this reason, three digital government best practice examples are presented in the following chapter.

14.4 Summary, Review Questions, Topics for Discussion, and Online Exercises

- A successful implementation of digital government should generally comprise at least two important parts: the pre-implementation analysis phase and the implementation phase including a robust audit and evaluation concept.
- In the first step, providers of digital government services must perform an analysis (SWOT) from both an internal and external point of view, including the customer perspective. The second step is designed to compare existing digital government services, processes, and deliverables with best practices from other digital government approaches in order to identify further optimization potential for the current digital government portal.
- The key task of the third step is to create a concept that summarizes current and expected user demand and preferences. The fourth phase then combines the results of the previous three phases into a basic digital government concept.

- In the implementation phase, the developed target concept is transferred to the reality of the organization. An integrated digital government business model analysis (first four steps) serves to define the final requirements for the business model process. In step five, the draft of the new digital government master plan is derived and a corresponding strategy is determined.
- The sixth step refers to the evaluation and selection of the digital system including the identification of relevant IT systems and applications by evaluating different digital government IT systems and applications. The aim is to compile a list with a narrow selection of IT systems in order to then select a suitable system.
- Step seven includes in particular the design, setup, and optimization of organization-specific IT systems and applications. The step also includes the derivation of target states with a milestone plan for implementation. Finally, an integrated implementation plan must be created.
- Step eight is dedicated to data migration, pilot testing, and training to successfully implement the system. Therefore, it is necessary to involve all relevant stakeholders. Furthermore, findings and user feedback from this step should be incorporated into the new digital system.
- In the ninth step, the digital government business model and its applications are put into practice, i.e., the system is used in the working environment. It makes sense to start with a pilot project and then to connect further departments to the new system in a step-by-step rollout.
- The last step of the implementation process—monitoring and audit—is of particular importance as it aims at the long-term success of the project and needs a systematic approach in deploying a respective monitoring system. Therefore, the audit approach is divided into two main components of evaluation: assessment areas and assessment levels.
- Targets of a successful implementation process particularly include target orientation, a suitable project team, sensitive culture orientation, top-down management support, a supportive change management strategy, respective training and practice, an inclusive open innovation approach, and finally, an adequate equipment of resources.

Chapter 14
Review questions, topics for discussion and online exercises

Review questions

1. Explain all four phases of the pre-implementation analysis phase model.
2. Describe all of the six implementation phases of the implementation phase model.
3. Name some of the key targets of a successful digital government implementation according to the targets of digital government implementation model.
4. Describe the three assessment areas and the associated feedback loops of the digital government 3+3 audit and evaluation system model.
5. Explain the three levels of assessment of the digital government 3+3 audit and evaluation system model and identify relevant key indicators.

Topics for classroom discussion and team debates

1. Discuss whether an implementation phase always requires a pre-implementation analysis phase. What are the advantages and disadvantages of a pre-implementation analysis phase for successful implementation?
2. Discuss whether the six phases of implementation must necessarily be carried out in the described manner and which are particularly important for ensuring implementation success.
3. Discuss to what extent the 3+3 system covers all relevant monitoring and audit areas that are important for implementation and whether, in your opinion, relevant ones are missing.

Online Exercises

1. Visit https://read.oecd-ilibrary.org/governance/benchmarking-digital-government-strategies-in-mena-countries_9789264268012-en#page1. What can you learn from these examples with regard to Step 2 Benchmarking? In which areas does benchmarking take place in this study? Are these areas conclusive, or what other areas might be important for benchmarking in the digital government context?
2. Enter https://www.canada.ca/en/government/system/digital-government/government-canada-digital-operations-strategic-plans/digital-operations-strategic-plan-2021-2024.html#toc04# and look at Appendix D "Progress report on 2018-2022 DOSP strategic actions." Which of the 10 steps of digital government implementation can you identify in the list? Discuss whether the Canadian government's approach is reasonable.
3. Explore https://www.nao.org.uk/sector/digital-government. According to the digital government 3+3 audit and evaluation system model, are all assessment areas and assessment levels addressed? Which areas or levels are falling short?

References

Homburg, Vincent (2008): Understanding E-Government. Information Systems in Public Administration. London, New York: Routledge.

Wirtz, Bernd W. (2010): Electronic business. 3rd ed. Wiesbaden: Gabler.

Wirtz, Bernd W. (2021): Digital Business and Electronic Commerce. Cham: Springer International Publishing.

Wirtz, Bernd W. (2022): E-Government. Wiesbaden: Springer Gabler.

Wirtz, Bernd W.; Daiser, Peter (2015): E-Government. Strategy, process, instruments. 1st ed. Speyer.

Wirtz, Bernd W.; Daiser, Peter (2017): E-government. Strategy, process, instruments. 2nd ed. Speyer.

Wirtz, Bernd W.; Piehler, Robert; Thomas, Marc-Julian; Daiser, Peter (2016): Resistance of public personnel to open government: A cognitive theory view of implementation barriers towards open government data. In Public Management Review 18 (9), pp. 1335–1364. DOI: https://doi.org/10.1080/14719037.2015.1103889.

Part IV

Digital Government Cases and Outlook

Digital Government Case Studies 15

Contents

Learning Objectives

By working through this chapter, you will be able to:

1. Describe the London City portal in terms of its services offering structure.
2. Describe the New York City portal in terms of its services offering structure.
3. Describe the Hong Kong City portal in terms of its services offering structure.
4. Outline the key insights of the three case studies.

In the previous chapters, essential digital government concepts, strategies, processes, and instruments are outlined.[1] To enrich these rather conceptual explanations with practical illustrations, offer additional public managerial insight on digital government portals in practice, and provide further context from best practice examples, three case studies of top-tier digital government portals—London, New York, and Hong Kong—are presented in the following.

A case study is a detailed analysis of a specific case that deals with the particular characteristics of the case in question and allows an examination of the respective setting (Bryman 2012). It usually provides a supplementary context for observed phenomena (Eisenhardt 1989), which in this particular case should provide public managers with inspiration and best practice suggestions on how to make the best of their public sector organization's digital government offering.

[1] See for Chapter 15 Digital Government Case Studies also Wirtz and Daiser (2015, 2017); Wirtz (2022).

B. W. Wirtz, *Digital Government*, Springer Texts in Business and Economics,
https://doi.org/10.1007/978-3-031-13086-1_15

Since local digital government portals provide a wide range of services and are often the first point of contact between the digital government user and provider (Wirtz and Nitzsche 2013; Wirtz et al. 2015, 2017), the selected best-in-class digital government portals are regarded as suitable for this purpose.

15.1 London

London is a leading global city and the capital of England as well as the United Kingdom. The city is home to 9.0 million people, sharing its area of 1.12 square miles. Given these figures, London is also the UK's most populous city, showing a diverse range of people, languages, and cultures.

Its long history, its influence in arts, commerce, education, entertainment, fashion, and finance, as well as its high metropolitan GDP, being the fifth or sixth largest in the world depending on the measurement, make London a world societal and cultural capital (Wikipedia contributors 2022).

The landing page of the City of London presents three dominant menu bars (two at the top and one at the bottom), which provide the visitor with direct links to the particular website content, and a collection of most popular links, which is prominently positioned on the top page. This way, the visitor has several opportunities to choose or locate her or his desired content.

Similar to the digital government portals of Hong Kong and New York City, London has an integrated search function on the middle top of the landing page. In the middle, the portal provides a message selection function, an overview of selected city information, current notes on Covid 19, current event information as well as notes and a link to London's Twitter channel.

At the bottom of the landing page, a third menu bar is applied which provides direct links concerning further website information, jobs, news and media, safe space online, and other additional links. Please visit London's official website to get an overview. You can use the link https://www.cityoflondon.gov.uk/ or the QR code in Figure 15.1 for this purpose. The landing page of the City of London is presented in Figure 15.2.

Fig. 15.1 QR-Code to visit London's official website

QR Code London

Fig. 15.2 Landing page of the City of London portal. Source: City of London (2021b)

At the top of the landing page, visitors of London's digital government portal find two menu bars. The first menu bar is divided into three sections: "Things to do," "Services," and "Supporting Business." The second menu bar may be divided into seven sections: "COVID-19," "About us," "Events," "Contact the City Corporation," "Accessibility statement," "Councillors, committees and meetings," "Report, Pay, Apply." The last button leads the user to an overview of payment services as well as reporting and application forms. Figure 15.3 shows the first and second menu bars of the landing page.

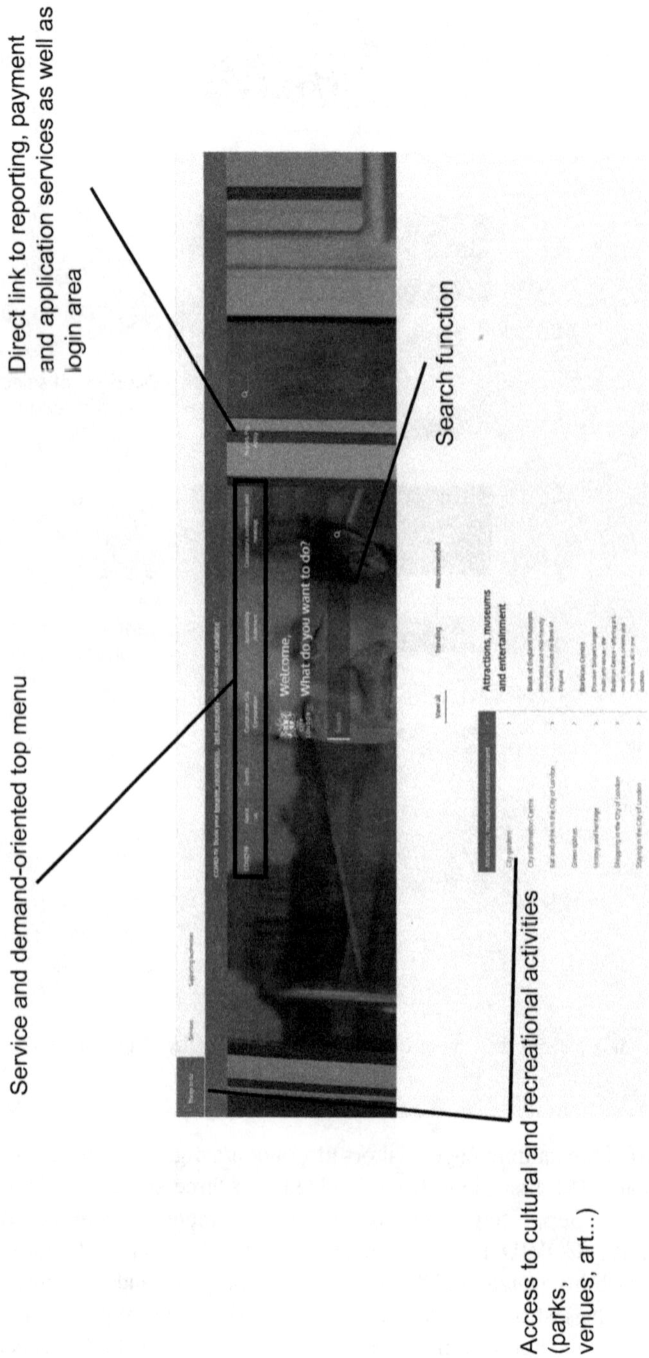

Fig. 15.3 First and second menu bar at the top of the portal. Source: City of London (2021a)

The respective sub-content, to which the visitor is directed, is presented and structured in several categories. The sub-content of the digital government service for citizens, for example, is arranged according to a set of umbrella terms, including health, libraries, housing, council tax, and so on. Here, the visitor can select the associated category to reach the desired information or service.

The third menu bar at the bottom of the landing page provides direct access to the following content items: further website information, jobs, news and media, safe space online, and other additional links. Thus, this represents a further option for supplying a common housing for particular website content.

Summarizing, what stands out of the digital government offering of the City of London is its search-oriented structure that presents various types of information and service classifications in striking positions. This is underlined by the particularly visible set of most popular information and service requests, helping many users to find current topics instantly.

Concerning mobile integration, the number of available mobile applications is interesting. London provides no mobile apps on its digital government portal and maintains a mobile version of the website.

Compared to Hong Kong and New York City, London's digital government offer also provides a broad range of useful information—albeit not as extensive—to its visitors, but possesses a considerable smaller full online service portfolio.

In an analysis of the sustainable success of various cities from a demand perspective, London, New York, and Hong Kong were described as "balanced innovators." These are characterized by convenience and security, among other things, as well as an advanced technological infrastructure, whose importance for improving service quality will increase in the future. In the context of digital government, the two core aspects of "automated" and "sensing" stand out in particular. The former refers to the ever-increasing use of automated processes and AI. The latter refers to the employment of integrated sensors to manage municipal services (Arcadis 2018). Figure 15.4 summarizes the key insights from the analysis of the digital government platform of the City of London.

cityoflondon.gov.uk digital government key insights

- Search-oriented structure of the digital government portal
- Offering several menu bars that guide the visitor
- Provision of a personalized user account, which is required for particular transactions and supports customized digital government access
- Prominent position of most popular links at the top of the website
- Broad range of useful information and services
- Innovative full online digital payment system
- Comparably little integration of mobile solutions

Fig. 15.4 Key insights from the cityoflondon.gov.uk digital government offering. Source: Wirtz and Daiser (2015, 2017)

15.2 New York City

With round about 8.5 million inhabitants, New York City is the most populous city in the United States of America. It exerts a significant impact on worldwide commercial, cultural, societal, political, and technological trends and thus, has also been described as the cultural and financial capital of the world. The city spreads over a total area of 468.9 square miles and accommodates as many as 800 languages that are spoken in this municipality.

Please visit New York City's official website 311 to get an overview. You can use the link https://portal.311.nyc.gov/ or the QR code in Figure 15.5 for this purpose.

Fig. 15.5 QR-Code to visit New York City's official website 311

QR Code New York

When entering the portal, the visitor finds a user-oriented and service-oriented structure that is divided into several sections and that provides an overview of and direct access to the particular topics. Right at the top, digital government portal visitors encounter a link with customized offers, actual information concerning Covid 19 and have the possibility to switch between 109 languages. This is followed by a search function next to the navigation.

In the next page section, a quick snapshot of important local news and developments as well as a direct link to upcoming events and service status of public utilities is provided. In addition a search engine, a sign-in and sign-up button, and the possibility for direct payment are offered. This is a convenient collection of information for the users, which provides a clear added value by summarizing relevant public local information in a single spot.

At the bottom of the landing page, visitors find digital government offers sorted by topic. These include, among others, courts and law related digital government offers, education related digital government offers, environment related digital government offers, and public safety related digital government offers.

At the end of the landing page, visitors see links to different social media offers, other digital government related offers, the official New York City apps, contact options, feedback opportunities, an overview of the most important language settings and copyright information.

Principally, mobile integration is a vital factor that is considered in the entire process of digital government service provision. With the 311 app, for example, users of the portal have far-reaching mobile access possibilities, allowing them to use public services whenever and wherever they want. Apart from that, New York City offers apps free of charge for finding restaurants, second-hand exchange, local discount programs, health care, environmental protection, building search, locating drinking water, waste and recycling information, as well as police and emergency services.

A further important aspect is the high degree of full online service provision. There are manifold services that already can be handled completely online, e.g., notification of a street festival, application for a parking permission, or application for building a garage or house rebuilding.

Of particular importance is the sophisticated complaint management system, which is already presented on the landing page. Here, users can complain online about various public services (e.g., damaged infrastructure, vandalism, pollution, animal welfare) and can provide detailed online feedback on the public service offering. It is used as an important monitoring and controlling system to enhance public and digital government service provision.

Summing up, New York City's digital government portal provides an extensive set of public services and a wide range of useful information to public stakeholders. The entire service provision shows a clear user-orientation and aims at providing full online offers within a vast multichannel offer. Against this background, New York City's digital government offering shows a very strong social media presence. They make use of eleven different social media applications: Facebook, Flickr, Foursquare, Google+, Instagram, LinkedIn, Tumblr, Pinterest, Twitter, YouTube, and

WordPress. In total, nyc.com applies 333 social media channels for communicating and interacting with their digital government stakeholders (New York City 2021b).

Moreover, New York City's digital government portal possesses an innovative full online digital payment system and already provides various participative services and suggestion systems for the users (e.g., suggesting new bus stops, fire hydrant positioning, collectively building up databases that show defibrillator locations). Although the portal shows a high degree of innovative full online services, the digital government provider runs a comprehensive call center support, which provides help for the users in 175 languages (New York City 2021a).

This demand-driven approach is also reflected in the results of the analysis on the sustainable success of various cities from a demand perspective. Its results underscore the service orientation of New York City (Arcadis 2018). For this reason, New York City is a shining example of a user-oriented and service-oriented digital government offering. Figure 15.6 shows a summary of the key insights from New York City's digital government portal.

nyc.gov digital government key insights

- Very broad range of useful information that is provided on the portal
- High availability of services, especially full online services, that are centrally available through the digital government portal
- Extensive provision of highly developed, interactive services
- Provision of participative services and suggestion systems
- Innovative full online digital payment system
- Far-reaching complaint and satisfaction management, which is directly presented at the landing page
- Very strong presence in social media channels. In total, nyc.com uses 340 social media channels

Fig. 15.6 Key insights from the nyc.gov digital government offering. Source: Wirtz and Daiser (2015, 2017)

15.3 Hong Kong

Hong Kong, which is officially denominated as Hong Kong Special Administrative Region of the People's Republic of China, is an autonomous territory and represents a major business and trade gateway to China. It covers an area of 687 square miles that is shared by 7.51 million inhabitants. Thus, Hong Kong is one of the most densely populated areas in the world, which is characterized by free trade, low taxation, and minimum government intervention. Chinese and English are the official languages and approximately 89% of the population speak Cantonese—only 4.3% are English speakers, English is widely used in the public, legal, and professional sector (Hong Kong 2021b).

Similarly to the digital government offering of New York City, Hong Kong possesses an appealing, comprehensive, and professional digital government presence. Please visit Hong Kong's official digital government portal to get an overview. You can use the link https://www.gov.hk/ or the QR code in Figure 15.7 for this purpose.

Fig. 15.7 QR-Code to visit Hong Kong's official digital government portal

QR Code Hong Kong

Looking at the landing page of Hong Kong's digital government portal, the visitor is presented a clear structure that provides direct access to the different service categories, to mobile apps and mobile services, as well as to important news and data. What is special about the presentation of the digital government service offering are its strong target group orientation and its personalization feature, which allows to set up a personalized user account. These two characteristics are positioned right at the top of the website.

Apart from these two features, Hong Kong takes special care to provide a mobile digital government service offering (at the time of the analysis, Hong Kong provided, for example, 121 mobile apps) (Hong Kong 2021a). In the middle part of the landing page, a selection of mobile apps is given, which leads the visitor directly to the mobile digital government offering.

Coming back to the strong target group orientation of Hong Kong's digital government offering, the initial menu bar of the landing page allows the visitor to select between four customized digital government service offerings: residents, business & trade, non-residents, and social groups.

Concerning residents, business & trade, and non-residents, the respective link leads the visitor to a sub-website that provides digital government information and services tailored to the needs and requirements of the specific user group. The menu item social groups presents five different links to websites that particularly consider the needs and requirements of specific social groups (women, youth, family issues, senior citizens, and people with disabilities).

The social community groups are a special offer of Hong Kong's digital government service, which provide specific content and services for the respective social group. CyberAble.net is an online community that provides information and services to people with disabilities.

The social community eElderly is particularly designed for senior citizens. Happy Family provides citizens with various information concerning children, family, and education issues. Youth.gov.hk is a social platform for young people and the Women's Commission deals with gender-relevant issues.

Furthermore, Hong Kong's digital government offer shows an extensive integration of mobile services and websites as well as mobile applications. At the time of the analysis, the portal provided links to 121 mobile apps. Apart from the official GovHK app, which allows the user to access the digital government portal from a mobile device, many further apps are supported. Examples are event search, family education, information on buildings and locations, health topics, and so on.

Summing up, what stands out of the digital government offering of Hong Kong are its special target group orientation, its social group community offers, its personalization possibilities that support customized digital government access and interaction, and the extensive mobile support. Similarly to the digital government offering of New York City, Hong Kong provides a broad range of target group-oriented information as well as a comprehensive set of advanced digital government services. These also include innovative transaction and integration services, such as full online services for driving licenses and online complaint management, and an innovative full online digital payment system.

The subject-related structure allows ongoing interaction and collaboration on topics, while at the same time being a reference point for knowledge search. For this reason, online forums are regarded to possess considerable potential as participation and collaboration tools (Meijer 2011). Figure 15.8 summarizes the key insights from the analysis of Hong Kong's digital government offering gov.hk.

gov.hk digital government key insights

- Very high target group orientation of the digital government offering
- Three-way division of digital government offering (residents, business & trade, non-residents)
- Offering of special social group communities (people with disabilities, family issues, women, youth, and senior citizens)
- Provision of a personalized user account that supports customized digital government access and interaction
- Very broad range of target group-oriented information
- High availability of services, especially full online services, that are centrally available through the digital government portal
- Provision of innovative transaction and integration services
- Innovative full online digital payment system
- Extensive integration of mobile offers and websites as well as mobile applications (e.g., 121 apps available free of charge)

Fig. 15.8 Key insights from the gov.hk digital government offering. Source: Wirtz and Daiser (2015, 2017)

15.4 Summary, Review Questions, Topics for Discussion, and Online Exercises

- The digital government offering of the City of London is characterized by its search-oriented structure. For example, popular, current information, and service requests are presented in a particularly visible way.
- Unlike the digital government portals of New York City and Hong Kong, London's digital government portal does not offer any mobile applications. However, a mobile version of the website is available.
- New York City's digital government portal has a strong demand orientation and offers a wide range of online services via a variety of social media and other applications, as well as an innovative, fully digital payment system. The demand orientation is demonstrated, for example, by demand-driven, participatory services or call center support.
- To improve public and digital government services, New York City's digital government portal uses a differentiated complaint and feedback management system as a monitoring and control system.

- Hong Kong's digital government offering is distinguished by several characteristics: a specific target group orientation, social group community offerings, personalization capabilities that support tailored digital government access and interaction, and extensive mobile support.
- Similar to New York City's digital government offering, Hong Kong provides a wide range of target group-oriented information as well as a comprehensive range of advanced digital government services (e.g., full online services for driver's licenses, an online complaint management system, an innovative, fully digital payment system, and extensive integration of mobile services and apps).

Chapter 15
Review questions, topics for discussion and online exercises

Review questions

1. Describe the London city portal in terms of its service offering structure.
2. Describe the New York city portal in terms of its service offering structure.
3. Describe the Hong Kong city portal in terms of its service offering structure.
4. Outline the key insights of the three case studies.

Topics for classroom discussion and team debates

1. Compare the three case studies. Discuss differences and similarities.
2. Discuss international differences in city portals. Evaluate the importance of adapting city portals to the regional culture.
3. Based on the three case studies, develop a draft for a city portal in your hometown.

Online Exercises

1. Visit https://www.cityoflondon.gov.uk/ and explore the London city portal.
2. Visit https://portal.311.nyc.gov/ and explore the New York city portal.
3. Visit https://www.gov.hk/ and explore the Hong Kong city portal.

References

Arcadis (2018): Citizen Centric Cities. The Sustainable Cities Index 2018 Europe. Available online at https://creativehubfrankfurt.de/wp-content/uploads/2019/01/Arcadis-Sustainable-Cities-Index-2018-Europe.pdf, checked on 12/8/2021.

Bryman, Alan (2012): Social Research Methods. 4th ed. Oxford, UK: Oxford University Press.

City of London (2021a): Things to do. Available online at https://www.cityoflondon.gov.uk/things-to-do, checked on 7/26/2021.

City of London (2021b): Welcome. Available online at https://www.cityoflondon.gov.uk/things-to-do, checked on 7/26/2021.

Eisenhardt, Kathleen M. (1989): Building Theories from Case Study Research. In Academy of Management Review 14 (4), pp. 532–550.

Hong Kong (2021a): Government Mobile Applications. Available online at https://www.gov.hk/en/about/govdirectory/mobileapps.htm, checked on 7/21/2021.

Hong Kong (2021b): Hong Kong – the Facts. Available online at https://www.gov.hk/en/about/abouthk/facts.htm, checked on 7/20/2021.

Meijer, Albert Jacob (2011): Networked Coproduction of Public Services in Virtual Communities: From a Government-Centric to a Community Approach to Public Service Support. In Public Administration Review 71 (4), pp. 598–607.

New York City (2021a): About NYC311. Available online at https://portal.311.nyc.gov/about-nyc-311/, checked on 7/20/2021.

New York City (2021b): All 340 of NYC's official social media channels. Available online at https://www1.nyc.gov/connect/social-media.page, checked on 7/20/2021.

Wikipedia contributors (2022): London. Wikipedia, The Free Encyclopedia. Available online at https://de.wikipedia.org/wiki/London, checked on 2/24/2022.

Wirtz, Bernd W. (2022): E-Government. Wiesbaden: Springer Gabler.

Wirtz, Bernd W.; Daiser, Peter (2015): E-Government. Strategy, process, instruments. 1st ed. Speyer.

Wirtz, Bernd W.; Daiser, Peter (2017): E-government. Strategy, process, instruments. 2nd ed. Speyer.

Wirtz, Bernd W.; Nitzsche, Philipp (2013): Local level e-government in international comparison. In Journal of Public Administration and Governance 3 (3), pp. 64–93.

Wirtz, Bernd W.; Piehler, Robert; Daiser, Peter (2015): E-government portal characteristics and individual appeal: An examination of E-government and citizen acceptance in the context of local administration portals. In Journal of Nonprofit & Public Sector Marketing 27 (1), pp. 70–98.

Wirtz, Bernd W.; Weyerer, Jan C.; Thomas, Marc-Julian; Möller, Anke (2017): E-government implementation. Theoretical aspects and empirical evidence. In Public Organization Review 17, pp. 101–120.

Digital Government Outlook 16

Contents

The textbook starts with a historical retrospective:[1] "For some time, there has been an essential change within the economy and society induced by information technology. This change is mainly caused by increasing digitization: "With the beginning of the 'digital age', also called 'digital revolution', which evolved throughout the development of the multimedia market, there will be a fundamental change of existing structures in the telecommunication, computing, entertainment and media industries" (Denger and Wirtz 1995, p. 20). This assessment in 1995 aptly illustrates the impact of digitization (Wirtz 2019).

At that time, I worked as a consultant in the strategy consulting division of Accenture and was full of enthusiasm about the great potential and opportunities of the digital revolution. In the course of the digital journey towards the information society over the last two decades, my perceptions and views have also significantly changed.

The comprehensive and far-reaching digitization of our spheres of life provides a variety of benefits for our lives. However, there are also fundamental developments in the digital realm that give cause for concern. Figure 16.1 shows six future challenges of digitization for business and society.

[1] See for Chapter 16 Digital Government Outlook also Wirtz (2021, 2022).

B. W. Wirtz, *Digital Government*, Springer Texts in Business and Economics,
https://doi.org/10.1007/978-3-031-13086-1_16

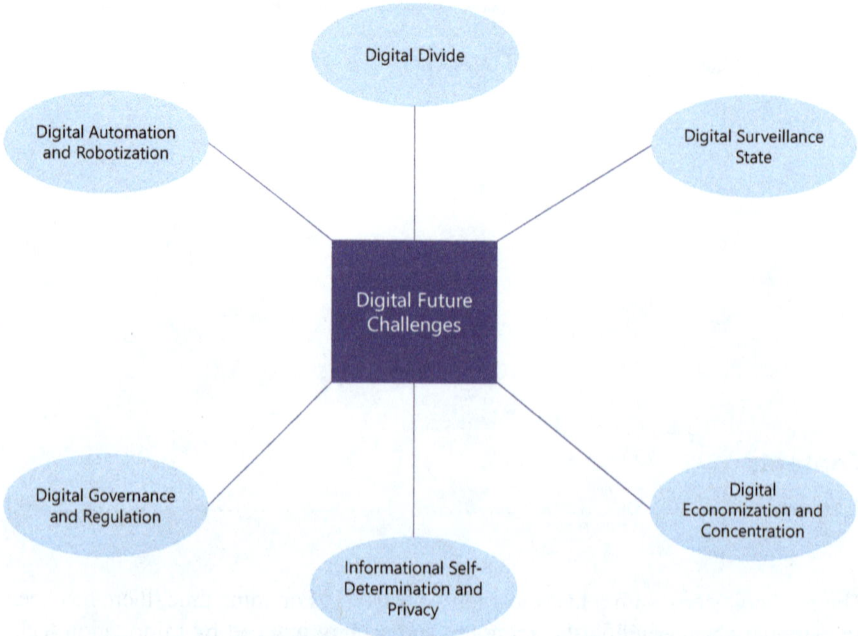

Fig. 16.1 Digital future challenges. Wirtz (2021)

- Challenge 1: Digital divide

A first important challenge concerns the digital divide in our society. Access to the Internet and the use of digital opportunities should be open and unrestricted for everyone in our society, regardless of social and economic circumstances. Today, education, information, and communication have largely become a digital commodity, which presupposes fundamental and fair equality of opportunity in terms of access and use. Digital open access is therefore constitutive of an open and democratic society.

- Challenge 2: Digital surveillance state

A second challenge refers to the danger of a "digital surveillance state." The possibilities of digital surveillance by government institutions are very pronounced in a digitally dominated and data-driven society. A large number of countries around the world already have very extensive digital surveillance of citizens in place. The analysis of widely established surveillance cameras with facial and motion recognition software in combination with the analysis of digital communication such as email, social media, blogs, or messenger chats by means of AI-based big data analytics enables government institutions to obtain a comprehensive picture of every citizen. On this basis, government institutions can carry out very restrictive behavioral control and sanctioning actions (e.g. based on a social credit system).

Here, the abuse of digital technology, for instance, by authoritarian regimes is an important topic of discussion in our society.[2]

- Challenge 3: Digital economization and concentration

A third challenge concerns digital economization and concentration. In the last two decades, very powerful digital champions such as Google, Facebook, Amazon, Microsoft, Apple, Alibaba, or Tencent have emerged worldwide. These global players pursue data-driven business models. Often, private data of users is collected to use it for the economic benefit of the organization.[3] Big data and AI technology are often used in combination to collect and analyze data about people's personal preferences and behavior in order to model predictive behavior patterns and influence them in a targeted manner (digital behavior modification). Digital search engines, large digital marketplaces, and social media are of considerable importance in this context. One example is the targeted influencing of voters in the 2016 U.S. presidential election by means of data from Facebook and Cambridge Analytica. Due to the enormous market power of digital companies, market developments that are dangerous in terms of competition law will increasingly arise in the future. Moreover, this digital market concentration and competition is leading to a significant profit and value migration in our economy and society in favor of a few highly profitable companies. In particular, digital intermediaries such as Uber or Airbnb are leading to disruptions of value constellations that will permanently change our economy and society.

- Challenge 4: Informational self-determination and privacy

A fourth challenge concerns the informational self-determination and privacy of citizens and consumers. The digital world and in particular the digital champions collect a myriad of data usually in exchange for providing free services, like Facebook or Google. The data is collected very intelligently and systematically from the "data owners" without their full understanding regarding the scope and commercialization of the data. In this connection, it is absolutely necessary to improve people's digital awareness of these processes through education and training, and to intensify digital governance.

- Challenge 5: Digital governance and regulation

This leads to the fifth important challenge in the form of digital governance and regulation. The digital world has been able to develop largely free of public governance and regulation over the past 20 years. In the meantime, the legal design

[2]For further reading, I recommend the book "1984" by George Orwell (2008).

[3]For further reading, I recommend the book "The Age of Surveillance Capitalism: The Fight for the Future at the New Frontier of Power" by Shoshana Zuboff (2019).

and regulation of the "Wild West" Internet has begun to some extent, for instance, with the European Union General Data Protection Regulation and the political debate on the regulation of the market power of digital champions, such as Google and Facebook. Here, particularly the governance of digital personal data, digital disinformation (fake news), and digital hacking (digital crime) are of paramount importance to our society, as well as the fair taxation of digitally generated corporate profits.

- Challenge 6: Digital automation and robotization

The sixth challenge that is of great importance for the future concerns digital automation and robotization. The interplay of big data, increasingly powerful AI and leaps in robotic development will dissolve considerable parts of our working world in the future. Previously human tasks will be carried out by AI and intelligent robots. This workforce substitution will lead to an unprecedented release of labor. The mass unemployment that may arise in this context will lead to significant problems for our society that will require forward-looking and intelligent governance. In a not-too-distant future, the question of how our society should deal with (independent!) intelligent machines and robots will also increasingly arise. Not only James Cameron's Terminator movies show the dangers of AI-based autonomous technology. The so-called cyberwars are a scenario that can occur in a real-world context today, given the fundamental work such as that of the world's leading robotics organization Boston Dynamics.

Against the background of these six important aspects, social and governmental institutions must comprehensively and integratively accompany and actively shape the future digital development in an open and democratic social context. Only the greatest possible transparency, participation, and fairness will make an information society viable.

References

Denger, Katharina S.; Wirtz, Bernd W. (1995): Die digitale Revolution. In Gablers Magazin 9 (3), pp. 20–24.

Orwell, George (2008): 1984. London: Penguin Books.

Wirtz, Bernd W. (2019): Medien- und Internetmanagement. 10th ed. Wiesbaden: Springer Gabler.

Wirtz, Bernd W. (2021): Digital Business and Electronic Commerce. Cham: Springer International Publishing.

Wirtz, Bernd W. (2022): E-Government. Wiesbaden: Springer Gabler.

Zuboff, Shoshana (2019): The age of surveillance capitalism. The fight for a human future at the new frontier of power. Paperback edition. New York: Public Affairs.

GPSR Compliance
The European Union's (EU) General Product Safety Regulation (GPSR) is a set of rules that requires consumer products to be safe and our obligations to ensure this.

If you have any concerns about our products, you can contact us on

ProductSafety@springernature.com

In case Publisher is established outside the EU, the EU authorized representative is:

Springer Nature Customer Service Center GmbH
Europaplatz 3
69115 Heidelberg, Germany

www.ingramcontent.com/pod-product-compliance
Lightning Source LLC
Chambersburg PA
CBHW061639240826
50353CB00003B/30
9783031130854